WORKS MINIS
IN DETAIL

WORKS MINIS
IN DETAIL

By Robert Young

Herridge & Sons

ACKNOWLEDGEMENTS

I have been interested in the Abingdon works Minis for many years, and have studied and analysed these little cars to the point of obsession in my quest to discover as much as I possibly could about their build, the stories behind the events, the people involved… Everything. Along the way I also amassed several-thousand images of works Minis and a large archive of material, including a vast number of contemporary magazines and newspapers, all of which have allowed me to be in a position to write this book.

However, it could not have been written without the kind help and assistance of many people. I have to thank in particular Bill Price, who made available to me all of the Abingdon build sheets that he rescued from Abingdon when the department closed and his vast collection of his BMC photographs. Peter Browning also kindly made available his collection of BMC photographs.

Thanks also to Stuart Turner for his advice, good humour and encouragement, along with Graham Robson, both of whom were a great help to me. Guy Smith and Chris Spennewyn shared their personal collection of works photographs that they, like me, have collected over many years. Mike Wood also generously allowed me the use of his unique photographs taken at the time from these fabulous adventures. Paul Easter was a great help in commenting on the many events he competed on with the great Timo Makinen; his memory of these events is encyclopaedic. He also made available his personal archive of press cuttings from each event while at Abingdon.

I am indebted to Peter Barker for his contribution in reading much of what I have written. Paul Stanworth, Pete Flanagan and David Taylor were particularly helpful with information relating to racing Minis. In addition, David Taylor contributed to the rallycross chapter. Tony Salter and David Dyson were a great help with early 850 works Minis information. Kelvin Sparrowhawk on the Mk2 cars and also many of the current owners of these fine works cars for commenting on the scripts I had written about their cars. They include Bernard Griffin, Chris Spennewyn, Alistair Vines, John Littman, Peter Moss, Simon Joslin, Mike Mark, David Brazell, Mike Hyrons, John McIntosh, Guy Smith, Paul Sulma, Andrew Bond and Simon Wheatcroft.

I must also thank the patience, understanding, support and encouragement offered to me by my publisher Herridge & Sons, who were always so understanding when yet another finish date came and went. For a book that is now four years late, I'm thankful for the trust given to me in writing this book.

I'm sure there are those who I have forgotten to mention, for which I apologise.

Finally, I must acknowledge the great help and encouragement that my long-suffering wife, Lesley Young, gave me throughout the long six years this book took to compile. She proof-read, corrected and made suggestions to improve the book, when really I'm sure she would have rather been doing other things. Lesley, I could not have done it without you.

Robert Young
April 2020

Published in 2020 by
Herridge and Sons Ltd
Lower Forda, Shebbear
Devon EX21 5SY

Reprinted 2021

Designed by Ray Leaning, MUSE Fine Art & Design

© Robert Young 2020

All rights reserved. No part of this publication may be reproduced in any form or by any means without the prior written permission of the publisher and the copyright holder.

ISBN 978-1-906133-96-2
Printed in China

CONTENTS

INTRODUCTION 6

CHAPTER 1 8
THE EARLY DAYS – THE MINI 850
YOP 663 – 10, TJB 199 – 11, TMO 559 – 12, TMO 560 – 17, TMO 56 – 22, 617 AOG – 27, 618 AOG – 28, 619 AOG – 31, 363 DOC – 34

CHAPTER 2 36
THE MINI COOPER
737 ABL – 38, 407 ARX – 43, 977 ARX – 48, 477 BBL – 51, 17 CRX – 57, 18 CRX – 59

CHAPTER 3 62
THE MK1 MINI COOPER S
8 EMO – 64, 277 EBL – 68, 33 EJB – 73, 569 FMO – 79, 570 FMO – 82, AJB 33B – 86, AJB 44B – 93, AJB 55B – 100, AJB 66B – 105, BJB 77B – 112, CRX 88B – 116, CRX 89B – 119, CRX 90B – 126, CRX 91B – 131, AGU 780B – 134, DJB 92B – 139, DJB 93B – 147, EJB 55C – 156, EBL 55C – 160, EBL 56C – 164, GRX 5D – 173, GRX 55D – 188, GRX 555D – 193, GRX 195D – 200, GRX 309D – 211, GRX 310D – 219, GRX 311D – 233, HJB 656D – 243, JBL 172D – 252, JBL 493D – 258, JBL 494D – 262, JBL 495D – 267, JMO 969D – 275, LBL 6D – 283, LBL 66D – 290, LBL 666D – 297, LBL 606D – 308, LBL 590E – 315, LRX 827E – 319, LRX 828E – 331, LRX 829E – 335, LRX 830E – 341

CHAPTER 4 346
THE MK2 MINI COOPER S
ORX 7F – 346, ORX 77F – 351, ORX 777F – 358, ORX 707F 364, OBL 45F – 369, OBL 46F – 374, OBL 47F – 381, OBL 48F – 382, RBL 450F – 382, RJB 326F – 388, RJB 327F – 389, URX 550G – 395, URX 560G – 398

CHAPTER 5 402
THE MK3 MINI COOPER S & MINI CLUBMAN
XJB 308H – 403, YMO 881H – 407, YMO 885J – 408, YMO 886J – 410, SOH 878H – 411, OBL 991F – 413, NBL 126D – 413

CHAPTER 6 – RALLYCROSS 414

CHAPTER 7 – EPILOGUE 422

INTRODUCTION

The 1966 RAC Rally, with Simo Lampinen and Tony Ambrose aboard JBL495D.

When the humble Mini was introduced by BMC into the world in August 1959, with its front-wheel drive and gearbox slung below the engine sloshing around in engine oil, nobody knew what a superb competition car it was soon to become. The Mini was radical and a revolution in car design.

No British car had been built in volume with front-wheel drive. Suspension, for the day, was always via metal springs, whereas the Mini used rubber. Transverse engines were rare, and none had the engine over the gearbox sharing its oil. Ten-inch wheels were unheard-of and the diminutive size of the Mini, at just 10ft long, could comfortably seat four adults. To top it all, the car had a respectable turn of speed and was very nimble.

However, Alec Issigonis – who designed the Mini with district nurses in mind – saw no role for his Mini in speed events, even though he was an experienced competition driver. The writing had actually been on the wall during the car's design stage, when the original engine at 948cc was detuned to 850cc, as it was reasoned that the Mini was just too fast with the larger engine fitted. This reduced the top speed from a very respectable 90mph down to a more moderate 72mph. So it was obvious, once the superb handling of the car was exploited, it wouldn't be long before engine modifications would follow.

Once the competition potential of the car was discovered, John Cooper was soon on the scene and it is to BMC's eternal credit that it was receptive to John's overtures to go into production with a high-performance Mini. John had a strong ally at BMC in the shape of George Harriman, the managing director, who when presented by John's ideas for his high-performance Mini, gave him the go-ahead to build the prototype. This was to be called the Mini Cooper, with a twin-carb 997cc engine and many special internal parts.

It was followed, two years later, in 1963 with the all-conquering Mini Cooper S. Initially in 1071cc form, it was followed another year later by the 1275cc Cooper S, which was to become the mainstay of the BMC competition department at Abingdon for the next six years. The 970cc Cooper S was also produced, for a short period, to enable the car to compete in the European 1-litre class, which showed just how successful John Cooper was in convincing BMC management to enter the car in world competition.

This book covers, in detail, all of the works Minis built and campaigned on the world stage by the BMC competition department based at the MG Works at Abingdon in Oxfordshire. These cars were all called 'works Minis', being owned, prepared and competed by the factory between 1959 and the department's ultimate closure in 1970.

During that period, 77 works Minis were built and competed by Abingdon in nearly 300 events, the vast majority of these little cars being painted in distinctive red and white

The Abingdon Competition workshop in 1967.

paintwork, nearly all devoid of any sponsorship decals.

In this book is each and every works Mini, from early 850s through to crossflow-headed 1275 Cooper Ss, the events they entered and the people involved. These Abingdon-built cars concentrated largely on international rallies and only ventured onto racetracks in later years, when they pitched themselves, rather unsuccessfully, against the Cooper Car Company race Minis. These Cooper Car Company machines were only partially funded by BMC, and for the purpose of this book are not considered works Minis.

The aim of this book is to cover in detail every works Minis built and run from the world-renowned BMC competition department at Abingdon, without reference to the build of previous cars. This has, however, meant some inevitable repetition in details when cars were built at a similar time and did the same events.

It will become obvious that a good number of works Minis had numerous bodyshells during their competition history. Identities of cars were swapped for numerous reasons, one of which was when a specific car was entered for a rally months in advance (and paperwork dispatched accordingly), the car may well have been damaged on another rally or recce in the intervening time and rendered unsuitable. Rather than go through the tedium of changing paperwork and shipping details, the car's identity was swapped for that of another Mini.

The life cycle of a works Mini was generally that a new car was built for an event, it was used for a recce or two, then rebuilt and entered into another event. This would continue until it was either damaged or considered tired and in need of replacement. It was then either sold off as an entity or a new car was obtained and its identity transferred. Replacement cars, fresh from the factory, were often Cooper S models but on occasions Mini 850s were delivered instead and built into rally cars.

It has to be recognised that it was often easier to rebuild a damaged or worn-out rally Mini into a new car, rather than rebuild or repair a tired or damaged body. It was also financially expedient to do so rather than procure and register a new car (due to the prevailing UK taxation at the time), which was a practical method repeated by other competition departments the world over.

It is also apparent that, over time, a good number of ex-works cars we see today no longer retain their original Abingdon bodyshells – largely because they were used and abused once sold. They were, after all, competition cars, designed to be used in a harsh environment.

But this is not to detract from any of these beautiful cars we see today – most have been restored into period bodyshells to a very high standard. However, this book will restrict itself to the Abingdon days and covers all of the competition department-built works Minis made between 1959 and 1970.

CHAPTER 1:
THE EARLY DAYS – THE MINI 850

Abingdon, early 1961. Peter Garnier and Rupert Jones in TMO 559, Tom Christie and Nigel Paterson in TMO 560, Derek Astle and Saville (Steve) Woolley in TMO 561, all destined for the 1961 Monte Carlo Rally.

The BMC competition department at Abingdon was really the brainchild of MG managing director John Thornley, who in 1954 persuaded the top men at BMC that they should relocate their competition department from Longbridge to the MG factory at Abingdon in Berkshire. MGs were steeped in racing and record-breaking attempts both in the pre- and post-war era, and had in place all of the right people in the right departments to make up a successful competition department.

Initially the new competition department was under the control of MG designer Syd Enever, who had three main tasks: MG development, customer tuning and competitions. With MG work taking most of his time, he decided to find a competition manager – the job fell to Marcus Chambers, who was appointed in 1955. This set in place the foundation stone for what was soon to become one the most revered and well-respected competition departments in the world, which will always be inexorably associated with the success of the works Minis.

Even in those early days, things were rapidly changing. Soon Abingdon would see the departure of gentlemen drivers, and in their place professional drivers, soon to be followed by professional co-drivers. The cars were now being prepared to almost aircraft standard, as many of the mechanics had seen national service and were highly trained, which showed in the cars they lovingly prepared.

By 1959 Abingdon was fast becoming a very well-respected outfit. It was larger than its rivals, better equipped and better run, and so had little difficultly in attracting the best people available, all wishing to be part of a successful team, which back then was largely centred around the Healey 3000, often affectionately known as the Big Healey.

However, BMC – at the time of the launch of the Mini – had a large number of cars still in the range (some would say far too many) and most, if not all, were assessed for their suitability for competition work. It was the competition department's job, as well as preparing numerous different cars for active competition, to assess any new car added to the line-up. And so it was that the humble 850 Mini was delivered to the factory gates at Abingdon for assessment. These 850 Minis, in common with all subsequent Minis entered by Abingdon, right to the end, were delivered to the competition department as standard road cars, be they Minis, Coopers or Cooper Ss. None were built up from bodyshells.

Initially, the Mini received a very cool reception. Nobody liked the little car. Whenever one of the mechanics needed to nip into town, the Mini was steadfastly avoided, most preferring to blast down the road in the Big Healey – and why wouldn't you? Most just didn't wish to be seen in such a diminutive little car. However, the Mini's superb handling slowly began to win over its many detractors. It was, of course, only a short while before an 850 Mini was being prepared for its first competitive event.

Preparation of those early cars was, by later standards, basic and rudimentary. It was also a learning process in trying to understand what parts were going to suffer stress and possibly failure under competition use, and not the least of which was how to protect the underside and the low-slung running gear on loose surfaces and damaging roads.

Suspension durability was very important, and early failure of damper mountings resulted in revised units being incorporated into mainstream production, designed by Abingdon. Rear radius arm bushes were soon to be replaced by needle rollers on the competition cars, soon to be followed by production changes.

The tiny Mini 10in wheels would also cause an early problem. When people started to race the little car, which could eclipse many more powerful cars simply because of its agility, problems soon surfaced when Minis started to shed wheels. It was quickly discovered that the wheels were just not strong enough, and the RAC acted quickly by banning all Minis from racing until the faults were remedied. Abingdon pressured the factory, and stronger wheels were produced, stamped with an MG octagon to differentiate them from earlier wheels. They were distributed freely to those racing to enable them to continue, and an improved standard production wheel soon followed. This was probably the first instance of the Mini's competition career improving that of the road cars.

Basic preparation of the 850 Mini engine consisted of carefully selecting the standard components and building the engine, utilising the maximum or minimum parameters of the design tolerances specified (which is known as blueprinting the engine). All such early engines were hand built at Abingdon.

Initially there were no special parts available and none were permitted when running in the standard touring class. With the little Mini being well able to hold its own for class awards and not outright wins, there was little need in obtaining a lot more power – mechanical reliability was what was needed. With no dyno or rolling road available, early engine testing was basic – a blast up the road to see what revs the engine would pull was all that was undertaken.

Soon, modified cylinder heads, initially built by Weslake and latterly by Don Moore, (which proved the better of the two) were incorporated on 850 engines. The heads had Speedwell valves of improved material but of a standard size and the compression raised to 9:1. The standard camshaft was later to be replaced by a new in-house design: the 630 camshaft. The crankshaft and flywheel were both just very carefully balanced. Twin engine breathers were also introduced to help the engine breathe more efficiently and to prevent it from discharging oil, which it had a tendency to do. Clutch oil seals, as we will see later, were a great source of trouble and it took a while to be properly rectified with a newly designed primary gear and bush. Steel timing chain gears were introduced, along with stronger idler gears. Early production Mini gearbox casings were manufactured in magnesium, which were soon replaced by aluminium. These much-valued lightweight magnesium casings were all snapped up by Abingdon for exclusive use.

With the development of improved parts, before they could be used in motorsport had to be homologated. Homologation is a Greek word meaning 'to agree', which in a motorsport context simply meant the granting of approval by an official authority – in the UK it was the RAC under the jurisdiction of the FIA (Fédération Internationale de l'Automobile) in France – to use the parts specified. The parts, however, had to be produced in minimum numbers to be eligible to compete in certain classes of motorsport. It would mean each car entered for an international race or rally had to have a set of homologation papers detailing the agreed modified parts that could be fitted before it could compete. This would be a necessary but time-consuming requirement, particularly as modifications became numerous.

However, despite the relatively basic level of modification, preparation (as we will see for all Abingdon cars) was both meticulous and exhaustive. Each car, for every event in which it was entered, had a build sheet, which consisted of up to a dozen closely-typed pages of everything that needed to be carried out on the car for its build. After every event, the process was repeated as if it were a fresh build all over again. Everything was covered, noting the engine, transmission, electrics, cooling system, fuel system, brakes, steering, and body including seats, seat belts, instruments and so on – even the kit carried in the car. Nothing was left out. Each car was assigned a mechanic who would religiously tick off each job until all were completed.

Sadly, not all of the build sheets survive. When Lord Stokes's axe fell on British Leyland, he decreed that all of Abingdon's records and paperwork should be disposed of – he saw no purpose in retaining any. It is only because certain forward-thinking Abingdon personnel rescued some of these valuable documents that anything survives today. I shall refer to these build sheets where necessary in the text.

Early cars were supplied in standard monotone paintwork. These were the days before the highly recognisable red-and-white livery was standardised at Abingdon. One feature that survived through the entire BMC competition department's life was the use of the Ecurie Safety Fast emblem, which was devised by Marcus Chambers, who took out a team entrant's licence in the name of Ecurie Safety Fast.

Decals with Ecurie Safety Fast were superimposed over BMC rosettes and attached to the side of the front wings of all works Minis. They were much coveted and were supplied only on works Minis, and were always removed when the cars were sold. It is also of note that nearly all works Minis, delivered to Abingdon, were registered in Reading, Berkshire and all showed in the car's log book that they were owned by MG Car Co Ltd.

In all, there were just nine works 850 Minis prepared and entered by the works. None of these early cars had any great success, and sadly – to my knowledge – none have survived, although there is an unconfirmed rumour that one may be in the Channel Islands; but at the time of writing it is just a rumour.

Registration Number	First registered	Chassis number	Engine	Engine number	Model
YOP 663	Aug 1959		850cc		Austin Seven

Not a works entry but YOP 663 was to be seen out on the 1961 RAC Rally on a typical rock-strewn forest track.

The very first works Mini was registered as soon as the first batches of Minis were off the production line and it was painted Tartan Red. YOP was registered in Birmingham, so was likely part of the original press fleet. As the cars were in need of competition assessment, Marcus Chambers, the then-competitions manager, took it upon himself to test the untried car in competition first hand. He was navigated by Peter Wilson on the Mini's inaugural competition event.

YOP 663 was entered in the Viking Rally in September 1959, a round of the European championship. Based in Oslo, the event consisted of seven special stages over the mountains and back to Oslo. The Norwegian event was tough and one that would be a good test for the new Mini. However, at this early stage in its assessment and development, the Mini was primarily entered as a following support car to Pat Moss in her works Austin A40, who was chasing the European Ladies' Championship. Servicing was not permitted on the rally but there was nothing stopping one competitor helping out another. And this Marcus duly did in YOP 663.

The car had very little preparation and was effectively a standard car with just a sump guard and a map light fitted, plus a few rudimentary creature comforts. Marcus nursed the car to the finish in 51st place, gaining valuable experience with the Mini. Along the way, the car managed to break its wheels – due in no small part to the large ruts it had to contend with. Failing Mini wheels would soon manifest themselves on the racetrack and would see the Mini banned from racing by the RAC until strengthened wheels were fitted. Abingdon became supplier of 'approved' strengthened wheels until production changes were made.

YOP663 also leaked badly on the Viking Rally, and again that would soon be rectified on the production line. So this early Mini was not only paving the way for an improved competition car, BMC was also improving the production car by entering cars into competition, on which BMC always prided itself.

Records show this was the one and only event the car was entered by the works, although it did compete on the 1961 RAC, probably once sold on from Abingdon, when driven by Jimmy Ray and J Hopwood. They finished seventh overall, were second in their class and were the highest-placed private entry – so no mean feat.

Competition Record

Date	Event	Crew	Number	Overall result	Class result
Sept 1959	Viking Rally	Marcus Chambers/Peter Wilson		51st	

Registration Number	First registered	Chassis number	Engine	Engine number	Model
TJB 199	Aug 1959	M/A2S4 675	850cc	8MB-U-H 899	Morris Mini Minor

This little Morris Mini Minor holds the honour of being the first Mini to win a rally outright. Well, to qualify that, the first works Mini. It may well be that a privateer won a local event in his own Mini but the contemporary records show TJB 199 was the first Abingdon-prepared car to win an event. The car appeared in standard monotone Cherry Red.

The event was the Knowldale Car Club's Mini Miglia in October 1959. A national event, it finished near the delights of Macclesfield and was won by Pat Moss, who was ably navigated by Stuart Turner (later to become BMC's competition manager). They won by a clear ten minutes. The Mini seemed underpowered compared with the Healey 3000 that Pat Moss was used to, and Stuart Turner complained of the car being uncomfortable and giving him wet feet.

Pat Moss never really warmed to the Mini, although she would compete in another five rallies in Minis. The car was, at this early stage in the Mini's development, still very basic, prepared with the bare necessities of a map light, sump guard and a couple of driving lamps.

As a test run and prelude to the forthcoming Monte Carlo Rally, TJB 199 was prepared for the Portuguese rally, which was run in December 1959. Entered again with a female driver, but this time Nancy Mitchell and navigated by Pat Allison, they were second ladies and were 54th overall. Nancy Mitchell was a very accomplished rally driver, being European Ladies' Champion in 1956 and 1957, but would soon be eclipsed by Pat Moss.

So far the new baby car was proving reliable and, if not fast, its handling was a big plus point; and whilst the car struggled uphill, for the brave it was very quick downhill. So the stage was set for Abingdon to send a team of Minis, with some confidence, to the following month's Monte Carlo Rally.

The last event for the car at Abingdon was the 1960 Tulip Rally, run in the May of that year. Yet again, the car was to be used for Mini development work, and this time entrusted to the very capable John Sprinzel, with Mike Hughes on the maps.

Nancy Mitchell in a Spanish filling station in a very standard looking but much travel-stained works 850 Mini.

By now, it had become apparent that the little 850 Mini needed much more power if it was ever to challenge for anything other than class awards. Fortunately, under the newly-introduced Appendix J regulations, two new classes had been created for production cars. The first, the touring car class, was basically a standard showroom class, later to become Group 1. The second, the improved touring class, allowed for cars to be modified; this was later to become Group 2.

This freedom allowed Abingdon to prepare Sprinzel's car with twin carburettors, a modified camshaft and reworked cylinder head. The car was considered to be the Mini Cooper

WORKS MINIS IN DETAIL

The snow on the high climbs helped the Mini, where its superior roadholding impressed many.

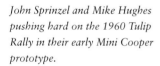

John Sprinzel and Mike Hughes pushing hard on the 1960 Tulip Rally in their early Mini Cooper prototype.

prototype, as many of the modifications that John Cooper had been using on his racing A-series engines were soon found on the GT-category Minis that Abingdon was using in competition.

On the Tulip Rally, because of the modifications, they were placed in the 1000cc GT category and had a long battle with Austin-Healey Sprites and Renault Gordinis but came home second in class, outdone in the end by the Gordini but beating all of the Sprites – which was actually not great publicity for Sprinzel's Sprite tuning business! John was, however, delighted with the car, which he felt was much improved with the extra power the modifications had produced. It was a good event for the Mini, as all three Abingdon Minis finished what was considered to be a gruelling rally. The car was sold to Alan Hutcheson, who was a renowned racing driver, usually at the wheel of a Riley 1.5.

Competition Record

Date	Event	Crew	Number	Overall result	Class result
Oct 1959	Mini Miglia	Pat Moss/Stuart Turner	29	1st	
Dec 1959	Portuguese Rally	Nancy Mitchell/Pat Allison	57	54th	2nd
May 1960	Tulip Rally	John Sprinzel/Mike Hughes	99	43rd	2nd

Registration Number	First registered	Chassis number	Engine	Engine number	Model
TMO 559	Oct 1959	M/A2S4 4258	850cc	8MB-U-H 2890	Morris Mini

This car was one of a group of three new Mini 850s delivered to Abingdon, all Morris Mini Minors, in late 1959, to be prepared for the RAC Rally in November that year. This car, along with its two sister cars, was used extensively over its 18 month stay at Abingdon.

These early cars were supplied in standard monotone paintwork. TMO 559 was painted in Clipper Blue, being a Morris. The car's first event was also the first team event for BMC with the Mini, the 1959 RAC Rally of Great Britain. The car was driven by Pat (Tish) Ozanne and Noreen Gilmour. Tish Ozanne, who hated being called Pat, was the most active of the early 850 Mini drivers, tackling five rallies in these early rather underpowered cars. Tish was perhaps always in the shadow of Pat Moss but was nevertheless a formidable driver.

CHAPTER 1: THE EARLY DAYS - THE MINI 850

Tish Ozanne and Noreen Gilmour prior to their retirement on the 1959 RAC Rally.

Tish Ozanne on an RAC Rally hillclimb, probably at Prescott; note the absence of the navigator.

The 1959 RAC Rally was the first time this important British event had moved its calendar date to November, in an attempt to attract more foreign entrants, as it was to be the final round of the European championship and to make the event more of a winter challenge. The rally also now concentrated on testing road sections rather than driving tests (later to be known as autotests). This date change resulted in severe weather throughout most of the event and was a tough test for the trio of works Minis.

RAC preparation, still in the early days of the car, was again rudimentary but thorough. A Weslake high-compression cylinder head was fitted and the engine carefully assembled in every detail. The car had its ride height raised to give it more ground clearance over the poor roads it was expected to traverse, and it was also fitted with a sump guard, two driving lamps on the bumper and wire-mesh headlight protectors. It is noted that these early cars were fitted with magnesium gearbox casings, which were later in production, soon replaced with cast aluminium. The damper brackets were strengthened and modified.

Crew comfort on this long event, the length and breadth of the country, was also well catered for. A screen heater bar was fitted to the driver's side, along with a Helphos lamp mounted centrally on the windscreen. The navigator also had the use of two Smiths aircraft-type stopwatches, as well as his map light fixed on the top of dash rail. To save weight, all the glass (except the front screen) was replaced with Perspex. Sadly, a slipping clutch – a common problem with early Minis – saw this car and all of the other works Minis retire. Oil seal failure around the primary gear resulted in oil seeping onto the clutch plate, rendering it useless. Despite applications of fire extinguisher and other chemicals into the clutch housing, no on-event cure was found and the car was retired. It would be another item that would soon be corrected on the production line of the Mini when the primary gear and bush were redesigned.

The 1960 Monte Carlo Rally saw the car again entrusted to Ozanne and Gilmour but they would again retire, albeit not due to clutch slip on this occasion. By the time of the Monte, the aforementioned primary gear had effected a potential cure for the leaking primary oil seal problem. Unfortunately, the car was already in Oslo for the start and a hasty on-site replacement of the primary gear was undertaken by Brian Moylan, one of the works mechanics. Brian had three Mini engines to take out, fix and then refit – a task completed just in time for all three Minis to take the start with the new gear in place.

The car was entered in the touring car class, so was

Tish Ozanne leaving the Paris start control on the 1960 Monte Carlo Rally.

13

Rupert Jones on 1960 Alpine loose-surface mountain climb.

David Seigle-Morris and Vic Elford on a skid-pan test on the 1960 RAC Rally.

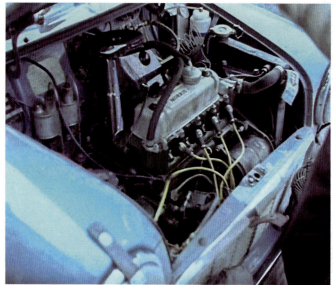

Rare shot of the works 850 engine of TMO 559 revealed on the 1960 Monte.

basically standard. However, for this gruelling winter challenge, much attention had been paid to the interior. The driver's instruments, in a separate pod fixed to the dash rail, held a Speedwell rev counter and a dual oil pressure and water temperature gauge. The navigator had a pair of Heuer clocks in front of him and a special calibrated speedo with an additional distance recorder that could be zeroed. Together with the customary map light and additional switches for the two extra driving lamps, things were looking quite different, but there were still no seat belts.

The car retained the electrically-heated bar to keep the driver's screen clear in the cold weather, plus it now had a Perspex deflector to channel the warm air from the demister vents straight up to the screen. A larger-capacity heater was also installed and the radiator was fitted with a Mory radiator blind, which could be raised or lowered from inside the cabin to adjust the temperature of the car. An external ice thermometer was fitted to the top corner of the windscreen to help the crew gauge if the outside temperature would result in the roads being ice-covered.

Externally, the sump guard disappeared from the car and the headlight stone-guards gave way to Perspex covers on straps that would be a feature on nearly all works Minis from then on.

TMO 559's non-finishing run continued on the 1960 Circuit of Ireland, when David Hiam and Tony Ambrose used it over the Easter weekend. The car had in fact been prepared for Erik Carlsson, who at the last moment was unable to start because of a leg injury, so David stepped in.

David was a determined driver, who so nearly finished the gruelling Liège Rally in his own Mini (16 BOJ) in 1961. He was also Dunlop's rally manager, so was an expert on Mini rally tyres. The car was repainted yellow and blue – Swedish national colours – especially for Carlsson. On the event, however, they incurred a great amount of penalties for booking in early at many controls, which was an uncharacteristic mistake by Ambrose on the finer points of the regulations.

The 1960 Alpine Rally in June saw the car handed to Reverend Rupert Jones and Ken James, but sadly the change of crew made no difference to the car's finishing record – it

Gerald Wiffen fitting the rear drive for the auxiliary speedometer, which was equipped with an odometer to accurately record distances without front wheelspin.

Rupert Jones and Peter Garnier depart a time control on the 1961 Monte Carlo Rally.

retired again due to a crash.

The car was being used for the development of the forthcoming Mini Cooper and was running the small 7in disc brakes, which were proving less than adequate over the Alpine mountain descents. An experimental Cooper prototype gearbox was also being tried. The crew was leading its class until the very last day of this gruelling Alpine marathon, when Ken booked into a control four minutes early; the error caused Rupert to attack the Col d'Allos even faster, with the ultimate result of going off and deranging the front end. Struggling to the finish, they were out of time and a good result was lost.

In October, the car was loaned out to David Seigle-Morris and Vic Elford, as an unofficial entry for the 1960 London Rally, which was a non-stop 600-mile road rally that started from four locations around the UK (Leeds, Birmingham, Taunton and London) to converge in Wales where the meat of the rally took place. The event attracted 240 cars but just 63 finished in the totally fog-bound route around Wales. Designed for private entrants, works participation was discouraged on the London, hence it being a private entry for Seigle-Morris.

The new pair of Seigle-Morris and Elford would both go onto greater things, Elford as a very successful works Porsche driver, and Seigle-Morris successful in Big Healeys and then with works Ford Cortinas.

The 2000-mile long 1960 RAC Rally at last saw a change of fortune for the car when David Seigle-Morris and Vic Elford took over and came a superb sixth overall (from 177 starters) and second in class behind the winning Saab of Erik Carlsson and Stuart Turner. This was despite persistent clutch slip towards the end of the event, which necessitated Doug Hamblin pouring fire extinguisher fluid into the clutch while in parc fermé at Brands Hatch. Nobody noticed and they got away with it!

It was a brilliant result and a boost to the team; the Mini won three of the seven special tests in its class, which clearly showed that the 850 Mini could do well on such a demanding rally against the best known British and continental crews.

After the RAC, expectations were high for the 1961 Monte

The wreck of TMO 559 with Rupert Jones trying to find the quickest way home.

Carlo Rally but once again the car failed to finish – along with all the other works Minis.

New for 1961 were the Appendix J regulations, which for series production cars were classed as Group 1 or Group 2, in effect the standard and modified classes. Grand touring cars were now pure sports cars like the Healey, Sprite and Porsche, but could also include heavily-modified saloon cars, which fell outside Group 1 or 2. These GT cars had the option of a Group 3 class, which was again a modified class and also permitted weight saving.

Tyres, always an important issue with the Monte, saw all the works Minis entered as Group 2 cars, using studded Dunlop Durabands for the snow and ice. These early studded tyres effectively had studs bolted through the tyre and, although few in number by modern standards, proved effective.

Another innovation for the Monte was the auxiliary Smiths speedometer with an odometer driven by the rear wheel. This clever innovation – designed to allow quick wheel changes – was devised by Tommy Wellman, the deputy foreman at Abingdon, in an attempt to eradicate inaccuracies in distance recording (vital for accurate average speed calculations) caused by the front wheels spinning on snow and ice. An extended stub axle with a modified hub carrier housed the right-angle drive, which could be removed easily by removing a split pin when changing tyres. However, the risk of damage to the vulnerable right-angle drive saw the idea dropped.

All this came to nothing when the car driven by Peter Garnier with Reverend Rupert Jones was involved in a road accident, when an errant French farmer's Peugeot assaulted the little Mini at a crossroads near Reims, leaving Peter with a few broken ribs and a very battered motor car.

With TMO 559 effectively destroyed in the Monte road accident, a new car was built for David Seigle-Morris and Vic Elford to tackle the 1961 Tulip in May. It was a formidable pairing, which in the end proved a bit of a disaster, with the car crewed by two very capable drivers, who would both rather be behind the wheel.

Entered in Group 2, it was prepared to the usual Abingdon high standard with modified head to raise the compression and by now, with the Mini Cooper due to hit the streets in the September – not four months away – the car was continuing to trial many Cooper parts, such as brakes and transmission, in addition to internal engine modifications that would soon find their way into production of the new car. The flexibility of Group 2 regulations allowed Abingdon the perfect test bed for the forthcoming car.

The Tulip turned out to be a long event short on competition but sufficient to allow Seigle-Morris and Elford to practice a new sideways style of driving they had developed in the hope of emulating or beating the Scandinavian style of sideways motoring. Seigle-Morris would steer the car into a bend and Elford would yank on the handbrake, leaving David to steer around the corner with the car in a drift. This didn't endear themselves to the mechanics, and not the least Marcus Chambers, who disapproved of Elford's wayward driving style. Nevertheless, the pair got the car to the finish to collect third in class and 23rd overall.

This was the final event for TMO 559 at Abingdon. The car was sold to Vic Elford.

David Seigle-Morris and Vic Elford departing for the 1961 Tulip Rally at Southend Airport, awaiting a Bristol Carvair transport plane.

Competition Record

Date	Event	Crew	Number	Overall result	Class result
Nov 1959	RAC Rally	Pat Ozanne/Noreen Gilmour	129	DNF	
Jan 1960	Monte Carlo Rally	Pat Ozanne/Noreen Gilmour	307	DNF	
April 1960	Circuit of Ireland	David Hiam/Tony Ambrose		DNF	
June 1960	Alpine Rally	Rupert Jones/Ken James	5	DNF	
Oct 1960	London Rally	David Seigle-Morris/Vic Elford			
Nov 1960	RAC Rally	David Seigle-Morris/Vic Elford	183	6th	2nd
Jan 1961	Monte Carlo Rally	Peter Garnier/Rupert Jones	254	DNF	
May 1961	Tulip Rally	David Seigle-Morris/Vic Elford	135	23rd	6th

CHAPTER 1: THE EARLY DAYS - THE MINI 850

Registration Number	First registered	Chassis number	Engine	Engine number	Model
TMO 560	Oct 1959	M/A2S4 1640	850cc	8MB-U-H 2886	Morris Mini

This car was the second of a group of three new Morris Mini 850s delivered to Abingdon, late in 1959, to be prepared for the November RAC Rally that year. This car too was used extensively over its 18-month time at Abingdon, competing in eight international rallies.

TMO 560 was turned out in monotone Cherry Red paintwork, the three cars being presented in different colours, which was a far cry from what was to become the almost-universal Abingdon war paint of red and white. Preparation was similar to the other cars with a modified head to raise the compression, strengthened damper mount and numerous crew comfort additions.

For the RAC Rally, a hard event on the car, a sump guard was fitted, and to try to keep the front drum brakes cool, the corners of the front panel were cut away with air deflectors. To keep the weight down, Perspex was used for all the glass except the front 'screen. Inside the car, a Helphos lamp was fixed to the screen, as was a heater bar on the driver's side. Two Lucas fog lamps were mounted on the bumper and front panel.

Entered in a three-car team for the RAC, TMO 560 was driven by Alec Pitts and Tony Ambrose. This was Ambrose's first event at Abingdon, and this marked the beginning of the professional co-drivers, as he brought a new level of professionalism to the team and went on to do 30 rallies for the works – equalled only by Henry Liddon as the most successful works co-driver. Coincidentally, this was also the first Abingdon drive for Alec Pitts.

With the event now moved to November, the severe weather conditions dished out made driving testing, and the car (along with the rest of the team) retired with clutch slip. As noted previously, this problem would continue until a remedy in the shape of a new primary gear and bush was developed to eradicate the oil seeping past the seal.

Along with the move to November, the rally also introduced the use of a Tulip road book for the first time, which had a series of symbols depicting road junction turning points – another attempt to encourage continental entrants who were often baffled by our maps and grid reference system.

Starting from Blackpool and journeying up to the Highlands before returning south, through Wales and finishing at the Crystal Palace race circuit in South London, the 2000 miles was certainly a huge challenge, which the new Mini was not yet up to. The rally itself, beset with bad weather, resulted in many crews not being able to reach the control at Braemar in Scotland. This marred the event, as the resulting protest (by Stuart Turner, no less, navigating in a German DKW) saw the results having to await the outcome of an FIA tribunal. Rallying was coming of age.

For the 1960 Monte, the car was again crewed by Pitts and Ambrose; they were entered in the modified GT class, so the engine received its customary high-compression head and modified camshaft, which produced around 42bhp. For the Monte the car was fitted with an external temperature gauge at the top right-hand side of the passenger's window, to detect the onset of ice on the roads. There was no sump guard, and

Alec Pitts and Tony Ambrose queuing to check in to a control in the Highlands on the 1960 RAC Rally.

Alec Pitts and Tony Ambrose in the snow at Dover before boarding the ferry for France for their Paris Monte start.

17

Alec Pitts and Tony Ambrose leaving the Paris start for the 1960 Monte Carlo Rally.

The much damaged car of Alec Pitts and Tony Ambrose on the Monte, sold for £10!

TMO 560 receiving service attention on the Monte - rather unsure where the fluid is being poured, perhaps to clean oil from the clutch? Seen is the external temperature gauge at the top corner of the windscreen.

gone was the cut-down front panel found on the RAC Rally, the car now reverting to a full skirt below the bumper.

A Mory radiator blind was fitted, which was operated from inside the car should the engine run too cold. The car was fitted with two Lucas 576 lamps, one spot and one fog fixed to the bumper and front panel. It was also fitted with removable Perspex headlight covers.

Starting from Paris, clutch slip started almost immediately but with liberal quantities of fire extinguishant and sand poured in, it helped Alec on his way. But in thick fog he hit the back of another competitor, damaging the radiator, and the resulting spin across the road deranged the rear wheel. Once on the move again, Alec came to grief by hitting a milk float just outside Monte.

By now the car was severely damaged, with windows missing and the body badly misaligned. Undeterred, Alec tackled the mountain circuit in a car held together with string, patched up with cardboard and tape, which was barely drivable.

But complete it he did, despite many stops to attend to the still-ailing clutch, which had been rendered solid by the use of resin bought from a Monte piano shop. Progress on the two classification mountain loops was further delayed by two more visits to the scenery and picking up various bits of the Mini that were falling off along the way. At the finish, now with the exhaust also dangling, Alec offered Marcus Chambers £10 for the car – which he gladly accepted! Alec's determination netted them 73rd place on what had been a torrid event.

Needless to say, a new TMO 560 had to be built up for Ken James and Rupert Jones for the next event, the 1960 Tulip Rally. Ken James was equally happy driving or co-driving, having navigated for John Gott in Big Healeys, and would soon swap seats and accompany Rupert Jones as co-driver.

Running in the improved series-production touring class – which allowed some modification of the standard car, but not to the degree permitted for the grand touring class – the Mini was therefore carefully modified from standard. However, it was running small disc brakes on an experimental basis for the new Mini Cooper, which caused trouble and failed several times. They also had repeated fuel pump problems. Housed outside in the elements on the subframe, the pump lost them six minutes when it failed, before being replaced at the next service.

When Jones took the wheel, feeling he could do just as well

CHAPTER 1: THE EARLY DAYS - THE MINI 850

Ken James and Rupert Jones had already damaged their new car on the 1960 Tulip Rally.

Alec Pitts and Tony Ambrose on a typical (for the day) loose-surface Alpine pass.

as James, he rather embarrassed himself by grazing the car along a bridge parapet but without loss of time. The Dutch rally was a long event, which went all through France and then down to Monte Carlo and over the snow-covered Col de Turini, then up and on into Germany to the Nürburgring to finish in Eindhoven – certainly no tiptoe through the tulips. The pair brought the car home to seventh in the tough class and 75th overall.

For the 1960 Alpine, TMO 560 was returned to the safe hands of Alec Pitts and Tony Ambrose. Pitts was another successful early campaigner of the Mini and was rewarded with four drives at Abingdon – this was his last, where he rewarded Marcus Chambers's faith in him by bringing the car home safely, 30th overall and fifth in the touring class. The Alpine Rally of 1960 was indeed a hard event of 1850 miles over the Alps with just one rest stop over the four days, so it was a very respectable result for what was basically a standard Mini on this particularly severe Alpine.

Tom Christie and Nigel Paterson were to drive the car on the 1960 RAC Rally, a 2000-mile route covering the length and breadth of the UK, starting at Blackpool and finishing at Brands Hatch. The car was again prepared to a high standard, with the now-overheating front brakes attended to by cutting away the ends of the full-width front skirt – this would ultimately find its way into standard production cars with a modified front panel. The car was also fitted with a Helphos sign-spotting lamp stuck to the windscreen, which could be swivelled by hand to any direction needed.

Christie was a successful clubman who had been rallying a Mini from the start, and was now having his first of just three drives for Abingdon. Sadly, he was not to finish, as the car's flywheel parted company with the rest of the engine, eliminating it on the spot. But it was not before Christie had put up a formidable challenge to Erik Carlsson's Saab that would eventually win the rally.

With David Seigle-Morris getting his works 850 up into sixth place at the finish, it was starting to show the Mini had pace, if not reliability, in several key areas. The dreaded clutch slip was a constant worry and, as we will see, a cure for that was still a few months away. Suspension reliability, on rougher events at least, was also still an issue that needed resolving.

Christie and Paterson were to use TMO 560 once more on the 1961 Monte Carlo Rally. The car was entered into the new Group 2 class, which allowed for homologated modifications. Still in the early days of the Mini's competition evolution, they were restricted to raising the compression with a modified cylinder head with a higher-lift camshaft. A sump guard was omitted but a rear-wheel-driven speedo drive was fitted, and inside was a heater bar on the driver's side of the windscreen,

Alec Pitts and Tony Ambrose speed past the expectant pair at a fuel station, the car again showing body damage.

WORKS MINIS IN DETAIL

Tom Christie brings the Mini into the controls on the 1960 RAC.

Jonny Organ with the 1961 Monte entry showing the auxiliary speedo with odometer, the pair of Heuer watches, additional switch panel, Watson rev counter, duel oil and water temp gauge, large oil warning light, screen heater and Les Leston steering wheel.

together with a Perspex deflector to ensure hot air from the vents kept the screen clear. A flat Les Leston steering wheel was added, and there was a central instrument panel for the extra dials and switches, including a Smiths-Weston rev counter. The navigator seat was modified to recline, and the car's front skirt was cut away on the corners to aid brake cooling.

New regulations for the Monte this year included the requirement to have a bracket, fixed to the engine via sealed bolts, with a 10mm hole, the purpose of which was to bond the engine to the chassis as one with a wire and seal arrangement, the idea being to stop either engine or car swapping.

Most of the Paris starters elected, because of the snow, to fit studded tyres – in the works Minis' case, tungsten-shod Dunlop Durabands.

However, the 1961 event would prove a disaster for the Abingdon Minis, which was a bitter disappointment after the encouraging results on the previous year's Monte.

This year all three works Minis failed to finish, for different but terminal reasons. Christie's car, starting from Paris, was in fact perfectly fine, but Christie went down with acute food poisoning and was unable to continue the event.

Alas, Abingdon's hope for a win had been thwarted: there was in place a rather controversial handicap system based upon weight of the car and its engine size, so a small-capacity car was odds-on favourite to win outright. Abingdon could so easily have pre-dated Paddy Hopkirk's 1964 win by three years if the team's luck had held. As it was, 848cc Panhards took the first three places.

Pat Moss's second works Mini drive was with TMO 560 on the Lyon-Charbonnières rally in May 1961, navigated by Ann Wisdom. This formidable pairing was invariably favourite for the Coupe des Dames whenever they entered. Moreover, they were always well up in the general classification.

Pat was to prove to be one of the very fastest behind the wheel

Tom Christie and Nigel Paterson early on the 1961 Monte Carlo.

of her favourite car, the Healey 3000. Being Stirling Moss's sister, she was bound to be quick and competitive no matter what she drove, and had driven every type of competition car Abingdon had at its disposal. She was ultimately tempted away to Ford in 1963 – a sad loss for BMC.

Despite the Mini being much slower than anything else she'd driven, even though it was a Group 2 car, she soon adapted to front-wheel drive and was well up the field on the rally, keeping pace with Erik Carlsson's Saab. Unfortunately, transmission failure scuppered Pat's fine efforts in TMO 560. The result, originally thought to be crankshaft failure, was traced to the idler gear bearing having collapsed – something else that would be changed later in the Mini's evolution.

TMO 560's final Abingdon event was as part of the three-car team to attempt the notoriously rough Acropolis Rally. It proved that the Mini was still under-developed for this type of event, with a litany of problems besetting all of the cars; the Greek terrain proved just too rough and demanding.

This was actually to be the last event Abingdon would be entering with the 850 Mini, as the new Mini Cooper was waiting in the wings, only a few months away. The car was assigned to David Seigle-Morris and Vic Elford, entered in Group 2, with the customary modifications that were allowed but now sporting a black-painted bonnet to keep sun glare to a minimum.

When Elford was driving, the car hit a large immovable rock, which sheared the tie-rod mounting on the subframe. Local welding effected only a temporary repair and the subframe soon broke again. With the repairs taking too long, the car was outside its time limit and they were forced to retire.

It was to be Elford's penultimate drive with BMC and the last in a Mini, when he was unceremoniously sacked by Marcus Chambers after the Alpine Rally a month later because of an unnecessary accident on a road section. This, with hindsight, was a big mistake by BMC, as Elford went on to be successful at Ford, and was invincible when he later joined Porsche and won the Monte Carlo Rally. He then graduated to Formula One and World Sportscars – so quite a loss to BMC.

Ultimately, TMO 560 hadn't been very successful, finishing only three of its eight events. The car was sold to Alec Pitts.

Ann Wisdom climbs into the car alongside Pat Moss having had her time card stamped on the 1961 Lyon-Charbonnières Rally.

David Seigle-Morris and Vic Elford before the start of the 1961 Acropolis Rally with alternative headgear. Elford would soon be sacked by BMC.

Competition Record

Date	Event	Crew	Number	Overall result	Class result
Nov 1959	RAC Rally	Alec Pitts/Tony Ambrose	135	DNF	
Jan 1960	Monte Carlo Rally	Alec Pitts/Tony Ambrose	284	73rd	
May 1960	Tulip Rally	Ken James/Rupert Jones	161	75th	7th
June 1960	Alpine Rally	Alec Pitts/Tony Ambrose	1	30th	5th
Nov 1960	RAC Rally	Tom Christie/Nigel Paterson	174	DNF	
Jan 1961	Monte Carlo Rally	Tom Christie/Nigel Paterson	227	DNF	
Jan 1961	Lyon-Charbonnières	Pat Moss/Ann Wisdom	81	DNF	
May 1961	Acropolis Rally	David Seigle-Morris/Vic Elford	125	DNF	

WORKS MINIS IN DETAIL

Registration Number	First registered	Chassis number	Engine	Engine number	Model
TMO 561	Oct 1959	M/A2S4 4336	850cc	8MB-U-H 2495	Morris Mini

The Morley twins, with gentlemen's hats, pressing on during the 1960 Monte Carlo Rally.

Erle Morley refills the car on the 1960 Monte.

This car was the last of a group of three Morris Mini Minor 850s delivered to Abingdon, in October 1959, to be prepared for the RAC Rally in November. This car was also used extensively over the next year-and-a-half, with seven international rallies to its credit. Continuing with the monotone theme of these early cars, TMO 561 was delivered in Old English White.

TMO 561 for the 1959 RAC Rally was prepared similarly to its sister cars, with a modified cylinder head to raise the compression, and strengthening to the damper mountings. The interior dashboard layout was, by later standards, rather haphazard but functional. The rev counter was a Speedwell Weston electronic with a duel oil and water temperature gauge alongside.

For the RAC Rally a sump guard was fitted to the car and the front skirt was cut away at the corners to aid brake cooling, which was assisted by deflectors. Meanwhile, the front grille was split down its centre to aid access. Two Lucas lamps were fitted to the bumper and front panel, and a small Lucas 494 reversing lamp was secured above the rear number plate.

A screen heater bar was fitted to the driver's side, and all of the glass was replaced with Perspex. A Helphos spotting lamp was fitted centrally to the 'screen, and the navigator also had the use of two Smiths aircraft stop watches. The car was also fitted with seat belts. These were, however, early days in works Mini preparation.

Ken James and Ian Hall got their hands on the new car for the RAC, which followed the pattern of the their sister cars – beset with atrocious weather conditions. They too were eliminated with the dreaded clutch slip, due to oil finding its way onto the clutch because of an ineffective primary gear oil seal.

For the 1960 Monte Carlo Rally the car was handed over to the Morley twins, Don and Erle, a pair of Suffolk farmers who were better known for their driving of works Healeys. Their rallying programme was often constrained by harvest times on their farm and they probably could have achieved more if they had not had other commitments. Erle was a fastidious co-driver, and Don a fast, determined driver. They were a great pairing, which was not often split up. This was to be their first competitive Mini drive.

The car was entered into the modified production touring class, which allowed for engine modifications. The tuned cylinder head effectively raised the standard compression ratio of 8.3:1 to a more useful 9:1. A four-blade fan was fitted to the engine.

CHAPTER 1: THE EARLY DAYS - THE MINI 850

The Morleys blasting through the night on the Monte.

Tish Ozanne and Pat Allison refuelling on the 1960 Tulip Rally at Barrême. TMO 560 in the background.

Pat Allison takes over the wheel on the Tulip Rally road section.

For the Monte the car lost its sump guard but was fitted with an external ice thermometer on the top of the windscreen. Two Lucas 576 auxiliary lamps were added to the front of the car, and it used Continental headlamps. The cut-down front skirt disappeared, replaced by a full-width skirt; a side-mounted radiator blind was fitted, which could be raised or lowered from inside the car should the engine overcool. In common with the six works Minis on the event, the twins would have exclusive use of the latest Dunlop Duraband tyres fitted with tungsten steel spikes. By later standards they had few spikes, but were nevertheless effective on the snow and ice.

The Morleys acquitted themselves well, considering it was their first competitive Mini drive, by getting the car up to 33rd overall, despite delays on the mountain circuit from regularly having to stop to replenish their radiator. They were the second-placed Mini behind Rupert Jones, both in the modified class.

The next event for the car was due to be the Sestriere rally in Italy, in February 1960, where the car was to be driven by Tish Ozanne. Nancy Mitchell was also to take a sister car for a two-pronged attack for the ladies' prize on the event. Sadly, the rally was cancelled at the last minute due to the Italian highway authority deeming the winter roads too dangerous. This was also the end of the Sestriere rally as a European championship event.

Tish Ozanne and Pat Allison were next to use TMO 561 on the Tulip rally. This was a really tough event in 1960 and was a fitting test for the car over the 2000-mile route.

Running in the improved series-production touring class, and hence modified to give more power, Tish got the car up to 72nd overall, despite losing time booking into a control late due to searching for fuel. The Tulip did prove that the Mini was becoming reliable, if not that quick, as all three works 850s finished the gruelling event.

For the 1960 Alpine, Tommy Gold and Mark Hughes took over the car and achieved a great result, getting the car to 14th overall and winning the GT category. Although they were the only finishers in that class, it shouldn't detract from what was a very good result from an entry of the best 77 cars and crews from all over Europe. The 1960 event was considered by many to be a vintage Alpine, which was tough and demanding, testing cars and drivers over many of the best climbs to be found in France and Italy.

So the Mini showed itself well, as did all the works Minis on

TMO 561 on BMC's favourite event, the Alpine Rally.

Mike Sutcliffe and Derek Astle on the starting ramp of the 1960 RAC Rally.

A very travel-stained TMO 561 at Brands Hatch for the speed test at the circuit.

Tommy Gold and Mike Hughes on a climb on the 1960 Alpine Rally.

the event, putting up astonishing performances. Surprisingly, after such an impressive drive, this was Tommy Gold's only drive at Abingdon. He went on to drive very successfully in Sebring Sprites.

Back home, the car was re-prepared for yet another pairing to take over on the RAC. Mike Sutcliffe and Derek Astle would use TMO 561 as part of a three-car team of TMOs to hopefully do well on BMC's home event.

Sutcliffe had shown well on the Acropolis Rally earlier in the year in 618 AOG, his first Abingdon drive, so was expected to go well on home soil.

They were entered into the touring car class (basically standard) because the only eligible grand touring class for the Mini was for cars of up to 1300cc, so the decision was clear. The standard engine was blueprinted, with no head- or port-polishing permitted, let alone a high-compression head.

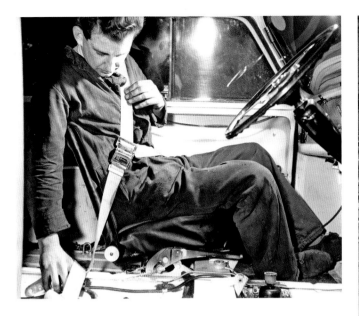

Den Green tries the seat belts on TMO 561 prior to the 1961 Monte; the lines running down the centre of the car with the starter switch clearly shown.

Derek Astle and Saville Woolley packing TMO 561 with all the equipment carried in the car - the extra weight must have been quite a handicap.

Derek Astle and Saville Woolley leave a time control on the 1961 Monte Carlo Rally.

The 2000-mile event from Blackpool to Scotland, finishing at Brands Hatch in Kent, was challenging, with the added introduction of a few special stages to sort out the winners. These were to prove important, so it was disappointing that Sutcliffe suffered time loss on the very rough stage near Inverkirkaig. Many others did likewise but the penalty was worse for Sutcliffe and Astle as they were high up in the general classification. Sutcliffe still managed to get the fastest time of the day on the Wolvery sprint.

Of the seven stages, the little works Minis between them won four. Erik Carlsson, the eventual winner, won the other three. So the Mini was showing that it had the performance, if well driven, which could mix it for high honours. Sutcliffe and Astle finished eighth overall.

Derek Astle would continue with the car for the following year's Monte Carlo Rally, this time as the driver and with Saville Woolley on the maps. Astle's drive was a one-off in the Mini but he would be in a works MG Midget later in the year on the RAC. Sadly, he was tragically killed in an ex-works Big Healey on the 1963 Tulip.

The Monte would see numerous changes to TMO 561: the sump guard was deleted and the front skirt reverted to a cut-down version to cool the brakes. The battery cable was run inside the car, along with the brake pipe down the centre tunnel sides. The navigator's seat was modified to recline, and both crew had the use of Britax seat belts. A central panel was fitted below the speedo for extra switches, and a rear-wheel-driven Smiths auxiliary speedo was installed with an odometer. The navigator had the use of two Heuer Autavia stopwatches; the driver had a Weston rev counter and a large oil warning light.

After the encouraging results on the RAC, hopes were high for the Monte, only for it to fall to pieces, with all three works Minis failing to finish. Astle's car was built to Group 2 regulations, allowing Abingdon to fit a high-compression cylinder head. But it was all for nothing, as he was eliminated when the car was hit by a landslide. This was a bitter disappointment to Abingdon, as it was clear from the Monte regulations that a small-capacity car, because of the handicap system, could so easily have won that year's Monte.

The final event for TMO 561 was the 1961 Tulip Rally. Unlike the previous year's event, the 1961 edition was far less of a challenge. That shouldn't detract from the superb 12th

WORKS MINIS IN DETAIL

TMO 561 being loaded onto a Channel Air Bridge Bristol Freighter to transport the team to the start of the Tulip Rally.

Peter Riley and Tony Ambrose on a stage of the 1961 Tulip Rally.

Peter Riley and Tony Ambrose all smiles with their class-winning laurels for their fine finish on the Tulip Rally.

place that Peter Riley and Tony Ambrose achieved in the car, as well as winning their class as Group 2 Appendix J car, even more so when you consider there were 132 cars entered that year.

The car appeared much as it had on the Monte, other than sporting an additional spotlight along the front bumper, and the door squares for the Tulip were black instead of white. Apart from losing their exhaust at one point, the Riley-Ambrose partnership worked well.

The Mini was beginning to make its mark, and with the Mini Cooper only a few months away, spirits were high at Abingdon about the prospects of the Mini soon becoming an outright winner – in the right hands.

TMO 561 was the most successful of the batch of three TMOs that had served well for a year-and-a-half. The car was sold to Ann Wisdom.

Competition Record

Date	Event	Crew	Number	Overall result	Class result
Nov 1959	RAC Rally	Ken James/Ian Hall	126	DNF	
Jan 1960	Monte Carlo Rally	Don Morley/Erle Morley	263	33rd	
May 1960	Tulip Rally	Tish Ozanne/Pat Allison	159	72nd	6th
June 1960	Alpine Rally	Tommy Gold/Mark Hughes	19	14th	1st
Nov 1960	RAC Rally	Mike Sutcliffe/Derek Astle	170	8th	4th
Jan 1961	Monte Carlo Rally	Derek Astle/Saville Woolley	226	DNF	
May 1961	Tulip Rally	Peter Riley/Tony Ambrose	136	12th	1st

CHAPTER 1: THE EARLY DAYS - THE MINI 850

Registration Number	First registered	Chassis number	Engine	Engine number	Model
617 AOG	Nov 1959	A/A2S7 7024	850cc	8A-U-H 6487	Austin Mini

The second batch of three 850 Minis to be delivered to Abingdon, all Austins, to balance the corporate requirement to use both Austin and Morris cars at Abingdon, arrived a month later, in November 1959. These three cars were registered in Birmingham, not Oxfordshire as many cars were. As all three were Austin cars, they would have been produced at Longbridge and registered locally before being dispatched to Abingdon.

These three cars were delivered whilst the first batch of TMO cars were being prepared for the forthcoming RAC Rally. The three AOG Austins would be prepared new for the Monte Carlo Rally the following January, and make up a six-car entry with the three TMO Morrises re-prepared after their RAC outing.

617 AOG had a relatively short stay at Abingdon and, unlike many of the early cars that did a lot of service over 18 months, it was used for just six months.

Its first event was the 1960 Monte Carlo Rally, crewed by Nancy Mitchell and Pat Allison. It was decided that the car would be prepared for the standard touring class, which – other than the additional crew and navigational equipment and a couple of extra fog lights – meant the car was basically standard. The engine's only treatment was the careful and selected assembly to optimise the standard components. The car was in fact first used as a recce car by Alec Pitts for the 1960 Monte Carlo Rally, so was not only quickly prepared, it was re-prepared in double-quick time once returned from the recce in time for the rally itself.

The troublesome primary gear oil seal had at last been cured, albeit the parts only became available after the car had left for the start in Oslo; Brian Moylan was dispatched from Abingdon and flew out to Norway to change the primary gear and block off an oil hole in the crank on all three of the works cars. To Nancy Mitchell's annoyance, her car was the last to be modified with the new parts but it was done in time for her to make the start.

The weather once out of Oslo was poor, and despite being fitted with the latest Dunlop Duraband studded tyres, progress was slow, made worse by numerous jackknifed lorries littering the main roads. Eventually, over an hour late, they went over their time limit (OTL) at Chambéry because they had earlier become marooned on a completely blocked Autobahn.

Tish Ozanne was given the car for the Geneva Rally in April; Pat Allison was again to co-drive, and the car now appeared in red bodywork indicating that perhaps the car or the body was changed. Making up a three-car team of AOGs, Tish was runner-up in their class behind the Morley twins' sister car,

Nancy Mitchell smiles at the crowd at the start of the 1960 Monte Carlo Rally with 617 AOG.

A determined Tish Ozanne and Pat Allison pressing on during the 1960 Geneva Rally.

and 27th overall.

Clearly the Mini's performance, now with some improved reliability, was beginning to make its mark. The car still being not a year old – not to mention the challenge of keeping a car designed for the distinct nurse (according to Alec Issigonis the designer) together and competitive over demanding terrain – was work in progress for the Abingdon team, but they were making progress.

With the good results from the Geneva Rally and further development in keeping the suspension together, particularly

Tish Ozanne talking to other competitors at a control on the Geneva Rally, with Tony Ambrose behind in 619 AOG.

Tish Ozanne and Pat Allison using their works car as a private entry on the 1961 Monte but in the BMC team.

until a passing bus took them (and the broken ball joint) to the next village, where a local blacksmith made good a repair and got them a lift back to the car – well outside their time, but mobile again.

Tish Ozanne was to buy 617 AOG from Abingdon, and went on to do the 1961 Monte Carlo Rally in the car, and again with Pat Allison but this time as private entrants in their ex-works car; they also tackled the Alpine Rally later the same year. On both occasions they were co-opted into the factory team and helped along the way with Abingdon service.

in retaining dampers in the place they were designed, Abingdon entered the Acropolis Rally with some optimism.

Sadly, the Greek terrain proved just too much for Tish Ozanne and Pat Allison's 850, and they retired early in the rally. Whilst the dampers stayed in place and the unit itself broke, it was the ultimate failure of the front suspension ball joint that saw the crew retire. They had to sleep in the car

Competition Record

Date	Event	Crew	Number	Overall result	Class result
Jan 1960	Monte Carlo Rally	Nancy Mitchell/Pat Allison	18	DNF	
April 1960	Geneva Rally	Tish Ozanne/Pat Allison	47	27th	2nd
May 1960	Acropolis Rally	Tish Ozanne/Pat Allison	120	DNF	

Registration Number	First registered	Chassis number	Engine	Engine number	Model
618 AOG	Nov 1959	A/A2S7 7045	850cc	8A-U-H 6603	Austin Mini

The second AOG car rather jumped the gun for the 1960 Monte for which it was being prepared, as the car was quickly prepared and dispatched to compete on the 1959 Portuguese rally.

Painted Farina Grey, 618 AOG was to be driven by the pairing of Peter Riley and Tony Ambrose to accompany Nancy Mitchell and Pat Allison in TJB 199. These two cars were extensively carrying out pre-Monte testing on a live event, and both cars finished the rally. With the cars on the Monte being entered in both the standard production touring class and the modified touring class, Peter Riley's was the tuned modified car and Nancy Mitchell's was the standard production car. In these early days, the difference between the output of the standard engine and that of the tuned unit was but 8bhp, with the standard 850 Mini producing 34bhp and the modified car 42bhp – but this represented nearly 25 per cent more power, so in Mini terms it was significant.

Before the Monte, however, 618 AOG was used for the recce, being driven by Don Morley and Erle Morley. It was then handed over for the Monte to Peter Riley who was teamed with Rupert Jones – no mean driver in his own right. As indicated above, the car was entered into the modified class

CHAPTER 1: THE EARLY DAYS - THE MINI 850

Peter Riley with Rev Rupert Jones on the 1960 Monte Carlo Rally in 618 AOG at the Gorges du Cians.

Peter Riley consults with Don Morley as they wait for their correct time at the Monte control.

with its engine's compression raised to 9:1 with a polished and ported cylinder head. It was one of the three works Minis that started from Oslo, and – in common with the other two Oslo starters – received the revised primary gear and crankshaft mod, which would hopefully alleviate the oil-onto-clutch problem that beset early Minis. To get in some practice before the Monte, Peter and Rupert spent time training on a skid pan back in the UK, which boosted their confidence for the snow and ice they were to meet once they had left Oslo.

Running the entire event on Dunlop Durabands, with their bolted in studs, was to make a significant difference to the car. However, the cold weather from Oslo also resulted in the carb icing up, which was resolved by Peter fixing a metal can to the air intake to allow hot air from the exhaust into the carb; this was another early change to the production of the Mini, brought about by competition in extreme environments. They arrived at Monte to be classified to take part in the mountain circuit, which entailed two loops up into the mountains behind Monte Carlo, with each loop having to be completed in the same time. They were soon delayed by helping the Morleys who were losing water in TMO 560 but got their time back and finished the event in 23rd place overall, which became the highest placing for an 850 Mini on the Monte Carlo Rally.

It was estimated that the cost to BMC for the seven-car assault on the Monte (six Minis and an A40 for Pat Moss) cost £10,000. No doubt money well spent.

Rupert Jones borrowed 618 AOG straight after the Monte to enter the Cambridge University Motor Club's Mini Monte and took Dunlop's David Hiam with him as navigator. In the terrible rain and snow conditions in Yorkshire and the Lakes, with 618 AOG still equipped with the Duraband spiked tyres from the Monte, he was at a distinct advantage and should have won the event, had he decided not to attempt part of the route that the organisers said was impassable – yes, he got stuck and lost sufficient time to relegate him to second place.

The next event that 618 AOG was prepared for was due to be the Sestriere Rally in Italy, a month after the Monte, where the car was to be driven by Nancy Mitchell. Tish Ozanne was also to take another works car for a dual attempt for the Coupe des Dames. Sadly, the rally was cancelled at the last minute due to bad weather – the Italian highway authority deeming the winter roads just too dangerous.

For the Geneva Rally in April, always a BMC favourite, 618 AOG was handed over to the Morley twins. Still entered into modified production class, the Morleys scored the Mini's first class win, including beating Erik Carlsson's Saab, and came 14th overall. Following on from the Monte, they were

The Morleys take a break on the 1960 Geneva Rally.

29

Don Morley waits to punch his time card in the Longines machine on the Geneva Rally. Tony Ambrose also waits, wearing two wristwatches.

618 AOG parked up by the Parthenon awaiting the start in Athens for the Acropolis Rally

encouraging results for a car so young in its competition development.

Hopes were high for a good result on the Acropolis Rally the following month, when 618 AOG was to be driven by new team members Mike Sutcliffe (who had previously competed in a works Riley 1.5) and Derek Astle. Disaster struck on the first stage when the car left the road; back on the road with help from the locals, it had lost 12 minutes – and with a mark lost per second, it was a loss they were unable to recover.

That didn't stop Mike Sutcliffe putting on a splendid performance on the last stage, a 30-minute race round the Tatoi circuit, Mike hurling the little Mini around the track, to the delight of all of the many spectators. Their reward was 31st overall and fifth in class, which reflected the penalty for going off early in the event.

One final duty for 618 AOG was for it to be used, once again, as a recce car, this time for the 1961 Monte and driven by Derek Astle. It was to be the last Abingdon appearance for 618 AOG, which had proved to be quite successful. The car was sold to Mike Sutcliffe.

The final stage on the Tatoi race circuit.

Competition Record

Date	Event	Crew	Number	Overall result	Class result
Dec 1959	Portuguese Rally	Peter Riley/Tony Ambrose	59	64th	
Jan 1960	Monte Carlo Rally	Peter Riley/Rupert Jones	110	23rd	
April 1960	Geneva Rally	Don Morley/Erle Morley	44	14th	1st
May 1960	Acropolis Rally	Mike Sutcliffe/Derek Astle	122	31st	5th

CHAPTER 1: THE EARLY DAYS - THE MINI 850

Registration Number	First registered	Chassis number	Engine	Engine number	Model
619 AOG	Nov 1959	A/A2S7 7046	850cc	8A-U-H 6492	Austin Mini

The final car of the three AOGs was delivered to Abingdon in November 1959 to be prepared for the Monte Carlo Rally the following January, along with its sister cars. The car was delivered in Speedwell Blue but would later reappear in Tartan Red monotone.

Being entered on the Monte into the standard production class meant 619 AOG was permitted few modifications, other than carefully building the engine to exacting standards in an attempt to achieve maximum performance. The car had a Helphos lamp attached to the windscreen, which was an additional lamp that could be moved from inside the car to find road signs or used to add extra light to the edge of the road. Later they were replaced by a movable lamp fixed to the roof of the car, until they were prohibited by the regulations.

Also of note on this car was the provision of an external thermometer fixed to the upper left corner of the windscreen, which was useful as a warning of the potential of ice on the road. The car also had the customary two auxiliary Lucas fog lamps, on brackets, fixed to the bumper and the front panel.

For the 1960 Monte, the car was driven by Tommy Wisdom, father of Ann Wisdom, Pat Moss's co-driver. Tommy was a

Gentleman Tommy Wisdom, with his trademark trilby hat, checks the oil on 619 AOG, where the external ice thermometer can be seen at the top corner of the windscreen.

Tommy Wisdom and Jack Hay leaving the Paris start on the 1960 Monte Carlo Rally.

619 AOG leaving a time control during the night, fitted with the Duraband tyres with bolt-through studs.

Alec Pitts and Tony Ambrose at full speed on the 1960 Geneva Rally.

Alec Pitts on the timed improvised slalom track with a very clean 619 AOG.

A very dapper John La Trobe and John Huntridge at the start of the 1960 Liège Rally with 619 AOG with its singleton spotlight in front of the offside indicator.

well-respected motoring journalist who, no doubt with one eye on publicity, Marcus Chambers signed up for the Monte drive. He was partnered by Jack Hay, and the pair had an eventful rally, finishing 55th overall despite rearranging the rear of the car against the scenery.

The Geneva Rally in the April saw Alec Pitts and Tony Ambrose take over a new car. Alec was an enthusiastic and determined privateer who was an early campaigner in the 850 Mini. This was his third drive for Abingdon, but once again an accident with Pitts at the wheel of a works Mini saw the car into retirement when they crashed into a mountain side. Charging around a blind bend at night, they were confronted with their path blocked by another competitor broadside across the road. Pitts had no option but to hit the side of the mountain, rather than going over the edge. The car was badly damaged and replaced by another 619 AOG, this time in monotone red.

Once again, 619 had a new crew for the demanding Acropolis Rally a month later. John Milne was getting his one and only drive in a Mini for Abingdon and was co-driven by Bill Bradley. Milne was a Scot, well-known to Marcus Chambers from his HRG days.

The cars for the Acropolis faced some of the roughest roads in Yugoslavia and Belgrade, so – starting in Trieste – all three of the AOG Minis faced a tough challenge. The cars were prepared for the worst, with attention to damper mountings and underside protection.

The special stages, mostly dry and dusty, caught out many, and Milne suffered a time-consuming puncture and was unable to claw back his time (despite overtaking many cars), due in no small part to the thick dust.

Milne got 619 AOG to the finish, just, but had no brakes left at all when the car was taken from the parc fermé to tackle the race circuit at Tatoi. The car was withdrawn but was nevertheless classified 16th overall out of just 35 cars that made it to the finish in Athens. This was a fine result for a rather low-slung car on such a rough event.

Next, 619 AOG was assigned to John La Trobe and John Huntridge to attempt the toughest rally in Europe, the Liège. Le Trobe was another successful driver in his own BMC car, who was given a one-off works drive. The 1960 event was a 3000-mile dash across Yugoslavia, Austria, Italy, Germany

John La Trobe on the 1960 Liège-Rome-Liège Rally, where we see a different-coloured 619 AOG.

Mike Sutcliffe and Derek Astle attending to suspension problems on the 1961 Acropolis.

and France, to be completed virtually non-stop in 90 hours.

Now appearing with red paintwork, 619 AOG had a new bodyshell after the Acropolis rally. The BMC works Healey team conquered the event, with Pat Moss winning outright, but of 83 crews that started the rally, a mere 13 were classified at the finish. Needless to say, the Mini wasn't one of them, as it expired in Yugoslavia with a failed fuel pump.

The car was loaned out in October to the Morley brothers, as a private entry, for the 1960 London Rally. A 600-mile road rally, it started from four different locations around the country (Birmingham, Taunton, Leeds and London) to converge in Wales where the real competition of the rally took place.

The event attracted a large field of 240 cars but the fog-bound route saw just 63 make it to the finish. Designed for private entrants, works participation was discouraged, and although a few works cars were loaned out by manufacturers to favoured drivers, it was officially classed a private entry for the Morleys.

Another new bodyshell was given to 619 AOG in the summer of 1961, as the existing bodyshell was hastily given to Don Moore to rebuild for Christabel Carlisle, who had written off her race car CMC 77 in practice at Silverstone in early July 1961. The work to reshell Carlisle's car was completed in a day, and she raced the next day at Silverstone in 619 AOG's bodyshell – but now with CMC 77 on the bonnet – and came 12th overall.

The final event for 619 was again the Acropolis, a year later in 1961, where the car was handed over to Mike Sutcliffe and Derek Astle. Development of the 850 Mini, with the Mini Cooper now about to be launched, had effectively stopped, although these later cars were in effect Mini Cooper prototypes, testing numerous bits and pieces that would find their way into the production Cooper.

Their event was a litany of problems, when early on a damper mounting failed, and – despite several attempts – was unable to be properly repaired. With the almost-ineffective damper, the steering ball joint eventually collapsed, but with a great deal of improvisation they effected a roadside repair – only to have the head gasket fail within striking distance of the finish. The car was sold to Arnold Farrar.

Competition Record

Date	Event	Crew	Number	Overall result	Class result
Jan 1960	Monte Carlo Rally	Tommy Wisdom/Jack Hay	229	55th	
April 1960	Geneva Rally	Alec Pitts/Tony Ambrose	45	DNF	
May 1960	Acropolis Rally	John Milne/Bill Bradley	124	16th	4th
Sept 1960	Liège Rally	John La Trobe/John Huntridge	54	DNF	
Oct 1960	London Rally	Don Morley/Erle Morley			
May 1961	Acropolis Rally	Mike Sutcliffe/Derek Astle	115	DNF	

WORKS MINIS IN DETAIL

Registration Number	First registered	Chassis number	Engine	Engine number	Model
363 DOC	March 1961	A/A2S7 97971A	850cc	8AM-U-H 136551	Austin Seven

Don Morley and Ann Wisdom all set and ready to go on the 1961 Acropolis Rally.

Delivered to Abingdon in March 1961, 363 DOC, painted Tartan Red, was registered in Birmingham – unlike nearly all of the cars that followed, which were registered in Oxfordshire. This Austin Mini was prepared for a three-car attempt on the 1961 Acropolis, an event for which the Mini seemed unsuited but one that they kept plugging away at. The rough terrain was often the undoing of the Mini, with its poor ground clearance, and the car was basically under-developed for such a rough event. All three Minis failed to finish.

Don Morley was assigned to drive the new car, partnered this time by Ann Wisdom rather than his brother Erle. This was to be only the second time the brothers wouldn't compete together in more than two-dozen rallies during their time at Abingdon.

Entered in the modified class, this gave the car some extra power but it was suspension strengthening and protection that was badly needed. A broken top damper mounting was repaired, but Don and Ann's ultimate departure from the Acropolis was dramatic and frightening: travelling very fast and trying to overtake a much slower Alfa Zagato, when the Alfa braked hard for an approaching corner, the Mini shot off the road and rolled seven times down a near-vertical slope, coming to rest some 75ft below. Ann, who was wearing full harness, was quite unharmed, while Don – secured by a lap belt – sustained a small cut and a black eye. Result: one scrapped Mini.

By then, Marcus Chambers had departed Abingdon to run the service department at Appleyards in Yorkshire. His replacement was Stuart Turner, who took over the reins on 1 September 1961, which coincidentally was the official launch date of the Mini Cooper. Great timing!

With the Mini Cooper now in full production and available for Abingdon to use, it was strange that the team continued to campaign the 850 Mini, albeit on just a few more events. As a new 363 DOC was needed to replace the rolled car from

It all ended in a massive accident, flying off the road and landing 75ft below.

Reverends Rupert Jones and Philip Morgan by 363 DOC before their departure for the 1962 Monte Carlo.

Greece, it is even more surprising that it was replaced with another underpowered car.

However, the attraction of a class win was the motivation for the car being entered in the 1962 Monte Carlo Rally. The handicap system for 1962 seemed to favour a standard small-engined production car, but 363 DOC was entered into the GT class (for modified production cars) as, once again, many Cooper parts were fitted to increase its performance.

This also had a good publicity potential, as the car was to be driven by Reverend Rupert Jones and accompanied by fellow vicar Philip Morgan as co-driver. Philip had done a little rallying but was a Mini driver, so time was spent getting him his international licence by accompanying Rupert on smaller events in the UK prior to the Monte. The sight of two dog-collar-wearing clergymen in a works Mini, albeit an 850, on the Monte was just too good an opportunity to miss. Abingdon did its bit to fuel the publicity by painting a dog-collar stripe on the bonnet and a halo on the roof!

The BMC works entry for the 1962 Monte was diverse in the extreme, which must have made servicing a nightmare. Apart from the lone 850 Mini, Abingdon entered seven other cars, two of which were new Mini Coopers but also an A110 Westminster, MG Midget, MGA, Healey 3000 and finally a Riley 1.5. Stuart Turner must have had a migraine for the entire rally...

Starting from Glasgow to get maximum publicity, the pair of vicars had a relatively easy run to Monte Carlo. However, on arrival they were informed that their class had been amalgamated with the class above because one in their class failed to start. This rather negated their plans for a class win, as they had arrived leading their class by a good margin.

They finished third in the amalgamated class and 77th overall, which was still a very good result. To add to the publicity, Rupert Jones completed the final Grand Prix circuit wearing his dog collar – it was not actually planned but he had to complete some religious duties in the morning at the local church, and didn't have time to return to his hotel to change clothing.

The final event for 363 DOC, and the very last event for a works 850 Mini, was in May 1962 on the Tulip Rally, where David Seigle-Morris was partnered with Tony Ambrose. The car was entered into the touring class, so did not have the benefit of a modified engine. The handicap system on the Tulip favoured standard production cars, which BMC was certain would secure a win. But the car did not last long,

The vicars charged through the night on their studded tyres on ice-covered tarmac.

having been withdrawn after the first special test around part of the Nürburgring when it left the road and managed to get stuck. Extricating the Mini took ages, and the great loss of time rendered any further participation futile, so 363 DOC was withdrawn.

It was rather a sad end to the car's rather odd time at Abingdon, where it was largely being overshadowed by the new Mini Cooper.

Rupert Jones pushes the car hard on the Grand Prix circuit at Monaco.

Competition Record

Date	Event	Crew	Number	Overall result	Class result
May 1961	Acropolis Rally	Don Morley/Ann Wisdom	117	DNF	
Jan 1962	Monte Carlo Rally	Rupert Jones/Philip Morgan	97	77th	3rd
May 1962	Tulip Rally	David Seigle-Morris/Tony Ambrose	142	DNF	

WORKS MINIS IN DETAIL

CHAPTER 2:
THE MINI COOPER

737 ABL was the most successful Mini Cooper, driven by Pat Moss to two outright wins (seen here winning the ladies' award on the 1962 Monte Carlo Rally) and Pauline Mayman. There were only six works Mini Coopers – all 997cc.

The Mini Cooper was officially launched in July 1961, with deliveries being made in September. It was just what Abingdon wanted: a more powerful Mini. Whilst the handling of the Mini was unrivalled, it lacked the power to be an outright winner.

The concept of the Mini Cooper had been in gestation for a good while, with Abingdon trying and testing modified parts on the Mini whenever regulations allowed. However, it was John Cooper who, as a successful constructor of Grand Prix cars – having won two constructors' championships – was to give his name to the new machine (and get £2 royalties per car).

John had already gained experience in designing and building single-seater Formula Junior race cars with A-series BMC engines, and it was this experience that would be used in the new Mini Cooper. Using his knowledge, he had tried to persuade the Mini's designer – his great friend of Alec Issigonis – to make a high-performance Mini, but Issigonis was indifferent to the idea, still insisting his Mini was designed as a people's car for a family of four to go on holiday and for the district nurse to get about in. It was not meant to be a sports car.

However, John Cooper would not be put off and went to the top – to BMC's managing director George Harriman – to convince him that a high-performance Mini would be in demand. Harriman gave John a car to take away and modify as he thought fit, which effectively involved fitting a modified Formula Junior engine into the car, along with some experimental small disc brakes that he'd persuaded Lockheed to supply.

John took the finished prototype back to Harriman at Longbridge, who test-drove the car and agreed there and then to put it into production. John did warn him that they would need to produce 1000 to get the car homologated, which, despite early misgivings, was easily achieved once the car was successfully introduced.

In no time at all, the humble Mini went from a 34bhp basic road car to a 55bhp sports car with a top speed of 85mph (and which soon turned into a 70bhp rally winner once it had been tuned and modified by Abingdon). There was also an added bonus that the engine was more reliable than that of the 850 Mini.

Its size was increased to 997cc, neatly just under the one-litre class category, using a basic block with reduced bore but an increased stroke on the crank. The engine now had twin carburettors, a tubular exhaust manifold, a camshaft with an increased overlap, and the cylinder head was modified with larger valves and double valve springs. All this was topped off with a close-ratio gearbox, and it also saw the end of the 'magic wand' gearstick, as a neat remote shift was made for the Mini Cooper. With the extra power came the need for better brakes, which was served by novel little 7in discs on the front wheels. Back then, disc brakes were still the preserve of sports cars.

A happy coincidence (or just good planning) also came into play during September 1961, when the Mini Cooper was released to the public, because it saw Stuart Turner take over the reins at Abingdon from Marcus Chambers. Stuart Turner was, at the time, a very successful navigator, both at club and international level, and had won the 1960 RAC Rally alongside Erik Carlsson.

Trained as an accountant, the lure of motorsport got the better of him, and he became the rally correspondent at *Motoring News*; from there he was approached by John Thornley, the general manager at MG, to take over the mantle at Abingdon. Marcus Chambers was instrumental in Stuart's appointment, having recommended him for the position. With a scant handover during September, when both Stuart and Marcus journeyed out on the Liège Rally to enable Stuart to see the team at work first-hand, he was, come October, at the age of just 28, in charge of what was to become one of the most successful competition departments in the world.

By this time, now under the stewardship of Stuart Turner, Abingdon had more or less standardised red and white as the preferred colour scheme for works Minis. The story goes, according to Willy Cave (one of the most experienced co-drivers), that the colour scheme had been chosen because Italian level-crossing operators (gates were manually-controlled back then) would open the gates for red rally cars (as they were assumed to be Italian) and shut them for all other colours, thus delaying them… Maybe not entirely true, but it sounds plausible.

The white roof was used as it kept the inside of the car cooler than a black roof would. This colour scheme, of course, had been used on works Healeys for a long while. It should also be noted that red and white was not a standard colour option back then, and most Abingdon Minis were delivered from the factories – be it from Cowley for a Morris or Longbridge for an Austin – in Tartan Red with a black roof, the roof colour being repainted Old English White at Abingdon.

Abingdon was soon to begin its own development on the 997 Cooper engine, although it was certainly powerful enough to start with, after the little 850 Mini. Different camshafts were experimented with, using a 731 cam, which gave more power but at the expense of low-down torque, while still allowing the engine to rev to 7000rpm. The standard 948 camshaft was generally used to give better low-speed pick-up.

All six works Mini Coopers – and there were only six – were Morrises, and all were 997cc cars. Abingdon did not use the later 998cc Mini Cooper, which was not announced until January 1964.

Cliff Humphries was beginning to take over the responsibility of building the works engine, once the domain of the mechanics building the cars, and in conjunction with Eddie Maher (who was chief of engines, based in Coventry) the pair explored, modified and developed the engine to produce a reliable 70bhp. Eddie Maher would continue development work on the Cooper and the Cooper S, which was soon to follow, right through the Abingdon era, including much work with the race Coopers used in the 1969 season.

The Cooper was launched to the press at the military test track at Chobham in July, where numerous Grand Prix drivers were on hand to demonstrate the car's potential – and at £680, it was well received. History will show that the Mini Cooper appealed to a different group of people to that of the 850 Mini and, apart from proving to be a very useful competition car, it became fashionable to own and be seen in a Cooper – which did the sales of the car no harm at all. Furthermore, being used by Abingdon in competition was a superb shop window for the new wonder car, dubbed the 'ten-foot tornado' by Wilson McComb, the editor of *Safety Fast!*, the MG Car Club magazine. It was just the start of the Mini Cooper's meteoric rise.

WORKS MINIS IN DETAIL

Registration Number	First registered	Chassis number	Engine	Engine number	Model
737 ABL	Nov 1961	KA2S7 165317	997cc	9F-SA-H 617	Morris Cooper

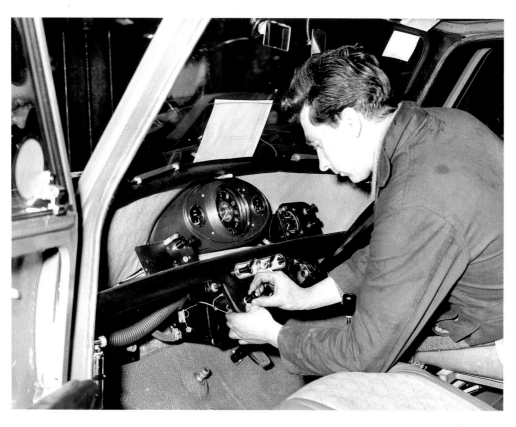

Gerald Wiffen fitting up the rather basic dashboard arrangement for 737 ABL for the 1962 Monte Carlo Rally.

Pat Moss on the Monaco Grand Prix Circuit with her class-winning Mini Cooper.

With the new much-awaited (by Abingdon at least) Mini Cooper being announced in September 1961, it was a surprise that it took until the following January for the car to be blooded in active competition, with Abingdon seeming to use the Big Healey, almost exclusively, since May when the last of the 850 Minis appeared on the Acropolis Rally.

With Stuart Turner now in place at Abingdon, replacing Marcus Chambers, it was a doubly exciting new dawn for the competitions department. Its first Mini Cooper, a Morris, was delivered to Abingdon and registered in November as 737 ABL. The car was dispatched from Cowley in standard Tartan Red bodywork with a black roof (which is correct, by the way, despite a well-known model of the car being widely sold with green and black paintwork; how did the manufacturer make such a mistake?)

With a car that now had 55bhp in standard form, it was in percentage terms a massive increase in power from the 34bhp 850 Mini, which even when tuned and modified was reaching only 42bhp. The Mini Cooper, on the other hand, when tuned and modified, was soon producing 70bhp, which, it should be noted, was the same power output as the 1071cc Cooper S that was to follow in March 1963. However, we are getting ahead of ourselves here, but it just illustrates how powerful the works Mini Cooper was.

Having extolled the amount of power available from the Mini Cooper, it was decided that because of the prevailing handicap system for the 1962 Monte, Abingdon would enter an unmodified car in the series-production one-litre class for Pat Moss and Ann Wisdom. Pat Moss was once again favourite for the Coupe des Dames, which she had won for the past two years, and winning it again would mean she would retain the trophy for good.

It was only Pat's second drive in a works Mini and the first for the Mini Cooper. Although in the standard production class, where no modifications were allowed, the car was stripped out of much of its trim to save weight, as the sum of the extra rally equipment still meant the car was within the specified homologated weight of 585kg (1289lbs). The car also ran a right-hand fuel tank with quick-lift Aston filler caps. Inside the car, by now the familiar Abingdon dash tins were being fitted to house the extra gauges and switches that the driver and co-driver had at their disposal It also had a

Pat Moss and Ann Wisdom collecting their Coupe Des Dames at the prize-giving ceremony on the 1962 Monte Carlo Rally.

Pat Moss having the spark plugs changed whilst pushing the car into the time control on the Tulip Rally.

Pat Moss giving an interview after the Tulip Rally win. Note the radio aerial in the rear above the boot - most unusual.

sump guard and three additional lights.

Starting from Oslo, the uncharacteristically good weather meant they would begin with non-spiked tyres but had reserve tyres waiting at Frankfurt, Liège and Chambéry. Much to Pat Moss's annoyance, on the very first stage, the Col du Granier, the car's throttle cable broke loose and for part of the stage Pat had to operate the throttle by pulling a piece of improvised wire. It was thought that hasty preparation had been at fault – something not typical of Abingdon. The delay in fixing the throttle cost five minutes and dropped the pair out of contention, finishing 26th but still winning the Coupe des Dames. Without the throttle problem they would have been 4th overall, which would have been a brilliant result for the new car.

For the Tulip Rally in May, Pat Moss and Ann Wisdom were again to use 'Able' (as 737 ABL was often known). The car, with the standard full-width skirt beneath the bumper, appeared at the start with metal removed at the ends to aid brake cooling. This would appear on production bodyshells but not until late in 1964.

Before the event, Pat's life was turned upside down when Stirling Moss was seriously injured in a Goodwood accident in April, which would end his career. Pat decided it best to continue the Tulip Rally, which she dominated by being fastest in her class on every one of the 18 stages.

This year's Tulip was again using the class improvement scheme, which was not much liked by most competitors, and open to be manipulated. It is also quite likely that the sharp brain of Stuart Turner turned it to BMC's advantage: to their surprise, because of the system, Pat and Ann discovered they had won the event outright. They, of course, also won the Coupe des Dames, and at last the Mini had won its first international rally. The Mini had come of age.

It was to be the last event for the pairing, as Ann Wisdom, who had recently married Peter Riley, had already decided to retire after the Tulip because she was pregnant and did not feel it was right to risk the life of her unborn child as well as her own. What an event to finish her career on – a fitting end to a great partnership.

With Ann Wisdom now in retirement, a new female co-driver was needed. Stuart Turner suggested to Pat Moss that Pauline Mayman would be a good choice. Pat was initially reluctant because she considered Pauline a driver, not a

Pat Moss changed navigators to Pauline Mayman for the Baden-Baden Rally, which she won, making it two in a row for ABL.

Pat Moss and Pauline Mayman waiting at a start control for the 1962 Geneva Rally.

for the Baden-Baden rally in September. Despite the rally being badly organised and subject to the class improvement handicap system, Moss stormed through the event, and by finishing fourth on scratch, the handicap elevated them to overall winners. In the process they outwitted the calculating Mercedes team, who had tried to manipulate the class improvement system, only to have it backfire when it rained on the last stage, preventing the Merc from putting in the time it needed. The girls once again won the Coupe des Dames and their class. This was the second international win for the works Mini.

The Geneva Rally in October saw Able with the now-familiar red-and-white livery, the roof colour having been changed from black to white. It is suggested that the reason that the roof was painted white was to reduce the heat inside the car when the car was used in hot climates. However, works Healeys and MGs had white hard-tops years before. Certainly, under Stuart Turner's tenure, the roofs had been painted white, but quite who initiated the idea is open to debate.

On arrival at the start, the crew was disappointed to learn that because of low numbers in their class, they were to be amalgamated into the next class. Undeterred, Pat Moss still put in a fine performance and won the amalgamated class anyway, despite strong opposition from more powerful cars, and came home third overall, plus winning again the Coupe des Dames. This fine result also meant Pat was also crowned as the European Ladies' Rally Champion.

It was, however, the last time Pat Moss was to drive a works Mini – a car with which she was never really happy. She did the RAC Rally in a Healey, and by the end of the year her name was on a Ford contract, despite Stuart Turner's best efforts – but the £7000-a-year offer from the Blue Oval was way above the £2000 ceiling Turner was able to offer.

Not to be outdone, Turner was quick to sign up Val Domleo from Ford, who was Ann Hall's co-driver, thus depriving Pat Moss of a top navigator at Ford. This change at Abingdon saw Pauline Mayman swap over to the driver's seat and Val Domleo become her regular navigator. To sweeten the deal, Val, who was having difficultly getting time off from her employer to go rallying, was taken on at BMC as a materials researcher and thus could freely have all the time off she needed. Quite a neat bit of rallymanship by Mr Turner, as Pat Moss had a new employer but now no co-driver. She was not best pleased!

The new pairing of Pauline Mayman and Val Domleo took Able to the Monte Carlo Rally in early 1963. For the Monte at their Paris start, the car had grown a set of headlight washers and, from the Abingdon trim shop, a full grille muff. It also had demister bars on each half of the windscreen in addition to the Perspex heat deflector fixed to the top of the dash rail – all in an attempt to keep the front 'screen clear in the cold weather.

navigator, but she agreed to try the partnership, which proved to be very successful. Pauline, although having started out as a club navigator, had raced single seaters, saloons and sports cars before taking up rally driving, so Pat's doubts were not without foundation. Pauline, however, showed she was very competent on the maps and could be relied upon to drive well when needed.

The new partnership had now competed in four rallies in Healeys and 1100s by the time they took Able to Germany

Pauline Mayman with Val Domleo on the Col du Turini on the 1963 Monte Carlo Rally.

All the BMC cars this year were carrying snow chains and the crews had practised putting these fiddly things on the wheels. With 1963 being such a bleak winter, poor weather was anticipated throughout the route and BMC carefully selected differing routes to hedge their bets, should one area be adversely affected by heavy snow. Once again, the Monte had invented its own handicap system called 'factor of comparison' based on engine size and group, the net result being Group 3 GT cars had to achieve times about eight per cent faster than a standard production car, so a small-capacity standard car was favoured for the win.

It was sensible, therefore, that Able was prepared and entered in the standard-production Group 1 class, as effectively an unmodified car. Even so, there was much that Abingdon could still do to improve the standard car. Built by Cliff Humphries, who would soon become responsible for most of the engines that came out of the comps department, Able received all the usual attention to detail to obtain the maximum out of the car. The cylinder head was slightly skimmed to raise the compression to 9.2:1 from 9:1 (every little helps); twin 1½ SUs were used, with MME needles and red springs; the transmission was standard, apart for having straight-cut gears, plus the Abingdon-preferred 4.1 diff; the suspension was raised with 3/16in washers and Armstrong dampers, with the front subframe carefully rewelded.

Once again, the car used the Mory radiator blind and also an external grille muff. The electrics, still powered by a dynamo, received the full Abingdon treatment, with the battery turned around, with the terminals away from the tank and the cable lengthened. The all-important lights were Lucas 700 fog lamps with yellow bulbs and a single Cyclops 576 spot lamp – also with a yellow bulb. The car was fitted with both a brake and rear light cut-off switch, obviously designed

The Grand Prix Circuit race at the end of the Monte was always a crowd puller.

Pat Moss and Pauline Mayman about to collect more silverware after the class win on the 1962 Geneva Rally.

WORKS MINIS IN DETAIL

Pauline Mayman with Val Domleo finished 21st on the 1963 Tulip Rally.

to fool following cars over the stages.

The exhaust, specially made by Abingdon, was held in place by Healey gearbox mounting rubbers. Quick-release Aston caps were used on the twin tanks, which had the standard single pump on the subframe protected by a small plate – the fuel lines ran outside protected by metal channelling; the brake line, however, ran inside the car. Restall reclining seats were fitted for both the ladies, with Britax lap and diagonal seat belts; Mayman also used a wooden steering wheel. The bonnet and boot lid were lightened, and Perspex windows were used to save weight. Extra equipment carried included a shovel, ice pick and a jemmy bar. They were obviously expecting trouble!

As predicted, the vast majority of the route was either snow or ice-covered and proved a real challenge. The girls came home 28th overall and fourth in class but unscathed – nearly 250 cars had retired, with just 94 at the finish. All four works Mini Coopers finished and dominated their class entirely.

On their return to Abingdon, the girls reported that the car handled superbly well and the only real complaint was that the heating system was just not up to the freezing conditions they experienced, making visibility through the frozen 'screen a real problem – even reporting items in the door pocket froze together!

After the cold of the Monte, the Tulip Rally in April was a welcome change, and Mayman and Domleo were again entered in Able. By now the car was becoming well used, and with the Abingdon cycle of building a car new for an event, then using it on a recce and rebuilding for the next event, it had spent extensive time with the Abingdon mechanics.

Cliff Humphries again prepared the girls' car, this time as a Group 2, which allowed for more modifications. Compression was further raised to 9.5:1, this time with polished ports and inlet manifold. Cliff, when testing the car, reported that it would do 0-to-60mph in 9.2 seconds and pull 7200 revs. The headlights were now tripod type, and they reverted to white bulbs after complaints on the Monte about the yellow bulbs – no surprise there. Nevertheless, the new headlights were not well received, and were soon abandoned after the event due to their poor light output.

However, Able was proving to be one of the most reliable cars Abingdon would have. The Tulip was again using a handicap system but this seemed to work well, as there appeared no manipulation or withdrawal by Mercedes this time and the rally was won by a big Ford Falcon. Nevertheless, three stages had to be cancelled because of snow – such was the winter of '63 all over Europe. Mayman and Domleo had a trouble-free run on the Tulip and, other than breaking the navigator's seat, they had an uneventful run, finishing 21st overall and fourth in their class. In truth, Mayman was finding it hard to match the successes that Pat Moss achieved in the car.

The last event for this much-used works Mini was the Trifels Rally in Germany in the May. On this event, it all came good for Pauline where they won their class and the Coupe des Dames plus the award for the best foreign crew. Able was to be used once more, this time as a recce car for the 1963 Alpine where Terry Hunter and Denise McCluggage drove.

So Able was retired on a high, and sold to P Anton, who was the secretary of the Wolverhampton and District Motor Club.

Competition Record

Date	Event	Crew	Number	Overall result	Class result
Jan 1962	Monte Carlo Rally	Pat Moss/Ann Wisdom	304	26th	7th, CdD
May 1962	Tulip Rally	Pat Moss/Ann Wisdom	104	1st	1st, CdD
Sept 1962	Baden-Baden	Pat Moss/Pauline Mayman	85	1st	1st, CdD
Oct 1962	Geneva Rally	Pat Moss/Pauline Mayman	135	3rd	1st
Jan 1963	Monte Carlo Rally	Pauline Mayman/Val Domleo	58	28th	4th
April 1963	Tulip Rally	Pauline Mayman/Val Domleo	129	21st	4th
May 1963	Trifels Rally	Pauline Mayman/Val Domleo			1st, CdD

CHAPTER 2: THE MINI COOPER

Registration Number	First registered	Chassis number	Engine	Engine number	Model
407 ARX	March 1962	KA2S4 222450	997cc	9F-SA-H 4203	Morris Cooper

Two Mini Coopers were delivered to Abingdon to be registered in March 1962, both Morris Coopers. Delivered in Tartan red with a black roof, 407 ARX was soon changed to have an Old English White roof, as this was now the normal colour scheme for works Minis.

The first event the car entered was the Alpine Rally in June. It was also the first works Mini drive for Rauno Aaltonen, who had impressed Stuart Turner several years before when he watched him drive a big Mercedes with great skill and speed. He was also co-opted into the works team for the 1962 Monte Carlo Rally when he was co-driving with Geoff Mabbs in 11 NYB, Geoff's Mini Cooper that had been prepared at Abingdon. Although Aaltonen was listed as a co-driver, he did in fact drive most of the stages to great effect and was heading for a good finish when he clipped a protruding rock on the Col de Turini with the sliding tail of the car, which flipped it onto its roof. The car was soon ablaze, and it was only due to Geoff Mabbs's bravery that he managed to extract Aaltonen from the burning Mini.

From that accident, Abingdon revised its seat belts because the melting belt had prevented Geoff from extracting Aaltonen quickly. It was felt the car caught fire because the fuel tank shorted out across the battery, but it is also likely that the fuel pump continued to pump and sprayed petrol onto the hot exhaust; it may have been both reasons.

However, Stuart Turner signed Aaltonen on the strength of that performance, and his first event was in a works MGA on the Tulip Rally in April. Rauno Aaltonen would prove to be the most successful works Mini driver, becoming European Champion in 1965, and competing in 41 rallies in works Minis.

For the Alpine, always a favourite with many drivers, Abingdon entered the lone Mini Cooper amongst a four-car Healey onslaught on the event. Aaltonen was co-driven by Gunnar Palm, who would in turn become one of the great co-drivers, although not with BMC.

Prepared as a Group 2 car, 407 ARX was allowed a good number of modifications, which would see it pushing out 70bhp. With the handicap, it was still expected that the Mini Cooper could do well, especially with the very fast young Finn at the wheel. Sadly, the car ran into trouble early in the first leg out of Marseille on the Mont Ventoux, with gearbox problems due to overheating, which was often a problem with transmissions on the Alpine. However, the opposition had time to note the car and driver's startling performance before they retired, as they had been second fastest touring car on the Col de l'Espigoulier. BMC won the rally and the team prize with the Healeys – still the best weapon in Abingdon's arsenal for such events.

For 407ARX's next event, Rauno Aaltonen was teamed with Tony Ambrose, a co-driver he would stay with until Ambrose retired in 1966 after the Monte – a formidable partnership. The 1000 Lakes in Finland, tackled in August, is a very fast and specialised event, dominated by Scandinavian drivers, so hopes were high for Aaltonen to do well. He had won the rally the previous year, driving a Mercedes 220, so the nimble

Rauno Aaltonen and Gunnar Palm on Mont Ventoux during the 1962 Alpine Rally.

Timo Mäkinen teamed with John Steadman for the 1962 RAC Rally.

Mini Cooper was expected to shine. The car was prepared to sustain the pounding of high jumps and landings, but 407 ARX posted another DNF when it retired with mechanical problems.

The 1962 RAC Rally saw Abingdon enter a large team of eight cars for the home event, including three Mini Coopers. Again, 407 ARX was prepared as a Group 2, given to a new signing to BMC: Timo Mäkinen. He was teamed with John Steadman to guide him through the 2200-mile route from Blackpool, up to Inverness and back down to Bournemouth; and with the RAC using (for the first time) 300 miles of forest stages, it was to be a good test for Mäkinen.

At the time, Timo spoke virtually no English, so Steadman invented 'Finglish' to communicate. Timo was just told to drive the car around, get some experience and bring it back to the finish. He did just that and returned in seventh place, winning the class.

Mäkinen proved to be without doubt the fastest Mini driver and, although very hard on his car (particularly on the transmission, due in no small part to his left-foot braking

A cheerful Paddy Hopkirk with fancy headgear with Jack Scott at a control on the 1963 Monte Carlo Rally. Note the snow shovel on the rear parcel shelf and twin heater elements on the windscreen.

407 ARX being prepared for the 1963 Monte Carlo at Abingdon by Tommy Wellman, with 977 ARX in the foreground with Brian Moylan.

necessitating clutchless gearchanges), he would either win any event he entered or retire with a mechanical problem. He hardly ever crashed a Mini – he was just scintillatingly quick and a trail blazer, which would often result in the opposition crashing out or breaking their cars trying to catch the original flying Finn. As an aside, because of contractual obligations with a Finnish BMC importer, Timo always drove a Morris during his time at Abingdon.

The Monte Carlo Rally in 1963 saw Paddy Hopkirk take over the car with Jack Scott in the co-driver seat. Jack Scott had been a regular navigator with Paddy in Ireland and the two Irishmen got on very well. Jack's business, however, meant he retired in 1963. This was to be Paddy's first works Mini drive, which would be the start of a massively successful career, making him a household name.

Paddy actually joined BMC to get his hands on the works Healey: he'd tried Pat Moss's car and had been so impressed with it that he wrote a pleading letter to Stuart Turner in June 1962, asking for a BMC drive. Aided and abetted by pressure from John Thornley, history will show Stuart Turner offering Paddy a contract was a brilliant move. Paddy had two drives with the Healey since joining the team in September 1962 but Turner decided to try him in the Mini for the Monte the following January – and it would be the first of many.

The actual car prepared for the Monte, despite its registration number, was in fact a brand new Mini – 17 CRX, registered in December 1962. As Abingdon had decided to enter the car in Group 1, and to ease the preparation schedule, it was easier to use a new car that hadn't been modified for Group 2, as indeed 407 ARX had been for Mäkinen on the RAC. In addition and, more importantly, the car would have sustained a great deal of wear and tear on the RAC with 300

Hopkirk charging through the mountains with studded tyres on what looks like dry tarmac.

Hopkirk on the final race around the Monaco Grand Prix circuit.

miles of forests, and it is likely the car was sold off.

Hopkirk's car for the Monte was built by Brian Moylan and, although a Group 1 car was, as always, built very carefully to get the most out of the little Mini Cooper, using slightly-raised compression and larger 1½ SUs (being a permissible alternative in Group 1). The gearbox was straight-cut and was mated to a 4.1 diff. The front mounting for the Armstrong dampers still used a modified bracket, and the suspension was raised at the front by using a rocker cover distance piece. Microcell bucket and recliner were used, with Britax lap and diagonal belt and a full harness belt for Scott. Hopkirk also kept his wood-rim steering wheel.

Perspex windows and a lightened bonnet and boot were used, which allowed the car, including the rally equipment, to keep within the homologated weight of 584.8kg (1289lbs). The new car was prepared almost identically to 737 ABL for the Monte, having a set of headlight washers and a full grille muff plus the demister bars on each half of the windscreen, with Perspex heat deflector on the top of the dash. The car was also carrying snow chains.

The weather on the '63 Monte was very cold, and despite starting from Paris, the roads were challenging. With the Monte Carlo handicap system (based on engine size and group) it was prudent that it was entered in the standard production Group 1 class, as effectively an unmodified car. Europe's severe winter of 1963 meant the vast majority of the route was either snow- or ice-covered, which eliminated all of the entrants from Athens and Lisbon.

Hopkirk took to the Mini immediately and finished a creditable sixth overall, and was fastest on the manoeuvrability test at the finish – skills honed on Irish driving tests (later to be called autotests). Hopkirk's only complaint of the car was the poor heating and demisting – and he also suggested that bigger diameter wheels, as fitted to the 1100 range, could be an advantage. He was astonished at the car's handling and performance, being totally convinced on front-wheel drive in poor conditions.

After the Monte, the London Motor Club organised what was later to become known as a rallycross event at Brands

The birth of rallycross way back in 1963 - 407 ARX still with its Monte plate comes close to Pat Moss's Anglia.

Timo Mäkinen with Logan Morrison at the start of the 1963 Tour de France.

Hatch for the BBC Grandstand sports television programme; the concept was thought up by Raymond Baxter, so he can be credited with inventing rallycross. The course, down one of the access roads and back behind the pits, was a great hit, and much fun was had by the many British Monte Carlo Rally entrants who were invited. Hopkirk, with his Monte car, had a race-long battle in 407 ARX with Pat Moss in her works Anglia, but came second behind a hard-charging Mäkinen in his works Healey 3000, who won this inaugural rallycross event.

The Scottish Rally in the June was the next event for 407 ARX, where Logan Morrison, navigated by Donald Brown, took not Hopkirk's Monte car (and the BBC Grandstand car) but the 407 ARX that Mäkinen had used on the previous RAC Rally for his home international. The Scottish was now an all-stage event, which was very hard on the cars, so to use Mäkinen's stronger (albeit hard-driven) RAC car was a sensible choice.

The crew crashed out in spectacular style whilst comfortably leading the rally. Morrison had been fastest on all seven stages in 407 ARX when on the eighth, the Culbin Sands forest stage, the car suffered suspension failure that caused a driveshaft to seize. The car rolled several times as it came out of a corner, scattering its windscreen and windows along the track. Fortunately, neither Morrison nor Brown was hurt but they landed in the trees in a much deranged and narrower Mini. The car was not used again.

The Tour de France saw the car in Mäkinen's hands again, this time with Logan Morrison sitting alongside. The Tour was one of the toughest events in Europe, of around 3600 miles journeying around most of France on racetracks and hillclimbs. For the event, the car had identification stripes painted on the bonnet and boot lid, to aid recognition from the pits as all of the works Minis looked the same as they steamed past. There was a single stripe on the driver's side of 407 ARX, and – for the spectators' recognition – the crew names were written in a large script on the wings. Another visual difference to the car was the positioning of the driving lights, which were attached to bumper overriders to allow more air into the engine. New on the car for the event was the first edition of the quick-lift jacking points, which were fixed to the edge of the subframe and painted white.

The car was entered into the touring category. However, now that the Cooper S had been introduced, Mäkinen was at a distinct disadvantage with the 997cc Cooper, albeit with 70bhp at his disposal. The Cooper engine was fitted with a 731 cam and the compression ratio rose to 11:1, plus the fitting of 1½in

The result of the Logan Morrison's massive accident with 407 ARX when leading the 1963 Scottish Rally when the suspension failed.

Mäkinen at one of the many race circuits on the Tour de France.

407 ARX having a brake pad change - note the small disc brakes.

SUs gave much-needed extra power. Straight-cut gears and a longish 3.7 diff was fitted because of the large amount of circuit work the car would have to do on the event, and because of that the suspension was not raised. Armstrong dampers were used throughout, whilst weight was saved by fitting Perspex glass and having lightened bonnet and boot lids.

Mäkinen showed very well compared to the Cooper S that Hopkirk was using, and was lying second on handicap behind the Irishman. Having replaced a loosened crank pulley, disaster struck on the next stage when the 997cc engine let go and a rod came through the side. It was a problem that would befall another of the works Minis on the event – due in no small part to the sustained high revs the engines were pulling on the circuits.

As was the norm with works cars, 407 ARX was pressed into recce duty for the following 1964 Monte Carlo Rally after being rebuilt. For that event, Raymond Baxter had been teamed with Ernest McMillen, so they were sent to recce together in 407 ARX. The car was also used in France for ice note duties on the forthcoming Monte.

The final event for 407 ARX was the 1963 RAC Rally, where Logan Morrison moved over to the driving seat, his place now taken by fellow Scot, Ross Finlay. The car was prepared as Group 2, and it appeared much as it had on the Tour de France, complete with the singular bonnet strip. The car also sprouted a roof lamp and a heavy-duty Dural full-length sump guard, plus two Lucas 700 fog lights and a single Cyclops 576 spot light in the centre at the top of the grille. There was a grille muff, and 'screen clearance was aided by an electric demister bar on the inside. Abingdon was still using dynamos to power all the lights and electrical equipment, which despite being reworked were really at the limit of their

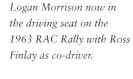

Logan Morrison now in the driving seat on the 1963 RAC Rally with Ross Finlay as co-driver.

Morrison battles on to 19th overall with sparse spectators in the sunshine.

output.

On the event, the new sump guards needed attention as the strengthening strips were wearing through – despite the suspension being raised to its maximum with spacer washers. They also crushed their exhaust at one stage and, because they couldn't get at the clamp protected by the sump guard, they had to break the exhaust to continue.

The very wet and muddy event, of some 2200 miles with 400 forest-stage miles, from Blackpool to Bournemouth via Inverness, took its toll on many cars. But all the works Minis finished, and Morrison got the car home in 19th place, winning the Group 2 up-to-one-litre class, which was an impressive result.

The car was then sold to Peter Riley, who with his wife Ann Wisdom, continued to use the car as a private entrant on several international events, including the 1964 Tulip Rally.

Competition Record

Date	Event	Crew	Number	Overall result	Class result
June 1962	Alpine Rally	Rauno Aaltonen/Gunnar Palm	63	DNF	
Aug 1962	1000 Lakes	Rauno Aaltonen/Tony Ambrose	35	DNF	
Nov 1962	RAC Rally	Timo Mäkinen/John Steadman	38	7th	1st
Jan 1963	Monte Carlo Rally	Paddy Hopkirk/Jack Scott	66	6th	2nd
Feb 63	BBC Grandstand	Paddy Hopkirk		2nd	
June 1963	Scottish Rally	Logan Morrison/Donald Brown		DNF	
Sept 1963	Tour de France	Timo Mäkinen/Logan Morrison	27	DNF	
Nov 1963	RAC Rally	Logan Morrison/Ross Finlay	36	19th	1st

Registration Number	First registered	Chassis number	Engine	Engine number	Model
977 ARX	March 1962	KA2S4 226727	997cc	9F-SA-H 4582	Morris Cooper

Rauno Aaltonen and Tony Ambrose at the Blackpool start for the 1962 RAC Rally.

The second Mini Cooper to be delivered for registration in March 1962 was 977 ARX, painted Old English White with a black roof. It seems odd that the car apparently languished at Abingdon from March through to November without being used, but there are no records of a white Mini Cooper until the November, so it can only be concluded that it remained unused and was a new car for Rauno Aaltonen and Tony Ambrose on the RAC Rally.

The car was prepared as Group 3 in the GT class, which meant opposition would be tough, as it had to enter the up-to-1600cc category. With 300 miles of forest stages in its 2200-mile route from Blackpool to Bournemouth via Inverness, it was a hard rally made worse by the constant wet weather. Aaltonen could be seen at the start with hand-cut drainage channels in his Dunlop SPs.

Being a Group 3 car, 977 ARX was stripped of excess weight as much as it was safe to do so – even to the extent of removing the stiffening to the underside of the bonnet. The engine was up to the 70bhp expected out of the 997cc lump.

Left-foot braking was still the preserve of the Scandinavians, and Aaltonen was one such exponent of this technique for front-wheel-drive cars on loose surfaces. Using the brake

Aaltonen and Ambrose check into a time control on their way to a class win and fifth overall.

977 ARX receiving service by the Abingdon mechanics.

1963 Monte Carlo Rally with Rauno Aaltonen and Tony Ambrose pushing hard.

pedal with the left foot, with the accelerator flat to the floor with the right, allowed the car to lock its rear wheels to drift into the corner – effective but very demanding on the transmission (because of clutchless gearchanges) and the front brakes, which always needed attention.

Aaltonen brought the car safely home in fifth place, despite having to replace the exhaust manifold in Scotland and sliding off on a liaison section between two stages in Wales. He also won the GT 1600cc class, so BMC had a very successful home event, with Hopkirk coming second in a Healey.

The Mini was reprepared after the rigours of the RAC and dispatched to do a recce of the 1963 Monte route with Pauline Mayman at the wheel. The second time the car officially appeared, on the 1963 Monte, we saw a red-and-white 977 ARX at the start – in fact it was 18 CRX, which had been built as Group 1 car. For the Monte, because of the favourable handicap system, it was reckoned that the winner would be a standard production car.

The preparation of a Group 1 car, which allows few modifications, largely centres on optimising the standard parts and by careful assembly. Built by Jonny Lay, the engine components were all standard, although it did have a distributor that would end up on the Cooper S. The compression ratio was 9:1 with 21.1cc combustion chambers, and care was taken to match the inlet and exhaust manifolds to the head, none of which was polished. Larger 1½in SU carbs were used with MME needles and red springs with fork-and-peg linkage and float chamber extensions.

The gearbox had straight-cut gears, with a 4.1 diff ratio.

Aaltonen and Ambrose arrive at the finish in Monte Carlo winning their class and third overall.

An unusual entry for the 1963 Police Rally when Stan Goody and Dick Couling took over the car - and won the team prize.

The ride height was raised by using packing washers on the struts and by Mini van rear struts. Special Armstrong dampers were used, along with bump stops on the rear arms.

Inside the car, the driver had a Microcell bucket with a lap-and-diagonal Britax belt, and the co-driver a Microcell recliner with a Britax full harness. The dashboard had two panels either side of the middle speedo binnacle (which was in kph) to house the numerous switches and instruments they each needed. Padding was fitted to the door and the locks.

Externally, the car had twin tanks with quick-release Monza filler caps and three additional lamps: two Lucas 700s and a 576 Cyclops. The car ran a dynamo and used an HA12 coil. The brakes were standard other than using Ferodo DS11 pads and VG95 linings at the rear. The competition numbers, incidentally, were painted on the doors; the number plate was stick-on.

Aaltonen started from Stockholm, the most northerly start, which more or less guaranteed snow-and-ice-covered roads – as in fact it did for all of the start points, such was the severity of the winter across Europe in 1963. These conditions, of course, were ideal for Aaltonen, who finished a superb third overall and won the class. Only 100 cars finished out of the 342 that entered, which was an indication of just how bad the conditions were. Aaltonen was lucky not to be one of the retirements, as the Mini was soon to lose oil pressure and eventually fail completely on the journey home.

After the Monte, the car, back at Abingdon, was reprepared for Paddy Hopkirk to take on a recce of the route for the 1963 Tulip in the April. The original white-and-black 977ARX was rolled out next for the 1963 International Police Rally, loaned out to PC Stan Goody and PC Dick Couling to compete against other police forces around the world. This was at the behest of John Gott, who was the Abingdon team captain in the Healey day and was also the chief constable of Northamptonshire. The rally was, however, not an easy event as it was a 24-hour nonstop blast from Liège and back over very demanding terrain. Goody and Couling brought the car back in one piece but at a rather lowly 65th place.

The fourth appearance of the car saw it reappear with all-white bodywork, including the roof. John Sprinzel was to return to the Mini for the Alpine Rally, this time with Willy Cave on the maps. John was more accustomed to driving his famous Sprite but could turn his hand to driving anything. The Alpine as always was a big event for BMC, the 2300-mile route from Marseille and back again had eight hillclimbs and 24 selectives thrown in to challenge the 87 entrants.

Built by Ernie Giles, 977 ARX was entered into the GT category as a Group 3 car, allowing many more modifications outside the confines of Group 1 or Group 2. Although the car was the same as on the Monte, it had a lot more power for the Alpine. It was also as light as possible, and with the compression raised to 9.5:1 with polished ports and inlet manifold, with the usual bigger H4 carbs and 4.1 diff, the car made much use of the extra power.

The suspension was raised in height and fitted with Armstrong dampers on modified brackets and the subframe rewelded. For the warmer climate, the inner wing was cut out by the radiator and wire mesh used instead; it also used a four-bladed fan.

The electrics were once again powered by a dynamo, and with three extra lamps and other equipment, it was near the limit for a C40. Restall reclining seats were fitted to the car

John Sprinzel and Willy Cave on the 1963 Alpine Rally.

The aftermath when the steering bolt came adrift on the Col de Trébuchet near Entrevaux, just a few hours from the finish of the Alpine Rally. John Sprinzel looks on, standing by Willy Cave.

and Britax belts, together with a wood-rim steering wheel, which were the popular choice in the early '60s. Willy Cave had the use of an 8-day Smiths clock (but no Halda trip meter) rather than a pair of Heuer clocks now being regularly used in the cars. Brakes, as were common of the day, used DS11 disc pads and VG95 linings at the rear, but without a servo.

The car retired in spectacular fashion, when only four hours from the finish and in second place in their class when they lost their steering on the Col du Trébuchet near Entrevaux. The car came to rest on its side and was severely damaged.

It was quickly discovered by Terry Mitchell, who was soon on the scene, that the pinch bolt was still in position at the bottom of the steering column and concluded that the column must have just been pinched by the clamp rather than the bolt passing over the groove on the protruding part of the steering rack. This resulted in the column being pulled upwards and becoming detached from the rack.

Despite the car's alarming departure, Sprinzel was happy to report that the steering column connection should be wire-lock-secured, and said he would have preferred DA3 pads rather than the DS11s. Reassuringly he reported that the seat belts were superb, causing no injury during their crash.

Competition Record

Date	Event	Crew	Number	Overall result	Class result
Nov 1962	RAC Rally	Rauno Aaltonen/Tony Ambrose	6	5th	1st
Jan 1963	Monte Carlo Rally	Rauno Aaltonen/Tony Ambrose	288	3rd	1st
May 1963	Police Rally	Stan Goody/Dick Couling	75	65th	
June 1963	Alpine Rally	John Sprinzel/Willy Cave	24	DNF	

Registration Number	First registered	Chassis number	Engine	Engine number	Model
477 BBL	April 1962	KA2S4 221347	997cc	9F-SA-H 4432	Morris Cooper

The next and fourth Mini Cooper to be delivered to Abingdon was again a Morris, registered in April 1962, and it was soon painted with a white roof over the production black, to appear in the works red-and-white colour scheme.

The car was initially prepared and dispatched to be a support car for the 1962 Liège Rally in the September, not so much as a recce car but more as a travelling emergency service vehicle for this notorious dash across to eastern Europe and back.

Logan Morrison was then assigned the car for the 1962 RAC, which was to be his first works Mini drive. Until then, Logan had been a successful Scottish privateer who was often drafted into the works team to support class results in his own car.

WORKS MINIS IN DETAIL

Logan Morrison starting the 1963 Monte Carlo Rally with Brian Culcheth in the navigator's seat.

Logan Morrison and Ross Finlay get their time at a time control on the 1962 RAC Rally.

Logan Morrison and Ross Finlay waiting for their time before the start of a rocky section in Scotland during the RAC Rally.

For the 1962 RAC Rally, 477 BBL was entered in the GT category, as a Group 3 car. This allowed far more extensive modification than in Group 1 or 2, but for the RAC it meant the car was in the up-to-1600cc class. Morrison acquitted himself well on this long, wet and wintry rally of some 2200 miles, including 300 miles on Forestry Commission land.

It seemed that the Mini Cooper, particularly with the extra power that could be extracted from the engine if it were entered as a Group 3 car in the GT class, could do very well against more powerful cars, especially when well-driven – and the nimble handling of the Mini could be exploited to the full. Getting the car home in 13th overall and third in class also meant, along with Aaltonen and Mäkinen, BMC won the manufacturers' team price, so Morrison did all that was asked of him.

Logan Morrison took another new member of the BMC team with him on the 1963 Monte Carlo Rally: Brian Culcheth. Brian would later become a mainstay as a driver in the British Leyland days, with the TR7 until 1979. Unlike the other Abingdon cars entered for the Monte, 477 BBL was again in the grand touring class rather that Group 1 production touring like all of the others. This was likely expedient as the car had been prepared and modified as Group 3 in the GT category for the previous RAC Rally, and whilst it was often the case that new cars were supplied for the Monte, Morrison kept his RAC car for this winter classic.

The car was built by Peter Bartram for the Monte and, in common with all the other works cars prepared for the event, now had headlight washers and a full grille muff, in addition to the usual Mory radiator blind. These early blinds were clever devices that were operated from inside the car but proved rather ineffective, so were eventually abandoned in favour of a removable grille muff, which had a couple of opening sections that could be opened or closed as desired. The car also had a couple of electrical demister bars on the windscreen and a Perspex hot-air deflector, while the heater vents were fed by slightly enlarged air ducts and the heaters themselves were uprated to give as much hot air to the screens as possible – and into the car.

Logan Morrison and Brian Culcheth hurry through the mountains with the studded tyres clearly visible on the dry tarmac.

A very picturesque vantage point on the Monaco Grand Prix circuit for the last test on the Monte Carlo Rally.

Restall seats were used, along with a Britax lap-and-diagonal belt and a Britax full harness belt for each crew member, but still a wood-rim steering wheel was used. Also, to save weight, Perspex replaced the heavy glass, along with a lightened bonnet and boot lid.

To get as much power as possible from the Group 3 car, the engine was fitted with twin H4 carbs and an MG 1100 cylinder head, which when reworked by Weslake gave a 10:1 compression. A four-bladed fan kept things cool. The usual straight-cut gears and 4.1 diff were of course fitted, and the suspension was raised to the maximum height with spacer washer, used with Armstrong dampers and special front mounting brackets.

From the Stockholm start, along with Aaltonen in 977 ARX, they finished 44th overall and won their class, so the decision to enter Morrison in a different class paid off. The works Minis had a clean sweep in the Group 1 category for one-litre cars, taking the first three places and netting the team prize.

Timo Mäkinen took Christabel Carlisle on the 1963 Rally of the Snow in 477 BBL with the car much as it was when it finished the Monte, other than using very heavily studded tyres. This event, in Finland, was instigated by Stuart Turner as a thank you to the Morris dealer in Helsinki, Raoul Falin, who had introduced Timo to Stuart. This allowed Stuart to launch Timo so successfully onto the world stage, with his first works Mini drive on the 1962 RAC. It was also as a thank you for Timo and Christabel's superb drive in the works Healey on the 1963 Monte.

The Rally of the Snow (or more correctly the Hankiralli) was, as its English name suggests, run entirely on snow. Starting in Helsinki, the 1000-mile route took a northerly loop from Helsinki, where it ran very close to the Russian border, and with 33 stages, studded tyres were vital. To prevent works-supported cars having multiple tyre choices, cars were restricted to just six – these being branded and marked to ensure compliance. The stages varied from narrow

Timo Mäkinen and Christabel Carlisle on the 1963 Rally of the Snow.

Rauno Aaltonen with Tony Ambrose at the Reims circuit on the 1963 Tour de France. Note the white jacking points on the rear subframe.

forest tracks to fast, wide snow-packed roads. In between the stages the timing of the road sections was sometimes tight, and with the event being spread over two long days, accumulated time loss took its toll. To add to the fun, four of the stages consisted of an ice race, carved out of the many snow-covered lakes that abound in Finland, and something with which Mäkinen was very experienced, having raced D-Type Jaguars on ice! A fast and largely trouble-free run saw him finish in a creditable sixth place.

Rauno Aaltonen and Tony Ambrose took over 477 BBL for the Tour de France. This ten-day annual 3600-mile hillclimb and race circuit thrash around France was always a big challenge for the Mini. With exotic GTs such as Ferrari GTOs, Jaguar 3.8s and many other high-powered sports cars entered, the Mini would always only be able to do well in its handicap class. The main contenders were after the general classification prize or the touring car classification – none of which were in the Mini's grasp... yet. However, France was a big market for BMC and the Mini – and the sight of works Minis tearing around their circuits in a Mini train, inches from each others' bumpers, was a spectacle much appreciated by the many French spectators.

Peter Bartram again built the car, which for the Tour de France was generally quite different to the build of a normal rally car because the event involved so much race circuit work. The cars needn't be as strong but they had to be able to sustain constant high speed and, of course, weight saving was high on the list – within the rules, of course. To get as much top speed as possible, the 'standard' Abingdon 4.1 diff was replaced by a longer 3.7:1, giving much-needed extra top speed at the expense of acceleration. New on the car for the event was the first edition of quick-lift jacking points, which were fixed to the edge of the subframe, being moved to beneath the bumpers some months later.

All the works Minis on the event had identification stripes on the bonnet because one red-and-white Mini looks much the same as the next when they flash by. They also had their crew names painted in a large script on the wings, so spectators could identify who was driving.

Aaltonen's car had a single broad white stripe on the nearside of the bonnet and a thinner vertical stripe on the boot lid. The car also carried two extra fog lights, which were fitted to the bumper overriders. These unique features were used only on the Tour de France works Minis. Aaltonen was destined to retire near half way of this gruelling event.

Used for testing prior to the 1963 RAC Rally, 477 BBL also appeared after the Tour de France in a different guise, when it was taken to forest tracks near Basingstoke. The car, still

477 BBL being used as a test-bed prior to the 1963 RAC Rally, now with a roof lamp.

Rauno Aaltonen with the car on the Tour de France. Note the windscreen heater bar, tripod headlights and white jacking points on the front subframe.

with its Tour de France-striped bonnet, had sprouted a roof lamp and the bonnet was held with two straps either side of its Morris Cooper badge.

For the 1964 Monte Carlo Rally the car was assigned to Raymond Baxter, who was a well-known BBC reporter and later would become BMC's director of PR. It was his first works Mini drive although had used a works MG 1100 on the '63 Monte, and he had Ernie McMillan as co-driver.

By now the Cooper S was readily available to the team, and four other works Minis for the 1964 event had 1071Ss at their disposal. But as a last hurrah for the 997 Mini Cooper, 477 BBL was retained as a one-litre car (it would be the last entry for the little Mini Cooper; from then on, Abingdon would contest the one-litre class with the 970 Cooper S). Baxter's car for the Monte, again built by Bartram, was entered as a Group 3 car, so that it could take full advantage of the extra power Group 3 modifications would permit, and the car could also be pared down in weight. Despite this, a Group 1 car was favoured to win because of the handicapping system in place.

The Monte preparation for the cars was now moving up a gear, as more additional equipment was added. As was standard practice the car was rewired by the resident Lucas technicians – either John Smith or Stan Chalmers – who would incorporate, within reason, the driver's preference with switches and layout.

The dashboard was standardised and consisted of a full-width panel in three sections: the driver's side contained the rev counter and a dual oil and water temperature gauge plus numerous switches for the additional lamps; the co-driver had a pair of Heuer clocks and a Halda distance recorder behind a magnifying lens, and he too had numerous switches for instrument lights, map light and so on. Cars of this era alternated between Heuer watches and the Smiths 8-day clock, at the co-driver's preference. The centre panel around the speedo, which had a separate zeroing trip, had just this and various switches for the reverse light and cigar lighter. A Microcell bucket and Microcell relining seat were fitted, and a wood-rim steering wheel was used.

The demand on the electrical system during the Monte, with extra lights and constant heating and demisting needs, had the dynamo working at its limit, so for the Monte this was a special 28amp unit with roller bearing. Iodine bulbs were used on all the lights, but these were the days before dipping QI bulbs, so the headlight dipped beam had to be served by the small 576 fog lights, positioned where the indicators were located, which would switch on with the dip switch and the main beam-only headlights would be extinguished. A good deal of effort was also taken to provide spray-type washers for the headlights, with a separate water supply.

One innovation for the Monte was the introduction of a heated front 'screen – a Triplex invention, which consisted of a gold film within the laminate that carried current through

Resident Lucas Racing technician John Smith wiring a new 477 BBL for the 1964 Monte Carlo Rally, which is an 850 Mini bodyshell without vinyl on the dash rail. Note also the brake pipe close to the hot tunnel.

John Smith at work in the car with the engine exposed on 477 BBL with the vertical heater by the offside wing and fitting bracket for the Cyclops spot lamp.

to warm and demist the glass – although it was only on the driver's side due to the high electrical demand, as works cars were still using a dynamo. Unfortunately the 'screens were not that popular with drivers as they felt they were distracted looking thorough the gold film, and Baxter changed his to a standard laminated windscreen on arrival at Reims (as did Paddy Hopkirk), where the common route began.

Starting from Minsk (a new starting point in Russia), the roads were dry, so 477 BBL was fitted with standard Dunlop SP tyres but carried two studded Dunlop SP44s in case the weather deteriorated. Once in range of the Dunlop tyre trucks and BMC service, the tyre choice was much wider, although patches of ice were catching the car out on the summer tyres before the studs were fitted. Baxter finished well in 43rd place in what was by now an underpowered Mini Cooper. The car was also narrowly beaten into second place in its class. It was then sold to Mike Wood.

Raymond Baxter pressing 477 BBL very hard on the Grand Prix circuit. Note the offside tyre.

Raymond Baxter with Ernest McMillan asleep with his pillow in the passenger seat on their way to Monte Carlo.

Raymond Baxter and Ernest McMillan congratulating themselves in their second-in-class win.

Competition Record

Date	Event	Crew	Number	Overall result	Class result
Nov 1962	RAC Rally	Logan Morrison/Ross Finlay	32	13th	3rd
Jan 63	Monte Carlo Rally	Logan Morrison/Brian Culcheth	155	44th	1st
Feb 63	Rally of the Snow	Timo Mäkinen/Christabel Carlisle	10	6th	
Sept 1963	Tour de France	Rauno Aaltonen/Tony Ambrose	24	DNF	
Jan 1964	Monte Carlo Rally	Raymond Baxter/Ernie McMillan	39	43rd	2nd

CHAPTER 2: THE MINI COOPER

Registration Number	First registered	Chassis number	Engine	Engine number	Model
17 CRX	Dec 1962	KA2S4 318992	997cc	9F-SA-H 14732	Morris Cooper

Two sister cars, 17 and 18 CRX, both Morris Coopers, were the last of the small batch of six 997 Mini Coopers used by Abingdon; with the new 1071cc Mini Cooper S only a short while away, there was little appetite for the diminutive 997 Mini Cooper.

The first, 17 CRX, was registered in Berkshire in December 1962. Painted once again with a white roof, 17 CRX was in fact soon prepared and dispatched for the 1963 Monte Carlo Rally but was actually to carry 407 ARX's registration plates on that event – because 407 ARX had just completed a very hard RAC rally and moreover was a Group 2 car, the new 17 CRX was used instead. It was also prepared as a Group 1 car. For practical reasons, as the entry and custom paperwork would have been in place for the worn-out RAC car, it was easier to swap cars rather than struggle with changing the entry and other paperwork.

So the first official entry for 17ARX was on the 1963 Tulip Rally with Paddy Hopkirk and his new co-driver Henry Liddon, who had taken over Jack Scott's seat, the latter having retired to concentrate on his business interests. Henry Liddon was the most active of all of the regular co-drivers at Abingdon, who competed in 38 rallies whilst at BMC in works Minis, chiefly with Paddy Hopkirk and later Rauno Aaltonen; a most fastidious co-driver.

For the Tulip Rally, the car was built by Jonny Organ as a Group 2. This allowed twin 1½in SUs, running MME needles and red springs with float chamber extensions, plus a 948 camshaft and high-compression Weslake cylinder head, giving 9.5:1 ratio. A straight-cut gearbox and a 4.1:1 diff was used – vital for climbing out of uphill Alpine hairpin bends. The suspension was raised slightly to give a bit more ground clearance but was helped by the use of a Moke sump guard. Armstrong dampers were installed throughout, with special modified brackets to the front. Twin tanks with quick-release Aston filler caps were used, with the standard pump on the subframe protected by an aluminium plate. The fuel line was outside, shielded by metal channels, but the brake line ran inside.

Two additional fog lights were fitted on drop-down brackets fixed to the bumper and front panel; it also had a Cyclops spot lamp at the top of the grille, all run from a modified C40 dynamo and an RB310 control box, along with twin Mixo Minor horns. A wood-rim wheel was specified, much favoured by Hopkirk back then. A Microcell bucket was used by Hopkirk, alongside a Microcell recliner for Liddon, plus Britax harnesses. The car also featured Perspex windows and had a lightweight bonnet and boot lid; the front panel below the bumper was cut away at the ends to allow cooling for the brakes.

Hopkirk's performance on the Tulip was remarkable, managing to beat most cars on the climbs and impressively beating all of his old Rootes teammates. He was even quick around the Nürburgring circuit test, and also faster than the

Paddy Hopkirk and Henry Liddon waiting at the start line of a hillclimb stage on the 1963 Tulip Rally with Hopkirk looking particularly cheerful on his way to second overall.

Hopkirk and Liddon hard-charging in 17 CRX on the Tulip Rally.

Denise McCluggage and Rosemary Sears look pensive before leaving a time control on the 1963 Alpine Rally.

Denise McCluggage and Rosemary Sears screech into a time control as Sears leaps from the car to get their time card stamped.

winning Ford Falcon on several stages. Even Julien Vernaeve, in his Group 3 Mini, could not match Hopkirk in 17 CRX. At the finish, Hopkirk was a superb seventh overall on scratch, which with the handicap class improvement system elevated him to second overall and winning his class.

The car had performed well, with early overheating problems solved by the complete removal of the Mory radiator blind, although Hopkirk reported that the car was jumping out of first gear almost from the start of the rally. After Pat Moss winning the rally the previous year, second in 1963 was another good result for Abingdon on this popular event.

For the 1963 Alpine, 17 CRX was taken over by colourful American journalist Denise McCluggage and navigated by Rosemary Sears. This was a one-off drive for McCluggage, who had raced at Sebring in an MGB with Christabel Carlisle. The car was entered in the touring car category as a Group 2, much as it was for the previous Tulip Rally and was virtually unchanged. Interestingly, however, after the cooling problems experienced on the Tulip, the grille on the inner wing protecting the radiator was cut out and a wire mesh used instead. The car also lost its headlight washers, and its twin Heuer watches were replaced by the Smiths 8-day clock.

This particular Alpine was extremely tough, with just 24 cars arriving back at the finish in Marseille from the 85 that left there six days earlier – but 17CRX wasn't one of them. Whilst leading both their class and the Coupe des Dames, the crew suffered terminal driveshaft failure when the rubber coupling failed. Nearing Beaufort, Brian Moylan at the BMC service diagnosed the mechanical noise that the girls had been experiencing for many miles was a collapsed engine mount and that the drive coupling was fast breaking up. The crew pressed on tentatively, hoping to get to the next service to get the problem fixed; sadly they never made it, with the joint failing just before the next selective, where they were forced to retire. Subsequently all the joints were replaced on the remaining works Minis as a preventative measure.

The drive coupling problem would persist, made worse with the increased power the engines were now producing, until the cars were changed to the more robust Hardy Spicer universal joint. In the meantime, the Abingdon mechanics became very adept at changing the drive couplings in double-quick time.

Returning to Abingdon after the Alpine, the car was used as a recce car for the forthcoming Tour de France in the September and was subsequently loaned out for the 1964 Police Rally. It was sold to Stuart Turner.

Competition Record

Date	Event	Crew	Number	Overall result	Class result
April 1963	Tulip Rally	Paddy Hopkirk/Henry Liddon	130	2nd	1st
June 1963	Alpine Rally	Denise McCluggage/Rosemary Sears	64	DNF	

Registration Number	First registered	Chassis number	Engine	Engine number	Model
18 CRX	Dec 1962	KA2S4 318988	997cc	9F-SA-H 15276	Morris Cooper

The very last Mini Cooper to be supplied to Abingdon, 18 CRX, was registered, along with its sister car (17 CRX) in December 1963. By now Abingdon was preparing for the arrival of the new 1071 Cooper S, and with eyes now focused on outright wins, the need for a class winner in the shape of the 997 Cooper was no longer at the top of the list. It is therefore no surprise that, on paper at least, 18 CRX languished until the following June before being used on the 1963 Alpine Rally. In fact, the car was used prior to that Alpine, first appearing as 977 ARX on the 1963 Monte as a new car for Rauno Aaltonen.

For the final fling of the Mini Cooper, which had proved to be a car more than capable of winning its class (and one outright win with Pat Moss on the 1962 Tulip), the car was handed to the women's crew of Pauline Mayman and Val Domleo with the hope of a good result on the Alpine Rally.

Entered in the one-litre touring class and as a Group 2 car built by Peter Bartram, 18 CRX had twin 1½in SUs, a high-compression (9.5:1) cylinder head, and used a 948 camshaft, which would give around 70bhp. The customary straight-cut gearbox and 4.1 diff was fitted. The suspension, using Armstrong dampers, was also raised to its maximum height.

Once again, the inner wing grillage was cut away to aid

Pauline Mayman and Val Domleo at the start on the 1963 Alpine, which will give them a class win and sixth overall.

Pauline Mayman and Val Domleo charge through a French village on this fast and furious event.

The stunning scenery of the Alps make a superb backdrop of the girls on the Alpine Rally.

Jack Thompson and Frank Hays on a one-off Abingdon drive leave for their start in Paris of the 1964 Monte Carlo Rally.

cooling, and wire mesh used to protect the radiator. The car now also sported a pair of larger Lucas 700 fog lights, replacing the smaller Lucas 576 fog lights previously used on most works cars. These heavier lamps required steady stays to be provided below the bumper between the lower apron and the drop-down brackets to which they were mounted, as the lights tended to vibrate. The rather unpopular Tripod headlights were replaced by European headlights, considered to be far superior in use. However, all the electrics were powered by a high-output dynamo.

There was no provision for headlight washers but the car was fitted with a 'screen demister bar, while the accompanying Perspex deflector on the dash rail had disappeared. The wood-rim steering wheel was still used, together with Microcell seats. The seat belts were, however, specially made, along with grey-coloured early Irvin belts. The car was also lightened, with Perspex windows and a lightweight boot lid.

The Alpine Rally was a resounding success for Abingdon and indeed the two girls, who not only won their touring car class, they also won the Coupe des Dames and – more significantly – won an Alpine Cup for an unpenalised run on the road. And, to cap it all, they finished in sixth place overall.

Other than a puncture on the climb up the Col de Rousset, where they had to stop and change the wheel, they had a trouble-free run. BMC won the team prize and the manufacturer's prize - plus another Alpine Cup with Rauno Aaltonen, who also won the touring category outright. In fact,

BMC as a company did exceedingly well, with eight Coopers at the finish out of the lowly 24 cars from an initial field of 84 starters.

After the Alpine and its safe return to Abingdon, 18 CRX was reprepared for Pauline Mayman to take out and recce the route for the Tour de France scheduled for September, where she would get her hands on a Cooper S – 277 EBL.

For the 1964 Monte Carlo Rally, the very last event for the Mini Cooper in Abingdon's hands, 18 CRX was given to Rhodesian Jack Thompson for a one-off drive with Frank Heys in the hot seat.

The car was now much changed from the Alpine Rally – it was fitted with a 1071 Cooper S engine and, in common with the other Abingdon Mini entries on the Monte, the headlights had been upgraded to single-filament iodine lamps, necessitating the dipped beam to be provided by a Lucas 576 fog lamp mounted directly below the headlights, which in turn meant that the indicator/sidelight was relocated a little further around the wing.

Because of the handicap system on class improvement on the Monte, it was decided to enter the car as a Group 1, in the hope for one last class win for the Mini Cooper. Prepared visually the same as the other works entries for the Monte, with its battery of seven lights on the front, half-heated front windscreen, grille muff and such like, it was rather a sheep in wolf's clothing, being in the standard production class.

Starting from Paris, the crew got as far as St Claude on the fifth day, when they rolled the car. Struggling to get the rear lights working, they lost ten minutes at the Chambéry control and promptly rolled the car again, a few kilometres down the road – and into retirement. Rather an ignominious end to the short career of the Mini Cooper at Abingdon.

After the car's competition career was over, another 18 CRX was used for destruction testing at Strata Florida in Wales, where Abingdon would regularly go to test suspension modification or sump guards or any number of items that the harsh environment at the test site threw at the car. It was a good opportunity to put the cars through their paces to see just what would break or fall off rather than let it happen on an international rally.

A car bearing the registration 18 CRX was sold to Paul Easter, who at the time was a keen active club rally driver who was entering numerous international events in his own car. It would be only a matter of nine months before Paul would join the works team as a regular co-driver to the great Timo Mäkinen.

18 CRX being tested to destruction in Wales to evaluate suspension and sump guard designs.

The easiest way to inspect the underside whilst testing was to tip the car onto its side. Stuart Turner looks on with Geoff Mabbs showing interest in the damage he's inflicted on 18 CRX.

Competition Record

Date	Event	Crew	Number	Overall result	Class result
June 1963	Alpine Rally	Pauline Mayman/Val Domleo	73	6th	1st
Jan 1964	Monte Carlo Rally	Jack Thompson/Frank Hayes	187	DNF	

CHAPTER 3:
THE MK 1 MINI COOPER S

Monte Carlo Rally-winning Mk1 Cooper Ss: 33 EJB Paddy Hopkirk and Henry Liddon; 1964: AJB 44B Timo Mäkinen and Paul Easter; 1965 and the disqualified GRX 555D; also Timo Mäkinen and Paul Easter. Missing is LBL 6D of Rauno Aaltonen and Henry Liddon, 1967.

It had taken only three-and-a-half years from the introduction of the little Mini 850, in August 1959, for the car to grow horns and turn into the 1071 Cooper S of March 1963, via the 997 Cooper in July 1961. It was a meteoric change, with the cars going from 34bhp to 70bhp in their respective standard form. Much of the impetus for these changes was driven by competition and, in no small part by Stuart Turner at Abingdon, aided and abetted by the redoubtable John Cooper.

With the new 1071 Cooper S, Abingdon could challenge for outright wins and would no longer be content to be a class winner. However, the 1071cc was a rather inconvenient size, as the European Championship had an up-to-1300cc category and an up-to-1000cc class. It would take only a short while, after the introduction of the new 1071, for it to be usurped by the bigger 1275cc Cooper S a year later, in February 1964. If that was not enough, come June 1964, a 970cc Cooper S also became available. These two new cars produced 75bhp and 65bhp respectively, and Abingdon would use all three to good effect.

The experience gained by John Cooper and Daniel Richmond at Downton in Formula Junior racing was the technical inspiration behind building the Cooper S. Many quite exotic materials were used in the Cooper S engine, virtually unheard of in a sports car, let alone for a small family saloon. The nitrided EN40 steel crankshaft, specially treated to increase its hardness, was one of the strongest production crankshafts at the time. Because all three engine blocks shared the same bore diameter at 70.64mm (considered to be the maximum the original A-series block could be safely bored to), the three Cooper S engines all had different strokes; and although the 1071 and 1275 shared the same conrods, the 970 rods were longer to give the three different capacities.

It was Eddie Maher's job (and his team at BMC's experimental department in Coventry) to make it all work on what was basically a Morris Minor 803cc engine block. The bores were offset and moved out as far as possible to safeguard the waterways. For the bigger engine, the only solution was to cast an extra lump of metal onto the top of the block.

The 1071 engine had a slightly oversquare configuration, in that the bore was larger than its stroke, which allowed the engine to rev freely. The 970 had an even more oversquare configuration with a really short stroke, and would pull exceedingly high revs; although less powerful and with less torque, in the right hands it was a potent engine. The 1275 engine was not, however, oversquare, having a relatively long stroke compared to its bore, and although more powerful was a rougher engine that was less willing to rev, but its better torque and larger capacity saw it as the one everyone wanted.

The cylinder heads had Nimonic 80 steel valves with Stellite stem tips and ran in Hidural valve guides with stronger double valve springs, together with forged rockers. The valves were also considerably increased in size, with much work being carried out in the shape of the ports and combustion chambers. A new camshaft was designed for the engine, which was common to all three, and all had a duplex timing chain and gears. The Cooper S also had a unique gearbox, and a selection of no less than five different final drives could be ordered. When an optional close-ratio gearbox was specified, together with another two final drives, it can be seen just how many combinations were available for the competition-minded motorist. It was no accident that the Cooper S was to become the competition car of choice for many an aspiring driver.

With the extra power the Cooper S delivered, it was sensible that the car was given better brakes – up from the tiny and largely ineffective 7in discs of the Mini Cooper, to thicker 7½in discs together with a brake servo. Stronger driveshafts were used but initially retaining the troublesome and short-lived rubber crucifix driveshaft couplings; they were to be replaced, and much later, with solid Hardy Spicer universal joints (although the works team was to use the parts long before being included on the production car).

Wider road wheels were provided and, with twin fuel tanks being offered as an optional extra (before being a standard fit on all Cooper Ss), the car looked much sportier on the road and appealed to the rich and famous. It was soon to become an object of fashion.

With all these special parts, it made the transition from production car to effective and powerful competition car so much easier. Without doubt, none of it could have happened without John Cooper – he certainly deserved his royalty.

Abingdon would of course not stop there, as the team sought to improve upon production cars, specifying and installing many performance-enhancing parts. Bill Price, who joined the competition department as Marcus Chambers's assistant in 1960, was responsible for ensuring all of these special parts were homologated and accepted by the RAC, and were therefore allowed to be used on the car in international competition. This saw the 75bhp (which the standard Cooper S produced) increase to around 100bhp and beyond – and, in later years, way beyond.

During the four-and-a-half years that the Mk1 Cooper S was in production, just under 20,000 cars left the production line, of which 42 were destined to be delivered to Abingdon for competition work (plus a good number of replacements lost within the system), all of which will be covered in this chapter.

One area of production development on the Cooper S that didn't please Abingdon was, a year-and-a-half after the car was launched, the abandonment of the rubber cone suspension in preference for new fluid hydrolastic suspension. This system, developed way back at the Mini's inception, was shelved as being too expensive but was now felt, with further development, to offer a more pleasant ride.

Unfortunately, for competition use at least, it was not well received, as pitching between front and back caused unfavourable handling. Ways were developed by Abingdon to restrict the flow of the fluid front to back and to add dampers to reduce the often unpleasant pitch. The system, in the early days, was also unreliable compared to the dry rubber cones, and would cause numerous on-event dramas with collapsed suspension.

It is on record that Timo Mäkinen disliked Hydrolastic suspension, and many of the early works cars he drove at Abingdon continued to use the dry rubber suspension, until eventually he too was obliged to use Hydrolastic. When you are as good as Mäkinen you can, presumably, make such demands! But as you can see, apart from Mäkinen, Abingdon didn't always get its own way with the cars.

It is perhaps worth mentioning the categories in which the Cooper S competed internationally, which were within the rules laid down by the Commission Sportive International (CSI), and on January 1966 new regulations were published outlining the respective groups cars could compete within.

Appendix J of the Sporting Code was rewritten and cars divided into two main categories: homologated cars and special cars. Homologated cars, in which the Mini fell, were divided into specific groups. Group 1 was for standard production cars of which 5000 had to be made within a year, and the only modifications permitted being those in the existing Appendix J Group 1 rules. Group 2 cars would be for those of which 1000 had been built in 12 months, and they too could be modified only within existing Appendix J regulations. Group 5 cars would be those deemed to be special touring cars, and that allowed a wider range of modifications to be permitted, all of which could fall outside the Appendix J rules for Groups 1 and 2. The only caveat was that to be a Group 5 car it had to have been originally homologated in Group 2. Group 3 was for GT cars and Group 4 for sports cars, so not applicable to the Mini.

Abingdon would generally enter Group 2 cars, and when it was felt the regulations were favourable for standard cars, it would also field a Group 1 car. Latterly, when the pressure from opposition became very strong and the events permitted Group 5, these highly-modified cars were built. There was also a Group 6 prototype category, which Abingdon used when competing in rallycross.

During the four-and-a-half years Abingdon was using and developing the Mk1 Cooper S, many changes and improvements took place to make the car faster, more reliable and – of course – more competitive. The car in the autumn of 1967, when the Mk1 was replaced with the Mk2, bore little resemblance to the more simple cars of 1963 – so much had be improved and developed through hard competition. Great achievements were recorded: three outright Monte Carlo Rally victories plus one very public disqualification on the 1966 Monte due to a squabble over the lighting used on the cars, a European Championship, and more than two-dozen outright international victories.

However, whilst they worked away, the competition was not standing still. With the introduction of the Ford Escort at the end of 1967 and Porsche finally realising it had a potential rally winner in the shape of the 911, the Cooper S had likely peaked. Whilst development on the Mk2 Cooper S continued, it was reaching the end of its potential, and the heady days of the many wins gathered by the Cooper S were now on the decline.

Stuart Turner, surely the mastermind behind the brilliant results Abingdon achieved with the Mk1 Cooper S, was due to leave for a PR job with Castrol in March 1967, to be replaced by Peter Browning, who would steer Abingdon through its most troubled times when doing battle with Lord Stokes and his wielding of the axe to shut down the department.

During the competition life of the Mk1 Cooper S, nothing else captured the imagination more, and no car achieved more, than the little red-and-white bricks from Abingdon.

Registration Number	First registered	Chassis number	Engine	Engine number	Model
8 EMO	May 1963	KA2S4 384848	1071cc	9F-SA-H 19754	Morris Cooper S

Paddy Hopkirk and Henry Liddon push on hard as a spectator casually watches the car fly around the corner.

The first of a batch of three new 1071 Cooper Ss officially delivered to Abingdon, 8 EMO marked the start of an exciting chapter in the competition department's history. Abingdon had at last got its hands on a Mini that could challenge for outright wins and not have to be content with class wins.

With the experienced line-up of top drivers now assembled, together with the new breed of professional co-drivers, the stage was set for Abingdon to take the world by storm.

Although 8 EMO waited in the wings whilst its two sister cars were used on the Tour de France and the Alpine (it did the Tour de France as 277 EBL), after six months it was assigned to Paddy Hopkirk and Henry Liddon to tackle the 1963 RAC Rally.

Entered in the touring car class as a Group 2, it was a broad class for cars from 1000cc to 1600cc, so the little S was at a disadvantage. The car was prepared by Gerald Wiffen with the 1071 engine bored out by 0.040in to give 1101cc. With a 731 camshaft, a polished high-compression head of 11:1 and a pair of H4 carbs, the car was going to be quick enough to perhaps halt the Scandinavian domination of the event that had existed for the last two years.

As was normal practice, the gearbox used straight-cut gears manufactured from special material, a 4.1 diff and rubber driveshaft couplings – which would, as always, need constant attention through out the rally. Abingdon had become adept at changing these couplings in double-quick time at the roadside, often by rolling the car onto its side to gain easy access to the joints buried beneath.

The car was lightened with a lightweight bonnet and Perspex glass. Microcell seats were used, with a lap-and-diagonal belt for Hopkirk and full harness for Liddon. For the RAC a 3/16in Dural alloy-sheet sump guard was used, which would need additional rubbing strips to be welded to the guard as it progressively wore away.

Lighting – always important on the poor weather the event tended to experience – was served by Lucas Tripod headlamps with washers plus two 700 fog lights and a single 576 Cyclops spot light fitted with iodine bulbs; the car also sprouted a roof lamp, and all were powered by a modified C40 dynamo.

The suspension, although standard, was raised to its maximum and had Armstrong heavy duty dampers. Aston quick-release fuel caps were used on the twin tanks, and the duel fuel pump was fitted to the subframe, protected by an alloy plate. The fuel line was protected with metal channelling,

Paddy Hopkirk on a rain-soaked racetrack on his way to a fine fourth place on the RAC Rally.

Paddy Hopkirk and Henry Liddon crash through the terrible conditions found on the 1963 RAC Rally.

8 EMO was used extensively in Strata Florida in the Cambrian Mountains in Wales testing Hydrolastic suspension and sump guard design for the 1964 RAC Rally.

as was the external battery line; the brake lines, however, ran inside the car.

The 1963 RAC Rally was now a mammoth 2000-mile event, covering much of the UK. Starting in Blackpool and finishing Bournemouth via the Highlands of Scotland and deepest Wales, the 400 miles of mostly forest stages would decide the event, which the Scandinavians had now started to dominate.

Trouble hit 8 EMO even before the start, when the car failed scrutineering because the exhaust was deemed too noisy, which meant a new system was fitted. Once under way, Hopkirk was very soon recording quick times in the car and was a match for the Scandinavians' sideways style. Hopkirk's smooth and more conventional style was both quick and effective and he was the only British driver in the top ten, dominated by Scandinavians, at the halfway point. He was still in fourth place at Bournemouth, despite a spin in Wales, and had been constantly swapping times with Mäkinen's Healey and Pat Moss's Cortina.

Fourth place at the finish was a fine result for the Cooper S and had cemented Hopkirk as a great Mini driver. The car came through relatively unscathed, with just a pair of dampers being changed, along with a set of drive couplings. Paddy did note, however, that the car leaked badly and was very draughty.

The car would have to wait over a year – until 1965 – to be used again in competition, as it was consigned to recce work for most of 1964, being used for practice on the Monte Carlo Rally, the Tulip Rally in April, the Alpine in June and finally the Tour de France in the September. It was not unusual for cars used on the hard and damaging events (such as the RAC Rally) to be pensioned off or used as recce cars before being sold. However, more was in store for 8 EMO.

The career of 8 EMO as a competition car was put on hold even longer as it became a test mule for the soon-to-be-introduced Hydrolastic suspension, which underwent a great deal of assessment by Abingdon – particularly prior to the 1964 RAC Rally, when 8 EMO was relentlessly pounded over rough tracks to establish how the new wet suspension system would stand up to the rigours of hard competition.

Abingdon was corporately committed to using the new

The twin bottles are for normal washer fluid and one for alcohol to prevent screen wash freezing (not for personal use!). Note also the intercom box fixed to the roof.

Engine details of the new build for the 1965 Monte Carlo Rally.

suspension system, despite its shortcomings. Numerous modifications were carried out, even experimenting with isolating the front suspension fluid from the back with shut-off taps, together with the addition of dampers to try to control the pitching on rough roads. However, Hydrolastic on a rally car was never a great success, although it was used extensively – except by Mäkinen, who simply refused to use it in the early days, insisting on a dry-suspension car. This dispensation, reportedly sanctioned by Alec Issigonis himself, was an indication of Mäkinen's influence – but it was much to the annoyance of Issigonis' great friend and the designer of the system, Alex Moulton.

An all-new 8 EMO was rolled out for Raymond Baxter and Jack Scott to enter the 1965 Monte Carlo Rally. This time, however, despite being a Cooper S, it was built from a Mini 850, as was evidenced by the monotone red interior and the absence of chrome finishers around the doors. Built by Brian Moylan, this was a very lightweight car entered as a Group 3, and with over a year's improvements on the Cooper S at Abingdon, it jumped quite some way in development.

Fitted with a 970S engine, with a 731 camshaft and an 11.1 compression ratio cylinder head, it was also equipped with a very short 4.26:1 diff. The engine block was fitted with core plug retainers, which would hopefully stay intact in the freezing weather expected at Baxter's Minsk start.

The car was fitted with hydrolastic suspension with yellow-band displacers. To combat the eternal problem of the rubber fracturing at the rear of the remote shift, Terry Mitchell had designed a new rubber mount, which contained a movable joint, so it was now virtually indestructible. It became known as the Mitchell mounting and would be used on every works car from then on.

Timken needle roller bearings were now used on the rear hubs, brought about by the difficulty of removing the roller bearings in the field – particularly if they seized. Now all the lines were fitted inside the car: battery, fuel and brakes. By this point, the cars were sporting seven QI lights, and their demand, plus the heated front windscreen, saw the change to an alternator with a separate regulator.

Weight saving on the car was extensive, with over 50lb removed. Perspex windows were installed (apart from the front heated 'screen), there were alloy bonnet, boot and doors, and a large number of 2in holes were drilled under the rear parcel shelf and rear seat back to remove surplus metal. Lightweight Rivington thin carpet was specified, and there was an alloy heater. A lightweight front grille, cut from an Austin A110 grille, was fitted, and the only addition was a set of lovely Abingdon fabricated alloy wheel spats. Every surplus bracket was removed, and even fibreglass headlight bowls were made to save every precious pound.

However, all of the effort came to nothing, as the car didn't even make it to the start of the Monte. Shipped to the Port of Gdynia in Poland, some 480 miles to the start in Minsk, the

CHAPTER 3: THE MK 1 MINI COOPER S

engine threw a rod through the side once in Russia, and all the best efforts of BMC were unable to get permission from the Russian authorities to fly a new engine out to the stricken car – so it was forced out of the event before even turning a wheel. Despite the disappointment of losing 8 EMO so early, BMC was rewarded with Mäkinen winning the rally outright, in atrocious conditions, in AJB 44B.

The final appearance of 8 EMO was on the annual Police Rally in May 1965, when Baxter again took the wheel. This event was a favourite of BMC at the time, as John Gott, the one-time team leader of BMC, was also the chief constable of Northamptonshire; he would enter a BMC car or two on the event, which was mainly a competition between numerous police forces around the world.

It was, however, no easy event as it was a 24-hour non-stop blast from Liège and back over demanding terrain. The last duty 8 EMO would perform was as a recce car for the 1966 Monte Carlo Rally, where Henry Liddon and Paul Easter shared the car. It was then was sold to Oswald Tillotson, where Mike Wood was a salesman. This would be one of several works cars that found their way to the Tillotson dealership over the years.

8 EMO on recce duties for the 1966 Monte Carlo Rally nearly coming to grief with a Citroën van full of hay.

Beautiful hand-crafted aluminium wheelarch extensions, later to be replaced by fibreglass items.

The dashboard arrangement on the new bodyshell for the car for the Monte Carlo Rally. Note this is an 850 Mini body.

Competition Record

Date	Event	Crew	Number	Overall result	Class result
Nov 1963	RAC Rally	Paddy Hopkirk/Henry Liddon	21	4th	2nd
Jan 1965	Monte Carlo Rally	Raymond Baxter/Jack Scott	91	DNF	
May 1965	Police Rally	Raymond Baxter/Jack Scott			

Registration Number	First registered	Chassis number	Engine	Engine number	Model
277 EBL	May 1963	KA2S4 384611	1071cc	9F-SA-H 19243	Morris Cooper S

Rauno Aaltonen and Tony Ambrose leaving the start on the 1963 Alpine Rally, which they would win outright.

Dashboard of 277 EBL at the start of the Monza test on the Alpine Rally with tape to pull off for each of the required laps completed.

The second of the three early 1071 Cooper Ss delivered to Abingdon was 277 EBL, which would enable BMC to run at the front of the field. Chasing class wins would be a thing of the past; with the increased power of the Formula Junior-based race engine, the Mini had become a real force to be reckoned with.

Abingdon would not have to wait long, as the car was entered for Rauno Aaltonen and Tony Ambrose to do the Alpine Rally in the June of 1963, always an Abingdon favourite. It was the first event for the Cooper S in the hands of the works, and much was expected.

Prepared by Jonny Lay, the car was entered in the touring category as a Group 2 machine. It was customary for one mechanic to be solely responsible for the build of each car, including, in these early days, the engine and gearbox. It would be later that Cliff Humphries became Abingdon's chief technician and responsible for engine builds and development. The individual mechanics were justifiably very proud of their workmanship, and it was one of the reasons Abingdon was so successful – with Doug Watts, the Abingdon foreman, encouraging friendly competitiveness between mechanics, who would always be striving to build the next winner for their driver.

With the engine of the car being mostly standard, other than a special camshaft and a polished cylinder head, the resulting 10:1 compression ratio was thought to produce sufficient power to propel the Cooper S up the Alpine climbs, helped no end by the 4.13 diff and straight-cut close-ratio gearbox.

The suspension was raised by the use of packing washers front and back, and using Mini van rear suspension trumpets with bump rubbers on the radius arms. Armstrong heavy-duty valve-type dampers were fitted all round, and the front mounting modified with a special bracket. The subframes also received extra welding to add strength.

Cooling received extra attention, with the removal of the inner wing radiator grille to be replaced with wire mesh. Additionally, the heater outlets were modified into ducts, which were routed out through the floor, so that the heater could be used at full blast in the hot climate and not stifle the crew (not exactly legal for a Group 2 car, but effective nevertheless).

Electrics, still fed by a modified C40 dynamo, had an HA12 coil bolted on top and an RB310 regulator box fitted up on the bulkhead. The car retained a single-speed wiper motor but with special deep-throated wheel boxes. Lighting featured European headlights with two Lucas 700 fog lights on quick-release brackets, with a single Lucas 576 Cyclops spot light on a special bracket on the front slam panel; bulbs were white tungsten. Aaltonen also had a single heated demister bar on his side of the screen.

The car ran twin Mixo Minor horns, which were additionally operated by a foot switch in Ambrose's footwell. As was common with all works Minis, the cars were

Aaltonen arrives at the end of a descent of one of the many climbs with smoking brakes, with the Morley brothers close at hand having just retired, so near the end of the rally.

277 EBL receives a rubber drive coupling change to keep in the running.

completely rewired with a unique wiring loom, handmade in the car by the two semi-resident Lucas technicians John Smith and Stan Chalmers.

Crew comfort was served by a Microcell bucket and Microcell recliner with a lap-and-diagonal and full harness belts respectively. Weight was saved by using Perspex in place of glass (other than the laminated front windscreen); the bonnet was also lightened, and sound-deadening material was removed behind the trim. Padding was fitted to the sides of the door pockets, and covers to the door locks and a grab handle fitted over the passenger's door. Of course, special dash panels were fabricated for each side of the fascia to suit the additional switches and instruments, notably a special Halda distance recorder behind a magnifier for the navigator and also a pair of Heuer watches. Only the brake line was run inside the car; the battery and fuel lines ran outside but, along with the fuel pump, were protected.

The 1963 Alpine, starting and finishing in Marseille was a five-day 2300-mile tough rally, a third of which was in darkness. It included 17 laps of the Monza circuit and eight speed hillclimbs over mountain passes, the longest of which being 84 miles. For these the roads were closed but for the other 24 special sections of over 480 miles, timed to the second, they were not.

Of the 87 starters, only 24 finished – one of which was Aaltonen, who won the touring category and an Alpine Cup for a penalty run. BMC also won the team prize. Aaltonen posted some stunning times in the Cooper S – five times beating the GT category winner's Alfa Romeo on the speed hillclimbs, such was his pace.

However, the ever-troublesome rubber drive couplings presented problems, being changed at the roadside as preventive measures because one other Mini had already been lost due to their failure far away from the attendant BMC service crews. Aaltonen was also sensible enough to nurse his car when necessary, and was noticeably slower through towns and villages when needed – a complete contrast to his laughingly fast style on the speed sections. The only sadness for BMC was the Morley twins being denied their Gold Alpine Cup, for three consecutive clean sheets, when their Healey's diff failed so near the end. Tears were shed.

For the car's next event, the Tour de France in the September, 227 EBL was to be driven by the crew of Pauline Mayman and Liz Jones. Jonny Lay was again responsible for the preparation of the car, and again as Group 2 in the touring class. Contemporary photos of the car for the Tour de France

Pauline Mayman with a different 277 EBL on the Tour de France with the fog lights removed from the overriders.

The numerous race circuits meant the car only had the driver on-board for much of the competition but Liz Jones was still needed for the hillclimbs and to guide the car over the 3600-mile route.

would indicate, however, that it was likely a different car from the Alpine Mini that Aaltonen had previously used. This was largely due to the different positions of the Lift-the-Dot fixings for the straps on the Perspex headlight protectors, which were quite different and always a giveaway for a changed car, as it is exceedingly unlikely a car would ever have two front wings and a front panel replaced. Additionally, the number plate on the bonnet was also very different. However, there is no documentary evidence to support this notion.

With the Tour being heavily based on race circuit work, the car's build was more about outright top-speed performance. With the compression raised to 11:1, the cylinders over-bored by 0.040in and with the full-race 648 camshaft, the engine had more power available, and to get more top speed out of the car, it was fitted with a long 3.75 diff ratio. Using their usual twin H4 SU carbs on ram pipes, the needles chosen were MMEs with red springs, after thorough testing to ensure the mix was not lean at the top end.

Again, because of the racetrack work, the suspension trumpets were lowered at the front by 4mm but standard at the rear. Extra bump-stops were also fitted to the rear, and the car now sported quick-lift jacking brackets front and rear. These were early jacking points, which were fitted behind the lower panels and not onto the front as they were later.

Novel for the Tour de France was the fitting of fog lights onto the car's two front overriders, which was to allow a better airflow through to the engine. In fact, these lights were often removed during the daylight sections, only to be replaced at night. European headlights were fitted and, once again, a C40 dynamo. Electrics for the Tour de France were essentially simpler than for other rallies.

Microcell seats were used with Britax lap-and-diagonal belts on both sides. Pauline Mayman also preferred the then-fashionable wood-rim steering wheel. Weight saving was again evident, with only one spare wheel being carried, Perspex rear windows and a lightened bonnet. There was also minimal trim in the car – and crew padding was to be found on the door locks only.

Starting from Strasbourg, the 3600-mile, ten-day tour around France was a popular event for BMC because France was considered to be an important market; the Tour, sponsored by *L'Equipe* (a French sports newspaper), always guaranteed the event received great press coverage. It was, however, a fearsome test for the cars, where a dozen races from one to two hours long greeted the cars as they toured around France, visiting racetracks and hillclimb courses.

It was not to be a good event for Mayman and 277 EBL, when the car retired before Le Mans, at not half distance on day three, with a rod through the side. Just 30 cars out of the 122 that started finished the gruelling event back in Nice, so the Mini was in good company.

Pauline Mayman would keep the car again, this time with Val Domleo as co-driver, to tackle the 1963 RAC Rally. However, once again there was a car swap, this time back to the original Mini used on the Alpine Rally, as the RAC car used by Mayman here I believe to be the original 277 EBL and not the Tour de France car.

Johnny Organ was trusted with the build of the Group 2 car for the event and, as was always the case, strength and reliability were high on the list of priorities for this demanding and damaging event for the little low-slung cars.

The engine build was similar to the car's previous specification, apart from reverting to the favoured short 4.1 diff to give better acceleration on the forest roads. For the RAC the car had a 3/16in Dural sheet sump guard, which would prove to be somewhat ineffective as it progressively wore away on the abrasive tracks. Once again, competition dampers were fitted but it was noted that no body strengthening was undertaken, probably due to more diligent scrutineering being expected on Abingdon's home event. To keep the engine warm and dry, a grille muff, made in the MG trim shop, was fitted. This had opening flaps to let in air, in part or full, and was fitted with Lift-the-Dot studs that were screwed to the outside of the grille moustache.

Electrics were still supplied by a C40 dynamo, and Abingdon was now standardising on using two large Lucas 700 fog lights, which would be standard-fit on almost all of the works Minis, right to the end. A single spot light was secured on the centre of 277 EBL's slam panel, and it also ran a roof-mounted spotter lamp, again a Lucas 700, which was variously used to point the way around corners and also as a means of picking out road signs. It was rotated by the co-driver via a large handgrip dangling from the roof, but these lamps were soon to be outlawed by the rule makers and would disappear from the cars.

The other noticeable addition to the car for the RAC was the provision of headlight washers, which consisted of a brake

The Alpine car used by Aaltonen was now used by Pauline Mayman on the 1963 RAC Rally.

A deserted forest stage, somewhere in the Lake District on the 1963 RAC Rally, where the car would finish in 30th place.

Bundy tube with a stopper end fitted near to the lower quarter of the headlight rim. This was fed by a separate washer bottle and was, in truth, only marginally effective at keeping the headlights clear. Otherwise the car was equipped much as it was on the Alpine Rally.

Mayman did not get off to a good start on the 2200-mile RAC Rally with its 400 miles of mainly forest tracks, when she slipped off the road and landed in deep mud. It took the rally marshals some considerable time before they could extract the ladies and send them on their way – but fortunately without recording any loss of time.

Along with the other works Minis, rubber driveshaft couplings were changed and the sump guards reinforced as they were progressively worn away. Mayman ended in 30th position overall at the finish in Bournemouth, after five days' hard motoring with only one night's rest back at Blackpool. The crew was also third in the Ladies' Award behind Pat Moss and Ann Hall – two very fast women, both in Ford Cortinas. With Hopkirk coming home fourth in his Cooper S and Mäkinen fifth in the Healey, it was a good event for Abingdon – but the Scandinavians still held their strong hold on the event, with Tom Trana in his Volvo clearly leading the field.

The merry-go-round for 277 EBL continued for the car's final event, the 1964 Monte, when a new-build 569 FMO was rebadged to be entered as 277 EBL. The 'new' car now also appeared as an Austin and not a Morris, as it was originally. This swapping around of cars was not unusual and easy to understand, and despite the RAC car 277 EBL being much used, it was thoroughly re-prepared and plate swapped for Aaltonen to use as 569 FMO for the 1964 Monte. However, as an entry was already in place for 277 EBL for Mayman for the Monte, where customs paperwork had to be completed well in advance, it was pragmatic to rebadge another car rather than go through the tiresome process of changing the required customs documents.

Thus we saw an all-new 569 FMO replated as the 277 EBL Monte car, to be crewed again by Mayman and Val Domleo, with Johnny Organ once more responsible for the build. The big change for this – and the other six works Minis prepared for the Monte (not all Cooper Ss) – was the use of a heated

277 EBL fully prepared and ready for the Monte Carlo Rally, seen here prior to the 569 FMO plate swap.

The sidelights needed to be relocated around the wing to accommodate the fog lamp used as the dipped beam. The car was rebadged as 569 FMO.

A completely different dashboard now on the car (which soon became 569 FMO) with a full-width dash and the small Halda behind a magnifier. Note the servo under the dashboard.

The two studded tyres carried in the boot, held down by bungee straps. Note the 'clear view' on the rear window, protection to the tank sides with Aston filler caps.

Pauline Mayman illustrated the Elwell car shovel carried in the works cars to dig themselves out on the Monte if needed. The car is actually the new 569 FMO badged as 277 EBL.

front windscreen for the very first time. These early screens had a gold film in the laminate through which current was passed to heat the 'screen, which was operated only on the driver's half, such was the current drain. These screens, however, were not universally popular with all of the drivers, and BMC made provision to change back to standard windscreens along the route, should the drivers prefer. Several did.

Also new for the Monte was the fitment of iodine headlight bulbs. However, these early bulbs did not have a dip facility, so it was served by the use of two small Lucas 576 fog lamps mounted below the headlights where the indicators lamps were located – which in turn were moved further outboard.

The electrical system, always heavily stressed on the Monte with the demands for extra powerful heaters and a battery of extra lights, would still see Abingdon stuck with the old C40 dynamo, albeit reworked to produce 28 amps. The cars now, with the extra dip fog lights below the headlight, had an array of eight lamps including the roof lamp – certainly enough to challenge the dynamo.

Despite the best preparation of the car, no account can be made for the unforeseen, as happened to the girls just outside Maastricht from their Paris start. They were unceremoniously hit by an errant farm vehicle, which lurched into the main road without warning and straight into the new car. The Mini was badly damaged and the girls were only just able to get clear before it burst into flames, completely destroying the car; such was the inferno that the carburettors melted onto the upturned bonnet. They crew were both taken to hospital, where it was found Mayman had suffered a broken rib and cuts about her head, whilst Domleo, who had been asleep at the time, was badly shocked but otherwise unhurt.

Despite this setback, the 1964 Monte was a fabulous success for BMC where Paddy Hopkirk won the event in 33 EJB. BMC also won the manufacturers' team award with a clean sweep, and in the touring car class with Hopkirk, Mäkinen and Aaltonen. Not a bad result for Abingdon but sadly not for 277 EBL.

The burnt-out wreck of Pauline Mayman's car on the Monte Carlo Rally. The photo was used by Britax to illustrate the benefit of its seat belts.

Competition Record

Date	Event	Crew	Number	Overall result	Class result
June 1963	Alpine Rally	Rauno Aaltonen/Tony Ambrose	63	1st	1st
Sept 1963	Tour de France	Pauline Mayman/Liz Jones	39	DNF	
Nov 1963	RAC Rally	Pauline Mayman/Val Domleo	38	30th	
Jan 1964	Monte Carlo Rally	Pauline Mayman/Val Domleo	189	DNF	

Registration Number	First registered	Chassis number	Engine	Engine number	Model
33 EJB	May 1963	KA2S4 384627	1071cc	9F-SA-H 19269	Morris Cooper S

The last of the three early 1071 Cooper Ss delivered to Abingdon, 33 EJB was soon to become one of the most famous of all works Minis. It is retained at the Heritage Museum at Gaydon, Warwickshire, along with the two other Monte Carlo Rally winners: AJB 44B and LBL 6D.

Although the car is highly prized and much revered, it is sadly not presented in the museum exactly as it was when it won 1964 Monte Carlo Rally. Students of the Mini should therefore be aware when noting details of this and the other three cars held at Gaydon that, at the time of writing, they are not 100 per cent correct.

However, we are jumping ahead of ourselves, as 33EJB was first to be prepared for Paddy Hopkirk and Henry Liddon to tackle the Tour de France in the preceding September. Built by Jonny Organ, for the touring car class, the engine was over-bored +040in with a 11.1 compression ratio gained from a polished and gas-flowed cylinder head, which was modified by the in-house engine branch. It also had a full-race 648 camshaft and a long-ish 3.7 diff in an attempt to get a high top speed out of the car (at the expense of acceleration), which would be better suited to the predominantly circuit work the Tour dished out on its journey around much of France. The twin H4 carbs, fitted with MME needles and a red springs, were also found to give an extra 5bhp when fitted with ram pipes rather than air filters when put on the rolling road – every little helps.

WORKS MINIS IN DETAIL

Paddy Hopkirk lifting a wheel with 33 EJB on the 1964 Tour de France.

Service on the car, attending to the two leaking fuel tanks the car experienced. Note the standard passenger seat.

The car was lowered by removing 4mm off the suspension trumpets front and back, and special lowered shockers were used all round.

To aid cooling, the heater had the heat ducted out of the car through the floor, so it could be used even in the heat of the day. Additionally, the inner wing, by the radiator, was cut away and replaced with wire mesh to get a bit more airflow. For the Tour minimal extra lights were fitted to the car, other than two small fog lights fixed to the overriders.

Other unique features found on Tour de France cars were the identification stripes: 33 EJB carried two broad stripes, one on either side of the bonnet, and another slender pair on the boot. The other team cars had single stripes on either left or right, and one had no stripes at all. All was to aid identification as the cars sped past. Additionally, the crew names were painted on in a large script to help spectators see who was driving. Hopkirk was to use a Microcell bucket seat but Liddon had to content himself with a standard Mini seat. Paddy also used a wooden steering wheel.

The Tour de France, being an event that was very important to BMC, generally saw a four-car team from Abingdon tackle the 3600-mile event around France, visiting many famous racetracks and hillclimbs over a ten-day period in late summer. The French seemed to enjoy watching Minis tear around the tracks nose-to-tail, and Paddy was indeed a crowd favourite with his giant killing, driving against much bigger cars and often getting the better of them. Press coverage, in France at least, from one of the event's main sponsors *L'Equipe*, the French sports newspaper, was certainly guaranteed. Hopkirk continually hit the headlines with the great results he achieved with the Mini, many times beating quite formidable opposition, and he soon became untouchable.

Paddy had little trouble with the car on the event, apart from getting through two new petrol tanks, both of which sprung leaks, dumping fuel and fumes into the car. Paddy brought the car home in a brilliant third place overall in the touring car class on scratch, and of course winning the handicap class comfortably. He was certainly a big hit in France in the Mini, which did BMC France a great deal of good to sales figures.

The next event for 33 EJB was the 1964 Monte Carlo Rally. As was becoming Abingdon's standard practice, a new car was built for the Monte. This one event would cement Paddy Hopkirk as a household name and bring the Mini right to the front of the public's eye with this famous outright Monte win.

Hopkirk's Monte-winning Mini was built by Gerald Wiffen as a Group 1 car. As such, the engine was very standard, even

More service on the car - Stuart Turner looks on. Note the details of the rear of the car showing its identification stripes.

Paddy Hopkirk and Henry Liddon at the finish in a fine third place with a much travel-stained 33 EJB.

Engine detail of the new 33 EJB built for Paddy Hopkirk and Henry Liddon for the 1964 Monte Carlo Rally.

down to the fitting of a standard Cooper S camshaft, with the cylinder head being just cleaned (no polishing or flowing), giving 10.5:1 compression. However, a straight-cut gearbox was used and a 4.133 diff, ideally suited for climbing up and over the Alps. The suspension was also standard, with the ride height unchanged but using competition dampers all round.

All five of the other team 1071 Cooper Ss entered for the Monte were prepared to a very similar specification as 33 EJB, being entered into the standard production class, which heavily restricted the allowable modifications.

The all-new Triplex heated front windscreen fitted to the car was quite a revelation, and with its gold appearance caused a few problems; Hopkirk was soon to change his heated 'screen for a clear one, as he found looking through it a distraction. The gold film was early technology, borrowed from the aviation industry, where the film, inlayed in the laminate, carried a current that effectively demisted the driver's half of the 'screen.

The lighting on the car was also upgraded with the use, for the first time, of iodine bulbs. These, however, had the drawback of not having a dip facility when used in the headlights, so small Lucas fog lights were fitted where the indicators used to sit, and would be switched on when the dip switch was operated and the headlights went out. In all, with a new roof light, the car ran eight lamps, which put high demands on the uprated C40 dynamo.

As was common on all works cars, after the Aaltonen accident on the 1962 Monte in 11 NYB (when the car burnt out after the battery shorted out on the side of the fuel tank when he left the road), all cars had their batteries reversed with the terminals away from the fuel tank. This meant the battery cable, which ran outside the car, needed to be changed to a longer cable, but it was a small price to pay for a bit more safety. It was only the brake line that ran inside the car, as the fuel line also ran outside. Both, however, were protected with metal channelling.

Paddy's car was fitted was a Microcell bucket seat and a Microcell recliner. The trim was removed as much as possible, and in particular from the rear seat, as the rear bulkhead had to be modified to allow the fitment of two studded tyres stacked on top of each other, which meant the boot wouldn't shut without relieving the rear bulkhead; the simple solution was to cut a section of an oil drum and let it into the bulkhead! The fuel tanks were also protected from damage from the studded tyres by a plywood facing on the tanks.

The brake servo was also fitted inside the car, above the passenger's footwell, which allowed room for the larger heater to be fitted under the bonnet. Inside the car the dashboard was a fabricated aluminium three-piece affair, which housed all the extra switches and instruments, including a small Halda behind a magnifier lens and a pair of Heuer clocks – one recording the time of day and the other a stopwatch. These much-valued pieces were always removed from the cars and kept in a locked cupboard at Abingdon when not in use.

Starting from Minsk was never the easy option for Hopkirk. Temperatures were so low (at -26C) that many cars had to be tow-started. The severe Russian weather was just one of many problems, along with unreadable road signs and the expected Russian officialdom, with Hopkirk being reprimanded for taking too many photos of Russia!

But France proved to be worse, with Hopkirk being caught by a gendarme when driving the wrong way down a one-way street. Back then (and still the case on the Monte today) such traffic transgressions generally resulted in a time penalty, and in severe cases disqualification. A quick-witted Hopkirk explained to the gendarme that he had retired from the rally because he was rushing back home to his mother's funeral; the ruse worked, and he escaped the penalty and went on to win the event.

But not without a superb tussle with Bo Ljungfeldt in the mighty Ford Falcon. It was truly a David and Goliath battle, with the huge Ford Falcons dwarfing the little Minis. The 1071 Mini was beaten by the Ford by a small margin on the majority of the stages but on the final rush round the Grand Prix circuit (1964 would be the last running of this test) the Mini narrowly won on the handicap.

In the end, despite a somewhat advantageous handicap system favouring the Mini over the large-engined Falcon, Hopkirk was only 81 seconds behind the Ford on scratch times, which showed just how quick the Mini was.

BMC celebrated in fine style with the car's designer, Alec Issigonis, flying down to Monte to join in the party. The cars were all flown back to England in a chartered Carvair

Interior shot of 33 EJB from the driver's side showing the full-width dashboard and Microcell bucket seat.

Interior shot of the navigator's side showing the Halda distance recorder behind a magnifier.

Boot detail of 33 EJB with its fabricated spare wheel clamp and modified MGB jack. Tank sides protected with plywood.

CHAPTER 3: THE MK 1 MINI COOPER S

Paddy Hopkirk and Henry Liddon on their way to winning the 1964 Monte Carlo Rally. Not sure what the gentleman on his camping chair is doing!

Den Green and Paddy Hopkirk attend to the wipers on the car at a routine service on their way to victory.

Paddy Hopkirk and Henry Liddon in a snow-covered road - with warning sign of the hazardous bends on the road.

Paddy Hopkirk and Henry Liddon with all the silverware for winning the Monte Carlo Rally at the award ceremony. It would be the start of four wins in a row for the Mini (if you include the 1966 fiasco with the lighting).

33 EJB with Hopkirk and Liddon and much of the BMC team arrive victorious at Southend Airport, where a civic reception and the press greeted them.

and 33 EJB, along with the victorious crew, were to feature on the televised broadcast of Sunday Night at the London Palladium the following weekend, viewed by nearly half of the UK nation.

There is one more story to tell surrounding the often-incorrect rumour that 33 EJB was stolen whilst it was in London with Paddy Hopkirk, allegedly being taken by a soldier and crashed. There is some truth in that a car Hopkirk had taken to London was stolen but it was 569 FMO, Rauno Aaltonen's Monte car (not Mäkinen's car which has also been incorrectly reported). The Mini was stolen by an unemployed young man who admitted the charge at Bow Street Magistrates' Court, saying he just wanted to experience the car. The Mini was not damaged, and 33EJB, at the time, was safely tucked up on display at the Racing Car Show.

The car now resides in the British Motor Heritage Museum in Warwickshire, England.

Competition Record

Date	Event	Crew	Number	Overall result	Class result
Sept 1963	Tour de France	Paddy Hopkirk/Henry Liddon	38	3rd	1st
Jan 1964	Monte Carlo Rally	Paddy Hopkirk/Henry Liddon	37	1st	1st

CHAPTER 3: THE MK 1 MINI COOPER S

Registration Number	First registered	Chassis number	Engine	Engine number	Model
569 FMO	Nov 1963	CA2S7 482488	1071cc	9F-SA-H 26586	Morris Cooper S

Two new cars were delivered to Abingdon, both Austin Cooper Ss, in November 1963. This was likely to balance the three Morris Cooper Ss sent in May, as Abingdon was corporately obliged to use both marques in equal numbers.

But these Austins were destined to have a relatively short competition life at Abingdon: 569 FMO did but one event – the 1964 Monte Carlo Rally – in the hands of Rauno Aaltonen, and this was shrouded in some mystery and confusion. The contemporary build sheets indicate that in fact 277 EBL was used on that Monte, carrying the registration plate of 569 FMO, and although 569 FMO was an Austin, it was clearly displaying Morris Cooper badges screwed to the bonnet and boot.

This saga is further compounded by the actual entry for 277 EBL on the Monte for Pauline Mayman, which shows on its build sheet that the car entered was actually 569 FMO… So it would seem that the two cars were swapped around, with the newer car (569 FMO) given to Pauline Mayman (although badged as 277 EBL), with Rauno Aaltonen using the older machine, 277 EBL (badged as 569 FMO). However, for the Monte, the old 277 EBL was reused as 569 FMO but built to identical specifications.

One plausible reason behind the swapping was that an entry was already in place for 569 FMO for Aaltonen, where customs paperwork had already been completed well in advance, and it was therefore easier to rebadge 277 EBL rather than go through the time-consuming process of changing the necessary customs documents. Likewise for Mayman, who had likely already been entered in 277 EBL. Quite why Abingdon started off building the 'wrong' cars for each driver is a mystery, but it was simply resolved by swapping number plates.

So we will describe here the build of the car that became 569 FMO. Constructed much along the lines as its sister cars for the 1964 Monte, 569 FMO was put together by Bob Whittington as a Group 1 standard production-class car, and as such was not heavily modified. The engine had a standard bore of 1071cc but with flat-top pistons to up the compression to 10.6:1 from an unmodified cylinder head of 21.5cc capacity. The engine block, because of the anticipated cold weather, had core plug retainers to ensure they could not fall or blow out.

The straight-cut gearbox (with a 4.133 diff) was protected by an RAF-type guard with an alloy extension plate. The oil cooler was noted to be an MGB type, which varied only in that the top mounting ears were not there but the flexible pipes were wire-locked in place for added security. The carburettors were twin 1½in H4 SUs with float chamber extensions, MME needles and red springs, and modified to 'fork and peg' throttle control but without air cleaners, so fitted with ram pipes. Cooling was helped with a four-bladed fan, and should it become too cold, the MG trim shop had tailored a grille muff, which had sections that could be opened or closed to allow some or no airflow over the engine. It was secured around the grille moustache with Lift-the-Dot studs.

The suspension was standard, apart from the fitting of additional bump rubbers to the rear and competition dampers on special brackets at the front. Quick-lift jacking brackets were fitted front and back below the bumpers, which enabled the mechanics to quickly raise the car with their own fabricated over-centre jacks that were carried on the roofs of their service barges, which were invariably large Austin A110 Westminsters. The brake line was the only pipe run inside the

Engine shot of 569 FMO - again similar to that of 33 EJB but with two angled relays on the top left of the bulkhead.

WORKS MINIS IN DETAIL

Interior of 569 FMO - very similar to 33 EJB but devoid of the fusebox on the navigator's side.

Rauno Aaltonen and Tony Ambrose slide 569 FMO through the summit of the Col du Turini.

car, as both the fuel and battery lines ran outside but protected by channelling. The twin fuel pump was fitted in the standard position on the rear subframe but protected by an alloy plate.

The electrics, always stretched to the full on the Monte because of the high demands for heating and lighting, were still fed by a modified 28amp C40 dynamo. The battery was reversed, with the terminals facing away from the additional right-hand fuel tank, protected by thin plywood glued to the tank face, in case the studded spare tyres punctured the thin steel. A two-speed wiper motor was fitted but not wired through the ignition.

Lighting on the Monte was always very important and by now Abingdon was using newly-developed quartz iodine bulbs. But these early bulbs did not have a dipping facility, so the dipped beam was provided by a small Lucas 576 fog light fitted below the headlight where the indicators usually sat; these in turn were moved further around the lower wing. The headlights also had washers directed onto them via a small tube, in a vain attempt to keep them clean. Additional lighting came from two large Lucas 700 fog lights and one long-range Cyclops spot light fitted on the slam panel. A roof lamp was not fitted to this car.

Other electrical additions included, for the first time, a heated front 'screen, albeit only on the driver's half. It had a gold film in the laminate, which when a current was passed through it, heated up and demisted the windscreen. Aaltonen was happy with the 'screen, unlike other drivers who complained about their vision being distracted through the glass; he used it throughout the rally, whilst others reverted back to the standard clear 'screen.

Inside the car, Aaltonen used a wooden steering wheel and a Microcell bucket seat, with a Microcell recliner for Ambrose. The dashboard was a three-piece continuous panel right across the parcel shelf, which contained all of the additional switches and instruments together with a Halda distance recorder, behind a magnifier, and a pair of Heuer watches, which completed the navigation tools.

The brake servo was fitted under that dash rail, and a clear Perspex heat deflector was fitted to the top of the dash rail to direct as much heat from the demister vents as possible to the screen. Padding was supplied to the door locks and, although the carpet was retained, as much trim as possible was removed to save weight. In the boot, there were two spare wheels and a modified MGB side jack, with the boot externally having a Lucas 576 fog light as a reversing light.

Starting from Norway, Aaltonen faced the longest haul from the most northerly point of the route on their 2800-mile journey to Monte Carlo. As the sole works Mini starter from Oslo (the other works Minis started from Minsk and Paris), the expectation was for bad weather. But not only was it mostly devoid of snow and ice, they arrived in good time at Reims for the common run to Chambéry, having journeyed the whole way on standard Duraband road tyres.

The common run was divided into four sections, all to be achieved at 37mph for the first 500 miles, which proved easy enough; it was only on the higher ground that Aaltonen used studded tyres just on the front. Once at Chambéry the pace picked up dramatically, and this is where the competition really began, with five flat-out stages over the last 400 miles to Monte. Here the conditions worsened, with the ever-present danger of patchy ice to catch out the unwary. With the often-high-speed descents testing the very brave, Aaltonen was heard to comment that it was the most dangerous rally he'd ever driven. These five stages, of around 85 miles, effectively decided the event, as all that remained was for the top 120 crews to take on the circuit race around the streets of Monte Carlo the following day.

Much confusion was caused when Aaltonen was called in one lap too early by the marshals, with the result that they had to average his earlier laps to get his final time. Aaltonen was rewarded with seventh place overall and was part of the winning BMC team. With Hopkirk winning the rally, Abingdon was now on a real high, having achieved what was without doubt the most prestigious of all rallies to win.

The Monte Carlo Rally was 569 FMO's one-and-only event.

Aaltonen and Ambrose arrive at the finish of the 1964 Monte Carlo Rally in seventh place overall.

Aaltonen on the Monaco Grand Prix circuit's final timed test of the Monte.

WORKS MINIS IN DETAIL

569 FMO with 37 on the door prior to being mocked up as 33 EJB to do the publicity rounds for the press and dealerships, such was the demands to see the winning car of Hopkirk's.

A youthful Rauno Aaltonen looking pensive along the harbour front of Monte Carlo.

Its only other appearance was straight after the Monte as a press loan car, where it was badged up to look like 33 EJB, the victorious Monte Mini – such were the demands of the press to get their hands on the 'winning' car that Abingdon cloned it. However, as all of the Monte cars were virtually identical, it was an easy and convincing operation, driven largely by expediency.

The car was sold to Mike Wood, who managed to buy several works Minis during his time at Abingdon as one of the top co-drivers.

Competition Record

Date	Event	Crew	Number	Overall result	Class result
Jan 1964	Monte Carlo Rally	Rauno Aaltonen/Tony Ambrose	105	7th	

Registration Number	First registered	Chassis number	Engine	Engine number	Model
570 FMO	Nov 1963	CA2S7 482499	1071cc	9F-SA-H 26606	Morris Cooper S

The second of the two new Austin Cooper Ss delivered to Abingdon in November 1963, 570 FMO arrived in time to be prepared for the 1964 Monte Carlo Rally the following January. This car, along with its sister 569 FMO, would have a relatively short competition career of just two events, the latter of which was a monumental achievement that no other Mini before or since ever managed – to finish the fearsome Spa-Sofia-Liège Rally.

But first the new car was entrusted to Brian Moylan to prepare for Timo Mäkinen and Patrick Vanson for the Monte. Patrick was semi-domicile in France and spoke fluent French, and was a regular co-driver with Mäkinen in these early days.

Built as a Group 1 standard production class car, it was not heavily modified or lightened, so despite its outward appearance was relatively ordinary. The engine capacity was kept standard at 1071cc but with flat-top pistons increasing the compression to 10.6:1 from an unmodified cylinder head, which had not been polished but just 'cleaned'. The engine block had core plug retainers (to ensure they stayed put in possibly freezing conditions) in the form of lovely crafted circular plates screwed over the core plug aperture.

One other interesting Abingdon touch to the engine was to 'blue' the end of the dipstick. This was done by heating the end to turn it blue, before it went red hot, then quenching it.

Once blued, it made the oil level on the dipstick much easier to read.

The carburettors were twin 1½in H4 SUs with float chamber extensions, MME needles and red springs, and the linkage modified to 'fork and peg' throttle control. This arrangement, copied from earlier SU carbs, allowed the special throttle cable, with a nylon insert, to have some safe slack to avoid early failure. However, with no internal springs on the shaft, external spring hangers were needed (one for each carb) to shut the throttles. The carbs also did not use air cleaners, so were fitted with open ram pipes.

The radiator core had 16 gills per inch and the header tank was fitted with a 13psi cap, which, together with a four-blade fan, kept things cool. A spare fan belt was fitted around the timing chain cover in case of failure, which meant easier refitting when in a hurry. A thermostat was fitted into the cooling system and the drain plug was also wire-locked shut for added security, as was the engine drain plug.

A straight-cut gearbox with a 4.133 diff was fitted into a specially-selected gear casing. This explains why the gearbox was always left unpainted (unlike production cars, which were painted mid bronze green BS223). The flywheel housing was also specially selected and also unpainted. Both of these components were as perfectly matched as possible and were carefully selected from the vast stock at Abingdon's disposal.

For the Monte, a lightweight RAF sump guard with an alloy extension plate was used, as that rally, although often snow bound, was not considered to be a rough event.

The suspension was standard, with Cooper S cones front and back without packing washers to raise the ride height. Other than the fitting of additional bump rubbers to the rear and competition dampers on special brackets at the front, it was all very standard. Quick-lift jack brackets were fitted front and back below the bumpers, which allowed the mechanics to quickly raise the car at service halts. The tie rods used castellated nuts and split pins at each end to ensure they stayed put. Brakes were standard Cooper S but fitted with Ferodo DS11 front pads and VG95 rear shoes – borrowed straight from the race track. Mäkinen was notoriously hard on his brakes with his left-foot braking.

On this car both the fuel and battery lines ran outside but were protected by channelling; the brake line was the only pipe run inside the car. The twin fuel pump was fitted in the standard position on the rear subframe but protected by an alloy plate. A lovely Abingdon-made grille muff was fitted over the front grille and equipped with Lift-the-Dot studs to the front panel, as the grille moustache was removed. This clever muff had opening panels to allow little or no airflow over the engine should the weather deteriorate.

The car's electrics, still fed by a modified 28amp C40 dynamo, were on the absolute limit, such were the demands on the electrical system on the Monte because of the extra heating and lighting requirements. The battery was reversed, with the terminals now facing away from the fuel tank. Both tanks, fitted with quick-release Aston filler caps, were both protected by thin plywood sheet glued to the tank face to prevent the studded tyres in the boot from puncturing the tanks.

Lighting was now much improved, and the cars used newly-developed quartz iodine bulbs. Unfortunately, these early bulbs had only single a single filament, so the dipped beam was provided by a small Lucas 576 fog light fitted below the headlight, where the indicators were usually fitted. The headlights also had rather primitive washers directed onto them via a small bent metal tube. Additional lighting was provided by two large Lucas 700 fog lights and a long-range single spot light fitted on the slam panel. A roof lamp was also added to this car to allow the navigator to pick out corners for the driver. The boot had a Lucas 576 fog light as a reversing light. In all, a lot of extra lamps!

Other electrical additions included, for the first time, a heated front windscreen that had a gold film in the laminate, which when a current was passed through it, heated up and demisted the screen. Mäkinen was pleased with the 'screen, unlike Hopkirk and Baxter who complained about their vision being distracted through the glass. Mäkinen used it throughout the rally.

Inside the car, Mäkinen used the popular and fashionable Moss wooden steering wheel and a Microcell bucket seat, with a Microcell recliner for the navigator. The dashboard, similar to the other Monte cars of the time, was a three-piece continuous panel across the parcel shelf; this contained all of the additional switches and instruments, together with a Halda distance recorder, housed behind a magnifier, plus a pair of Heuer watches. The brake servo fitted under that dash rail made room for a high-capacity heater under the bonnet. Despite the fitting of a heated 'screen, the car still had an internal Perspex heat deflector mounted on the top rail of the dashboard.

A push-button starter on an extension rod was fitted onto the lower dash rail on the right-hand side to allow Mäkinen to restart the car without reaching to the centre ignition key. Mäkinen also had a two-speed wiper motor fitted but this was not wired through the ignition. Padding was fitted to the door locks and the carpet was retained, but as much trim as possible was removed to save weight.

Starting from Paris on their circuitous route to Reims, which took over two days, going anti-clockwise up to Arnhem, Boulogne and over to Angoulême, Mäkinen arrived at the Reims control feeling under the weather, with food poisoning. However, the relaxed time schedule of 37mph for the 1800-mile journey had allowed the crew to arrive in good time.

From Reims, the rally started with the common run to Chambéry divided into four sections, which got tighter as the route progressed. Fortunately, largely devoid of snow, the time schedule was cleaned by many. The real action started at

WORKS MINIS IN DETAIL

Timo Mäkinen understeering around a snow-covered stage with Patrick Vanson calmly reading the pace notes.

Mäkinen and Vanson with the awards at the finish ceremony in Monaco.

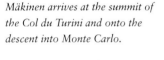

Mäkinen arrives at the summit of the Col du Turini and onto the descent into Monte Carlo.

Chambéry with five special stages, timed to the second and varying in length from 11 to 29 miles. These would decide the rally.

The slippery conditions on the high passes were indeed a handicap for the hard-charging Ford Falcons but favoured the little front-wheel-drive Mini with its studded tyres fitted for the ice. Mäkinen used 'pop in' studs in Dunlop Weathermaster tyres on the front for the Col de Turini, Dunlop SPs being used almost through out the rally. Mäkinen, now recovered from his illness, was swapping times with the other works Minis and keeping the Falcons within reach.

Of the 299 starters, 163 arrived at Monte Carlo, 73 of them penalty free. Mäkinen was in fourth place, and with only the three laps of the Grand Prix circuit to tackle the next day, his position was secured. BMC won the event with Paddy Hopkirk and also the team award with Aaltonen. Many celebrations followed, and this rally marked the start for Mäkinen as a front runner on only his third event for Abingdon; it would soon be his turn to win this prestigious of all rallies. Above all, the Mini Cooper S was now a winner.

The next event for 570 FMO, the gruelling Spa-Sofia-Liège Rally, went down in history as the only time a Mini was ever to finish the event. The car was reprepared after the Monte with the addition of a large heavy-duty sump guard to combat the very rough roads the event always threw at competitors, and it also received a 1275 Cooper S engine, bored out to 1293cc to give as much power as possible.

The car was assigned to John Wadsworth, on his one and only works drive, after winning a coveted Alpine Coupe on the 1964 Alpine in his own Cooper S. Accompanying John was Mike Wood, the canny Lancastrian, who was a master on the maps and would prove his worth on this incredibly demanding rally. John had completed a partial recce of the route with other BMC crews, and having done the 1963 event, was under no illusion about the challenge in front of them.

The Liège was really more of a race than a rally, with a 3500-mile route over four days and nights, non-stop. And other than a one-hour rest halt at Sofia, before they turned round and raced back to Spa, it was all flat-out motoring. Maurice Garot, the colourful organiser, only really wanted to see one car finish his event. BMC wanted that to be a Healey and the Mini was, at best, a stop-gap entry. It was not expected to finish, and accordingly BMC carried no Mini spares at all.

The Liège had its own unique timing, which got faster and faster as the event wore on, and with the rough roads in

CHAPTER 3: THE MK 1 MINI COOPER S

Mike Wood and John Wadsworth posing by the rebuilt Monte car before the start of their epic run on the Spa-Sofia-Liège Rally. The toughest of all rallies.

Yugoslavia still set at an average speed in excess of 70kph, it was expected that all the cars would always lose time – up to their three-hour permitted lateness – after which was exclusion.

Needless to say, service time was at a bare minimum, with fuel for the car and sustenance for the crew paramount. The constant pounding of the car over the rough roads eventually sheared the front sump guard mountings, and the Mini came into service with the guard dragging on the ground. Fortunately, Bill Price managed to lash the guard back in place with nylon rope, which miraculously held to the finish.

By then, with two unscheduled detours thrown into the mix, with no time addition, the crew was dangerously near exclusion. Fortunately, once into Sofia for their one-hour rest, the times for the detours were added and once again they had a chance to get the car to the finish.

Only half the field made it to Sofia. The rough roads continued back into Yugoslavia but the lateness limit was also being progressively reduced by the organisers, so again it got faster and faster. By now the terrible bashing the car had sustained started to show itself in a failing drive coupling outside Split. With no service time, let along spares, John had to reduce his pace to save the car. They had also run out of tyres, but fortunately Dunlop had provided spares for BMC.

Despite John's careful driving, with the inevitable time loss, the other drive coupling was also starting to fail. As the crew entered their fourth night out of bed and with still the dreaded Gavia and Stelvio to tackle, good luck came their way, when they found Peter Bartram at the next service point; he, when packing his service barge, had thrown a pair of drive shaft couplings into the car. So if they could make up enough time on the steadily improving roads and slightly more relaxed average speed they could change the couplings.

By then, because all other BMC cars were out (other than Aaltonen, in what was to be the winning Healey) there were two service barges shadowing them to the finish. With more time made up, the joint finally let go, and within minutes the BMC barges drew up behind the stricken Mini. Gaining access to the driveshafts was difficult without a ramp, and the idea was hatched to tip the car on its side to easily get at the joints. This is believed to be the first of many times this process was carried out by the works on numerous rallies over the years.

With the car repaired, all the crew had to do was blast to the finish, some 350km away in Spa. Despite other delays due to traffic congestion, they made it, second to last, in 20th

Wood and Wadsworth about to start the Liège that nobody expected them to finish, so much so that scarce service provisions were laid on for the car. A casual Stuart Turner walks by.

570 FMO receives a new driveshaft coupling by the roadside from the following service barge, which was now attending the Mini as all the other BMC entries had failed.

WORKS MINIS IN DETAIL

An exhausted crew receive the flowers and champagne for finishing the gruelling rally, which covers 3500 miles in four days with only one hour's break. They finished second to last - but finish they did.

570 FMO safely back at the MG Abingdon plant after finishing the Liège, badly cleaned but in one piece. The competition department is on the far left.

place. They had accumulated nearly six hours' lateness, but entered the history books as the only Mini ever to finish this notorious road race.

The car, or what must have been left of it, was sold to Ken James.

Competition Record

Date	Event	Crew	Number	Overall result	Class result
Jan 1964	Monte Carlo Rally	Timo Mäkinen/Patrick Vanson	182	4th	2nd
Aug 1964	Spa-Sofia-Liège	John Wordsworth/Mike Woods	168	20th	

Registration Number	First registered	Chassis number	Engine	Engine number	Model
AJB 33B	Feb 1964	CA2S7 487712	1071cc	9F-SA-H 927680	Austin Cooper S
			1275cc	9F-SA-Y 38155	
			970cc	9F-SA-X 29032	

Timo Mäkinen taking a break from his recce for the 1964 Alpine Rally, which he did with Don Barrow, complete with bald nearside tyre.

This car was one of four new 1071 Cooper Ss delivered to Abingdon in February 1964, all sequentially registered AJB 33, 44, 55 and 66B, two Austins and two Morrises. However, despite being registered as 1071 Cooper Ss, they were all to have 1275cc engines fitted before they entered competition.

With the 1275 Cooper S being officially launched on 11 March 1964, it was logical that 1071s should be farmed out to Abingdon for conversion into 1275s. Abingdon would no longer use the 1071, and although the 1071 would remain available until August 1964, the team would not be restricted to the small engine size again – crews could now compete fully in the up-to-1300cc class with the 1275 Cooper S.

The first event for AJB 33B was to be the Acropolis Rally in Greece, where the new Mini was built by Gerald Wiffen for

Paddy Hopkirk and Henry Liddon to use in the May rally as a Group 2 car. It was fitted with a 1275 engine and presented as a Morris, not an Austin, using a Morris grille and badges.

The engine ran a standard capacity of 1275cc but with a gas-flowed and polished cylinder head to give an increased compression ratio of 10:1. It also featured the Abingdon standard full-race camshaft, the evergreen C-AEA648, generally known as the 649 simply because of the number stamped on the casting. Twin H4 carbs were used with ram pipes and float chamber extensions. The engine didn't run a thermostat but a blanking insert, which eliminated potential thermostat problems and also allowed the engine to run cooler due to less-restricted coolant flow.

The gearbox used straight-cut close-ratio gears, coupled to a 4.133 diff with the output to the driveshafts using special drive couplings. The gearbox and underside of the car was protected by a large full-length 3/16in thick Duralumin sump guard to combat the many rough tracks found in Greece.

The suspension was standard, apart from extra bump stops at the rear and the obligatory competition dampers fitted all round, where the front mounting brackets were also tack-welded for extra strength. Brakes were all standard, apart from competition Ferodo DS11 pads and VG95 linings; the lines ran inside the car.

The electrics, still with an uprated C40 dynamo, powered the additional two fog lights and centrally mounted spot light, all with iodine bulbs. Other additions were two-speed wipers and twin Mixo horns that could also be operated by a foot switch by the co-driver's feet. As was now customary, the battery was turned around with its terminals facing away from the side of the fuel tank, the cable of which still ran outside the car, protected by metal channelling.

Crew comfort was provided by a pair of Microcell seats: a bucket for Hopkirk and a recliner for Liddon; both used Irvin seat belts. Additional padding was provided to the door locks plus the door pockets, and Hopkirk again used a wooden steering wheel. The instrument panels consisted of two flat plates where a 10,000rpm rev counter was provided on the driver's side, together with the additional switches and controls. The speedo was a special unit with an internal trip, and for the navigator, along with a pair of Heuer clocks, his distance recorder was a single Halda unit housed behind a magnifier lens.

The 12th running of the Acropolis Rally was part of the European Championship and was an event in which Abingdon regularly took part. It was an extremely tough event where the roads took their toll on many cars, and was reckoned to be a challenge just to finish, second only to the infamous Liège Rally. Seventy-two cars lined up for the evening start at the foot of the Acropolis in Athens for their three-day 1800-mile dash around Greece – just 19 of which would make it back to the finish.

Hopkirk was quick out of the blocks and was setting a blistering pace with the powerful 1275cc engine, which saw him well into the lead. By half way he was holding off Erik Carlsson's Saab and Tom Trana's Volvo. But as the event wore on, so did the damage to the car that the roads were inflicting. Within just two hours of the finish, and still with a comfortable lead, disaster struck the car when the constant abrasions of the road surface wore through the metal channelling that protected the external battery cable, with the inevitable results that the cable shorted out with the body and burnt out the cable. With little time available to replace the damaged cable, the car was retired, leaving the works Volvo to take the honours. It questioned the sense of having a battery cable on the outside of the car, particularly on such a rough event – something that would soon be changed on all subsequent works Minis.

Soon after the Acropolis Rally, AJB 33B was quickly pressed into service again as a recce car for Timo Mäkinen for the Alpine Rally, due to take place at the end of June. He would be accompanied by Don Barrow, who was summoned at the last minute to accompany Mäkinen on the recce, but would be co-driven by Patrick Vanson on the rally itself.

The next event for this busy car was the 1000 Lakes in Finland in August 1964, where it was handed over to Timo Mäkinen and local co-driver Pekka Keskitalo; they were hoping to do well in Timo's home event, where he was very experienced.

The car was prepared by Tommy Eales and Johnny Evans, including several experimental additions (despite it being Group 2) to be tried during this high-speed race through the

Timo Mäkinen and local co-driver Pekka Keskitalo took AJB 33B to fourth place on the 1964 1000 Lakes.

undulating Finnish forests. Engine capacity was enlarged to 1293cc and fitted with a full-race camshaft; the compression ratio was raised to 11.6:1 with a polished and gas-flowed cylinder head. The distributor was changed to the latest 40979 together with a heavy-duty condenser. The final drive was a very low 4.26:1 and the driveshafts were fitted with Hardy Spicer couplings, in preference to the unreliable rubber. The car produced 80bhp at the wheels on the Abingdon rolling road.

A heavy-duty Scandinavia sump guard was used and the bulkhead steady bracket was safety-welded. In addition, both subframes were seam-welded and the rear subframe had strengthening plates added to the webs. The rear hubs now had Timken roller bearings fitted in place of the standard ball bearing setup, which had proved troublesome to change quickly. The exhaust received extra attention, with it being fully skidded with a turned-up tailpipe, and each joint having a bracket at both sides and a locating bar to ensure it didn't come apart. All lines, fuel, brake and battery were now run inside the car. The suspension was Hydrolastic, with single-red and double-red displacer units front and rear, and despite the common belief that Mäkinen refused to drive a Hydrolastic car, this Mini had the new system.

Abingdon had at last abandoned the use of the ancient C40 dynamo to power the electrics and was now using a Lucas 11AC alternator with a separate 4TR control box. This would make life much easier running the numerous additional lamps and electrical items found on the cars. Also abandoned was the small Halda behind a magnifier for the co-driver, as his distance recorder, with the new Halda Twinmaster now readily available. Gone too were the Microcell seats, replaced by an Abingdon-built recliner and fibreglass bucket seat. It was in essence a much-modified car built to sustain the high speed jumps found on this unique event.

The fast and furious pace saw Mäkinen home in a fine fourth place, behind the winning Saab and the runner-up Volvo; the third-placed Saab was driven by Rauno Aaltonen, which must have rankled with Mäkinen and BMC.

AJB 33B would again revert to recce duties and was used in late October 1964 for tyre testing in preparation for the 1965 Monte Carlo Rally. The car was used by Mäkinen and Easter, and in addition, Henry Liddon and Paul Easter compiled pace notes – which were interrupted by a huge landslide that blocked their progress. The testing and early preparation allowed Mäkinen and Easter to go on to win the 1965 Monte convincingly in what turned out to be atrocious conditions.

The next event for this, by now, much used car was the Swedish Rally in the March. Actually, as AJB 33B was now rather tired, it was swapped for the all-new DJB 92B, which was originally earmarked for Timo Mäkinen but – as we shall see – was built as a 970, while Mäkinen was put into another DJB 92B but a 1275. So Hopkirk was now put into

Mäkinen and Henry Liddon tyre testing for the forthcoming 1965 Monte Carlo Rally.

Henry Liddon surveys the huge rockfall blocking their path with Paul Easter doing route recce for the Monte Carlo Rally.

Paddy Hopkirk and Henry Liddon at the start of the 1964 Swedish Rally.

the original DJB 92B but badged as AJB 33B, which is the car we cover here.

Built by Robin Vokins for the Swedish as a Group 1 car for Paddy Hopkirk and Henry Liddon, albeit originally for Mäkinen, it was a 970S despite the production of the 970 Cooper S ending in the January – BMC having produced (in theory) the 1000 cars needed to satisfy homologation requirements.

Being a Group 1 car and therefore extensively a standard showroom car, there were few modifications allowed. Provision had to be made to provide a seal to the cylinder head, the engine and the gearbox, so that the scrutineer would be able to see if any of these parts had been changed on the rally. The bore was kept to the standard size, and with just an unpolished cylinder head the compression was a modest 9.5:1. However, the engine was still fitted with a full-race camshaft and ran twin 1½ SU carburettors, and with an ultra-short 4.26 diff ratio and straight-cut gears, it was far from a showroom example.

The rear of the remote gearshift was fitted with a 'Mitchell mounting', which was designed by Terry Mitchell, the chief chassis designer at MG. It was a clever solution that replaced the troublesome standard solid rubber mount, which would invariably fail under the constant acceleration and deceleration loads that a competition engine inflicted on the standard part. The mounting, identical externally, had within the rubber a simple universal joint, which when bolted to the remote and its retaining bracket, could not part company. Also of interest is that despite a new anti-rattle gearstick now being fitted as standard on all production cars, the car had reverted back to the early gearstick with its domed gaiter and the resultant rubber hose down the shaft to keep it quiet.

Hydrolastic suspension was used with competition displacers, and the subframes were rewelded for added strength. The car was also fitted with a heavy-duty Scandinavian guard and a battery-box skid plate, as despite the Swedish being a snow-covered event, it was hard on the underside of the car. Additionally, all of the lines – battery, fuel and brakes – were run inside the car.

Despite Abingdon's usual thorough preparation, all four works cars that were entered for the Swedish did not finish. They all succumbed to differential failure, which was likely due to lubrication problems caused by the intense cold.

In April a new AJB 33B appeared on the Tulip Rally for Timo Mäkinen and Paul Easter to be entered in the touring class, which was to Group 2 standards. Built by Bob Whittington, it was put together around a new 850 Mini shell, devoid of chrome trim around the doors, and with dry suspension. It was also back with a 1275 engine, albeit overbored by 0.20in to give 1293cc – as close as possible to the 1300cc class capacity limit. With the pistons brought to within 10 thou of the deck and a polished-and-flowed Downton cylinder head, the engine had an 11.6:1 compression ratio. With a full-

race camshaft and twin H4 SU carburettors, the engine was pushing out just under 86bhp at the wheels on Abingdon's rolling road.

Once again, the gearchange reverted to the older-type gearstick and the car was also fitted with special white spot rubber drive couplings but with modified driveshafts by Hardy Spicer. After the recce, it was decided not to fit a sump shield and the diff was selected as 4.133; the gearbox had straight-cut gears and was also close-ratio. The rubber cone dry suspension was set at the standard ride height but with competition Girling dampers, the front mountings were tack-weld reinforced, and subframes were rewelded for added strength and reinforced around the bump rubbers.

As the car was built around a standard Mini shell it only had one fuel tank, and this was not changed for the customary twin tanks for the Tulip, which must have considerably reduced the range between fill-ups. To combat the heat inside the car, generated by the hot manifold and exhaust, the front carpet had an asbestos blanket placed underneath, and the bulkhead below the front crossmember also had an asbestos plate covered with aluminium screwed to the bulkhead. The rear bulkhead had two access holes cut in to allow access to the top of the damper mountings, which made removal much easier behind the twin fuel tanks.

Despite the Tulip being a smooth event, all lines were run inside the car, although the twin fuel pump was fitted outside on the subframe. The wipers also received attention, where 'deep-throated wiper wheel boxes' were fitted to the car. These were far stronger than standard wiper wheel boxes,

Timo Mäkinen surveys the underside of AJB 33B at scrutineering for the 1964 Tulip Rally.

WORKS MINIS IN DETAIL

Mäkinen and Easter prepare to drill the bonnet of AJB 33B to accept their Tulip Rally plate. These were invariably riveted down to prevent trophy hunters removing the plates.

Mäkinen having his racing tyres removed and studded tyres fitted to the car for the snow-covered summits found on the Tulip Rally that year.

which tended to strip if a heavy snow load was deposited on the screen.

The lighting was subtly different from that used on previous events – gone was the Cyclops lamp up high on the slam panel, replaced by a single Lucas 700 Continental driving lamp placed on a quick-release bracket centrally between the two similar Lucas 700 fog lamps. The two Lucas 576 lamps remained on the bonnet to act as the dipped beam.

The Tulip was an uncharacteristically tough event in 1965, primarily because of the treacherous weather, with deep snow, blizzards and fog that made even the easy road sections a difficult challenge for the large entry of 157 cars, only 47 of which made it to the finish. The 1900-mile dash through Belgium, Holland, Germany, Luxembourg and France over three days was similar in nature to a cut-down Tour de France with race-circuit timed sections and hillclimbs; the rally was considered a relatively easy event – but not this year. Many of the elimination sections had to be shortened or cancelled due to deep snow but not before Mäkinen had put up some extremely fast times on the uninterrupted tests, resulting an easy class win, third in the touring car category and sixth overall.

Abingdon had been the only team to have prepared for the eventually of snow and had at its disposal sufficient studded tyres for the cars, meanwhile using race tyres for the dry sections. Despite the car consuming a lot of oil towards the end of the rally and dying at one stage and needing a fresh set of points, it proved to be extremely fast. In fact, Mäkinen and Easter were second overall on scratch times, just nine seconds behind the Morley brothers' Healey 3000; but such were the complications of the event's class improvement marking system that they were relegated to sixth overall, and outright victory went to Rosemary Smith in her 998cc Hillman Imp.

Mäkinen and Easter, with their car strewn with winning tulips, whilst being directed to the finishers' park, winning their class and coming third overall on the Tulip rally.

CHAPTER 3: THE MK 1 MINI COOPER S

Mäkinen and Easter setting off on the 1965 Alpine Rally.

Mäkinen and Easter near the summit of the barren waste of Mont Ventoux.

The 1965 Alpine, always a favourite event for the Abingdon team, saw AJB 33B fielded again, still in the hands of Mäkinen and Easter. This time the car was prepared by Brian Moylan and again as a Group 2; apart from being completely rebuilt, it was very similar to how it appeared on the Tulip Rally some four months earlier. It managed to achieve 84bhp at the wheels on the Abingdon rollers, once rebuilt, so 2bhp less than previous. It was, as customary, effectively a full-race engine.

The car was again run on dry suspension, on Mäkinen's insistence. The only significant change was the abandonment of the potentially unreliable rubber driveshaft couplings for the new needle roller Hardy Spicer universal joints with larger diameter driveshafts. Mäkinen had also elected to use an even shorter diff ratio of 4.26:1, and because of the route being rough in parts, a full sump guard was also fitted. To help cooling, being a summer event and the 1275 engine tending to run hot, the radiator fan was changed from the standard four-blade fan to a six-blade export fan. The car also now sprouted a second fuel tank.

The Alpine, starting from Marseille and finishing in Monte Carlo, some six days and 2200 miles later, saw the 93 crews tackle most of the big climbs in the region. The route was divided into three sections of 500, 800 and 900 miles, and with two lengthy stops of half and one full day at Grenoble, the rally was not as tiring as it once was, largely because the organisers were striving to save their event from extinction.

Despite the more relaxed format, the rally proved a tough challenge over its 13 special speed tests and its high-speed road sections that required a lofty average to keep on time.

Just 32 cars were classified as finishers, eight of which achieved clean sheets with no road time lost, and hence were awarded a coveted Alpine Cup. One was Mäkinen, who came home in second place in the touring class, just 1.7 seconds adrift of the winning Lancia Zagato of René Trautmann after over two hours of time tests. Mäkinen had started the last leg 28 seconds behind the Lancia and was confident that he could easily pull back that deficit, especially with two climbs of the Allos ahead of him. He drove conservatively (for him) and was dismayed at the finish to have done so, missing the win by such a small margin.

Apart from a broken rear light, Mäkinen had no trouble with the car – other than with the French owner of a Mini from which Mäkinen was trying to remove the rear lamp... Abingdon had a successful rally, with both Mäkinen and Hopkirk getting Alpine Cups and winning the Coupe des Dames with Pauline Mayman.

The final rally for this much-used car was the 1965 1000 Lakes in August 1965. Mäkinen again took the experienced local co-driver Pekka Keskitalo with him in preference to Paul Easter. The Mini, very similar to the Alpine car, was

Mäkinen and Pekka Keskitalo with a rather clean AJB 33B on the opening stage of the 1965 1000 Lakes. Note the blanked-off holes for the bonnet lamps.

91

A jubilant Mäkinen and Keskitalo sit on their winning car with Aaltonen and Hopkirk either side.

A much battered and travel-stained AJB 33B with tape over the exposed lights to prevent damage from flying stones from the many cars Mäkinen caught.

additionally reprepared in Finland by his mechanic Antti Kytola in Voimavaunu, at the local Helsinki BMC importer (Mäkinen's personal sponsor), before the event.

A driver's wing mirror was fitted to comply with Finnish road traffic laws, there were Morris-logo mud flaps front and back, and the customary heavy-duty Scandinavian sump guard. The lighting was changed slightly, in that the central Continental headlight unit in the central Lucas 700 case was replaced by a Marshall spotlight by the BMC importer. The car was also adorned with much advertising material, placed there by the event organisers, which was quite a novelty at the time.

Mäkinen dominated his home event and after three attempts won the rally outright, beating his teammate Aaltonen into second place, with Hopkirk sixth. The Thousand Lakes was better known in Finland as the Jyväskylä Grand Prix, so fast was the rally with its many jumps and crests that were, for the brave and well-practised, flat-out blind.

Before the start at Jyväskylä, scrutineering caused a problem for the works Minis as they were all fitted with iodine headlamps, which were prohibited in Finland. After much negotiation, it was accepted that they could be used as they were legal in Britain – however, because Aaltonen was Finnish, he had to change his headlamps to the old tungsten bulbs. Mäkinen escaped, as he (along with Hopkirk) was running on a British licence.

Once the rally started and the route entered the forests, Mäkinen was soon in the lead and stayed there, despite Aaltonen giving him a good run for his money. Their lead became so dominant that they were able to slow on the few rougher stages to avoid unduly damaging the cars. Come the second half of the rally, Mäkinen and Aaltonen pulled away further as the opposition collapsed by the wayside. Abingdon was rewarded with the team prize, and with that the Mini really had made its mark on this unique event.

The car was bought by Timo after the rally and he continued to use it on home events.

Competition Record

Date	Event	Crew	Number	Overall result	Class result
May 1964	Acropolis Rally	Paddy Hopkirk/Henry Liddon		DNF	
Aug 1964	1000 Lakes Rally	Timo Mäkinen/Pekka Keskitalo	50	4th	1st
Mar 1965	Swedish Rally	Paddy Hopkirk/Henry Liddon	25	DNF	
Apr 1965	Tulip Rally	Timo Mäkinen/Paul Easter	124	3rd	1st
July 1965	Alpine Rally	Timo Mäkinen/Paul Easter	70	2nd touring car	
Aug 1965	1000 Lakes Rally	Timo Mäkinen/Pekka Keskitalo	28	1st	1st

Registration Number	First registered	Chassis number	Engine	Engine number	Model
AJB 44B	Feb 1964	KA2S4 488512	1071cc 1275cc	9F-SA-H 27647 9F-SA-Y 31815	Morris Cooper S

The second car of the AJB batch is one of the most famous rally cars, now housed permanently at the British Motor Heritage Museum at Gaydon in Warwickshire after it won the 1965 Monte Carlo Rally in the hands of Timo Mäkinen and Paul Easter. However, prior to that, the car had three non-finishes.

The first duty for AJB 44B was for it to be dispatched in April to Greece as a recce car for the Acropolis Rally in May. The car, still as a 1071 Cooper S, was prepared by Cliff Humphries for Tony Ambrose to compile recce notes for a two-car BMC team, these being Hopkirk and Aaltonen in AJB 33B and 55B respectively.

Despite AJB 44B still retaining its small engine, it was built to rally standards as a Group 2 car with a full-race camshaft, overbored engine, straight-cut close-ratio gears and a 4.133 diff ratio. Needless to say, for the rough going found in Greece, the car was fitted with a thick Duralumin sump guard and a set of competition dampers. To keep things cool in the heat often found in Greece, the car ran an extra-large 15-row oil cooler and a six-blade export radiator fan.

Crew comfort extended to Microcell bucket and reclining seats, and all of the usual padding to the door locks and door pockets; the car ran standard trim and carpets. It also had a full complement of lights, with a high-capacity dynamo powering the electrics. In essence, the preparation of the car was just as thorough and exacting as if it were to be used in competition, right down to every last detail. This is entirely understandable, as it was important that the recce was completed without any mechanical breakdowns disrupting the task in hand, and although it was usual for a used rally car to be consigned to recce duties, on this occasion, due to pressure on other cars, this new car was dispatched for the job.

After the Acropolis recce, the car was reprepared by Tommy Eales for Paddy Hopkirk and Henry Liddon to tackle the Alpine Rally in June 1964. Now fitted with a 1275 engine, replacing the original 1071 unit, it was kept to its standard bore but still ran an AEA-648 full-race camshaft, as indeed did almost every works Mini built at Abingdon. This camshaft was often termed a '649' cam, derived from the number stamping on the camshaft, which by BMC convention was always one digit in advance of the actual part number. The cylinder head saw the engine's compression raised to 10:1, with the head being gas-flowed and polished. Carburettors were the standard Abingdon fit of twin H4 SUs with ram pipes and

Paddy Hopkirk and Henry Liddon posing by the car in Marseille prior to the start of the 1964 Alpine Rally.

float chamber extensions, which ran CP4 needles and blue springs, linked together with a 'fork and peg' linkage. The gearbox used the customary straight-cut close-ratio gear set, driven through a 4.133 diff running yellow-marked rubber drive couplings.

As the Alpine was not considered a rough event, the suspension was kept very much as standard, other than the use of competition dampers. However, the suspension cones were renewed after their hard work on the Acropolis; the subframes were replaced, as were all four hubs and bearings. Also changed after the trip to Greece was the oil cooler, which reverted to a 13-row unit, and the radiator fan reduced to four blades.

The electrics, still powered by the uprated C40 dynamo, saw the lights fitted with iodine bulbs and set up with the two small fog lights acting as dipped beam on the bonnet, with the single Cyclops spot lamp in the middle of the slam panel, accompanied by two larger fog lights on quick-release brackets on the lower panel and bumper. Wipers were two-speed but without electric washers; the headlights were

Hopkirk and Liddon at full speed on one of the many Alpine climbs.

Hopkirk and Liddon just failed to finish the Alpine, retiring near the end of this demanding rally.

also devoid of washers. The battery was reversed with the terminals away from the tank as a safety measure, and the battery cable ran outside the car but was protected. Only the brake line ran inside the car.

The twin tanks had Aston quick-release filler caps fitted and the fuel delivered via a twin-SU fuel pump fixed in the standard position to the subframe; although it was a twin-ended pump, only one was wired to work at any one time. However, should it fail, the cable was simply reconnected to the dormant pump.

Hopkirk used a wooden steering wheel, and Microcell seats were fitted for both crew members: a bucket and a recliner with Irvin safely harnesses. Special care was taken to ensure that the heater was capable of being completely closed off. Being a Group 2 car, with regulations now being tighter than they once were, all glass was retained; no longer would we see Perspex being used in Group 2. All the trim, underfelt and carpeting was also retained, and together with the extra padding and protection, the cars were now heavier than they once were.

The driver's dashboard was a flat panel, mirroring the navigator's flat panel. This housed a rev counter, numerous light switches and a long headlight flasher switch. A starter push, on an extension, was fixed to the right-hand side of the lower dash rail, which made restarting the car easier than reaching for the ignition key, should the car stall. The navigator had a pair of Heuer clocks and a Halda distance recorder behind a magnifier lens in addition to numerous other control switches at his disposal. He also had a foot-operated horn switch by his feet, should someone not hear the screaming Mini coming.

The 25th Coupe Des Alpes ran for five days over 2100 miles, starting in Marseille and finishing in Monte Carlo. The rally visited most of the famous Alpine climbs – 90 in all, split into three legs from Marseille to Cannes, Cannes to Chamonix and finally finishing in Monte Carlo, with overnight stops in between. Hopkirk had flown to the start, straight from Le Mans, where he'd shared an MGB with Andrew Hedges to 19th place, so he was perhaps just a little tired come the 10pm start the following Monday. From the relatively low entry of 73 cars, only 25 made it to the finish – and one of them wasn't Hopkirk in AJB 44B, who retired when running well, with collapsed suspension due to a broken ball joint.

Hopkirk had a very time-consuming problem on the first leg. At the service in Sigale, his car needed new rear brakes and, because of a bad batch of rear hubs, they too were to be changed. Although a routine task, there was little time in hand to complete the job. The new bearing refused to go back on, largely because of the heat of the shaft, and despite asbestos gloves, there were burnt and bloodied fingers before the bearing was eventually refitted. Hopkirk had been leading the touring class comfortably but was two minutes late at the next control, despite clawing back 18 of the 20 minutes delay – and with that went his Alpine Cup, which was awarded for

Hopkirk and Liddon about to start the 1964 Tour de France, Liddon checking his time card. Note the one identification stripe on the driver's side of the bonnet.

Hopkirk chases Mäkinen at the Rouen circuit with privateer Geoff Mabbs forming an effective Mini train.

an unpenalised run. Nevertheless, Hopkirk still carried on to put up some fantastic times, in the hope that others may fall by the wayside, and was well up the leader board before he retired on the last leg from Chamonix to Monte.

The next showing of AJB 44B was on the Tour de France in September 1964. The car was again crewed by Hopkirk and Liddon, with car preparation being shared between Den Green and Tommy Eales. For the Tour, Abingdon decided to enter this and two other works Cooper Ss in the one-litre class as 970Ss, reasoning they would do better in the smaller capacity class. Accordingly the engine was overbored by 0.040in to give a capacity of 999cc, and with the use of flat-topped pistons and its gas-flowed and polished cylinder head, the compression was up to a respectable 11:1. As the weather in France was expected to be hot, and the engine would be running at high revs for long periods (as the short-stroke 970 engines were designed to), a large 15-row oil cooler was fitted, together with a six-blade radiator fan.

For the predominantly race circuit work found on the Tour de France, the straight-cut close-ratio gearbox was fitted with a slightly longer diff ratio to get a bit more top speed at the expense of some acceleration, so a 3.94 diff was used and, for the first time, Hardy Spicer drive couplings now replaced troublesome and unreliable rubber drive couplings. After the experience of numerous failures of the remote-shift rubber mounting, the car was fitted with a new Mitchell mounting, which was designed with a joint within the rubber to eradicate failure for good and all. The body was also strengthened with strapping, spreading the load where the mounting bracket fitted into the tunnel of the bodyshell.

The suspension was lowered by the removal of 4mm from the struts, and the car was fitted with a rear anti-roll bar. This was a forward-facing unit, unlike modern parts, which customarily trail rearwards. Competition Girling dampers were used with additional bump rubbers preventing the radius arm dropping too far. The rear hubs were fitted with Timken taper roller bearings after the issues experienced with the car on the Alpine Rally.

Demands on the electrics were somewhat less on this event, as few additional lights and equipment were fitted; accordingly, the car was rewired, reflecting the lesser demand on the electrics. It still used a dynamo and, other than two small Lucas 576 fog lamps uniquely fitted to the overriders, and headlights reverting to vertical-dip tungsten bulbs, no extra lamps were fitted. Even the customary reversing lamp was removed.

Gone too was the wooden steering wheel, replaced by a thin-grip Springall steering wheel. The steering arms were thicker than standard, and they would soon find their way onto standard production cars, albeit mated to a steering rack with a slightly larger turning circle. Tracking was set as 1/8in toe out, and the lock nuts were replaced with castellated nuts and split pins for added security, as were those fitted to the front tie bars.

The appearance of the car, to distinguish it from other team cars around it, saw the addition of a single white bonnet stripe on the driver's side, mirrored by a similar broad stripe on the nearside of the boot lid. Other team cars had different arrangements, so they too could be recognised as they sped by.

The Tour de France was an important event for BMC and

Hopkirk and Liddon on one of the hillclimb stages on the Tour de France.

Scandinavian crew Carl Orrenius and Rolf Dahlgren took over AJB 44B for the 1964 RAC Rally - they failed to finish, making three events in a row the car had not finished.

after Hopkirk's fine performance on last year's event and his Monte win, expectations were high. Starting from Lille, the 3780-mile route, running basically anti-clockwise around France, was for the first time classed by the FIA as a race due to the eight circuit races of up to two hours in duration and eight hillclimbs dispersed over the week-long event. Taking advantage of the event's handicap system, Hopkirk's Mini was soon creeping up the leader board, swapping places with Mäkinen is his similarly-powered 970S. Mäkinen, Hopkirk and Geoff Mabbs, in a private 1071 Cooper S, delighted the crowds by running nose-to-tail on every racetrack, swapping places to get the best possible times for each other, even going around hairpin bends nose-to-tail. With Mabbs having more power than the two little 970s he was of great assistance towing them around.

With big Ford Mustangs leading the touring car class, BMC's hopes were pinned on the handicap and playing a waiting game for the faster cars to break down. Hopkirk excelled on the hillclimbs, which were better suited to the Mini, and was again trading places with Mäkinen. But it was not to last, as Hopkirk retired with driveshaft failure on the Col de la Croix, and he was out. All would have been well if the spare driveshaft that Pauline Mayman had been carrying had been for the correct side (they were of unequal lengths). Mäkinen was soon to follow suit, and with Aaltonen long since retired, it was left for Pauline Mayman to save the day by winning her class.

For AJB 44B's next event, the RAC Rally, it was handed to the Scandinavian crew of Carl Orrenius and Rolf Dahlgren. This was to be a one-off Abingdon drive for Orrenius, although he was a regular member of the BMC Sweden team. The car was reprepared to take on what was always considered to be a rough event, with more than 400 miles of special stages largely through the British forests on a 2500-mile route around Great Britain.

For this home event, a reliable but powerful 1293cc engine was built with a gas-flowed cylinder head (giving 11:1 compression), an AEA 648 race camshaft and twin SUH4 carburettors. It had a straight-cut close-ratio gearbox and 4.133 final drive, which used special driveshafts and Hardy Spicer universal joints. The sump was protected by a screwed-on sump plate in addition to an alloy sump guard. It was also fitted with a battery box guard.

The remote gearshift was fitted with a Mitchell mounting, and the body strengthened around the bracket mounting. The suspension was dry cone, with small spacer washers used to increase the ground clearance. The subframe was strengthened plus gussets were welded to the front tie rod brackets. Rear hub bearings were changed to Timken taper roller bearings rather than the standard ball-race bearings, which had proved troublesome to service when very hot.

The car had five additional lamps on the front plus a roof lamp and headlamp washers. It was also fitted with a back-mounted Lucas fog lamp, fixed to the boot lid, acting as a powerful revering lamp. Inside the car, demister bars were added to the 'screen, there were comfortable seats and padding to the door pocket and door locks. Two flat dash panels were fitted for the extra switches and instruments.

A large entry of 180 cars assembled in London at the Duke of York's Barracks for the 7am start, and as the cars headed off towards the West Country on their five-day journey, entrants were already falling by the wayside on the early stages.

BMC had entered a team of four Cooper Ss on the home event; sadly, none were to finish. The first retirement was AJB 44B, when at near midnight in Wales on the first day, it succumbed in the Brechfa Forest stage – Orrenius hit a tree and into instant retirement. It was now three retirements in a row for the car.

Needless to say, for AJB 44B's next event, the 1965 Monte Carlo rally, a new car was prepared. It was often the case that new cars would be built for the Monte, it being the most important rally of the year, despite being the start of the season. For this winter classic, AJB 44B was driven by Timo Mäkinen with Paul Easter and built by Peter Bartram as a lightweight Group 3 car in the improved touring class. This involved saving as much weight as possible, starting with using aluminium doors, bonnet and boot, and then reducing the weight of the structure of the car – undertaken by cutting a large number of 2in holes in the rear seat pan and rear bulkhead, the rear parcel shelf and even the dash rail.

Additionally the glass was replaced by Perspex, the heater was contained within an aluminium housing, and the exhaust specially made in thin-gauge material. Brackets on the bonnet hinges were drilled, and all surplus brackets removed. There was a stick-on rear number plate with a much smaller light, and even the front grille was replaced by a lightweight mesh grille from an Austin A110. The underseal was also laboriously removed, as were the carpets, to be replaced by lightweight Rivington thin carpet.

The bodyshell had a set of lovely Abingdon-fabricated wheelarch extensions to cover wider wheels, but the idea to use fibreglass headlight bowls was abandoned. The overall weight saving was 50lb.

Much of the other preparation was similar to the current Group 2 cars of that time. Mäkinen was again using the full-race camshaft and his preferred ultra-short differential of 4.26:1 – ideally suited for climbing the Alps. The cylinder head was polished and flowed and had 0.040in skimmed from it to raise the compression to 11:1. The rocker pillars also had 0.055in removed because of increased valve lift. The engine produced 75bhp at 6500rpm at the wheels. Strangely, the drive couplings reverted to the rubber joints and the gearchange went back to the early type, pre anti-rattle mechanism but with the indestructible Mitchell mounting at the rear of the remote. Standard suspension was used and, as was usual for Mäkinen, the car was not Hydrolastic but dry.

The electrics now had the benefit of an alternator, replacing the dynamo. The lighting all had iodine bulbs, with the usual two large fog lamps and one driving lamp on drop-down brackets on the bumper, with two small fog lamps acting as dipped beam on the bonnet.

The car had a new Triplex heated front windscreen, which replaced the earlier gold film 'screens used on the 1964 Monte. These screens were clear laminated glass with the heat being generated by small wires connected between the silver conductor strips at the top and bottom. The 'screen could be heated as half or entirely, and could be left on at reduced power, being controlled by a specially-made four-way rotary

Dashboard of AJB 44B in its second incarnation for the 1965 Monte Carlo Rally, now fitted with a heated front 'screen, Springall steering wheel and a Halda Twinmaster distance recorder.

Abingdon fibreglass buckets seat fitted to an existing Mini lower frame and covered in early Mini cloth trim.

control switch. The 'screens were universally popular with the drivers, unlike the gold film they replaced. The windscreen washers used two Tudor bottles, both fixed inside the car on the rail below the driver's-side rear window. One had normal washer fluid with de-icer and the other alcohol (for the screen not the crew), The wipers also had deep-throated wheel boxes, which were more robust than the standard items and better able to cope with a snow load.

All the lines for battery, fuel and brakes were run inside

Mäkinen and Easter flat-out at night on the snow-covered road where they totally dominated the entire entry and atrocious conditions.

Timo Mäkinen and Paul Easter at their start from Stockholm on the 1965 Monte Carlo Rally.

the car but the twin fuel pump was still situated on the rear subframe in the standard position, albeit protected by an alloy plate. Quick-release Aston filler caps were used, and the twin tanks were protected against damage from studded tyres. The retaining straps for the tanks were fitted on the outside in order to keep the tank in position should the car have a heavy side impact. Additionally, the battery was reversed with the terminals away from the side of the tank, as added security in case the tank moved.

Despite the weight-saving campaign, the car still had extra padding to the door locks, door pillars and door pockets. However, now the Microcell bucket seat was replaced with a lightweight fibreglass bucket seat made for Abingdon and trimmed in early Mini fabric cloth. Mäkinen was also using a Springall thin-grip leather steering wheel. Paul Easter had a newly-introduced Halda Twinmaster distance recorder, replacing the small Halda odometer housed behind a magnifier. The new Halda had the advantage that it could be adjusted by replacing the internal gears for different tyres and was infinitely more accurate than the earlier offering,

AJB 44B receiving service by the Abingdon mechanics. Note the quick-lift jack and the spare fan belt fixed to the bonnet stay.

Mäkinen and Easter between stages on the Monte as they are without crash helmets; the car snow-covered, indicating the severity of the weather.

reading to 1/100 of a mile.

Mäkinen elected to start from Stockholm, along with teammate Paddy Hopkirk. It was, with hindsight, to prove one of the better starting points. A relatively small field (by previous standards) of 237 cars started on their respective 2600-mile journeys from eight starting points around Europe, converging on St Claude in mid France for the common run to Monte Carlo. The event had for the first time lost its final stage around the Grand Prix circuit at Monaco, to be replaced by a 380-mile final night loop into and over the mountains around Monte Carlo. The weather, however, was to have its turn in decimating the entry with blizzards, deep snow, ice and drifts beating most of the entry once in the Massif Central area. As the field headed down towards Monte, the weather closed in further still, and of the 211 cars that safely reached St Claude, only 35 made it to Monte within their allowable one-hour lateness – Timo Mäkinen was fastest on three of the five stages down to Monte and was significantly the only car to arrive without any time penalties. A truly outstanding achievement.

Once in Monte Carlo the following morning, after a night of atrocious weather, the depleted field prepared for the all-new mountain circuit that night. That too was to prove decisive, and despite the organisers having some misgivings about actually sending the cars out, Mäkinen stamped his authority on the field and was fastest on five of the six mountain stages. He took the win by a considerable margin. Only 22 cars finished the mountain circuit, even after an extra eight minutes had been allowed at the first control, and because of the weather, the maximum lateness was also extended a further 15 minutes. The only drama for the car was towards the end of the last night, when it died on a road section through Puget Théniers. This was quickly traced by the crew to a broken heel on the distributor's points, which Easter changed with spares carried

Final service for the car and fresh studded tyres for Mäkinen.

Mäkinen and Easter at the harbour front in Monaco with their winners' trophies.

in the car, and they were soon speeding on their way.

The 1965 Monte Carlo Rally has become, over time, notorious as having had the very worst weather conditions ever encountered. On this event Mäkinen slaughtered the opposition in what were appalling conditions, demonstrating his considerable skill on the snow and ice. This result, despite Hopkirk's victory in 1964 being the first Mini win, was probably the most decisive ever and probably Mäkinen's finest hour. Just to put it into perspective, Mäkinen beat the second-place Porsche 904GTS of Böhringer by 20 minutes on the stages, such was his dominance. Timo Mäkinen's win in AJB 44B in 1965 is regarded by many (particularly Stuart Turner) as the Monte win and the finest drive of all time of any rally driver.

As already stated, the car is now retained in the British Motor Heritage Museum at Gaydon, Warwickshire. However, those interested in studying this car should be aware that despite it being externally accurate, as is much of the interior, the engine is sadly incorrect, as it was removed and replaced with a modern engine for Paddy Hopkirk to tackle the Golden Fifty Rally in 1982. Unfortunately, there are no plans to reinstate the correct Monte Carlo engine.

Competition Record

Date	Event	Crew	Number	Overall result	Class result
June 1964	Alpine Rally	Paddy Hopkirk/Henry Liddon	18	DNF	
Sept 1964	Tour de France	Paddy Hopkirk/Henry Liddon	19	DNF	
Nov 1964	RAC Rally	Carl Orrenius/Rolf Dahlgren	37	DNF	
Jan 1965	Monte Carlo Rally	Timo Mäkinen/Paul Easter	52	1st	1st

Registration Number	First registered	Chassis number	Engine	Engine number	Model
AJB 55B	Feb 1964	CA2S7 487640	1071cc	9F-SA-H 27614	Austin Cooper S
			1275cc	9F-SA-Y 31399	

The third AJB car to be registered in February 1964 was AJB 55B, an Austin and, like its sister cars, a 1071 Cooper S. It was soon to be built up with a 1275cc engine just like the others. The car was delivered, of course, in production Tartan Red with a black roof, which was also soon changed to the Abingdon standard Old English White roof.

For the Acropolis Rally in May, Aaltonen and Ambrose had recced the route in AJB 44B, so had a fresh AJB 55B built by Bob Wittington for the Greek round of the European Championship. The 1275 engine kept its standard bore but had a full-race camshaft, which along with a polished and flowed cylinder head, raised the compression to 10:1. The engine block also had core plug retaining plates fitted to ensure they stayed in place. In an attempt to keep the engine oil cool, an extra-large oil cooler was added, although the radiator only had a four-blade fan.

Gears were straight-cut but, as was usual, they were made of a material somewhat better than available over the counter. The driveshafts had rubber couplings but again of an improved material. The diff was the almost-standard Abingdon fit of 4.133. The rough roads on the Acropolis also demanded a substantial sump guard to protect the engine and gearbox: a full-length Duralumin guard of 3/16in plate fabricated by Abingdon.

Despite the rough roads the suspension was standard, as gone were the days when the suspension would be raised for

CHAPTER 3: THE MK 1 MINI COOPER S

AJB 55B, brand new outside the competitions department at Abingdon.

The rather untidy light arrangement of the early works cars. Note that the car appears to have been a Morris Cooper, and also how the lower apron is pushed upwards to allow more air to the gearbox.

Dashboard of AJB 55B with two flat panels in front of each crew member. Note also Microcell seats and dip control for the headlights on the left of the steering column, a feature favoured by Aaltonen.

rough events. After much debate, and testing with Dougie Watts, it was found that the raised ride height was putting extra strain on the driveshafts because they were working at an unfavourable angle. The move to help the life of the driveshaft was therefore at perhaps the expense of damage inflicted to the underside of the car.

Gone too were modified front damper brackets. These were now standard items but tack-welded for reinforcement. The dampers were competition Girling units and the only other addition was the provision of extra bump stops at the rear – provided to prevent the rear radius arm dropping down too far. Brakes were likewise standard but used DS11 front pads and VG95 rear linings – race specification Ferodo offerings, which would take the continual left-foot braking for which Scandinavians were renowned. Brake lines were run inside the car.

Electrics, always the hallmark of a works Mini, saw the car fitted with the special uprated C40 dynamo, which had a roller bearing in the end plate rather than a bronze bush. It also had a larger pulley fitted to reduce the speed of the dynamo at high revs. This special dynamo meant the car was also fitted with a RB340 regulator box.

The car was completely rewired by the in-house Lucas competition department technician. Abingdon had at its disposal two Lucas technicians, who would spend the majority of their time wiring the cars. It was common practice, to ensure reliability, that cars were completely rewired between events. Looms were all handcrafted to account for the driver's preference of ancillaries and lighting. Until weight became an issue, much later in the works Mini's history, all cars were wired with cloth-covered cable together with soldered copper spade connectors or soldered bullet connectors. The wiring was always of an exemplary standard.

Headlamps were fitted with iodine bulbs, which did not at that time have a dip facility, this being provided by two small fog lamps on the bonnet. Two larger fog lamps were fitted, together with a single spot lamp. There was also a small fog lamp fitted to the boot lid to act as a reversing light, operated by a special illuminated switch on the dashboard and not automatically by a switch in the gearbox.

Inside the car, Aaltonen was using a wooden steering wheel, Irvin seat belts and a Microcell bucket seat; Ambrose used a Microcell recliner. Being a Group 2 car, AJB 55B retained its glass rather than having lightweight Perspex. All the trim was retained, and additional padding was fitted to the door locks and doors. The car was also fitted with an intercom and Ambrose had the use of a small Halda distance recorder fitted behind a magnifier lens. He also had a pair of Heuer watches, a stopwatch and a time-of-day clock arranged around a pair of Abingdon-fabricated dashboard panels.

The 1964 Acropolis Rally, being the 40th anniversary, was to prove an even more demanding event than usual. The organisers were determined that the rally would be the toughest yet; Aaltonen commented that the event came second only to the Spa-Sofia-Liège for sheer speed and severity. Of the 72 crews who started the rally from beneath the Acropolis in Athens, only 19 made it back after their 1750-mile thrash around Greece. Aaltonen was not one of them. AJB55B was retired, when highly placed, just before half way on the second night, when the car spun around completely out of control because the steering had broken. Abingdon was using racing tyres for the hard and rutted stages, which were thought to have contributed to the strain in the steering and its premature failure.

The car was reprepared for the 1964 Alpine Rally, built again by Bob Whittington. This time Aaltonen would have at his disposal AJB 55B as a Group 3 lightweight for this very fast event, entered into the GT class. The engine was still kept at its standard bore, with a full-race camshaft and the compression set at 10:1. The gearbox retained its 4.133 diff and straight-cut gears. The suspension cones were replaced after the hard work on the Acropolis, as were the suspension trumpets. Both the front and rear subframes were also replaced – and the latest steering arms used and carefully checked after the Acropolis failure. Being a tarmac rally, Dunlop R6 racing tyres with tubes on wide rims were used all round, and two spares carried.

The electrics were much as before, but now saw the addition of a hand-operated dip switch fitted to the left-hand side of the steering column, opposite the indicator stalk, which alleviated the need for the use of the cumbersome foot-operated dip switch. This was at Aaltonen's instance, and one of the many innovative ideas he brought to Abingdon to improve the works Minis.

The fuel system saw the addition of a twin SU fuel pump rather than the single unit. This was, however, still located outside the car in the standard position on the rear subframe but protected by an aluminium plate. The fuel line (and battery line) was run outside the car, protected by channelling, although the brake line was run inside.

The weight saving began with the fitting of aluminium door skins, together with the bonnet and boot. However, trim, underfelt and carpets were all retained. Perspex windows were fitted, other than the laminated front 'screen, replacing the heavy glass. No structural body lightening was carried out. AJB 55B was in essence a Group 2 car but with lightweight panels. Nevertheless, the overall weight saving was considerable and guaranteed to improve the car's performance and handling.

The 25th Coupe des Alpes, starting in Marseille, was fought out over the Alps using most of the famous climbs on the demanding 2100-mile route. Seventy-two cars started, with only 25 making it down to the Monte Carlo finish five days later. Throughout the rally, Aaltonen's performance was simply astounding, being incredibly fast on all of the stages. Aaltonen recorded quicker times than the GT-winning Alfa Romeo on five of the eight stages. So fast was Aaltonen that he nearly came to grief on the descent of the infamous Col du Granier, when he missed a sharp left-hand bend, slid off and over the edge, and dropped 30ft. Fortunately, other than collecting bits of fencing and without damage to the car, he was able to regain the road from the field in which he had

Rauno Aaltonen and Tony Ambrose on their abortive attempt of the 1964 Acropolis Rally, sidelined at halfway when the steering broke.

Aaltonen corners hard on one of the many hillclimbs on the Alpine Rally.

Aaltonen and Ambrose at the start of the 1964 Alpine Rally heading out of Marseille.

Stuart Turner getting his hands dirty helping service AJB 55B. Note no quick-lift jack lifting the car.

Aaltonen about to start the 3800-mile rally whilst Ambrose checks his time card before departure from Lille.

landed, via a goat track, and back up to the tarmac, with only six minutes wasted but happily no marks lost. Aaltonen and Ambrose won their up-to-1300cc GT class and finished a creditable fourth overall on scratch times, behind the winning Alfa, the Morley brothers' Healey and a Porsche 904GTS.

Aaltonen and Ambrose would again use AJB 55B for the Tour de France, in the September, with once again Bob Whittington building it for them. The engine specification was unchanged other than the compression was raised to 11:1 by skimming the cylinder head. To keep things cool, the engine was given a six-bladed cooling fan. To get as much top speed as possible on this mostly-circuit-based event, the diff ratio was changed to 3.7:1. The driveshaft now had Hardy Spicer couplings replacing the troublesome rubber joints that had so plagued the team. Another addition was the provision of the Mitchell mounting at the end of the remote shift. This special replacement rubber joint had a movable joint within, designed by Terry Mitchell, and was now virtually indestructible. The body was also strengthened with straps around a reinforced bracket that carried the Mitchell mounting.

The suspension was lowered by reducing the trumpets by 4mm, and the car used special Girling competition dampers. The rear hubs were now fitted with Timken taper roller bearings, which were easier to deal with in the field than the standard ball bearing type. Also a new addition was the provision of quick-lift jacking brackets below the bumper, front and back, which would mean quicker and easier tyre changes and servicing on the rally. Abingdon also fabricated its own tubular steel quick-lift jacks, which were carried in the service barges.

Unique to the Tour de France was the provision of mounting the fog lights onto the front overriders on the bumper. Unlike the other works Minis on the event, ABB 55B carried no identification white stripes on the bonnet or boot lid – that in itself distinguished it from the other three works Minis taking part, which were carrying identification strips of various combinations.

With less demands on the electrics, the car was rewired by Lucas. The only addition from the Alpine was the provision of demister bars for the front 'screen. All the extra lamps were removed, as were the reversing lamp and headlamp washers. Changed also was the wooden steering wheel, replaced by a Springall thin-grip leather wheel. Whilst Aaltonen used a Microcell bucket seat, Ambrose now had a special reclining seat fabricated by Tommy Wellman. Also inside the car, the speedo was changed, reflecting the change to a 3.7 diff.

As the car was entered as a Group 2, the lightweight aluminium panels from the Alpine were removed and replaced with standard steel panels, and the Perspex was replaced by standard toughened glass. Certainly, the preparation for the Tour de France was quite different from the other rallies Abingdon regularly entered, as the event was more a series of circuit races and was classed by the FIA as a race and not a rally.

Starting from Lille, the 3780-mile route ran anti-clockwise around France, taking in numerous race circuits and hillclimbs on the week-long event. Aaltonen had been going well but was forced into retirement relatively early in the event at the Le Mans circuit test, when all the oil escaped after the oil cooler came adrift, which in turn resulted in permanent bearing damage due to the lack of oil. John Wadsworth, in a private Cooper S, took oil to Aaltonen stranded out on the circuit, but the damage was done; once back at the Le Mans pit, the car was retired with irreparable damage to the engine.

The car was sold to Swede Ragnavald Haakansson, who was Harry Källström's regular co-driver.

Ambrose topping up the car with fuel from the BMC rubber fuel bag. Note two spare racing tyres carried in the boot.

Aaltonen at Le Mans when he lost all of his oil when the oil cooler came adrift. Brian Moylan informing Aaltonen that the car would go no further.

Competition Record

Date	Event	Crew	Number	Overall result	Class result
May 1964	Acropolis Rally	Rauno Aaltonen/Tony Ambrose	64	DNF	
June 1964	Alpine Rally	Rauno Aaltonen/Tony Ambrose	70	4th	1st
Sept 1964	Tour de France	Rauno Aaltonen/Tony Ambrose	30	DNF	

CHAPTER 3: THE MK 1 MINI COOPER S

Registration Number	First registered	Chassis number	Engine	Engine number	Model
AJB 66B	Feb 1964	KA2S4 488503	1071cc 970cc 1275cc	9F-SA-H 27154 9F-SA-X 29001 9F-SA-Y 31360	Morris Cooper S

AJB 66B outside the Abingdon competition department newly built as a 1275cc car.

Interior shot of the unique curved sides to the dashboard of AJB 66B. Note the small Halda behind the magnifier, Microcell seats, navigator's horn block on the floor and small fire extinguisher.

The fourth and final car of the AJB batch to be registered in February 1964 was AJB 66B, which was logged as a 1071cc Morris Cooper S in red and black, and – like its sister cars – was repainted with a white roof and fitted with a 1275cc engine.

Its first task, in April 1964, was for Timo Mäkinen and Tony Ambrose to compete on the Tulip Rally. As a 1275S it had just been homologated in time for the event, and built as Group 2 car by Cliff Humphries. The engine retained its standard bore, and the camshaft selected was the 948 (the standard 997 Cooper camshaft) in preference to the 648 full-race cam, which had become effectively the standard-fit camshaft on works Minis. The 948 was fitted for its better low-down torque characteristics over the full-race cam. The distributor was also changed to the latest 40979 model, which had an asymmetric cam designed to alleviate points bounce at high revs. The cylinder head was standard other than being gas-flowed and polished, and the compression kept to 10:1. Carburettors were twin H4 SUs with CP4 needles, running open ram pipes, with fork-and-peg linkage. To get the best from the more-or-less standard engine the straight-cut gearbox was fitted with the low 4.1 diff. The gearbox was protected by a lightweight RAF sump guard.

The brakes were all standard apart from using DS11 racing pads and VG95 rear brake shoes. AJB 66B was lowered for the Tulip, by removing 1/8in from the suspension trumpets (which effectively decreased its height by around 1/2in) and used competition dampers all round.

The electrics, which always received a great deal of attention, saw an uprated C40 dynamo used to power the electrics, along with a large pulley to reduce its speed at high revs. The headlights, protected by Perspex covers, used early iodine bulbs without a dipped beam, this being provided by small fog lights on the bonnet. Two large fog lights were also fitted on drop-down brackets on the bumper, and a single spotlight placed centrally on a bracket at the top of the grill. Headlight washers were fitted to the car and twin Mixo Minor horns were used, which could additionally be operated by the navigator via a foot-switch on the floor.

Microcell seats – a bucket and recliner – were fitted but only fixing eyes for the Irvin seat belts, as the belts were not initially used by the crew. The now-standard wooden steering wheel was fitted and, being a Group 2 car, all of the toughened glass was retained, as was all the trim, carpets and underfelt. Additional padding was supplied for the door locks and doors to aid crew comfort. Uniquely, the car was fitted with

Engine details and light arrangement of AJB 66B.

Boot detail of AJB 66B. Plywood protection to the fuel tank and the Elopress Tyre and Fire fixed to the boot board.

Timo Mäkinen and Tony Ambrose preparing for the start of the 1964 Tulip Rally, which they won outright.

sculptured dash panels curved around each side of the oval central binnacle, which housed the usual array of switches and controls, together with a Halda distance recorder behind a magnifier lens, a pair of Heuer watches and a 10,000rpm rev counter.

The Tulip Rally was, for 1964, a more compact event condensed into 48 hours, starting and finishing in Noordwijk in Holland with the route meandered over its 1750 miles through Holland, France, Belgium, Luxembourg and Germany, with the competitive element being 19 tests of just under 90 miles covering race circuits, hillclimbs and Alpine-style climbs.

The event attracted 174 starters, 95 of whom made it back to the finish. The organisers had devised a class system where the winner would be the one who had the best advantage over winners in the classes both above and below. Complicated and time-consuming to calculate but it was felt that Mäkinen, in the new 1275 Cooper S, would stand a good chance. With superb times being set on all of the timed tests, Mäkinen revelled in the predominantly-wet conditions, often beating the bogey times by some margin. At the finish, after protracted calculations, Mäkinen had the lowest percentage score and won the touring car class, and scored the lowest percentage compared to other class winners – and although there was no official overall winner, Mäkinen had the best result. The event

CHAPTER 3: THE MK 1 MINI COOPER S

Mäkinen and Ambrose in AJB 66B on the 1964 Tulip Rally.

Mäkinen and Ambrose pulling into a time control on their way to first place.

Pauline Mayman and Val Domleo in AJB 66B, now with a 970cc engine, take the start on the 1964 Alpine, which will give them a class win and sixth in the touring class.

therefore marked the first international win for Mäkinen and the 1275 Cooper S.

In the May of 1964, the car was reprepared and dispatched to Greece for the Acropolis Rally. AJB 66B was crewed by Henry Liddon, whose duties it was to make notes for the rest of the BMC team.

For the car's second event, the 1964 Alpine Rally, AJB 66B was handed over to the female team of Pauline Mayman and Val Domleo. Built by Roy Brown, the car was entered as Group 2 but as a 970S and so received the first of just three 970S engines dispatched without close-circuit breathing, all assigned to Abingdon. The engine was overbored by 0.040in to bring it to 999cc, just within the one-litre class, and fitted with a full-race camshaft. The compression was raised slightly to 10.3:1 with a gas-flowed and polished cylinder head, and the rocker assembly had 1/16in removed from the pillars due to increased valve lift. It also had two fume pipes to help the engine breathe, an extra-large oil cooler and a four-bladed radiator fan. The Abingdon standard diff of 4.133 was fitted to the straight-cut gearbox, which had rubber driveshaft couplings.

New subframes were fitted to the car and the entire suspension was completely renewed after the hard work in Greece, now set at the standard ride height with competition dampers. The electrics and electrical ancillaries were unchanged from the previous event with the same five-additional-lamp arrangement; the only revisions were that the reversing lamp, a small 576 fog lamp, was fitted lower down on the boot lid and the car was now fitted with a twin-ended fuel pump on the subframe. No changes were made to the interior other than the Microcell reclining seat, which was modified and made stronger.

Abingdon entered a four-car team for the Alpine, always one of its favourite events. Mayman was accompanied by three

1275Ss but she was the lone works Mini in the one-litre class. Starting from Marseille, a small field of 73 cars undertook the 2100-mile event over five days. This was split into three legs, with 90 tests, and took in most of the famous Alpine climbs. Less than a third of the entry made it to the Monte Carlo

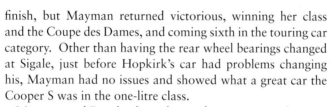

Mayman and Domleo pressing on to their class win on the 1964 Alpine.

The same crew entered the car on the 1964 Tour de France, again with a 970cc engine. Note the double identification stripes on the bonnet also repeated on the boot lid.

finish, but Mayman returned victorious, winning her class and the Coupe des Dames, and coming sixth in the touring car category. Other than having the rear wheel bearings changed at Sigale, just before Hopkirk's car had problems changing his, Mayman had no issues and showed what a great car the Cooper S was in the one-litre class.

Mayman and Domleo kept the car for next event, the Tour de France in September, where AJB 66B would be entered as a 970S in the one-litre touring car class as a Group 2. Built again by Roy Brown and also Ernie Giles, the engine was rebuilt from the Alpine and left unchanged other that having the compression raised further to 11:1. The four-blade radiator fan was replaced with a six-blade to increase

Mayman in AJB 66B on the Tour de France. Note the large crew names on the front wings.

cooling efficiency. Because of the need for as much top speed as possible, the diff was changed to a 3.9, and the straight-cut gearbox was now fitted with Hardy Spicer joints, in deference to the rubber couplings of old. The car also used the new Mitchell mounting (with a knuckle joint cast within it) to the rear of the remote to eradicate premature failure of the weak rubber joint.

The suspension was lowered by turning 4mm from the trumpets, and the car was fitted with a rear anti-roll bar (they were proving a benefit on race Minis, and as the Tour de France was mainly fought out on race circuits, it was decided that the works Minis should have them). Timken taper roller bearings were fitted to the rear hubs, after the problems experienced on the Alpine removing the older ball-bearing type. The car was also fitted with quick-lift brackets below the bumpers, which made servicing quicker and easier, although it meant the service crew had to carry a pair of large over-centre jacks on the roof racks of their A110 Austin Westminster service barges.

For identification purposes, AJB66B carried two broad white stripes, one on either side of the bonnet and on the boot lid – this to distinguish the car from the other three team cars on the race circuits, reasoning that one red-and-white Mini looked much the same as the next as they sped by.

The Tour de France placed less demand on the electrics of the car, and with only two auxiliary lamps (in the shape of two fog lamps fixed to the overriders) the C40 dynamo was not overstretched; even the reversing light was removed. The headlights reverted to vertical-dip tungsten bulbs and the headlight washers were also removed. With little nighttime running, lighting was not as important as experienced on most rallies. By now, the unique sculptured dash panel had been replaced with a boxed-out driver's panel and a flat dash for the navigator, which would become the standard design

for the majority of works Minis from here onwards. The special speedo, with its zeroing trip, was changed to reflect the higher diff ratio from that used on the Alpine Rally. Also at this time, wooden steering wheels disappeared from works cars, to be replaced with the Springall thin-grip wheel. It is also worthy of note that thicker steering arms were used, and castellated nuts and split pins for security.

The 1964 Tour de France, lest we forget, was for the first time classified as a race by the FIA and not a rally. The event visited almost every race circuit in France as it journeyed around the country from Lille to Nice, in an anti-clockwise direction, and ventured down into Italy to visit Monza. With nine speed hillclimbs thrown in for good measure, it would be a strong car that survived the demanding 3800 miles of competition and ten hours' racing. Fortunately, with Shell being one of the main sponsors providing fuel and *L'Equipe*, the French motoring paper also sponsoring the event, publicity was assured.

It would, however, be the GT class that grabbed the headlines, with works Minis contesting the touring category. Nevertheless, Mayman won the one-litre class, despite having been unceremoniously shunted off the road on the second lap of the Circuit de l'Auvergne at the hairpin. She spent most of the race trying to get the wing off the tyre; the driver's-side front corner was badly deranged but was made good enough by the service crew for her to carry on. Mayman was trying right to the end and was the fastest on handicap up the Col de Turini and second on the Col de Braus – enough to secure her the class win.

After the Tour de France, AJB 66B was dispatched for recce duties for the forthcoming Monte Carlo Rally, then loaned out to John Gott – the Northamptonshire chief constable and one-time team captain of the Abingdon works – to enter the annual Police Rally in May 1965. This was a competitive rally, mainly between numerous police forces. It was, however, no easy event, as it was a 24-hour non-stop blast from Liège, around the hills and mountains, and back over demanding terrain to Liège.

Timo Mäkinen and Paul Easter were to take over a new AJB 66B for the Rallye Vltava, better known as the Czech Rally, some ten months later. After the damage sustained by the car on the Tour de France, a new version was built by Robin Vokins for Mäkinen. This time, however, it was built up from a new red 850 Mini, not a Cooper S, as was customary. The car therefore had standard red Mini interior trim (not grey brocade) and was devoid of chrome finishers around the doors.

Being the summer of 1965, works Mini specification had progressed and much had changed from the car's original build from early 1964. Now a Group 2 1275 Cooper S,

the engine was overbored 0.020in to give 1293cc, with the crankshaft cross-drilled to increase lubrication. The more-or-less-standard full-race camshaft was fitted with lightened drive gear. The compression was raised to 11.6:1 with a polished and gas-flowed Downton cylinder head, while the rocker shaft pillars were machined down by 0.055in due to increased valve lift. The latest Lucas 40979 distributor was used, along with an MGB oil cooler. Replacing the core plug

Mayman and Domleo with the slightly battered AJB 66B at the finish in Nice on the Tour de France.

A new AJB 66B was built for Mäkinen and Easter for the Czech Rally. As can be seen the car is based on an 850 Mini bodyshell. It now has a different dashboard arrangement; gone are the curved panels.

AJB 66B with EJB 55C behind a very overloaded BMC service barge and trailer arriving for the start of the 1965 Czech Rally.

retaining plates, Abingdon now simply glued them in place with epoxy cement.

The carburettors were the normal twin H4SUs with float chamber extensions modified to allow for a fork-and-peg operation. The fuel banjo bolts were now wire-locked to the float chamber bolts to secure them from loosening. An asbestos shield was also provided on the lower bulkhead to keep heat away from inside the car from the now-extremely-hot exhaust manifold.

Another modification was to the engine steady bar, which now a spacer and bolt at the bulkhead end, to allow for ease of changing the rubber, should it fail; the bracket on the bulkhead was also rewelded for added strength.

The gearbox had special crack-tested straight-cut gears and Mäkinen elected to use an ultra-short 4.26 diff ratio. Enlarged driveshafts were used with special Hardy Spicer flanges and joints. Interestingly, the old type of gear lever was used in preference to the latest anti-rattle mainstream item.

Being for Mäkinen, it was built as a 'dry' car with rubber cone suspension in deference to Hydrolastic, which was now fitted to road cars. The suspension was standard other than having additional bump stops at the rear and Girling competition dampers, plus the subframes were rewelded for added strength.

The electrics now received an 11AC alternator, with a remote regulator and race-type battery, fitted in the customary way with the terminals away from the fuel tank. A two-speed wiper motor was fitted, driving deep-throated wheel boxes, which replaced the flimsy standard Mini items. Lighting, still in the early days of iodine bulbs, meant the non-dipping iodine headlight had to have small Lucas 576 fog lights fitted to the bonnet acting as the dipped beam, again with iodine bulbs. Two Lucas 700 fog lamps on quick-release brackets were fitted along the bumper, and gone was the single Cyclops lamp to be replaced with another Lucas 700 lamp on the bumper but with a Continental driving lens – all with iodine bulbs. The car now also carried an intercom, with the control box being attached to the roof via a Lift-the-Dot fixing – not forgetting, this was before the days of roll cages, to which the intercom box would subsequently be secured.

The car also had a document bag made into the roof headlining. Navigational instruments now consisted of a Halda Twinmaster replacing the small Halda distance recorder behind the magnifier in addition to the kph speedo having a zeroing trip.

Mäkinen now had the use of a fibreglass bucket seat, which had been introduced to the team by Rauno Aaltonen and would replace the Microcell buckets seats used in the past. He would also use an Irvin lap-and-diagonal belt, whilst Easter had an Irvin full harness. All trim, glass and carpet was retained but with the addition of an asbestos mat placed under the front carpet, again to keep heat from the exhaust out of the car.

The exhaust itself, now a fully-skidded system, with security joints, also had the tailpipe turned up rather than straight – done due to difficulties when being driven up steep ramps with a straight exhaust pipe grounding out.

Timo Mäkinen and Paul Easter on the cobblestones on the Czech Rally. Note the small Austin Healey reversing lamp and now the car had an upswept exhaust pipe.

The body had access holes cut in the rear bulkhead, to allow easy access to the top of the dampers, should they need changing. This was preferable to moving over the fuel tanks and all the effort involved in taking off the Aston fuel caps, with their threaded bosses that were driven onto the tank necks.

The event, however, was not to be successful for Mäkinen and Easter, as they retired on the first night with numerous maladies. The Rally Vltava attracted 83 entrants for this round of the European Championship, and an indication of how tough the 1400-mile event was that it saw only 12 cars make it back to the finish. It was made even harder for the crews as no service was permitted and, worse still, they were allowed only six wheels, which were marked so they couldn't be changed. Ironically, they could change tyres – if the crews changed them themselves – but not the wheel rims.

This was also a very fast event and with the national speed limits relaxed at night, it meant an average speed of over 50mph in places. So other than topping up with fuel, there was little time to do anything, should something go wrong. And this is what befell Mäkinen and Easter: first, they had trouble with a leak from the union on the oil cooler, which they stopped to tighten. Ten miles down the road, they were stopped with no oil pressure – only to discover that the union had broken off the cooler. Time was spent effecting a bypass but once on the road again, the fan belt failed. Once replaced and on the move, it was only a few miles down the road when a nut holding the radius arm came adrift. After fitting a new nut, it was decided to cut to the next passage control, to try to keep in the rally. Sadly, they arrived too late and were excluded.

AJB 66B was finally wheeled out in the October of 1965 for its final event as a works car, handed to new boy Tony Fall, teamed with experienced co-driver Ron Crellin, for the Three Cities Rally. Fall was a young car salesman at Appleyards in Leeds and was a successful club driver in Yorkshire. Having won a Coupe des Alpes in his own car in 1965, he was offered this one off-drive for the factory team. The Munich-Vienna-Budapest Rally, known as the Three Cities Rally, saw Fall return the faith expressed in him by Stuart Turner by bringing the car home to a creditable second in class and winning the team prize. It marked the start of a successful career for Fall with the Abingdon works team.

Fall's role on the event, however, was initially to drive as

Tony Fall and Ron Crellin on the Three Cities Rally for AJB 66B's final works appearance.

slowly as possible, as the rally was to be decided on the class improvement system. As it was the penultimate round of the European Championship that Rauno Aaltonen was leading, it gave him the best chance of winning, if he outshone others in his class. Fortunately, the organisers decided to abandon the idea and run it on scratch results, so Fall was free the do his best – providing he finished behind Aaltonen. Paul Easter and Henry Liddon, in Paul's own Cooper S, BON 44C, acted as Aaltonen's service crew, shadowing him and carrying all the spares and tools because servicing was not permitted on the event – but there was nothing preventing fellow competitors helping each other. Aaltonen duly won the Czech Rally and went on to win the European Championship.

AJB 66B was sold to Hugh Piggins via John Cracknell, Paddy Hopkirk's partner in his Mill Accessories Group, who had obtained the car from Abingdon.

Competition Record

Date	Event	Crew	Number	Overall result	Class result
April 1964	Tulip Rally	Timo Mäkinen/Tony Ambrose	119	1st	1st
June 1964	Alpine Rally	Pauline Mayman/Val Domleo	8	6th	1st CdeD
Sept 1964	Tour de France	Pauline Mayman/Val Domleo	20		1st
May 1965	Police Rally	John Gott/Bill Shepherd			
July 1965	Czech (Vltava)	Timo Mäkinen/Paul Easter	100	DNF	
Oct 1965	Three Cities	Tony Fall/Ron Crellin	65		2nd

Registration Number	First registered	Chassis number	Engine	Engine number	Model
BJB 77B	June 1964	KA2S4 489078	1071cc	9F-SA-H 33200	Morris Cooper S
			1275cc	9F-SA-Y 31360	
			970cc	9F-SA-X 29003	

A brand new BJB 77B poses besides the works Healey at Abingdon with the export MGBs behind, all made at the Abingdon plant.

Tommy Eales working on the dashboard of BJB 77B. Note the early Halda and the fire extinguisher, Springall steering wheel, rope grab handle and Microcell seat.

BJB 77B was built in April 1964, dispatched in May and registered in June 1964. Unfortunately it could not carry the number AJB 77B as hoped – to keep the serial of numbers 33, 44, 55, and 66 running – as that registration had already been allocated. Delivered some four months after its sister cars it was, like them, also a 1071 Cooper S. It was also a dry car and, just like the others, BJB 77B was soon to receive a 1275 engine for its first event – the Alpine Rally – with Timo Mäkinen and Patrick Vanson.

Built by Peter Bartram as a Group 2 car, it was kept at the standard 1275 bore but fitted with the more-or-less-obligatory full-race 648 camshaft and a slightly flowed and polished cylinder head, giving 10:1 compression. Twin SU H4 carbs, with 'fork and peg' linkage with ram pipes were fitted, plus the inlet manifold was polished internally. Core plug retainers were fitted to the front of the block, these being cylindrical plates screwed over the core plug to ensure they stayed in place. No water thermostat was fitted, and the bypass hose omitted and blanked off at the cylinder head and water pump. A four-blade fan was used on the radiator with a 13lb cap. The ARO9794 oil cooler was fitted onto a nicely crafted platform set into the front panel.

The gearbox was fitted with close-ratio straight cut-gears, had a 4.133 diff and drove through yellow-marked rubber drive couplings; it was protected by a small RAF-style sump guard – often termed the 13-hole guard, for obvious reasons.

The electrics, fitted with a dynamo, fed five auxiliary lamps, all with iodine bulbs, with dipped beam being supplied by two lamps on the bonnet; there were two extra fog lights and one small spot lamp in addition to a small fog lamp mounted on the boot lid as a reversing light. Two-speed wipers were fitted, and twin Mixo Minor horns were used, operated by the driver by the horn-push and the co-driver by a foot-operated button fitted into a wooden block up on the front bulkhead. Headlight washers were also supplied. The battery was reversed, with a longer cable run so that its terminals were away from the fuel tank. Both fuel tanks were fitted with quick-release Aston fuel caps and protected with thin plywood, should studded tyres or anything else in the boot damage the tanks. Fuel lines were run outside the car but protected by metal channelling.

Microcell seats were used with Irvin seat belts, although only the fixing eyes were supplied for Mäkinen, as he preferred not to use a belt. He also used a wooden steering wheel and the handbrake was modified to operate as a fly-off type. As the

Timo Mäkinen and Patrick Vanson posing by BJB 77B in Marseille prior to the start of the 1964 Alpine Rally.

Mäkinen high up in the mountains with stunning Alpine backdrop.

car was a Group 2, all glass, trim, underfelt and carpets were retained, and extra padding supplied to the doors and door locks. Scotchlite red reflective tape was also placed on the door shuts and rear bumper, which showed up in headlights at night. Instruments consisted of a kph speedo with a trip, together with a small Halda distance recorder behind a magnifier. A 10,000rpm rev counter was used, along with a special capillary temperature gauge, as well as the standard oil pressure gauge. Two Heuer watches were also fitted.

Brakes were standard, other than DS11 pads and VG95 racing linings. The brake limiting valve, apportioning brake pressure front to back, was changed to a 325lb item and the brake lines were run inside the car. The suspension was also essentially standard, other than the addition of extra bump stops at the rear and the use of competition dampers, with the front fixing brackets being tack-welded for added strength. The wheels were shod in 500L Dunlop R6 race tyres.

There was mixed success for the four-car team that entered the 1964 Alpine. Two cars finished, two didn't. The Alpine ran for five days over 2100 miles, starting in Marseille with three legs from Marseille to Cannes, Cannes to Chamonix and finally finishing in Monte Carlo using most of the classic Alpine climbs – 90 in all. Seventy-three cars started but only 25 made it to the finish; sadly, Mäkinen wasn't one of them.

After setting a good early pace, although not on par with those set by Aaltonen in the lightweight Group 3 car, Mäkinen was forced into retirement towards the end of the first full day. Disaster struck on the Col de Valberg when the rubber mounting at the end of the gearshift remote failed. With the resulting thrashing about of the engine, the exhaust then broke and one of the carburettor's float bowls fractured on the bulkhead. The resultant petrol dripping down over the hot exhaust and a terrible misfire saw the car withdrawn once down off the Col. After the failure of the rubber mounting, and the resulting problems it caused, attention was centred on finding a permanent answer to this perennial problem. A solution was not that far away.

BJB77B was then reprepared, again by Peter Bartram for its next event, the Tour de France the following September. The car was to be crewed by Timo Mäkinen and Don Barrow, but illness, contracted whilst on the recce, forced Barrow to withdraw, and at the very last minute Paul Easter was summoned to Abingdon by Stuart Turner's secretary and offered the seat. He was told to report to Abingdon to collect some driveshafts and some money, and jump on a plane to France – everyone else was already in Lille preparing for the start.

It was initially a strange choice, as Easter was a driver of some repute and not a navigator. As a successful private entrant on national events he had started to gain valuable experience on European rallies, so he was well known to Abingdon. Having also won his class on the 1963 Acropolis Rally, he had on occasions been drafted into the BMC team – but always behind the wheel, not a map. However, the combination of Mäkinen and Easter gelled instantly, despite

Timo Mäkinen and Paul Easter before the start of the 1964 Tour De France where they so nearly won the touring category. Note the fog lights on the bumper overriders and single identification stripe.

BMC Service for the three works Minis out on the Tour de France, Timo Mäkinen in BJB 77B at 18, Hopkirk at number 19 and Pauline Mayman at number 20.

Turner's misgivings that Paul was better suited as a driver. History will show that Mäkinen and Easter went on to become one of Abingdon's more successful partnerships.

For the Tour de France the car was to be entered as a 970S in the one-litre class. The engine was bored 0.040in to give 999cc, just within the class limit. With flat-top pistons, a full-race camshaft and 11:1 compression from the modified cylinder head, the engine was extremely powerful for a one-litre car. To keep things cool a six-blade fan was used, plus a large oil cooler.

The straight-cut gearbox had a slightly longer 3.938 diff to allow for a little more top speed at the expense of acceleration. The solution to the failure of the gearshift remote rubber was now at hand, in the shape of a so-called Mitchell mounting. Designed by MG chassis designer Terry Mitchell, the new rubber had cast within it a movable joint; when bolted to the remote shift and the bracket on the body, it could not come apart. The bracket was also reinforced and strapping provided inside the car to spread the extra stress on the body. These joints never failed again. Also new on the car for the Tour de France were Hardy Spicer drive couplings, replacing the troublesome crucifix rubber couplings, which had dogged the car from the early days.

Another change was to fit a larger-diameter interconnecting pipe between the fuel tanks to make refuelling faster and more reliable, as often, in a rush, cars left service only partially fuelled, as it took time for the fuel to balance between the two tanks.

As the Tour de France mainly centred on race circuit work, the car was lowered by shortening the struts by 4mm, fitted with competition Girling dampers and, of course, Dunlop R6 race tyres. All the works Minis prepared for the tour were fitted with quick-lift jacking points front and rear to speed up service and (in particular) tyre changes, should they be needed during timed races. This would become a standard Abingdon fit from then onwards and, other than the inconvenience to the service crew of having to lug around cumbersome over-centre jacks on their roof racks, they were a welcome and time-saving addition.

The electrics, being much simpler for the tour, meant less demand was placed on the system, and without an array of extra lamps the car was rewired accordingly. Other than two fog lamps mounted on the overriders, no extra lamps were used. Even the reversing light was abandoned – as were the headlight washers. The fuel pump was upgraded to a twin-end pump but still located outside on the subframe, albeit protected by an aluminium plate.

Also changed was the wooden steering wheel, replaced by a Springall thin-grip leather wheel. The Microcell seats were retained but were now covered in early Mini cloth trim. Despite the desire to save weight, nothing could be removed as the car was in Group 2, so all trim had to be retained, as did the heavy glass. To help identification from other works Minis on the race tracks, BJB 77B had a broad white stripe painted on the co-driver's side of the bonnet and boot lid. Other AJB team cars had either two stripes, no stripe or one on the driver's side – reasoning that one red-and-white Mini flashing by looked much the same as the next.

The 1964 Tour de France, now classed as a race by the FIA, visited almost every race circuit in France from Lille to Nice, in an anti-clockwise direction, and also went down to Monza in Italy. The 3800 miles of competition on this week-long event included nine speed hillclimbs and eight circuit races of up to two hours in duration, and represented a big challenge. It was also a key event for BMC, as France was a significant market for the manufacturer – good publicity was important.

Service for BJB 77B with the car up on the quick-lift jack and the rear wheel bearing being attended to, and the service barge in the background.

Mäkinen leading a Mini train with Hopkirk and Mabbs very close behind. This method used to improve each other's lap times.

Mäkinen and Easter on one of the numerous hillclimbs on the mammoth Tour de France. They would retire so near the end.

During the race, Mäkinen and Hopkirk were neck-and-neck, were both in a good position in the handicap and showing well in the touring car class on scratch. The works cars of Mäkinen and Hopkirk, with the assistance of Geoff Mabbs in his private 1071 Cooper S, entertained the crowds by forming a slipstream train, running nose to tail, lap after lap, to improve their times – at every track for the first three days. To get an edge on his team rival (and others, of course) Mäkinen undertook a 200-mile round trip during a night halt at Aurillac, when he travelled with John Sprinzel and Andrew Hedges, in a hire car, to Clermont-Ferrand for a quick practice of the very twisty circuit. But it was all to no avail, as Mäkinen had a driveshaft let go on the test and earned himself a fail, despite repairing it out on the circuit, and slipped way down the order.

Journeying down to Italy, to the famous Monza race circuit, saw the end of Mäkinen's challenge. Whilst leaving the Monza circuit test, Easter took over the wheel, and on the outskirts of Monza the car was attacked by a Fiat 1100 taxi from the right, which hit the car in the rear corner, spinning it across the road and into a kilo-stone. The car was damaged, with the driver's-side rear wheel being out of line, and so it was retired. Easter felt sure that his new job at Abingdon was over almost before it had started. Mäkinen just looked upon it as an opportunity to retire to the nearest bar...

Their adventure, however, did not end there, as although still drivable, the car was somewhat crablike as it went down the road. Undeterred, Easter drove the car all the way back from Italy, only to be arrested by the police once on UK soil. Ordered to drive no further, he was charged with driving without due care and attention, and the car was left at a nearby garage. At the subsequent court case, early the next year, Doug Watts presented the offending rear radius arm and satisfactorily demonstrated to the three magistrates that the car was not dangerous, and the case against Paul was therefore dismissed. The arresting police officer was most apologetic to Paul, having realised that he and Timo had just won the Monte Carlo Rally a few weeks beforehand.

The car was purchased by the MG plant maintenance foreman 'Drummer' Longshaw.

Competition Record

Date	Event	Crew	Number	Overall result	Class result
June 1964	Alpine Rally	Timo Mäkinen/Patrick Vanson	19	DNF	
Sept 1964	Tour de France	Timo Mäkinen/Paul Easter	18	DNF	

Registration Number	First registered	Chassis number	Engine	Engine number	Model
CRX 88B	Oct 1964	CA2S7 552400	1275cc	9F-SA-Y 32170	Austin Cooper S

Tony Ambrose and Rauno Aaltonen with CRX 88B in Athens preparing for the start on the 1965 Monte Carlo Rally. Note the four studded tyres on the roof.

Aaltonen takes CRX 88B into scrutineering. Note the blanking tape over the oil cooler and lightweight grille.

CRX 88B was one of four new Cooper Ss registered in October 1964: two Austins and two Morrises in line with BMC policy to promote both marques. By now, all cars supplied to Abingdon were 1275 Cooper Ss, and as Hydrolastic suspension was fitted to Cooper S road cars, these too were all Hydrolastic – although not all stayed that way. Two cars were prepared for the forthcoming RAC Rally straight away; the other two were to christened on the Monte Carlo Rally in the following January. CRX 88B was to be saved for the 1965 Monte.

For the Monte, it was entered as a lightweight Group 3 car, to be driven by Rauno Aaltonen with Tony Ambrose, and built by Bob Whittington. As the Monte this year did not penalise Group 3 cars over the less-modified Group 2 class, it was obvious that a lightweight car would stand a good chance of winning the rally. The engine was kept at its standard bore but with a 648 full-race camshaft and a polished and flowed cylinder head to give 11:1 compression. Valves were standard but the rocker shaft pillars had 0.055in removed due to increased lift. It used the latest 40979 distributor, while the carburettors were standard Abingdon-fit of twin SU H4s but with float chamber extensions, blue springs and CP4 needles. Power output was estimated to be around 100bhp.

The gearbox had a close-ratio straight-cut gear set with an ultra-short 4.26 diff and a set of special driveshafts modified by Hardy Spicer, together with 'white' marked couplings. The gearshift remote received an indestructible Mitchell mounting, with its bracket and body also being strengthened. All this was protected by an Abingdon-made full-width Dural sump guard.

The Hydrolastic suspension was standard other than the rear displacers being yellow-banded and the front units having 2mm spacer washers added to raise the ground clearance. The subframes were rewelded front and back for added strength, and the rear hubs were fitted with Timken taper roller bearings. Brakes were standard but had racing pads and linings fitted, namely Ferodo DS11 and VG95s. The rear brake limiting valve was changed to having a 325lb pressure spring.

An alternator was fitted to the car, replacing, at last, the heavy dynamo that had always been fitted to works Minis; the extra power and reliability was much welcomed. Lighting was the familiar pattern of two large fog lights mounted on quick-release brackets with a single smaller spot lamp on the slam panel and the headlights dipping onto two small fog lamps fitted to the bonnet. All lamps had iodine bulbs and, to save weight, the headlamp bowls were fibreglass instead of steel. To save more weight, only a single Mixo horn was used and the rear number plate replaced with stick-on digits on a painted background. The reversing lamp was a Healey 3000 sidelight, mounted on the boot lid.

A two-speed wiper motor was fitted with deep-throated

CHAPTER 3: THE MK 1 MINI COOPER S

wheel boxes that were better able to cope with snow loads than the standard items; they were fed by two washer bottles: one with normal fluid and the other with alcohol, and hence the car also had four washer jets. The washer bottles were fitted inside the car, under the driver's-side rear window, stopping them from freezing and allowing them to be refilled on the move. Gone, however, were the headlight washers. The battery was again reversed away from the fuel tank and the cable run inside the car, along with the brake and fuel lines, although the twin fuel pump was still located outside on the rear subframe. The twin fuel tanks were protected from damage from spiked tyres by alloy plates fitted to the sides of the tanks.

The weight-saving continued with the use of alloy doors, bonnet and boot lid. A new front grille was made from an Austin Cambridge part, while the front wings had handmade alloy wheelarch extensions to cover the wide wheels. Perspex replaced all of the heavy glass, other than for the heated front laminated windscreen. Even the heater was replaced with one with an aluminium body.

The bodyshell also had large 50mm holes cut in the rear seat pan and the back bulkhead, together with the rear parcel shelf. The carpet was replaced with special lightweight Rivington thin carpet but with an asbestos blanket under the front to keep away heat from the manifold. No sound deadening was fitted to the car. The exhaust was also lightweight, and all surplus brackets and tabs, unused, were removed from the shell. Finally, a lightweight fibreglass bucket seat was used by Aaltonen. It was estimated that some 50lb had been shaved off the car.

Ambrose had the use of a Halda Twinmaster, reading in kilometres (as did the speedo), replacing the small distance recorder fitted behind a magnifier; he also used two Heuer timepieces: a stopwatch and a time-of-day clock. There was a map pocket fitted into the roof lining, plus the customary extra padding fitted on the door locks, door pockets and now also the door pillars. The driver's instrument panel was extended forward by 75mm and now appeared more vertical; it no longer mirrored the navigator's panel, still set into the parcel shelf at an angle.

For the Monte, the car started on Dunlop SP3 road tyres but would use special Dunlop snow tyres with 'pop-in' tungsten studs fired into the tread and others with special spiral spikes forced into the tyres, designed for heavy snow. The car carried a modified MGB jack to allow quick wheel changes away from the service crews.

The car was also kitted out with a full roof rack, which enabled the crew to carry sufficient tyres for its journey across Europe before the serious competition started at St Claude in France. The roof rack was removed at Chambéry prior to St Claude. The crew, along with the other team members, were also told that great efforts had been made to save weight on the cars, so were instructed not clutter the car with junk and that all excess baggage was to be offloaded at Chambéry for the service crews to carry on to Monte.

Queuing up for the Athens start in front of Geoff Mabbs and John Davenport. Ambrose sorting his equipment in the car. Note the door lock and pocket padding, also the reflective Scotchlite tape on the door shut and rear bumper.

Starting from Athens, on their own (other BMC works cars, in pairs, started from Stockholm, Paris and Minsk) meant service arrangements would be stretched but Stuart Turner was gambling that some routes would be less snowbound than others – plus BMC achieved wider publicity starting from various locations. In fact, Brian Moylan was the only BMC mechanic in Athens, having transported the car to the start. Aaltonen had asked to start from Athens, as generally the roads out of Greece to Italy, at this time of year, were always passable. Despite Aaltonen's logical preference for the Athens start, only eight cars elected to start from the Greek capital.

A field of 237 cars started the Monte on their respective 2600-mile journeys from nine starting points around Europe, converging on St Claude in mid-France for the common run to Monte Carlo, three days later. Gone for 1965 was final stage

Aaltonen and Ambrose pull into a time control, still with tarmac tyres fitted. No snow yet, which was soon to follow. Note the grille muff to keep out the snow and cold from the engine.

WORKS MINIS IN DETAIL

On their way to Monte Carlo, where trouble with a blown head gasket and ultimately a failed condenser connection saw the car arrive too late at Gap.

CRX 88B dressed up as the Monte winner for the Geneva Motor Show. Note carefully this is not AJB 44B: the Lift-the-Dot studs for the headlight protectors are in a different place, even though the car has been changed to a Morris.

CRX 88B on display at the Berlin Motor Show on the Lucas stand expounding the merits of the Lucas alternators fitted to the car.

around the Grand Prix circuit at Monaco, which was replaced by a 380-mile final night loop over the mountains around Monte Carlo. However, the weather was to prove decisive in 1965 and decimated much of the field when the route got into central France on the Monday evening; the terrible weather of blizzards, deep snow, ice and drifts eliminated many cars once in the Massif Central area. As the depleted field headed down towards Monte, the weather closed in further still, and of the 211 cars that safely reached St Claude, only 35 made it to Monte within their allowable one-hour lateness.

None of the Athens starters made it to Monte Carlo. Aaltonen's run from Athens had started well but he ran into mechanical problems before leaving Greece, when the head gasket leaked. With no service having been planned for this leg of the route, a phone call to England resulted in a mechanic flying out to Milan with a new head gasket and a fresh cylinder head (with a budget of £15,000 assigned to the 1965 Monte, the additional cost was relatively small). The new cylinder head was fitted when the crew were met at a local BMC agent in Alessandria.

Once on the move again it was easy running on the Yugoslav Autoput and the Italian Autostrada, both being free of snow. However, they ran into snowdrifts and blizzards near Sestrière and had to stop and fit studded tyres that were carried on the roof. Soon after, between Sestrière and Gap on the Col de Monte Montgenèvre, the car spluttered to a halt. It took a long while to find the fault, which was simply caused by the screw holding the condenser in the distributor coming adrift. With still over 30km to the next control and only 15 minutes of time left, Aaltonen and Ambrose arrived at the next control in Gap over their one hour of permitted lateness and were eliminated.

The remaining cars that made it down to Monte Carlo the following morning, after a night of atrocious weather, prepared themselves for the mountain circuit that night. That too was to prove decisive, with the organisers themselves being uncertain about actually sending the cars out. Brilliant driving in terrible weather saw Timo Mäkinen come through the clear winner – he had simply dominated the event in another works Mini.

After the 1965 Monte, CRX 88B was not used again as a competition car, mainly because it had been built as a Group 3 and most European events favoured Group 2 cars. However, it was used at the Geneva Motor Show, dressed up as the Monte winner AJB 44B. It was later used on the Lucas stand at the Berlin Motor show as the company actively promoted the new alternator that BMC was then using on works cars. It was also used as a service support car on the 1965 RAC Rally.

Competition Record

Date	Event	Crew	Number	Overall result	Class result
Jan 1965	Monte Carlo Rally	Rauno Aaltonen/Tony Ambrose	273	DNF	

CHAPTER 3: THE MK 1 MINI COOPER S

Registration Number	First registered	Chassis number	Engine	Engine number	Model
CRX 89B	Oct 1964	CA2S7 552318	1275cc	9F-SA-Y 32562	Austin Cooper S

The second of the four new CRX cars delivered to Abingdon in late 1964 was, like the first, registered as an Austin: CRX 89B, prepared for Rauno Aaltonen and Tony Ambrose for the 1964 RAC Rally.

The new car was reprepared to take on what was always a rough event. For the RAC, a powerful 1293cc engine was built with a gas-flowed cylinder head, giving 11:1 compression, a race camshaft and twin SUH4 carburettors, all sitting on a straight-cut close-ratio gearbox and 4.133 final drive. It also used special driveshafts with Hardy Spicer universal joints. The sump was protected by a sump plate screwed on, in addition to an alloy sump guard. It was also fitted with a battery box guard. The remote gearshift was fitted with an indestructible Mitchell mounting and the body strengthened to carry its bracket. The subframe was strengthened and gussets welded to the front tie rod brackets. The rear hub bearings used Timken needle rollers rather than ball race bearings.

The car was equipped with five additional lamps on the front plus a roof lamp and headlamp washers. It was also fitted with a back-mounted Lucas fog lamp, fixed to the boot lid and serving as a reversing lamp. Under the bonnet saw twin Mixo horns, a dynamo, a six-blade fan, and plates screwed over the core plugs to ensure they stayed in place. As always, the car was prepared to a very high standard.

It was uncertain if Aaltonen would actually make the London start for the RAC Rally in time, as he had been given a free entry on Grand Prêmio d'Argentina, a 3000-mile road race from Buenos Aires to the Bolivia border and back again, which finished just 24 hours before the RAC was due to start. Aaltonen had been invited to take part in an MG Magnette, prepared by the local MG agent Siam di Tella, as a thank you for winning the Spa-Sofia-Liège Rally. Unfortunately, having spent two hot and dusty weeks practising for the event, it was cancelled at the last minute due to floods, and Aaltonen was able to make the RAC start comfortably.

The 1964 RAC was the last and deciding round of the European Championship, and the rally followed the recipe of fast forest stages and relatively undemanding road sections. At 2500 miles the route included about 400 miles of stages, mostly in British forests. A field of 180 cars assembled in London at the Duke of York's Barracks for the 7am start, with the route heading off towards the West Country and on into Wales, northern England and up to Scotland. With an overnight halt at Perth, before a loop back to Perth and then heading south to finish back in London some five days later, the event was indeed a formidable challenge. BMC had entered a team of four Cooper Ss on the home event but sadly

Brand-new engine being fitted to CRX 89B for Rauno Aaltonen's attempt on the 1964 RAC Rally. Note a dynamo fitted, two washer bottles, 150-degree wiper motor and the engine still has lifting brackets fitted.

Rauno Aaltonen and Tony Ambrose depart from London on the 1964 RAC Rally.

none was to finish, despite three of them challenging for the lead at some point.

From the start, Aaltonen was immediately up with the leaders and by the time the crews reached Wales on the first night, where the roads were very icy, he was up to second overall. BMC had devised a novel way to service and inspect the underside of the works Minis by using a Lansing Bagnall fork lift truck to hoist up the cars. This caused quite a stir, with much interest and publicity – despite which, the idea was never used again. Perhaps moving a fork lift truck around the country was not the easiest thing to do.

Through the night and into the next day, Aaltonen was swapping times with Hopkirk and Källström in the other works Minis, as the weather deteriorated. However, it was not all plain sailing, as once up in Scotland near Turnberry, Aaltonen had a puncture, left the road and collected a

CRX 89B crashing through a rock-strewn stage at unabated speed.

Aaltonen leaping CRX 89B at the Carron Valley Bridge in Perth on the RAC Rally.

maximum, it taking too long to extract the car – and it was only the efforts of the Morley brothers (running late in the works Healey) hauling them back on the road that kept them in the rally. But after the overnight halt in Perth, the next morning's run out of Perth and back again saw Aaltonen retire with a broken gearbox on the Blackcraig stage, and the Mini could go no further. With the failure of the three other works Minis, it was not a memorable RAC Rally for the Abingdon record books.

After the RAC, CRX 89B was repaired and dispatched, just before Christmas, for recce duties for the forthcoming Monte Carlo Rally, crewed by Paddy Hopkirk and Henry Liddon.

For the car's next event, the 1965 Circuit of Ireland, CRX 89B was handed over to Irishmen Paddy Hopkirk and Terry Harriman to compete on their home international. A new car was built, after the rigours of the RAC, prepared by Johnny Evans as a lightweight Group 3 machine for what was a fast and furious mostly-tarmac event. The engine was overbored 0.020in to bring the capacity to 1293cc and the crankshaft cross-drilled to aid lubrication at high revs. The cylinder head was polished, gas-flowed and skimmed to give an 11.8:1 compression ratio. The rocker shaft pillars were also skimmed by 0.055in due to the extra valve lift with the full race camshaft that was fitted. The car had a reported 78bhp at the wheels on the Abingdon rolling road.

The gearbox was straight-cut close-ratio and fitted with an ultra-short 4.26 diff for extra acceleration, and the driveshafts were fitted with special couplings. All this was protected by a strong Scandinavian sump guard, which stopped damage caused by heavy landings on the bumpy Irish roads.

The Hydrolastic suspension, pumped to 500psi, was retained but used competition displacers and was also fitted with spacer washers added to the struts to raise the ride height, and the hydro lines were run inside the car. The subframes, front and back, were rewelded for added strength and a skid plate fixed to the rear subframe to protect the exposed battery box. The external fuel pump was also protected by an alloy plate. Clever protection plates were fitted by the front tie rods to add strength. Quick-lift jacking plates were fitted, as were towing eyes, front and back. Brakes were standard but used racing linings.

The electrics, now with the luxury of an alternator, fed the five additional lamps, all with iodine bulbs. There was also a roof lamp over by the navigator's side of the car. As the car was lightweight, an Austin Healey sidelight was used as a reversing lamp on the bootlid. The battery cable was run inside the car and, as was customary, the race battery was fitted with the terminals away from the fuel tank. The brake and fuel lines were also run inside the car, although the twin fuel pump remained outside on the subframe. And those fuel tanks now had their retaining strap fitted inboard to prevent the tank being pushed into the boot area and over the battery should the car have a heavy side impact.

As this was a Group 3 car, weight-saving was at a premium, so Perspex replaced the heavy glass, other than the laminated front 'screen. The bonnet, boot lid and doors were all made from aluminium. Inside the car, most trim was removed, and lightweight carpet was used in the front; none in the rear. However, extra padding was fitted to the doors, door locks and pillars. The heater was replaced with a lightweight alloy-cased unit, and alloy wheelarch extensions also made to cover the wide-rim wheels. The exhaust was also lightweight and it was about this time that Abingdon changed the design, abandoning the straight pipe and using the upturned tailpipe that was to become a familiar sight – designed, it was said, to aid getting on and off ferries without damaging the end of the exhaust.

The Circuit of Ireland, held over the Easter weekend, offered the 100 starters a 1370-mile route, with 33 timed stages over five days and two nights throughout Ireland, mostly on closed public roads. There were just two nights in bed at Killarney. Setting off on Good Friday evening from Bangor, Hopkirk and Harryman were front-runners all through the night and next day, and held the front of the field. At the first night halt in Killarney on the Saturday evening Hopkirk was in the lead. Soon after, on the classic Sunday run the following morning over the Kerry Mountains, Hopkirk was to relinquish his lead to a hard-charging Vic Elford in the works Cortina, but after the famous Moll's Gap climb – where Hopkirk changed onto racing tyres – the Mini took back the lead from the Ford, which it was not to lose.

After the Easter Monday restart, heading north, Hopkirk dived straight into a local garage at Doon, where BMC mechanics put the Mini onto its side, removed the sump guard and changed drive couplings in less than 12 minutes – and he retained the lead with no time loss. Through the night on the dash down to the Larne finish on the Tuesday morning, Hopkirk and Elford continued to fight it out until the Ford flew off the road and lost valuable time. By Larne, half of the field had retired, such was the rate of attrition, Hopkirk was a clear winner and Elford had to settle for second place. It was Hopkirk's fourth Circuit of Ireland win but the first in a works Mini. The car, when back from Ireland, was put back onto the Abingdon rolling road to recheck the power and it gave 76bhp, slightly down on when it started.

After the success of the Circuit of Ireland, Paddy Hopkirk was dispatched to take part in the Luxembourg Slalom at the invitation of the local Morris dealer. This was an international event, albeit of a rather low key. The slalom course was laid out with hay bales in a huge car park with minimal safely precautions. Paddy, being a past master at driving tests (now known as autotests) won the saloon car category and brought the Mini home in seventh place overall after two spirited runs in damp conditions, which rather suited the Mini's handling.

Keeping with the theme of using the car for home internationals, CRX 89B was next entered on the Scottish

Paddy Hopkirk and Terry Harryman on the 1965 Circuit of Ireland Rally, a rally they would win outright.

Hopkirk cornering hard in CRX 89B, where the roof lamp has moved from the position on the RAC car, as has the position of the headlight protection straps, indicating a bodyshell change.

International in June of 1965, driven again by Paddy Hopkirk but this time navigated by Henry Liddon. The successful lightweight Group 3 car from Ireland was reprepared by Mick Legg for the event, with few changes. The Hydrolastic suspension now had double-red rear displacers at the back and single-red at the front because of the rough terrain it was to be used on. Oddly, the all-new engine had the compression lowered slightly from the Circuit of Ireland unit (to 11.6:1) but it now produced 84bhp on the rollers instead of 78bhp. The only other change to the engine was the replacement of the standard Cooper S distributor for the latest Lucas 40979, which had an asymmetric cam; plus the six-blade fan was replaced by a four-blade. So perhaps these two changes did

Paddy Hopkirk and Henry Liddon took CRX 89B on the 1965 Scottish Rally. Seen here with auxiliary lights removed for daylight running and to allow more cooling to the engine.

give that extra 6bhp. Other small alterations to the car were the provision of an asbestos plate fixed to the front bulkhead above the subframe, which was designed to keep excessive heat from the manifold away from the inside of the car. The exhaust, because of the anticipated rough Scottish forests, had brackets welded either side of the joints, with a security bolt fixed between to ensure the system stayed together. Gone was the roof lamp, and a document bag was fitted into the headlining above Liddon's head. Finally, the car now carried a modified MGB jack, which was faster to use than the standard Mini side jack, as it had a cranked wooden handle.

Held over the Whitsun holiday, the Scottish was now regarded by many as a very tough event, and most competitors thought it as tough as the RAC Rally. Starting from Glasgow

Hopkirk and Liddon with some damage to the rear of CRX 89B, where they failed to finish the Scottish Rally.

on the Monday, the 108 starters faced a 1700-mile route containing 52 special stages, amounting to over 300 miles of rock-strewn forest tracks. Only 42 cars would make it back to the finish, but sadly Hopkirk wasn't to be one of them.

Heading southwards and back on the first day, before a day into the hills to the west during the first night, Hopkirk fought for the lead with BMC teammate Mäkinen in the Healey 3000 and Roger Clark in a works Ford Cortina. Trouble struck Hopkirk after the early stages when a non-competing car had brake fade and smacked into the back of the works Mini, denting the rear quite badly. With Mäkinen in trouble with a worn out sump guard, Hopkirk was now in second place behind the Cortina.

The following day, to the north east Highlands, the pace was relentless. Hopkirk's Mini suffered a broken driver's seat, which resulted in Liddon forsaking his seat and taking up residence on the rear seat for several stages, until Hopkirk's seat could be repaired by the BMC mechanics. However, it was all to no avail as on the third day's loop eastwards, the final drive disintegrated, spewing oil all over the car and into retirement. It was not a good event for BMC as Mäkinen too retired, with a failed pinion, so the spoils were left to Clark in the Cortina.

For the Polish Rally the following month, a new car was prepared for Rauno Aaltonen and Tony Ambrose, built as a Group 2 by Tommy Eales and Johnny Evans. This was to be the third CRX 89B thus far; the RAC car was not seen again, and the Circuit of Ireland and Scottish car – being a lightweight Group 3 and now badly damaged – was not used again either.

The new Mini was a 1293cc Hydrolastic car with the usual full-race camshaft and with new distributor. The straight-cut gearbox now had the benefit of the new and much more reliable Hardy Spicer needle roller drive couplings but still retained the ultra-short 4.26 final drive. This new car was likely to have been a standard Morris Mini as it was clearly devoid of Cooper chrome trim around the doors and it is noted that the Austin Cooper badge on the bonnet had two telltale screws either side, which would indicate that the bonnet, at the very least, had come from a Morris; this is also reinforced by a clumsily-fitted 'S' badge above it. It also had standard Mini interior trim.

As CRX 89B was now a Group 2 car, it retained all of its toughened glass and kept its standard trim. The lighting arrangement was slightly different on this car, in that the long-range Cyclops lamp, mounted high by the bonnet release, was replaced by a larger Lucas 700 lamp mounted centrally on the bumper and front apron on a quick-release bracket. This was fitted with a Continental headlight. It was, however, removed during daylight running to give more cooling to the engine compartment.

Aaltonen also did not like the foot-operated dip switch, so a column-mounted dip switch was fitted, which came from a

Riley Pathfinder. We also saw the departure of the Mixo horns, to be replaced by Maserati air horns; these were to become standard-fit on works Minis. However, at this stage, they were fitted externally on the front apron by the indicators, before being moved under the bonnet on later cars.

The Polish Rally, being an Eastern European event, was blessed with lenient local laws, which allowed very high average speeds to be set on public roads at night, and the organisers also allowed smaller cars to have a slightly more generous time allowance. On conventional European rallies, the time allowed to complete the road sections is the same for all cars and they are not generally designed so that competitors should lose time on road sections, which means a rally is usually decided either on special stages or hillclimbs on closed roads. The Polish Rally did use closed roads for special stages, but the most important parts of the rally were the road sections – where any failure to drive quickly would result in time penalties.

Aaltonen's and Ambrose's preparations for the event did not go to plan, as their rather tired recce car, having already been used on the Alpine, let them down. The good sportsmanship of René Trautmann in the works Lancia, who was Aaltonen's main rival for the European Championship, took Aaltonen and Ambrose around in the back of his practice car to complete their recce – which Aaltonen found quite revealing on how his main opponent was going to tackle the rally.

On the event, Aaltonen nearly came to grief on wet cobbles, through a village; he swerved to miss a cat and hit the kerb, bending the rear wheel and rear radius arm. The wheel was soon changed, and the slightly deranged car saw them to the finish –but not before Aaltonen severely burned his arm whilst removing the radiator cap to check the suspected low water; the resulting torrent of boiling water scalded him badly, and he was patched up at the roadside by a spectating nurse. Ambrose took the wheel until the next stage, after which Aaltonen and Ambrose made no more mistakes, and by virtue of being the only car to finish the rally unpenalised on the road section, won the rally outright.

By now the 1275 Cooper S was becoming a dominant force on international rallies and this marked the third win by Aaltonen in 1965 – in so doing making him a strong contender for the European Championship.

The Munich-Vienna-Budapest Rally, usually called the Three Cities Rally, saw CRX 89B used again by Aaltonen and Ambrose in the October, largely unchanged from the Polish Rally. Brian Moylan was responsible for re-preparing the car to Group 2 regulations, and the fresh 1293cc engine now produced 87bhp at the wheels. Other than the car being thoroughly rebuilt, it appeared much as before, complete with a large Finnish flag on the side of the front wings to denote Aaltonen's nationality.

The Three Cities this year was the penultimate round of the European Championship, which Aaltonen was battling

with René Trautmann to win. Stuart Turner entered two other works Minis, one driven by new boy Tony Fall with Ron Crellin, and the second by Geoff Halliwell with Mike Wood – plus he roped in Paul Easter with Henry Liddon, in Paul's own car, to support Aaltonen. Easter and Liddon were assigned the role as travelling service crew; they would shadow Aaltonen over the entire route, carrying his spares, tools, tyres and fuel. This made Aaltonen's car as light as possible and, as organised service was not permitted, Easter and Liddon were always close at hand should anything go wrong.

The Three Cites was based on a class improvement system of marking, so in theory the other two works Minis needed to go

Rauno Aaltonen and Tony Ambrose on the Polish Rally as a young boy looks on – a rally they won. Ambrose was either asleep in the passenger seat, or he took the photo.

Aaltonen and Ambrose on the Munich-Vienna-Budapest Rally, often known as Three Cities Rally, which Aaltonen won again. This despite what appears to be a Weathermaster tyre on the offside and a racing tyre on the nearside of the car.

Aaltonen and Ambrose were shadowed on the entire event by Paul Easter and Henry Liddon in Easter's car to act as their service car and bag carrier, as official service was prohibited.

as slowly as possible, in their class, to allow Aaltonen to forge a big class lead. However, just before the start, the organisers abandoned that idea and declared that the winner should be decided on scratch, so Fall and Halliwell were free to try as hard as they wanted, providing they didn't beat Aaltonen.

Starting from Munich at 4am in poor weather, the 101 entrants set off in the gloom in a north-easterly direction towards Czechoslovakia. Of the six special stages, Trautmann's Lancia won the first, but Aaltonen was fastest on the rest. Into Austria the damp weather continued, and the pace increased. Heading back into Czechoslovakia for a short rest halt, Aaltonen was in the lead. Onwards to Vienna

and into Hungary, the average speed upped to 90kph. As they entered Budapest it was too much for Trautmann's Lancia, which retired with piston failure, which left Aaltonen with an unassailable lead and valuable points towards the championship. At the finish, not only did Aaltonen win the event, the three Minis also won the team prize. It was Aaltonen's fourth international win of the year and the ninth for Abingdon.

After the Three Cities Rally, the car was loaned out to Valerie Pirie to compete on a new event, the Rally Trofeo Jolly Hotels. Valerie was Stirling Moss's secretary and personal assistant, and Stuart Turner was persuaded to lend the car to her as a personal favour to Stirling. Pirie had not driven a works Mini before but had driven several works Triumph Spitfires on the Alpine, Tour de France, RAC, Tulip and Monte Carlo Rally – and she hadn't finished any... Perhaps Stirling thought she may fare better in a Mini. She was co-driven by the very experienced Val Domleo and the car was entered under the SMART banner – Stirling Moss Automobile Racing Team – but as CRX89B was still a works car at the time, it is considered a works entry all the same.

The rally, run in Italy at the end of October, along similar lines to the Tour de France with hillclimbs and racetrack work, was sponsored by the Jolly Hotels group, which came with the added advantage that at the end of each day, the route conveniently finished at a fine hotel. Split into five legs, starting from Palermo and finishing in Trieste, there was minimal navigation for the 87 starters and a low average speed on the road liaison sections resulted in a leisurely pace. The winner was effectively decided on the faster race circuits, as the smaller manoeuvrable cars, such as the Mini, were unable to gain much back on the twisty hillclimbs. However, Pirie continued her non-finishing record by putting the car off the road and into

Gerald Wiffen re-preparing CRX 89B for the 1965 RAC Rally at Abingdon for Tony Fall and Ron Crellin. Note all of the rally plates on the back wall.

Stirling Moss's secretary and personal assistant Valerie Pirie took CRX 89B on the Jolly Hotels Rally with Val Domleo.

CHAPTER 3: THE MK 1 MINI COOPER S

Fall and Crellin head into the November sunshine on the RAC, where they would finish 15th place after several visits to the scenery.

Tony Fall and Ron Crellin looking happy on the 1965 RAC Rally in CRX 89B.

retirement relatively early. The event was won by De Adamich in an Alfa Romeo Giulia TZ2. The Jolly Hotels Rally ran for a few more years before fading from the calendar.

The final event for CRX 89B was the 1965 RAC Rally, when it was pressed into service one more time and handed to Tony Fall and Ron Crellin. Rebuilt by Gerald Wiffen and Tommy Eales, it was again prepared as a Group 2 car and was substantially the same as when it appeared on the Polish, Three Cities and Jolly Hotels Rallies, other than it now appeared as a Morris Cooper S. There were, however, minor changes, largely because the RAC was such a tough event. Much work had gone on in designing and testing sump guards at Strata Florida in Wales. This had resulted in a new sump guard being fitted to the RAC cars and the floor under the driver's feet was also double-skinned so as not to distort by the throttle pedal. Special guards were made up to protect the flexible hoses fitted to the front brake callipers, and the exhaust now had two boxes – a large rear box and a smaller expansion box in the middle.

The fresh engine, on the Abingdon rolling road, was reported to give 84bhp at the wheels, and because of the expected cold weather, an 82C thermostat was fitted and a new radiator muff had been made by the MG trim shop, which fitted over the grille moustache and was held on with Lift-the-Dot studs. The two-speed wiper motor was also now held in place by a quick-release bracket (meaning a defective unit could be swiftly changed without removing half the dashboard), and because the rally was in the UK, the speedo was changed to read in mph. All small changes but significant ones specifically made for the RAC Rally.

The 1965 RAC, starting from London Airport, saw a field of 162 crews head off towards the West Country on their 2350 mile journey to Scotland and back over five days with just one night's rest in Perth. Fifty-eight stages in all were to be tackled, mostly on forest roads, and the weather before the event had been very wet, so the early stages were tricky.

At the Bristol Airport control, Fall was up in fourth place and going well. As the route headed into Wales the weather deteriorated, and in Northern England, snow and ice caused major problems in the Yorkshire forests. Many crews suffered badly in Pickering where a particular hill became nearly impassable for the early numbers. With studded tyres not being permitted, Dunlop SP44s were all that could be used.

Fall had several off-road excursions on the drive north and

Practice for the 1966 Monte Carlo Rally with Rauno Aaltonen and Terry Harryman in CRX 89B on the Fontbelle stage meeting a works Triumph coming the opposite way - a common problem when practising stages numerous times.

125

his problems got worse in the Lake District when a driveshaft failed on the stage start line. Fortunately, he was able to roll back to the waiting BMC service crew and have the driveshaft changed, albeit with much time lost. The rather battered CRX 89B arrived back at the finish at London Airport in a creditable 15th place – but 100 cars hadn't even made it.

One final outing for this much-used Mini was as a recce car for the 1966 Monte Carlo Rally. After the RAC Rally, CRX 89B was quickly repaired and sent on its way with Rauno Aaltonen and Tony Ambrose to compile notes for the BMC team. The car was sold to successful privateer Geoff Mabbs.

Timo Mäkinen and Rauno Aaltonen put out a warning sign that BMC are practising on the road. The roof rack, with its numerous spiked tyres, used as a prop for the paper tablecloth notice from a nearby restaurant.

Competition Record

Date	Event	Crew	Number	Overall result	Class result
Nov 1964	RAC Rally	Rauno Aaltonen/Tony Ambrose	2	DNF	
Mar 1965	Circuit of Ireland	Paddy Hopkirk/Terry Harriman	2	1st	1st
May 1965	Luxembourg Slalom	Paddy Hopkirk		7th	1st
June 1965	Scottish Rally	Paddy Hopkirk/Henry Liddon	3	DNF	
July 1965	Polish Rally	Rauno Aaltonen/Tony Ambrose	55	1st	1st
Oct 1965	Three Cities Rally	Rauno Aaltonen/Tony Ambrose	72	1st	1st
Oct 1965	Jolly Hotels	Valerie Pirie/Val Domleo		DNF	
Nov 1965	RAC Rally	Tony Fall/Ron Crellin	36	15th	3rd

Registration Number	First registered	Chassis number	Engine	Engine number	Model
CRX 90B	Oct 1964	KA2S4 552445	1275cc	9F-SA-Y 32706	Morris Cooper S

Paddy Hopkirk and Henry Liddon, with all smiles, leave the London start on the 1964 RAC Rally. Note the heater bars on the lower 'screen.

The third of the CRX cars delivered to Abingdon in 1964 was registered as a Morris, it being first prepared for Paddy Hopkirk and Henry Liddon to tackle the 1964 RAC Rally.

The car was made to take on what was always a rough and demanding event. A powerful but reliable engine was built and a 1293cc engine was put together with a high-compression gas-flowed cylinder head, a race camshaft and twin SUH4 carburettors, and placed on a straight-cut close-ratio gearbox with 4.133 final drive. It used special driveshafts and Hardy Spicer universal joints. The sump of the gearbox was protected by a sump plate screwed directly to the underside in addition to a sump guard. A battery box guard was also used. The remote gearshift mounting was fitted with an indestructible Mitchell mounting, and the body strengthened around the tunnel to carry the bracket.

The suspension was dry cone with the addition of small

spacer washers to increase the ground clearance; the subframe was also strengthened with gussets welded to the front tie rod brackets. The rear hub bearings used Timken needle rollers rather than ball race bearings. The car was equipped with five additional lamps on the front plus a roof lamp over the right-hand side and headlamp washers. It was also fitted with a back-mounted Lucas fog light, fixed to the boot lid serving as a reversing lamp. Inside the car, demister bars were fitted to the 'screen, along with the normal two flat dash panels – one in front of each crew member.

The RAC was now a fully-fledged stage event with over 400 stage miles, mostly on Forestry Commission land, to decide the winner. A large entry of 180 cars assembled in London for the start at the Duke of York's Barracks. Being the final round of the European championship, many crews from abroad had entered, the favourites of which were the Scandinavians; Tom Trana, in his Volvo, was hoping to win the title by the time the rally returned to London after the five-day 2500-mile journey the length and breadth of the country. It was to be a tough event.

Four works Minis were entered, with Hopkirk seeded at number one. He was, however, the only British driver in the team, the other three being Scandinavian - such was Stuart Turner's faith in their abilities on loose surfaces.

As the route headed out to the West Country in fine weather, Hopkirk was immediately posting top times. As they entered Wales, with the weather deteriorating, the icy forests saw him matching the Scandinavians' times and lying in fifth place just behind them. The fog-bound stage at Oulton Park saw Hopkirk stamp his authority with the fastest time, as many found their way gingerly around the circuit. Hopkirk's progress through Northern England and on into Scotland was only tempered by him reporting a completely collapsed driver's seat as they entered the Turnberry control on the Ayrshire west coast.

At the Perth overnight stop, the only one on the event, Hopkirk was just 40 points behind the leading Volvo of Trana, with Källström just ahead of him and Aaltonen just behind. Heading out from Perth, Hopkirk was immediately in trouble with a puncture on the second stage and was further delayed with a crushed fuel line, damaged on the Scottish rocks. The Blackcraig stage brought his rally to an end when he misjudged a corner after a long straight and went flying off the road, a long way, until he was stopped by a stout tree. This stage was to be a BMC jinx, as Aaltonen was also to retire with a broken gearbox almost in sight of Hopkirk. It was not a good RAC for Abingdon, as despite much promise, none of the four works cars finished.

After the rough treatment CRX 90B received on the RAC, a new car was built for the 1965 Monte Carlo Rally. It was handed to Don Morley and his brother Erle, who were, if truth be told, far happier in the Healey 3000, but their experience was much valued and they formed part of a six-car works

Hopkirk leaps CRX 90B over the Carron Valley Bridge in Perth on the RAC Rally.

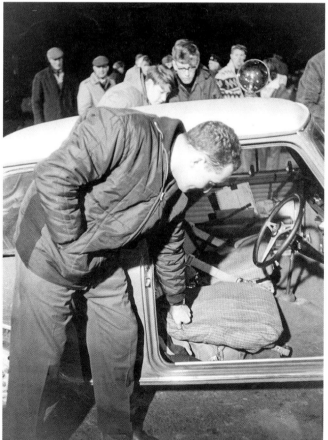

Hopkirk looks at the collapsed seat on CRX 90B - perhaps caused by the heavy landing in Scotland.

New for the Monte Carlo Rally in 1965 was the fitting of a Lucas 11AC alternator replacing the less powerful dynamo setup. Note also black backs to the Lucas 700 lamps, these being rarely used industrial units.

Mini entry for this winter's classic.

Built by Johnny Organ as a Group 2 car, the standard-bore engine ran the customary AEA648 full-race camshaft and the block was fitted with core-plug retaining plates (should the cold weather do its worst) and the latest 40979 distributor. The compression was raised to 11:1 by skimming 0.040in from the cylinder head and flowing and polishing the internals. The rocker pillars had 0.055in shaved off due to increased valve lift. Power output was reported to be 70bhp at the wheels.

The gearbox was the usual Abingdon fit of a straight-cut close-ratio gear set with a 4.26 final drive, and the remote shift was secured by a Mitchell mounting, which ensured the mounting stayed in one piece. The driveshafts retained the rubber couplings, and the entire engine and gearbox was protected by an alloy sump guard (crafted by the MG press shop), which had five large air holes punched into the front to allow air to cool the sump.

The Hydrolastic suspension was standard apart from being raised slightly by the use of 0.080in packing washers under the struts on the yellow displacers and extra bump stops at the rear, which meant the subframe was strengthened. Front tie bars and track rod ends were security bolted with castellated nuts and held in place by split pins. Towing eyes were fitted front and back, as were quick-lift jacking points. Cooling was helped by a six-blade fan and an 82C thermostat. The car also had a grille muff, made by the MG trim shop.

The electrics, now with the benefit of an alternator, made life easier for the battery of lights. Keeping with the familiar five-lamp set-up, which included two small fog lights on the bonnet to act as the headlights' dipped beam (which were needed because the iodine headlight bulbs were devoid of a dipped beam). The two large fog lamps were on quick-release brackets on the bumper, and the centre spotlight mounted high on a bracket around the top of the grille moustache.

A laminated, heated front windscreen also made demands on the electrics but the improvement in visibility was considerable in cold weather. The two-speed wipers had deep-throated wheel boxes to replace the standard wheel boxes, which tended to fail shifting a heavy snow load. The battery cable was run inside the car and the battery reversed with the terminals away from the fuel tank. The fuel and brake lines were also run inside the car.

The Morleys had the use of a fibreglass driver's bucket seat and a special Tommy Wellman-made reclining seat. Being a Group 2 car, all glass and trim was retained, although the heater was replaced with a lightweight alloy-cased unit. An asbestos blanket was placed under the front carpet to keep away heat from the lightweight exhaust. The speedo was marked in kph and the car also ran two washer bottles, both fixed inside the car the on the rear side window rail – one with washer fluid, the other with alcohol. Headlight washers were not fitted. There was an intercom to help communication between the crew in the noisy car, and they also stowed four tyres in the cabin: a pair with spiral spikes and a pair with pop-in studs so they could be equipped for any weather conditions. The car, at the start, sat on Dunlop SP3 tyres.

With a works team of six Minis entered for the 1965 Monte, expectations were high, with the entry spread over four starting points of Athens, Paris, Stockholm and Minsk. CRX 90B was to start in Minsk, where hopefully the Russian venue would gain BMC some publicity.

A field of 237 cars departed from the nine starting points on their 2600-mile route to join together at St Claude in central France for a common run to Monte Carlo. More stages had been promised for this year, and with the very bad weather crews found once in mid France, the challenge of just getting to Monte Carlo was a real one. From Minsk, the Morleys were soon in trouble with damp electrics hampering their progress; it was compounded by a faulty fuel pump, which, being on the rear subframe, resulted in them lying in sub-zero conditions trying to fix it. This was followed with severe overheating and the resultant loss of water. Once at the Brest control, some 215 miles down the road, the thermostat was removed and the problem went away.

Don Morley and Erle Morley hurl CRX 90B around one of the many hairpin bends on one of the few snow-free climbs early in the event.

The Morley brothers storm off from the stage start on the Monte Carlo Rally with their new CRX 90B.

From St Claude, the timed stages began, and over the Col du Granier the Morleys posted a top-ten time. However, on the following stage, over the snow-covered and twisty Chamrousse, they left the road, losing 35 minutes extricating the car. On reaching Monte Carlo they were still in 20th place. As the weather in the Massif Central area closed in, just 35 cars made it to Monte within their time allowance. More was to come. The newly-designed 380-mile mountain circuit, set to replace the dash around the Grand Prix circuit, to be tackled the following night, saw the snow and ice continue in the Alpes-Maritimes. Six stages were tackled, with the Turini no less than three times.

But BMC had done its homework and had supplied the cars with detailed ice notes, compiled just hours before the roads were closed, together with fuel and service points strategically placed over the mountains north of Monte Carlo. The works Minis also had at their disposal special Dunlop snow-and-ice tyres, consisting of Dunlop Weathermasters with up to 600 studs fired into the rubber of different designs to bite through the snow and ice.

Once again, however, the Morleys were in trouble straight away, when the fuel pump failed when leaving the restart, losing them another 11 minutes whilst replacing it and dumping much of their fuel on the tarmac. It was all to no avail, as on the first stage of the mountain circuit, the nearside drive coupling let go and they were out – but fortunately they were still classified in 27th place as finishers. This was to be Don and Erle's last works Mini drive, as they returned to their familiar Healey 3000 for the rest of their works career.

After the Monte, the car languished at Abingdon until it was used for recce duties on the Geneva Rally in the June of 1965, crewed by Aaltonen and Ambrose, who were to do the event in a brand-new EBL 55C.

CRX 90B on the last night of the Monte in the snow-covered stage with Erle Morley calling out the pace notes just before a driveshaft broke – but would still finish in 27th place.

Nobby Hall changes the broken driveshaft on CRX 90B, in far from ideal conditions – such are the joys of a rally mechanic.

Geoff Halliwell with Mike Wood press on during the Three Cities Rally with a new light arrangement on the car.

Paul Easter with Henry Liddon used CRX 90B for BMC's recce duties for the 1966 Alpine Rally.

For CRX 90B's last competitive event at Abingdon, the car was handed over to Geoff Halliwell and Mike Wood for the Munich-Vienna-Budapest Rally – more commonly know as the Three Cities Rally – in the October. Halliwell was a successful club rally driver and the general manager at Tillotson's Commercial Vehicles in Burnley, Lancashire, who just happened to employ Mike Wood as sales manager. Halliwell had a good relationship with Abingdon and would, over the years, along with Wood, purchase numerous ex-works Minis.

Halliwell, in this one-off drive, was entered by Stuart Turner, along with Tony Fall, to support Aaltonen in his bid to secure the European Championship. The rally was to be decided on a class improvement system, so Halliwell and Fall were there to go as slowly as possible to exaggerate Aaltonen's undoubted class win. As it transpired, the organisers relented at the last minute and changed their minds and decided the event on scratch results, freeing Halliwell and Fall to do the best they could – providing they didn't beat Aaltonen.

CRX 90B was prepared by Johnny Evans as a 1293cc Group 2 car. The compression was raised now to 11.6:1 and the troublesome rubber crucifix drive couplings, which had been the problem on the Monte, were replaced with the latest Hardy Spicer needle roller universal joints. As this event was considered to be rougher than the Monte a heavy-duty sump guard was fitted. The Hydrolastic suspension was again raised by using 0.080in spacer washers in the front, but now with double-red displacers at the rears and single-red displacers at the front. Both subframes were renewed, rewelded and strengthened.

The lighting setup was changed, in that the small central Cyclops lamp high up by the bonnet release was replaced by a larger Lucas 700 lamp, with a Continental headlight unit now located in the middle on the bumper with a quick-release bracket. However, because the headlights were fitted with single-filament Iodine bulbs, the dipped beam was still served by two small fog lamps on the bonnet. The two-bottle washer system used on the Monte was abandoned and now just a single Lucas electric bottle was used. However, much as on the Monte, the car carried four spare tyres, largely this time because on the Three Cities no organised service was allowed, so they had to carry all the tyres they needed. New on the car for the event were fabricated guards fitted to the front brake callipers to protect the vulnerable hoses, although skin plates, attached to the rear handbrake brackets, had been used for some time to protect the rear brake tubing from damage.

The Three Cities started in damp weather that would persist for the entire rally, and despite being a round of the European Championship, which attracted over 100 crews, it contained only six special stages to decide the winner – and none of those very long. The average speeds were nevertheless high and it was on the fourth of these six stages that Halliwell came to grief on the hillclimb near Eisenstadt in the extreme east of Austria. Halliwell and Wood were using pace notes that they hadn't compiled, and either through some confusion or an error Halliwell misjudged a corner and they had a heavy accident against the bank. They were both hospitalised and Wood was badly concussed – largely attributed to not having used his seat belt – waking on his way to hospital. Halliwell was just badly bruised but both missed the prize-giving where Aaltonen won and BMC took the team prize.

It is unlikely that this version of the car was used again because of the severe damage it suffered on the Three Cities Rally. However, records show that CRX 90B continued to be used as both a recce car and a test car for over a year at Abingdon. Henry Liddon and Paul Easter used the car for recce duties for the 1966 Alpine Rally, and Aaltonen and Ambrose used it as a recce car for the 1966 Czech Rally.

Its final recce was for the 1000 Lakes in 1966, for Aaltonen and Väinö Nurmimaa to practice this unique event. It was by then a white car and, although carrying CRX 90B registration, it is extremely unlikely to have been a repainted car. Its last appearance was as a chasing service car on the Monte Carlo Rally. There are also records which show that the car was also used as a test car, which was a fate that befell many works cars when they were taken to Wales for destruction testing.

CRX 90B was eventually sold to Paul Easter – in red and white!

Competition Record

Date	Event	Crew	Number	Overall result	Class result
Nov 1964	RAC Rally	Paddy Hopkirk/Henry Liddon	1	DNF	
Jan 1965	Monte Carlo Rally	Don Morley/Erle Morley	72	27th	2nd
Oct 1965	Three Cities Rally	Geoff Halliwell/Mike Wood	71	DNF	

Registration Number	First registered	Chassis number	Engine	Engine number	Model
CRX 91B	Oct 1964	KA2S4 552446	1275cc	9F-SA-Y 32341	Morris Cooper S

The fourth and final Mini in the CRX batch, registered in October 1964 as a Morris, was also a Hydrolastic car. Whilst two of its sister cars were sent out on the RAC Rally in the November, CRX 91B, along with CRX 88B, were saved for the 1965 Monte Carlo Rally the following January and both cars were very similar. Built as a Group 2 car by Gerald Wiffen, CRX 91B was assigned to Paddy Hopkirk and Henry Liddon, with hopes of repeating their 1964 win in 33 EJB.

The 1275cc engine was kept at its standard bore and fitted with the AEA648 full-race camshaft, although an AEA731 rally camshaft was initially specified. By now the ultra-strong standard Cooper S nitrided steel crankshaft was double-drilled to increase lubrication to the bearings – another competition modification that would find its way onto production crankshafts. The cylinder head was gas-flowed and polished, and the engine's compression raised to 11.1 by skimming 0.020in off the block and 0.050in off the cylinder head.

Carburettors were twin 1½in H4 SUs, using both float chamber extensions and ram pipes with the linkage modified to a fork-and-peg arrangement, which relieved tension on the throttle cable. They also had a heat-collecting box made to fit over the ram pipes to capture hot air from the manifold, which prevented the carbs from icing. The engine produced 74bhp on the Abingdon rolling road.

To keep the engine cool, despite the expected cold weather, a six-bladed fan was used and – as added security – core plug retaining plates were fixed to the block. To ensure the engine didn't get too cold, a fabricated grille muff was made by the MG trim shop, which fitted over the grille moustache. This had an opening panel to allow air to the oil cooler, or not, if needed. It was secured by Lift-the-Dot fixings. Subsequently

Paddy Hopkirk and Henry Liddon leave the Stockholm start on their long journey to Monte Carlo in an attempt to repeat their 1964 victory.

on the Monte, the muff was cut away from the radiator end to allow more air to the radiator but still restrict airflow to the other half of the engine bay.

The straight-cut close-ratio gearbox was fitted with a very short 4.26 final drive, and the modified driveshafts used rubber couplings. Despite Cooper Ss now being fitted with a revised gear lever with an anti-rattle mechanism, the car was built with the old gear lever, which simply had a rubber hose fitted over the shaft to keep it quiet. The rear gearbox mounting was equipped with the indestructible Mitchell mounting, and the entire gearbox was protected by an alloy sump guard fabricated by the MG press shop.

Hopkirk and Liddon on the snow-free lower climbs of the Alps during the 1965 Monte.

Hopkirk and Liddon about to start the stage with their studded tyres - note the witness marks on the road left by the studded tyres.

The Hydrolastic suspension was fitted with yellow-band displacers all round and raised at the front with a 0.050in packing washer under the strut. The subframes were rewelded to add strength and had additional plating added where the larger rear bump stops would strike. Timken needle roller bearings were fitted to the rear hubs. Brakes were standard but fitted with DS11 racing brake pads and VG95 racing brake shoes at the rear.

The electrics, now with the benefit of an alternator that replaced the outdated dynamo, were better able to cope with high demands – especially on the Monte with the extra lights and now the addition of a new heated front windscreen. This 'screen, replacing the disliked gold-tint 'screen used on the previous year's Monte, had the heating elements embedded within in the laminated glass middle layer. The alternator was a Lucas 11AC unit with a separate regulator box, which was screwed to the bulkhead. Five additional lights were still fitted, all with iodine bulbs, which still meant, as the headlight didn't dip, that the dipped beam had to be served by two small fog lamps on the bonnet. Two large Lucas 700 fog lamps were fitted on quick-release brackets on the bumper, and a single small spot light mounted on a special bracket by the bonnet release; these lights were protected by red Lucas covers.

Two screen washer bottles were used, one with washer fluid and the other with alcohol. It also had four washer jets: two singles in the standard position and a double jet in the centre. The wipers were fitted with deep-throated wheel boxes, being stronger than the standard items, which had been known to fail when shifting heavy snow loads.

The main battery cable, along with the fuel and brake lines, was run inside the car and the battery reversed with the terminals facing away from the side of the fuel tank. The fuel tanks were fitted with Aston quick-release filler caps, and inside the boot the tanks were protected against damage from studded tyres with plywood glued to their sides. A twin fuel pump was located on the rear subframe but protected by an alloy plate.

Inside the car, Hopkirk used a leather-covered steering wheel and sat in a lightweight fibreglass bucket seat. Liddon had a more comfortable Tommy Wellman-fabricated reclining seat, and both were trimmed in speckled grey cloth, first seen on early Minis. As the car was built as a Group 2, all standard glass and trim had to be retained and in addition, to help crew comfort, the car had additional padding fitted on the door locks, pockets and pillar. It also carried an asbestos blanket under the front carpet to keep heat from the exhaust at bay. The heater was in a lightweight alloy body. Instruments and switches were arranged on two individual alloy dashboards; the driver's dashboard extended out by 3in at the top and was therefore nearly vertical. The speedometer and Halda were calibrated in kilometres.

With the selection of many Dunlop Weathermaster tyres, fitted with either pop-in studs, Kelhu spirals or Rengas-Ala chisels at the team's disposal – in addition to standard Dunlop SP3s – deciding what tyres to carry in the car needed consideration. The chisel tyres, with over 600 pieces of tapered tungsten steel sunk in, provided great grip in biting through the ice and snow to the road below. They were also very effective in scrabbling through the deep snow and would prove a great choice for the prevailing conditions. The car therefore carried a pair of studded tyres and a pair of spirals, and started on SP3 road tyres. This allowed the car to cope with most conditions if out of reach of the service crews or Dunlop's service vans.

BMC had high hopes of winning the 1965 Monte after Hopkirk's victory the previous year. A team of six Minis was entered, spread over four cities: Athens, Paris, Stockholm and Minsk. CRX 91B was dispatched unaccompanied from Felixstowe and into the care of BMC Sweden, as Hopkirk, along with Mäkinen, was to start from Stockholm. The large field of 237 cars set off from their respective starting points on their 2600-mile journey to descend on St Claude before heading off together for Monte Carlo. The weather, however, would make things very difficult, especially for the later numbers, as no sooner had the early crews arrived in mid France, the weather rapidly deteriorated and the challenge soon became just getting to Monte Carlo.

With the weather in the Massif Central area closing in fast, just 35 cars made it to Monte within time. Come the next day they faced a new innovation – a 380-mile mountain circuit. Here six stages were tackled in deep snow and ice, which by now had completely covered the Alpes Maritime. BMC had, however, produced detailed ice notes, just before the cars went over the stages, which allowed the team to make the right tyres choice from the large stock of Dunlops exclusively available.

Hopkirk's event, despite the weather, was going well as he was posting good times. He was in second place on the first stage from St Claude, the famous Col du Granier, just behind Mäkinen (in a sister car and eventual winner). He was second again, behind Mäkinen, on the next and just behind him again on the third stage, despite going off on the very last corner, deranging his front suspension and splitting the front subframe mounting from the tie rod – but he was still placed fourth and managed to continue. Tommy Wellman, at their next service, managed to weld the subframe back together in the middle of a blizzard, but it took 34 minutes to repair. Hopkirk continued, managing again to be just behind Mäkinen on the next stage. All these stages had been very badly affected by snow and ice but the last stage before Monte Carlo was miraculously dry, which saw the more powerful cars feature well.

On arriving in Monte Carlo, Hopkirk was classified second on scratch after the first five stages behind the incredible Mäkinen, but entering the overnight parc fermé, the suspension broke again. Needless to say, he was second overall once the handicap had been applied and by reaching Monte Carlo was now officially classified as a finisher. Fortunately, because of the poor weather conditions, the organisers allowed more road time for the next section – the mountain circuit of six stages – so Hopkirk was able to get his subframe rewelded as soon as he departed on the mountain circuit the next evening. This the BMC mechanics did in the comfort of a garage in Menton, taking just 14 minutes this time.

However, this repair didn't last and a few kilometres down the road, it failed again. Once more to it was rewelded, this time just outside the control at Sospel. Now, because of all their repairs, the crew left the control right on their maximum lateness. Despite their best efforts and pulling back a few minutes of time, it was to finally fail again on the third stage

CRX 91B in service on the Monte with Stuart Turner rushing around the car as Hopkirk directs operations whilst the mechanic peers under the car.

and this time the car was retired, there being just no time left to make a repair. The car limped down to Monte Carlo with its two front wheels pointing at odd angles. However, despite the resulting penalties, Hopkirk was still to finish in 26th place and also won his class. With Mäkinen winning the event and combined with all of Stuart Turner's detailed planning, BMC's large budget (reportedly of £10,000) was entirely justified.

After the Monte Carlo Rally, the car was initially seen dressed up as AJB 44B, the winning 1965 Monte car, with 52 on the door, as a replica. This was likely simply to satisfy press requirements – much as other 1964 team cars had been replicated to appear as 33 EJB in the wake of the 1964 Monte win.

CRX 91B was then loaned to Timo Mäkinen, who, supported by the BMC dealer in Helsinki, Oy Voimavaunu Ab, did several events in Finland. The first of these was the Hanki Rally in the winter of 1965, where the car carried the local registration number A-1800. Timo was co-driven by Pekka Keskitalo. The

Timo Mäkinen and CRX 91B with AJB 44B's competition number on the door, publicising his win on the 1965 Monte, whilst the actual car was on other PR duties elsewhere.

Timo Mäkinen with Pekka Keskitalo on the 1965 Hanki Rally where the car carried the local registration number A-1800. The CRX 91B plate can just be seen underneath.

Geoff Mabbs at Strata Florida in Wales, testing with CRX 91B for sump guard and suspension modifications, in preparation for the RAC Rally in November.

event, based in Helsinki, used multi stages over frozen ice lakes where huge spiked tyres were the order of the day. The car was much as it appeared on the Monte other than the lighting arrangement, with the removal of the two small fog lights on the bonnet and the centre Cyclops Lucas spot lamp replaced by a Marshall unit. The headlamps and fog lamps carried large 'eyebrow' light shields, and the car sprouted a wing mirror on the driver's side, required to comply with Finnish traffic laws. The car also did the Riihimäki rally and the Finland winter rally in the hands of Timo Mäkinen.

Once repatriated to the UK, the car was used for development work, where testing at the Strata Florida test site in Wales took place over very rough tracks, and various parts such as sump guards and suspension were tested to destruction in preparation for the forthcoming RAC Rally in November 1965. The car was sold to Rauno Aaltonen

Competition Record

Date	Event	Crew	Number	Overall result	Class result
Jan 1965	Monte Carlo Rally	Paddy Hopkirk/Henry Liddon	56	26th	1st

Registration Number	First registered	Chassis number	Engine	Engine number	Model
AGU 780B	Nov 1964	CA2S7L 551892	1275cc	9F-SA-Y 31798	Austin Cooper S

This car is rather unique in Abingdon's history in that it was prepared by the competition department for BMC Sweden, being registered in London as part of the BMC export scheme and not registered in Berkshire as all the other works cars. It was also unusual in that it was green and white, which more closely matched BMC Sweden's colour schemes. Further, the car was left-hand drive and also, throughout its works career, driven only by Harry Källström – his first drive for the Abingdon team.

The RAC engine was built as a powerful but reliable 1293cc unit, with a gas-flowed cylinder head with 11:1 compression, a race camshaft and twin SUH4 carburettors. The engine sat on a straight-cut close-ratio gearbox with a 4.133 final drive and special driveshafts with Hardy Spicer universal joints. The sump was protected by a sump plate screwed to the sump in addition to an alloy sump guard. It was also fitted with a battery box guard.

An indestructible Mitchell mounting was fitted to the remote gearshift mounting and the body strengthened to carry its bracket. The suspension was dry cone, set to increase the ground clearance by using small spacer washers to the trumpets; the subframe was strengthened and gussets welded to the front tie rod brackets. Rear hub bearings were changed from ball race bearings to Timken needle roller bearings.

The car had five additional lamps on the front and a roof lamp plus headlamp washers. It was also fitted with a back-

AGU780B was left hand drive and this shot shows the car in build with the wiring in place and the driver's panel built but not fixed. The fixings for the navigator's panel can be seen and the two fuse boxes below. It was dragged out to test the heated windscreen.

mounted Lucas fog lamp, fixed to the boot lid serving as a reversing lamp. Inside the car, demister bars were fitted to the windscreen, and there were two flat dash panels, with the chrome not receiving the customary coat of matt-black paint. In green and white, it did look quite different from the rest of the works cars.

The RAC Rally, now more or less an all-forest rally, was well suited to the Scandinavian drivers such as Källström, who were very experienced on loose surfaces. The 1964 rally was a highly competitive event, to be decided over 400 miles of special stages within the 2500-mile route, which started in London and travelled all around the UK, from the West Country to Scotland and back, over five days with just an overnight halt in Perth. As a round of the European championship, the event attracted a large foreign contingent; Källström was expected to challenge the leaders, and with this being BMC's home event, hopes were high of success from the four-car team of Cooper Ss, three of which were driven by Scandinavians.

A large crowd saw the field of 180 cars head off in fine weather from the Duke of York's Barracks in London towards the West Country. After the tarmac stage at Porlock, Källström was soon making his presence felt. As the cars got into Wales, where the roads became slippery and icy, Källström was lying in second place behind Tom Trana's Volvo, which was heading the European Championship. By Llandrindod Wells, Källström had grabbed the lead and would continue to post fast times, swapping them with Trana, Aaltonen and Hopkirk in the other works Minis. Fog was now an issue as the route headed into Northern England; Oulton Park race circuit was particularly bad. Into Scotland and with Källström still contesting the lead, the overnight halt at Perth was a welcome break.

With Hopkirk and Aaltonen retiring soon after the restart, it was left to Källström to uphold Mini honours. Sadly, the car was never to get down to the North Yorkshire forest,

AGU 780B was also unique in works Mini history as it was green and white, not red and white. Seen here at the start in London for the 1964 RAC Rally.

Harry Källström and Ragnvald Håkansson led the RAC Rally before retiring with a broken transmission.

as the pinion on the diff came adrift after the second Wark stage, and his event was over. It was a great disappointment, as with only six stages to go, he had been leading the event – so the lead passed back to Trana's Volvo, which he was not to relinquish. Embarrassingly, the RAC ended with all four works Minis retiring. It was left to Mäkinen, who had elected to forsake the Mini in preference for the Healey 3000, to save Abingdon's bacon by getting the Healey across the line in second place.

After the RAC, AGU 780B was reprepared for the Monte Carlo Rally. It was generally Abingdon's practice to supply new cars for the Monte but in this case the well-used RAC car was pressed into service again. Tommy Eales was assigned to rebuild the car for Källström and Håkansson, which was entered into Group 2 and would form part of a six-car team that were hoping to repeat their 1964 win on this most prestigious of all events.

The engine retained its standard bore and was fitted with a full-race AEA648 camshaft in deference to the AEA731 rally camshaft originally specified. Core plug retainers were fitted as an insurance against losing them in possible freezing conditions. The crankshaft had, by now in the Cooper S evolution, been cross-drilled to help oil distribution and would soon be a production feature. Compression was raised to 11:1 by removing 0.045in from the cylinder head, which was flowed and polished and, whilst retaining its standard valves, had 0.055in removed from the pillars due to valve lift.

Keeping things cool was a six-blade fan and an 82C thermostat, a 13lb cap, plus a 13-row oil cooler mounted on a fabricated platform let into the front panel. The Lucas 40979 distributor was the latest competition item, replacing the 40819 standard units; it had a better advance curve and an asymmetric cam to lessen the chance of points bounce at high revs. The exhaust system was specially made and importantly light in weight, with a straight pipe. Carburettors were twin 1½ H4 SUs with float chamber extensions, and with CP4 needles the engine produced 75bhp at the wheels on the Abingdon rolling road.

Transmission had, as usual, a straight-cut close-ratio gear set and was coupled to a short 4.26:1 differential – invaluable for climbing out of tight uphill hairpins. Driveshafts were modified by Hardy Spicer and special white-flash rubber couplings were used. The car still retained the old-style gearstick, despite a revised anti-rattle item now being in standard production (the old shaft was simply quietened by slipping a rubber hose down the shaft). This older type was preferred as a more direct method of changing gear, as the shaft was solid without an intermediate rubber median. The remote housing for the gearchange was fitted with a Mitchell mounting, which was designed not to break under the most arduous conditions, and the body was strengthened around the remote bracket to dissipate the strain.

The suspension reverted to dry cone rather than Hydrolastic, which was by then fitted to production cars. The ride height was kept standard. Extra bump stops were fitted to the rear arms and hard Healey Sprite bushes used in the front wishbones. The car also used Girling competition dampers. Security welding took place on both subframes at joints, webs and where the bump stops hit. Tie rods and track rod ends were further secured by split pins and castellated nuts. The rear hubs used Timken needle roller bearings in place of the standard ball bearing joints, as these had proved troublesome to change in a hurry. Brakes were standard other than using a special limiting valve and changing the pads and linings to racing specification items. The brake line was run inside the car and rerouted around the rear radius arm out of harm's way.

There were quite a few changes when it came to the electrics on the car for the Monte, notably that there was now an alternator in place of the dynamo, which meant the electrics had an easier life. The alternator did cause some concern with the scrutineer in Paris but a reference to the homologation papers soon solved the issue. The first change was that the windscreen heater bars could now be replaced with a heated front 'screen – the first use of the heated 'screen with silver bus bars visible in the laminate; the brief use of gold-film heated windscreens on the 1964 had proved unpopular with most of the drivers.

Gone were the headlamp washers and gone too was the roof lamp, which was now deemed illegal to use. However, the lighting arrangement remained the same with the familiar five external lamps, with the two small fog lamps on the bonnet acting as the dipped beam, as the headlamps used non-dipping iodine bulbs. The two large fog lamps were fixed on quick-release brackets. The reversing lamp was an Austin Healey sidelight unit fixed to the boot lid and operated automatically from the gearbox. The battery cable was run inside the car and the battery itself, being a lightweight racing

Källström removes his crash helmet whilst Håkansson gets his time from the confused marshal who was expecting the navigator to be on the other side.

unit and wrapped in foam to keep out the cold, was reversed with its terminals facing away from the fuel tank.

Inside the car, the navigator now had the use of the new Halda Twinmaster distance recorder, replacing the relatively ineffective single Halda unit fitted behind a magnifier lens. Källström used a thin-grip Springall leather steering wheel and sat in a lightweight cloth-covered fibreglass bucket seat, whereas Håkansson had the comfort of a specially-made reclining seat. Källström also uniquely had a rear-view mirror fixed to the top rail of the dashboard as well as the one attached to the top of the windscreen.

Being a Group 2 car all the glass, trim and carpets were retained, and it was bolstered by extra padding to the door locks, B-post and door pockets plus an asbestos blanket laid under the front carpet to keep the manifold heat at bay. Interestingly, to save weight, the heater was remade in aluminium and the rear number plate board was simply painted on.

Needless to say, for the Monte, provision was made to safely stow a pair of studded tyres in the boot. Both tanks were protected by boards fixed to the sides, and both had quick-release caps. The fuel line was run inside the car but the twin fuel pump was outside on the subframe, protected by an alloy plate.

AGU 780B started the 1965 Monte from Paris, where the service crew of Bob Whittington, Nobby Hall and Robin Vokins took the car, along with their A100 Traveller service barge, over to France and were met by the crew who had flown up from Nice, having just finalised their final recce. Although the Paris start was popular with UK entrants, Källström and Håkansson were in the only works Mini to start from there – Stuart Turner wisely distributing his cars over the various starting points to hedge his bets on some getting better weather than others. As it turned out, this proved a good move as the severe weather decimated the entire entry from Athens and Lisbon, most of those from Frankfurt, Paris and also Monte Carlo. The other works entries started from Athens, Stockholm and Minsk.

From an entry of 275 cars 237 made the start on their respective journeys across Europe to descend upon St Claude in mid France for the common run to Monte Carlo some three days later. Once in Monaco, and after a day's rest, the all-new 380-mile mountain circuit was undertaken the following evening. Here six stages, over the mountains above Monte Carlo, would decide the winner. The weather, however, was to prove decisive and eliminated many of the cars once the route got into central France. The early numbers leaving St Claude did have a slightly easier time but the severe weather of deep snow, drift, ice and blizzards eliminated many cars once in the Massif Central area. Of the 211 that safely reached St Claude, only 35 made it to Monte within their allowable one-hour lateness.

However, Harry Källström and Ragnvald Håkansson

Källström and Håkansson all smiles as they get their Lucas lights adjusted by the Cibie people before the start of the 1965 Monte Carlo Rally.

were not among them, having retired with terminal clutch failure after the fifth classification stage before Monte Carlo. Källström started in relatively mild but wet weather from Paris on Dunlop SP tyres; their route headed north east towards Liège before going westwards around the coast and south all the way down to Montauban, where the weather deteriorated and their studded tyres were fitted. They headed on north eastwards towards St Claude, which they, along with many others, made on time. The 580-mile common run to Monte Carlo would now prove decisive, where the field

Källström and Håkansson pose in the rain in Paris before the start on the 1965 Monte in AGU 780B.

AGU 780B on the snow and ice, territory very familiar for Källström. However, the clutch failed after just five stages and the crew were out.

Harry Källström and Ragnvald Håkansson at the start of the 1965 Swedish Rally with team of three Scandinavian drivers, Aaltonen, Mäkinen, all expected to do well in the frozen conditions. All retired with broken diffs due to freezing oil.

was decimated by the appalling weather.

Trouble hit Källström and Håkansson nearing Chambéry, when they had to stop and remove a bent fan blade, which left the car in a state of imbalance and saw them late at the next control. With the fan imbalance, it made driving the car quickly very difficult as the engine couldn't be revved very hard. They decided to remove the fan entirely at the Chambéry control. Without the cooling fan the engine boiled on the climb up the Col du Granier stage, and soon the pistons were seizing and copious quantities of snow were heaped in and around the radiator to try and reduce the temperature. They eventually arrived at Gap very late but still in the rally. Finally the clutch failed, probably as a result of the severe overheating, allowing oil past the main seal and onto the clutch. They would go no further.

The third and final event for this car would be the Swedish Rally, where AGU 780B was prepared as a Group 1 car and again built by Tommy Eales. Converting a Group 2 car back to a Group 1 car always meant taking off modified parts and putting back standard parts, as Group 1 cars were presented as a showroom class and relatively standard.

The standard-bore 1275cc engine still had a full-race AEA648 camshaft but the cylinder head was unmodified, unpolished and not skimmed, retaining the standard 9.5:1 compression ratio. The rocker pillars were, however, skimmed due to increased valve lift. The gearbox was much as used on the Monte, still retaining the low 4.26:1 diff ratio and special driveshafts. The carburettors had a change in needles from CP4s to XH92, reflecting the less modified engine. Despite the perceived standard engine, it still produced 70bhp at the wheels on the rolling road, just 5bhp down on the more modified Monte engine.

Standard suspension, albeit still dry and not Hydrolastic, was used with Girling competition dampers. To aid access to the rear dampers (should they need to be changed in a hurry), two access holes were cut on the rear bulkhead behind the seat back, which meant the fuel tanks would not have to be disturbed to gain access to the top mountings. The subframes also received extra welding at the joints and webs, with special attention around the tie rod mounting at the front after Hopkirk's problem on the Monte where he split the subframe. To add extra strength, skid brackets were fabricated and fitted to the subframe where the tie rods mount. Another skid plate was fabricated to protect the battery box, much as seen on the RAC car, plus a heavy-duty Scandinavian-style sump guard was also fitted to protect the gearbox.

Despite the obvious cold weather, the car was still fitted with a six-blade fan but it also retained the MG trim shop-made grille muff. However, in addition, and not seen on works cars since the 850 days, was a radiator blind fitted between the radiator and inner wing. The electrics remained unchanged, the only addition being a metal plate placed behind the grille to keep rain and snow away from the distributor, which had also reverted to the standard 40819 type. The grille was now held on by new knurled buttons, manufactured by Paddy Hopkirk. Of course, tyre choice and selection was paramount and special studded tyres were used throughout the event, all of which were special Scandinavian tyres locally-sourced.

The Swedish Rally was previously called the Midnight Sun Rally, where it was run in the long daylight hours of the Swedish summer. But from 1965 the event switched to the frozen Swedish winter to make it more of a challenge. It was, however, run on the class improvement handicap system, whereas many rallies in Europe were by then won or lost on scratch times – the fastest wins. So in 1965 the Swedish Rally was held a couple of months after the Monte Carlo Rally, in early March, when ice was still very evident in Sweden and where high-speed races over frozen lakes took place in routes ploughed out through fresh snow over the packed ice; the rest of the route was on hard-packed frozen roads. Abingdon sent a team of four cars to the event, driven by three Scandinavian drivers, Aaltonen, Mäkinen and Källström plus Paddy Hopkirk. Sadly, all four cars retired at the end of the first day, three of which, including AGU 780B, were due to differential failure, which with the severe cold weather meant that the oil was not working as it should and the diffs failed.

This rather unsuccessful car was sold to Harry Källström.

Competition Record

Date	Event	Crew	Number	Overall result	Class result
Nov 1964	RAC Rally	Harry Källström/Ragnvald Håkansson	42	DNF	
Jan 1965	Monte Carlo Rally	Harry Källström/Ragnvald Håkansson	176	DNF	
Mar 1965	Swedish Rally	Harry Källström/Ragnvald Håkansson	23	DNF	

Registration Number	First registered	Chassis number	Engine	Engine number	Model
DJB 92B	Dec 1964	KA2S4 553382	1275cc	9F-SA-Y 134628	Morris Cooper S

DJB 92B was one of a pair of new 1275 Cooper Ss registered in December 1964, this one a Morris and the other, DJB 93B, being an Austin. By now Hydrolastic suspension had been fitted as standard to all production Cooper Ss but it was still not accepted by all of the works drivers – notably Timo Mäkinen, who insisted his cars were built with dry rubber cone suspension.

With the Swedish Rally entry for Timo Mäkinen and Paul Easter being in Group 1, the car was relatively standard, and to ensure no major parts were changed during the rally, sealing points for the cylinder head, engine block and gearbox had to be provided, which would allow the scrutineer to see if any part had indeed been changed.

The engine bore for this 1275 was standard and the cylinder head unpolished, with the resulting compression ratio being down to 9.5:1 - but with a full-race camshaft, a pair of 1½ H4 SU carburettors and a short 4.26:1 final drive to the straight-cut close-ratio gearbox, the performance was nevertheless high. Suspension was also virtually standard, apart from the use of Girling competition dampers and the change to rubber rather than Hydrolastic suspension. The subframes, however, did have reinforcing welding on the seams and webs for added strength and stiffness. A heavy-duty Scandinavian sump guard was fitted to the car when it arrived in Sweden. It also had a battery box skid fitted on the rear subframe.

Despite the 1965 Swedish Rally, for the first time, being a

Timo Mäkinen with the brand-new DJB 92B preparing for the start of the 1965 Swedish Rally.

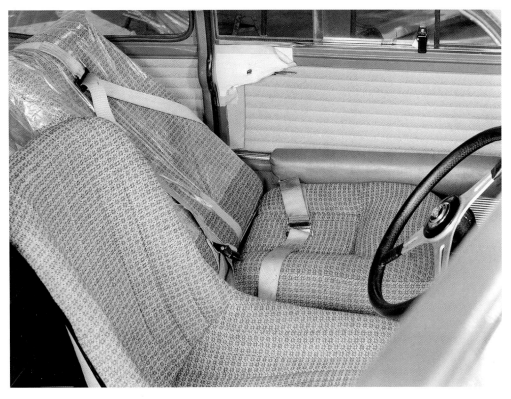

Timo Mäkinen and Paul Easter leaving the Gothenburg start on their abortive attempt on the Swedish Rally - they retired from second place when the crankshaft pulley came adrift.

A lovely pair of works seats trimmed in early 850 Mini cloth material, showing the fibreglass bucket seat and reclining seat with full-harness seat belt for Paul Easter.

mid-winter event (its predecessor, the Rally of the Midnight Sun, ran in the height of summer) the car still ran a six-blade fan to keep things cool; DJB92B also had a grille muff to keep out the snow and freezing cold air. New for the 1965 season and, first seen on the Monte the previous month, was the laminated heated front windscreen. This was a major improvement on the earlier gold-film 'screen, which was not popular with some drivers. This new 'screen, operated by a special rotary switch, allowed the heater to be used at full power, half power over the entire 'screen or just power to the driver's half. The current draw was high, and it was just as well that its introduction coincided with the fitting of an alternator, which replaced the dynamo that had been used since the Mini 850 days. This also allowed the customary array of extra lamps to be used without fear of draining the battery.

Tyre selection, vital for such an event, consisted of entirely studded or spiked tyres, most of which were locally sourced and especially suited to the severe weather conditions. Protection in the boot was therefore needed in the shape of alloy plates in the tyre well and plywood sheeting glued to sides of both fuel tanks. Mäkinen was very experienced at this sort of event, as he had been racing D-Type Jaguars in ice races in Finland before he became a works Mini driver, so was very used to racing with spiked tyres on ice. He had also convincingly won the Monte Carlo Rally, in atrocious conditions, just two months before.

The 1965 Swedish Rally was based in Gothenburg and was on either snow- and ice-covered tracks or routes carved out by a snow plough on the frozen lakes. Three such races on the ice were scheduled; the rest, and these were often very long stages, were over packed snow and ice tracks. Virtually no practice was possible, as the tracks used for the special stages were not ploughed free of snow until a few days before the rally. The BMC works team of four cars, three with Scandinavians at the wheel – Rauno Aaltonen, Timo Mäkinen and Harry Källström, with Paddy Hopkirk being the lone non-Scandinavian in the team – started with high hopes.

It soon transpired that the entire works team had retired by the first night, although Mäkinen in DJB 92B did get to the 11th stage and was lying in second place behind the eventual winner, Tom Trana's Volvo, when the lower pulley came adrift from the crankshaft - and the car went into retirement. But not before Mäkinen had covered one 70-mile stage on snow and ice in a staggering 68 minutes.

After the Swedish Rally in March, DJB 92B was loaned out to compete in the 1965 International Police Rally in Liège, Belgium in May. This had been a popular event in which Abingdon took part over the years, largely at the behest of John Gott, who was not only once the BMC team captain but also the chief constable of Northamptonshire and naturally a great supporter of this event. The Mini was built by Robin Vokins as a Group 2 car with a 1293cc rally engine.

The Nordrhein-Westfalen Rally was the next event for DJB 92B, allocated to Paddy Hopkirk and Henry Liddon. The car that appeared on the rally was likely not the same as Mäkinen used in Sweden four months earlier; now, amongst other

The German Rally saw Paddy Hopkirk and Henry Liddon take over DJB 92B but this was a different car to that used by Mäkinen on the Swedish Rally.

things, badged as an Austin Cooper S, although it carried a Morris Cooper grille. As the Abingdon entry was requested by the German Austin importer in Düsseldorf, to be badged as an Austin was hardly unexpected.

The lighting was also different, and although it still retained the five-light setup, the mounting of the lamps had changed. The car reverted to using the small Cyclops lamp, up by the top of the grille, as opposed to the large Lucas 700 Continental driving lamp fitted down between by the fog lamps on the Swedish car. It had also lost its Union Jacks on the front of the wings by the headlamps and the grille moustache was different where the muff would have been fitted. All of this would indicate that a different car was entered. Also of note is that, oddly, the car (along with all the others on the event) didn't carry competition door numbers – only those on the bonnet, along with a rally plate.

Starting from Cologne in West Germany, the Nordrhein-Westfalen Rally, often called the German rally, was based on a rather outdated handicap system that was not very popular, as many European events were now being decided on scratch results. The rather poorly organised event consisted of nine special tests plus five laps of the Nürburgring race circuit and ten laps of the Zolder track in Belgium. The tests were in fact rather Mickey Mouse, with short slaloms, hillclimb sprints and even a timed Le Mans start. The controls were very difficult to find and it was only Liddon's expert navigational skills that saved the day – local knowledge seemingly being paramount.

Tommy Wellman and Robin Vokins serviced the car from their Westminster barge and, other than Wellman resetting the ignition timing to cure a loss of power that Hopkirk had complained about at half way, the car ran without much attention. In retrospect, Hopkirk was lucky not to be penalised for allowing Wellman to go charging up and down the road to test the car but so lax was the event's organisation that it went unnoticed.

Despite Hopkirk, along with Andrew Hedges in the works MGB, winning every stage between them (Hedges the circuits and Hopkirk the tests), Hopkirk was relegated to sixth overall and Hedges 11th, with the winner being a German Opel. So incensed was Hopkirk at the finish that he said he'd never do the event again – the organisers retaliated by saying they'd not accept his entry anyway. Nevertheless, the saving grace of the rally was that Paddy was awarded a barrel of local beer at the finish, in recognition of his performance on the special tests. This was duly rolled down the hill into their hotel to be shipped back to Abingdon, where it was quickly consumed by the entire competitions department.

Late in the autumn of the 1965, DJB 92B was fully prepared by Dudley Pike (one of the many MG apprentices who would stay in the competitions department) for Rauno Aaltonen and Tony Ambrose to do their recce for the forthcoming Munich-Vienna-Budapest Rally in October. As is common with most of the recce cars, it was built up as a fully-competitive rally car with a 1293cc rally engine and all the usual Abingdon modifications. Both reliability and performance were very important here and the car was much as it appeared in Germany in July. Once again, however, special requirements to suit the driver were incorporated. Aaltonen did not care for the foot-operated dip switch found on Minis and so had asked for a dip switch to be provided on the steering column. A search through the Lucas parts book found a suitable dip switch sourced from a Riley Pathfinder; these dip switches found their way onto all of Aaltonen's cars.

For the car's next event, the RAC Rally in November 1965, it was handed to Finnish star Jorma Lusenius who had been offered the drive after putting up a brilliant performance for BMC Sweden against Timo Mäkinen on the 1965 1000 Lakes Rally, where he came fifth behind Mäkinen and Aaltonen, just ahead of Hopkirk. He was to be partnered on the RAC with Mike Wood, who would no doubt impart much of his local knowledge and experience to help Lusenius on this challenging event. Stuart Turner was continuing the pattern of signing Scandinavian drivers and partnering them with first-class British navigators – Turner himself being a championship-winning navigator was only too well aware of the valued contribution a top-rate navigator can bring to a team.

Badged once again as an Austin Cooper S, DJB 92B was built as a Group 3 lightweight car for the RAC with Perspex replacing the heavy glass all round (apart from the front laminated windscreen). Alloy bonnet, boot and doors replaced heavy steel and it also carried a lightweight front grille, crafted from an Austin Westminster part. Another special feature on the car was the alloy wheelarch extensions that were handmade at Abingdon.

The engine, bored out to 1293cc, ran the usual full-race

Jorma Lusenius with Mike Wood took DJB 92B on the 1965 RAC Rally, which started at London Airport. The car was again badged as an Austin Cooper S. Note air horns above the bumper.

camshaft, with the compression raised to 11.6:1 by skimming the cylinder head – which was gas-flowed and polished by Downton and had a capacity of 19cc. Downton was by now taking on more and more of Abingdon's engine work, once the sole domain of the Abingdon mechanics, although Cliff Humphries was still very much in control of engine work at Abingdon. Downton was also responsible for the special exhaust and inlet manifold modifications – also supplying special inlet valves for the team.

Carburettors were twin H4 SUs, with float chamber extensions and open ram pipes, which were fitted with AZ needles and blue springs. Power, on the rolling road, showed 84bhp at the wheels.

As usual, a straight-cut close-ratio gearbox was used and coupled to a 4.26:1 differential. Gone for the RAC were the troublesome rubber driveshaft couplings, replaced by the latest Hardy Spicer needle roller joints. These joints, which would soon find their way onto production cars, were far more reliable and less likely to break up under severe load. Their only down side was they were harder on the gearbox because the give imparted by the rubber joints took some of the strain from the transmission – however, with less power loss and the increased reliability, it was a welcome improvement to the powertrain. The gearbox was protected by a very heavy-duty full-length sump guard that had been developed by destruction testing in Wales earlier in the year.

Along with the heavy sump guard, both of the subframes were security rewelded, with strengthening plates and double-skinned skid plates on the rear subframe. The floor under the driver's feet was also double-skinned to avoid it buckling around the accelerator pedal. The front subframe had a cut let into it to clear the oil filter bowl. The suspension was Hydrolastic with small 1/10in spacers to raise the ride height without increasing the fluid pressure, and shock absorbers were not fitted. Steering arms and tie rods all had castellated nuts and split pins to ensure they didn't part company – with dire results.

Now with the benefit of an alternator, the strain on the electrics was much lower, and for the RAC the car didn't have a heated front windscreen. The lighting setup was similar to the Swedish car but different from the German car. The arrangement reverted to three large lamps on quick-release brackets on the bumper, with the centre lamp being a driving lamp between the two fog lamps. The two small fog lamps, on the bonnet, were there to act as dipped beam for the headlights, which being iodine, did not have a dip facility. The car was also fitted with a set of powerful Maserati air-horns, which were mounted externally next to the fog lamps on the front panel by the bumper.

Inside the car, a fibreglass bucket seat and a specially-made reclining seat were fitted. Both had Irvin seat belts but only Wood's was a full harness; Lusenius had to make do with a lap-and-diagonal belt. Extra padding was provided to the door pockets, locks and B-posts; the carpet was retained, with an asbestos blanket placed underneath to keep exhaust heat away from the crew. Special dash panels were made up to carry the rev counter and numerous extra switches on the driver's side, with a similar panel on the navigator's side housing twin Heuer clocks, Halda Twinmaster trip meter and other switches. The navigator also had a control panel in his door pocket, housing his map light, two-pin plug and other switches.

All lines were run inside the car – fuel, brakes, battery and Hydrolastic – although the twin fuel pump remained outside on the rear subframe and protected by an alloy plate. Twin fuel tanks with quick-release Aston filler caps were fitted, with plywood protection on their sides plus retaining straps to the outside of the tanks – primarily to prevent the tanks from moving onto the battery, should the rear corner take a side swipe against something substantial.

For the 1965 RAC the 2350-mile route was a massive challenge, with more than 400 stage miles spread over 58 stages, starting and finishing at London Airport and journeying all the way up to Perth via the West Country, Wales and the Highlands, then back to London. A challenge that attracted 162 hopefuls, of which 100 fell by the wayside on this five-day event with only one night in bed – and that was all the way up in Perth. BMC fielded a team of five Cooper Ss, with Timo Mäkinen electing to use the Healey 3000, which he felt stood a better chance over the forest tracks than the Mini.

The weather was wet and foggy for the early stages of the RAC but as soon as the route headed northwards, snow and ice became a major problem, with many stages becoming ice-

Lusenius and Wood head into the brief winter sunshine on the early stages in the south of England.

A bent nearside wing shows evidence of Lusenius going off the road as the conditions worsened. Lusenius and Wood finished a fine sixth place, repaying Stuart Turner's faith in giving him the drive.

bound and, in some cases, virtually impassable; Yorkshire was particularly badly hit.

With Lusenius being well versed in such conditions, having been a successful ice racer in his native Finland (the downside of which was he spoke virtually no English, so communication with Wood was a little difficult) he was doing very well over these treacherous stages. He was up to third place by the second night, despite having experienced alternator failure in Wales that night. Driving through the stage with minimal lights, he was soon caught by the car behind, which fortunately happened to be Tony Fall in CRX 89B. Fall swiftly overtook Lusenius and guided him, at great pace, to the finish of the stage with little loss of time, where the BMC mechanics were waiting and soon replaced the offending alternator.

With a ban on studded tyres, all that was available were Dunlop SP44s, and although snow chains were permitted, they were generally considered unsuitable for front-wheel-drive cars. However, as BMC hadn't provided any chains at all, the crews hastily set about making sets by buying dog-collar neck chains and leads at every pet shop they could find – such was their inventiveness.

By Tuesday's breakfast halt, with Mäkinen holding a five-minute lead in the Healey over Aaltonen, Lusenius was nudged down to fifth place just behind Källström, and BMC was very pleased with four cars in the top five places. However, there were still another 1000 miles to go and by then only 86 cars were still in the running, such was the rate of attrition. It would get worse, and at the finish, a mere 62 cars remained. Lusenius, on his first works drive, despite bashing the front nearside corner and tearing off the wheelarch, finished a creditable sixth overall and won his class, beating Hopkirk into second place. A brilliant drive, which justified Stuart Turner's preference for using Scandinavian drivers for such conditions.

After the RAC rally the car was quickly but thoroughly rebuilt and dispatched for Mäkinen and Easter to undertake their recce for the 1966 Monte Carlo Rally. As is usual for Abingdon, the car was fully prepared for the recce, treated as if it was being built for a full event. Much work was carried out tyre testing with Dunlop on the recce, trying numerous different tyre and stud combinations - in addition to making pace notes and practising the stages at high speed.

However, the car suffered terminal damage on the recce when it came into sharp contact with a kilo-stone (after some New Year revelry) and retired hurt. DJB 92B was left in Switzerland at Garage Auber in Geneva, to be recovered at a later date. It was therefore not available for ice notes and service duties on the event as planned.

It was back to Sweden for the car's next event, and with the FIA bringing in new rules for Appendix J in January 1966, the specification had to change. The rules on modifications were

DJB 92B was used for recce work in late 1965 for the 1966 Monte. Here Timo Mäkinen and Rauno Aaltonen meet headlong with the works Citroen of Pauli Toivonen and Ensio Mikander, who would go on to win the controversial 1966 Monte.

Timo Mäkinen and Terry Harryman removing the heavy roof rack with the spiked and studded tyres of DJB 92B for some serious fast practice for the 1966 Monte. Note the open boot with two spare wheels, MGB jack, tool bag and Elopress.

Another new DJB 92B reverts to a Morris Cooper S for the 1966 Swedish Rally, now with the new lighting arrangement along a lamp bar. This shot in the UK before its departure. A broken driveshaft saw the car retire.

much tighter, in particular the Group 1 regulations, which now stipulated 5000 of a model had to be produced within one year – and with that, few modifications were allowed, this being termed a showroom class. These new rules also affected cars prepared in Group 2 and Group 3.

So it was that after the severe battering the lightweight Group 3 car received on the RAC Rally, a new group 2 car was built for Timo Mäkinen and Paul Easter to tackle the 1966 Swedish Rally. This, let us not forget, was just three weeks after the disqualification of the team of 1966 Monte Carlo rally – and Timo in particular was most aggrieved at being thrown out from his winning position. Car preparation therefore was undertaken very much with these new rules in mind.

The most striking feature with the car externally was the disappearance, at last, of the cluttered five-light arrangement on the front, replaced by four lamps all in a line. These were fitted to a chromed lamp bar on the front panel above the bumper in front of the grille; it housed four large Lucas 700 lamps, two fog lights on the outside and two Continental driving lamps in the middle. This iconic pattern would largely stay with the works Minis to the end.

For the Swedish the car was fitted with a heated front windscreen and narrow 3½J steel wheels to help cut through the expected snow. Gone too were the Aston filler caps and, being a Mäkinen car, it reverted to being a Morris Cooper S. Also to avoid possible problems with scrutineers, the ritual welding-up of bung holes in the floor to keep out the water, which Abingdon had always done to bodyshells, simply had the bungs stuck down and sealed.

Now that the Swedish had settled on its winter date, the temperature was expected to be minus 26C, and as it had been snowing continuously for days in Örebro, where the event started, the temperature had dropped to minus 40C. Practice had been virtually non-existent (much as last year) due to the prevailing conditions, so re-ploughing of much of the route was needed just before the start. There were 27 stages totalling 680 miles, one of which was 60 miles long with 30 miles on a frozen lake – all this with only one five-hour rest stop in 51 hours of competition.

First, however, scrutineering had to be overcome, and with the new regulations in force, much debate and arguments ensued over what was and was not permissible within the new Group 2 rules. Abingdon was initially told its cars couldn't run with their fuel lines inside, nor with a reversing light (as it was one light too many). Fortunately, in both cases, common sense prevailed.

But it all came to nothing, as Mäkinen, leading at the time, retired on stage five with failed transmission when a driveshaft broke. As last year, the other remaining Abingdon cars also failed to finish. Just 48 cars completed the 1966 Swedish from a field of 120, where the severity of the conditions caused many to be eliminated with frozen carburettors or by hitting concealed objects within huge vertical snow banks.

For the next and penultimate event for this now much-used car, DJB 92B was handed to Tony Fall for the Circuit of Ireland over the Easter of 1966. He was teamed with the vastly experienced Henry Liddon and, although the Circuit had departed from being a rather navigational event to one where the route was depicted entirely by Tulip road book, Liddon's map-reading skills would certainly still be much valued.

Built as a Group 2 car by Robin Vokins it was similar to the specification of the Swedish Rally car, being 1293cc with a high-compression cylinder head, a full-race camshaft and a 4.26 differential. As before, most of the engine modifications were carried out by Downton. The car put out 87bhp at the wheels on the rolling road.

Tony Fall and Mike Wood took DJB 92B to Ireland for the Circuit of Ireland, seen here outside the Gallaher building at the start.

Fall and Wood cornering hard in the Irish hills. They would beat all of the local crews and win the event outright. The car now fitted with wheelarch extensions.

Much as the Swedish car had the new lamp bar arrangement for the four extra lamps, the car now also sprouted black fibreglass wheelarch extensions for the first time. These were now deemed necessary under the new Group 2 regulations to keep the wider 4½J wheels covered.

Other noteworthy fitments to the car were bolt-on skid plates to protect the front of the tie bars and protection plates on the brake callipers to stop the brake pipe from being hit. These had also appeared on the Swedish car. Needless to say, for the bumpy Irish tarmac a substantial sump guard and battery guard were fitted. Because the event was mostly on tarmac, Fall used predominantly Dunlop R7 race tyres, with SP44s for the forest tracks. And in the interest of health and safety, the plywood protection plates fixed to the sides of the fuel tanks in the boot were replaced by sheets of asbestos. The fuel pump, still fitted outside on the subframe, was protected by an alloy plate, and the exhaust received special attention with each joint having a securing locating bar welded on to ensure it did not part company.

The Hydrolastic suspension used double-blue front displacers and single-blue at the back, with orange 30lb helper springs at the rear but no shock absorbers, other than extra Aeon bump stop rubbers. The coloured banding for the displacers was there to designate the stiffness of the units, and this varied dependant on the amount of compliance the suspension was needed to provide, considering the terrain to be driven over and also driver preference. However to ensure that the scrutineer's attention wasn't drawn to any modified parts, all had their special paint marks removed. The final changes from the Swedish car were the replacement of the heated front 'screen with a standard laminated version, and the speedo and Halda distance recorder recalibrated to read in miles rather than kilometres.

Ninety cars started from Ballymena on Good Friday for the 1966 Circuit of Ireland. It was a five-day, 1500-mile event containing 50 stages, mostly on closed public roads – and to try and limit the amount of service the cars could have by the ever-attendant works mechanics, the Ulster AC decided to have time controls situated every ten miles or so throughout the route. With a maximum lateness of 30 minutes, any major problem on the car would mean collecting large time penalties or being excluded.

Paddy Hopkirk was favourite and was looking to repeat last year's win, but a massive end-over-end roll on the Lough Eske stage, which totally destroyed the car, dashed that hope. So all BMC's efforts were concentrated on Tony Fall whose early pace meant he was up to third place behind the two works Lotus Cortinas when they reached Sligo. Fall would continually swap leading times with the Fords and was still holding third place at Killarney until Roger Clark's car ran its bearings on the Borlin stage and he was now up to second place. Fall went on to take the lead on the Healy Pass stage, which he held to the finish in Larne on the Easter Monday. This was Tony Fall's first international win and it was also the first time a non-Irish driver had won the rally. It also meant BMC had a hat-trick of wins in Ireland following Ronnie McCartney's and Paddy Hopkirk's wins.

DJB 92B's final Abingdon rally was the Austrian Alpine in mid May where the car was assigned to Paddy Hopkirk and his new co-driver Ron Crellin, who had replaced Henry Liddon; this was to be their second event together. The car was again entered as a Group 2 and built by Mick Legg. It appeared very much as it had been on the Circuit of Ireland other than the twin fuel pump was relocated under the rear seat from its

The interior of DJB 92B just before the Austrian Alpine. Of note are the three fuseboxes, tape over the Halda windows, Mini cloth-covered fibreglass bucket seat and the small fire extinguisher.

rather inconvenient and rather exposed location on the rear subframe. The speedo and Halda distance recorder once again had to be recalibrated, this time to again read in kilometres. With the engine likely having just the top end refreshed, the recorded power on the rolling road had dropped to 85bhp, having lost 2bhp over the Irish roads.

Despite the Austrian Alpine being early in the year and with some of its route high up in the snow line, an additional benefit of the new lamp bar was that it could be easily and quickly removed, complete with the lamps attached, to allow more air into the engine and keep the lights free from possible damage when running during the daylight hours. And so it was that DJB 92B was to be seen during the day without any additional lights.

Hopkirk discussing his tyre choice with the man from Dunlop as Crellin looks on. Stuart Turner in conversation behind.

A contrast in climate experience on the Austrian Alpine and DJB 92B threads its way through deep snowbanks.

Hopkirk now with Ron Crellin on 1966 Austrian Alpine kicking up the dust in the hot conditions. Note the lamps bar and lights removed.

The rally, which started in Velden, attracted only 78 starters but did include two works Porsches determined to beat Hopkirk and not allow him the repeat of his 1964 win. Two works Minis were entered for Paddy Hopkirk and Tony Fall and, despite the event not officially allowing any service, BMC sent down a new Vanden Plas 4 litre R to service the cars. These new barges, powered by Rolls Royce engines, were very powerful and soon proved ideal for the job and very popular with the mechanics.

As part of the strict 'no service' rules there were additional restrictions on the number of wheels. The car had to carry all the rims it was allowed to use and all of the rims were marked, and this was further compounded by the stipulation that if a tyre needed to be replaced, it had to go back onto the original rim. Nevertheless, Abingdon still managed to service Hopkirk, out of sight and just off route, prior to the car going into the highly policed official area, where only the crew would service the car.

Split into two loops, the first starting at dawn, Hopkirk was soon in the lead. After 15 hours' motoring and a half-night's sleep, the next-day restart at 2am saw Hopkirk extend the lead with the Porsches still in his wake. He would go into Yugoslavia to consolidate his lead, being fastest on all the remaining six stages, including the five-lap blast around Klagenfurt airfield where Hopkirk benefited from fitting racing tyres to his rims. Fortunately, the organisers permitted service personnel to change the tyres, provided the crew took the wheels off and put them back on again. So Hopkirk won again, with just 37 other cars making the finish.

However, DJB 92B's work at Abingdon was not yet finished, as the car went direct from Austria to Greece for Timo Mäkinen and Paul Easter to do their recce of the 1966 Acropolis Rally at the end of May. Once their recce had been completed they left the car in Greece to act as a press car on the Acropolis Rally. It was assigned to a *Motor* magazine journalist Roger Bell and MG's Wilson McComb who, whilst covering the event, just happened to stop between two stages, when Mäkinen suddenly appeared in his works car (HJB 656D) with its rear suspension torn off – the bracket holding the rear suspension arm to the subframe had sheared in half. The matching bracket was removed from DJB 92B to repair Timo's car and the pair were left in the middle of nowhere with a three-wheeled Mini. By luck, a passing bus driver came across the pair and kindly found a local blacksmith to repair the offending bracket. This was soon put back on the car and saw them on their way again.

The car was sold to John Sprinzel, who being a canny car dealer at the time, as well as a sometimes BMC works driver, quickly sold the car on, but not before he did the 1966 Coupe des Alpes in it.

Competition Record

Date	Event	Crew	Number	Overall result	Class result
Mar 1965	Swedish Rally	Timo Mäkinen/Paul Easter	31	DNF	
July 1965	German Rally	Paddy Hopkirk/Henry Liddon	58	6th	1st
Nov 1965	RAC Rally	Jorma Lusenius/Mike Wood	44	6th	1st
Feb 1966	Swedish Rally	Timo Mäkinen/Paul Easter	35	DNF	
April 1966	Circuit of Ireland	Tony Fall/Henry Liddon	4	1st	1st
May 1966	Austrian Alpine	Paddy Hopkirk/Ron Crellin	58	1st	1st

Registration Number	First registered	Chassis number	Engine	Engine number	Model
DJB 93B	Dec 1964	CA2S7 662044	1275cc	9F-SA-Y 34709	Austin Cooper S

DJB 93B was the second of a pair of new 1275 Cooper Ss registered in December 1964, this one being an Austin, although it would manifest itself as a Morris later in life. The brand-new car was hastily pressed into service for recce duties for the 1965 Monte Carlo Rally before it would bloody its nose in competition, when the Morley twins took over DJB 93B just before Christmas for their recce. The car was left in France to act as an ice notes car for the team.

For DJB 93B's first event, the Swedish Rally in the frozen Scandinavian winter, it was entered as a Group 1 car for Rauno Aaltonen and Tony Ambrose. Unlike its sister car, DJB 93B used Hydrolastic suspension, which Aaltonen preferred and which had by now been fitted as standard to all production Cooper Ss, replacing the dry rubber cone suspension. The car was built by Brian Moylan.

For the Swedish, the planned 1275cc engine was changed to a 970cc unit because the organisers decided, at short notice, to amalgamate Group 1 and 2 classes in the up-to-1300 class, so Aaltonen would have been at a distinct disadvantage in a Group 1 1275. He therefore entered the up-to-one-litre class.

Rauno Aaltonen posed by DJB 93B for the 1965 Swedish Rally - the driver's seat looks like it is still covered in polythene. The event was not a success, where the transmission failed early on.

Aaltonen kicking up the snow on the early stages before failure of the diff caused premature retirement.

So, for the Group 1 car the one-litre engine bore was kept to standard but fitted with the almost-standard-Abingdon-fit of a full-race camshaft, the AEA-648. The cylinder head was also kept unmodified with standard compression ratio of 9.6:1 but the carburettors were a larger set of twin H4s with CP4 needles – these being free, even for the showroom class back then. For the Swedish, the engine and gearbox needed to be sealed, to ensure replacements were not fitted, so the cylinder head, rear of the engine case and gearbox sump were all sealed (to seal the cylinder head, two barrelled head nuts were fitted with a small hole in each to allow the scrutineer to wire lock the unit).

To ensure the core plugs in the block stayed in place in the extreme cold, they had Isopon filler placed around the edges. Despite the anticipated very cold weather, the engine was fitted with a six-blade fan, a radiator blind and a grille muff. This, together with an 82C thermostat, was an attempt to keep things warm inside the car. For protection of the engine, for what was expected to be a hard event for the underside of the car, inevitably sledding over packed snow and ice, a heavy-duty Scandinavian sump guard was fitted. In addition, a skid plate was added to the rear subframe to protect the vulnerable battery box, which sat below the body and was rather exposed on rough terrain. The car was also fitted with a special and much-skidded exhaust system with an upswept tailpipe.

The gearbox, with straight-cut close-ratio gears, was fitted with a 4.26:1 diff ratio together with a set of modified and strengthened driveshafts. The rear of the gearbox used the indestructible Mitchell mounting, designed with a movable joint: where the standard production solid rubber joint would invariably fail, this Abingdon design was very robust. Abingdon was still, despite road cars now being fitted with anti-rattle gearsticks, using the old type direct gear levers, which was what the drivers preferred.

The Hydrolastic suspension had special competition displacers fitted with the addition of 2mm thick spacer washers to raise the suspension. The car was, however, devoid of any shock absorbers. For added strength (not strictly allowed) both subframes were rewelded and the front frame had protection plates bolted around the front tie bars, which of course added much strength. Castellated nuts and split pins were used on the steering arms and tie bar ends, to ensure they couldn't come undone.

Brakes were standard, only receiving racing linings and pads, but did have a 325psi limiting valve to change the brake balance. The brake lines were all run inside the car and small shields made up to protect the rear fitting to the wheel cylinder, as they too were vulnerable to damage and being torn off.

As usual, the electrics received expert attention from the resident Lucas racing electricians, the car being completely rewired to suit the needs of the event – and would invariably be completely rewired for subsequent events. Reliability was paramount. Switches were likewise habitually replaced. At the heart of the electrics was now an alternator, replacing the heavy and underpowered dynamo.

The light configuration was a five-light setup with a small centre spot lamp mounted centrally on the slam panel and two large fog lamps on quick-release brackets low down by the bumper. Two additional small fog lights, mounted on the bonnet, acted as the dipped beam for the non-dipping powerful iodine headlamps. Aaltonen had the tiresome foot-operated dip switch removed and a hand-operated stalk fitted to the steering column. A small Austin Healey sidelight, with a powerful bulb, was fitted to the boot lid to act as a reversing lamp.

The battery cable was run inside the car and the battery was reversed in the boot, with its terminals facing away from the side of the fuel tank. Gone were the electric demister bars, often seen on the cars on cold events, to be replaced now by a fully-heated front windscreen, specially made by Triplex. Special dashboards, for each crew member, had their switches and controls arranged accordingly and the all-new Halda Twinmaster distance recorder was fitted to the navigator's panel.

Inside the car, Aaltonen had a fibreglass bucket seat, with Ambrose having a special reclining seat designed and made by Tommy Wellman. Both crew members had specially-made Irvin seat belt harnesses. Being a Group 1 car, all of the glass and trim was retained and no lightweight panels were permitted, but additional padding was fitted to the door locks, pillars and door pockets, as was an asbestos blanket under the carpet to keep heat at bay from the exhaust manifold.

Access holes were cut in the rear bulkhead, behind the rear seat squab, to allow quick access to the top of the springs, should the displacer units need changing – removing the twin tanks, with their quick-release Aston filler caps (and not-so-quick to remove from their filler necks...) is not a swift process. Both tanks were protected against puncturing from the spiked tyres carried in the boot, with plywood stuck to their faces and – as an added safety feature – the right-hand tank, by the battery, had the holding strap repositioned on the inside of the seam, hence preventing the tank being moved across over the battery should the car receive a heavy side impact. To speed up wheel changes, a modified MGB jack was now carried in the car, which made it much quicker to raise the car via a cranked handle. The car, of course, had quick-lift jacking brackets front and rear for use by the service crew with their racing jacks.

The 1965 Swedish Rally, once called the Midnight Sun Rally because of its mid-summer timing had, for the first time, moved to a mid-winter event. This was largely to keep the vast crowds under control, reasoning less would venture out in deep midwinter but also to curb practising, as many of the proposed stages were not ploughed until just before the rally was due to start. So the concept of the rally changed dramatically – now being a very fast race over frozen ice stages, often ploughed on frozen lakes. These stages were interspersed with road sections, again on packed snow and ice, making quite a challenge. The only gripe of the event was that it was to be decided on the unpopular class improvement marking system and not on scratch times.

Aaltonen sadly, along with all the other BMC works entries, retired very early on the Swedish when, halfway through stage two, he lost all drive. This was subsequently discovered to be the pinion on the end of the layshaft coming adrift and therefore losing all drive, although the initial diagnosis was diff failure due to oil feed problems brought on by the extreme cold.

From the cold of Scandinavia, the car's next task was in the Alps where it was used by Timo Mäkinen and Julien Vernaeve to assess the benefits and suitability of having a limited-slip differential fitted to works cars. Robin Vokins came along as a travelling mechanic and Paul Easter was also there, as the time was also used for a recce of the forthcoming Tulip Rally in April.

The next event for DJB 93B was in the heat of Greece for the Acropolis Rally in May 1965. The car was handed to Timo Mäkinen and Paul Easter and, as is usual with cars for Mäkinen, the car was rebadged as a Morris. It was rebuilt as a Group 2 car by Peter Bartram and Gerald Wiffen and was much changed from the Swedish car. Notably it now had a 1275cc engine, overbored by 0.020in to give 1293cc and still with the full-race camshaft. The cylinder head was much modified, being gas-flowed by Downton with the compression raised to 11.6:1. The straight-cut close-ratio gearbox retained its short 4.26:1 ratio. Oddly, for the hotter climate in Greece, the cooling fan was reduced from six blades to four.

Timo Mäkinen and Paul Easter at scrutineering for the 1965 Acropolis Rally where the car reverted to a Morris. The car now fitted with large forward-facing mud flaps.

WORKS MINIS IN DETAIL

Mäkinen high up in the hills on the Volos loop on the Acropolis Rally.

However, despite Mäkinen's dislike of Hydrolastic suspension, the car retained its wet suspension but with double-red displacers at the rear and yellow on the front but still with a 2mm spacer. These colour markings were there to denote the different stiffnesses of the units and hence spring rate. For the anticipated rough roads the subframe was rewelded and stiffened plus the body was plated for the extra bump stops.

The lighting arrangement was changed for the Acropolis – gone was the Cyclops lamp on the slam panel, to be replaced with a large driving lamp fitted centrally, mounted down by the bumper, where the two large fog lamps were also mounted. All three lamps were fitted on quick-release brackets. However, the headlights, still without dipping iodine bulbs, had the dipped beam served by small fog lamps on the bonnet. A roof lamp on the nearside front corner of the roof appeared. Headlamp washers were fitted and the heated front 'screen disappeared.

The car also sprouted large mud flaps at the front corners of the bumper by the overrider bars, designed to lessen water and mud splashing up towards the headlamps. It carried large white numbers (number 60 in this case) on the bonnet in addition to the rally plate and the normal black-painted numbers on the doors, sign-written at Abingdon.

The Acropolis Rally saw 85 cars line up for the traditional start for a 48-hour thrash over what were to prove demanding roads. Mäkinen had a long battle with the powerful Mercedes 230SL of Böhringer and would be leading comfortably once the German retired. This allowed him to build up sufficient time to change the troublesome drive couplings, carried out in the traditional way of tipping the car onto its side.

Further on, however, the Mini was soon to be delayed again as the couplings needed changing once more. With only one service barge in attendance (and that too was delayed due to it colliding with a bus) Paul Easter was forced to change the coupling on the ferry at Patras, despite protestations from the ship's captain as oil and fuel spilled onto the ship.

Things got worse. In their haste there was insufficient time to replace the heavy sump guard that was promptly dumped into the back of the Mini. Timo was forced to drive slowly, over the rough ground, but soon the sump was leaking and, to make matters worse, on their way to the very last stage the

Disaster struck when the car was tipped on its side for hasty service to weld the broken subframe. The escaping fuel was ignited by the welding sparks but the fire was quickly extinguished and Mäkinen carried on until the engine cried enough.

The blacked rear and collapsed suspension are clearly visible but the engine also had a piston fail.

A new DJB 93B appeared, in an 850 Mini bodyshell, on the 1965 Alpine Rally for Pauline Mayman and Val Domleo. The car behind is AJB 33B, crewed by Mäkinen and Easter.

carpets caught fire and, delayed as they were, Paul was forced to act as fireman as they sped along.

Once they had found the service crew, the car was again tipped onto its side, as by now the subframe had also split. In the rush to weld the repair, the fuel leaking from the fuel tank ignited and the car was quickly engulfed in flames. Fortunately, the fire was soon extinguished, and Mäkinen was able to speed to the last stage – but he would not make it. Running on just one carburettor and, because of the loss of oil, a piston gave up. Mäkinen was out, and the dishevelled Mini was uncermoniously towed back to the finish.

After the battering from Greece, a new car was supplied, this time prepared by the special tuning division next-door to the competition department. The car supplied was a base 850 Mini rather than a new Cooper S and retained its standard red interior trim rather than the grey unique Cooper S brocade.

The new car was handed to Pauline Mayman and Val Domleo to tackle the 1965 Alpine Rally. Mayman had actually retired from international rallying at the end of the previous season but was keen to try and get a hat-trick of wins in the Coupe des Dames, so decided to have one last crack at the Alpine.

The new car, reverted to an Austin once more, lost its roof lamp and front mud flaps, and the air horns were now mounted outside the car below the indicator/sidelights by the bumper. One major change was the abandonment of the potentially unreliable rubber driveshaft couplings, replaced by new needle-roller Hardy Spicer universal joints. This would herald a new era of reliability for this often unreliable part of the Mini's drivetrain.

The Alpine Rally, starting from Marseille and finishing in Monte Carlo some 2200 miles and six days later, was a great favourite of Abingdon, which entered a team of four Minis with high hopes. Ninety-three cars took the start to tackle most of the famous Cols in the Alps.

The route was divided into three legs of 500, 800 and 900 miles and, with the luxury of two stops of half and one full day at Grenoble, the rally was not as hard as it once was. This relaxation was to appease the public, as the organisers were desperate to save their event from disappearing altogether. Despite the more relaxed format, the rally proved as tough a challenge as ever, with 13 special speed tests and demanding high-speed road sections, which required the cars to achieve a high average just to keep on time.

Such was the rate of attrition that only 32 cars were classified as finishers, eight of which did achieve clean sheets, meaning no road time lost, and hence were awarded a coveted

Mayman speeds through a village in the mountains, such is the relentless speed on the Alpine to stay on time. The girls would finish 13th overall and win the ladies' prize.

Alpine Cup.

Always favourite to win the Coupe des Dames, Mayman didn't disappoint and won her class but missed out on an Alpine Cup by just a few seconds. With a badly overheating car, it was decided at their service that the engine was just too hot to top up with water, so they pressed on. Having lost most of its water, the car started to seize, when the girls stopped by a small stream. They dammed the stream and filled their washer bottle with water to quench the hot engine. Sadly, it took just a few moments too long and their Alpine Cup was gone. Mayman finished a creditable 13th overall and, with two of the other team cars being awarded Alpine Cups, it was a very successful event for Abingdon.

The Alpine car was then rebuilt for Rauno Aaltonen and Tony Ambrose, this time to tackle the RAC Rally in November, and it changed yet again back to a Morris Cooper S. Prepared as a Group 2, unlike its sister car, DJB 93B had to keep all of its steel panels and heavy glass and was without fabricated wheelarch extensions.

The engine, however, was very similar, in that it was a 1293cc with a high-compression polished and gas-flowed cylinder head prepared by the skilled hands at Downton. The usual full-race camshaft and straight-cut gearbox with a 4.26 diff were fitted, as were the all new Hardy Spicer needle roller drive shaft couplings – which were a welcome improvement over the troublesome rubber couplings that invariably needed frequent changing. The only down side was that they were a little harder on the transmission. The car showed 85bhp at the wheels, which would equate to approximately 105bhp at the flywheel. With the low diff ratio and a self-imposed 7300rpm maximum, the car would go no faster than 94mph flat out – but of course, torque and acceleration were all that was needed, especially for a forest event.

Hydrolastic suspension was fitted, which Aaltonen had spent a lot of time improving and re-specifying to his own taste. This meant fitting uprated units that partially negated the soft see-saw motion associated with standard units, especially when used on rough roads. For the RAC they were designated as single-red units at the front and double-red at the rear with added helper springs.

Despite the RAC being a winter rally, the new heated front windscreen, first seen on the Swedish Rally, was not fitted to the car. But as usual, the electrics, now driven by an alternator, received their usual high attention. Lighting was the same as used on the Alpine Rally but with the addition of a roof lamp by Ambrose's left side. This was used as a spotter lamp and could be swivelled over a wide arc by hand from inside the car. It was also useful for picking up corners. Iodine bulbs were used all round, and the headlamp dipped beam was served by two small fog lamps mounted on the bonnet. We again saw a powerful set of air horns mounted externally by the front bumper.

Inside the car, Aaltonen had his customary fibreglass bucket seat, whilst Ambrose had the comfort of a specially-made reclining seat. Both had Irvin seat belts, with the driver's being a simple lap-and-diagonal belt, which anchored on the rail below the rear side window. Ambrose had a full harness. He also had the use of a pocket let into the headlining to carry documents and time cards.

For the RAC a very substantial sump guard was fitted and all lines were placed inside the car. Both subframes received additional security welding and some double-plating reinforcing plates. With studded tyres not allowed, Dunlop SP44s were used extensively, with Dunlop SP3s for road sections and Dunlop R7 race tyres for the few tarmac stages.

This year the RAC Rally was the last round of the European Rally Championship, which Aaltonen was the frontrunner to win, such had been his dominance throughout the year – but he still had to beat René Trautmann's Lancia, the only driver who could unseat him. However, the late withdrawal

Rauno Aaltonen with Tony Ambrose were again in DJB 93B, this time for the 1965 RAC Rally, and it reverted back to a Morris.

Aaltonen checking for some paperwork in the roof document pocket of the car that some of the cars were fitted with.

of Trautmann's Lancia meant Aaltonen was effectively the champion when he took the starting ramp at London Airport's Forte Hotel. Alec Issigonis was there himself to congratulate Aaltonen and wish him well for the rally.

The 1965 event had 58 stages in its itinerary, totalling over 400 miles in its 2350-mile route, covering most of Great Britain over its five hard days – with but one night in bed. The weather was to largely decide the outcome of the 162 hopeful starters. Only 62 would make it back to London. Flagged off at the start by Graham Hill, who would himself drive a works Mini on the RAC Rally the following year, the cars headed out in continuously wet weather – 3in of rain had fallen the days before and, as a result, the first stage was cancelled. As dusk fell, the cars headed through the West Country and by nightfall were into Wales, where snow began to fall, making for treacherous driving conditions, which not only favoured the Scandinavian drivers but also suited the Mini.

At the Devil's Bridge breakfast halt, Mäkinen's Healey 3000 was in the lead with Aaltonen close behind. Aaltonen's only problem was a broken navigator's seat, which had to be welded by the service crew. However, he slipped from the leaderboard on the first stage after breakfast when a puncture on the stage cost him three minutes. Heading northwards, the weather deteriorated further with many stages being covered in snow and ice. Mäkinen, despite going off the road for five minutes in Dovey Forest, was still in the lead at Oulton Park. Aaltonen was clawing his way back, having been fastest on Dovey Forest. On into the night and Yorkshire beckoned, with deep snow and ice covering many roads and the stages; Mäkinen was struggling in the Healey and even Aaltonen was in difficulty.

Onwards up to Perth and the battle continued. The weather and road conditions worsened, and for many just keeping up the 30mph average speed of the road sections was proving an insurmountable challenge. By the overnight halt at Perth, half the field had already retired. Aaltonen had climbed back into second place and was the lead works Mini, all of which were still in the hunt – but Mäkinen had a comfortable four-and-a-half-minute lead in the powerful, if much battle-scarred Healey.

Into the Lake District and back into Wales, the battle continued with Mäkinen still ahead but it was not to last, as the icy conditions proved just too much for the Healey. Deprived, as all cars were, of studded tyres for the British forests, grip in Clocaenog was beyond the Healey and the sure-footed Mini of Aaltonen squeezed past Mäkinen – literally. Mäkinen was stuck for five minutes and his lead was gone. Aaltonen brought the Mini home in first place, two minutes clear of Mäkinen. This was the first real rough road win for the Mini Cooper S and concluded a superb year for Abingdon. Aaltonen had won the European Championship and the car, to celebrate, appeared on the stage of the London Palladium in front on BBC television cameras.

Soon after the RAC Rally, *Motor* magazine tested the car and

Tyre service stop for DJB 93B on the RAC Rally. Both Healey wheels and Mini wheels available.

Aaltonen celebrates winning the RAC Rally by pouring champagne over the car, with Ambrose intervening to prevent such waste.

– other than being impressed with the car – the performance figures were revealing: its 0-to-60mph time was recorded at 13.4 seconds, which was around two seconds slower than a standard Cooper S. However, the magazine did note that the time was recorded with two people in the car and with all the rally equipment still on-board.

Soon after the *Motor* road test, Aaltonen was obliged to take his British driving test and, to further aid publicity (and after a change to a more docile camshaft), DJB 93B was used by Aaltonen to successfully gain his British driving licence. This was much to the disappointment of the waiting press, who would no doubt have been delighted to report that the winner of the RAC had failed.

After the RAC, the car remained unseen for six months until DJB 93B appeared for the Scottish Rally in June 1966, to be driven this time by Tony Fall and Mike Wood. It was extensively rebuilt after the rigours of the RAC and it is very likely that if it had been any other event other than the Scottish Rally, a new car would have been built. Changes included the roof lamp being removed and plated over and the two fog lamps, which acted as dipped beams, being removed from the bonnet. The car had also by now sprouted black fibreglass wheelarch extensions to legally cover the wide 4½J steel wheels now that the 1966 Appendix J regulations had been implemented. The car was, for the second time in its career, prepared and supported by the special tuning department, largely because of the proximity of the Acropolis Rally that finished a day before the Scottish and the Geneva Rally that started a week after, both of which were stretching Abingdon's resources.

DJB 93B was rebuilt for Tony Fall and Mike Wood for the 1966 Scottish Rally. The subframes have both been removed to be replaced with new items.

The interior of DJB 93B clearly showing the standard 850 Mini plain door trim. The dashboard arrangement typical of the period.

The Scottish, run in early June, invariably meant a hot, dusty and a damaging event, as Scottish forests were notoriously rough, and for 1966 the entry was depleted of many works cars. This was largely for the reasons stated above but it still attracted 100 starters for the 1800-mile, five-day charge around Scotland. On offer were 64 stages, which was enough to tempt both BMC and Ford to send a car each for Tony Fall and Roger Clark, who was looking for his hat-trick of wins on the event in his Lotus Cortina. Jerry Larsson, in a works Saab, would also be a contender, but the Saab faded with failing suspension and, without a full service crew, was effectively out of contention. Roger Clark, despite leading early on, retired when his limited-slip diff failed, so it left Fall to get the car's second win in a row.

But it was far from plain sailing for Fall as the rear subframe broke after the first 40 stages just before the Grantown-on-Spey halt. However, it was rewelded and all was well, Fall holding first place ahead of the ailing Saab of Larsson. More trouble befell the car, with severe overheating problems,

Kicking up the dust on the very dry stage on the Scottish, which Fall and Wood would go on to win.

DJB 93B at the start of the Gulf London Rally, sandwiched between the works Cortina and works Saab.

due to the loss of water, which was eventually traced to a broken heater that unceremoniously dumped itself in pieces on the floor. Before the end, the subframe failed once again on the notoriously rough Culbin stage and had to be repaired. Fortunately, Fall's lead was unassailable and he finished the event more than five minutes clear of the Saab.

The final event for the car was the Gulf London Rally, and DJB 93B was again crewed by Tony Fall and Mike Wood, reverting to an Austin Cooper S for its swansong. This was, however, not that same car that had won the Scottish; nor the RAC, and despite Abingdon looking for a hat-trick of wins for a car that had endured two very demanding events, it was sensibly replaced with another DJB 93B. This time the car appeared without a roof lamp plate, so it was definitely a different and perhaps new car for the rally. DJB 93B now sported a new auxiliary four-lamp setup on a chrome-plated badge bar, which was fitted just above the bumper on the lower panel. The bar consisted of two continental driving lamps in the middle and two large fog lamps on the outside. The bar was designed to be quickly released and could also be swung out to the side, should access to the engine be needed, whilst still keeping the lamps electrically connected. It was to feature on all Abingdon cars from then on. The car also ran fibreglass Group 2 wheelarch extensions and was also fitted with a very heavy full-length sump guard.

The Gulf London was a relatively new event and, as this was only its third running, it was not possible for UK manufacturers to advertise success on the event should they win (because it was not established, it was not on the Society of Motor Manufacturers and Traders' list of accredited events). UK works entries were therefore so low-key that BMC didn't actually enter but loaned DJB 93B to Fall and Wood – but, of course, they had the use of a BMC works car all the same.

Paddy Hopkirk and Ron Crellin also entered themselves and were loaned the works Mini JBL 495D. Despite the loan of two works cars only one service barge was sent, and it proved insufficient.

The Gulf London was a very demanding rally, which circumnavigated most of Great Britain and even eclipsed the RAC Rally of the day in terms of endurance. The event ran continuously, day and night for three days, with virtually no rest stops to speak of, and only two one-hour breaks – it was the British equivalent of the Liège Rally. It was run and devised by David Seigle-Morris, who was part of the BMC works team back in the Healey days, and he was a great exponent of massive endurance rallies. The event also had the unique feature of supplying free Gulf fuel and oil to all competitors. Obviously, Gulf petrol stations were well used but in remote areas, Gulf fuel tankers were to be seen topping up competitors' cars.

The event was also incredibly fast, as Seigle-Morris had carefully devised a timing system that included 50mph stage timing within the road schedule, and with little rest, the pressure was on. The 120 starters were mainly British clubmen, attracted by the low entry fee and free fuel but it was nevertheless an international event with a large contingent from Sweden, where Gulf Oil was very prevalent. The 1200-mile route, starting and finishing near London Airport, saw the crews not turning south until they reached Kielder Forest deep into Scotland. The 300 stage miles decimated the entry down to just 44 cars at the finish.

Tony Fall was running well and in the lead in the Mini when, during the last night in Wales, he overdid it on the fast Dovey Forest and put the Mini onto its side, fortunately finishing on a grass bank, which allowed the crew to get out and push it back on its wheels; with only superficial damage, they were able to carry on, albeit no longer in the lead.

Sadly it would get worse: whilst trying to claw back lost time, and within sight of the finish, disaster struck in the Forest of Dean on the Speech House stage. Fall misjudged his speed over a narrow disused railway crossing, got the car out of sequence on the fast undulating road and dramatically rolled it end-over-end. Once the car had stopped rolling, Fall was all for continuing but it was soon obvious the battered car was going nowhere. So spectacular was the accident that a spectator had to be taken to hospital having collapsed with shock.

This brought the curtain down on one of the most used works cars.

The sad end to DJB 93B after Fall had a massive high-speed end-over-end roll on the 1966 Gulf London Rally.

Competition Record

Date	Event	Crew	Number	Overall result	Class result
Mar 1965	Swedish Rally	Rauno Aaltonen/Tony Ambrose	22	DNF	
May 1965	Acropolis Rally	Timo Mäkinen/Paul Easter	60	DNF	
July 1965	Alpine Rally	Pauline Mayman/Val Domleo	66	13th	1st
Nov 1965	RAC Rally	Rauno Aaltonen/Tony Ambrose	5	1st	1st
June 1966	Scottish Rally	Tony Fall/Mike Wood	2	1st	1st
June 1966	London Rally	Tony Fall/Mike Wood	4	DNF	

Registration Number	First registered	Chassis number	Engine	Engine number	Model
EJB 55C	March 1965	CA2S7 675795	1275cc	9F-SA-Y 35826	Austin Cooper S

EJB 55C in the UK ready to go to Czechoslovakia for the 1965 Czech Rally. Note the stays below the bumper for the lamp brackets.

This was the first new car for 1965, one of only three that year despite Abingdon still undertaking 15 international rallies during 1965 and winning the European Championship. EJB 55C, registered in March, was an Austin and was built by Jonny Evans for Rauno Aaltonen and Tony Ambrose to compete on the car's first event, the Czech Rally in July.

Built as a Group 2, 1275 Cooper S, the engine was bored 0.020in to give 1293cc, with the crankshaft cross-drilled for increased lubrication. The full-race camshaft was fitted with lightened drive gear and the compression was raised to 11.6:1 with a polished and gas-flowed Downton cylinder head. The pillars of the rocker shaft were machined down by 0.055in because of the extra valve lift.

The carburettors were twin H4SUs with float chamber extensions, and the linkage was modified to allow for a fork-and-peg operation; in addition the fuel banjo bolts were now wire-locked to the float chamber bolts.

The latest Lucas 40979 distributor was used with a large competition condenser. An MGB oil cooler was fitted with special hoses, and gone now were the core plug retaining plates – Abingdon simply gluing them in place with epoxy cement. The engine steady bar was modified by using a spacer and bolt at the bulkhead end, which allowed for easy changing of the rubber, should it fail. The bracket on the bulkhead was also rewelded for added strength.

Aaltonen used an ultra-short 4.26 diff ratio and the gearbox had special crack-tested straight-cut gears. Large-diameter driveshafts were used with special Hardy Spicer flanges and joints. The old type of gear lever was installed in preference to the latest anti-rattle mainstream item.

An asbestos shield was fitted on the lower bulkhead to keep heat away from the inside of the car from the now extremely hot exhaust manifold. All lines were run inside the car, although the twin SU fuel pump was located in the standard position under the car on the rear subframe but protected by an aluminium plate. The exhaust, now a fully skidded system, with security joints, also had the tailpipe turned up rather than being straight.

The Hydrolastic car had double-red displacers at the front and single-reds at the rear but without any dampers and with the front raised by using 2mm spacers below the struts. Unlike Mäkinen, Aaltonen was not averse to Hydrolastic suspension. The subframes were rewelded for added strength and the car also had tie-bar protection plates fitted to the front of the subframe, which were effectively just strengthening plates. The car also wore a heavy-duty sump guard fabricated by Abingdon.

The electrics were now fed by an 11AC alternator, which had a remote regulator and a race-type battery, fitted in the customary way with the terminals away from the fuel tank. There was a two-speed wiper motor with deep-throated wheel boxes, which replaced the flimsy standard Mini items. Lighting, with iodine bulbs, meant the non-dipping iodine headlights had small Lucas 576 fog lights fitted to the bonnet acting as the dipped beam, again with iodine bulbs. Three large Lucas 700 fog lamps on quick-release brackets were fitted along the bumper – all with iodine bulbs. Twin Maserati air horns were fixed externally either side of the fog lamps just below the sidelights on the lower front panel, rather than in the crowded engine bay.

Aaltonen had the use of a fibreglass bucket seat, which he had brought to the team to replace the popular Microcell bucket seats. He would also use an Irvin lap-and-diagonal belt, with Ambrose using an Irvin full harness. All the trim, glass and carpet was retained, with the addition of an asbestos mat placed under the front carpet, again used to keep heat from the exhaust out of the car. The rear bulkhead had access holes cut in to allow easy access to the top of the helper springs, should they need changing. This was easier than having to remove the fuel tanks.

The Rally Vltava, as the Czech Rally was often known, attracted 83 entrants for this round of the European Championship but it saw only 12 cars make it back to the finish, which was an indication of just how tough the 1400-mile event was. This was compounded for the crews as no service was permitted, although it didn't stop BMC having works mechanics as bystanders offering advice should it be needed. Further still, cars were allowed only six wheels and these were marked so couldn't be changed. Oddly, they could change tyres – if they changed them themselves – but not the

wheel rims. Random checks ensured compliance.

The rally was a very fast event, and with national speed limits relaxed at night, it allowed an average speed of up to 50mph on some sections. Time was therefore always short and, other than topping up with fuel and oil, there was little time to do any servicing.

Navigation on the event came in for much criticism as the described route just gave names of villages to pass through, with a supplied set of organisers' maps simply showing all the villages in Czechoslovakia. The maps, woefully out of scale, meant unless you had local knowledge or had carried out a full recce, navigation was very hit-and-miss. This was badly received, especially as it replaced a Tulip road book of the past year, the organisers only placating the competitors by

Rauno Aaltonen with Tony Ambrose corners EJB 55C hard on the Czech Rally, which they would go on to win.

Service for Aaltonen and Ambrose with EJB 55C; Bill Price supervises.

using a large number of directional arrows around the route. BMC had, of course, carried out a full recce but it was still an issue trying to locate some of the controls in larger villages.

Ahead of the crews lay 14 speed tests, including a two five-lap races around the street circuit in Liberec at the start and finish. The main route began in the evening, winding its way around the hills close to Liberec, and as night fell, the national speed limits were relaxed and the speeds increased considerably; and with damp, misty conditions, the challenge grew and many crews were already running out of time.

Only three crews would finish with no road penalties. Aaltonen would have no problems with the car, which would inevitably have caused time delays, and despite the event being based upon an out dated class improvement system the pair were still fastest on scratch. The final five-lap blast around the street circuit saw Aaltonen consolidate his lead by getting within one second of the lap record; he was back in parc fermé whilst the last cars were completing their final lap. Aaltonen won by a comfortable margin from René Trautmann's Lancia.

After the success of the Czech Rally the car was reprepared by Johnny Organ for the Danube Rally. The car was largely unchanged from the previous successful specification, the only slight alteration was that the diff ratio was changed from 4.26 to 4.133 to allow just a little more top speed at the expense of some acceleration.

After the Czech Rally there was additional strenghtening added to the rear subframe and the cooling fan was now just a four-blade rather than six.

The Castrol Danube Rally was the next event for the EJB 55C, in September, which started in Ingolstadt in Germany, traversed through to Romania and finished back in Vienna in Austria. This fast and demanding event was sponsored by Castrol (which serviced any car that requested help) and was an up-and-coming rally, which in truth was not that well suited to the Mini, largely because of the terrain. But local interest meant Abingdon was encouraged to enter and, with that, support a local driver. The two local men entrusted with

Walter Pöltinger and Kurt Schwingenschloegl were trusted with EJB 55C for the Castrol-Danube Rally. They retired before getting too far.

EJB 55C were Walter Pöltinger (an Austrian rally driver) and an Austrian speedway ace, Kurt Schwingenschloegl in the navigator's seat. This crew was part of a BMC entry that also included a Vitafoam Cooper S (AAC 853B) that Harry Radcliffe had prepared for Rupert Jones and John Clegg, and a works MGB (BRX 854B), driven by Tubmann and Stefanoff.

Service, not afforded to many on the rally, was provided by the local Viennese Austin dealership. Rupert Jones came in second overall after a superb drive against much more powerful opposition, with the MGB in 13th place.

EJB 55C failed to finish, being in trouble before the very first stage with signs of one of the infamous rubber universal joints breaking up. This meant nursing the car through the early miles in Romania until it was replaced near Brasov. However, engine maladies were soon to see EJB 55C sidelined near the Hungarian-Romanian border some 700km short of the finish. The rally was won by a BMW 1800 TiSA driven by Dr A Pilhatsch. It was tough event, which saw just 14 finishers from a field of 46 hopefuls.

For the car's third and final full event, it was converted into a Group 3 lightweight for Harry Källström and Nils Björk to use on the RAC Rally in the winter of 1965. Brian Moylan, one of the most experienced of the Abingdon mechanics, was assigned to prepare the car, which needed much changing from the Group 2 specification used on the Czech and Danube Rallies.

The engine was much the same, with 1293cc capacity, running a full-race camshaft and a high-compression cylinder head, with the diff reverting to the favoured short 4.26 ratio. The fresh engine produced 84bhp at the wheels on the Abingdon rollers. The drivetrain saw the fitment of Hardy Spicer needle roller couplings replacing the troublesome rubber couplings, which often required frequent on-event replacement.

The Hydrolastic suspension retained double-red at the front and single-red displacers at the rear, and it was again raised at the front with even more spacers, now up to 3mm, which would give the car around 10mm extra ground clearance. The new subframes were rewelded and strengthened, with the front subframe being relieved to clear the oil filter bowl.

The electrics, rewired, were largely unchanged and the lighting arrangement remained with the five-light setup, having dipped beam provided by fog lamps on the bonnet but the central fog lamp replaced with a driving lamp. The heater, very important on a cold RAC Rally, was a standard unit but had enlarged demister pipes. The pair of Heuer clocks was replaced by a single Smiths 8-day clock, largely at the navigator's preference.

But it was the body that received the most changes. Converting the shell from Group 2 to Group 3 primarily meant shedding weight, starting off with replacing all of the heavy glass with Perspex (except the windscreen). The rear side windows were rendered non-opening and the chrome-hinged frames replaced with rubber seals retaining the Perspex

Harry Källström and Nils Björk now took over EJB 55C for the RAC Rally. John Gott stands by on the ramp.

Källström stuck in a typical British traffic jam on the RAC Rally. Note the pale-colour Lucas light covers.

instead. The doors, bonnet and boot lid were all replaced with aluminium panels and the car also sprouted lovely crafted alloy wheelarch extensions to cover the wide wheels. Even the standard front grille was replaced with a lightweight offering, crafted from an Austin Westminster grille, and the chrome trim surrounding the doors was also removed. The carpets were retained and also had an asbestos blanket under the front to keep heat from the hot exhaust and manifold away from the cabin.

However, weight was added by double-skinning under the driver's footwell to prevent buckling under the pedals. The car also carried a very substantial sump guard, and skids were made up to protect the front brake hoses on the brake callipers, and the car again used front skids that protected the front tie bar location, which in turn added much strength to the front of the car. It also carried the now-normal extra padding on the door pillars, door locks and door pockets.

The RAC Rally, being Abingdon's home event, always meant it produced a strong team. This year a five-car entry was put in for the November event: two Group 2s for Aaltonen and Fall and three Group 3s for Hopkirk, Lusenius and Källström in EBJ 55C. Abingdon desperately wanted to break its duck and win the home event.

As usual, the rally received a full entry and 160 starters were flagged off from London Airport by Grand Prix driver Graham Hill, who would himself contest the RAC the following year. In front of them were 2350 miles including 58 stages in the week-long battle up to Scotland and back. The weather in the previous week had been monsoon-like and it was no surprise that as the crews headed towards the West Country the first stage was cancelled. Onward into dusk and the weather deteriorated markedly, and by nightfall the crews had entered Wales and it was snowing. The bad weather continued, and with ice and snow covering many roads, progress was often slow and perilous. It would, however, suit the Scandinavian drivers, and BMC crews were doing well.

Källström and Björk in Scotland on the route back to London. The crew retired from fourth place when the gearbox failed in the Lake District.

Källström was holding fourth place at Oulton Park in EJB 55C with some impressive stage times in Wales. Mäkinen in the Healey 3000 was leading, with Aaltonen, the eventual winner in DJB 93B, in second place. In the snow and ice, and with studded tyres being outlawed, all the cars struggled for grip, particularly in Yorkshire. But by the time the crews reached breakfast at Peebles on the third morning, Källström was up into second place.

Just over half of the now-depleted field reached Perth, before the route headed south again, where Källström held fourth place. However, it was not to last when the gearbox failed in the Lake District just after the Grisedale Forest stage, and with just seven Welsh stages to go, the car was out. Abingdon's honour was saved with Aaltonen's win and Mäkinen second. And with all the other works Minis finishing the gruelling event, it was a great result for the team.

This would be the last competitive rally for the car but it was used soon after the RAC, once it was reprepared to undertake recce duties for the 1966 Monte Carlo Rally where Rauno Aaltonen and Tony Ambrose made route notes for the team. EJB 55C was again used after the Monte when Tony Fall and Henry Liddon used the car on their recce for the 1966 Flowers Rally. Its final showing was in Strata Florida in Wales when it was extensively used for testing.

Competition Record

Date	Event	Crew	Number	Overall result	Class result
Mar 1965	Czech Rally	Rauno Aaltonen/Tony Ambrose	102	1st	1st
Sept 1965	Danube Rally	Walter Pöltinger/Kurt Schwingenschloegl	28	DNF	
Nov 1965	RAC Rally	Harry Källström/Nils Björk	37	DNF	

Registration Number	First registered	Chassis number	Engine	Engine number	Model
EBL 55C	April 1965	KA2S4 675665	1275cc	9F-SA-Y 35595	Morris Cooper S

EBL 55C, first registered in April of 1965, was the second of three new Cooper Ss delivered to Abingdon that year, this one a Morris. It was driven on all three of its events by Rauno Aaltonen, the first being the Geneva Rally in June 1965, teamed by his regular co-driver Tony Ambrose. The car was built by Roy Brown who was also lay preacher, so perhaps not the typical stereotype one would expect to become a works mechanic.

Entered as a Group 2 car and overbored by 0.020in to 1293cc, this gave the maximum capacity in the 1300cc class. And with the Cooper S now being established as a potential overall winner – and not just one hunting for the class awards – the 1300 class was very competitive, with everything being done to extract as much power as possible from the diminutive A-series engine. It was fitted with an AEG648 full-race camshaft with a high-compression Downton 11.6:1 cylinder head and twin SU H4 carburettors. The engine produced 84bhp at the wheels on Abingdon's rolling road, and it was kept cool with a four-blade fan. It was specifically noted on the build sheet that the engine had to have at least 1500 miles on the clock before the rally.

The gearbox, with straight-cut close-ratio gears, had a reported 4.2 diff ratio, and would have been achieved by the use of a 63-tooth crown wheel and a 15-tooth pinion – a most uncommon ratio for a Mini. The enlarged driveshafts had white-spot rubber couplings fitted with special GKN interference-fit nuts to the U-bolts.

The Hydrolastic suspension was fitted with yellow front displacers and double-red at the rear, with the front struts being raised by 2mm packing washers, which effectively raised the front suspension by just over 25mm. The rear was kept at the standard ride height and dampers were not used – just the standard helper springs – and to gain access (should the rear suspension need attention) the rear bulkhead had holes cut

Rauno Aaltonen and Tony Ambrose lining up with EBL 55C before the start of the 1965 Geneva Rally.

just above the shocker absorber mounting points.

Timken needle roller bearings were used in the rear hubs as these had proved more durable and easier to change than the standard ball race bearings. The front tie roads were secured by castellated nuts and split pins as these, on occasions, had been known to part company with the front of the subframe, with disastrous results. This also applied to the lock nut on the steering arms. The subframes were rewelded and strengthened at the location of the bump stops.

Brakes were kept standard other than changing the front pads to racing DS11s and the rear shoes to hard VG95 linings. The servo was retained and a higher-than-normal pressure limiting valve (at 325psi) was fitted, which shifted the brake bias.

Twin fuel tanks, with quick-release caps, were protected by plywood shields. They also had the securing straps relocated to the outside of the tank, which meant the straps were inboard. This was primarily to prevent the tanks, especially the one near the battery, from moving across the boot, should the car suffer a heavy rear side impact. The twin fuel pump, located on the rear subframe, was protected by an aluminium plate but the fuel line was run inside the car. Brake lines and the Hydrolastic lines were also run inside the car to save them from damage. The car also ran a substantial sump guard.

Inside the car, Aaltonen used a fibreglass bucket seat, whilst Ambrose had an Abingdon-fabricated high-back reclining seat. Both were cloth-covered and both crew members used special Irvin seat belts. All the carpets and trim were retained, as it was a Group 2 car. Additionally, an asbestos blanket was placed under the front carpet to keep exhaust heat out of the cabin. Extra padding was fitted to the door locks, door pockets and B-posts, which over the years had proved essential for crew comfort from the bumping around in a fast-moving rally car. Extra dash panels were fitted in front of the two crew members for the necessary switch controls and instruments plus navigation equipment respectively. Ambrose also had his door pocket divided for maps and a small additional switch panel.

Under the bonnet, the engine steady was modified with a bolt and spacer where it located on the bulkhead so that it could be quickly changed. The carburettors' float chamber bolts were wire-locked to the fuel banjo bolts for added security, and it was noted that Aaltonen asked that the speedo hole be blanked off with an aluminium plate to keep some noise and fumes out of the car.

The electrics, now with an alternator (Abingdon having seen the back of dynamos), were rewired to suit by the resident Lucas technicians. Lighting, all with iodine bulbs, featured five auxiliary lamps – two large fog lamps on quick-release brackets on the bumper, with a small Cyclops spot lamp fitted centrally on the slam panel. Two additional small fog lamps were used for the dipped beam, mounted on the bonnet, as the headlights were unable to dip, being fitted with

Aaltonen and Ambrose on the early stages on the Geneva Rally.

early non-dipping iodine bulbs. Two powerful Maserati air horns were fitted externally to the front of the grille. A two-speed wiper motor was used and Aaltonen had the dip switch changed to a column-operated version, while Ambrose had a foot-operated horn button by his feet. The crew also had the use of an intercom.

The Geneva Rally, run in early summer, was a popular event, using many of the famous Alpine climbs, and was also a round of the European Championship. However, due to several fancied crews non-starting, only 80 starters lined up to

Aaltonen and Ambrose pressing on to victory on the Geneva Rally.

The winners' trophies on EBL 55C, with Stuart Turner, Don Morley, Tony Ambrose and Rauno Aaltonen.

be flagged off in Geneva, and Aaltonen headed for a relatively unchallenged win. With an interesting handicap system, which clearly favoured the smaller cars (particularly as the route devised by the organisers was primarily on narrow twisty roads) the handicap system also allowed entrants to delete their worst timed section.

Once under way, the rally headed for France and the customary Alpine climbs. This was interspersed with often very tight road sections between the timed tests, which were traditional on this rally and, as a result, the rally was soon taking its toll. Aaltonen, however, was posting very quick times, despite the weather being wet and misty, often with fog lingering over the tops of the climbs. Once the handicap was applied Aaltonen was comfortably in the lead at Uriage, the first stop the following morning. It had been a hard night, and by the end of the day at Chamonix, only 37 cars remained.

The route ran back and forth between Switzerland and France but the second night brought better weather, and many sections were cleaned by the top crews, including Aaltonen. Aaltonen went on to retain his lead, effectively unchallenged, to the finish in Geneva and valuable European Championship points.

After the success of the Geneva Rally, Aaltonen and Ambrose were again assigned the car to take on one of Abingdon's favourite events, the Alpine Rally. The car was reprepared by Roy Brown, who again looked after the car for Aaltonen. Once again EBL 55C was entered as a Group 2 car and was largely unchanged from its Geneva Rally build.

Notable alterations were that the driveshafts were fitted with the latest Hardy Spicer needle roller joints, replacing the troublesome rubber crucifix joints, and the transmission had a slightly shorter 4.26 diff ratio. The engine was kept cool with six-blade export fan because the high climbs of the Alpine made heavy demands on the cooling system, and the sump guard was changed to a lighter version, as the Alpine was expected to be less rough. The suspension was swapped to double-red Hydrolastic displacer units to the front and rear, and the rear subframe was further strengthened. Visually, the car was also slightly different, as the auxiliary lights were changed – gone was the Cyclops spot lamp, which was replaced with a large continental driving lamp placed in line with the two large fog lamps mounted on quick-release brackets on the bumper and lower panel.

Starting from Marseille and finishing in Monte Carlo six days and some 2200km later, climbing many of the famous cols in the region, the Alpine Rally was always a tough challenge. It still attracted 93 hopefuls, of which only 32 would be classified as finishers at the end of this very fast event.

The Alpine was, in theory, only based on road time but such was the fast time schedule that many failed to get a clean sheet on the road. Average speeds in excess of 60kph over the cols were not uncommon, and with the organisers' mileage often being stretched in reality, the actual average speed required was considerably higher. There was often little time for service other than to top up with fuel. Those that didn't drop any road time were awarded a coveted Alpine Cup; only eight were awarded this year. Ties, for those on equal road time,

A new lighting arrangement on the front of EBL 55C, as seen on the car at the start of the 1965 Alpine Rally.

were decided by the 13 climbs over demanding Alpine climbs.

Aaltonen, having won an Alpine Cup over the last two years for his clean sheets, was in line for a Gold Cup awarded for three clean runs in a row, an achievement few have managed. Sadly, due to a navigational error, Aaltonen was deprived of the Gold Cup. Leaving Chamoux towards the end of the second of the two legs, he was directed by a gendarme down a road that conflicted with the BMC route notes. By the time the error was discovered and their steps retraced, they were two minutes late at the next control near Grenoble. This was particularly galling as Aaltonen had been in the top ten in all of the stages and would have finished third overall, just behind Timo Mäkinen in AJB 33B, who himself was just under two seconds behind the winning Lancia Zagato of René Trautmann.

But despite Aaltonen having to settle for 14th place, Abingdon had a very successful Alpine, winning three Alpine Cups in the hands of Mäkinen, Hopkirk and Fall. The team also won the Coupe des Dames with Pauline Mayman, and the team prize to boot.

The final event for EBL 55C was the 1000 Lakes, just four weeks after the Alpine Rally, and the car was once again prepared by Roy Brown for Rauno Aaltonen, but this time forsaking Tony Ambrose for local navigator Anssi Jarvi. The car received extra attention because of the hard landings to be experienced on the many high-speed jumps found on the fast flowing Finnish forest roads. EBL 55C remained in Hydrolastic form but the double-red displacer units were all renewed, as were the driveshafts and drive couplings. New wheel bearings, ball joints and all bushes were replaced, as were the steering arms and track rod ends. The engine was fully stripped, cleaned and checked, with most reciprocating parts renewed, such as piston rings, bearings and valves. With most of the works cars running open ram pipes on the carburettors, engines were always subject to premature wear from the ingress of dust. However, the engine and gearbox specification remained unchanged.

The lighting arrangement differed yet again, this time with the deletion of the two small fog lamps on the bonnet that delivered the dipped beam. Finnish law did not permit the use of iodine headlights, so Aaltonen, pulled up at scrutineering before the start, had to resort to standard dipping tungsten headlights, which meant he no longer needed the dipped-beam fog lamps on the bonnet. The two other team cars, for Hopkirk and Mäkinen, because they were both using British driving licences, were exempt from the iodine headlight ban, so ran five lights. EBL 55C only ran with three auxiliary lamps. There was, however, the addition of a compulsory (by Finnish road traffic law) mirror fixed to the driver's front wing. There were other additions in the shape of much advertising material placed on the cars by the organisers, which at the time was a most unusual happening.

Even the driver's fibreglass seat received extra strengthening webs welded to the frame to ensure Aaltonen didn't end up sitting on the floor of the car. Inside, the modified MGB jack would find itself located on the side of the offside rear pocket, which made finding the jack swifter and removed it from potentially damaging the tanks in the boot. Finally, the exhaust received special attention by having locating brackets welded to each joint and the jubilee clips holding up the exhaust were replaced with steel collars welded in place, such was the risk of the exhaust being torn away.

The 1000 Lakes, often referred to as the Jyväskylä Grand Prix, is a special stage event run over fast, undulating Finnish forest stages, interspersed with a couple of 'sand races' for

Aaltonen and Ambrose finished in 14th place after losing their Alpine Cup by two minutes due to a navigational error.

Aaltonen took local navigator Anssi Jarvi with him for the 1965 1000 Lakes Rally. Note the local registration plate over the Berkshire plate and the mandatory wing mirror fitted to the car.

added entertainment. Starting and finishing in Jyväskylä, the 1965 rally was a works Mini whitewash, with Aaltonen having a long battle with eventual winner, Timo Mäkinen. Despite both having a sizeable lead, there was no letting up, as both were trying to outdo each other. They led right from the start, which they were not to relinquish.

Aaltonen had eventually to settle for second place and it wasn't until towards the later part of the second half that the two works drivers took things a little easier, both sensibly deciding to save their cars, especially over the rougher sections. Privateer Jorma Lusenius in his own Cooper S had been giving the Abingdon stars a run for their money and it was only because of a tightening engine, due to overheating, that he had to slow, but still finished just ahead of Hopkirk in fifth place. So impressed was Stuart Turner with Lusenius's performance that he offered him a drive in the forthcoming RAC Rally in a works Mini. At the finish, Abingdon was rewarded with the team prize.

This successful rally car stayed in Finland and was sold to the BMC dealer in Helsinki, Oy Voimavaunu Ab, who had helped prepare the car when it arrived in Finland and supported and helped with service for the works cars.

Competition Record

DATE	EVENT	CREW	NUMBER	OVERALL RESULT	CLASS RESULT
June 1965	Geneva Rally	Rauno Aaltonen/Tony Ambrose	64	1st	1st
July 1965	Alpine Rally	Rauno Aaltonen/Tony Ambrose	56	14th	
Aug 1965	1000 Lakes	Rauno Aaltonen/Anssi Jarvi	26	2nd	2nd

REGISTRATION NUMBER	FIRST REGISTERED	CHASSIS NUMBER	ENGINE	ENGINE NUMBER	MODEL
EBL 56C	MARCH 1965	KA2S4 676062	1275CC	9F-SA-Y 35953	MORRIS COOPER S

EBL 56C was the third and last new works Mini to be registered from Abingdon during 1965. It was a Morris Cooper S and it would do more events than its two sister cars put together. It would also stay at the works for nearly two years.

Paddy Hopkirk and Henry Liddon line up for the start of the 1965 Alpine Rally.

The first event for EBL 56C was the 1965 Alpine Rally, where it was built by Mick Legg for Paddy Hopkirk and Henry Liddon as a Group 2 car with a 1293cc engine and full-race AEA648 camshaft, coupled to a high-compression cylinder head; crafted by Downton and with twin SU H4 carburettors, the engine produced 85bhp at the wheels.

A Lucas competition 40979 distributor was used, which had a better advance curve than the standard Cooper S item and also had an asymmetric cam to ease the closing of the points at high revs. Other modifications to the engine included removing 1.4mm from the rocker pillars due to the extra valve lift. The engine was kept cool with a six-blade export fan, and no thermostat was used – it was replaced by a blanking sleeve.

An ultra-short diff ratio of 4.26:1 was used, which made climbing the steep Alps and accelerating out of tight hairpin bends easier and quicker – albeit at the expense of top speed. The straight-cut close-ratio gearbox helped maintain the engine at the right rev range to give of its maximum power. The car was still fitted with the old-style direct gear lever, without the anti-rattle rubber (which was much preferred by the drivers), at the expense of some noise - which was simply dampened by placing a rubber hose over the gearstick.

Enlarged driveshafts and the latest Hardy Spicer needle roller universal joints ensured all the power was transferred to the road. The abandonment of the rubber universal joints was much appreciated by the team, as considerable service time was spent changing the unreliable rubber joints that tended to fail under extreme use.

The suspension on the car was Hydrolastic with single-red displacers at the front whilst at the rear were double-red displacers. The rear bulkhead had two access holes cut into it, just above the shock absorber mounting points, to allow quick access to the top of the helper springs should the rear suspension need attention. The front suspension was also raised by placing a 2mm packing washer under the struts, which because of the lever effect raised the front by just under 15mm. Both front and rear hubs were fitted with Timken needle roller bearings, rather than ball races, and were packed with high-temperature grease. The tie rods and track rod ends were securely fastened with castellated nuts and split pins to ensure they could not become detached.

Lighting on the car was served by five auxiliary lamps: two large fog lamps on quick-release brackets down by the bumper with a single central spot lamp up by the bonnet's slam panel. Two additional small fog lamps were fixed to the bonnet to act as dipped beam for the non-dipping iodine headlamps. The reversing light was a Healey 3000 sidelight with a powerful bulb.

To drive the high electrical demands, the car was fitted with an 11AC alternator with a remote regulator box. A pair of Maserati air horns were fixed externally, low down either side of the fog lights, replacing the puny standard horn, which was just too quiet. The wiring harness was specially made by one of the two Lucas technicians and was unique to the car, incorporating all of the specific requirements the driver had for additional switches and equipment. The main battery cable was run inside the car, and the battery was reversed with its terminals away from the fuel tank, in case the tank become dislodged in an accident. As added security, the straps holding the twin tanks were fitted inboard.

Hopkirk sat in a fibreglass cloth-covered bucket seat, with an Irvin lap-and-diagonal seat belt, whereas Liddon had the comfort of a special Abingdon-modified reclining seat with a full-harness Irvin seat belt. Hopkirk also used a Springall leather-covered steering wheel. All the trim, glass and carpets had to remain, being a Group 2 car, and an asbestos blanket was placed under the front carpet to keep heat from the exhaust at bay. This was in addition to an asbestos plate, which was aluminium covered, being fixed to the front bulkhead above the subframe to keep the manifold heat away from the cabin.

The car also had additional padding fixed to the door locks, door pockets and B-post, and both occupants had special dash panels – Hopkirk's housing a rev counter and numerous control switches, and Liddon's housing his navigational equipment, which consisted of a Halda Twinmaster and a pair of Heuer watches plus duplicated switches. Liddon additionally had his door pocket divided for maps and for an additional control panel, while his map light and a grab handle were above the door.

Brakes were uprated by using competition disc pads and brake linings, DS11s and VG95s respectively, with the servo retained and an uprated rear brake limiting valve, which changed the brake bias. The brake lines were run inside the car and a special shield was fabricated to protect the front and rear hoses from damage. Tyres were exclusively Dunlop R7 race tyres but after the event Hopkirk felt Dunlop SP3s would have been better suited due to the large amount of loose gravel on the roads.

For the Alpine Rally, Abingdon entered a full and strong team because this, along with the Monte Carlo Rally and the RAC, were the top three events in the calendar. The Alpine was a very fast event and it was, in truth, on borrowed time, with the authorities less sympathetic to cars charging around the Alps during summer months. This was compounded by the event being effectively decided on road time – in that the winner would come from the often small number that hadn't dropped any road time. No mean feat, as the high average speed, coupled with mileages that were often stretched, resulted in the average speed being much higher than published. The timed-to-the-second hillclimbs, up and down the Alps, were only there as a tie decider. Those who did clean the road section were awarded a much-prized Alpine Cup – three in a row and you got a gold one.

Hopkirk, in line for a Coupe D'Argent for three non-consecutive Alpine Cups, was one of the 93 competitors that lined up on a late evening in Marseille for the first of three sections and a 2200-mile thrash around the Alps, ending

A very travel-stained EBL 56C with the beautiful Alpine backdrop.

Hopkirk and Liddon blast off the line at the start of the hillclimb outside Die. Hopkirk finished fourth overall and won an Alpine Cup for a clean time sheet.

in Monte Carlo six days later. Along the way they were to undertake ten classic Alpine climbs against the clock, in addition to keeping to the demanding road time schedule.

The first leg to Grenoble saw Hopkirk running well – just outside the top ten but still on time on the road, despite the fuel pump failing, which being located under the car on the subframe, meant Liddon had to crawl under the car to swap the pump. Unfortunately, as the car was being fuelled at the same time, the attendant, distracted, allowed the tank to overflow and Liddon suffered petrol burns through his soaked shirt. Liddon continued on shirtless.

The second leg from Grenoble and back again, where only 39 cars restarted, had Hopkirk still on time but outside the top ten on stage time. Come the final leg to Monte Carlo, several of the top runners dropped by the wayside and Hopkirk, still with his clean sheet, was classified fourth overall, one of only seven cars to receive Alpine Cups for their clean sheets.

Just 29 cars made it to the finish, which included all of the works Minis, with Mäkinen losing out on the top honours by just 1.7 seconds from the winning Lancia. BMC also won the team prize and the Coupe Des Dames. Once again, the Alpine was a successful event for Abingdon.

For EBL 56C's next event, the 1000 Lakes in Finland just under a month later, the car was again to see Hopkirk at the wheel. This time he decided to take a local co-driver, Kauko Ruutsalo, the service manager of the BMC dealer in Helsinki, Oy Voimavaunu Ab, who would hopefully help with his local knowledge. Hopkirk had gone to race a works MGB in North America straight after the Alpine and dashed back in time for a week's practice for the Finnish event, again using an MGB.

For the Finnish event the car was reprepared by two mechanics, probably as time was short, Gerald Wiffen and Bob Wittington. It was rebadged as an Austin Cooper S for Finland and it was also fitted with an obligatory wing mirror on the driver's side, required by local traffic laws. The car was also much adorned with advertising supplied by the organisers, so looked quite different from the Alpine Mini.

The engine and gearbox specification remained unchanged, and the rebuilt unit now punched out 86bhp on the Abingdon rollers. The suspension, renewed all round, was also the same as for the Alpine. No other changes were made to the car other than being extensively rebuilt by replacing most reciprocating parts to ensure reliability – especially as the 1000 Lakes is notoriously hard on the cars with its many jumps through the high-speed forests.

All was not well at scrutineering in Jyväskylä, just before the start, when the car was initially thrown out because it was illegal to run iodine headlights in Finland. However, a tribunal – convened on the spot – ruled that cars from outside Finland could have any lighting system that was legal in their country, which meant Hopkirk (and Mäkinen – but not Aaltonen) with a British driving licence, in a British registered car, could run iodine headlights. So the car was permitted to start with its five auxiliary lamps and powerful headlamps, which had been changed from the Alpine Rally – gone now was the single small spot lamp high up on the slam panel, now replaced with a large driving lamp positioned low down by the bumper with the two large fog lamps.

Always popular, the 1000 Lakes attracted a field of 126 starters for what was mainly a very fast three-day stage event over closed forest roads, with a couple of spectator stages in the shape of a few laps of a sand track plus a slalom test. The slalom test was just up Hopkirk's street, being an expert at driving tests (autotests) and a past champion in Ireland. Despite high speeds in the forests, adherence to the speed limits away from the stages was rigorously enforced by the police.

Hopkirk, with his local navigator, put in a very impressive

Hopkirk with local navigator Kauko Ruutsalo used EBL 56C on the 1000 Lakes. The car now an Austin Cooper S and with a revised lighting setup. Note also the mandatory (for Finland) wing mirror.

Kicking up the loose surface found in Finland, which is like running on small ball bearings. They finished in sixth place despite shooting off the road backwards.

Hopkirk and Liddon retained the car for the 1966 RAC Rally, where it reverted to a Morris Cooper S.

performance, as the rally had always been won by Scandinavians; outsiders were never expected to do well. Hopkirk's stage times were very respectable but he couldn't match those of Mäkinen and Aaltonen, who were brought up on these roads. Hopkirk finished a creditable sixth overall, despite going off backwards and hitting one of the many huts that adorn the Finnish forest. Breaking the rear window and denting the fuel filler, the crew had to construct a temporary cardboard rear window to keep out the exhaust fumes. Hopkirk was nevertheless the first non-Scandinavian home and Abingdon was rewarded by Mäkinen winning, just ahead of Aaltonen, and also by winning the team prize.

After the 1000 Lakes, EBL 56C was thoroughly rebuilt once more, now being converted into a lightweight Group 3 car by Bob Whittington. Again it was for Paddy Hopkirk and Henry Liddon, this time to tackle Abingdon's home event, the RAC Rally. The rebuilt engine was much the same specification as in the car's previous two events, being a 1293cc engine running a full-race cam with a 11.6:1 high-compression Downton cylinder head with twin SU H4 carbs. The gearbox was again straight-cut and close-ratio with a 4.26 diff ratio, running enlarged driveshafts and Hardy Spicer needle roller universal joints. Power was recorded as 83bhp on the rolling road.

Visually, the first notable change was the car reverted to being a Morris Cooper S once more, having been an Austin in Finland. The work involved in making the car a lightweight included replacing all the heavy glass, except the laminated front 'screen, with Perspex and the rear side windows were non-opening with just a rubber seal in place. The bonnet, boot and doors were replaced with aluminium skins, as was the front grille, this being replaced with a lightweight mesh, fabricated from the front grille of an Austin Cambridge. The car also now had fabricated-aluminium wheelarch extensions to cover the wide steel wheels. However, the car retained its trim and carpet – probably in the interest of crew comfort. Also new on the RAC car was the addition of a roof lamp, operated from inside the car and placed over by the co-driver's door. At the rear of the car, for the first time, the boot lid was additionally secured by the use of a Moke bonnet rubber, where previously the boot catch itself had been modified.

The suspension, all renewed again, was the same specification as the 1000 Lakes build, with Hydrolastic double-red and single-red displacer units front and back. The new subframes were additionally welded along all of the seams and had strengthening plates added where the rear bump stops hit. The front subframe was also cut to clear the oil filter bowl, which made changing it easier and quicker with the sump guard in place.

The floor was double-skinned under the driver's feet to prevent it from buckling under the throttle pedal. The exhaust also received special attention, now with two exhaust boxes, which had skids welded to the underside and all the joints and locating bars welded to the joints to prevent the exhaust being torn away. It was also held onto the car with welded steel clips rather than Jubilee clips. All lines were run inside the car but the fuel pumps remained outside on the subframe, protected from damage by an aluminium plate.

The RAC Rally that November, being the UK's premium rally and last round of the European Rally Championship, attracted 162 starters for the 2350-mile route around Great Britain, which included 400 stage miles, nearly all 58 stages

Henry Liddon checks the marshal's time as he clocks into a control on the RAC Rally, ensuring his road book is correctly signed.

Hopkirk at Oulton Park stage where his racing experience stood him in good stead. Due to numerous mechanical issues, he finished in 13th place.

being on forest roads. With just one night in bed – once reaching Perth some 48 hours later – the rally was a massive challenge that saw just 62 finishers. The severe weather was largely responsible for decimating much of the field. Abingdon entered five Cooper Ss, four of which finished, with Aaltonen winning outright.

Setting off from London Airport to the West Country in wet weather saw Hopkirk going well, with the conditions soon deteriorating once in Wales, where snow and ice greeted the crews on the journey northwards. Half of the field had fallen by the wayside by the time the cars arrived at Perth. The snow and ice meant that the Dunlop SP44s, without studs, were struggling to cope. Abingdon even tried to cobble together makeshift snow chains from dog leads. On the very icy Pickering stage in Yorkshire, Hopkirk was the first car through and had to be helped uphill by spectators, such was the difficulty in gaining any traction on the ice.

Hopkirk had a troubled rally, with a catalogue of woes along the way. Near the Scottish boarder a tie-rod nut became detached from the subframe, with the result that the front wheels became independent of each other. Fortunately it happened just 50 yards from the end of the stage where spectators had gathered – and very soon an appropriate nut was removed from a willing spectator's car, who in turn had to wait for the BMC service crew to fix his car. This problem of the nut detaching itself had been well known, and as such Abingdon always fitted castellated nuts and a spit pin in place of the common Nyloc – inexplicably, the split pin must have been lost and the nut turned itself off.

More was to follow when, nearing the end of the Loch Achray stage, the engine lost oil pressure; on stopping, a split oil cooler was found. Topping up with oil, they continued, only for the oil to continue to be lost. Fortunately the oil cooler was bypassed and a very co-operative Ford works service crew topped up Hopkirk's engine.

With most of the rally behind him and with all his delays, Hopkirk checked into the Devil's Bridge time control in Wales just minutes from exclusion, only to have a driveshaft coupling begin to fail. It eventually broke on the Pantperthog stage; fortunately the ever-attentive BMC service crew replaced the joint in double-quick time and Hopkirk was able to continue, trouble free, to finish a rather lowly 13th place.

After the RAC Rally, Hopkirk and Liddon were dispatched to France in the car during December, to carry out their first recce for the Monte Carlo Rally in mid-January 1966. However, the RAC car was to prove unreliable as the crown wheel shed its teeth, probably due to the driveshaft failure on the RAC, putting undue strain on the crown wheel. The car was left in Geneva and a new gearbox and diff were fitted in time for Hopkirk and Liddon to return just after Christmas to complete their second recce. They found much snow and ice in the Alps, which they hoped would suit the Minis on the rally in a few weeks' time but they were not looking forward to the prospect of running an effectively a standard Group 1 car on the event.

After the rigours of the RAC Rally and the previous 1000 Lakes Rally, a new EBL 56C was seen on the 1966 Geneva Rally for Tony Fall and Henry Liddon in June 1966. This time the car was a Group 1 1275 Cooper S, entered in the showroom class and built by Bob Whittington. This class, under the new rules, meant 5000 identical examples of the car had to have been built and to be unmodified in almost every way. With Abingdon still smarting from its exclusion on the Monte Carlo Rally, the car was meticulously prepared within Group 1's very restrictive regulations.

CHAPTER 3: THE MK 1 MINI COOPER S

A new Group 1 EBL 56C appeared for the Geneva Rally for Tony Fall and Henry Liddon.

Fall, in the Group 1 car with its skinny wheels and just two extra lights, sweeps past the vineyards

A rear shot of the car showing the small Austin Healey sidelight used as a reversing light, the clear view rear window and Moke rubber toggle securing the boot lid.

The engine was fitted with the Cooper S's standard AEG510 camshaft and twin 1¼ SU carburettors. The engine was kept down to 9.75:1 compression and everything was kept to standard, although all parts were carefully selected. The clutch diaphragm, an orange rally clutch, even had the orange paint rubbed off. Straight-cut gears were used, as they had been homologated; the diff ratio was 4.1 to help acceleration, and the car used Hardy Spicer couplings on the enlarged driveshafts.

The car ran a standard exhaust system and even a single fuel tank – the right-hand tank being removed and the filler blanked off. The Hydrolastic suspension had double-blue displacers at the rear and single-blue displacers at the front but all had rubber covers. The rear suspension was further fitted with Aeon bump stops, with standard helper springs.

The electrics reverted to a dynamo, with the coil fitted in the standard position on top. Just two additional lamps were used on the badge bar-type lamp bar, which now replaced the brackets fixed to the bumper and front panel. The headlights had the latest dipping iodine bulbs, meaning the offending dim-dip system used on the Monte Carlo Rally, which caused so much trouble, was no longer needed. To cap all of the standard fitments, the car ran on narrow 3½J wheels but had the use of Dunlop R7 race tyres as well as Dunlop SP3s.

The Geneva Rally was a relatively short rally with just two legs: one to the north and west of Geneva and the second, after a day's sleep, a more interesting route to the south and west, which included many of the favourite Alpine passes. The event was designed to favour Group 1 cars, as the result was to be decided on a handicap system and not on scratch times, as many rounds of the European championship now were. The road timing for Group 1 cars had a more generous time allowance, and the three hillclimb selectives were there only as a tie decider. Abingdon therefore entered Fall, fresh from winning the Scottish Rally, in a very standard-looking Group 1 car. As predicted, the first six places went to Group 1 cars but this didn't detract from a rally-long battle Fall had with eventual winner Gilbert Staepelaere in his semi-works Lotus Cortina, finishing in a well-earned second place overall. BMC further won the team prize and two class awards; Fall, however, had to settle for second place in his class.

For EBL 56C's next event, the Czech Rally in July, a virtually unchanged car for local crew Sobieslaw Zasada and Zenon Leszczuk was prepared again by Bob Whittington, still as a Group 1. The specification and build details were unchanged from the Geneva Rally other than the car now had twin tanks.

Local crew of Sobieslaw Zasada and Zenon Leszczuk took the Group 1 EBL 56C on the Czech Rally and rewarded Abingdon with a fine fourth place.

Tony Fall with EBL 56C, still in Group 1 trim, on his recce for the German Rally.

The Castrol Danube Rally saw EBL 56C as a Group 2 car for Tony Fall and Rupert Jones leaving the Ingolstadt start in Germany.

This did cause a stir at scrutineering, as the twin tanks were due to be homologated on 1 July, the start date of the rally, and, as it was still only 30 June, head-scratching ensued – but common sense prevailed and the twin tanks stayed. Sobieslaw Zasada, the Polish Rally champion, had been given the seat by Stuart Turner as he had been impressed with his superb driving for Steyr-Puch, so he had hopes of him doing well for BMC too. Zasada was teamed with Aaltonen and Mäkinen, both of whom had Group 2 cars at their disposal.

Starting and finishing in Prague, the route on often tight and twisty lanes wound a 1500-mile circular path around the city. With 26 time controls, 14 special stages and high-average-speed road sections, it was all that was needed to sort out the winner. Two of the special stages were regularity races, both at the start and finish of the rally at the Prague Strahov Sports stadium. Zasada, in the Group 1 car, put up very impressive times on the track, coming fifth. Out into the late afternoon, the tight twisty stages began. Zasada was going well and on the fourth stage got within four seconds of Mäkinen's high-powered Group 2 car.

With no speed limits in force at night, three very fast and long road sections were next – 60 miles, 55 miles and 50 miles in length – over twisty and often gravel-covered roads and through small villages. Zasada remained clean but few did, and 20 were forced into retirement. More stages followed into the following day, with Zasada still within reach, posting times generally in the top five.

The following night saw more high-speed road sections, with even more retirements, then more stages with Zasada still on Aaltonen and Mäkinen's heels. The final regularity race, where competitors had to beat or equal their first race times, saw Zasada finish a remarkable fourth place overall and also gave BMC the team prize. One wonders what might have been if he'd had been given a Group 2 car to drive.

After the Czech Rally, the car was quickly pressed into use again for Tony Fall to do a recce for the German Rally at the end of July, still in its Group 1 guise. This would be the last time EBL 56C would appear as a Group 1 car.

The Danube Rally in September was the next event on the agenda for EBL 56C, crewed by Tony Fall with Reverend Rupert Jones in the co-driver's seat – no mean driver himself; the car was now upgraded to Group 2. The Cooper S had fibreglass wheelarch extensions covering its wide steel wheels and ran four auxiliary lamps along the front, as well as those twin tanks, plus with a much more modified and powerful engine. The car was sponsored by British Vita.

As the Castrol Danube Rally was not a round of the European Championship, works entries were minimal but Abingdon took the opportunity to send Fall to Ingolstadt to gain knowledge of the event, as the following year it would be a round of the European Championship. The depleted entry of 40 starters set out on the four-day event, which was a mixture of tarmac and gravel roads where tyre choice was to prove paramount. Apart from navigational difficulties because the crew hadn't been able to complete a full recce of the 2800-mile route, the lone British crew was forced to retire through lack of tyres – the service car being nowhere to be seen. Just 11 crews made it to the finish in Wien; the winner Walter Pöltinger was in his own VW 1500.

The final event for EBL 56C was the 1966 RAC Rally, when this rather well-used car was once again pressed into service. With BMC's eye on the ladies' prize, the car was handed to Rauno Aaltonen's sister, Marjetta, who had been relatively successful in her native Finland driving a Saab 96. She was paired with Caroline Tyler as her co-driver, who it was hoped would be able to impart some local knowledge, as she was an experienced competitor in the UK.

Abingdon assembled eight works Minis for its home event, all Group 2 cars and all, for the first time, fitted with roll cages. These cages, supplied by Simplex (latterly to be taken over by John Aley), were made from alloy and not steel, to save weight. They were a simple hoop over the B-post, behind the crews' heads, with a back stay going onto the rear parcel shelf; over the years, they would prove a valuable addition to crew safety. This was no more so than the entry on this RAC when Simo Lampinen rolled JBL 495D comprehensively in Wales but was able to drive on, thanks to the roll cage – albeit into retirement, with a badly bent car.

The RAC engine in EBL 56C, fresh for the event, was overbored 0.020in to give 1293cc, with the compression raised to 11.4:1, the cylinder head being modified by Downton and fed by twin SU H4 carburettors. The significant change to the engine (from the normal Group 2 car) was the fitting of a standard Cooper S camshaft – the AEG510 rather than the normal full-race AEG648. This was in an attempt to get more low-down torque for the anticipated muddy conditions. Cliff

Marjetta Aaltonen (Rauno Aaltonen's sister) and Carolyn Tyler took over EBL 56C for the 1966 RAC Rally. This is the first time a roll cage was fitted to a works Mini.

Servicing of EBL 56C. It can be seen that the car has a 'piggy back' additional wiring loom laid above the Group 1 standard loom.

The girls finished in 37th place as Aaltonen took time to get used to British forests tackled without pace notes.

Humphries, who now looked after all of Abingdon's engine work, had carried out some development to keep the power loss for this camshaft change down to an acceptable 12bhp less than the normal 85bhp. The car ran Abingdon's usual 4.26 diff, had a lightened steel flywheel and a competition clutch, with a close-ratio straight-cut gearbox.

EBL 56C now had a heated front 'screen for the expected cold weather and it also ran a full detachable grille muff. The electrics on the car, having been a Group 1, had two front looms: the standard pattern loom with an additional loom piggy backed above it to serve the requirements of the extra electrical equipment, such as the four extra lamps along the front of the car. The car ran an alternator, despite it still retaining its dynamo regulator box on the inner wing, which was a hangover from its days as a Group 1 car – the regulator simply serving as a jointing box.

A special competition exhaust was fitted with two boxes and stronger mounting points. Needless to say, a very strong sump guard was added and the subframes were strengthened and rewelded. The car ran Hydrolastic suspension with all lines inside the car, and the twin fuel pump was located under the rear seat. The car ran on Dunlop SP44 tyres, other than for the two tarmac stages, where Dunlop R7s were used.

As the rally was sponsored by the *Sun* newspaper, the customary large numbers on the doors were replaced by large orange roundels, representing the *Sun*, with small competition numbers on the bottom. This caused a deal of confusion as it became difficult to read the small door numbers once the car became mud-splattered, so much so that some cars started to appear with improvised numbers on their doors.

The 1966 RAC Rally was a mammoth event and matched, if not exceeded, any continental rally of the day, other than perhaps the Acropolis in Greece. With over 400 stage miles, mostly on forest roads, the route covered most of the United Kingdom. Starting from the Excelsior Hotel at London Airport, it headed for the West Country before going through Wales, the Midlands, Northern England and up onto Scotland before turning round at Aviemore, after a night in bed, to journey back down the east side of the country to the finish back at London Airport some five days and 2400 miles later – and all with just one night's sleep. The event attracted 144 hopefuls to the start; just 63 made it back to London for the finish.

Marjetta finished well but had a couple of off-road excursions, fortunately without mechanical damage, or much loss of time. As there were no spectators visible when going off, she started to yell for help, which rather alarmed her co-driver Carolyn Tyler – but it worked, and spectators soon came running through the forest and helped them back to the road. Being more accustomed to her Saab, the Mini had taken her time to get used to and driving on the often-twisty British forest roads was new to her – she being more familiar with the fast flowing Scandinavian forests. So after a relatively uneventful five days, Marjetta finished in 37th place but outside the top ladies' prize – that being won, not unsurprisingly, by Pat Moss.

The car was sold to British Vita in July 1967, which had looked after the car on the RAC and also supported the car on the Geneva Rally earlier in the year. British Vita was a long-standing works-assisted racing team run by Brian Gillibrand, who went on to rallycross the car, occasionally with Paddy Hopkirk.

Competition Record

Date	Event	Crew	Number	Overall result	Class result
July 1965	Alpine Rally	Paddy Hopkirk/Henry Liddon	60	4th	2nd
Aug 1965	1000 Lakes	Paddy Hopkirk/Kauko Ruutsalo	22	6th	
Nov 1965	RAC Rally	Paddy Hopkirk/Henry Liddon	8	13th	2nd
June 1966	Geneva Rally	Tony Fall/Henry Liddon	75	2nd	2nd
July 1966	Czech Rally	Sobieslaw Zasada/Z Leszczuk	16	4th	1st
Sept 1966	Danube Rally	Tony Fall/Rupert Jones	25	DNF	
Nov 1966	RAC Rally	Marjetta Aaltonen/Carolyn Tyler	117	37th	

CHAPTER 3: THE MK 1 MINI COOPER S

Registration Number	First registered	Chassis number	Engine	Engine number	Model
GRX 5D	Jan 1966	CA2S7 820483	1275cc	9F-SA-Y 39689	Austin Cooper S

GRX 5D was one of four new cars built for the 1966 Monte Carlo Rally. GRX 5D was also to become the most used works Mini of all time, competing in no less that eleven international rallies spanning 27 months. It was additionally used on five recces during that period. Needless to say, with all that hard work, it received several bodyshells over that time.

For its first event, GRX 5D was meticulously prepared as a Group1 car for Paddy Hopkirk and Henry Liddon for the 1966 Monte Carlo Rally. For the 1966 event the organisers had decided, in their infinite wisdom, to heavily penalise Group 2 cars by some 18 per cent, with the view of allowing private competitors in standard, less-modified cars a better chance. All that happened, of course, was that factory teams soon realised that a Group 2 being heavily handicapped could not win, so inevitably they all prepared Group 1 cars. This in effect left the majority of private competitors rather stuck with their now rather uncompetitive Group 2 cars.

BMC's task, together with that of other manufacturers, was also made more complicated because 1 January 1966 heralded the introduction of new regulations that governed what could or could not be done to a car to compete within the various groups. These regulations were not published until August 1965 with the proviso that clarifications would follow, which entailed many exchanges of documents between the various manufacturers and the FIA, which governed motorsport.

A vast list of questions was forwarded to the governing body in the intervening months to ensure the cars were prepared according to the new rules. This was further complicated, if not already, by the rules being exclusively in French and, despite translations being made available, the French text had precedence over the translations. Nevertheless, after many discussions, scrutiny and several visits to the FIA in Paris, Stuart Turner from BMC, Henry Taylor from Ford and Marcus Chambers from Roots had all satisfied themselves that they understood just what the new rules entailed. So preparation at Abingdon got under way in late 1965 to build three identical Group 1 Mini Cooper Ss, one of which was GRX 5D.

With the strict new Group 1 rules much in everyone's mind and with the rules effectively ever-changing due to clarifications, it resulted in several false starts in the preparation of the car. Nevertheless, the standard 1275 engine was meticulously assembled, with everything perfectly matched and balanced but not lightened in any way. The camshaft selection was the new-to-production AEG510, which gave good low-down torque plus good top-end power and was well suited to a standard engine, especially as the cylinder head was unmodified. With standard twin 1¼ SU carburettors and standard exhaust manifold, the power achieved of around 67bhp was considered acceptable, albeit 20bhp down on a Group 2 engine.

Cooling, not so much a problem for the Monte Carlo Rally, was served by the now-standard 16 fins-per-inch radiator and a 16-blade fan. Additionally, to keep things warm, a grille muff was fitted around the grille moustache. An oil cooler was installed with special heavy-duty hoses, the engine had a thermostat, and the core plugs were bonded in place with epoxy glue.

Fortunately, a straight-cut gearbox had already been homologated for Group 1 use, along with a desirable short diff ratio of 4.133, which would make climbing the cols much easier. The new-to-production larger driveshafts were also used, coupled with solid Hardy Spicer couplings, replacing the rather unreliable rubber couplings. This was a risk, as the 5000 production target had yet to be reached for homologation into Group 1.

Despite the relatively low power of the engine, the car was still fitted with Ferodo racing DS11 disc pads and

GRX 5D, car 230 being prepared for the 1966 Monte Carlo Rally at Abingdon. Paul Easter talking to the mechanic, Gerald Wiffen with Lucas Racing's John Smith on his right. The car was to be driven by Paddy Hopkirk with Henry Liddon.

WORKS MINIS IN DETAIL

Paddy Hopkirk and Henry Liddon in the rather standard-looking Group 1 GRX 5D.

Service stop for the car. The very standard-looking engine with dynamo regulator and small carburettors clearly visible.

VG95 brake shoes – such were the demands put on the brakes because of left-foot braking favoured at least by the Scandinavian drivers.

Hydrolastic suspension was fitted to the car but with export heavy-duty single-red and double-red displacers front and back. The suspension was raised slightly with 0.01in packing washers, and it was also stiffened slightly by using heavy-duty bump stops, which attempted to reduce the customary Hydrolastic suspension pitching, experienced under hard acceleration and deceleration. Other mandatory standard items that needed to be fitted were 3½J wheels in deference to the wider 4½J wheels, which were still just an option – as was the right-hand fuel tank, so only the standard left-hand tank could be fitted. This in itself was to produce refuelling logistical problems for the team, with such a short range of the car only 5½ gallons of fuel on board. All fuel, brake and battery lines remained outside the car but all were protected with metal conduit. The fuel pump was also retained on the rear subframe but covered by an aluminium skid plate.

The problem of Group 1 restrictions was probably felt just as much inside the car, as standard Mini seats had to be retained, which meant no bucket seat or comfortable reclining seat for the navigator. Instead, the standard seats had slip-over Karobes rally seat covers, and the only departure from standard was the fabrication of a larger removable headrest for the co-driver. However, it was permitted to fit safety padding to the door pockets, door locks and B-posts, which was customary for works Minis. The team was also permitted to fit additional dash panels for instruments and navigational equipment.

With the maximum number of auxiliary lights being restricted to just two extra lamps, under the new Group 1 rules, the demands on the electrics were lower than normal. However, even the electrics were not immune from the Group 1 regulations restrictions in that the standard wiring loom had to be retained although an additional loom alongside was permitted.

Nevertheless the car was, as always, completely rewired by one of the two resident Lucas competition technicians. It was fitted with a dynamo rather than an alternator, as this too was another Group 1 requirement – but with only the heated front windscreen as the other high-consumption addition, it was considered acceptable. This nevertheless had its power consumption reduced from 14amp to 5amp by having only the driver's side operational. Despite this an uprated 28amp unit and regulator was fitted.

In an attempt to get the maximum from the restrictive lighting on the car, Lucas devised a dim-dip system for the quartz iodine single filament headlights. This involved providing a large rheostat that was fixed to the front bulkhead near the master cylinders, which allowed the headlamps to be dimmed when the dip switch was operated. The alternative was for the dip switch to simply extinguish the headlights and have the dipped beam provided by the two auxiliary fog lamps. The driver could select, by the use of a three-way switch on the dashboard, which he preferred. History will show this was the car's undoing.

For this 35th running of the Monte Carlo Rally, between 14 and 20 January, the Minis were expected to do well and BMC's hopes were high in achieving the Monte hat-trick, following Paddy's 1964 win and Mäkinen's in 1965. This year's route contained, for the first time for many years, no tests from the nine starting points on the route down to Monte Carlo. It was hoped this would ensure a maximum number of cars that would actually make it to Monte to support the hoteliers and restaurants. Stuart Turner had selected different starting points for each of his four Minis, with Hopkirk starting from Warsaw, favouring an Eastern Bloc start as he did 1964. This would dictate an easterly journey down through France, and only 15 cars elected to start in Warsaw – which proved not to be an inspired choice, as they had to battle through heavy snow and blizzard conditions once they had left.

At the various starts on the Friday were 192 cars, of which 171 would arrive safely in Monte Carlo. The route down was relatively undemanding (albeit with a good deal of snow in Poland and Yugoslavia) but was nevertheless in marked contrast to the 1965 event when only 28 cars actually made it to Monaco in time. This year, few lost time and most arrived in good time on the Sunday evening. Facing them the following Monday morning was a 24-hour dash to Chambéry and back – over 900 miles and including six special stages, which 88 crews completed within time.

The leading 60, after a night's rest in Monte, then tackled the mountain circuit on the Wednesday night, with another 380 miles and six special stages. Thursday morning saw the victors descend once more onto the seafront of Monte Carlo after a total of 155 stage miles over the two loops.

Hopkirk was to finish the common route, up to Chambéry and back, in fifth place, which considering the problems he had was a good result. On the 30-mile Col du Granier stage, a wrong tyre choice hampered his progress. Running quite a way down the running order, the packed snow for the front runners (in particular for Mäkinen running number at number 2) meant using full chisel-stud tyres. Unfortunately, by the time Hopkirk went through, this hard-packed snow had turned to powder and his tyres were woefully unsuitable. Matters got worse when the car developed a misfire, resulting in no power below 4000rpm. A quick plug change on the road section failed to cure the problem – fortunately and mysteriously, the misfire went away a while later.

Dissatisfied with his tyres, he removed the front chisels and replaced them with short pop-in studs. This proved to be a disaster as the car oversteered wildly due to such poor grip on the rear compared to the front. This resulted in a huge amount of very sideways motoring and the inevitable happened: Hopkirk clouted the scenery. In the circumstances, to be just over three minutes adrift of Mäkinen's lead, on his return to Monte Carlo Tuesday morning, was a good position.

Back in Monaco, rumours had already surfaced that the officials were questioning the legality of the headlights used by the works Minis (and other British contenders) and an official notice was posted to that effect. After many discussions, all the cars in question were released to attack the mountain circuit on Wednesday evening.

The mountains north of Monaco were mostly covered

The Mini as always dominates in the poor snow and ice conditions where Hopkirk and Liddon initially finished in third overall until disqualified.

in hard-packed snow, and with a clear night, temperatures plummeted. Hopkirk was running well and was seven minutes up on his road time when he visited the service area in Saint-Sauveur for fuel, to adjust his rear brakes, inspect his pads and change tyres. But before he was due to leave it was discovered that his head gasket had failed... Doug Watts quickly threw a can of Wondarweld into the radiator and sent him on his way. The car continued and still recorded stage times in the top six.

Back in St Sauveur for the second time, still with time in

Hopkirk powering out of a hairpin bend. The blanked-off right-hand tank can be seen. The extra tank, at that time, was not homologated for Group 1. It was a struggle with just a small single tank.

The abortive attempt by Tony Fall and Henry Liddon on the 1966 Flowers Rally, which unusually required a number painted on the boot lid. They were excluded almost before the start when the air filter element was found to be missing from the air box.

GRX5D still as Group 1 car took Timo Mäkinen and Paul Easter to a class win on the 1966 Tulip Rally. The narrow 3½ J wheels and just two extra lamps were the order of the day. The car still retained its Austin grille but was now badged as a Morris Cooper.

hand, a vibration was reported by Hopkirk but it only proved to be a loose sump shield. The head gasket was still dripping water but it got the car back to Monaco in a strong third place, behind Aaltonen and the storming Mäkinen.

Once in parc fermé, the officials, having posted yet another notice regarding the potential illegality of the Minis' headlights and their dipping system, proceeded to take the cars apart in an attempt to find something that contravened Group 1 regulations. After Nobby Hall had spent eight hours stripping the car and the officials weighing and measuring everything, nothing was found. Then, with a tape measure, an official proclaimed that Hopkirk's front track was too wide – which, after further examination with the car reset at its correct ride height, showed to be correct. So in the end it was just down to the headlights. Ultimately, the officials prevailed, deeming the single-filament bulbs used by the Minis were not as manufactured (which, of course, was a twin-filament bulb) and therefore the entire team was disqualified. Citroen was the beneficiary and declared winner – in a car that was over nine minutes behind Mäkinen.

BMC, however, gained more publicity from the exclusion, and the public support and condemnation was huge. The cars were flown back to England and shown on *Sunday Night at The London Palladium* TV show at the weekend, to huge patriotic chants. But it still left a very unsavoury taste in everyone's mouth.

The Flowers Rally, the following month, was another event that was to favour a Group 1 car. However, the Automobile Club of San Remo, somewhat oblivious to the fallout from the Monte Carlo Rally, had stuck to its guns and told all entrants that the top three cars would all, after the event, be taken away and stripped to check compliance with the latest Group 1 regulations. Abingdon, having had its cars already put through very rigorous scrutineering, just reprepared the car – and of course changed the offending headlights – and sent Tony Fall and Henry Liddon on their way to San Remo. The car was almost identical to the Monte specification, complete with narrow wheels and one fuel tank. The only distinguishing feature was the competition number being painted onto the top left side of the boot lid.

Their recce did not go well. Fall was practising the route, on one particular 50km section that was tightly timed and would be used on both directions (at different times, of course). Unfortunately, pressing on very hard, he encountered Pauli Toivonen in his works Renault practising coming the other way. Both took evasive action, but Fall had no choice than to leave the road of his side, Toivonen having no escape on his side. The result was that Fall rolled the car, four times, down a steep bank and was only stopped by some stout trees preventing an even worse accident. The car was a mess; it was GRX 55D.

The rally itself would serve Fall no better. The first part was an easy run up to Alexandria, then onto San Remo in the afternoon to assemble for a ceremonial restart. Sadly, Fall found himself unceremoniously excluded. Upon routine inspection of the cars at the San Remo restart, from the various starting points, the organisers discovered that the paper element was missing from his car's air filter box. The element was actually in the car, having been removed by the service crew during carburettor adjustment. Despite Fall's offer to refit the air cleaner, the organisers were having none of it. Two exclusions for the car on the trot was not a great record.

For the car's next event, it returned to the hands of Mäkinen and Easter, this time to tackle the Tulip Rally in April. GRX 5D was still in Group 1 trim, with its narrow wheel rims, single fuel tank and just two auxiliary lamps, but as Mäkinen was at the wheel, the car was badged as a Morris, albeit it still retaining its Austin front grille. Mäkinen drove only Morris cars due to a personal contractual arrangement with the BMC importer Voimavaunu back home in Finland. Mäkinen had lost the toss with Aaltonen, as to who would drive the faster Group 2 car on the rally – Aaltonen being the beneficiary, with Mäkinen stuck in the Group 1 car.

The Tulip Rally, starting in Noordwijk on the Dutch coast, was still a favourite with many amateurs, largely because of the generally good fast tarmac roads used for the numerous hillclimbs the event was famed for, but was now being contested, in good numbers, by professional teams, especially as it counted towards the European Championship.

To appease the works teams, the unpopular class improvement handicap system was axed, with the results being based on scratch times in each capacity class; however, each class would also have separate amateur awards to keep the privateers happy.

At the start in Holland were 116 crews lined up for a 1750-mile four-day route journeying through Luxembourg, Belgium and France, and as far south as Geneva and back to Holland. With good weather and just 18 tests of 55 miles of special stages on offer, including a lap around the Zandvoort race circuit, it was power that decided the outcome, with Aaltonen picking up the winner's laurels. Mäkinen, in the underpowered Group 1 Mini, was having a trouble-free run until the car started to burn copious quantities of oil, which meant Easter having to frequently clean oiled-up spark plugs in addition to constantly replenishing the car with oil. Nevertheless, they came home a very creditable ninth overall and won the class by the narrowest of margins of just seven seconds from Bengt Söderström in a Lotus Cortina.

Post-event scrutineering consisted of spot-checking three cars, one of which was Mäkinen's. It was swiftly passed, the organisers having little appetite for the scrutineering disputes experienced on other events, notably the Monte. BMC went away contented with the good results, having also won the team prize.

After the Tulip Rally, the Group 1 car undertook numerous recce duties for much of the year. The first was in May 1966 when Tony Fall and Mike Wood used it for their recce of the Acropolis Rally. This was followed by Tony Fall again, but this time with Henry Liddon to do a recce of the Geneva Rally in late May. The car was again used in late July for Rauno Aaltonen and Henry Liddon for their recce of the Polish Rally in early August. Finally, Tony Fall again got his hands on GRX 5D with Henry Liddon in late August for a recce of the Alpine Rally in September. Sadly, this would result in a coming together with a Renault Dauphine and the Mini was effectively sidelined.

For the car's next event, GRX 5D was presented as a Group 2 car for Timo Mäkinen and Paul Easter to compete on the RAC Rally, and here it changed to being a Morris Cooper S for Mäkinen's contractual arrangement. It is quite likely the car was a new build for this important event, where Mäkinen was seen as one of the favourites to win. Eight works Minis were prepared for their home event, all Group 2 cars.

Mäkinen and Easter with the winners' tulips always given to the crews. They finished ninth overall in addition to winning the class.

The RAC engine in GRX 5D, fresh for the event as always, had a capacity of 1293cc with the compression raised to 11.4:1; the cylinder head was modified by Downton and fed by twin SU H4 carburettors. Mäkinen insisted on running a full-race camshaft, in deference to all the other works cars, which for the RAC ran standard AEG510 camshafts (incidentally, Mäkinen's car did not have a roll cage, unlike all the others, which for the first time had John Aley-manufactured alloy cages). GRX 5D ran Abingdon's usual 4.26 diff, had a lightened steel flywheel and a competition clutch with a close-ratio straight-cut gearbox.

Tony Fall and Henry Liddon again had problems on their recce, this time for the Alpine Rally, when they came together with a Renault Dauphine on the road with the resultant damage to both cars.

Mäkinen and Easter in GRX 5D set blistering times and were leading until succumbing to engine and then transmission problems.

GRX 5D was now converted to a full Group 2 car for Mäkinen and Easter for the 1966 RAC Rally. Here are some of the BMC Mini crews. From left to right: Marjetta Aaltonen (Rauno's sister), Rauno Aaltonen, Timo Mäkinen and Simo Lampinen.

Somewhere in a Welsh forest Mäkinen and Easter crash through the rough track. The car survived but the engine and gearbox did not.

Mäkinen also decided not to run a heated front 'screen for the expected cold weather but did have a full detachable grille muff to keep the cold and wet out of the engine and to help raise the engine temperature.

The car ran four extra lamps along the badge bar lamp bracket, and featured an alternator with a separate regulator fixed to the front bulkhead. It also had headlamp washers, and front-facing mud flaps fitted to the front bumper corners to try and keep mud off of the headlights. In fact, they proved troublesome as they partially blocked to airflow to the overworked front brakes. Also seen for the first (and likely only) time on a works Mini was a piece of leather-cloth protecting the small bonnet release aperture; the distributor was generally protected from the elements by fixing an aluminium plate behind the grille but water could still get in by the bonnet release, hence the flexible cover, which was fixed to the grille moustache with three screws.

A special competition exhaust was fitted with two exhaust boxes and stronger mounting points, and the subframes were also strengthened and rewelded. Fuel, brake and the battery line were run inside the car and the twin fuel pump was now safely located under the rear seat out of harm's way. Dunlop SP44 tyres were used, other than for the two tarmac stages, where Dunlop R7s were fitted; being a Group 2 car, fibreglass wheelarch extensions were added to cover the wider 4½ J steel rims.

Protecting the engine and gearbox was a new Scandinavian sump guard constructed of spring steel, which was lighter and stronger than the very heavy guard of the past. With the front of the guard extending up the front panel to the bumper, it meant the fitting of quick-lift jacking brackets to the leading edge of the sump guard, with additional channels welded on and painted white so they could be easily identified when servicing at night. Nevertheless, Mäkinen still managed to bend the guard and break the back of the gear extension.

The 1966 RAC Rally was, as always, a challenging event, with over 2400 miles and 67 stages coving 400 miles, nearly all on loose-surface forest roads. The route covered most of the United Kingdom. Starting from the Excelsior Hotel at London Airport it took in the West Country, Wales, the Midlands, Northern England, then up into Scotland and Aviemore for the one-and-only night in bed. From Aviemore the field journeyed down the east side of the country, taking on Kielder Forest and the fast Yorkshire stages and eventually back to London Airport, to the finish five days later.

At the start were 144 crews but only 63 would make it back to London. A reported 1,000,000 spectators turned out to watch the event, no doubt boosted by the event's sponsor, the *Sun* newspaper.

Roger Clark in a works Lotus Cortina took an early lead but his swift demise heralded Mäkinen taking fastest time on most of the early stages. This was repeated through Wales and into the Lake District and onto Scotland where he held a comfortable six-minute lead at the night halt in Aviemore. More than 50 crews had by now retired, after what had been over 50 hours of non-stop motoring. After the restart Mäkinen's car was soon in trouble – first needing to have a tie-rod replaced, and at service the car was tipped onto its side to attend to the gearbox remote, which had been damaged due to the sump guard's extension plate working loose. The sump guard was also beaten straight, so rough had been the many bolder-strewn Scottish stages.

Mäkinen was still leading at Dumfries but was now complaining of low oil pressure and transmission noise, which was diagnosed as transfer gear bearing problems. The car nearly succumbed in the notorious Kielder Forest, when Mäkinen arrived at the finish with the rear brakes on fire after a wheel cylinder had burst – but he still set the fastest time. But it was not to last, as the car was by then nursing a cracked sump and needing lots of oil.

The car eventfully retired after 51 stages, with only 16 to go, having set 26 fastest times. GRX 5D now had no clutch and no drive – after the transfer gears failed – and a very sick engine. The RAC Rally win had again eluded Mäkinen, and he hitched a lift back to London, consuming a bottle of whiskey on the way, to drown his sorrows.

After the RAC, with the 1967 Monte Carlo Rally looming, the car was rebuilt and used extensively for practice and tyre testing for this most important rally for Abingdon. Tyres being of utmost importance, Dunlop was actively involved in developing special SP44 tyres for the forthcoming rally. Timo Mäkinen and Paul Easter also used the car for their recce and it was again utilised as an ice note car on the event.

GRX 5D (with GRX 555D in the background) receiving attention whilst tyre testing for the 1967 Monte Carlo Rally. Henry Liddon looks on as the BMC Westminster service barge attends to the car.

Easter at the wheel of GRX 5D pulls out of a time control whilst Mäkinen sleeps in the reclining seat.

For the car's next competitive event, the 1967 Circuit of Ireland, GRX 5D was handed to Paddy Hopkirk and Terry Harryman for this Easter weekend classic in March. It is very likely, after the severe battering the car sustained during the RAC Rally, that it was replaced rather than rebuilt. Now a full Group 2 car with a very powerful 1293cc engine, and despite the Circuit of Ireland being almost entirely on tarmac (albeit rather bumpy tarmac), the car was again fitted with a heavy-

Paddy Hopkirk with Terry Harryman took GRX 5D on the 1967 Circuit of Ireland. Here at the Gallaher factory start in Ballymena.

Hopkirk and Harryman came through numerous problems to win the Circuit of Ireland, this being the fifth Circuit win for Hopkirk.

duty sump guard. It also used lightweight magnesium Minilite wheels, first seen on the Monte Carlo Rally in January.

Seeded at number 1, in a field of 94 cars, Hopkirk set off on Good Friday evening from the start near Ballymena in Northern Ireland for an all-night thrash. This year, the 1500-mile rally was held in atrocious weather with rain, gale-force winds and, in places, snow, making the tight, twisty lanes even more challenging. Hopkirk, however, was straight on the pace and at breakfast in Carlow after nine stages, he had a comfortable lead. Very tight road timing between the stages meant the pressure was relentless. To discourage servicing, most stages also had a time control near their finish, resulting in very little time to attend to ailing cars. Further, practising had been specifically excluded, all in attempt to make it easier for private entrants.

Disaster nearly struck Hopkirk at the end of the second day in Killarney: when leaving the last stage, he took a wrong turn, being misdirected by the garda, and as the fuel pump ticked crazily away, he promptly ran out of fuel – fortunately right outside a petrol station. With the tight road timing, Hopkirk just made it to the final control with only two minutes in hand.

The circular Sunday run of 300 miles and 14 stages back to Killarney saw snow on the hills and, with that, Dunlop SP44s were the order of the day rather than R7s. By good fortune, BMC had taken along a set of studded tyres, which Hopkirk made good use of as he extended his lead further still. Again, the snow continued for the next day over to Sligo where Hopkirk continued his dominance. Where others were sliding off, he, apart from a minor graze to the car, extended his lead. The final day, with 12 more stages back up to Larne in Northern Ireland, saw Hopkirk ease back slightly. Still with a comfortable lead, he was the clear winner. And with his fifth win on the Circuit of Ireland under his belt, he quickly departed to the USA to take part in the Sebring races, leaving Harryman to pick up the trophy. GRX 5D had run faultlessly throughout.

GRX 5D's next event, still as a Group 2 car, was the Tulip Rally a month later at the end of April. The car was rebuilt and handed to David Benzimra, and again Terry Harryman occupied the co-driver's seat. David Benzimra was a director and son of the managing director of Benbros Motors, which was the BMC importer in Nairobi, East Africa. Benbros Motors had been particularly helpful to Abingdon when Rauno Aaltonen competed on the East African Safari Rally – the first and only time a works Mini contested this formidable rally. Its reward was the use of a works Mini for the Tulip Rally.

The Circuit of Ireland car had its heavy-duty Scandinavian sump guard removed and replaced with a much lighter, short 13-hole guard just covering the front of the sump, supplemented with a Moke sump plate screwed to the bottom of the gear casing. The battery guard, spanning the rear subframe, was also removed. All this weight-saving was sensible because the Tulip Rally was an all-tarmac event and not considered a rough event. Otherwise, the car was very similar to how it appeared in Ireland.

The Tulip Rally was a popular event with many British crews, being relatively easy and with the innovative Tulip road book, using diagrams to describe junction turns, which is now universally used for nearly all rally road books. The event is no longer run with the class improvement system but now, to fall in line with the majority of European events, is run on scratch times – meaning, basically, the fastest wins.

The 1967 version consisted of 18 timed-to-the second tests and all bar two were classic hillclimbs. These tests were interspersed with numerous timed selectives with a bogey time to beat, mostly set at 45mph. The 2000-mile route went

CHAPTER 3: THE MK 1 MINI COOPER S

Terry Harryman was again in GRX 5D for the 1967 Tulip Rally where David Benzimra would be his driver. Benzimra was a director of Benbros Motors, a BMC importer in Nairobi, East Africa, which helped Abingdon with Aaltonen's East African Safari entry.

Benzimra had not competed on any tarmac rallies and the Tulip was probably not the best to start with but he was nevertheless accrediting himself well.

Frozen water run-off that turned to ice, caught out many on one corner, including Benzimra who planted GRX 5D against a rock face. He retired with clutch problems, having been in the top ten.

from its start at Noordwijk on the Dutch coasts, into Belgium, Luxembourg, then to the mountains of western France to arrive at Annecy for a 12-hour stop. The route then returned back to Noordwijk via a three-hour stop at Rumilly on a northern route, mirroring the outward-bound southern path. Heavy snow before the rally had meant some rerouting, which rather cut some of the rally's competitive content, particularly near Annecy. Undeterred, 108 starters lined up on a bright sunny Monday morning to take on what was offered.

Benzimra was competing in his first tarmac rally and the first time using racing tyres, so he was rather thrown in at the deep end, but was soon to surprise everyone with his fast and consistent pace. He was never too far from the top ten and was even cleaning some of the tests. With a high-calibre entry, not the least of which with Mäkinen and Aaltonen in brand-new cars plus a good smattering of works Porsche 911s to contend with, his performance was very creditable. As it would turn out, the Porsche of Vic Elford won every stage except two and came out the winner.

Benzimra did not bring back his trusty workhorse unscathed, however, as he, like so many others, succumbed to a very icy corner in the Croix Fry tunnel, which was encountered on the night section out of Annecy. A left-hand bend, in the middle of the tunnel, had a cascade of water across the road, which had frozen just before the apex. Benzimra, like many others, understeered off and straight into the waiting rock face, bending the entire offside of the car, and then lost three minutes while he and Harryman changed a punctured wheel.

Sadly, despite his best efforts, Benzimra would not finish the rally: just two tests from the end and lying well up in his class, he had the misfortune to lose his clutch. Despite all the BMC mechanics' best efforts of pouring cola over the clutch, it refused to work and the car was sadly retired. Abingdon honours were upheld, however, with Mäkinen and Aaltonen coming first and second in the touring car class, and second and third overall.

After the rather severe body damage inflicted on GRX 5D on the Tulip Rally, it is unknown if this car was used again. It is more likely, as its next event was to be the Scottish Rally, a non-European Championship round and a notoriously rough event, that rather than build a new car, another works car was used for Tony Fall and Mike Wood on this rally. It should be noted that the car had changed from a Morris Cooper S to an Austin Cooper S since the Tulip Rally and the number plate now appeared as a square plate on the right-hand side of the bonnet, which tends to support the notion of a new or swapped car. Nevertheless, an immaculate GRX 5D was presented at Blythswood Square in Glasgow on 4 June.

GRX 5D returned to being an Austin Cooper S for Tony Fall and Mike Wood to do the 1967 Scottish Rally, seen here at the Blythswood Square start in Glasgow. The car would soon retire with a dropped valve before the first stage.

Tony Fall and Mike Wood would use GRX 5D again, unchanged for the Gulf London Rally. Route organiser David Seigle-Morris ensures Fall doesn't leave the start before his allotted time.

Because of the congested competition timetable, with the Scottish being sandwiched between the Acropolis Rally and the Geneva Rally, this was the only works car entered by BMC in Scotland. Further, the car was prepared by the special tuning division, managed by Basil Wales, which was conveniently situated next-door to the competition department at Abingdon. This group's aim, however, was different from the comps department as it dealt with the preparation of private entrants' cars and existed primarily to manufacture and sell competition parts to the public. Special tuning was to have its hands full on the Scottish, as it had also prepared and was looking after cars for Lars Ytterbring and Jerry Larsson – both very quick Scandinavian drivers.

Taking place in early June, the Scottish was a challenging five-day rally with 66 mostly forest stages in the four legs. The crews had the first night out of bed, where the meat of the rally was undertaken, consisting of 35 stages in 800 miles. The other three legs were in daylight, with a night in bed and a party in the evening.

It was indeed a popular event. Ninety-six cars lined up for the Sunday afternoon start, which headed out for the long run towards Dumfries. Starting at number 1, in recognition for his win the previous year, Fall's car soon objected to this rather long road section and promptly dropped a valve, which instantly holed a piston and he was out on the spot. It was the first of what would be numerous retirements on this rough event. Special tuning's hopes were further dashed when during the night Larsson cracked open his sump and also into retirement. However, Ytterbring saved blushes by coming home in a fine second place behind Roger Clark's Ford Lotus Cortina.

With a freshly rebuilt engine, GRX 5D was again rolled out, this time for the Gulf London Rally. The car was little changed from its abortive and short attempt on the Scottish three weeks prior. Tony Fall and Mike Wood would again take the wheel for what was a very long, hard and challenging rally.

The event was envisaged by David Seigle-Morris, once an Abingdon works driver in the Healeys, where he had the aim of putting on a rally just like the Liège Rally – long, tough and unrelenting. The event, which started at Manchester Airport, ran continuously for three nights and three days, with just one three-and-a-half-hour rest and two short one-hour stops. During that time, 2000 miles with 61 forest stages of 500 miles were on offer. Only 120 cars were accepted because the rally was not designated as a 'trade supported event' by the Society of Motor Manufacturers. This meant a restricted size of entry; it also meant, more significantly, that (in theory at least) entrants could not be from a motor manufacturer and had to be private entries – so works service had to appear a little low key.

The rally had another attraction for the 120 hopefuls: being sponsored by Gulf, free fuel was available to all entrants. It also attracted 40 Scandinavian entrants, who were encouraged by Gulf to enter, and free entries were supplied to many as previous awards.

On Tuesday evening of 27 June, the first car headed off for a long all-night anti-clockwise loop around Wales, with 18 stages, before heading to the Forest of Dean for another three stages, completed by lunchtime. It was then up to Oulton Park for a rest stop, early the following evening. Fall was fast on these early stages, being second fastest on the third stage, Clocaenog 1. He was fifth on the next, and a fourth on the final of the five Clocaenog stages. Many cars were experiencing punctures with the dry, dusty summer conditions in the forests, and Fall was not immune, receiving a puncture on the Machno stage and finishing on the rim – but not before winning the Betws-y-Coed stage.

He was second fastest on the next two stages, then suffered a very time-consuming puncture on the next stage, the 30-mile-long Dyfi, where he collected a puncture very early on but pressed on regardless. Thanks to the very strong Minilite wheels, he finished the stage with practically nothing of the wheel rim left.

He made up some of the lost time by claiming fastest time on the very next stage, Pantperthog. However, once again he came unstuck, this time in the Crychan Forest stage when he flew off the road and lost five minutes getting the car back onto the track after becoming entangled in some wire fencing. Once untangled, the car slid backwards into a ditch – it was the only thing holding it back – and more time was lost. Fortunately, the car was not badly damaged.

There was much activity at the service area once the car arrived at Oulton Park for the welcomed rest halt. Fall went to a local hotel for a hot meal, bath and some sleep. With Fall and the car refreshed, he headed to Penrith and the Lake District some four hours later. It was to be a long drag up the motorway in mist and rain. Many crews were thankful for the welcome sight of the Gulf fuel tanker dispensing free fuel after so many miles – the third free fuel stop for the crews. It was now well into the next night and Fall recorded third fastest on the Dodd Wood stage.

Into South West Scotland and it all finally came to an end for Fall, just as dawn broke, where on stage 29, Dalbeattie, he slid wide and side-swiped a tree on the offside, which deranged the rear suspension and bodywork; and although the car was driven out, it was too badly damaged to continue.

It was a sad end to a great challenge, overcoming numerous time-delaying punctures and excursions. He hadn't yet completed half of the route. Many others also fell by the wayside, and just 47 cars made it back to Manchester Airport on Friday lunchtime. Honours went to Ove Andersson and John Davenport in a works Lotus Cortina. The Gulf London, now sadly no more, was one of the greatest challenges.

The ninth event for this much-used car was the Marathon de la Route, held in late August. For this event, which was a cross between a race and a rally (more correctly it was a regularity event on a racetrack), the car was assigned to a three-driver team, as they would have to drive continuously for three-and-a-half days and nights around the Nürburgring. Tony Fall would again use GRX 5D, teamed with Julien Vernaeve and Andrew Hedges. Hedges was an experienced racing driver who was a regular partner to Paddy Hopkirk with MGs at Le Mans, Sebring and Targa Florio.

After the severe damage inflicted on the car on the Gulf London Rally, the GRX 5D that was prepared for this next event was a different car and it is probable that the bodyshell was an 850 Mini. There was an absence of chrome surrounds to the doors and the rear side windows were non-opening but it did bear reference to having an Austin Cooper bonnet

The Gulf London Rally was a tough event around much of the UK and was attractive to many as Gulf issued free fuel to competitors. Fall and Wood relished the relentless and demanding route.

Another GRX 5D bites the dust. Fall planted the car against a very stout tree and into retirement from a strong position, despite numerous off-road excursions and punctures with the car.

A three-driver team of Julien Vernaeve, Andrew Hedges and Tony Fall would share the driving of the regularity endurance race around the Nürburgring.

Another GRX 5D appeared for the 1967 Marathon de la Route. The car is displayed with its sister car and transporter in the UK before departure. GRX 5D was fitted with a 970S engine.

Andrew Hedges at the wheel of GRX 5D, clearly displaying the very large oil cooler and auxiliary radiator. The one-litre car would win the class and finish a fine second place overall.

badge. The car was built more as a race car than a rally car, befitting the event ahead. The engine was built as a 970S, bored 0.040in to give 999cc – just within the maximum capacity for the up-to-one-litre class. The inside of the car was devoid of much trim, with the rear seat removed and the exposed metal covered in red Rivington thin carpet. Perspex windows were fitted, replacing the heavy glass. Padding was applied to the driver's door pillar, door lock and pocket pad only. Outside, the car's appearance was quite striking: a clear view was fitted to the rear windscreen and the front laminated 'screen had an electric heater bar fitted by the driver's side to help keep it clear.

The bumpers were removed, the fixing lip taken off the front panel and the rear covered in a rubber tube. To aid identification, two lime green flashes were painted on each corner on the front panel. A large 16-row oil cooler was fitted prominently where the grille once lived. It also ran an auxiliary radiator alongside the oil cooler. Two large air holes were punched on the lower panel by the oil filter, also to help keep things cool.

The car ran four auxiliary lamps: two Lucas 576 spot lamps and two fog lamps but fitted where the grille moustache was fitted – all to allow as much uninterrupted airflow to the engine.

Quick-lift jacking points were fitted but painted red, rather than white as they customarily were. Quick-release Aston petrol caps were added to help speed up refuelling. Large white roundels were painted onto the bonnet and doors rather than the usual white door squares. The bonnet was held fast by two Moke rubber toggles, and the number plate painted low on the bonnet where the Austin badge was once fitted.

The bonnet also had a short Perspex insect deflector on the driver's side. The car was indeed very distinctive.

The format for this rather complicated event was to see who could travel the furthest within the three-and-a-half days around the race circuit. Each class had its own target time for one lap, and provided they did that time, they were credited with one lap; if not, no lap was credited. One-litre cars were allowed 18 minutes to complete each 17.5-mile lap. To allow for refuelling, an extra three minutes every 12 laps were allowed, and for periodic servicing, an extra ten minutes every 75 laps were allowed. Further still, in darkness, an extra two minutes per lap were allowed. If any car was more that 30 minutes late on one lap, he was excluded; likewise if a car had accumulated 60 minutes' delay. Yes, it was complicated, but Peter Browning was not only the BMC competition manager but also and accredited RAC time keeper, so he was well placed to keep a careful watch on progress.

Browning had entered GRX 5D in the up-to-one-litre class as its target lap times were more generous than the 1300 class, and he was also hoping that poor weather at night, for which the Eifel Forest was renowned, would equalise the car's lack of overall speed. An MGB would not be able to match cars in the two-litre class.

As it transpired, only one night was foggy. The event started, with the pretence of a regularity event, at Chaudfontaine, some eight miles from Liège, and then onto the Nürburgring 80 miles further on (some even got lost or broke down on this road section). Three-and-a-half days later, they drove back to Chaudfontaine. The flag fell at the Nürburgring at midnight. The schedule was that each driver would do a three-hour shift at the wheel and then take a six-hour break.

GRX 5D ran more or less faultlessly the entire time and, other than a short delay with a wheel bearing change, which proved difficult to replace after two-and-a-half days' motoring. The car was generally restricted to 5000rpm to preserve the engine, which proved sufficient to lap within its target time. The team consistently lapped two-and-a-half minutes below their target time to ensure any slight problem would not result in a lost lap.

After 12 hours the team was up to fifth place, and as the days wore on and the car kept going, others retired for numerous reasons and progressively the car made its way up the leader board. With problems hitting the leading Porsche, GRX 5D found itself in the lead with just 14 hours to go. However, the hard-charging Porsche was soon clawing back the lost time, and in the end, the Mini had to settle for second place. It consumed just ten tyres and covered 316 laps, the equivalent of some 5500 miles on the 17.5-mile lap. The trio justifiably won the one-litre class and were second overall behind a works Porsche 911, which was in the end only 12 laps ahead after three-and-a-half days' racing.

The next event for this car was the Tour de Corsica, held on the island of Corsica in early November. Often called 'the rally of 10,000 corners' and renowned as being a very fast, tight, twisty rally using narrow mountain roads that were slippery and potentially dangerous. Because of the threat now being faced by Abingdon from more potent cars, it needed to build a very powerful and lightweight car to stay in touch with the Porsche 911, Alpine Renault and now Lancia with the Fulvia – which meant a Group 6 car.

Therefore Brian Moylan built a very powerful and lightweight Cooper S for Paddy Hopkirk and Ron Crellin for this demanding rally. The power came from a 1293cc engine fitted with a full-race camshaft and a high-compression Downton cylinder head, which gave 12.6:1 compression ratio – just as much as the engine could take. The engine was coupled to a straight-cut close-ratio gearbox with a 4.2:1 final drive and straight-cut drop gears. As it transpired, this low ratio proved far too high and Hopkirk never got into top gear, and said a 5:1 ratio would have been more suitable.

As the car was entered in Group 6, it was free to fit a large 45DCOE Weber carburettor, adding slightly more top-end power than the customary twin SU H4 units fitted when in Group 2. On Abingdon's rolling road, the car produced 104bhp at its wheels.

An ongoing issue with a highly-tuned Cooper S engine was keeping the engine cool, so the car ran a small front-mounted radiator on the right-hand side behind the fog lamps. This could be switched on or off as required. It also had an 1100 radiator, which was a little taller and wider, so a small bulge had to be let into the bonnet and the inner wing was pressed out inside to clear it. An 11-blade fan was used and an overflow expansion tank fitted inside the car by Crellin's feet.

To save as much weight as possible, the car was devoid of bumpers and chrome trim around the doors; all of the glass, bar the front laminated windscreen, was replaced with Perspex. The bonnet, boot and doors were made of aluminium and internally, the rear seat was removed and covered in lightweight carpet. The headlining was also removed. Despite the extra weight, four auxiliary lamps were fitted with steady bars to the central lamps, connected with a quickly removable rubber plug and socket fitted below the headlamp. The car carried forward-facing front mud flaps and wheelarch extensions.

A Moke sump guard was used but with the addition of

GRX 5D was now produced as a Group 6 car for the Tour de Corsica. The window stickers show the car was perhaps used on the Marathon de la Route. The bonnet bulge is for the enlarged radiator to clear the bonnet. Knock-off Minilites were also used.

Paddy Hopkirk and Ron Crellin settling into GRX 5D before the start of the Tour De Corsica. This is an 850 bodyshell and the Bowden cable for the makeshift Group 6 mandatory twin-braking system can just be seen by the starter push.

A bothersome journalist interrupts Paddy Hopkirk as he waits for Ron Crellin to get his time card stamped on the Tour de Corsica.

Overheating problems caused by defective fan belts saw the early demise of GRX 5D (and sister cars), which caused much embarrassment to Abingdon. Just visible here are the air ducts to the front brakes.

an alloy plate extended to protect the gearbox. The remote shift was fitted with a Mitchell mounting and the floor strengthened accordingly. The subframe seams were all rewelded and double-skinned top and bottom with extra steel blocks welded to the rear radius arm brackets. Hydrolastic suspension was fitted but with the addition of Koni adjustable dampers (set at their softest setting) just to the front. This had proved beneficial to stiffen up the suspension when it was used for the first time by Hopkirk on the Southern Cross Rally the previous month. Another first for the car was the fitting of Minilite wheels with knock-off spinners, which – in theory – makes the numerous tyre changes as quick as possible, as the Dunlop race tyres using were lasting under 90 miles before they needed changing.

The front brakes had asbestos blocks inserted into the front callipers to keep as much heat away from the fluid as possible, and for the same reason the rear wheel cylinders where held in place by threading the boss rather than using a circlip. In addition the backplates were drilled, as were the brake drums to allow extra cooling. And to help cool the front brakes, ducts were cut into the front skirt to allow in extra air. To comply with Group 6 regulations, the car also had to have a twin braking system. This was made possible by a makeshift method of using a Bowden cable to the handbrake (which operates the rear brakes) off the brake pedal. This was sufficient to satisfy the scrutineers and, once passed, was quickly unadjusted so as to not affect the rear brakes.

In rainy conditions, the rally started at Ajaccio on the west coast of Corsica on Saturday evening and would be a 22-hour non-stop race back to Ajaccio. Ninety-eight cars headed off for 800 miles of tight, twisty roads, intermixed with 80 miles of four timed-to-the-second stages. Fortunately, all of the roads were tarmac and they were closed to other traffic but with an average speed of nearly 40mph throughout, it meant many would retire simply because they ran over their one-hour allowable lateness.

A short run to the first 15-mile stage saw Elford's Porsche record a time of just over 18 minutes. Hopkirk was going well, albeit not in the top six, but was already in trouble with the engine overheating and the knock-off Minilites coming loose. This was to happen twice, and on one occasion, the wheel jammed on and they couldn't change it. The overheating also got worse, despite stopping to top up the hot engine with water from a stream. At service, where they had just two minutes to change tyres, the fan belt was found to be loose, so was tightened. This had meant the water pump had not been properly driven, nor had the alternator.

Once tightened, he set off again but the problems persisted and yet again the fan belt was tightened. This also meant that not only was the engine running very hot, the lights were also fading as the battery ran down, so Hopkirk was having to use just one spot light in the poor conditions. Hopkirk was now losing lots of time. The problem was not solved, and shortly Hopkirk was out with a completely flat battery and a very hot engine – he had not made it through the night. Only 14 cars would arrive at the finish, and the event was won by Sandro Munari in a Lancia Fulvia. This heralded the shape of things to come, as the days of Mini dominance were now mostly over.

Once the car was returned to Abingdon, the fan belts were sent to Ferodo for examination and it was discovered they had come from a faulty batch. This was little embarrassing for Browning, who had to explain to the BMC management that the retirement was due simply to a failed fan belt.

A new GRX 5D appeared in June 1968 for its final event for Abingdon. This would be the car's 11th event, to be driven in Canada by Paddy Hopkirk on the Shell 4000 Rally. This was a very technical rally, requiring accurate distances and times to be recorded, which meant Hopkirk used experienced

CHAPTER 3: THE MK 1 MINI COOPER S

Mike Kelly checks his Halda, which was driven off of the rear wheel for accuracy, as Hopkirk collects the time card at Fort William checkpoint.

GRX 5D now appears as a Mk2 Cooper S for the Shell 4000 Rally in Canada. Paddy Hopkirk took local navigator Mike Kelly with him, being experienced in this very technical rally.

local co-driver Mike Kelly as his navigator. The entry was supported by BMC Canada.

GRX 5D appeared as a Mk2 Cooper S, due to the Mk1 being phased out in October the previous year; the Mk2 was mechanically identical to the Mk1, the changes being simply cosmetic: the front grille, rear lights and badges were revised, the rear 'screen was 6cm wider, plus the interior trim was now in black vinyl.

For the Shell 4000, the car was built as Group 2 by Tommy Wellman and was very distinctive in appearance owing to its very large forward-facing front mud flaps. It was also fitted with a pair of MGB reversing lamps low down on the boot lid.

Another addition to the car was a Halda distance recorder driven off of the rear nearside wheel, which was last seen on a works Mini on the 1961 Monte Carlo Rally. This was fitted to eradicate inaccuracies in distance recording due to the front wheels spinning. Other small changes from the Mk1 cars was the fitting of slightly wider wheelarch extensions, which in turn were painted red rather than left black.

The Shell 4000 was often known as the Cross Canada Rally, it being 4000 miles from the start in Calgary and finished six days later in Halifax – making it one of the longest rallies in the world. Run between 1 and 7 June, the event was unlike European rallies but was tough all the same, being a very complex regularity event. It was interspersed with ten very fast and long stages through military locations, forest reserves and national parks, all of which were timed to the nearest second and required the co-driver to leap out and punch the time cards to record the times.

The rally stopped at the end of each day and restarted the next morning, making it a rather fragmented and stop-go event. The entry was varied amongst the 69 starters, many of which were in big-engined American cars, and these were the fancied top runners. However, each of the six classes had their stage times multiplied by a coefficient to try and even out the power advantage that the large-capacity cars had on these fast open stages.

Hopkirk started at number 119, the starting order drawn by lots within classes, and he headed off in the evening for the only night section. Hopkirk would clean the road section and would arrive on time in Regina the following evening in the lead. But he was in trouble with the car, as it was overheating badly. In an attempt to cure the problem, the car appeared for the restart the next morning, for its 900 mile section to Lakehead, with a spare Mini radiator (complete with its own mesh protection grille) fixed onto the lamp bar on the front of the car. This had the desired effect and Hopkirk continued to

GRX 5D sprouted an additional front radiator to try to cure severe overheating problems. The scrutineers were not impressed and Hopkirk was disqualified whilst in the lead.

show that the Mini was a match for the big American-engined cars and stayed in the lead.

At the end of the leg in Lakehead, the organisers questioned the legality of Hopkirk fitting the second radiator to his car. Continuing on, still in the lead, into the third day, the organisers consulted the homologation forms and decided the radiator was illegal but allowed Hopkirk to continue for the fourth day whilst they consulted other manufacturers and then put in a call to the FIA in Paris for guidance.

Eventually, at the end of the fifth day, after much procrastination, they reached their decision and Hopkirk was disqualified. The unseasonably dry road meant 55 cars arrived at Halifax in the evening of the seventh day, with the winner being Scott Harvey in a 4.7-litre Chrysler Barracuda. It was a sad end to the competition career of the most used, if not the most successful of all works Minis.

The car was sold to Press Steel Fisher, where it was used by the apprentices to autocross, then acquired by Bob Freebrough.

Competition Record

DATE	EVENT	CREW	NUMBER	OVERALL RESULT	CLASS RESULT
Jan 1966	Monte Carlo Rally	Paddy Hopkirk/Henry Liddon	230	disqualified	
Feb 1966	Rally of the Flowers	Tony Fall/Henry Liddon	15	disqualified	
April 1966	Tulip Rally	Timo Mäkinen/Paul Easter	100	9th	1st
Nov 1966	RAC Rally	Timo Mäkinen Paul Easter	12	DNF	
Mar 1967	Circuit of Ireland	Paddy Hopkirk/Terry Harryman	1	1st	
April 1967	Tulip Rally	David Benzimra/Terry Harryman	73	DNF	
June 1967	Scottish Rally	Tony Fall/Mike Wood	1	DNF	
June 1967	Gulf London	Tony Fall/Mike Wood	8	DNF	
Aug 1967	Marathon de La Route	Tony Fall/Julien Vernaeve/Andrew Hedges	39	2nd	
Nov 1967	Tour de Corsica	Paddy Hopkirk/Ron Crellin	79	DNF	
April 1968	Shell 4000	Paddy Hopkirk/Mike Kerry	119	disqualified	

REGISTRATION NUMBER	FIRST REGISTERED	CHASSIS NUMBER	ENGINE	ENGINE NUMBER	MODEL
GRX 55D	JAN 1966	CA2S7 820482	1275CC	9F-SA-Y 39688	AUSTIN COOPER S

Rauno Aaltonen and Tony Ambrose pose by their brand-new GRX 55D prior to their start in Athens for the 1966 Monte Carlo Rally.

The second of the three new cars to be built for the 1966 Monte Carlo Rally was GRX 55D, assigned to Rauno Aaltonen and Tony Ambrose as an Austin Cooper S. Like its sister cars it too was prepared to standard showroom class as a Group 1 car.

The new FIA rules governing the cars came into force on 1 January 1966, so the regulations were as yet untested, and this resulted in much head-scratching by all manufacturers. Stuart Turner spent days poring over the French text to establish what could – and more importantly could not – be done to the cars. It was all too much for Saab, which decided to pull out of the Monte.

The decision to run in Group 1 was taken early (as soon as the Monte regulations were published) as the organisers, in an attempt to encourage private entrants back to the event, decided to handicap Group 2 cars (a regulation under which most works cars were built) by inflicting stringent time penalties. However, it backfired, as most manufacturers decided, not surprisingly, to enter standard Group 1 cars, as it was clear that a Group 2 car could not win the event.

So it was that GRX 55D was prepared and built as a

virtually standard car. But to do so, the new car was completely stripped of all of its components and fastidiously rebuilt, checking and matching everything to get the very most from the homologated standard Group 1 specification.

The 1275cc engine was balanced but not lightened, and fitted with standard twin 1¼ SU carburettors, an unmodified cylinder head, standard production exhaust manifold and the latest AEG510 camshaft. This new camshaft was ideally suited to the virtually standard engine and gave good power yet proved very tractable at low revs. With the compression ratio fixed at 9.75:1 the engine produced 67bhp at the wheels and was mated to a straight-cut close-ratio gearbox with a usefully short diff of 4.133 – both of which had been accepted as being produced in sufficient numbers to already comply with Group 1 regulations, which required 5000 units to have been manufactured and fitted to the car. Outside this figure were the enlarged driveshafts and new Hardy Spicer couplings that were fitted to the car, although these were now to be seen in standard production, so it was a gamble that they would be accepted.

Standard 3½J wheels had to be fitted because wider wheels were just an option and couldn't be used on Group 1 cars. The Hydrolastic suspension was more or less standard other than the fitting of uprated export single-red and double-red displacer units front and back. The suspension was also raised slightly by the use of thin packing washers and was also assisted by heavy-duty bump stops to arrest the pitching found with Hydrolastic suspension.

Despite the relative low power output and the almost standard suspension, Aaltonen had the brakes improved by fitting DS11 front pads and VG95 brake linings because his driving style of left-foot braking placed huge demands on the braking system, which generally overheated. These were the only available brake materials that could cope with the relentless heat build-up of habitually braking the front wheels that were still being driven hard. This problem was complicated further by the Group 1 regulations stipulating that the front brake dust covers had to be retained.

The other unfortunate standard item that had to be kept was the single fuel tank – the optional right-hand tank was not permitted, as this too was just an optional extra. This severely hampered the refuelling programme due to the car's very restrictive range. The small 5.5-gallon tank was protected, in the boot, with an asbestos sheet glued to its face. This protected against potential damage caused by carrying upwards of three spare studded tyres. The fuel pump was retained in its original position on the subframe and it too was protected, as were all of the fuel, battery and brake lines, which also remained outside.

The lumbago-inflicting standard seats had to be retained and so the only option to increase comfort, and offer some support, was to use rally seat covers. However, additional safely padding on the door locks, door pockets and door pillar

GRX 55D leaves the Athens start on their long journey to Monte Carlo before the real competition would start.

were permitted, as were the customary additional dash panels. Even the oversized standard steering wheel had to be retained.

The lighting on the car, which was soon to prove the car's downfall, had a unique dim-dip feature. With the restriction of just two auxiliary lamps, it was decided to dim the single-filament quartz iodine headlamps when the dip switch was operated, which entailed Lucas locating a large resistor on the bulkhead for the purpose. The alternative was to simply extinguish the headlights when dipped and turn on the fog lamps for the dipped beam. This was also incorporated in the wiring and was selected by a switch on the dashboard.

A reduced-power heated front windscreen was the only other heavy demand placed on the electrics – which was just as well, as the car had to run a dynamo rather than an alternator; nevertheless an uprated 28amp unit was used. Being in Group 1, the car also had to retain its standard wiring loom, but Lucas supplied a piggyback additional loom for the auxiliary equipment.

The Monte Carlo Rally, run between 14 and 20 January, featured 150 stage miles within its 1800-mile route, but this year's route contained no tests from the nine starting points on their respective runs down to Monte Carlo. This at least did ensure many got to Monte unscathed.

BMC's hopes were high following Mäkinen's 1965 win and Hopkirk's in 1964, and with Aaltonen now being the European champion, a hat-trick was on the cards – something that hadn't been achieved since 1932.

Aaltonen flies GRX 55D up the mountain climb on the first of the competitive loops to Chambéry and back – 900 hard miles in 24 hours.

Stuart Turner had selected different starting points for all his cars, with Aaltonen starting from Athens (along with just eight other crews). The Friday saw 192 cars make one of the nine starts, and we would see 171 reach Monaco by Sunday evening.

The competition proper started on the Monday morning, with a 24-hour non-stop 900-mile loop to Chambéry and back, which included six stages. This demanding route eliminated many, and only 88 crews made it back to Monaco on Tuesday morning. The mountain circuit, run on Wednesday night, was restricted to the top 60 finishers, who faced an even more demanding run over the mountains above Monaco, with a 380-mile route with six stages before the finish on the quayside at Thursday breakfast time.

Monday morning's Monaco-Chambéry-Monaco loop was to prove defining for Aaltonen. Running late in the order, he dropped two valuable minutes to Mäkinen over the Col du Granier stage. This 47km stage had hard-packed snow over most of the route when the ice notes crews went over, meaning chisel studs would be required, but this soon turned to powdery snow with the passing of many competitors. With incorrect tyres, the inevitable time loss was one Aaltonen could not claw back on the hard-charging Mäkinen. Nevertheless, Aaltonen was in a second position on his return to Monte Carlo on Tuesday evening.

What greeted him back in Monte, and most of the British cars, was a notice posted by the officials that they were looking into the legality of the headlights fitted to their cars. As the day dragged on, the organisers relented and allowed all cars under suspicion to undertake the mountain circuit on Thursday evening.

The weather for this final leg was cold and clear, with the Alpes Maritime being covered in packed snow on all but the first stage. The infamous Col du Turini would be visited three times and the Col de la Couillole twice in the two circular routes around the mountains. Aaltonen on his second assent of the Turini briefly came to grief and smote the nearside wing of his car. This resulted in slightly wayward handling but also meant that he wrecked a tyre scrubbing away into

Aaltonen lost time over the Col du Granier stage due to tyre choice.

The decisive mountain circuit, where the Col du Turini was visited three times, saw Aaltonen hit a wall on his second visit. It was all to no avail, as and the entire BMC team were excluded because of their headlights. Aaltonen had finished in second.

the wing. A quick change of tyre and temporary wing-pulling resulted in a one-minute loss of road time and his quest was effectively gone.

Back in service, at St Sauveur, much hammering had the wing clear but Aaltonen still felt the car was swaying around. Despite the little excursion Aaltonen was matching Mäkinen for stage times and was never out of the top five, and was rewarded by returning to Monaco still in very secure second place.

History will show that Aaltonen wasn't awarded his second place, as all of the works Minis, and many more besides, were disqualified. This was because of the use of single-filament headlight bulbs in deference to the Group 1 regulations that stipulated (after some clarification) that headlights must be as manufactured, which in effect dictated they be twin-filament. It was a last-ditch attempt by the organisers to find some illegal parts on the Mini because the French press and others seemed unable to accept that a Group 1 Mini could outperform a Porsche 911.

Try as they might, no illegal parts were found, despite stripping the car to its bare components. The scrutineers did at one stage question the front track on Aaltonen's car, as this appeared outside the specified dimensions. However, when the damage to the corner of the car was pointed out with the resultant damage to the subframe and suspension alignment noted, the subject was dropped.

Rumours abounded that BMC had actually swapped cars somewhere up in the mountains for more powerful versions, and when challenged by a French journalist, a standard Mini Cooper S was taken from a Nice showroom and driven over one of the stages – and it was quicker than Mäkinen's rally time. Without doubt, BMC's performance was due to meticulous preparation, superb pace notes, which were actually practised at the same time of day as the rally would take place – plus the team had the best drivers in the world. In the end, BMC received massive publicity due to the unjust disqualification – far more than if a Mini had won. Small consolation nevertheless for the crews involved.

After the Monte, GRX 55D had its nearside wing hastily bashed into line and the car was used for testing duties in Wales, still in its Group 1 condition. The Strata Florida area used by Abingdon was ideal for testing suspension and for general rough-road development. The wet tracks were both very bumpy and twisting and were a great testing ground for the car, where Tony Fall did his best to break it.

The car's next event was the Circuit of Ireland, held over the Easter weekend of 1966. The car was assigned to Paddy Hopkirk and Terry Harryman who, being last year's winners, were hoping to repeat their success and had been seeded number 1. GRX 55D was prepared as a Group 2 car and built by Peter Bartram. This was, however, very likely to have been a new build as the GRX 55D damaged on the Monte, used for testing in Wales and having been reprepared,

GRX 55D being tested in Wales straight after the Monte. Note the nearside wing hastily straightened after Aaltonen's accident on the Monte.

was used by Tony Fall for his recce for the Flowers Rally. Unfortunately, Fall rolled the car whilst practising and the car was badly damaged, meaning we had a different GRX 55D for the Circuit of Ireland

Free from the constraints of Group 1 regulations, the 1293cc engine was fitted with a full-race camshaft (the AEG648); coupled with a high-compression Downton cylinder head resulting in 11.6:1 compression, and now breathing through twin 1½ H4 carburettors, it produced 82bhp on the Abingdon rollers. This was a marked improvement from the standard Monte engine.

Straight-cut close-ratio gears were used in the gearbox, as

Stuart Turner and Henry Liddon overseeing a mechanical repair on GRX 55D whilst testing at Strata Florida.

WORKS MINIS IN DETAIL

A change of drive coupling to get the car back home. Note the large resister above the master cylinders, which provided a dim-dip function for the offending headlights that had excluded the car on the Monte Carlo Rally.

was a low 4.2:1 final drive, mated to modified Hardy Spicer driveshafts and flange couplings. Keeping the engine cool was a four-blade fan with the blades reduced by ¼in – and to ensure a little more clearance, the water pump had 1/16in turned off its face. The radiator bottom cowl was solidly bolted down and was also double-skinned. The car ran an 82C thermostat and also a radiator muff fitted to the grille moustache.

The car was again fitted with Hydrolastic suspension, with single-blue and double-blue displacers front and back, together with orange helper springs. The front suspension also used Aeon bump rubbers, whilst the rear ran MGB rubbers. The front tie bars were protected and their mounting strengthened by bolting protection brackets to the subframe. The nuts on both ends of the tie rods were secured by using castellated nuts and split pins, as were the nuts to the track rod ends.

Free from Group 1 restrictions, the car ran wider 4½J steel wheels, now with fibreglass wheelarch extensions to cover the resulting wider track. Two spare wheels were carried and the car ran Dunlop R7 race tyres, although crews had the option of SP Weathermasters for the few loose surface sections on the route. Brakes were all standard other than using race pads and linings and a 325 psi limiting valve to allow more braking to the rear.

The electrics were served by an 11AC alternator with a remote 4TR regulator, which produced enough power to run the four auxiliary iodine lamps – two outer Lucas 700 fog lamps and two centre Lucas Continental driving lamps. These four lamps were mounted on the now-standard badge bar mounted on the front panel just above the bumper and stabilised by a thick centre strap around and underneath the bumper.

The battery was a race type with its terminals facing away from the side of the fuel tank and the cable run inside the car. The exposed battery box was protected by a metal shield under the car, fixed to the subframe. The twin fuel pump was still located outside the car on the subframe, and this too was protected by a metal plate, but with the fuel line run inside the car.

Hopkirk and Harriman sat in lightweight fibreglass bucket seats, in deference to the normal and heavier reclining passenger seat. These were covered in early Mini 850 speckled cloth trim. Irvin seat belts, a lap-and-diagonal and full harness were used, and each had the customary supplementary dashboards in front of them to mount additional instruments and navigational equipment – the Halda distance recorder and speedo were set to read in miles rather than kilometres. Full padding and extra protection to the door locks, door pillars and door pockets were provided. The heated 'screen was gone and replaced with a plain laminated windscreen – Hopkirk not being a fan of heated front 'screens. However, to keep the windscreen clear, the heater was fitted with larger-diameter demister pipes and funnels.

For the 1966 Circuit of Ireland, the Ulster AC had devised a really challenging rally: covering 1500 miles with 50 stages over 300 miles, mostly on closed roads, the event would be fast and furious. The format departed from their more traditional navigational event and fell into line with most European events, which centred on special stage times and tight road sections in between. Time controls situated at almost every ten miles throughout the entire route, with a

Paddy Hopkirk and Terry Harryman start the 1966 Circuit of Ireland Rally, where a new GRX 55D was provided for the all-Irish crew hoping to repeat last years win.

maximum lateness of 30 minutes, meant any major problem on the car would mean collecting large time penalties or being excluded. This also seriously reduced the amount of service time that could be spent on cars before penalties piled up.

Starting from Ballymena in County Antrim on Good Friday evening, the 84 entrants faced a 250-mile run through rain and fog throughout Northern Ireland, with seven stages before a short stop for breakfast at Sligo – but Hopkirk never made it that far.

On the sixth stage, around Lough Eske in Donegal, disaster struck. The very fast stage had within it a blind brow, which at practice speed was noted as flat, meaning it could be taken flat out. Approaching the brow at around 80mph at rally speed, the car took off and landed badly at an angle. It bounced on its sump guard and landed again, this time slewing to the left and rolling over and onto its side, demolishing a tree with its roof. This inverted the car, which spun down the road on its roof, with sparks flying everywhere. The roof collapsed and Hopkirk's door was torn off (the door was later found wedged in the branches of a tree), scraping his shoulder along the ground. Fortunately, the car had so much momentum that it flipped back onto its wheels.

When it had all stopped, the crew were able to unbuckle their seatbelts and extricate themselves on Hopkirk's side because Harryman's door had jammed and the roof was down to the front 'screen. So badly had the rear of the roof been crushed that the top of the fuel tanks had been ground

Harryman gets back into the car, having clocked in with his time card. The weather is atrocious and it would soon see the car crash end-over-end and into retirement.

away and were now leaking fuel. Fortunately, Harryman still had the presence of mind to turn the ignition off. Mindful of the works Lotus Cortina of Vic Elford being right behind him, Hopkirk grabbed a torch and ran back to slow him down – only to discover, in all their spinning around, he'd run the wrong way!

Elford hit the Mini and shoved it further off the road. The car was a total mess, having not only rolled sideways but also end over end – all without a roll cage. Hopkirk admitted his mistake but felt that the Hydrolastic suspension had contributed to the accident.

Competition Record

Date	Event	Crew	Number	Overall result	Class result
Jan 1966	Monte Carlo Rally	Rauno Aaltonen/Tony Ambrose	242	disqualified	
April 1966	Circuit of Ireland	Paddy Hopkirk/Terry Harryman	1	DNF	

Registration Number	First registered	Chassis number	Engine	Engine number	Model
GRX 555D	**Jan 1966**	KA2S4 820484	1275cc	9F-SA-Y 39690	**Morris Cooper S**

The third brand new car to be built for the 1966 Monte Carlo Rally was GRX 555D. This was to be driven by Timo Mäkinen and Paul Easter, both looking to follow up on their 1965 Monte success.

The car, in common with its two sister cars, was built as a Group 1 standard production car that had to comply with the new Appendix J regulations, which came into force on 1 January 1966. Because of the severe handicap placed upon Group 2 cars for the Monte Carlo Rally by the organisers, it soon became evident that the winning car would inevitably be a Group 1, so the decision was made to enter the car in Group 1.

Needless to say, very careful scrutiny of the new regulations was needed before the cars could be built – with Stuart Turner spending many hours deciphering the French text to ensure that the cars complied. Bill Price had also worked tirelessly to get the car homologated as a Group 1 by early December 1965, when the FIA signed off the relevant papers.

With the car having to be relatively standard, much attention was given to the careful selection of parts to optimise the normal 1275cc engine. It should also be noted, so worried was Abingdon of drawing attention to any non-standard parts on the car, that all special identification paint marks were completely removed.

GRX 555D being prepared for the 1966 Monte Carlo Rally at Abingdon with Paul Easter looking on.

Under the engine of GRX 555D showing the short 13-hole sump guard and the Moke sump plate screwed directly onto the underside of the gearbox.

The underside of GRX 555D showing all of the lines outside the car protected by metal channelling. The plate on the rear subframe is protection for the fuel pump.

Everything was perfectly balanced in the engine, but of course nothing could be lightened, so no lightened flywheel or backplate could be used. The engine was fitted with an AEG510 camshaft, which had just been put into standard production for the Cooper S and would remain so for more or less the entirety of the car's production life; it had proved to be a very versatile and effective camshaft. The cylinder head, again unmodified, retained its standard compression ratio of 9.75:1.

Standard 1¼ twin SU carburettors were used but with red springs and M needles. The exhaust also had to be standard, which precluded the much-used long centre-branch exhaust manifold. Power, as recorded in the Abingdon rolling road, showed a peak of just 67bhp at the wheels at 5500rpm.

Fuel was supplied only via a single tank because the twin tank option had yet to be homologated. Abingdon had envisaged fitting a right-hand tank, so the shell was already punched for the extra tank neck, which in the event had to be blanked off. All the fuel lines were run outside the car and were protected with metal channelling. The SU fuel pump was also located in the standard position, on the subframe, outside the car but protected by an alloy plate. The fuel tank was protected, in the boot, by gluing an asbestos sheet to its exposed side. This was because of the risk that spiked tyres, in the boot, might puncture the tank. The car often carried three spare wheels.

The gearbox was fitted with straight-cut close-ratio gears, as these had been previously homologated for use in Group 1. The diff ratio was a homologated alternative, so the short 4.133 was used. Driveshafts were somewhat of a concern, as the car was fitted with the new solid Hardy Spicer driveshaft couplings, replacing the troublesome rubber couplings, together with enlarged shafts and modified splined ends. These parts had only just gone into standard production and had certainly not reached the 5000 production run required to satisfy the homologation requirement – but fitted they were.

Mäkinen was obliged to forsake his preferred dry-

Being a Group 1 car, GRX 555D had to retain the relatively unsupportive standard seats, so Abingdon used Karobes seat cover over the standard seats and the navigator had a fabricated high-back headrest placed over the seat.

suspension setup, as it had not been homologated for Group 1, so the car retained its wet suspension. The Hydrolastic suspension was raised slightly by the use of 0.01in packing with double-red rear and single-red displacers at the front, which had both been homologated as heavy-duty export suspension options. Additional Aeon bump stops were also fitted to stiffen the suspension further and reduce the pitching found with Hydrolastic suspension. These non-standard items were hastily added to the Special Tuning catalogue.

Timken needle roller bearings were used in the rear hubs, which would eventually find their way into standard production but were not, at this time, strictly homologated for 1966. Wheels had to be restricted to skinny standard 3½J rims as the optional 4½J wide wheels were not yet homologated for Group 1. Brake material has always been free as far as regulations are concerned, so the car ran DS11 racing pads in the front callipers and VG95 race linings in the rear drums, but the brake lines had to run outside the car.

The electrics, as always, meant a completely rewired car, albeit the standard loom had to remain. Running a C40R 28amp dynamo in conjunction with a RB310 regulator box was all that was needed to keep the mandatory two additional lamps and the heated front 'screen fed with juice.

The headlamps, fitted with single-filament quartz iodine bulbs, were designed to dip by both extinguishing themselves and turning on the fog lamps or, as an alternative, to be just dimmed via a rheostat. Lucas supplied a large rheostat, encased in a metal shroud and fitted near the brake master cylinder. This option was selected via a three-way switch on the dashboard, with the dip switch operating in the normal fashion; the 'dim-dip' was the preferred option. Additional

Lucas Racing technician Stan Chalmers finishing the wiring of GRX 555D. Note the additional wiring loom laid under the standard loom.

lighting was from two large Lucas 700 fog lamps fitted on quick-release brackets, with quartz iodine bulbs. This would be a step backwards into the dark by losing the two large auxiliary driving lamps that drivers had become used to.

Because of Group 1 restrictions, the car also had to be fitted with standard seats – even the optional-extra reclining seats couldn't be used. To afford the crews some additional comfort and support, Karobes rally seat covers were fitted over the seats and, in the case of the navigator seat, a large headrest was fabricated and attached to the back of the seat frame. Additionally, because Mäkinen was always keen to grab as much sleep as possible on the road sections, the mechanics made him a removable plywood-covered bed once at the Lisbon start. This replaced the passenger seat, which of course was ultimately refitted when the competition started in earnest and the bed ditched.

Protection padding was fitted to the door pockets and door pillars, and the customary auxiliary dash panels fitted either side of the speedo binnacle, together with a switch panel in the navigator's door pocket, which housed his map light and other control switches. The Halda Twinmaster, Heuer clocks and switches on Paul Easter's side and the rev counter, route card holder and numerous switches on Mäkinen's side were all much as usual in the two auxiliary aluminium panels.

The car was also equipped with a roof rack, carrying additional spare tyres for the journey down to Monte Carlo, before the meat of the event began. This was then removed.

Timo Mäkinen with Paul Easter busy reading his pace notes. The intercom system can be clearly seen on both crew members' crash helmets.

Raymond Baxter in discussion with Timo Mäkinen whilst a mechanic checks the car. The large resistor for the dim-dip function can be seen above the master cylinders.

Tyre choice, for all of the four works Minis, amounted to around 500 tyres of various stud patterns down to dry-tarmac race tyres – all supplied by Dunlop. They were generally ferried around the route in the back of the Cooper Car Company transporter.

Run from 14 to 20 January, the 1966 Monte Carlo Rally was, for the first time for many years, virtually uncompetitive from the nine starting points down to Monte Carlo. No stages were scheduled; this with the hope of getting as many competitors to the principality as possible unscathed – after pressure from the hoteliers, when in 1965 only 28 cars made it to Monaco.

BMC was looking for a hat-trick and Mäkinen was keen to repeat his 1965 success, starting from Lisbon. Turner selected four different starting points for his Minis, as a hedge against one or other having bad weather. As it was, their westerly route was easy, apart from a good deal of rain through Spain. Paul Easter reported that Mäkinen slept for 27 hours on the journey whilst he did most of the driving.

On the Sunday evening, 171 cars made it to Monte Carlo within time, from the 192 hopefuls who set off during Friday. The meat of the rally started on Monday morning with a 900-mile loop up to Chambéry and back, which including six stages. Just 88 crews made it back and of those, the first 60 were selected for the mountain circuit starting on Wednesday evening. This entailed a 380-mile high-speed dash over the ice-covered mountains, with another six stages to undertake before heading back to Monte Carlo on Thursday morning.

Mäkinen soon threw down his marker on the Chambéry loop, known as the common route, where he was putting up fast times and despite the snow-covered ground, was leading on the road even before Castellane. He took on new tyres at Laborel and during the freezing night, when the temperature dropped to -25C, he consolidated his lead. He was fastest on the very quick and dangerous stage into Gap, which was covered in ice, and also fastest on the Col du Granier/Col de Porte stage where packed snow prevailed and saw him take a clear two-minute lead over Aaltonen. It was here on this 47km stage, which he covered in just over 37 minutes, where the event was won. The two-minute lead that he took back to Monte Carlo the next morning was never lost.

However, all was not well come Tuesday evening when a notice was posted by the officials concerning the legality of the light-dipping used on numerous cars, including all of the works Minis. Undaunted, Mäkinen set off on the mountain circuit as rally leader on Wednesday evening, leaving the arguments behind him. He was greeted with light snow on the short Sospel stage and on the Col du Turini there was packed snow, as there was on all of the remaining mountain stages.

BMC's refuelling plans were now in full swing, with the cars being topped up from jerry bags at regular intervals; with high consumption, their range was only safe for around 70 miles. By St Sauveur Mäkinen had nine minutes in hand on the road and took on new tyres and four gallons of fuel.

Back at the same service again later than night, Mäkinen had managed to pull a 15-minute buffer and again took on new tyres and fuel. His stage times had been equally impressive, being fastest over the first of the three trips over the Col du Turini and second and third over the other two visits. Mäkinen rolled back into Monte just after dawn on Thursday, with a comfortable lead of just over two minutes on Aaltonen.

The last night of the Monte, where they visited the Col Du Turini three times. Here, they head off after a quick stop.

Mäkinen and Easter, in snowy conditions, power the Group 1 car up another Alpine climb.

Come Thursday evening, a second notice was posted, again concerning the lights of the Minis. At the post-event scrutineering, which took place on the Friday, all of the Minis were taken apart, literally piece by piece – even down to counting gear teeth, such was the thoroughness, but nothing against the regulations could be found (they missed the non-homologated Hardy Spicer drive couplings).

The organisers were still intent, however, on finding something and after much debate, concluded (to the amazement and disgust of all present) that the Minis' headlights were illegal. This, in the end, was upheld under appeal that the Mini's headlight bulbs had contravened the Group 1 regulations, which stated, albeit not clearly in the English translation, that headlights must be same as manufactured. As they were using single filament bulbs, they did not comply, because production Minis were fitted with twin-filament bulbs (which would also allow them to dip).

History was to show that BMC and the Minis received far more publicity from their disqualification than they could ever have hoped for, even for a hat-trick of wins. Citroen was awarded the winner's laurels and its driver, Pauli Toivonen, was forced by Citroen to attend the prize giving – but never drove for the team again. Prince Rainier didn't attend the prize giving either. Mäkinen had been a clear ten minutes ahead of Toivonen and the light bulbs can have made only a marginal difference. In any case, Citroen was using the same bulbs but changed them before arriving at the finish. The repercussions for that exclusion reverberate even today.

After the bitter disappointment of being disqualified from winning the Monte Carlo Rally, Abingdon pressed the car into recce duties – rather than keeping the car for posterity, as with the previous two Monte-winning cars. However, before

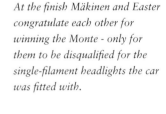

At the finish Mäkinen and Easter congratulate each other for winning the Monte - only for them to be disqualified for the single-filament headlights the car was fitted with.

The scrutineers deciding that GRX 555D's headlights were illegal, having failed to find anything wrong with the car, disbelieving that the Group 1 could have been that fast!

After the Monte Carlo Rally disqualification fiasco, Julien Vernaeve took GRX 555D to the Neige et Glace Rally near Grenoble. It was said to be as a thank you for his efforts with the team on the Monte.

Paul Easter repairing GRX 555D on their recce for the Acropolis rally. The Abingdon tool kit, carried on the rear seat, providing all the tools needed for the job.

Timo Mäkinen and Paul Easter's GRX 555D lines up at the start of the Polish Rally between Roger Clark's Lotus Cortina and Sobieslaw Zasada's Steyr-Puch 650TR, which finished third, behind the Minis of Fall and Mäkinen.

this, the car was loaned to Julien Vernaeve as a measure of the team's gratitude for all of the ice notes and assistance he gave the team on the Monte Carlo Rally. Vernaeve used the car to take part in the Neige et Glace Rally near Grenoble. The car was unchanged and still in Group 1 form for this rally, where Vernaeve finished 16th overall and sixth in the Group 1 class.

The car was next used for the recce of the Tulip Rally by Mäkinen and Easter, which took place in April, and used again by them for the Acropolis Rally held in May. Sensibly, the ex-Group 1 car had been fitted with the almost-obligatory right-hand fuel tank and suitably tuned in line with Group 2 specifications – and strengthened for the rough Greek roads where the car received a great deal of punishment.

The Polish Rally in early August was the car's next event. Timo Mäkinen and Paul Easter were again to crew the car, which was built by Gerald Wiffen to full Group 2 specifications. It is very likely that this was another car, reprepared for the Polish and its identity swapped or possibly a new build – as the car used on the Polish Rally was not the Monte 'winning' car.

The engine, bored to 1293cc using a 11.6:1-compression Downton cylinder head, and with a full-race camshaft, produced 86bhp at the wheels. This, coupled with the normal straight-cut close-ratio gearbox and the 4.133 diff, made for a very quick car.

Keeping the engine cool was a four-blade fan, which had the blades reduced by 5mm to aid fan belt changes. The radiator was also rigidly bolted down at the bottom, negating the rubber bushes on the lower mounting bracket. Stopping the car was entrusted to Ferodo DS11 racing disc pads and VG95 rear brake linings, always overworked with the constant left-foot braking employed by Mäkinen.

By now the Hardy Spicer drive couplings with larger diameter driveshafts were fitted as standard but, as always, Abingdon's were specially selected and checked thoroughly. Being a potentially rough event, the car carried a full heavy-duty sump guard and had a Moke sump plate screwed directly to the sump. The car also ran a battery skid plate fitted under the rear subframe, protecting the vulnerable battery box.

A special Mitchell mounting remote rubber was fitted to the end of the gearbox remote shift and the mounting bracket was strengthened by welding and further reinforced by straps inside the car. The gearstick was replaced with the standard-fitting anti-rattle type, forsaking the preferred solid early stick used for so long on works Minis.

Despite Mäkinen's dislike for Hydrolastic cars, this Mini was indeed a wet car with single-blue and double-blue displacers front and back with helper springs. The suspension was further assisted by the fitting of heavy-duty Aeon bump stops. The rear radius arm brackets on the subframe were strengthened and the subframe itself was double-skinned on its top face. Further, the front of the tie rods were protected where they mounted onto the front subframe with fabricated brackets (which also the strengthened the subframe).

Inside the car, the battery line, brake lines and fuel lines were all routed inside and the twin fuel pump now found itself located under the rear seat, rather than out in the damp and cold screwed to the rear subframe. Mäkinen sat in a special fabric-covered fibreglass bucket seat that had to be porta-powered apart to fit his rather large frame (the seat was brought to Abingdon by Rauno Aaltonen, who was somewhat slight compared to Mäkinen). Irvin harnesses were fitted. Apart from the customary padding inside the car to add comfort and protection, the car jack now found its way inside the car, fixed vertically behind the driver on the companion box side.

The 1966 Polish Rally got off to a bad start for Mäkinen and Easter when the clutch broke on their recce Mini and the only car they could avail themselves of was a Trabant. This was loaned to them by the one chap in Poland who seemed to have a Mini clutch-puller tool. There were compensations, however, as they did the recce three-up with Miss Poland in the back seat, which Mäkinen unsurprisingly seemed to rather enjoy.

Fifty-two cars lined up for this round of the European Championship. On offer were 22 special stages, two races, two hillclimbs and a driving test over the 1700-mile route. A very high average road speed meant clean sheets would be difficult and the weather over the three days event was also not kind, with wind and rain prevailing.

The organisers had followed the lead set by the organisers of the Monte Carlo Rally and adopted a similar class handicap system, and with Mäkinen in the 1300 class he had an advantage over the works Cortinas that had to go 0.8 per cent faster to beat him. But he was at a disadvantage to the one-litre cars that had a 1.7 per cent buffer – plus they had five per cent more time on the very tight road sections. And a minute lost on the road equated to three minutes of stage time penalty.

The event started and finished in Krakow, and the first night soon saw Mäkinen making his mark, with the weather taking its toll on the less-experienced and numerous local crews. So hard was the rally that only 11 crews made it back to Krakow within time.

Mäkinen was not, however, incident-free and on one very slippery stage he shot straight on and missed the finish completely, necessitating Easter to run back to get the time card stamped. As the rally progressed, Mäkinen was posting very fast times, leading the event and, despite being number 37, was soon running first on the road – still unpenalised. But this would prove their undoing.

The organisers had employed a brand-new electronic timing system, both untried and untested on one show stage. At the finish Easter recorded a stage time that showed he'd finished the stage before he'd actually started… At the end of the rally, this was brought to the organiser's attention by Easter, and it was assumed it would be corrected. Come the final results, Mäkinen was relegated to second place behind Tony Fall in the other works Mini. Stuart Turner, despite pressure from

Mäkinen sliding the now Group 2 GRX 555D over the cobble stones on the Polish Rally.

Mäkinen, did not protest the result, content that a BMC car had nevertheless won the rally. Mäkinen was so incensed that he refused to go to the prize-giving and vowed never to do the Polish Rally again. Unfortunately, yet again GRX 555D was relegated from its rightful top spot on the winner's podium.

The car was once again pressed into service for recce duties for the Alpine Rally in September and used for the Monte recce for the 1967 event, where it was used by Aaltonen and Liddon in preparation for their win on the winter classic. Its final Abingdon outing was a recce for the Rally of the Flowers in February 1967 for Fall and Wood. The car was sold to Les Lambourne, who was the MG plant director at Abingdon.

GRX 555D blasts off the line on the single driving test of the Polish Rally. Mäkinen finished a disappointed man, having been given a wrong time on one stage, handing the win to Tony Fall in GRX 309D.

Competition Record

Date	Event	Crew	Number	Overall result	Class result
Jan 1966	Monte Carlo Rally	Timo Mäkinen/Paul Easter	2	disqualified	
Feb 1966	Critérium Neige et Glace	Julien Vernaeve/Jean-Marie Jacquemin	81	17th	
Aug 1966	Polish Rally	Timo Mäkinen/Paul Easter	37	2nd	

Registration Number	First registered	Chassis number	Engine	Engine number	Model
GRX 195D	Jan 1966	KA2S4 799887	1275cc	9F-SA-Y 39495	Morris Cooper S

GRX 195D in the lanes around Abingdon before the 1966 Monte Carlo Rally, where Raymond Baxter and Jack Scott would have a Group 2 car at their disposal – all the Abingdon star drivers had Group 1 cars, which was the favoured class to win overall.

GRX 195D was the fourth new car built and prepared for the 1966 Monte Carlo Rally, and assigned to Raymond Baxter and Jack Scott. Baxter, then a BBC commentator, was competing on his third Monte Carlo Rally for BMC. It was, of course, good publicity for BMC to have a BBC reporter in one of its cars, and the bonus being Baxter was quite effective at the wheel.

Unlike the other three cars being prepared at Abingdon as Group 1 cars, GRX 195D was built as a full Group 2, with a time handicap of 18 per cent over a Group 1 car. This was indeed a tall order and likely insurmountable, which is why Turner had elected to put his three star drivers in Group 1 cars. Nevertheless, just to hedge their bets, if nothing else, a Group 2 car was built by Bob Whittington and Robin Vokins for Baxter.

With the new Appendix J rules coming into force on 1 January 1966, BMC, along with other manufacturers, had to carefully interpret the new regulations, and much time was spent ensuring the car's build complied with the new rules – and just because this was a modified Group 2 car, it was not exempt from close scrutiny.

Being Group 2, the engine could be highly tuned, and Baxter had at his disposal a 1293cc engine that produced 92bhp at the wheels – a vast increase on the Group 1 engine of its sister cars, which had 25bhp less to play with. Would it be enough to offset the 18 per cent time handicap?

The engine was built with a full-race camshaft, a lightened steel flywheel and camshaft gear. A high-compression Downton modified cylinder head, giving 11.6:1 compression, was used, together with a modified rocker shaft and pillars; this was fed by twin H4 SU carburettors with modified linkages, blue springs, AZ needles, float chamber extensions and ram pipes replacing the air filters.

Modified driveshafts with Hardy Spicer couplings were fitted and the transmission was via a straight-cut close-ratio gearbox with a 4.133 final drive. This was protected by an RAF-type sump guard with an additional sump plate screwed to the bottom of the gear casing.

Hydrolastic suspension was used with single-red and double-red displacers front and rear, with 0.100in packing rings below the struts. The suspension was further modified with additional heavy-duty bump stops. However, the subframes were not strengthened or rewelded, nor were any additional shock absorbers fitted.

The electrics and lighting, as always, received much attention from the resident Lucas racing technicians and the new car was completely rewired. An 11AC alternator was fitted, together with a remote 4TR regulator, being necessary for the extra demands on the electrical system. Lighting, with only single-filament iodine bulbs in the headlights, meant the fitting of two small fog lamps on the bonnet for the dipped beam. The car, in addition, had two large Lucas 700 fog lamps mounted on quick-release brackets on the bumper. An Austin Healey 3000 sidelight was used as a reversing lamp, fitted low down on the right-hand side of the bootlid. The car was also fitted with a Triplex heated front windscreen, and the wipers with deep-throated wheel boxes to add the strength needed to shift heavy snow off the screen.

A twin electrical fuel pump was fitted to the subframe, in the standard position, protected by an alloy plate, and all lines were run inside the car, with the main battery cable being fixed to the battery with large terminals, and the battery being turned around with its terminals facing away from the side of the fuel tank in case it got shoved sideways in an accident. The twin fuel tanks were protected from potential damage from studded tyres by gluing thin asbestos sheets to their sides – this replaced the normal thin plywood that had previously been used. Standard fuel caps were used, retained by light chains to the necks of the tanks.

Inside the car, fabricated alloy dash panels were fitted in front of the driver and navigator to house extra switches and controls, and navigation and timing equipment respectively. A fibreglass driver's bucket seat and a fabricated reclining seat

CHAPTER 3: THE MK 1 MINI COOPER S

On the starting ramp at London Airport for their journey to Monte Carlo.

GRX 195D joins a relatively deserted M2 motorway on their way to Dover for the ferry to France.

were fitted, together with a lap-and-diagonal and full-harness Irvin seat belts. Additional padding was supplied to the door pockets, door locks and door pillars. Full carpet was used with an additional asbestos blanket under the front to keep engine heat away from the cabin, under which all the floor bungs were removed and welded over.

Being a Group 2 car, all glass was retained, as were the metal doors, boot and bonnet – no Perspex or aluminium being permitted. Additionally, for the Monte, the car carried a four-tyre roof rack with an extra set of studded tyres, should they be needed on its journey down to the South of France.

The Monte Carlo Rally was very prestigious, and because of that, the most important rally in BMC's annual calendar. The planning and logistics that went into the event by Stuart Turner cannot be understated – nor indeed the tyres required. BMC had over 500 tyres for the four Minis, which were distributed around the route mainly from the John Cooper Racing transporter. They were largely Dunlop SP44s, either part or fully pop-in studded tyres, plus special chisel tyres and spiral studded tyres, with a few race tyres for dry roads. As GRX 195D was the only Group 2 BMC entry, for simplicity it was fitted with narrow 3½J rims – the same as the three Group 1 cars. Five regular service cars were in attendance, being Austin Westminster A110 and Travellers plus four of the recce Minis used for ice notes and emergency service.

With Baxter starting from London (as Turner hedged his bets against the risk of poor weather from one starting point or another), he was the lone works Mini to do so, although ten private Minis would join him on the hoped-for relatively easy run down to Monte Carlo. For the first time, the 1966 event would have no competitive stages down to the principality – likely to ensure the maximum number of competitors would reach Monte to swell the hotels after the debacle the previous year, when snowstorms decimated the entry and left the hoteliers perplexed with so many empty beds. As it was, only 20 crews failed to make it to Monte this year.

So 170 cars set off for the 24-hours, 900-mile competitive loop to Chambéry and back, which included six timed stages. These stages, however, would take their toll, as nearly half of the field fell by the wayside. Of those who remained, the top 60 contenders, after a night's sleep, tackled six stages on the last night. Timed to the second, over ice- and snow-closed

Baxter pressing hard despite fatigue on the competitive Chambéry loop, costing him dropped road time.

The beautiful backdrop of snow, sunshine and mountains sees Baxter and Scott safely finish the 1966 Monte, only to be disqualified, along with all the BMC cars, for illegal headlamps.

Henry Liddon takes a break from recce work for the Czech Rally, with a tin of fish and bottle of milk.

roads on the 380-mile mountain circuit above Monaco, the circular route tackled the famous Col du Turini no less than three times before the finish back in Monte Carlo just after dawn.

But Baxter would not have an easy time on the event, and whilst he had a trouble-free run down to Monte Carlo, along with most others, the continuous 24-hours Chambéry loop would take its toll. Fatigue set in and he lost 18 minutes' road time.

Safely back at Monte Carlo, however, he was still classified to compete on the last night's mountain circuit. Despite the extra power the Group 2 car had available, his times were no match for the superbly-driven Group 1 Minis of the other team members. All this was to be of no avail, as Baxter, along with all of the other works Minis (and many other) were disqualified at post-event scrutineering, when it was eventually decreed that the lights used on all of the works Minis were illegal.

Despite Turner's best efforts to interpret the new Appendix J regulations, he had fallen foul of them. After many hours of arguments, the single-filament iodine headlight bulb was considered to have broken the rules, which stated that the lighting had to be as manufactured, which meant twin-filament bulbs. This was exacerbated by the dipping mechanism, which had also been frowned upon. So it was that GRX 195D was disqualified from the Monte Carlo Rally and, despite subsequent appeals to the FIA, the exclusion was upheld.

After the Monte fiasco, GRX 195D became a recce car for much of 1966, the first of which was for the Tulip Rally in April where the car was used by Aaltonen and Liddon. It was again used for a recce in May, for the Acropolis Rally, where the car received a lot of punishment over the rough Greek roads at the hands of Hopkirk and Crellin.

The next recce was for the Czech Rally in July, where GRX 195D was used again by Aaltonen and Liddon. However, as the Czech Rally entry was for a Group 1 car, this Group 2 modified car was not used for this recce and a fully-prepared Group 1 car was dispatched instead. It is very likely that one of the Group 1 Monte Carlo cars was sent out to Czechoslovakia with a change of registration number. The recce car was rebuilt by Nobby Hall for the recce.

The next competitive event for GRX 195D was in September for the Alpine Rally, when it was handed to Tony Fall and Mike Wood to contest this popular summer classic. Built by Robin Vokins, the car was prepared to full Group 2 regulations, which by now had been clarified and understood by all competition managers.

After the hard work meted out to the car in Greece, a new version was built for the Alpine. The car now had the latest door handles with safety boss, and the bonnet and boot lid arrangements were changed from the Monte car, with different locations for bonnet and boot straps. The car also now had fibreglass wheelarch extensions to cover the wider 4½J steel wheels, and the four auxiliary lamps were now fitted to a chrome badge bar attached to the lower panel just above the bumper. These lamps consisted of two long-range Continental driving lights in the middle, with two large Lucas 700 fog lamps to the outside and all fitted with iodine bulbs. European headlamps were fitted with all-new 60/40W iodine twin-filament bulbs – alleviating the exclusion problems suffered on the Monte the previous January.

Tony Fall and Mike Wood with a new Group 2 GRX 195D in Marseille at the start of the 1966 Alpine Rally. New lighting arrangement clearly seen, distinct from the Monte car.

Fall rounds the loose-surface hairpin bend high up in desolate high Alps.

The build of the car, although similar to the Group 2 build for the Monte, was different in numerous ways. Notably the 1293cc engine had a very high compression of 12.6:1 and an even shorter diff ratio of 4.2:1. Curiously, the engine produced 4bhp less than the Monte engine. Gone were the lightened camshaft gears but now the engine used lightened tappets. To increase breathing, the oil filler cap had holes drilled into the side slot and a larger 5/16in hole drilled in the middle of the underside.

The underside of the gearbox was protected again by a Moke sump plate but also with a full sump guard. Despite the remote gearshift being fitted with the virtually-indestructible Mitchell mounting, an additional strap was fitted underneath the remote casing.

The Hydrolastic suspension now had single-blue and double-blue displacers front and rear with orange helper springs plus Aeon bump stops, and the rear radius arm brackets were also strengthened. The top side of the rear subframe was double-skinned and the front of the tie bars had protection brackets, which in truth added much strength. To add further to the strength of the car, the crossmember inside the car was double-skinned.

The twin fuel pump was now located inside the car, under the rear seat – away from the inhospitable location on the rear subframe. The interconnecting pipework between the twin tanks was also increased in size to increase flow between them. The brakes, always very stressed on the Alpine, received much attention. Asbestos blocks were fitted into the callipers' pistons that were just in contact with the pads, which helped to dissipate heat away from the brake fluid. The rear backplates were also drilled to aid cooling, and the brake wheel cylinder was bolted to the backplate, again to dissipate heat – such were the demands inflicted on the system with constant left-foot braking, so favoured by the Scandinavians. These significant changes were all part of Abingdon's development programme – lest we forget the Monte was nine months ago.

The Alpine Rally was a BMC favourite because it was, at best, a thinly disguised road race using the very best mountain climbs in the Alpes Maritime. Starting in Marseille, the first of three legs was an 800-mile, non-stop thrash finishing in Aix-Les-Bains. After a rest day, there followed another 800-mile loop back to Aix. The last leg, after another day's rest, was a final 800 miles to finish in Cannes. Eighty crews started the late-September event, with just 19 making the finish and only seven winning a coveted Coup des Alpes, awarded for a clean run without road penalties. Fourteen high-speed climbs, timed to the second, would decide the winner. Tony Fall used Dunlop R7 race tyres throughout (although SP44s were available in the Dunlop van, should snow be found on the high climbs). At the time, BMC was the only team regularly using racing tyres, and not just for tarmac; it would take a while for other teams to catch onto the benefits of using race tyres whenever they could.

Much hope was placed on Fall, having won a Coupe des Alpes the previous year as a private entrant. But trouble hit the crew on the second timed climb over the Allos when he

Through a village where people stop to see the cars flash by and police usher the cars onwards. Such is the pace of the Alpine, cars are constantly hard driven and Fall still keeps his crash helmet on. They would retire almost at the very end of the rally.

hit some rocks and deranged the car's handling, and until it could be repaired he adopted a very crab-like passage down the road. At the end of the first leg, just 54 cars remained, such was the furious pace, with only 16 still clean on the road – but despite his problems, Fall was still in contention with a clean sheet. Many cars, even with experienced crews, were only just making the time controls early enough.

The second leg saw Fall's clean sheet lost when again, on the second climb of the day, this time over the notorious Mont Ventoux, he lost a front wheel just 200 yards from the finish. All four wheel studs had sheared, and it took over 20 minutes for Fall and Wood to extricate two studs from the other front wheel to effect a temporary repair. Now only 28 cars remained and the clean sheets numbered just 11. The final sting-in-the-tail last leg saw Fall into retirement when on the Allos again, with one stage to go to the finish, the front suspension ball joint broke one mile from the summit. The chasing BMC service barge changed the offending joint and Fall was mobile again – only for the other joint to fail an hour later. With no service crew nearby, he was out. The Alpine had lived up to its reputation as a unique, tough and fast event.

Next up for GRX 195D was the RAC Rally of Great Britain in November, where once again Tony Fall and Mike Wood used the car. This event probably formed the trio of top events for the team, so with two non-finishes for the car, the hope was that its luck had to change soon.

Abingdon had no less than eight cars entered on the rally – desperate to win the home event. Built by Bob Whittington, the Alpine car was thoroughly rebuilt for what was always a hard event. It was again a Group 2 car, the major difference in the engine being the abandonment of the usual AEA648 full-race camshaft in preference for what was to become the standard production Cooper S camshaft, the AEG510. This camshaft offered far more low-down torque, which was thought would be an advantage in the tight and often muddy forest tracks used on the rally. With the loss of the full race camshaft came a loss of almost 15bhp but with increased driveability.

The engine had the benefit of the latest thick-flange block for added strength – this too would eventually find its way into standard production. Also, the cylinder head was held down with stronger MGB studs, even though the compression was reduced slightly to 11.4:1. For these changes the carburettor needles were swapped to no 7s, still with a blue spring. The short 4.2:1 diff ratio was retained, with the enlarged driveshafts and Hardy Spicer couplings.

The other major change on the car for the RAC was the fitting of a roll cage, which was the first time they were used on works Minis and would, in future, be a permanent feature. These cages, manufactured by John Aley, in lightweight

Bob Whittington building up the subframe on GRX 195D for the 1966 RAC Rally, now with Hardy Spicer joints. Also behind is the car and the wiring, relays and plumbing can be seen.

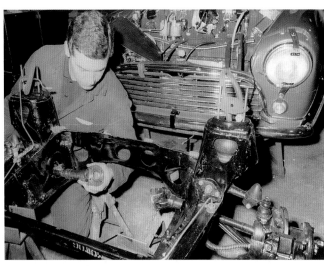

GRX 195D had front-facing mud flaps fitted to keep the lights and 'screen free of water splash. The car also has a grille muff fitted.

Tony Fall and Mike Wood leaving the start from London Airport's Excelsior hotel on the RAC Rally.

Fall cutting the corner in a drift on the loose shale surface in Wales, appearing to almost go over the edge.

aircraft-quality alloy were a simple loop behind the crew's heads, by the B-post, and with a single back-stay onto the rear parcel shelf. They were covered in foam and leathercloth to protect the crew still further. The cages would prove their worth, on this very event, when Simo Lampinen rolled his works Mini comprehensively.

For the RAC, unlike on the Alpine, where the weather was often freezing, the engine had a thermostat fitted and with that a bypass hose. Also to keep out the cold and possible snow from the engine, a leathercloth grille muff was made up and secured to the front grille moustache. A heated front windscreen replaced the standard laminated 'screen used on the Alpine, with the necessary operating switch fitted to the driver's auxiliary dashboard.

The electrics, apart from the screen switch, remained exactly as the Alpine car but all of the light switches were now routinely replaced to ensure reliability. This was to be common practice for each rebuilt car. The speedo and Halda were changed to read miles rather than kilometres to reflect the rally being in the UK. Tyres, of course, were more or less exclusively Dunlop SP44 for the forest tracks.

The RAC, being the UK's home international, was sponsored by the country's popular *Sun* newspaper, and all cars carried large orange roundels on the doors, mimicking the *Sun*'s logo. This was to prove a problem, as the small numbers became difficult to read once mud-splattered.

The event attracted 144 hopefuls, eager to tackle the 2400-mile route with 400 stage miles on mostly forest tracks. There were 62 stages in total. Starting at London Airport's Excelsior hotel, the route journeyed to the West Country, onto Wales, through the Midlands, up to Northern England and then to Aviemore, in Scotland, for the only night halt, before turning round down the east side of the country to the finish back at London Airport. Only 63 exhausted crews would make it back five days later.

Fall was amongst the finishers but he had numerous problems along the way. He collected a puncture on just the third stage at Lulworth, the hard surface causing many to puncture. Driving fast to catch back some of the lost time, he succeeded in going off on the very next stage – finding a ditch that numerous cars would end up in, including Aaltonen.

Once in the Lake District, Fall went off again, this time hitting a log pile, with resulting damage to the steering and

Fall takes a spin right in front of the camera but would go on to finish the RAC Rally in fifth place.

suspension, causing much work to the BMC service crew at the end of the stage. At the Aviemore night stop, Fall was lying a creditable fourth overall, four minutes behind Mäkinen in the lead but just ahead of Hopkirk.

Once the crews headed back south, Fall had a less fraught run, although he did mangle the radiator fan on one stage, needing a time-consuming change at the roadside by the service crew. To his delight, he caught and passed Pat Moss's Saab on a slippery uphill stage in Guisborough Forest – which unfortunately came to nothing, as the stage was cancelled for being too muddy. Fall's fine determined drive was rewarded with a creditable fifth place, and third in class behind Källström and Aaltonen in sister cars. A tough RAC, as always.

The next event for GRX 195D was the Italian Rally of the Flowers, in late February, the following year. Again, Fall and Wood were assigned to the car, which was rebuilt by Jonny Organ as a Group 2. The engine was back with a full-race camshaft, after the dalliance with the standard Cooper S cam for the RAC. The compression was also increased to 12.6:1, and the power increased to 96bhp – quite a leap from the RAC engine's lowly 76bhp.

Other changes included the heated front 'screen being replaced with a standard laminated windscreen and the headlight bulbs were now uprated to 80/60W from 60/40W previously. The intercom box was also refitted, having been removed for the RAC – not a pace-noted rally – which this rally certainly was. And the speedometer and Halda reverted to reading in kilometres.

The big change was the use of lightweight magnesium wheels manufactured by Minilite, which saved many pounds as they were under half the weight of the heavy steel wheels they replaced. They were also considerably stronger and could be run on should a tyre be lost. Additionally, they reduced the unsprung weight of the car and so improved the handling. They first appeared on works Minis on the Monte Carlo Rally the previous month.

The other visual change was the fitting of the front number plate – now painted on a square on the right-hand side of the bonnet. This was necessary because the front rally plate was deemed necessary to be secured in a vertical position, as opposed to flat on the bonnet, as was normal practice. This necessitated a back-stay for the rally plate, fixed to the bonnet. The car also sported large front mud flaps under the sidelights by the front bumper corners, designed to keep mud and water off the front windscreen; they did, however, tend to restrict air to the front brakes.

Because of the anticipated rough terrain, a heavy-duty Scandinavian sump guard was fitted to the car. This guard had the front quick-lift jacking points fixed to the protruding front edge of the spring steel sump guard as those on the front panel could no longer be reached by the racing jacks used by the service crews.

The rally didn't get off to the best of starts for Fall and Wood, as their planned recce was hampered by heavy snow, closing the majority of the roads that were to be used for the timed stages. Fortunately, a thaw just before the start allowed for some practising but the severe weather had taken its toll on the roads, which became very rough. Because of the snow and poor conditions, Fall ran more or less exclusively on lightly-studded Dunlop SP44 tyres.

Based in San Remo, the geographically-compact route of 1000 miles, to be covered in just 31 hours, meant numerous roads were used several times, which made the already-

Fall and Wood clatter through the rough roads on the rally. Despite damaging the rear of the car, they would finish in fourth place.

GRX 195D at the start of the 1967 Flowers Rally, where the car is now fitted with Minilite wheels, first used the month before on the Monte Carlo Rally.

CHAPTER 3: THE MK 1 MINI COOPER S

Fall about to tow the stricken car of Hopkirk's to their hotel despite its badly damaged suspension.

At the finish of the Flowers Rally, the very deranged rear suspension can be clearly seen.

Timo Mäkinen with Bill Price witness GRX 195D being lowered from the ship bringing the car from England to Helsinki for the start of the 1967 1000 Lakes Rally.

damaged roads even worse. Many roads were, at best, just goat tracks in the hills, and with steep drops to catch the unwary, pace notes were essential.

Fortunately, the majority of the road timing was generous, so the rally was decided on the 12 timed-to-the-second stages – which amounted to 100 miles of flat-out driving over very rough tracks. This would result in many cars being retired broken in some form or another.

Fall was not immune to problems, as the continual pounding on the rough roads broke the rear subframe (which had been double-skinned when built). He was also side-swiped by a bread van, with resultant damage down the nearside of the once-immaculate GRX 195D. This damage resulted in Fall doing the last third of the event with very severe negative camber on the nearside rear wheel, with the resultant detrimental effect on the car's handling. At the finish, he did well to bring the battered car home in fourth place, on what was a very hard event. It also marked the end of Stuart Turner's reign at Abingdon and it was now Peter Browning's turn to take over the helm.

After the Flowers Rally, Tony Fall kept hold of the car and entered it on the second round of the 1967 Motoring News Championship, the Filldyke Rally (a national rally, not an international). With its repaired suspension damage, the car appeared much as it had in Italy. It was to be the last appearance of this car, so Fall was no doubt allowed to use it freely.

The Motoring News Championship was the pinnacle of rallying in the UK at the time and the Filldyke Rally was no exception. Of the 160 cars that applied for a place, a full 120 started the event on Saturday evening in early March. Based in Yorkshire for the first time, this all-night stage event had 11 forest stages to contend, many of which were used on the RAC Rally, such as Wykeham, Dalby, Pickering, Cropton and Boltby Forests. Fall was no doubt familiar with most of them – he was fastest on six of these Yorkshire stages, and with that secured a fine first place overall.

For the Acropolis Rally in May, this Greek classic saw GRX 195D handed over to Timo Mäkinen and Paul Easter.

207

Timo Mäkinen and Paul Easter pose by GRX 195D, which now has a square number plate on the bonnet, which is propped open to increase airflow.

After the battering the car had received on the Flowers Rally and the RAC, it is very likely that this was a new version, it being very doubtful Abingdon would have repaired the badly-battered shell. Built by Mick Legg as a Group 2 car, the engine was – as always for a Mäkinen car – fitted with a full-race camshaft and a very short 4.26:1 diff ratio. It received a high-compression Downton cylinder head, but lower than usual, probably to compensate for lower-octane fuel being more prevalent in Greece. As a result, the engine was slightly down on power, to around 88bhp.

It should be noted that the gearbox casing was machined flat to enable a Moke sump plate to be screwed to it for added protection, as well as a heavy sump guard. Tie bar skids were also fitted. Additionally, an access hole was drilled in the clutch housing, over the starter Bendix, to allow lubricant to be sprayed in. Starter motors were becoming jammed in the flywheel, due to the starter Bendix not releasing properly, likely brought about by an excess of clutch-plate dust. These were now regularly removed and washed clean to increase reliability.

To keep the engine cool and increase the water capacity, an expansion tank was fitted to the radiator, routed inside the car by the navigator's left foot – it was covered and out of sight behind the carpet. A four-blade fan was used and, in addition, the bonnet was slightly propped open with a small block of wood by the bonnet safety catch to allow more airflow and encourage hot air out – all because of the anticipated heat in Greece.

Despite Mäkinen's dislike for Hydrolastic suspension, the car was indeed fitted with single-blue and double-blue displacers front and rear, together with orange helper springs and Aeon bump stops. The rear subframe was fully strengthened and the rear radius arm brackets were further strengthened. The electrics were largely as before but now all four auxiliary lamps had steady-bars fitted, securing them back to the grille moustache. The bars were crafted out of

Mäkinen, all smiles, leaves the start in Athens.

bicycle rod brake pulls.

Mäkinen also had a large back-mounted Lucas 576 fog lamp as a reversing lamp, fitted to the right-hand side of the boot lid. The tyre choice was confined to Dunlop SP44s and Dunlop R7 race tyres.

The Acropolis Rally had a fearsome reputation and was indeed a tough event where a reliable car was important. But now as speeds increased, a fast and reliable car was needed. Based in Athens, the continuous two-days, two-nights event was hard going. Two-thousand miles and 220 miles of stages greeted the relatively small entry of 72 cars. The stages were dry and dusty, all bar two on tarmac, albeit bumpy and of poor quality. These were up in the hills in and around most of Greece in very seasonally hot weather. The route also had a few hillclimbs thrown in for good measure – scored on scratch time.

However, the stages all had a target time to beat, and if cleaned, no penalty points were incurred. As it transpired, the fast cars cleaned most of the stages bar four and so in essence, they decided the rally – but only 18 cars would make the finish. And for the spectators, the final day had a 30-minute circuit race thrown it – but this had no effect on the rally result, provided competitors completed it.

The event had not got off to a good start for Mäkinen, as he was not happy with the gearbox on GRX 195D (and also its brakes). This kept the service crew busy the day before the start, swapping the gearbox from his recce car into the rally car. They also changed the brake servo.

The evening start in Athens saw Mäkinen, as usual, set a blistering pace, cleaning the stages and very fast on the hillclimbs. He was on top of the leaderboard as the rally charged through the first night.

The second day, once dawn broke, saw Mäkinen still ahead

GRX 195D is tipped onto its side at service in Volos to attend to a broken rear subframe.

Timo Mäkinen took Pekka Keskitalo with him on the 1967 1000 Lakes Rally, in yet another GRX 195D hoping for a hat-trick of wins on this classic rally.

Once again the car was on its side but this time into retirement with transmission failure. The rear gearbox mounting has just been cannibalised for Hopkirk's car and GRX195D is about to be towed back to Athens by the service barge with an A bracket tow bar.

Sideways as ever. Mäkinen slides GRX 195D in fine style on a demonstration run before the rally.

where the only loose-surface stages were tackled. Here he was just a second down on Aaltonen but still in the lead. By the second night, still in the lead, GRX 195D's gearbox was showing signs of complaining. Perhaps the gearbox, already overworked in the recce car, did not have enough miles left in it for the rally itself. Nonetheless, Mäkinen was still fast but now, in addition, the rear subframe was breaking up; at service in Volos, the car was tipped onto its side to have it rewelded. The Hydrolastic suspension was also pumped up. Soon the car was on its way again.

Sadly the gearbox finally broke, with a suspected layshaft failure. The car was dragged back to the service area and its gearbox mounting cannibalised for Hopkirk's car. Aaltonen had already retired in a road accident but Hopkirk won through to take first prize; so BMC was pleased enough.

GRX 195D's final event in August was the 1000 Lakes Rally in Finland, where Mäkinen would again take the wheel but this time with local co-driver Pekka Keskitalo. This was the preferred practice at Abingdon; taking a local co-driver on this much-specialised rally where it was felt local knowledge was paramount.

Once again, we saw a different car turn up for its next event. The Acropolis car would, despite being new for that event, have been very tired and with Mäkinen being the favourite for his home event and going for a hat-trick of wins on the event, a fresh car was prepared by Roy Brown. This was not, in fact, a new car but one in better shape than the Acropolis car, and was built as a full Group 2. However, unlike the previous cars, Mäkinen got his own way and the Hydrolastic suspension was replaced with his much-preferred dry rubber cone suspension. This was standard, other than 2mm being removed from the rear struts, ostensibly to slightly lower the rear and sit the car level; but it did have special Koni shock absorbers front and rear. As was customary, the rear swing-arm brackets had a steel block welded into them for added strength.

The engine, using the latest strengthened block and a 12.6:1 high-compression cylinder head, produced 87bhp on the rolling road. With the short 4.2:1 diff, the car's acceleration was considerable, with the close-ratio straight-cut gearbox being carefully built (it still being the car's weak point when driven so hard); the large driveshafts took all of the strain the punishing jumps the Finnish forests were renowned for. The heavy-duty Scandinavian guard, with the front jacking points secured to its leading edge, fully protected the engine and gearbox.

Cooling for the car, which was to prove an issue, was served by a four-blade fan and a 16-fins-per-inch radiator with a 13lb cap, but no thermostat – only a blanking sleeve. Brakes, with racing linings, had additional cooling in the shape of drilled backplates and brake drums, with the brake callipers using asbestos blocks. Further, the rear wheel cylinders were bolted to the backplates to help dissipate heat. Finally, the limiting valve was changed to a 325psi unit to send more braking to the rear.

Lighting was the customary four large Lucas lamps mounted on the chrome badge bar, with the two centre lamps held with steady brackets. The reversing lamp was changed from Lucas back-mounted fog lamps to a small and lighter Austin Healey sidelight. Also new inside the car was the headlight flasher, which was taken from the 1800 range of car and doubled as the indicator, dispensing with a separate flasher stalk on the dashboard that was used in the past. Maserati air horns were replaced by Mixo Minor horns – simpler and less weight.

In Finland scrutineering had been a problem for some; still with the lights disqualification hangover from the Monte Carlo Rally in mind, which was well over a year ago, the Finnish scrutineers insisted that cars using iodine bulbs had them only fitted to their fog lights. This was to accord with Finnish traffic laws – despite the fact the FIA rules allowed cars to run with the lighting system that was applicable in their country of origin. Nevertheless, having been bitten badly in the past, BMC elected to remove the iodine bulbs from spot lamps and replaced them with normal tungsten bulbs.

BMC was light in attendance in Finland, with Aaltonen electing to stay away and Bill Price being assigned to run the team whilst Peter Browning was away supervising on the Marathon de la Route. Nevertheless, with Mäkinen going for his third win in Finland, the pressure was on – and as it transpired, he had a long battle with Simo Lampinen in a V4 Saab.

The 1000-mile route around the 1000 Lakes (although nobody had really counted them) consisted of two large loops centred on Jyväskylä, with 24 stages to decide the winner. All bar a few were relatively short stages and made up just 100 miles of flat-out competition. Finland, however, had strict speeding laws and despite the nation's love of rallying, the 30mph speed limit between the stages was rigidly enforced. Of the 120 hopefuls who entered this round of the European Championship, only 70 would make it back to the finish.

Practising had been banned for the last two years, so great importance was placed on local knowledge. However, for the 1967 event, to make it fair to all competitors, practice was again being allowed – so Mäkinen's advantage with Keskitalo in the hot seat, with his local knowledge, was lost. Nonetheless, right from the start, in the rain, he was amongst the leaders.

The first stage, which was very fast around the streets of Jyväskylä, was a Porsche benefit, but once into the forest and the jumps, and it was still raining, Mäkinen and Lampinen were swapping fastest times. After the first loop of eight stages and back in Jyväskylä, Lampinen was in the lead, having won five to Mäkinen's three, who was in second place.

On the second loop, Mäkinen's car was starting to overheat. The service crew removed the four lamps and also propped open the bonnet in an attempt to let more air into the engine. They then tackled the longest stage of the event – 16 miles of fast-jumping forest, just south of Jyväskylä. With six miles to the finish, disaster struck as Mäkinen's bonnet flew open – in

Mäkinen throwing up the gravel surface. The car was overheating badly so all the lights had been removed to increase the airflow.

the rush at the service, the leather safety strap had been left undone. Undaunted, Mäkinen pressed on, looking out of the side window and still driving flat-out – so fast that he was second-fastest on this decisive stage and, more importantly, still beat Lampinen by five seconds.

But his problems were not over. All of the heavy landings had broken the remote gearshift mounting. Fortunately, the BMC service crew was quickly to hand and the car was ceremoniously tipped onto its side to effect a repair. It later transpired that the transmission case had also fractured but had held together.

On the final night, Mäkinen was 14 seconds faster than Lampinen on the last three stages, and at the finish back in Jyväskylä he had won by a slender eight seconds – and he'd got his hat-trick.

GRX 195D was retained by BMC as a publicity car for a while and then sold to Bob Martyn.

The bonnet flew up after six miles of a 16-mile stage, so Mäkinen drove 10 miles looking out of the side window and was still second-fastest on the stage, which was enough for him to win his third 1000 Lakes Rally.

Competition Record

Date	Event	Crew	Number	Overall result	Class result
Jan 1966	Monte Carlo Rally	Raymond Baxter/Jack Scott	87	disqualified	
Sept 1966	Alpine Rally	Tony Fall/Mike Wood	66	DNF	
Nov 1966	RAC Rally	Tony Fall/Mike Wood	21	5th	3rd
Feb 1967	Flowers Rally	Tony Fall/Mike Wood	82	4th	4th
March 1967	Filldyke Rally	Tony Fall/David Fawcett	6	1st	
May 1967	Acropolis Rally	Timo Mäkinen/Paul Easter	99	DNF	
Aug 1967	1000 Lakes	Timo Mäkinen/Pekka Keskitalo	29	1st	1st

Registration Number	First registered	Chassis number	Engine	Engine number	Model
GRX 309D	Jan 1966	CA2S7 799782	1275cc	9F-SA-Y 39462	Austin Cooper S

GRX 309D was one of a crop of six cars registered new in January 1966, eclipsing the meagre four new cars registered the previous year. Clearly, Stuart Turner's standing was increasing along with his budget, and with an extended rally programme and even more entries planned for 1966, it would be a busy year as Abingdon.

GRX 309D's first event was The Rally of the Flowers in Italy in late February, and saw the new car built by Brian Moylan as a Group 2 car for Paddy Hopkirk and Ron Crellin. This would be the start of a new pairing as Hopkirk had, with mutual consent, decided to part company with Henry Liddon, his co-driver since 1963. Crellin had been part of the works team for a while, doing ice notes and had also co-driven with Tony Fall. He was yet another very experienced British co-driver who had cut his teeth on navigational road rallies. He instantly gelled with Hopkirk and they too went on to become a successful team.

The build of the car followed normal practice for a Group 2 Mini but, mindful of their exclusion on the Monte Carlo Rally, it was specially noted that no parts should have special identifying marks painted on them. This, likely to automatically attract a scrutineer's attention, was not a path

Paddy Hopkirk and Ron Crellin with GRX 309D at the start of the San Remo Rally, known as the Rally of the Flowers.

Cars were required to carry their competition number on the boot lid, with just a single rally plate on the front of the car.

Abingdon wished to go down. Previously, Abingdon would, even for standard parts, carefully select them and often mark them accordingly (often with orange paint), but this practice was stopped. Further, it was also noted that no strengthening was to be carried out to the front subframe where the sump shield was fitted. Abingdon was clearly getting jumpy and sticking strictly to the rule book.

The engine, bored out to 1293cc, ran a Downton-modified cylinder head with 11.6:1 compression and a AEG648 full-race camshaft, and sat on a close-ratio straight-cut gearbox with a 4.2 differential. The carburettors were twin SU H4s, with float chamber extensions and AZ needles, being very slightly less rich than the normal BG needles used. As always, the car ran an oil cooler but now, as the bulky 11AC alternator was fitted, the oil cooler had to be moved over slightly, necessitating relocating its mounting brackets. Additionally, the diagonal front-panel steady bar was removed, modified and fitted vertically to clear the alternator.

Hydrolastic suspension was uprated by the use of single-red and double-red displacers front and back, and the suspension was raised by the use of 0.1in packing washers under the front struts, which increased the ride height by 1/3in. The car also ran larger bump stops and additional helper springs at the rear.

The Flowers rally used some loose gravel roads, which were often rough and hard on the cars – as a result, the car ran a heavy-duty sump guard as well as a battery guard on the rear subframe. The car also ran on standard 3½J wheels, not the optional wider 4½J-wide rims and, as a result, no wheelarch extensions. They were fitted with standard Dunlop SP3 tyres instead of Dunlop R7 race tyres.

Lighting, now using the badge bar for mounting the auxiliary lamps, consisted of the now-normal two large Lucas 700 fog lamps and a pair of Lucas 700 lamps with Continental lenses for driving lights all with iodine bulbs. The headlights were European vertical-dip units with 60/40-watt bulbs. The reversing lamp, fitted to the boot lid, was an Austin Healey 3000 sidelight unit equipped with a more powerful brake lamp bulb. These were nearly as effective as the Lucas 576 fog lamp often fitted but were of less weight and less likely to get damaged, being smaller and not as vulnerable.

As always, the electrics received detailed attention from the resident Lucas racing technicians, which resulted in a complete rewire from scratch, specifically designed for the car and the requirements of the crew regarding equipment, instruments and switches. Despite the common misconception, was never a works wiring diagram, the technicians relying on their skill and knowledge to wire the car, one wire at a time, to achieve what has always been a beautifully-presented wiring loom. The car was equipped with an intercom system and also, distinctively, had four washer jets by the wipers, in two banks of two – a very unusual feature. Furthermore, for the Rally of the Flowers, the competition number was painted onto the top left corner of the boot lid.

Inside the car, all the lines were run internally, although the twin fuel pump was located on the rear subframe outside but protected by an alloy pate. Gone were the Aston filler caps, replaced by standard fuel caps but held onto the car by a light chain. The twin fuel tanks were protected in the boot from damage by gluing asbestos sheets to their sides. A specially-fabricated reclining passenger seat was made from a Mini seat for the navigator, and a fibreglass bucket seat for driver. Both used Irvin seat belts – full harness and lap-and-diagonal respectively. The usual extra padding was fitted to the door pocket, lock and pillars, and the car retained its carpets but had an asbestos blanket placed under the front to keep exhaust heat away from the interior. Following on from Abingdon's jitteriness over modifying the body, the bung holes were not welded up, nor were access holes cut behind the rear seat to aid access to the helper springs. Beforehand, these modifications had been routinely carried out on most cars.

The Rally of the Flowers in Italy, later to be called the San Remo Rally, was a tough event run over two hard days in northern Italy, and held this year in unseasonably atrocious weather. At the start were 130 cars, and a mere 39 made it back to the finish. Hopkirk started well, swapping top times with Jean-François Piot in the works Renault 8 Gordini (who was eventually excluded).

However, it was not to last and Hopkirk, with his new navigator, didn't have the best of rallies, finishing a lowly 15th place. His trouble largely centred on the car losing water from the radiator and constantly overheating, boiling over on numerous occasions. This was caused by a stone deranging the fan blades, which in turn ground away at the radiator – bending the fan blades away made no difference, as the radiator was now leaking badly.

The serious water leak meant a change of radiator and a new fan but it made little difference, other than losing valuable time, and the car continued to overheat. The hard-pressed BMC mechanics had to effect the repair either side of the control to prevent the car being excluded by going over its time allowance. This meant taking the radiator off on one side of the control and fitting the replacement on the other side - leading to a 30-minute delay, which effectively meant Hopkirk slid way down the leaderboard. Matters got worse when the clack valve on the inlet manifold failed, and proceeded to gulp oil into the inlet tract, with a resulting chronic misfire. Not a great event for the new partnership.

After the Flowers rally, GRX 309D was used again by Hopkirk, this time as his recce car for the Circuit of Ireland scheduled for early April over the Easter weekend. Once completed and returned to Abingdon, Aaltonen used the car for his next recce, for the Acropolis Rally in late May. This would have taken a toll on the car, and it would not see active service again with Abingdon.

For the GRX 309D's next event, the Polish Rally held in August, the car was renewed. Built by Johnny Evans, GRX 309D appeared as a 970S. Assigned to Tony Fall and local Latvian navigator Atis Krauklis, the 970cc engine was overbored 0.040in to give 999cc – just within the one-litre class. Fitted with an AEG544 camshaft rather than the customary full-race cam, and with a high-compression cylinder head of

12.6:1, the car produced a maximum of 66bhp at the wheels on the Abingdon rolling road – much less than a 1293S, and also with considerably less torque. However, with a 4.26 diff ratio, the car was still capable of reaching 100mph.

The build of the car was very similar to that for the Flowers. However, now the subframe was strengthened by double-skinning to the top and rear of the frame and the rear suspension radius arm brackets were also strengthened. Hydrolastic suspension was used but this time with single-

Hopkirk and Crellin corner hard in GRX 309D on the Flowers Rally, as can be seen by the right-hand wheel almost tucking under the car.

GRX 309D was used by Rauno Aaltonen and Henry Liddon for their recce for the 1966 Acropolis Rally. The roads were often very rough and the car was badly damaged during the recce.

A new GRX 309D appeared for Tony Fall and Attis Krauklis for the 1966 Polish Rally. With a five per cent handicap bonus on time for one-litre cars on the rally, GRX 309D was fitted with a 970S engine.

Fall and Krauklis screech into a control. The speed of the one-litre car was amazing many people, including Mäkinen, whose times he was matching on many tests.

blue and double-blue displacers front and back, along with standard orange helper springs. As in Italy, the car ran narrow 3½J steel wheels without wheelarch extensions.

Inside the car, the fuel pump was mounted under the rear seat pan on the navigator's side, rather than outside on the subframe. It was still a twin SU pump but with only one pump wired, the second acting as a spare. The fuel lines were run inside the car but now, in the boot, the metal three-way connection between the tanks and pump was made larger to increase the rate of fuel delivery. Another addition was the provision of a steel safety strap fixed under the car at the end of the gear remote shift. Should the rubber mounting fail, the remote would fall no further than the strap. This was in addition to the special Mitchell mounting used in place of the standard mounting rubber for the remote. A touch of Abingdon belt and braces.

The Polish Rally was an event still behind the Iron Curtain in 1966, and despite it being a round of the European Championship, only a dozen European crews were part of the 52 entry, the rest being local Polish drivers hoping to make their mark. It had been a calculated judgement by Stuart Turner to enter Fall in a one-litre car, favouring the marking and class system employed by the organisers, which gave a more generous time allowance to the smaller-capacity cars on the road and also a beneficial handicap for their stage times. With the rally being set at a very high average speed – and including 22 stages, two hillclimbs and a couple of races during the three days – the 1700-mile event was to be a testing event.

Centred around Krakow, the unseasonably poor weather soon saw the field decimated, with only 11 crews making it to the finish. Fall was not without his problems, as the slippery conditions saw him fly off the road after a blind brow when the road turned sharp right. A full 360-degree spin on the well-placed escape road saw him rejoin without any great time loss. He also overshot the finish line of a particularly slippery stage, which resulted in Krauklis running back to clock in; this could have incurred a heavy penalty but fortunately the organisers decided not to enforce it because many others had done the same.

At service the BMC mechanics changed the rear radius arm, which had been bent in a slight mishap whilst Krauklis had been at the wheel when he slid off the road and damaged the rear corner. The second night section some 14 hours in duration, flat-out in streaming wet conditions, saw a furious pace over rough and stony woodland tracks. Fall was grateful for the 5 per cent handicap time bonus the one-litre car gave him, as everyone was dropping time.

The little 970S was posting remarkable times on nearly all the stages, even before the handicap adjustment. It was recorded that with the short 4.26 diff, the car was pulling 8500rpm on a long straight and was as fast as Mäkinen in the 1275S, where the 4.1 diff and 7800rpm netted similar

CHAPTER 3: THE MK 1 MINI COOPER S

terminal speed. So impressed was Mäkinen with the smaller-engined car he said he'd have been quite happy to have used the car himself. As the event wore on, Fall was in a strong second place, only to be promoted to first place once the results were posted. This was due to a timing error by the organisers robbing Mäkinen of the win. Fall, with his local co-driver, happily took the victory.

The car's next outing would again see Fall at the wheel, this time as his recce car for the Alpine Rally in early September. The next rally scheduled for the car was the RAC Rally of Great Britain, and Abingdon's home event. It was a coup that Abingdon managed to sign world champion racing driver Graham Hill to drive the car; he was to be navigated by BBC *Wheelbase* television presenter Maxwell Boyd and seeded at number five. Ford, not to be out gunned, signed Jim Clark, also a world champion racing driver, for a Lotus Cortina. He was close behind Hill at number eight. Both would benefit from smoother undamaged roads in the British forests compared to those behind.

Again, with GRX 309D, yet another car was prepared. It is probable that this car, built by Johnny Evans, was in fact a Morris Cooper S. The smaller Austin Cooper badge on the bonnet clearly showed screws, blanking off the larger mounting holes for a Morris Cooper badge either side. It's unclear if this was a new car delivered for preparation as a Morris or was in fact a used Morris rally car reprepared for Graham Hill. On balance, it is likely Abingdon built a new car for the world champion. So, in any event, this was the third iteration of GRX 309D.

The build of the car used one of the new strengthened engine blocks, which were customarily bored out to 1293cc. The car also had new forged oval pistons with special oil scraper rings. For the RAC, it was decided to fit a standard Cooper S camshaft, the AEG510, in preference to the normal full-race camshaft, despite it being built as a Group 2 car. It was

The race circuit test saw the little car put in a superb performance, enough for Fall and Krauklis to win the rally overall.

Graham Hill with TV presenter Maxwell Boyd, who would be his navigator on the RAC Rally, seen here at Bagshot military testing ground where Hill received driving tuition from Paddy Hopkirk. This was yet another GRX 309D.

reasoned that the need for instant low-down torque on the tight and often muddy British forest tracks was a reasonable trade off for a drop in peak power. Nevertheless, with a high-compression Downton cylinder head (held down with MGB cylinder head studs) the car produced a healthy 76bhp at the wheels – and with a low 4.26:1 diff, acceleration was still

GRX 309D early on the RAC Rally where Hill was eclipsed by the performance of Jim Clark in the works Ford Cortina.

215

WORKS MINIS IN DETAIL

Hill and Boyd did not feature well on the 1966 RAC Rally, having numerous mechanical problems and the world racing champion not taking well to forest rallying.

Hill looking very disgruntled having already damaged the car. He would retire in the Lake District with terminal transmission problems, probably much to his relief.

considerable. This was, however, 15bhp down on the car's customary expected power output. Straight-cut close-ratio gears were again used, as were Hardy Spicer drive couplings.

Once again, the car used Hydrolastic suspension with single-blue and double-blue displacers and orange helper springs. For the RAC, the subframes were strengthened front and back and the car carried a heavy-duty Scandinavian sump guard, made of spring steel, in addition to a Moke sump plate screwed to the underside of the gearbox casing. Wider 4½J steel wheels were used and therefore the car ran fibreglass wheelarch extensions. It was set at a standard ride height of around 13in from wheel centre to the edge of the wheelarch.

The car was fitted with external mud flaps fastened to the corners of the front bumper as an attempt to deflect water and mud away from the headlights and windscreen, which was a particular problem with the Mini as the front wheels are very close to the front of the car compared to more traditional designs. Nevertheless, the car also ran a headlight washer system and it had a heated front windscreen.

Strengthening continued inside the car, where a double-skinned crossmember was fabricated by the MG press shop and installed in the car to prevent it from breaking its back on the anticipated rough terrain. This had shown up on severe rough-road testing carried out in Wales prior to the event, where stress cracks appeared around the crossmember. Strengthening straps were used inside the car where the gearshift remote mounting bracket was fixed, and in addition the remote used a Mitchell mounting plus a safety strap should it fail.

Also inside the car, for the first time in a works Mini, it was fitted with a roll cage – a simple loop between the B-posts, going over the crews' heads, with a back stay and a coupling onto the rear parcel shelf. This relatively lightweight, simple cage was made from an aircraft-grade light alloy and not steel; unlike modern cages, it added little to the strength or rigidity of the car but added greatly to the crew's safety. The cage also made a suitable location to fix the intercom box. The other minor difference to the build of this car was that the speedometer and Halda were calibrated to read in miles and not kilometres as they generally were for European events.

For the RAC, it's unclear if Stuart Turner expected Hill to star on the event or simply be there to drum up publicity for BMC. Certainly Clark for Ford did both, while Hill sadly only achieved the latter, retiring somewhat disgruntled early in the rally. He did have several practice sessions to familiarise himself with a works Mini (in fact the car Hopkirk had used on the Gulf London Rally) and the art of rally driving prior to the event. Hill's training and familiarisation took place at the military proving ground at Bagshot in Surrey, tutored by Paddy Hopkirk; Hill was extricated from the scenery on several occasions.

The RAC Rally, by 1966, was becoming very popular, it being reported that over 1,000,000 spectators turned out over the five days that November – no doubt bolstered by the event's sponsor, the *Sun* newspaper. Starting at London Airport, the 2400-mile route included 67 stages, with all but one on forestry or military roads, amounting to some 400 miles. At the start were 144 crews, and so severe was the challenge that only 63 were classed as finishers.

From west London the route headed out westwards and on towards Bristol. Hill was soon a casualty ascending the Porlock Hill climb in the West Country, where a tooth from one of the differential planet wheels flew out through the gear casing and with that a great deal of oil. The car was summarily tipped onto its side by the BMC mechanics at the Bristol Airport service area – to effect a repair to the gear casing with plastic metal – and Hill was dispatched on his way and through the night into Wales. The car was finally to succumb to its injuries in the Lake District when it expired with terminal loss of drive on the twisty Grizedale stage where the final drive expired, due no doubt to the ailing planet wheel gear. Hill was soon on his way home, rather relieved it was all over, as unlike Clark, he'd not really taken to rallying.

Straight after the RAC Rally, the car was pressed into service again for Tony Fall and Mike Wood, this time to contest the Welsh International Rally in early December. The car was reprepared by Robin Vokins and Mick Legg – much the same as on the RAC other than the rebuilt engine now had the full-race camshaft fitted and, of course, the gearbox and final drive replaced after its RAC damage. The new Downton cylinder head was now at a higher compression of 12.6:1, so power output was again up to around 83bhp at the wheels. Also of note was that all the light switches were replaced on the car for every event to ensure 100 per cent reliability. So once again the resident Lucas technicians were kept busy.

The Welsh International, one of the four home internationals in the UK, was not often supported by Abingdon but it was decided to enter Tony Fall and Mike Wood to try to challenge Ford on the home event and to win the RAC Championship. Fall was, at the time, leading the RAC Rally Championship by one slender point from Roy Fidler in his Triumph 2000, so was hoping to do well to seal the championship.

Run in early December, the weather was cold, windy and very wet. Starting in Cardiff on the Friday evening, it ran more or less constantly until the Sunday lunchtime and, apart from two small breaks, the 650-mile route was a great test of stamina and resilience. Attracting the great and good of British rallying, it was always a popular event.

A third of the 124 hopefuls who started the rally didn't make it back to Cardiff by Sunday lunchtime. Sadly, Fall wasn't one of the finishers. He hadn't lasted past the first night, when in pouring rain he aquaplaned off the road on the tarmac military stages over the Epynt ranges north of Brecon. The car was well off the road and, with a badly bent rear subframe, was forced into retirement. This left Fidler to win the championship with a fine second place in his Triumph.

After the Welsh Rally, the car was patched up and once again quickly serviced and dispatched to France for Tony Fall and Raymond Joss to complete their recce for the Monte Carlo Rally, Fall having already spent time tyre testing in France before the RAC. Raymond Joss was to take over from Mike Wood on the 1967 Monte, as his services were now assigned to Simo Lampinen, on his second BMC works drive following the RAC.

The final event for GRX 309D was the Sebring 4 Hours race in North America, where it was driven by Paddy Hopkirk and John Rhodes. A new race car built up by Abingdon rather than converting a tired rally car for shipping to America. So, yet again there was a new GRX 309D.

The fourth GRX 309D was built for the Sebring 4-hour race in North America for Paddy Hopkirk and John Rhodes.

The new race car outside the yard at Abingdon. Abingdon was not experienced in building race cars but the car did look very purposeful with its roundels and side exhaust.

The long-range aluminium fuel tank sits across the top of the boot with the standard steel tank retained in the standard position.

Being a race car, it was quite different in appearance, with large white roundels on the bonnet, boot and doors. The exhaust was routed out underneath the driver's door and the car was fitted with Minilite magnesium wheels, which first appeared on the Monte Carlo Rally cars a few months earlier. These wheels offered a considerable weight saving and gave a far more responsive drive as the unsprung weight was drastically reduced. The car ran wheelarch extensions and sat on Dunlop race tyres.

Inside the car there was just a single boxed-out dash panel in front of the driver with rev counter, oil pressure and water temperature gauges. Hopkirk had elected to use a thin-grip Springall steering wheel, rather than the latest Moto-Lita wheels now on offer. The car was also equipped with a roll cage and one bucket seat. However, a standard passenger seat had to be retained. Inside the car was also a water expansion tank from the radiator, which had proved effective at retaining expanding water and allowed more coolant to be carried.

The race was a curtain-raiser to the main event, the 12-hour sports prototype race in which Abingdon had also entered a two-litre MGB. The four-hour Sebring race took place the day before and, despite the grid being largely populated by big saloons, seven Cooper Ss lined up in the field of 61 at the Florida racetrack.

A single dashboard was all that was needed on the race car, with oil temperature gauge and oil pressure gauge in front by the rev counter and a Springall steering wheel.

CHAPTER 3: THE MK 1 MINI COOPER S

Hopkirk and Rhodes qualified well in 36th place and were indeed the first Mini entry on the grid. The car ran well in the race and, other than a fuelling issue caused by a faulty refuelling rig in the pits, the car was well ahead in its class. As the four-hour mark came up, cruising to the finish, albeit eight laps behind the leading Shelby Ford Mustang, disaster struck just as the Mini approached the finish line and it spluttered to a halt, out of fuel. The mechanic hastily threw some fuel in to get the car going again, as the car had to be running at the end of the race to qualify as a finisher. Lancia protested BMC's action but Peter Browning successfully argued that the car was actually running at the four-hour finish mark, so it was rewarded with a fine class win and finished 20th overall, against a lot of heavy American muscle cars – a creditable result where only 36 of the original starters finished.

The Sebring car never returned to the UK, but stayed in North America and was sold to BMC USA.

Hopkirk and Rhodes won their class at Sebring's open airfield race track, despite running out of fuel on the finish line.

Competition Record

Date	Event	Crew	Number	Overall result	Class result
Feb 1966	Rally of the Flowers	Paddy Hopkirk/Ron Crellin	50	16th	
Aug 1966	Polish Rally	Tony Fall/Atis Krauklis	56	1st	
Nov 1966	RAC Rally	Graham Hill/Maxwell Boyd	5	DNF	
Dec 1966	Welsh Rally	Tony Fall/Mike Wood	3	DNF	
Mar 1967	Sebring 4 hrs	Paddy Hopkirk/John Rhodes	48		1st

Registration Number	First registered	Chassis number	Engine	Engine number	Model
GRX 310D	Jan 1966	KA2S4 799883	1275cc	9F-SA-Y 39485	Morris Cooper S

GRX 310D was the last of the six new Cooper Ss that arrived at Abingdon to be registered in January 1966. Four were assigned for the Monte Carlo Rally – GRX 5D, 55D, 555D and 195D – which left GRX 309D and 310D for other duties.

GRX 310D, a Morris Cooper S, would go on to have a long and successful career at Abingdon over a three-and-a-half year period and would end up as a race car after its rally duties were over. It would also do its fair share of recce duties along the way. Needless to say, over that period, GRX 310D would have several new bodyshells.

The first of the seven rallies the car was to tackle was the Swedish Rally held in February 1966. The event was on the snow-covered tracks of Sweden, where Rauno Aaltonen and Tony Ambrose were assigned the Group 2 car. Run now in the height of winter, the Swedish Rally – known locally as the KAK (Kings Automobile Club) Rally – was a different challenge from

GRX 310D was prepared for Rauno Aaltonen and Henry Liddon for the 1966 Swedish Rally under the new Appendix K rules. Aaltonen would retire with a seized engine.

most other rallies, as the air temperatures would always be well below zero for the whole event and the route would inevitably be entirely on snowbound roads and tracks.

With the new Group 2 Appendix J regulations now in place (which many teams were struggling to fully understand and comply with), the car was meticulously prepared. BMC, still smarting from its Monte Carlo Rally exclusion the previous month, had prepared the car strictly in accordance with the new regulations. Fresh for Abingdon for this event was a completely new auxiliary lighting arrangement on the front: gone were the cluttered five-light arrangements, to be replaced by four lamps in a line. These were fitted to a heavy, chromed badge bar on the front panel above the bumper ahead of the grill. This housed four large Lucas 700 lamps, with two fog lights on the outside and two Continental driving lamps in the middle.

Despite the car being entered into Group 2, narrow 3½J wheels were fitted, instead of wider 4½ J wheels, to help cut through the snow and ice. Studded tyres were used throughout on the always-snow-packed roads. Because of the obvious cold weather, a heated front 'screen was added, as was an uprated heater, together with a muff fitted to the grille moustache to keep out snow and the cold. The electrics were fed by an alternator, rather than a dynamo, and the powerful Group 2 engine was Abingdon's usual 1293cc engine, producing near 100bhp.

Scrutineering, feared by many with the new regulations, proved a time-consuming experience as ill-informed scrutineers interpreted the new rules incorrectly. Aaltonen's car was initially rejected as the scrutineers objected to the fuel line being run inside the car. Once the rules were re-inspected, it became clear under Group 2 regulations that lines could be freely placed anywhere. Normality resumed and the car was passed to start.

The organisers had allowed 'training' runs to let competitors get used to the stages but this proved of little value as the slow convoy through the first three stages only served to show that the ploughed stages were too narrow. They were all re-ploughed and widened come the start.

The stages formed the meat of the rally, as the road timing was so lax that even a calamitous stage time wouldn't result in any road time being lost. The event was split into two sections, the first a northerly route from the Örebro start (midway between Stockholm and Gothenburg) of almost 24 hours with 13 stages; the second, after six hours' rest back at Örebro, of 27 hours, where a further 15 stages were tackled. These retraced some of the northern route before heading southwards to return again to Örebro. In total, 680 stage miles were on offer, mainly over frozen lakes or frozen forest tracks.

At the start of the rally were 120 hopefuls, and with no snowfall experienced for two days, coupled with clear skies, the night temperature plummeted to -40C. All agreed that it was going to be a hard event.

And so it proved, as only 48 crews were classed as finishers, none of which were works cars. Aaltonen, on the sixth (very bumpy) stage, came across a rock that had been dislodged by a previous competitor nudging the bank. Aaltonen hit the rock and pushed the radiator onto the fan, losing all his water, and in little time the engine had seized and he was out. True to tradition, the rally was won by a Scandinavian driver, namely Ake Andersson in a works Saab.

Aaltonen was once again assigned GRX 310D for its next event, the Tulip Rally in April 1966, but would take on a new co-driver, Henry Liddon – the long-time partner of Paddy Hopkirk, with whom he had decided to part company. Hopkirk would then team up with Ron Crellin, and with Tony Ambrose (Aaltonen's regular co-driver) deciding to do fewer events, this new arrangement worked well and caused no disruption within the team.

GRX 310D was built as a Group 2 car for the Tulip and this had caused some discussion at Abingdon. The second car for the event was built as a Group 1 car, as BMC intended to challenge for as many class awards as possible, figuring it was all good advertising. Now that the unloved class improvement handicap system had been abandoned by the organisers at the last moment – brought about largely by pressure from works teams – the event would now be decided on scratch with the fastest winning. This would mean that the two star Abingdon drivers, Aaltonen and Mäkinen, would not be competing against each other for class awards. The decision as to who got the more powerful car was down to a toss of a coin – and Aaltonen won, grabbing the Group 2 entry whilst Mäkinen has to content himself with the lesser-powered car. This did not please Mäkinen one bit, especially after using a similar Group 1 car on the recent Monte Carlo Rally.

Although GRX 310D was registered as a Morris Cooper

The Tulip Rally saw Aaltonen and Liddon again in GRX 310D but this time as an Austin, although the front badge was initially covered over. Aaltonen would go on to win the rally.

S, it appeared early in the rally with an Austin Cooper badge on the front (with a Morris Cooper grille), which was swiftly hidden with masking tape. This leads to the conclusion the car was likely swapped for another Mini prior to the event and the badges were overlooked. The car appeared as a Morris in all subsequent events.

GRX 310D was fitted with a full Group 2 engine, which was reputed to be the most powerful engine produced by Abingdon for the Mini, reportedly putting out 100bhp at the wheels. The car was finished with Group 2 arches to cover the wider steel wheels and it used Dunlop racing tyres throughout. It also now had the customary four lights along the front, fitted with off-white-coloured lamp covers.

The Tulip Rally was always a favourite for privateers, and now with the inclusion of the Tulip road book, which clearly defined road junctions where a turn was needed, navigation for the less experienced was made much easier. The Tulip-style road book is, to this day, still used for a great number of rallies.

The previous class improvement system had given amateur drivers a better chance of an award and, despite the event now being decided on scratch, it still attracted an entry of 116 cars, largely made up of private entrants chasing amateur awards in all of the various classes. Even though the Tulip was a round of the European championship, few entries were works cars. Nevertheless, there was a strong but small contingent of contenders of works cars ready to take up the 1750-mile challenge.

Unfortunately for the organisers, the local police, at the last moment, refused a number of road closures, which meant the loss of eight hillclimb special stages. The meat of the rally was thus reduced to 55 miles of tests on 15 climbs, plus 80 miles of fast selectives on demanding twisty roads, and finally a couple of stages around an army camp and a blast around Zandvoort race circuit.

With the rally starting in Noordwijk on the Dutch coast, it ventured into Luxembourg, Belgium and France, in and around Geneva, before returning back to Holland. With no snow this year, the pace was fast and furious, and Aaltonen was soon posting fastest times on the climbs. The Cooper S with its low gearing, ideally suited to the terrain, ran faultlessly throughout. By halfway at Morez, in eastern France, he had a lead of 30 seconds over Vic Elford in a works Lotus Cortina – a lead he would keep and extend back at the finish in Noordwijk some four days later, winning by 45 seconds.

BMC was rewarded with the outright win of Aaltonen and also Mäkinen winning his class – but only just. BMC also won the team prize with privateer Bob Freeborough, who had been roped in. With no post-event scrutineering dramas, it was a successful event by any measure.

The following month, Tony Fall and Mike Wood took over the car to do the Austrian Alpine Rally. It was entered again as a Group 2 car with a 1293cc full-race engine with lightened flywheel and timing gear. Twin SU H4 carburettors

and an 11.7:1 Downton cylinder head were fitted, along with Abingdon's preferred camshaft, the AEA648. For the anticipated climbs, the car was fitted again with a very short 4.26:1 final drive, as well as a straight-cut and close-ratio gear set. A four-blade fan kept things cool and a heavy-duty RAC-type sump guard protected the gearbox underside.

The car was fitted with double-blue and single-blue Hydrolastic suspension and additional Aeon bump stops with orange 30lb helper springs, but no additional dampers. Fibreglass spats were fitted to the wheelarches to cover the

GRX 310D now with its Austin Cooper badge uncovered but still with a Morris Cooper grille.

Tony Fall and Mike Wood preparing for the start of the Austrian Alpine, clearly showing the co-driver's dashboard.

wider 4½J steel wheels.

Inside the car, Fall sat in a fibreglass bucket seat whilst Wood had a special reclining seat. Fall had a lap-and-diagonal Irvin belt whilst Wood had a full Irvin harness. All of the lines were run inside the car and now the fuel pump was located beneath the rear seat rather than on the outside on the rear subframe.

For the Austrian Alpine the car carried both numbers painted on the doors, as was Abingdon's usual practice, but in addition, the organisers supplied large numbers that also had to be stuck onto the bonnet of the car. This was in addition to the supplied rally plates that were also attached to the front and back of the car.

The Austrian Alpine, being run early in the year, often encountered snow on the high passes and this year, despite fine weather, still had snow to negotiate on the ground. However, with much of the 1000-mile route on twisty loose-surface roads, tyre choice was essentially Dunlop SP44s. Starting in Velden, just north of the Italian-Yugoslavian border, it visited the Alps of southern Austria and some of the Dolomites in northern Yugoslavia. The rally was, however, rather out of step with the way rallying was going, in that it didn't recognise an outright winner – only those who won their class or category.

The rally was still being aimed at privateers but being part of the European Championship, works entries were definitely in evidence – notably from Porsche and BMC. The aim of the rally was to remain clean on the road by not losing any time at the many time controls. Into the mix were 60 miles of speed tests (eight in all), which would only be used in the event of a tie. These tests consisted of hillclimbs and a blast around an airfield. To remain clean on the road, however, was no mean feat.

The Austrian maps were poor, and to do well a good navigator rather than a co-driver was definitely a requirement. The organisers were also keen to ensure that only the nominated driver attempted the timed tests, so each nominated driver had to wear a sealed wristband that was inspected at the start and finish of each test.

A further oddity of the rally was that service was not permitted. Further still, the cars were allowed only six wheels; tyres could be changed but not the wheels. BMC, however, still attended with one of its service barges to keep a watchful eye on the two cars entered – Hopkirk being the other car and the favourite to win, repeating his success from the previous year.

Scrutineering was expected to be difficult but, other than the Minis struggling to drive over a 4in block of wood – designed to ensure cars were not too low – no problems were encountered. And despite the strict restrictions on wheels, no special markings were carried out to ensure compliance.

The first loop from Velden, of 15 hours, saw a 4am start, and soon Fall was posting quick times only a few seconds behind hard-charging Hopkirk. Fall, however, dropped a valuable ten minutes on the third stage when he lost a rear wheel after the studs stripped. Now running on just two studs, he had a more serious front wheel puncture. Keen not to lose more time, he pressed on, only to flatten the steel wheel around the front disc and grind the car to a halt. Rebuilding the hub at the next time control fortunately resulted in no loss of road time and so his clean sheet was still intact.

The second leg restarted at Velden at 2am after half a night's sleep and, with another 17 hours of hard motoring ahead, the challenge was too much for many. After dawn broke, only three cars were still clean on the road. Fall, however, was not one of them as he hit a log pile on one of the fast sections through a forest and bent the steering arm into a U shape. With no service crew anywhere near, he retired. Only 37 cars made it back to the finish in Velden, and by the late afternoon, Hopkirk had been declared the winner, having run clean and won six of the stages.

After the Austrian Alpine, GRX 310D was assigned to recce duty. First in early June 1966 the car was used by Paddy Hopkirk and Terry Harriman to recce the forthcoming Geneva Rally, which the crew would tackle in JBL 495D. After its return, Timo Mäkinen and Paul Easter took GRX 310D into Czechoslovakia to recce that event, which took place in July where they would use the sister car, JBL 493D.

For GRX 310D's next event, the 1000 Lakes Rally in Finland in August, a new car was therefore built for Rauno Aaltonen, who would on this occasion take local co-driver Naino Nurmimaa in the hot seat. The 1000 Lakes, which didn't allow practice in 1966, relied heavily on local knowledge to safely and quickly tackle the many blind crests and twists through the Finnish forests – hence the need for a local navigator. Henry Liddon, who would normal accompany Aaltonen, was dispatched to recce the forthcoming Alpine Rally along

Fall and Wood retired near the end of the Austrian Alpine when they hit a log pile in GRX310D and bent the steering arm. With no service permitted, they were out.

with Paul Easter, who would also be giving up his regular seat alongside Timo Mäkinen, as he too took a local navigator on the 1000 Lakes.

The new Group 2 car was fitted with a very powerful 1293cc engine with a high-compression cylinder head of 12.6:1 and an AEA648 race camshaft. Twin H4SU carburettors were fitted with float chamber extensions and rich BG needles plus blue springs; ram pipes were fitted rather than air cleaners. Special pistons and a lightened steel flywheel, together with lightened tappets and timing gear, all made a very potent engine.

It drove through a straight-cut close-ratio gearbox, coupled to a 4.2:1 differential to get maximum acceleration. A very-heavy-duty spring steel Scandinavian sump guard was fitted underneath the car in addition to a Moke sump plate screwed to the bottom of the sump. A special Mitchell mounting rubber with a strengthened remote mounting bracket was fitted, together with further strengthening and strapping inside the car, intended to ensure the remote gear control didn't fracture away during the heavy landings over the many jumps that the cars always experienced in Finland. In addition, however, a safety strap was made up, fixed to the floor and supporting the underside of the remote control should all else fail. The internal crossmember was double-skinned internally for added strength.

The suspension, Hydrolastic with double-blue and single-blue displacers, was further strengthened with modified rear radius arm brackets. The rear subframe was also double-skinned on its top face. Front tie-bar skid plates were fitted, which also added strength, and the car was set with 13in from wheel centre to wheelarch, ensuring sufficient ground clearance. Wide 4½J steel wheels were used with wheelarch extensions, and the brakes were to racing standard with Ferodo DS11 front pads and VG95 rear linings. The apportioning limiting valve was set at 325psi.

Works cars' electrics, by now, were all fitted with Lucas 11AC alternators, with remote 4TR regulator boxes. The alternator also had a modified earth cable. Lighting was served by four large Lucas 700 lamps fitted to the sturdy lamp bar above the bumper. All four lights were wired with individual snap connectors and powered by iodine bulbs. The lamps were all separately switched, with the two middle long-range lamps being switchable to work with the headlights on high beam or stand-alone. A small Austin Healey sidelight was fitted to the boot lid, low down, to serve as a reversing lamp.

All lines were run inside the car, with the battery reversed with its terminals away from the side of the fuel tank. The twin SU fuel pump was now fitted inside the car under the rear seat but only one pump body was wired.

Aaltonen sat in his much-preferred fibreglass bucket seat with a lap-and-diagonal Irvin seat belt. Nurmimaa had the comfort of a special reclining seat and a full-harness Irvin seat belt. Additional padding was supplied to the door pocket sides, the B-post and the door locks. All of the carpets were retained, as was the glass, being a Group 2 car, and an asbestos blanket was placed under the front carpet. Abingdon-fabricated instrument panels were fitted in front of each crew member, housing additional controls and navigational equipment respectively. The car was also equipped with an intercom.

The 1000 Lakes Rally saw a team of three works Minis take part along with 113 other entries who lined up in Jyväskylä for this two-day tour on three loops in and out of the city. Twenty-seven stages were to be tackled but they were all relatively short, amounting to just 100 miles of competitive motoring and all, bar one stage, on loose surfaces. But at least the result would be decided on scratch, with no handicap system. Disappointingly for everyone, the very low average speed on the interlinking roads meant a rather processional event. Considering most of these transit roads were free of traffic and superb for driving, a really competitive European style of event could have been run, but the police refused to allow roads to be closed or speed limits to be compromised. Nevertheless, the benefit of the short stages meant those with problems were generally not heavily penalised.

Scrutineering was more to do with attaching sponsors' decals onto the cars than anything else – the 1000 Lakes being at that time unique in physically showing sponsorship on competing cars. Aaltonen ran into trouble as his car had been fitted with a steering column relaxer bracket and this was deemed illegal and had to be changed to the standard bracket. All cars also had to be fitted with mud flaps front and back. BMC was, however, fortunate in that it was permitted to run four auxiliary lamps whereas Finnish law dictates only three can be used, which saw a large proportion of the entry (being Finnish) restricted.

Being a non-practice event, the route was also kept secret until the morning of the rally, meaning local knowledge was

Rauno Aaltonen was back in a new GRX 310D with local navigator Naino Nurmimaa for the 1966 1000 Lakes. They would finish in third place.

most important. Good navigation was crucial, with the route information consisting only of a marked map trace, which gave neither positions of controls nor locations of stages – crews either knew where they were likely to be or simply stumbled upon them – but with the very relaxed time schedule, this caused little problems.

The midday start at Jyväskylä saw Aaltonen begin slowly on the early stages but by midnight he was up to seventh place and posting fast times. By the next morning he was up to fourth, only seconds behind Mäkinen, who was now in the lead – which he extended further after the breakfast halt with a five-lap race around a park in Kuopio, as he had the benefit of racing tyres, which Aaltonen didn't, being restricted to SP44 Weathermasters. Mäkinen had brought along his own tyres, knowing of the tarmac stage, which clearly he hadn't shared with Aaltonen...

Back in Jyväskylä and into the second night, Aaltonen continued to climb nearer with quick times but often just a few seconds down on Mäkinen. Three fastest times towards the end saw Aaltonen finish in third place but there was no denying Mäkinen's fine win by just over two minutes. BMC also won the team prize.

The next event for GRX 310D was the RAC Rally of Great Britain in November, and after the 1000 Lakes a brand new car was built for Rauno Aaltonen and Henry Liddon to tackle BMC's home event. Abingdon would be fielding eight works Minis for this very important event and Aaltonen was indeed one of the favourites to win, having won the previous year.

In common with seven of the other works Minis (Mäkinen's being the exception), Aaltonen's car was fitted with a standard Cooper S AEG510 camshaft. This effectively lost the car around 15bhp but it did provide more low-down torque, which was felt desirable in the muddy conditions so often found on the RAC Rally. The 1293cc engine with a slightly lower-compression (11.4:1) cylinder head produced just 75bhp but was partly compensated by the use of a very low final drive of 4.2:1, giving increased acceleration. The engine and gearbox were protected by a very substantial new Scandinavian sump guard made in spring steel, which had the front jacking brackets fixed to its leading edge.

For the first time in a works Mini, the car was fitted with a lightweight alloy roll cage, being a single hoop behind the driver with a stay onto the rear parcel shelf. It was also padded and it would, over the years, prove its worth.

Also fitted for the RAC were forward-facing mud flaps in an attempt to keep the water spray off the headlights and 'screen. This proved partially successful but to the detriment of overheating the brakes, as they restricted the airflow. Headlamp washers were fitted, as were lamp steadies to the two centre driving lamps. Also to improve vision in the cold damp conditions was a heated front windscreen, and to keep the engine warm, the front grille carried a muff that could entirely close off cold air to the engine should it be needed. The engine was also fitted with a thermostat and a heater with a higher output and larger-delivery trunking. The new car looked splendid on the start ramp at London Airport.

The RAC Rally of this era was a massive challenge and rated as one of the toughest rallies of the day. Sponsored by the *Sun* newspaper, which guaranteed public interest, it saw much of the route and many of the forest stages thronged with spectators. The 2400-mile route included 67 timed-to-the-second stages, which totalled almost 400 miles of mostly loose-surface forest tracks – all driven flat out.

At the west London start were 144 hopefuls, but only 63 would find their way back some five days later, after but one night in bed. The mid-morning start saw the crews head for the West Country before entering Wales for the first night and up into the Lake District, with Ayrshire being reached the following night, then a night in Scotland and the first overnight stop in Aviemore the following day. The return route, down the east side of the country through Dumfriesshire, the dreaded Kielder Forest and the fast tracks of Yorkshire, saw the tired crews, two days later, at Silverstone for the penultimate stage and then back to London Airport for the finish. A mammoth challenge.

The starters were flagged away by Jack Brabham, the reigning world motor racing champion, which was rather fitting as two of his contemporaries, Jim Clark and Graham Hill, were entered – Clark in a works Lotus Cortina and Hill in a works Mini, GRX 309D. Clark was in the lead straight away, as Aaltonen started steadily as usual. Aaltonen slid off on the third stage, Lulworth, and collected a puncture on the next stage, relegating him down the leaderboard. Things would

Yet another new GRX 310D was built for Rauno Aaltonen and Henry Liddon for the 1966 RAC Rally.

The rough roads often found on the RAC Rally were not kind to the Mini.

Aaltonen and Liddon in Wales with GRX 310D. The car was fitted, for the first time, with a roll cage.

get worse when, during the night in Wales, he punctured the oil cooler; a spare hose on board allowed him to bypass the cooler and continue. Aaltonen, however, was still in contention.

Steering deranged in the Lake District, through hitting some rocks, meant odd handling until it could be fixed, and the top engine steady bar also needed to be changed. The mishaps continued when on the Twiglees stage in the Lake District, which saw the marshal lean too far into Liddon's window as Aaltonen let the clutch out: the marshal's time clock, hanging around his neck, saw the strap catch in the door handle and rip it from his neck. The resultant loss (and damage) to the clock meant the stage was cancelled.

At the Aviemore halt, and a night's rest, Aaltonen was outside the top ten, behind Mäkinen (who was leading), Fall, Hopkirk and Källström. And with Lampinen and Hill retired, Aaltonen was the second-to-last works Mini running – but things would improve, with steady times and others falling by the wayside as he journeyed southwards. But his problems were not over, as he lost his fan belt on a long Yorkshire stage and struggled to the finish with a boiling engine.

By the closing stages Aaltonen had clawed his way up to third place but failing oil pressure, probably due to the engine boiling for so long, meant he had to ease his pace and eventually had to concede his third spot to Tom Trana's Volvo. At the finish back in London, his fourth place was happily topped by the news that his wife had just delivered him a son. So a memorable RAC Rally.

After the RAC Rally, GXR 310D was entered into a rallycross event in early February 1967 at Lydden Hill Race Circuit in Kent, organised by the 750 Motor Club. This was the first of what would become regular television viewing on Saturday afternoons in the UK, as rallycross became very

popular. Rallycross was a new concept, being a mix between autocross and circuit racing, using both loose surface and tarmac (which soon became very slippery with mud). This new form of motorsport was devised by driver John Sprinzel, journalist Barrie Gill and TV director Robert Reed. Entries were restricted to rally cars, so for this first event cars that had entered the Monte Carlo Rally in January were invited, with Porsche, Ford and BMC in attendance.

The rather tired 1000 Lakes GRX 310D was pressed into service and handed over to Bob Freeborough to drive. Freeborough had often been pressed into making up the numbers in the BMC works team, with his own Cooper S, and

Aaltonen at the Oulton Park racetrack test, with GRX 310D nicely cleaned for the occasion. Aaltonen would finish in fourth place, despite numerous problems.

was no doubt being rewarded for his services. Freebrough's run, however, didn't end well, with Freeborough comprehensively rolling the car and leaving it with very few straight panels; he'd simply nudged a bank at the exit to a shale-covered hairpin bend and inverted the car.

That would be the end of this particular works bodyshell, and rallycross would prove, over the coming years, to be a notable breaker's yard for tired works Minis to end their days in mortal combat. Vic Elford's Porsche 911 won this inaugural event, with Brian Melia's Lotus Cortina second. Tony Fall was third fastest behind the winners, in another rather tired works Mini.

After the rallycross damage, a new GRX 310D was entered for the 1967 Alpine Rally, held in early September that year, with Tony Fall and Mike Wood teamed to drive. Abingdon had entered four cars for this classic Alpine road race and had decided, as the event was so fast and with the now very prevalent threats from Alpine Renault and that of Porsche, the team needed a very fast Mini to try to stay on terms. To that end, Abingdon produced three Group 6 lightweight cars for Mäkinen, Aaltonen and Hopkirk. Fall missed the cut and had to be content with a Group 2 car.

That meant it had a 1293cc engine and a full-race camshaft, plus with a high-compression cylinder head, coupled to a low final drive, it was still very quick. However, it had to retain the twin SU H4 carburettors instead of using a Weber 45DCO of Group 6 cars, along with the extra weight the Group 2 car was required to keep. It was estimated to be around 10bhp less at the flywheel than the Group 6 car and, with the 100lb less weight removed, it was not as fast as the other three works cars entered.

GRX 310D was used for an early rallycross meeting at Liddon Hill where Bob Freeborough rolled the car comprehensively.

Externally, GRX 310D had one additional feature: the four additional lamps were now connected via a rubber plug and socket attached to the wing on the left-hand side between the headlight and sidelight. This was sourced from the Land Rover parts bin and would be a used on Abingdon Minis from then on. It made removing the lamps quicker and also made for a better connection rather than bullet connectors.

As the Alpine was not a rough event, a Moke sump guard and Moke sump plate were employed but with the addition of a duralumin sheet fixed to the sump guard to further protect the gearbox. Interestingly, the grille moustache had Lift-the-Dot fixings around its edge to allow for the fixing of a grille muff. Being a summer event, it is unlikely this would have been a requirement, so it poses the question that this was perhaps not a new car but one used previously on a colder event.

A new GRX 310D near Abingdon prepared for the 1967 Alpine Rally, now with a square number plate on the bonnet and the lamps connected by a rubber plug.

Tony Fall and Mike Wood in Marseille, about to start the Alpine Rally.

The Alpine was once about who remained on time over the entire route; those few who did would win a coveted Alpine Cup. The timed hillclimb stages were simply there as a means of classification. However, as speeds had increased, the organisers now decided that to keep on time, cars had to be within just two per cent of the fastest car in their class – so BMC had decided to build a powerful Group 6 car. The Mini was as fast as anything downhill but struggled against more powerful cars going uphill. Only three cars would remain clean on the road this year, such was the challenge.

This 2300-mile rally started from Marseille on 4 September on Monday evening for the first leg to Alpe d'Huez. This leg was a 900-mile blast over the Alps with 18 tightly timed selectives on the road, interspersed with four épreuves (timed-to-the-second hillclimb stages), with 110 cols to climb and descend, including the very tight and twisty selectives between Quatre Chemins, Sigale, Entrevaux and Rouaine, the Col d'Allos, the Col de la Cayolle and the dangerous Col de la Lombarde.

Elford's Porsche was soon leading but the Minis were close by. Fall was also to soon depart, when on the Sigale selective, he understeered on the loose gravel at a corner, clipped a rock, spun across the road and severely wrecked the nearside front suspension, and was unable to continue. Just 20 cars made it to the finish five days later in Monaco but BMC was rewarded with Hopkirk being declared the overall winner. Sadly, this international win would be the last for a works Mini, despite their best efforts – the opposition was now just too powerful. A final outing for this car was as a recce car for the forthcoming 1968 Monte Carlo Rally, when it and numerous other works Minis were pressed into recce duties for this winter classic.

A new GRX 310D appeared once again in May. Previously a Mk1 Cooper S, the car now appeared for the Acropolis Rally as a Mk2 Cooper S, although the bodyshell was not that of a Mk1 cosmetically changed to appear as a Mk2, as some were (the Mk1 had been phased out in October the previous year and Abingdon was now campaigning the Mk2 instead). The cars were mechanically and structurally identical, but with cosmetic changes. The front grille, rear lights and badges were the notable external alterations and the rear 'screen was now 6cm wider (far less noticeable). The interior trim was now in black vinyl and the instruments slightly different.

Things had moved on, both at Abingdon and with rallying. The opposition was now considerable: the Porsche 911 was formidable opposition, particularly on fast roads. The introduction of the Ford Escort Twin Cam was an equally worrying opponent. With the Lancia Fulvia and also the Alpine Renault in the mix, Abingdon was no longer the force to be reckoned with.

Abingdon had been exploring ways to get more power from the rather long-in-the-tooth A-series engine. When regulations permitted, Abingdon would enter a Group 6 lightweight car and would use a big Weber 45DCOE carburettor on a long inlet manifold, which would give an extra 5 or 6bhp. However, neither a lightweight car, nor one using anything other than a standard inlet manifold was permitted under Group 2 rules. Timo Mäkinen had seen in Finland a Mini fitted with twin Weber 45DCOE carburettors grafted onto a standard Cooper S inlet manifold and brought a set back to Abingdon for Cliff Humphries, Abingdon's engine guru, to test. These carburettors were soon adopted by Abingdon and were what Abingdon called 'prototype carburettors', being a pair of Weber 45DCOEs with one choke machined off each and the remaining chokes welded to a stub-tube. This, importantly allowed it to be bolted directly to a standard Cooper S inlet

Fall ran well on the Alpine Rally but retired when he hit a rock face and badly damaged the nearside suspension.

A new GRX 310D appeared once again for Timo Mäkinen and Paul Easter for the 1968 Acropolis Rally, now as a Mk2 Cooper S. This shot, of the car in the UK before departure to Greece, with the incorrect door number.

Mäkinen kicks up the dust as he charges through the stage but overheating problems and an inevitable blown head gasket saw the car sidelined.

manifold, and achieved the desired result, gaining a valuable 7bhp – although they were not without their controversy, as at their introduction on the 1968 Monte Carlo Rally, all of Abingdon's four works entries were under threat of exclusion. However, by the time of the Acropolis Rally in May, they were being accepted by scrutineers.

GRX 310D was now built as a Group 2 car for Timo Mäkinen and Paul Easter, with the 1293cc Morris Cooper S running what became known as split Weber carburettors. With the Abingdon almost-standard-fit full-race AEA648 camshaft, a high-compression Downton cylinder head and a short 4.2:1 final drive, the car was indeed very quick – but sadly, as time will show, not quick enough to keep up with the opposition. The 92bhp engine was fitted with straight-cut transfer gears in addition to a close-ratio straight-cut gearbox. These new transfer gears were used to increase reliability; they also had the advantage of having a roller bearing fitted on the idler gear, which had been prone to early failure.

The engine and gearbox were protected by a heavy-duty Scandinavian guard with the jacking points welded to its front edge. A wide battery box cover was also fitted at the rear of the car. Hydrolastic suspension, with a rear anti-roll bar, was used with single-blue and double-blue displacers front and back; there were no front dampers but it had orange helper springs at the rear.

The brakes were improved, with the brake callipers having asbestos blocks fitted into the pistons to take excess heat away from the brake fluid, and the rear wheel cylinders were threaded so they were fixed to the backplate with a large nut rather than a circlip to also take heat away from the brake fluid. Even wider wheelarch extensions were fitted to the car, now painted red. It was also fitted with forward-facing mud flaps under the headlights, in addition to rear mud flaps.

Lucas wired the car, running an alternator largely because of four additional lamps. The lamps – two fog lamps and two driving lamps fixed to a lamp bar – were connected by a five-pin rubber socket and the two driving lamps secured by steady bars. European headlamps with Perspex protective covers were fitted with iodine bulbs, as were the extra lamps. The driver's auxiliary dash panel now had the oil pressure gauge moved next to the rev counter and in its place in the binnacle was the water temperature gauge, with a circular fuel gauge where it used to live. As the car now had an expansion tank from the radiator located by the co-driver's feet on the inner wheelarch, the Tudor electric screen washer bottle was moved to the rear of the car on the driver's side. The co-driver also had a foot-operated horn switch.

A fibreglass bucket seat, now covered in black cord material for the driver, and a reclining high-back seat for the co-driver were fitted on modified seat brackets. There was an Irvin lap-and-diagonal seat belt for Mäkinen (which he rarely used) and full-harness Irvin belt for Easter. All standard trim and glass had to be retained under Group 2 regulations, including the carpets. All lines were run inside the car, with the fuel pump located under the rear seat. The number plate was now painted on the offside of the bonnet, held fast with a leather strap.

The Acropolis Rally, held at the end of May, was a hard, tough and relentless rally lasting 56 hours non-stop, over a 2000-mile route. On offer were 180 miles in 12 stages, all on scratch time, interspersed with 42 time controls. There were also three 'tests' (which were of less importance) the first of which was used simply as a tie decider should it be needed.

The severe weather the week before meant some remote roads had washed away, meaning the loss of three stages and a 100-mile loop around Volos. Starting at the foot of the Acropolis on Thursday lunchtime, the rally finished on the Saturday evening, with no service time, let alone any rest halts being scheduled – the only downtime was a ferry-crossing of the Corinth Bay.

Scrutineering, the previous day, was straightforward; with even the car's split Webers not causing any issues. The only disagreement, from some, was because the low entry of just 60 cars meant the organisers amalgamated classes. This was causing some complaints, especially within classes, as the seeding was decided by drawing lots. It also meant a good number of cars being bulked later in the event.

Just before the start, Mäkinen decided to have his Hydrolastic suspension hastily pumped up to increase its ground clearance – and he only just made the start. The first test, a simple one-mile sprint up the road, saw Mäkinen eighth fastest. Onto the first six-mile stage at Souli, it was now into the first night, where Mäkinen was sixth – but already a pattern was being set, with three works Ford Escort Twin Cams and two works Porsche 911s in the lead.

On the second stage Mäkinen was sixth at Kastanea but he was already complaining of the car overheating. His fan belt was tightened but the problem persisted. This was to get immeasurably worse as the night wore on, and before the next long stage, of over 30 miles just before Sparta, he was out with a blown head gasket on number four cylinder.

It was clear that the Mini was now struggling against much more powerful cars. Aaltonen finished fifth overall, as the best of the rest, and won the 1300 class, but it was a measure of things to come where the Mini simply could no longer beat top cars.

The year of 1969 came with many changes at the head of what had now become BLMC. This meant Abingdon was being forced to seriously cut back its motorsport activities. Lord Stokes, now at the head of the company, was not a fan of motorsport and felt it didn't sell cars. So this year the budget for such frivolous things was drastically cut; rallying was seriously curtailed, but racing survived and was to be the main visible motorsport activity from then on.

The downside of this was the racing contract with John Cooper, which had been so successful for so many years, was cancelled, as Stokes decided Abingdon would now enter its own cars in the British and European race championships. Although neither Abingdon nor Cooper would expect to win the BSCC races outright, the championship was fortunately decided upon class wins, so if the Abingdon team consistently won its class, the team could end up overall championship winner, as had been the case with the Cooper Car Company in the past.

Abingdon also had a reshuffle to accord with the new direction. Den Green would now be responsible for building the race cars, whilst Doug Watts would attend to the dwindling rally programme and Tommy Wellman would look after the rallycross car. Bill Price was promoted to assistant competitions manager and was placed in sole charge of the race programme.

Much pre-season testing was carried out to try and arrive at a competitive race car setup, as Abingdon was lacking the experience Cooper had gained over the years of Mini racing.

However, with John Cooper now out of contract, if he wanted to continue to race Minis, he would need alternative backers – achieved with Britax and Downton Engineering sponsorship. His cars would now be painted in bright yellow with black roofs and be driven by Gordon Spice and Steve Neal.

Abingdon managed to sign John Rhodes from Cooper and also secured John Handley from British Vita to race in its two-car team. It was to be a challenging 1969 season, with Abingdon pitched against the experienced and well-established Britax-Cooper-Downton cars but both teams would struggle

Mäkinen sits tight, looking exhausted as the tyres are changed on GRX 310D, the car being raised on the Abingdon-crafted quick-lift jack.

GRX 310D now changed, for 1969, into a race car as Abingdon concentrated on the BSCC. John Rhodes was the star driver, here at the second round at Silverstone.

against the more powerful Broadspeed Ford Escort 1300GT in their class.

After a debacle in the first round at Brands Hatch in mid March, where both works Minis were written off, new cars were wheeled out to replace them for the second round at Silverstone on 30 March, the Daily Express International Trophy. John Rhodes was given GRX 310D, now built as a new Group 5 race car and bedecked with numerous sponsors' decals.

The 1293cc power unit produced 128bhp on the Abingdon test-bed and had a 13:1 compression-ratio Weslake cylinder head running Lucas fuel injection with slide throttle and a 1247 Camshaft. Special idler gears were fitted to the close-ratio straight-cut transmission and the limited-slip differential was set at 65lb.

A 12.5-gallon flexible fuel tank was fitted with the fuel filler neck let into the bodywork. The suspension, with special tie rods, was fitted with Koni dampers with Hydrolastic top arms and Hydrolastic rear struts – however, the suspension was by dry rubber cone. The front wheels ran two degrees of negative camber, and 0.5 degrees negative to the rear. Brakes had the front standard shields removed and fitted with alloy Minifin brake drums to the rear. Ferodo DS11 disc pads were used with VG95 rear linings.

The car still had to run 10in wheels as the much-awaited homologation for 12in wheels was just days away, but not in time for Silverstone. This meant very high tyre temperatures and severe wear for the Dunlop race tyres. The bumpers were removed and quick-lift jacking points fitted to the front and rear of the car; wide wheelarch extensions were fitted with a chrome edge finisher.

Practice for the 20-lap race consisted of two one-hour sessions for the field of 34 cars, where Rhodes had to give best to Gordon Spice, who was the fastest Mini and broke the lap record. Rhodes was also just behind Steve Neal but ahead of Hadley who was three places back.

Come race day, where the track was both damp and oily following the featured sports car race, Rhodes started on wet tyres where it was hoped the slippery conditions would favour the Minis. Once under way, Rhodes got ahead of Neal but trailed Spice, then as the track dried he started to lose ground and was soon passed by first Neal and then by Handley. The two Abingdon cars were the last not to be lapped by the

John Rhodes, in typical stance, powering the Mini in his own distinctive style.

GRX 310D's next appearance, at Thruxton for the fourth round; the car was now fitted with 12in wheels, homologated only days before the Easter meeting.

eventual winner, Frank Gardner in the 1600 Escort TC. At the flag, the 1300 class win went to John Fitzpatrick in the Escort 1300GT, followed by Spice, Neal and Handley, with Rhodes bringing up the rear and finishing 11th overall. A rather disappointing result.

GRX 310D was next in action on the Easter Monday for WD & HO Wills Trophy International at the Thruxton Circuit. The car was the same GRX 310D that appeared at Silverstone for the second round the previous week but now with 12in wheels and tyres, which had just been homologated on 1 April; the wheels were of the Cooper Car Company's Rose Petal design. The only other difference was the bonnet was now secured by a central leather bonnet strap in addition to the two Moke rubber toggles.

Nevertheless, despite Abingdon's best efforts it would not be a memorable race for Rhodes. The 25-lap race saw Rhodes only qualify in 16th place, three behind Handley. The Cooper-Britax cars were in eighth and tenth place for Neal and Spice, with Spice in a spare car having blown up his race car. As the race progressed, Rhodes slipped further back down the field as he became plagued with oil surge problems due to excess oil consumption. He eventually finished dead last in 22nd place and an unsatisfying ninth in class, three laps behind the overall winner, Roy Pierpoint in a Falcon. The 1300 class was again won by Chris Craft in the Broadspeed Escort 1300GT, with Spice and Neal close behind.

June of 1969 saw the car entered in the six-hour European Touring Car Challenge round at the Kent circuit, Brands Hatch. Being a long race, Rhodes was teamed with rally driver Paddy Hopkirk, who was no slouch as a race driver, having had numerous outings with the Cooper race team in the past. As this was Rhodes's car, which he was now sharing with Hopkirk, his name was removed from the front wing and no crew names were used. The car also had a large number 4 race number on the boot lid. The car was prepared to the same specification as when it last appeared at Brands Hatch in March, except the cylinder head was now a modified Weslake version with modified waterways, the diff ratio was now 3.7:1 and the limited-slip differential was increased

Brands Hatch sees GRX 310D again in the hands of Rhodes but teamed with Paddy Hopkirk for the six-hour endurance race, a round of the ETCC. The car now fitted with knock-off Minilite wheels.

Rhodes in GRX 310D was plagued with high oil consumption, and the resultant oil surge meant he would finish dead last in the race.

Fuel stop at Brands Hatch as Rhodes looks on from the left, with Peter Browning with his back to the camera and Bill Price directing from the pit counter. Paddy Hopkirk at the wheel.

231

WORKS MINIS IN DETAIL

GRX 310D had a large number on the boot for the six-hour race at Brands Hatch; the pair would finish a distant seventh place after delays changing a rear radius arm.

to 85lb.ft. The wheels were 12in Minilites with knock-off spinners to make wheel changes quicker. The car was now fitted with twin filler caps. Only the offside cap was recessed, much as before. The nearside had a standard protruding neck on a standard fuel tank, which was fitted to increase its fuel capacity for the long race.

The endurance race was split into two divisions, with the up-to-one-litre cars racing each other the day before, where they had a two-hour race, leaving the remainder to race the following day over the full six hours. Practice, with all the cars together, saw Rhodes and Hopkirk qualify in ninth place on the grid behind the Spice/Neal Britax-Cooper-Downton in sixth – despite Neal having damaged the car in practice.

The plan was for Rhodes to take the first two-hour stint when the car would then be refuelled and the front tyres changed, and Hopkirk would do the next two hours with Rhodes taking the car for the last two-hour period. A rolling start saw Rhodes pass Spice, and the two remained very close for the first hour until Spice came into the pits to have his fuel pump changed, dropping him almost to the back of the field. By the time Rhodes handed over to Hopkirk, they were in sixth place, just ahead of teammates Handley and Enever.

The final race appearance for GRX 310D was at the Nürburgring for the six-hour ETCC race where Rhodes was teamed with Geoff Mabbs.

At nearly four hours, Hopkirk came in to have the rear radius arm changed, which had fractured. The mechanics replaced it in just seven minutes, then Rhodes took over the car but could do little to make up the three-lap deficit. Spice had by then retired after several delays and finally succumbed to a badly-handling car, perhaps due to Neal's practice accident. Rhodes/Hopkirk finished a distant seventh overall from Handley/Enever who were fourth. The class was won by John Fitzpatrick and Trevor Taylor in the Broadspeed Escort 1300GT.

The next outing for GRX 310D was to the Eifel Mountains for a round of the European Touring Car Challenge (ETCC). This was a six-hour race, on 6 July, using the fearsome Nürburgring circuit, where each 14.2-mile lap took the Mini well over ten minutes. This Group 5 car was driven by John Rhodes and Geoff Mabbs, bedecked now with numerous trade adverts, as was becoming the way at that time. In the absence of the troublesome Britax-Coopers, a good class result was hoped for. Mabbs was a successful club driver and had often been involved in testing rally cars for BMC. This would be the first of a couple of drives for Abingdon.

Abingdon was not contending the entire ETCC and Britax-Coopers had not entered any, both concentrating on the BTCC, but hopes were high with the absence of the Cooper team in Germany. The engine specification was very similar to that used at Brands Hatch on the last BTCC round but with raised compression, up to 14.5:1 on the Weslake Mk3 cylinder head. The final drive was also changed to 3.7:1 to try to get some higher top speed on this extremely fast but dangerous circuit. The car was fitted with two fuel tanks – a standard 5½-gallon steel tank and a long-range 12-gallon flexible tank in the boot. It was also fitted with an oil tank, with a hand-operated pump on the parcel shelf to allow replenishment of oil.

The setup of the car was again unchanged and used Armstrong adjustable dampers, and was fitted with Hydrolastic suspension pumped up to 250psi, with fixed bottom arms but adjustable tie rods. Knock-off Minilites were again fitted to the car to speed up wheel changes and Dunlop D15-232 tyres were used, which had a rather stiff sidewall, so the pressures were dropped to soften them, as it was feared the bumpy circuit may place extra strain on the suspension. This problem was exaggerated by the 12in wheels, and during practice these too gave problems by working loose. This was found to be the locating peg not having enough clearance and hence prevented the wheel from fitting the hub correctly.

At the 11am rolling start, Rhodes took the driving seat for the first stint but when he returned to handover to Mabbs after one-and-a-half hours, the car was showing signs of body damage, lying third in class behind teammates Handley and Enever and the eventual class-winning Alfa Romeo 1300 GTA.

As the race wore on the pair continued to circulate but now fearful of being delayed by the failed suspension that befell their teammates. Their only problem was a coming-together with a slower car, which promptly tore off the offside wheelarch. The car finished ninth overall and second in the 1300 class, having completed 33 laps in the gruelling six hours.

That was the end of what was one of the most well-used cars in the Abingdon fold. Bill Price, who was to eventually take over from Peter Browning, bought the car.

Competition Record

Date	Event	Crew	Number	Overall result	Class result
Feb 1966	Swedish Rally	Rauno Aaltonen/Tony Ambrose	16	DNF	
April 1966	Tulip Rally	Rauno Aaltonen/Henry Liddon	89	1st	
May 1966	Austrian Alpine	Tony Fall/Mike Wood	97	DNF	
Aug 1966	1000 Lakes	Rauno Aaltonen/Naino Nurmimaa	43	3rd	2nd
Nov 1966	RAC Rally	Rauno Aaltonen/Henry Liddon	18	4th	2nd
Feb 1967	TV rallycross	Bob Freeborough	S1	DNF	
Sept 1967	Alpine Rally	Tony Fall/Mike Wood	40	DNF	
May 1968	Acropolis Rally	Timo Mäkinen/Paul Easter	49	DNF	
March 1969	BSCC Silverstone	John Rhodes	14	11th	5th
April 1969	BSCC Thruxton	John Rhodes	23	22nd	9th
June 1969	BSCC Brands Hatch 6 hrs	John Rhodes/Paddy Hopkirk	4	7th	3rd
July 1969	ETCC Nürburgring 6hrs	John Rhodes/Geoff Mabbs	73	9th	2nd

Registration Number	First registered	Chassis number	Engine	Engine number	Model
GRX 311D	Feb 1966	KA2S4 820360	1275cc	9F-SA-Y 39837	Morris Cooper S

GRX 311D was one of seven new GRX cars registered in early 1966 – all in January other than GRX 311D, which was registered in February.

The car's first event was the Acropolis Rally in May, built by Dudley Pike as a Group 2 car for Paddy Hopkirk and Ron Crellin to tackle the rough, tough Greek event. The engine was at the usual 1293cc capacity, fitted with a race camshaft and a short 4.2:1 final drive. The compression was slightly reduced to 11.6:1 on the Downton cylinder head to reflect the lower-quality fuel generally found in Greece at that time. Carburettors were twin SU H4s with slightly less-rich AZ needles. Power on the Abingdon rolling road showed 88bhp at the wheels – perhaps 4bhp down on the most powerful works engine at that time.

The cooling system came in for additional attention – again because Greece can be very warm in May. The car was fitted with a 16-row Cooper S radiator with its cowl held in place with ¼in UNF bolts rather than small screws. The water pump had 1/16in machined off the face of the pulley to give more clearance and the bottom bracket was fixed solidly without the normal rubber mountings with special stepped bolts. A 13lb pressure cap was used and a 60 degree thermostat with a four-blade fan driven off a large pulley.

In anticipation of the rough roads the car was fitted with a very substantial sump guard, which had an additional plate fitted to its underside. The rear subframe was also double-

Paddy Hopkirk and Ron Crellin on the starting ramp under the shadow of the Acropolis for the start of the 1966 Acropolis Rally.

skinned and all of the tack welds on both subframes were welded over for added strength. The battery box also had its own skid plate, which was fitted on the rear subframe, and finally the front tie bars had protection brackets fixed to the side and the front of the subframe.

The exhaust was also skidded and its mountings bolted through the rubber. Fabricated guards were fitted to the brake callipers to protect the vulnerable brake hoses. The Hydrolastic suspension was equipped with single-blue and double-blue displacers front and back, together with helper springs and Aeon heavy-duty bump stops. The suspension was set at 13in wheel centre to wheels' arc edge, the steering set to 1/8in toe-out, and the car ran on 4½J steel wheels, covered by fibreglass wheelarch extensions. It was evident that the car was built in anticipation of some harsh treatment on the unforgiving Greek terrain.

The electrics were completely rewired by the Lucas Racing technician in line with the driver's requirements for additional switches. The car was fitted with an alternator, which required the front panel relieving to clear it, and because of that the Cooper S diagonal stiffener was relocated vertically further along the front panel. It was necessary to relocate the oil cooler (fitted on a platform on the front panel) away from the alternator an inch or so, which also meant relocating the vertical stiffening brackets. The car ran European headlights plus four additional lamps on a badge bar: two Continental driving lamps in Lucas 700 casings in the centre and two Lucas 700 fog lamps on the outside, all fitted with iodine bulbs. A Healey 3000 sidelight was used as a reversing lamp, switched by the gearbox.

All of the lines were run inside the car and the fuel pump was now located safely out of harm's way under the rear seat. The battery was reversed in the boot with its terminals away from the right-hand fuel tank. Both tanks were protected from damage by sticking a thin asbestos sheet to their sides. Standard filler caps, wired on, were now used. The car carried two spare wheels.

Hopkirk seems to question why GRX 311D has been tipped onto its side - he had split the sump on the very rough stages.

Inside the car were the customary black-crackle alloy dash panels for each of the crew. Crellin's panel contained clock, stopwatch and Halda Twinmaster distance recorder in addition to numerous control switches. Hopkirk had a rev counter and a multitude of switches to control lighting and other circuits. Crellin also had an additional switch panel in his door pocket, which housed his map-reading light. Hopkirk sat in a fibreglass bucket seat and had a lap-and-diagonal seat belt, whilst Crellin had a reclining seat and a full-harness Irvin belt. Additional padding was fitted to the sides of the door pocket, door locks and B-post.

As always, the new car appeared at the start in Athens in immaculate condition complete with an additional large competition number stuck on the bonnet – but most eyebrows were raised when it arrived on Dunlop R7 race tyres. Hopkirk and Crellin had come to the start straight from winning the Austrian Alpine in their winning car, DJB 92B, to use as their recce car for the Acropolis. As things transpired, for Mäkinen and Easter at least, this was to prove their salvation on the event.

The 1966 Acropolis of just less than 2000 miles was at the time on par with the Liège Rally in toughness, although in time duration it was shorter at just 50 hours' motoring spread over three days and two nights. The roads were in places exceedingly rough and the high average speed demanded over the 17 stages meant a huge challenge.

As it transpired, with good dry weather, keeping to the time schedule proved less onerous than in previous years.

On offer for the 118 entrants were the stages, three hill climbs and one circuit race. Unfortunately, the stages, although fast and of generally poor condition had a different bogey time for each class and moreover, despite the speed required, proved to be achievable by the majority of the top contenders, resulting in being of little consequence. The hillclimbs ,on the other hand, were very important. The fastest car set the bogey time and all others were penalised accordingly. The final circuit race around Tatoi airport roads was also of little consequence, providing a car started and finished it.

Many local crews were pitched against the works cars, attracted no doubt by the free hotel accommodation provided by the organising club. BMC fielded three works Minis to take on the three works Ford Lotus Cortinas, all of which were Group 2 cars – the event only being open to Group 2 or 3 cars.

Starting in early evening, at the foot of the Acropolis, Hopkirk sped off towards Corinth and the first stage some two hours away. On this he beat the bogey but was six seconds behind Mäkinen who was fastest. Into the night and the route headed southward and onto very rough roads.

On the second group of stages, Hopkirk was again upstaged by a hard-charging Mäkinen but both still kept clean sheets. It was just personal pride who was quickest. As the night wore on the Abingdon cars continued to set fastest times, and by morning at Patras many cars had fallen by the wayside. The short 15-minute ferry-crossing saw 73 cars head northwest across the central mountains to even rougher stages. The 35-mile fifth stage was exceptionally rough, and Hopkirk split his sump when a large rock punctured through the heavy sump guard. Hopkirk had to stop four times to top up with oil on the stage, and at the end had dropped only 19 seconds above the bogey time – while others had cleaned it by four minutes. Isopon was liberally applied on the offending sump by the service crew, and fortunately the easy road section that followed allowed it to set and stem the leak (mostly).

Back through Thessaloniki, the seventh group of stages greeted the remaining car; Hopkirk was again second just behind Aaltonen. Then came the all-important hillclimb at Portaria where Aaltonen was fastest, and Hopkirk was third just nine seconds adrift. Back at Volos, Hopkirk was lying third overall, 23 seconds down but of course 19 seconds of that was lost when he stopped for oil. The second hillclimb saw Mäkinen fastest and extend his lead. With just 300 miles to go, Aaltonen was out and Mäkinen was forced down the leaderboard due to the mechanical maladies, leaving Hopkirk now with a comfortable 40-second lead.

Just 40 cars made it back to Athens, and after a night's rest the final Parnis hillclimb and the half-hour race was all that was left. At the end, Hopkirk retained his lead and was greeted as the winner… But it was not to last.

When the results were posted, showing Hopkirk as the winner, all was well until, with less than four minutes to go before the results were declared final, Ford put in a protest, stating that Hopkirk had serviced within a time control area. It transpired that when BMC arrived to service, just before the time control area, as was normal practice, the area was very congested and they parked, unbeknown to them, a few meters inside the area. Hopkirk, on arriving, was being serviced when an official noticed their transgression. Pointing out the issue, the car was soon moved and the service work finished.

On further discussion, it was pointed out that the control area was not correctly marked and the matter was dropped. However, once the stewards became involved they decided to dock Hopkirk 420 marks for booking into the control early and a further 120 marks for servicing within the control. Despite an all-night sitting of the stewards and ultimately the matter being referred to the FIA, the penalties stuck and Hopkirk was relegated to third place – with the Ford Cortina of Bengt Söderström being declared the winner. It had been a most disappointing rally for BMC.

The next event for the car was the German Rally in July, where the Acropolis car was rebuilt by Dudley Pike for Paddy Hopkirk and Chris Nash. Ron Crellin, as a busy chartered surveyor, could not spare the time from work so Chris Nash, a well-known club navigator, was given his works seat alongside Hopkirk.

The engine had its compression raised back up to the more normal (for the time) 12.6:1 now that better fuel would be available, the final drive ratio was lowered to 4.26:1 and the twin SU H4 carburettors were fitted with richer BG needles. A stronger reinforced orange clutch diaphragm was fitted with a special thrust washer and the remote housing held in place with a Mitchell mounting – and, just to be sure, the car carried an emergency strap under the remote housing should that indestructible mounting at the end of the remote actually

Hopkirk and Crellin at the finish of the Acropolis Rally where they finished in third place despite numerous problems.

Tony Fall stands by JBL 172D, his drive for the 1966 German Rally, whilst Hopkirk and Tony Nash (standing in for Ron Crellin) will take GRX 311D.

Hopkirk damaged GRX 311D just behind Nash's door as can be seen at the Hockenheim race circuit, where he would ultimately retire with a blown piston.

fail. After the rigours of the Greek roads the Hydrolastic suspension was replaced, this time with blue displacers plus both subframes were replaced, strengthened and double-skinned.

The car, as developments continued, had numerous minor changes incorporated into its build to align it with how Abingdon was building new cars. The heater box was lowered on spacers to give more clearance under the dashboard, the interior mirror was now an MGB item, and the crew names were changed to incorporate the crew's national flag, replacing the Dymo names of the past and separate national flags. The inner wing by the front of the radiator was jacked out to allow more air around the radiators and the lamp bar had a stronger centre mounting bracket to keep the bar more rigid. Small changes but changes nevertheless.

The German Rally for 1966 had a rather depleted entry of just 50 cars, largely because the previous year's event had not been well received, plus the marking system based on the rather unpopular class improvement system was still being used by the organisers. There were, however, two long races included in the event, at the Nürburgring and the Hockenheim race circuit, which constituted more than three quarters of the competitive mileage. And with the 17 stages being based on a bogey time, which was achievable by the top crews, it was obvious the winner would come from the car that performed best on the two racetracks – meaning it would likely be a Porsche 911 or an Alfa GTV. Abingdon nevertheless entered two identical cars for Hopkirk and Tony Fall, being committed to the European championship.

The 1100-mile route, spread over just 42 hours, saw wet and windy weather for much of the time – rather uncharacteristically for July. The rally started in the Dolomites, south of Cortina in Italy, headed into Austria and then had the majority of the rally in Germany, with the finish in Düsseldorf. Despite the poor marking system, the road timing was fast, and with the adverse weather many struggled to keep to the time schedule.

Hopkirk was soon into his stride on the opening two stages in Italy but trouble hit when an alternator bolt came adrift, which meant the fan belt ran loose and the car boiled dry whilst Hopkirk was dashing the five miles to service. Further, Hopkirk had collected some bodywork damage on the second stage, where he had clouted a rock on an inside corner and deranged the rear panel behind Nash's door. Hopkirk, however, had lost little time, and at service the alternator was secured and the car was treated to water with some Radweld in the radiator plus a dose of Molyslip in the engine – and then all was well. This was despite the cylinder head and block having lost all of its paint because the engine had got so hot.

The third test saw Hopkirk second fastest ahead of his teammate. Into Austria with some very tight road sections, which very few cleaned, with two stages: the first suited the more powerful cars as it was open and wide, whilst the second suited the Mini, being tight and twisty. Into Germany with 40 cars remaining and onto the important Rossfeld hillclimb, effectively decided on scratch (as the fastest car set the bogey time for the rest), where Hopkirk was second fastest. From the hillclimb, things became rather frantic as the organisers hadn't specified a route to the next test, the race at Hockenheim. Many took a sweeping route on easier roads whilst the organisers had worked their timing on the shortest route on minor roads. The result of this saw many crews arriving late and several picking up speeding fines from the rather diligent German police.

On the Hockenheim circuit the crews had one practice lap and then a 30-minute race. Hopkirk started well but the hard flat-out pace started to take its toll on an engine that had been run red-hot the day before. Soon the car was on three cylinders and spewing oil out of the crankcase breather as the piston rings had clearly failed. It was only a matter of time and Hopkirk was out, having run out of oil and bearings. Disappointment for Abingdon continued as Fall's car seized on his very last lap, and both red-and-white cars were out. The rally was indeed won, as predicted, by a Porsche 911.

After the non-finish on the German Rally, more was hoped for on the Alpine Rally, which was in just seven weeks' time, in early September. Hopkirk, reunited with Crellin once again, retained the car and it was rebuilt by Dudley Pike. With the heavy body damage sustained to the nearside of the car behind the passenger door on the German Rally, it is likely that a different car appeared on the Alpine with the GRX 311D number on the bonnet, if not an entirely new car. The build of the car was identical to that of the German Rally, the only deviation being the fitting of a slightly longer diff ratio of 4.2:1, which would allow for a slightly higher top speed, so often demanded on the Alpine Rally, to the detriment of acceleration.

One of Abingdon's favourite events was the Alpine Rally, and for 1966 the event was run in blistering hot weather in early September, moved from its customary mid-July date, in an attempt to avoid tourist traffic in the area. Run over the very best cols in the Southern Alps, it was a monumental challenge of some 2400 miles, spread over three legs, driven at very high speed, and just keeping on time was a tall order – and for those that did, a coveted Alpine Cup was their reward. Starting in Marseille and finishing in Cannes, with two stops in Aix-les-Bains, 80 crews lines up for their first 24-hour thrash over the mountains. Ahead of them were also 14 hillclimbs, timed to the second, to decide the eventual winner.

Hopkirk's attempt didn't get off to a good start at scrutineering when Crellin collapsed with heat exhaustion and had to spend the day in bed. Once under way, with the car shod with Dunlop race tyres, Hopkirk was setting competitive times – but it was not to last. Hopkirk had been struggling with an intermittent electrical fault and, nearing the Swiss border on the Col du Noyer, worse was to come when the Mini lost most of its oil from a hole that had appeared in the diff housing. The crew weren't sure if something had hit it or something had come out... Despite attempts to stave off the massive leak with Gun Gum, it was no use and the car was retired.

Hopkirk was not alone: 26 other cars failed to finish the demanding first leg. So tough was the event that at the finish in Cannes only 19 cars were classified, with but seven clean sheets and Alpine Cups. As always, it was a tough Alpine Rally that hadn't been kind to Abingdon as three of the four works Minis retired, and although Aaltonen came home a creditable third, he missed his Alpine Cup by being just one minute late at a time control.

As an aside, the 1967 Scottish Rally has erroneously been listed, in numerous publications, as the next event for this car, driven by Lars Ytterbring. However, although he did the Scottish, running at number 10 and finished a fine second overall, the car was his private car, registered in Sweden as B8448 and was painted green and white. It was prepared and serviced on the rally by the factory's special tuning department under Basil Wales but it was not GRX 311D.

The 1967 Alpine, run in early September when the Alps were free of snow and slippery conditions, was a very fast and a relentless blast over the Alps. GRX 311D was to be driven by Timo Mäkinen and Paul Easter for the Alpine but was actually LRX 829E with its identity swapped over. The car was, however, much changed from when LRX 829E appeared on the Geneva Rally the previous June. It was now prepared as a lightweight Group 6 car. BMC viewed that this year's Alpine would be extremely fast and to try and keep up with Porsche 911s and Alpine Renaults, the car had to be much lighter.

Built by Nobby Hall, the engine was 1293cc with an AEG648 camshaft and a high-compression 16.4cc Downton cylinder head giving 12.6:1 compression ratio. The straight-cut close-ratio gearbox was fitted with a 4.2:1 final drive but without a limited-slip differential. The engine received more power, producing 125bhp at the flywheel, by replacing the customary twin SU H4 carburettors with a single Weber 45DCOE. This meant a small bit of metal bashing around the speedo aperture to accommodate the ram pipes and a suitable manifold.

To keep things cool, in addition to an oil cooler, the car ran an auxiliary front radiator fabricated from a Mini heater matrix. It was fitted on the right-hand side of the front grille, which was cut down to accommodate the extra radiator and the grille moustache was also deleted. An expansion tank for the radiator was located in the co-driver's footwell – this from a BMC 1100.

Hydrolastic suspension, with single-blue and double-blue displacers was used, much as Mäkinen preferred the dry rubber cone setup; it was set to give 13in from wheel centre to wheelarch. The subframes were seam-welded and the steering arms from the rack had nuts welded to them to make adjusting the steering easier. All nuts were further secured by split pins, and the top and bottom ball joints lapped in.

As always, the electrics received much attention and a new addition was the use of a BMC 1800 indicator stalk, which also now incorporated the headlight flasher. A small Healey sidelight was used as a reversing lamp, which was switched

The 1967 Alpine Rally saw GRX 311D again at the hands of Hopkirk and Crellin. Despite great expectations, the car retired early when the diff housing developed a large hole that could not be repaired.

The 1967 Alpine Rally has Mäkinen and Easter at the wheel of GRX 311D. Paul Easter checks his paperwork for the already battered car.

from the gearbox. Four auxiliary lamps, all with iodine bulbs were fitted: two fog lamps and two driving lamps on a badge bar where the two centre lamps used lamp steadies. They were connected via a rubber plug and socket attached to the wing on the left-hand side between the headlight and sidelight. This part, sourced from the Land Rover parts bin, would be a regular fit on Abingdon Minis from then on, which made removing the lamps much quicker. Mixo Minor horns were used rather than Maserati items. All lines were run inside the car and not within the sills as they had been on the previous build. The fuel pump was secured under the rear seat but only one pump was wired.

To save weight the car was fitted with lightweight panels to the bonnet, boot lid and doors. All of the glass, save the front laminated 'screen, was replaced with Perspex. The bumpers, front and rear were removed and as much trim as possible. Rivington thin carpet was laid where the rear seat once was. The weight saving was of some 100lb. The car used Dunlop R7 race tyres throughout but Dunlop had taken along SP44s Weathermasters just in case.

As the Alpine was not a rough event, a Moke sump guard and Moke sump plate were employed but with the addition of a duralumin sheet fixed to the sump guard to further protect the gearbox. A battery box guard was also fitted.

The bonnet was held down by two Moke rubber toggles, replacing the usual leather strap – as first seen on the Marathon de la Route cars. The boot lid was held securely shut by a single Moke toggle. The car, in Group 6 form, was very striking.

The Alpine traditionally had a strict time schedule on the road and only those who remained on time would win a coveted Alpine Cup. The timed stages were used simply as a means of classification. Now, as speeds had increased, the organisers deemed that to keep on time cars had to be within just two per cent of the fastest car in their class. The challenge was daunting and explains BMC's need to build a Group 6 car.

Starting from Marseille on 4 September after some very relaxed scrutineering, where being a Group 6 car meant almost anything goes, the 79 cars set off on Monday evening for the first leg to Alpe d'Huez of this 2300-mile event, with 110 cols to climb and descend. This leg was 900 miles long over the Alps, with 18 tightly timed road selectives; interspersed were four épreuves (timed-to-the-second hillclimb stages).

Traditional Alpine sections in the first leg included the very tight and twisty selectives between Quatre Chemins, Sigale, Entrevaux and Rouaine, the Col D'Allos, the Col de Cayolle and the fearsome Col de Lombarde. Elford's Porsche was soon leading but the works Minis were close by. Mäkinen was hard-charging and displaying red-hot disc brakes, to the delight of many spectators that night. Mäkinen arrived in the evening for a night's rest at Alpe d'Huez in third behind two Alpine Renaults. Elford had fallen to fifth. Hopkirk was in seventh place.

The second leg started the next morning, where 450 miles in 13 hours were undertaken with 13 selectives but no classification épreuves. It was all about fast, continuous speed. Mäkinen was now up into second place and his clean sheet on the road still in place – many had lost theirs. The 20-minute service at the end of the leg was well used by everyone. Mäkinen received new brake callipers again, as well as new brake pads.

The sting in the tail, the daunting third and final leg, was a 29-hour bash to just outside Monte Carlo at Menton. This

Mäkinen and Easter climbing one of the many cols on the Alpine Rally in the lightweight Group 6 car.

GRX 311D broke its throttle cable at the start of Col du Marocaz hillclimb; Mäkinen drove the stage on the key. At service, the new throttle cable can be seen on the floor, as can the split Weber carburettors.

Mäkinen was leading the rally when idler gear failure robbed the car of a fine result just two stages from the end of this gruelling event.

section was more than 1000 miles, with 18 selectives and six épreuves. It was both demanding and, with difficult navigation skirting north around Chambéry, it would prove defining. Mäkinen and Hopkirk were now pressing the leading Alpine as hard as they could but Mäkinen suffered a setback while leaving the start of the Col de Marocaz hillclimb when his throttle cable broke. With no time to replace it, Mäkinen jammed the throttle wide open and drove for the next couple of hours on the ignition switch. Road time was lost into Challes-les-Eaux and more time repairing the damage, so Mäkinen's challenge was effectively over as darkness fell on the last night, but he was not done, setting second-fastest time, with Hopkirk winning, on the foggy Col de l'Iseran épreuve, no doubt due to good pace notes.

At Guillestre, the leading Alpine blew up and Mäkinen was in the lead and hard-charging to make back his loss of time, but it was not to last. On the second-to-last épreuve, the Col de Restefond, his now-ailing engine, probably due to driving so long with the throttle wide open, finally succumbed, with his idler gears stripped, and he coasted downhill into Allos where the final test awaited. Hopkirk flew over the Allos and the three remaining selectives; he came through unscathed and cruised into Menton victorious. Only 20 cars followed him to the finish line.

GRX 311D was earlier used for recce duties, where Simo Lampinen and Mike Wood used the car for their recce for the forthcoming 1967 Monte Carlo Rally, where the pair would use HJB 656D. GRX 311D was equipped with a four-tyre roof rack, where a couple of pairs of heavily-studded tyres were stowed. They also carried two extra wheels and tyres inside the boot. The car was also used by Hopkirk and Crellin.

The next event scheduled for the car was to be the *Sun*-sponsored 1967 RAC Rally of Great Britain, but it was cancelled less than 15 hours before the start of the rally due to an outbreak of foot-and-mouth disease. The car was built to be probably the most powerful Cooper S rally car Abingdon had ever created, and it was to be driven by Timo Mäkinen and Paul Easter. It was a lightweight Group 6 car and was fitted with a crossflow eight-port cylinder head and Lucas mechanical fuel injection. It wasn't the first time this engine had been used, as it had been fitted to one of the recce

Simo Lampinen used GRX 311D for his recce with Mike Wood for the 1967 Monte Carlo Rally, Lampinen seen here carrying out essential maintenance on the car.

All dressed up with nowhere to go. A new GRX 311D, complete with fuel injection, ready to start the 1967 RAC, which was cancelled at the last minute due to foot-and-mouth disease.

Mäkinen and Fall ran number 18 on the impromptu televised rally stage, despite being number 24 for the cancelled RAC Rally.

One of the most used Mini photos, Mäkinen with Tony Fall in the passenger seat, performs for the television cameras due to the cancellation of the RAC Rally.

cars for the Tour de Corsica early in the month. The engine produced more power and more low-down torque. Because of the position of the fuel injection, the alternator had to be repositioned above the engine on the right-hand side, meaning a slight bulge had to be let into the aluminium bonnet to clear the fixing strap.

All of the preparation was to no avail but, as there was now a vacant television slot in the programming, a hastily-arranged TV stage was put together in Camberley forest, not far from the start at London Airport. Overnight the British Federation granted an application to sanction a single-venue event, on the proviso that it was closed to the public and open only to those invited – one of which was Mäkinen in GRX 311D.

Mäkinen and Hopkirk were both scheduled to drive and, whilst Hopkirk went out on the first run, he punctured on the rather rough bumpy stage and took no further part, not wishing to damage the car. Mäkinen, with Tony Fall in the passenger seat, drove with verve and the most publicised shot of a works Mini in action, airborne on the stage, was the result. This single event was to be the start of a new motorsport called rallycross, where the first event took place at Lydden Hill Race Circuit, with many RAC Rally competitors, the very next week.

The final event for this rather unsuccessful works Mini was on the Circuit of Ireland, held over the Easter weekend of 1969, where Paddy Hopkirk and Tony Nash would attempt to add to the five outright wins Paddy already had credited on this classic Irish event. By now the Mini was really struggling to match the pace of other more powerful machinery, notably the Ford Escort. It was therefore decided to build a very lightweight Mini for Hopkirk – fortunately, the Circuit of Ireland allowed Group 6 cars (a much freer formula than Group 5 and Group 2).

Roy Brown was instructed to take as much weight out of the car as was physically possible. Naturally, he fitted an aluminium bonnet, boot and doors plus Perspex windows. The vast majority of the trim was discarded, including the heater (which caused some discomfort in the cold night sections in Ireland) and radically, the body was de-seamed along the roof line and down the front and rear drain rails. This was no mean task.

Many steel brackets were replaced with fabricated parts crafted from aluminium, and he even cut off excess bolt lengths where they passed through nuts. The obligatory lamp bar was drilled for lightness and the Lucas 700 auxiliary lamps had large holes cut in the back to save even more weight. The door handles were let into the body, and the steel headlight bowls replaced with fibreglass units; the grille was also replaced with lightweight aluminium.

To protect the gearbox, Tech Del made a lightweight magnesium heavy-duty sump guard. It is reported that the car had shed over 100kg in weight. To finish the car off (as it had no roof gutter), the traditional white roof paint was extended down to the car's waistline, making it quite distinctive and radically different in appearance from any other Mini. It is said that nobody at Abingdon was prepared to add up just how much all of this extensive work had actually cost.

Hopkirk had previously tested a car at Thruxton race circuit to evaluate suitable wheels and tyres for the rally, and to also see if he was happy having a limited-slip differential fitted. It was decided to use an LSD, and both 12in and 10in versions were to be taken along to Ireland. The 10x5½J magnesium wheels were to be used with Dunlop R7 race tyres, and the 12x6J wheels fitted with Dunlop 236 race tyres. Additionally, if the weather was bad and for loose surfaces, Dunlop 175x12 SP44s were taken along.

The engine would also be as powerful as possible. However, it was to be a five-port, not an eight-port engine (now being used in Abingdon's race programme). It would therefore run split Weber carburettors and not fuel injection. Unfortunately, the new unit failed whilst being run-in, when a cam follower broke up. A hasty engine rebuild, just days before the start, did not bode well. Nevertheless, Cliff Humphries managed to run-in the new engine and get it onto the Abingdon rollers where, on split Webers, it showed 93bhp at the wheels.

Once in Ireland, Hopkirk was practising in his new car and was dismayed with the handling on 12in wheels, feeling it unstable. Further, a persistent misfire from the engine was defying all attempts to cure the problem. It was decided that the carburettors should be replaced, but no spare units had come over to Ireland – so a hasty call to Abingdon saw a new pair on their way, which wouldn't arrive until after the start.

The 1969 Circuit of Ireland was, by now, a thinly disguised road race of some 1500 miles, spread over four days with 56 stages (timed to the second) of some 500 miles and only 15 minutes lateness allowed between controls. This resulted in hard driving from start to finish and little time for servicing or mistakes.

The weather was superb for Easter in Ireland, and Roger Clark in the Ford Escort was to be Hopkirk's main opposition. He, like Hopkirk, was in a very special Group 6 car. His Escort was an 1800cc Twin Cam with enormous race tyres and wide arches to match – in truth, he had twice the power

A super lightweight GRX 311D was built for Hopkirk and Nash for the 1969 Circuit of Ireland, seen here with 12in wheels and race tyres.

of Hopkirk's Mini. At the start, at the Gallaher's factory in Ballymena, the field of 150 cars headed off into the Good Friday night to the first stage. What greeted them were classic Ireland stages such as Sally Gap before the breakfast stop at Blessington. The tired crews had tackled 11 stages in the dark and covered 300 miles.

Hopkirk and Nash had numerous problems, notably carburettors and importantly the poor handling on 12in wheels. The car seen here has reverted to 10in wheels and race tyres.

Hopkirk was struggling with the badly-handling car on its 12in wheels, which he changed onto the more familiar 10in variety after the seventh stage, but with that came lower ground clearance. His times were no better than in 1968 and at breakfast the new spilt Webers turned up. They were swiftly changed, sadly to no avail, as the misfire was even worse. In short order, the original set was replaced and the problem miraculously disappeared. It was later found the inlet flanges had not seated fully with the cylinder head, letting in air, weakening the mixture and causing the misfire. Now Hopkirk was flying again – but Clark was in a class of his own and leading the field by a sizeable margin.

The Saturday run from Blessington to Killarney of some 290 miles held another ten stages. By now Clark was running clear and Adrian Boyd in his ex-works Mini JBL 494D was the main challenger to Hopkirk, and was pushing him hard.

Despite his best efforts and that of Abingdon building a special car for the rally, Hopkirk and Nash had to settle for second place, unable to get on terms with Roger Clark's Ford Escort Twin Cam.

Fifty cars would find the pace too much and retired, with only 100 cars making it into Killarney.

The Sunday run, a round trip from Killarney and back, was the most spectacular and also the most challenging part of the four days, which saw the cars through the Cork and Kerry Mountains onto Kenmare and Bantry Bay.

Another 11 stages of some 90 miles were to be tackled, including Moll's Gap, Borlin and the superb Healy Pass (attempted twice), where Hopkirk had oil pressure problems. A change of the oil pressure relief valve didn't cure the problem, so the spring was packed with a few washers and the problem went away. The superb Ardgroom and Cod's Head stages followed.

By Easter Monday the field had been cut in half, with only 70 cars restarting. Facing them was 340 miles to Co Fermanagh for their supper halt. Hopkirk was slowly improving his times, masked by the fact that Clark, now in an unassailable lead, was starting to back off to preserve the Escort. The Ford was not without its problems and needed numerous welding jobs to its rear suspension.

Hopkirk, however, had all his hard work undone, as on the second stage of the day he spun and dropped time to Boyd, who now was in second place and ahead of Hopkirk. More trouble occurred at the end of the Knockanebane stage later in the day when the adjustable tie bar broke. It was soon replaced but the other side also failed soon afterwards and a standard unit was borrowed from a private entrant.

Their problems were not over, as a few stages further along, and having just left their service, the front damper failed. Nash ran back to the service barge, which had not departed, and a new unit was soon fitted. They now headed to the supper halt at Killadeas in County Fermanagh. With the last leg back to Larne still to do, Clark had a very large lead as the crews headed into the darkness for ten hours and ten more stages to the finish. With superb hard driving, Hopkirk managed to claw back the slender lead Boyd had over him, despite his engine now overheating – made worse by a sticking clutch master cylinder making gearchanges difficult.

At the finish, Clark had a 17-minute lead but Hopkirk was applauded for his fine second place, having been fastest on 13 stages. It was a good result, but the Mini could no longer be expected to be at the front.

The car was sold to Denis Cresdee.

Competition Record

Date	Event	Crew	Number	Overall result	Class result
May 1966	Acropolis Rally	Paddy Hopkirk/Ron Crellin	67	3rd	1st
July 1966	German Rally	Paddy Hopkirk/Chris Nash	42	DNF	
Sept 1966	Alpine Rally	Paddy Hopkirk/Ron Crellin	67	DNF	
Sept 1967	Alpine Rally	Timo Mäkinen/Paul Easter	103	DNF	
Nov 1967	RAC Rally	Timo Mäkinen/Paul Easter	24	Cancelled	
April 1969	Circuit of Ireland	Paddy Hopkirk/Tony Nash	2	2nd	1st

CHAPTER 3: THE MK 1 MINI COOPER S

Registration Number	First registered	Chassis number	Engine	Engine number	Model
HJB 656D	April 1966	KA2S4 821305	1275cc	9F-SA-Y 40412	Morris Cooper S

HJB 656D was one of two new Cooper Ss registered in April 1966: one an Austin and HJB 566D a Morris. With its first event being the Acropolis Rally the following month for Timo Mäkinen and Paul Easter, the car was built by Tommy Eales. It was the sister car to two other brand-new Minis destined for Greece, all built as Group 2 cars.

Built with Abingdon's customary 1293cc engine with race camshaft, the only deviation from standard practice was reducing the compression ratio slightly to 11.6:1 to reflect the lower grade of fuel available in Greece. The engine produced 88bhp at the wheels when fitted with AZ needles in the twin SU H4 carburettors. With the anticipated hot weather, the cooling system was carefully prepared, running a 60C thermostat. The radiator cowl was now affixed to the radiator with larger bolts and the bottom bracket was now solidly mounted, abandoning its rubber mounts. It also ran a small pulley on the water pump.

The rough Greek roads dictated much strengthening and protection to the underside of the car. The rear subframe was double-skinned and rewelded – as was the front subframe. The battery box had a skid fitted and at the front a heavy-duty sump guard was used. Also at the front, the tie rods had skid plates fixed to the subframe, and the brake callipers had protection plates fixed to their sides to prevent damage to the flexible brake pipe. The exhaust was also skidded and its joints had security bars welded to prevent them from being torn apart. All lines were run inside the car, with the fuel pump now located under the rear seat.

There was Hydrolastic suspension with double-blue and single-blue displacers, helper springs and Aeon bump stops but the suspension wasn't raised, set at its normal 13in between wheel centre and wheelarch. Steel 4½J wheels were used, necessitating fibreglass wheelarch extensions – and it sat on Dunlop R7 race tyres. The brakes were fitted with DS11 disc pads and VG95 shoes at the rear, and there was a brake servo.

The new electrical loom, built by Lucas Racing, unique to each car, was crafted to incorporate the additional switches, controls and auxiliary lighting. Driving this extra equipment was an 11AC alternator with a remote regulator. The extra lamps – two Continental driving lamps in the middle and two large fog lamps on the outside – were fitted on a low lamp bar above the bumper. A Healey 3000 sidelight was used for the reversing lamp, mounted on the boot lid.

Inside the car, Mäkinen had an alloy dash panel with a large rev counter and numerous switches. Easter had a similar panel with a Halda distance recorder and Heuer clocks,

together with additional control switches. In his door pocket was another switch panel housing his map light.

Mäkinen sat in a fibreglass bucket seat and Easter a more compliant reclining seat. Both had Irvin belts: a lap and diagonal for Mäkinen, and a full harness for Easter. To aid crew comfort, padding was fitted to the door pockets, door locks and the door pillar. An intercom was added, which was no doubt very necessary in a car being driven flat-out over rough roads.

A marathon 2000 miles of often-poor-quality roads in just 50 hours was going to take its toll on the 118 entrants for the 1966 Acropolis Rally; the expected finish rate was around 20 per cent. There were 17 stages, three hillclimbs and one race interwoven with a very high average speed, meaning a hard challenge. Unfortunately, the marking system of the stages, with a different bogey time to beat for each class, meant most of the top crews received no penalties – rendering them ineffective – unless they had a problem. The hillclimbs, however, were marked differently, in that the fastest time became the bogey time for others to beat, so these three hillclimbs effectively decided the rally. The race at the end was of little consequence and in effect only had to be completed.

HJB 656D, at start number 82, lines up with the other works Mini entries in Athens for scrutineering prior to the start of the 1966 Acropolis Rally.

Timo Mäkinen and Paul Easter in HJB 565D crash over a level crossing as the police wave them onwards.

Mäkinen and Easter set a blistering pace on the often very rough roads in Greece but it took its toll of HJB 656D.

Mäkinen started at the foot of the Acropolis towards Corinth and the first stage was some two hours away, where he was fastest. Into the first night heading south and onto more rough roads to the second group of stages, Mäkinen again set the fastest times. By dawn at the Patras ferry crossing he had beaten the bogey on all the stages but only 73 cars made the ferry.

Hopkirk and Aaltonen in the other team cars were also setting fast times. Much enthusiasm greeted Mäkinen wherever he drove, the Greeks cheering him on his way with great passion – too much on one road, where his windscreen was smashed from enthusiastic stone-throwing.

On the long 30-mile fifth stage Mäkinen beat the bogey time by four minutes and even Hopkirk, having holed his sump, only lost a small amount of time. Back through Thessaloniki to the seventh group of stages saw Aaltonen make his mark with Mäkinen just trailing Hopkirk. At the Volos service it became clear Mäkinen had suffered with brake problems; after the calliper was changed, he was on his way.

On the important Portaria hillclimb, Aaltonen won by just four seconds but on the next stage Aaltonen had ignition problems and Mäkinen sped into the lead, 11 seconds clear of Vic Elford in the works Ford. The very rough stages that followed saw Mäkinen lose his lead when a series of punctures (and running on the threepenny-bit-shaped steel wheel) broke the rear radius arm bracket. As luck would have it, Wilson McCombe, BMC's press officer, was spectating with a *Motor* magazine reporter in Hopkirk's recce car DJB 92B when Mäkinen came into view. Instantly Easter and Mäkinen set about cannibalising the recce car of its bracket. The bracket took a long time to remove and to replace on the rally car, costing 31 minutes – and their lead had gone. They left the stranded McCombe to try and get their now-broken bracket welded.

Mäkinen, however, was not giving up, and he simply stormed the next important hillclimb at Distomon, 28 seconds faster than anyone else. Fortunes would soon change, with Aaltonen out and Elford's Ford gearbox failing, promoting Hopkirk into the lead. But Mäkinen was again in trouble, as the engine started to overheat as he lost water, with the

Mäkinen helping to change the broken radius arm bracket removed from DJB 92D, which was out on press duties with Wilson McCombe.

cylinder head eventually cracking and losing power.

Just 40 cars made it back to Athens and, after a night's sleep, the final hillclimb and the race circuit around the Tatoi airport roads was all that was left. Mäkinen had to settle for a lowly tenth place, with his ailing engine, whilst Hopkirk was demoted to third place after picking up penalties for servicing within a time control area. It had not been the happiest of events for Abingdon.

For the car's next event, the Polish Rally in August 1966, the rather tired car was reprepared for Rauno Aaltonen and Henry Liddon by Tommy Eales and Peter Bartram. Needless to say, a fresh engine was built, to full Group 2 specification, bored to 1293cc using a 11.6:1 compression Downton cylinder head and a full-race camshaft, which produced 86bhp at the wheels. Coupled with the normal straight-cut close-ratio gearbox and a 4.133 diff, it made for a very quick car.

Keeping the engine cool was a four-blade fan, which had the blades reduced by 5mm to aid fan belt changes. The Cooper S radiator was also rigidly bolted down at the bottom, negating the rubber bushes on the lower mounting bracket. Stopping the car was entrusted to Ferodo DS11 racing disc pads and VG95 rear brake linings, and the servo was retained and fitted in the standard position under the bonnet.

Hardy Spicer drive couplings with larger diameter driveshafts were fitted as standard. As the Polish was generally a rough event, the car carried a full heavy-duty sump guard and had a Moke sump plate screwed directly to the sump. The car also ran a battery skid plate under the rear subframe, protecting the vulnerable battery box. A special Mitchell mounting remote rubber was fitted to the end of the gearbox remote shift, and the mounting bracket was strengthened by welding and further reinforced by straps inside the car. The gearstick was replaced with the standard-fitting anti-rattle type instead the preferred solid early stick used for so long on works Minis.

Hydrolastic suspension was fitted, with single-blue and double-blue displacers front and back with helper springs. The suspension was further assisted by the fitting of heavy-duty Aeon bump stops, also front and back. The rear radius arm brackets on the subframe were strengthened and the subframe was double-skinned on its top face. In addition, the front of the tie rods were protected where they mounted onto the front subframe with fabricated brackets, which also strengthened the subframe.

The battery line, brake lines and fuel lines were all routed inside the car, and the twin fuel pump found itself located under the rear seat, rather than out in the damp and cold screwed to the rear subframe. Aaltonen sat in a special fabric-covered fibreglass bucket seat, whereas Liddon had a comfortable reclining seat. Irvin harnesses were fitted. Apart from the customary padding inside the car to add comfort and protection, the car jack now found its way inside, fixed vertically behind the driver on the companion box side.

Held behind what was then the Iron Curtain, the 1966 Polish Rally centred around Kraków and used 22 fast stages of around 120 miles within its 1700-mile route. Split into two legs, a northern loop and southern loop, this round of the European Championship, which had very high (almost impossible) average speeds, attracted a small entry of 52 cars, most of which were local crews, and also works teams from BMC, Ford, Lancia and a few Eastern Bloc teams. The stages were mostly on tarmac and the rally also included a couple of races, two hillclimbs and a driving test (autotest). The rally

The 1966 Polish Rally saw Rauno Aaltonen and Henry Liddon take over the rebuilt HJB 656D.

Aaltonen had a really long battle with Mäkinen, swapping the lead but had to give best to his rival teammate when the transmission failed on HJB 656D.

was, however, also run on a complicated class and engine capacity system, now rather out of fashion, favouring small Group 1 cars (which was why BMC also entered Tony Fall in Group 1 970S).

Aaltonen was pitched against his old rival Mäkinen, both in 1275S Group 2 cars. Once under way, the first airfield race, held in torrential rains, saw Aaltonen second just behind Roger Clark's works Cortina and one ahead of Mäkinen. As the weather deteriorated further, the hard night began with a stage where Aaltonen was again second – this time to Mäkinen. Another stage saw Aaltonen fastest, and back at Kraków Aaltonen was leading. But the slippery roads were taking their toll on crews, with many overshooting junctions and – more importantly – stage finish lines, which incurred penalties.

Heading southwards, Aaltonen extended his lead with three fastest times to Mäkinen's two. After seven stages, Aaltonen was leading Mäkinen by just a single second but the fast and furious pace on the road was indeed a challenge. Both still held their clean sheets, with no road time lost, but it was not to last as the weather deteriorated further, and minutes started to be dropped by all the top crews. As the cars headed westwards, it all changed when Aaltonen had his transmission fail, and without gears he was out. Such was the rate of attrition that only 11 cars made it back to the finish in Kraków. Nevertheless, in the end, Fall won in the Group 1 970S, with Mäkinen having to settle for second place – such had been the vagaries of the marking system.

This now-much-used car was returned into the hands of Timo Mäkinen and Paul Easter to use on the Munich-Vienna-Budapest Rally in early October 1966, built this time by Bob Whittington, again as a Group 2 car. The engine was fitted with the latest strengthened block and high-compression (16.4cc) Downton cylinder head, which raised the compression to 12.6:1. The cylinder head used MGB head studs tightened down to 50lb.ft to ensure the head gasket stayed intact. It was also noted that the pistons were now fitted with special oil-control piston rings, as high oil consumption had started to become an issue with the oval pistons. With the now-customary race camshaft fitted, the car achieved 95bhp at its wheels on the rolling road. Mäkinen also specified a very short 4.2:1 final drive.

A notable change to the car was the fitting of the heavy-duty Scandinavian sump guard in addition to the Moke sump plate screwed to the underside of the gearbox. This new guard came up almost to the underside of the front bumper, covering the lower panel and also preventing the front quick-lift jacking points from being used. These were still retained but masked by red paint.

The suspension was Hydrolastic, despite Mäkinen's preference for dry cone suspension; it was fitted with the customary uprated blue displacers. The rear subframe was strengthened and, to add strength to the body, the crossmember was double-skinned internally. This was not strictly within the regulations but it was skilfully hidden within the existing box section and was never questioned. The only other change to the car was that the fibreglass buckets seat required a porta-power jack to widen it to allow Mäkinen's large frame to sit comfortably within the rather tightly fitting bucket seat.

Mäkinen's entry for the Munich-Vienna-Budapest Rally was to help him chase for the European Championship, which his rival Aaltonen had won the previous year – and with Aaltonen sitting this one out, it was a real opportunity.

This by-now much-used car was handed back to Mäkinen and Easter for the 1966 Munich-Vienna-Budapest Rally.

Service for the car, with the continual swapping of tyres between race tyres and SP44 tyres, was problematic, with the Dunlop tyres being delayed.

Counting for both Group 2 and Group 1 points, the rally, often known as the Three Cities Rally, attracted works entries form Saab, Ford Germany, Lancia and BMC. A strong entry of 104 assembled underneath a flyover in Munich for scrutineering. Nothing dramatic transpired, other than the scrutineers questioning Bob Freebrough's lights. Freebrough had been co-opted into the team using his 970S and would join Tony Fall as the three-car team.

For the first time this rally would be decided in scratch times – fastest wins – rather than the complex class improvement system used, and often exploited, in the past. European rallies were now nearly all using the scratch system as performance and speeds increased. Just seven stages would decide the winner, although once out of the rather regimented roads of Germany, the navigation became far more taxing, as did the average speed, and the roads more demanding.

Right from the start, on the first tarmac stage, Mäkinen was fastest. He had to give best to the works Lancia Fulvia on the second stage near the Czech border as he was unable to recce this forest stage, due to a large man with a big gun preventing him entering the forest to practice.

Into Austria the roads became twisty and narrow, where there were four more tests, mostly on loose surfaces, and the hard-worked BMC mechanics were busy switching between Dunlop SP44 Weathermasters and Dunlop R7 racer tyres for Mäkinen. This was also a headache for the Dunlop team, as the van carrying BMC's tyres was delayed at the border but arrived just in time. Mäkinen was fastest on all of the stages.

Very tricky navigation during the night near the Hungarian border still saw Mäkinen clean and well into the lead. As the average speed increased, it took its toll on many, with only 58 cars making Budapest. With only one rough stage remaining, Mäkinen was again fastest and maintained his lead, claimed his European points and quickly got on a plane back to Finland where he was competing in two championship races, which he also won. It had been a good few days.

It should also be noted that by this time, October 1966, BMC had just been amalgamated with Jaguar Cars and Pressed Steel to become British Motor Holdings Limited, with at its head Sir George Harriman. The company BMH would last for two years until it became British Leyland – more of which later...

With five team cars entered for the Monte Carlo Rally in January 1967, HJB 656D was reprepared for Simo Lampinen and Mike Wood; the other four cars would all be brand new, but Lampinen on only on his second drive for BMC (which would actually be his last) was not afforded a new car for this winter classic, which after exclusion the previous year, Abingdon was keen to avenge.

The Monte Carlo Rally's concentration run was rather tedious in the eyes of many professional drivers, where drivers had to endure two nights out of bed before they arrived at the competitive side of the rally. But this is where rallying gets its name: cars from various starting points around Europe would 'rally' on Monte Carlo for the main competition. Nevertheless, the publicity generated for such an event was huge, and that did not escape BMC, which was aware of the kudos of a Monte win.

The car, although not new and had by now seen a lot of hard work, was meticulously reprepared for Lampinen and Wood and built to the same specification as the four other brand new cars, LBL 6D, 66D, 666D and 606D. All had the same 1293cc engine, which with its high-compression Downton cylinder head, race camshaft and bigger carburettors produced

Mäkinen and Easter were the fastest on almost every stage in HJB 656D and would win the rally convincingly, improving Mäkinen's chances in the European Championship.

Simo Lampinen and Mike Wood were entered on the 1967 Monte Carlo Rally in HJB 656D. The car was still the same as had started the Acropolis Rally, not a new car as the other Monte works entries were.

Lampinen and Wood pull into a time control. Clearly seen here is the vertical rally plate fixed to the roof at the insistence that rally plates had to be fitted vertically.

A time-consuming flat tyre on the St Auban stage saw the crew lose time. Lampinen attends in the boot whilst Wood loosens the wheel.

around 95bhp on the rolling road. The straight-cut close-ratio gearbox was fitted with a 4.2:1 final drive and this, with the power, would have produced a very quick car.

Hydrolastic suspension was used with uprated displacers, and the brakes received racing pads and linings. New for the Monte was the fitting of Minilite magnesium wheels, which offered a considerable weight saving over steel wheels and were also very strong. This would be especially important as the car would be required to carry four extra wheels for the two competitive sections – due to the class that it was entered in, as identified by a yellow door square carrying its number. Additionally, these four wheels would see two secured onto the rear seat pan, meaning the seat cushion had to be held vertically with straps onto the back seat.

For the Monte, with the predicted inclement weather, the front grille of the car was covered with a removable grille muff. Also for the Monte, the front-facing rally plate was required to be fixed vertically rather than on the bonnet. This meant the rally plate was ultimately fixed up on the roof, by the front screen, on a couple of brackets and a back stay but had initially been fitted on the front bumper; a last-minute change when it became clear that the Monégasque scrutineers would be insisting on them being placed vertically.

Front forward-facing mud flaps to try and keep the 'screen and headlights clear were fitted but were removed at Monte Carlo through fear of the brakes being overheated due to restricted airflow. There was a heated front windscreen and the car carried four auxiliary lamps on a lamp bar. The headlights were protected by removable Perspex covers fixed to the wing. The electrics, to ensure total reliably, had all of the control switches replaced from the previous event.

Crew comfort, important on the long drive to Monte Carlo, saw two comfortable but heavy reclining seats fitted in the car. They were replaced at Monte Carlo for a lightweight bucket seat for Lampinen and a standard Mini seat, with a supportive cover, for Wood.

Lampinen would start his Monte Carlo Rally from Monte Carlo along with Rauno Aaltonen. This was often considered the easiest option, as the weather was often tranquil and if recce work was being carried out at the very last moment, as it often was, the Monte start saved extra travel to another far-flung starting venue. Nevertheless, Stuart Turner had dispatched four of his other works cars to those other far-flung destinations. Lampinen's route would see him travel out westwards to Bayonne in the south west corner of France and then up the west of France through Bergerac, La Rochelle and Poitiers before heading back south to Monte Carlo. His route would be in relatively good weather and he, along with 176 others, arrived in Monte Carlo in early afternoon. He had been on the road for just over 50 hours but arrived on time and without penalty, with the car going well.

This Monte was, however, going to be different because Lampinen, along with almost every other car, had decided to enter the eight-tyre category. In an attempt to encourage private entrants, the organisers had instigated a tyre limit in one category – the other category could have free choice of any number of tyres on the two competitive sections but they would incur a 12.5 per cent time handicap. This, most agreed, was too severe, so all bar 17 cars took the eight-tyre restriction. However, all tyres had to be with the car, so most had to accommodate at least two extra wheels and tyres – and the extra weight. Further still, these tyres had to be selected before each one of the two legs and, once chosen, could not be changed. The selected tyres were painted and branded with the car's number and heavy penalties were meted out should all the tyres not be with the car, or indeed any that had not be marked.

Apart from the burden of selecting tyres in advance, Dunlop had the added problem of producing tyres that would last the distance, bearing in mind a hard-driven works Mini could destroy a set of tyres very quickly should they be wrong for the conditions. Therefore Dunlop, along with BMC, had been testing different tyre compounds in the Alps since early November – stud retention was also a major issue. Once decided, Turner gave Dunlop a list of 420 tyres that he needed for his five works Minis – considerably less than in previous unrestricted years.

Once Lampinen had arrived back in Monte Carlo at the end of his two-day trip around France, he had to decide on tyres for the common run due to start the next day. This would be an 850-mile loop to Chambéry and back over 24 hours and would include six timed-to-the-second hillclimb stages. After consulting with other team members and Turner, he, along with the rest of the team (bar Hopkirk) elected to take four Dunlop SP3s and four half-studded SP44s. The weather looked to be set fair and with only ice reported on the top of the hills, it seemed a sensible choice.

The next morning the 176 crews, who had made it to Monte Carlo, set off on the common run. The first stage, Saint-Auban, was dry but Lampinen unfortunately punctured early, having hit a rock, so stopped to change the wheel and had to put on an SP44 rather than an SP3 tyre. He was now well down on time. His luck would get worse on the next stage, the hillclimb up Monte Ventoux, where he punctured yet again – this time he continued, running on the rim, arriving at the finish having completely lost the tyre. Fortunately, he was not penalised for not having all eight tyres on this occasion, despite initial suspicions from the officials. These losses of time would, however, be difficult to claw back. Lampinen was well down the field when he arrived back in Monte Carlo some 24 hours later, finishing just inside the top 30.

Undeterred, the next evening he had the Mountain Circuit in front of him – a 385-mile loop around the mountains above Monte Carlo. Along with just the top 60 crews allowed to start, he again had to select his eight tyres. The weather was now not as settled with rain forecast in Monte Carlo, which could only mean snow would appear on the top of the six climbs. Lampinen selected all SP44s this time, four plain and four half-studded. Ahead of them were no less than three visits to the Col du Turini and two on the Col du Couillole. The pace of the mountain circuit would be relentless, as although the schedule was not that fast, the time needed to service and continually change tyres meant that the pace was very fast. Lampinen, like others, was continually swapping his studded SP44s for plain SP44s, which he would use for the roads in between the stages – saving his studded tyres where he could.

The weather, as predicted, worsened and the last two

Lampinen and Wood power through one of the picturesque hill villages found in the Alps.

HJB 656D would finish in 15th place, as they pull into the final control at the end of the 1966 Monte Carlo Rally.

Many special features were built into HJB 656D. Here a Hydrolastic pump is provided to pump up the Hydrolastic suspension when and if needed.

Should the wipers fail, a hand-operated wiper could be operated from inside the car.

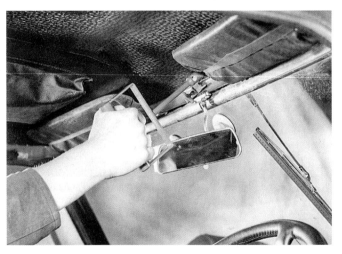

Rauno Aaltonen and Henry Liddon, as a prize for winning the Monte Carlo Rally, had HJB 656D prepared for the East African Safari Rally. Lifting handles on the wing, together with high-level fog lamps and bounce steps on the front can be seen here.

decisive stages were under a blanket of heavy snow. Lampinen was 15th fastest on the mountain circuit, and there he would finish in the final overall standings. Nevertheless, Aaltonen had won the rally and BMC had avenged the disappointment of 1966 when all Minis were disqualified.

As a reward for Aaltonen's Monte win, he was given a pair of free air tickets to Nairobi and free entry on the East African Safari Rally, which was held over the Easter holidays in March 1967. BMC was therefore only too keen to take advantage of this and built and entered a unique Mini Cooper S for Aaltonen and Liddon. The car was officially entered by Benbros Motors of Kenya, which was a BMC agent, to give extra publicity – and also involved in the final preparation and on-event servicing. Stuart Turner was making his very last trip with BMC as he decided to fly out with Den Green to see the country.

The car was quite unlike any works Mini ever built, before or since. This now-much-used car was again reprepared for what was to be its final event for BMC. The engine was rather tame, in that it was fitted with a standard Cooper S 510 camshaft, much as the works engines were on the previous year's RAC Rally. This was largely to give more low-down torque but to the detriment of its output. The engine produced 75bhp on the rolling road, compared to the 95bhp with the 648 race camshaft and a high-compression cylinder head. The carburettors were further constrained with the fitting of pancake air filters instead of open ram pipes. The prevailing dusty conditions would nevertheless see the car's early demise.

Because of the anticipated muddy conditions invariably found in East Africa, much work was centred on keeping the car dry and mobile. It was fitted with two pairs of lifting handles: two on the front wings and two on the rear of the roof – the idea being they would allow a pole (or heavy tree branch) to be slid through to allow helpers to lift the stricken car out of deep mud should it get stuck. Some comic suggested they were there for a helicopter to lift the car out of trouble – but Stuart Turner strongly denied such a plan.

The car also had a pair of 'bouncing steps' fitted to the front and rear above the bumper, this to allow the car to be bumped to increase grip and traction in the slimy mud so

For traversing deep water, a snorkel pipe was provided, which would be placed over the exhaust pipe; also seen here are the bounce steps provided at the rear of the car.

The dramatic scenery of East Africa might have been compensation enough for Aaltonen and Liddon as the car retired relatively early due to the ingress of dust choking the air filters and damaging the engine.

often encountered. Following the tradition of cars prepared for these tough events, two driving lamps were fitted on top of each wing, meaning if deep water obscured the headlights, these high-mounted lamps would still guide the way; they could also be kept clean by the crew leaning out of their side windows. An additional wiper was fitted above the driver, mounted on the roof, which could be hand-operated.

Large front-facing mud flaps were fitted, last seen on the Monte Carlo Rally, in addition to a pair of rear mud flaps. Needless to say, the car was fitted with the very heavy but strong Scandinavian sump guard and the subframes were also strengthened. To top off the car's striking external appearance, it had a matt black bonnet and wing tops to combat glare, plus it was fitted with removable fly-screen mesh ahead of the front grille. A similar removable grille was fitted under the wheelarch to help keep mud off the side-mounted radiator.

Inside the car, it was also rather special. Because the car retained its Hydrolastic suspension, it had a modified Hydrolastic pump fitted and plumbed into the system on the rear bulkhead behind the driver. This enabled the suspension to be raised or re-pressurised should it be needed. The fuel pump was also mounted inside but high up on the rear bulkhead to avoid it being drowned out, should the car be stuck deep in water. The rear seat was removed but the bulkhead carpeted instead.

Much as on the Monte, two spare wheels were carried inside on the rear seat pan with quick-release clamps. Also, as a precaution, should the car be stuck in deep water, a large document bag was fabricated and fixed into the headlining to keep vital documents, maps and time cards safe and dry. For the anticipated deep water, the exhaust was provided with a snorkel pipe, which could be attached to the already upswept tail pipe to clear deep water. The final piece of equipment that the car carried was a winch, this so that it could extract itself from almost any situation should it become stuck.

All of this preparation for wet, muddy conditions was to no avail, as an unseasonal dry Easter, the first in East Africa for many years, produced the hazard of constant dust over the 3000-mile route. Starting from Jamhuri just outside Nairobi, on Maundy Thursday at 8pm, a reported 10,000 spectators saw the cars head out on the first night towards the foothills of Kilimanjaro. Two loops, into and out of Nairobi greeted the 91 starters. For the first time, the cars were seeded, allowing the fancied drivers to head the field. The starting order was by ballot, which meant, very often, fast drivers being delayed by a blocked road due to an inexperienced driver becoming stuck.

The cars were set off at two-minute intervals, which was a bonus with the prevailing conditions, on a route that was invariably on very dusty roads or in most cases, no roads at all – with the added hazard of circumnavigating dried-up river beds, culverts and indeed large animals. Enthusiastic spectators were also an additional problem, as stone- and bolder-throwing seemed to be a common pastime.

Unfortunately, to many people's disappointment, Aaltonen was one of the early retirements. The Mini really was just too small, its wheels just not large enough, and the car fell into almost every dried-up mud hole that Africa could throw at it. The heavy dust was causing the engine to overheat and on an engine that is always susceptible to running hot, this was to prove an insurmountable problem. The air filters soon became clogged with dust, which resulted in the engine running lean on fuel, which soon overheated the engine – it eventually seized and, despite copious quantities of Molyslip being administered, which did free it off, the damage was done. Aaltonen crawled into the Lunga control, several hours late, then limped onto Mombasa and promptly retired. Aaltonen went off to bed.

Only 49 crews made it back to Jamhuri, just outside Nairobi, on Easter Monday. This had been a gruelling event. Peugeot dominated the result sheet, winning outright and having five cars in the top ten. The East African Safari was clearly an event totally unsuited to the Mini's attributes and Abingdon never repeated the experience.

This much-used car was destined not to return to the UK and was sold to Benbros Motors in Nairobi.

Competition Record

Date	Event	Crew	Number	Overall result	Class result
May 1966	Acropolis Rally	Timo Mäkinen/Paul Easter	82	10th	2nd
Aug 1966	Polish Rally	Rauno Aaltonen/Henry Liddon	29	2nd	1st
Oct 1966	Munich-Vienna-Budapest	Timo Mäkinen/Paul Easter	57	1st	1st
Jan 1967	Monte Carlo Rally	Simo Lampinen/Mike Wood	178	15th	
Mar 1967	East African Safari Rally	Rauno Aaltonen/Henry Liddon	8	DNF	

Registration Number	First registered	Chassis number	Engine	Engine number	Model
JBL 172D	April 1966	CA2S7 821287	1275cc	9F-SA-Y 40617	Austin Cooper S

Rauno Aaltonen and Henry Liddon in JBL 172D queuing for their start of the 1966 Acropolis Rally, where the cars all carried large black numbers on their bonnets in addition to door numbers.

JBL 172D was the second of two new Cooper Ss registered in April 1966, as an Austin Cooper S. The car was assigned to Rauno Aaltonen and Henry Liddon and was built by Brian Moylan to tackle the 1966 Acropolis Rally, where Abingdon was sending two other brand-new cars for this tough Greek classic.

Built to a very similar specification to its sister cars, the Group 2 car was fitted with a powerful 1293cc engine but very slightly detuned with a lower-compression Downton cylinder head because of concerns of low-grade fuel supplied in Greece. The car produced a peak power of 88bhp at 7200rpm on the Abingdon rolling road but, with the short diff ratio of 4.2:1, acceleration would have been very brisk. The transmission was fitted with a close-ratio straight-cut gear set and Hardy Spicer couplings on the latest driveshafts. It is also noted that the car was fitted with the latest type of anti-rattle gear lever, in spite of the drivers preferring the earlier non-rubber-mounted gear lever. Despite the anticipated dusty conditions, the twin SUH4 carburettors were not fitted with air filters but instead ram pipes.

For the expected rough roads, the car's Hydrolastic suspension received close attention, with the rear subframe being double-skinned and both subframes rewelded at their joints. The car was fitted with red displacers rather than blue but still used helper springs and heavy-duty Aeon bump stops. In addition to a heavy-duty sump guard, the battery box was also fitted with a skid plate and the front tie bars were protected by skid plates fitted to the subframe side and its front fixing bolt.

The front brake pipes on the callipers were sheltered with protection plates, as were the rear brake pipes. The exhaust, so vulnerable on rough roads, was skidded, locating bars were welded to each joint and special care was taken on its mounting, with the fixing bolt for the carrier being fitted through the rubber but then not overtightened.

The suspension was set at 13in wheel centre to wheel's arc edge and the steering set to 1/8in toe-out. The car ran on 4½J steel wheels with Dunlop R7 race tyres, which were covered by fibreglass wheelarch extensions. The brakes, always heavily used with Aaltonen's left-foot braking technique, saw

DS11 racing disc pads and hard VG95 brake linings. The car was also fitted with a fly-off handbrake and a brake servo.

For the expected hot weather, the cooling system received attention, with a six-blade fan and a 60C thermostat. To ensure the radiator was secure, the cowl was located with ¼in bolts rather than small screws and the lower bracket was solidly mounted, with stepped bolts rather than on rubber mounts.

As was customary, the car was completely rewired with an individual wiring harness in situ. Additional lights consisted of the now-familiar four lights fitted to the lamp bar, fabricated from a cut-down lump of angle iron fixed just above the bumper. Gone, thankfully, was the jumble of additional lamps fitted to the earlier cars. With the advent of dipping iodine headlamp bulbs, the need for a separate dipped-beam lamp had been removed.

The main battery cable ran inside the car along with the other lines, and the battery in the boot had its terminals facing away from the side of the fuel tank – which in turn was protected with thin asbestos sheets stuck to the exposed side. The car ran twin-speed wipers and was fitted with an 11AC alternator – this required some surgery to the car by removing the diagonal stiffening plate and relocating it vertically clear of the alternator. The top rail of the front panel was also relieved to allow easy adjustment of the fan belt, and the oil cooler was relocated a little further over for clearance.

Each wiring loom also specially catered for the additional switches and electrical equipment in the car. Aaltonen had a boxed-out instrument panel with a large rev counter and numerous switches for all of the extra lamps, two-speed wipers, electric washer and headlight flasher, all clearly labelled with Dymo tape. Liddon had a flatter panel housing his Halda Twinmaster distance recorder plus a pair of Heuer watches. He too had switches for washers and wipers and a map light in his door pocket. Both panels also had a cigar lighter.

Seating was the usual fibreglass cloth-covered driver's seat and a navigator's reclining seat with a lap-and-diagonal and full-harness Irvin seat belt respectively. They had the use of an intercom, and additional padding was fitted to the door pockets, lock and door pillar. The car carried two spare wheels and used a modified MGB side jack.

The Acropolis, in very dry hot weather for May, was always a tough rally – where it was not unusual to have over three quarters of the field fail to finish. Despite the rough roads and the high average speed needed to stay clean, the winner in 1966 would likely be the fastest on just the three hillclimbs. The 17 stages, with simply a bogey time to beat, were achievable by most of the top crews – which included the three works Minis and three works Fords. It was here the winner would come from.

Aaltonen and Liddon set off on the three-day and two-night rally from Athens, facing 2000 miles of hard driving and, despite the stages being far less important than they should have been, the pace was fast and furious. Lined up alongside

JBL 172D on the start ramp of the 1966 Acropolis Rally. It would not be a rewarding event for Aaltonen and Liddon, where they were forced to retire when the engine's timing chain broke.

were 118 cars, many of them locals and, true to form, only 40 crews would make it back to Athens; sadly, Aaltonen would not be one of them.

Heading out in the evening towards Corinth and the first stage, Aaltonen started steadily, as was customary for him, giving best to both of his teammates, Mäkinen and Hopkirk. On the twisty second group of stages, as the route headed southwards, Aaltonen was starting to have clutch slip problems and was still trailing the other Abingdon cars, but they were all still beating the bogey times. The slipping clutch was soon adjusted and he was third on the third stage. The route now turned inland north and onto even worse roads, where Aaltonen really got going and was fastest on the fourth stage.

By the morning at the Patras ferry crossing 73 cars remained, such had been the pace. The cars now headed to the central mountains and more rough stages. Back through Thessaloniki a seventh group of stages saw Aaltonen fastest again.

Then came the all-important Portaria hillclimb where Aaltonen was fastest and, with Hopkirk and Mäkinen in mechanical problems, he was reaping the benefit of a careful drive. However, it was not to last, as on the next stage, despite the dry weather, Aaltonen drowned out his electrics – with the loss of seven-and-a-half minutes and his lead gone.

More rough stages followed, and onto the second hillclimb. Mäkinen stormed that one, desperate to claw back lost time repairing his damaged car. Then disaster struck Aaltonen, when straight after the hillclimb, his timing chain broke and he was out. Hopkirk, despite holing his sump was now in the lead, which he held to the finish. This however, would be a short-lived victory, as he was penalised for servicing within a time control area and relegated to third place. Mäkinen, with the time lost fixing his car, could only come up to tenth place, with a very sick car. Ford won with Bengt Söderström in the Lotus Cortina. It hadn't been a very successful event for the team.

For the car's next event, the German Rally in July, it was rebuilt by Brian Moylan and assigned to Tony Fall, who would be with Henry Liddon. The engine was now fitted with a high-compression Downton cylinder head at 12.6:1 because better fuel was available in Germany. Other minor changes to the engine included removing the thermostat, and the ends of the four-blade fan were shortened slightly to allow easier fan belt changes. It was also noted that the nearside front wing's inside edge near the radiator was pushed out with a porta-power jack to give more clearance around the front corner of the radiator.

The engine, of course, had a new timing chain fitted after its premature failure in Greece. The clutch now used a reinforced orange diaphragm with a special thrust washer after the previous clutch issues. The diff ratio was changed to an even shorter 4.26:1 and the gearbox remote was secured using a Mitchell mounting, designed not to fail, as within the rubber block was a movable joint. The base of the gearbox was now additionally protected with a Moke sump plate screwed to its underside, in addition to a heavy sump guard. The twin SUH4 carburettors went back to using BG needles rather AZ.

Blue displacers were returned to the Hydrolastic suspension and the subframes were strengthened as before. The lamp bar holding the four large auxiliary lamps now had a heavier bracket securing the bar in the middle. Other small changes included the heater box being lowered slightly on its mounting to give more clearance, the interior mirror was now an MGB item with a large sucker, the navigator's seat now had a strap fitted to keep the full harness belts in place, and the modified MGB jack was stowed behind the driver's seat and fixed to the side of the rear companion pocket.

The German Rally – or to give it its full title, the Nordrhein-Westfalen Deutschland Rally – held in mid July, should have been blessed with good weather but it rained almost continually for the entire 42 hours of the competition, making the rally rather miserable for competitors. Only 50 cars started, due in part to the bad reception the previous year's edition had received. It was also a rally that was badly marked, in that it would be decided on the class improvement system and, as a large proportion of the competitive mileage of some 80 per cent took place on two long races at the Nürburgring and Hockenheim, the winner would likely be one of the fast Porsche 911s or Alfa GTVs. Nevertheless, Abingdon sent two cars, with Paddy Hopkirk in the other Mini.

The rally, of around 1100 miles, started in Italy in the Dolomites, went into Austria and for the meat of the rally and into Germany, finishing in Düsseldorf. The 17 stages were mostly short and undemanding – it was the two long races that would be the decider. The evening start in Italy saw the heavens open and on the first test, Fall was third fastest, with Hopkirk three seconds adrift but both clean. On the second, because of the weather, none was clean, with fortunes reversed – Hopkirk just pipping Fall by a second. Hopkirk then had engine issues but they were remedied and he took 20 seconds off Fall on the third stage. The night remained wet.

Into Austria and a very tight road section of 20 miles saw most crews drop time, which led to the fourth very fast stage – which was a Porsche benefit – with the Minis having to give best. But on the next stage, the steep and twisty Glockner Pass, which suited the Mini, Hopkirk led Fall by ten seconds.

Into Germany and daylight and still it rained. Forty cars were now left and, on the sixth stage, the Rossfeld hillclimb, Hopkirk was second fastest. The two continued to swap times and were both well up the leaderboard. After the next stage the field headed to the Hockenheim race circuit. The organisers did not specify a route from the last stage to the circuit, but their timing was based on the shortest route on minor roads of around 150 miles; the logical easier route, which most took, of nearly 100 miles further, meant many were struggling to make it on time and the German police were having a field day issuing speeding tickets.

At Hockenheim, the crews had one practice lap and ten timed laps, meaning around a half-hour race. Both Abingdon cars started well but soon Hopkirk was in trouble and retired, and on the very last lap Fall retired with a seized engine due to oil starvation. Within ten minutes both works Minis were out. The rally was won, unsurprisingly, by Gunther Klass in a Porsche 911 – who was rewarded with a Fiat 850 for his troubles. Abingdon would go home empty-handed.

The next outing for the car was for a couple of recces, where Mäkinen and Easter used it for their recce for the Polish Rally in August 1966. The car was then used again in September 1966, this time by Hopkirk and Liddon for their respective recces for the Alpine Rally where Hopkirk would be with Ron Crellin and Liddon with Aaltonen. JBL 172D was also loaned out in May for the 1967 Police Rally, where Cliff Wrigley and Michael Wise used the car for this annual event in Belgium, largely for police officers. Despite hitting a large pothole, whilst leading, which damaged the gearbox meaning they had to do 120 miles in second gear, they finished the rally but lost

The German Rally in 1966 saw JBL 172D handed over to Tony Fall but still with Henry Liddon as navigator. Heavy rain hampered the rally, which was decided on two long circuit races. The car was retired at the end of one of the races with a seized engine.

JBL 172D was loaned out to Cliff Wrigley to compete on the 1967 Police Rally in Belgium, which he was leading until he damaged the gearbox.

The 1967 Alpine saw a much-changed JBL 172D for Aaltonen and Liddon, here on the starting ramp in a lightweight Group 6 car. Aaltonen was sidelined relatively early in the rally when idler gears failed in the transmission.

their lead.

Leaping forward to September 1967 for the Alpine Rally, it was one of the last great road races left in the rally calendar and a favourite amongst the BMC team. Run in early September, the Alps were free of snow and slippery conditions and free of tourists. JBL 172D was handed to Rauno Aaltonen and Henry Liddon, and it was very different from how the car appeared on the German Rally over a year ago; it is unclear quite what happened to the car in the intervening 12 months.

It was now prepared as a lightweight Group 6 car. BMC viewed, as did most other competition departments, that the 1967 Alpine would be extremely fast and, to stave off the extremely fast Porsche 911s and Alpine Renaults, the car had to shed much weight and get a bit more power.

The car was fitted with lightweight panels to the bonnet, boot lid and doors. All of the heavy glass, apart from the front laminated 'screen, was replaced with Perspex. The bumpers, front and rear, chrome around the doors, and side-window hinged frame were all removed, as was as much interior trim as possible, including the rear seat. The engine received a power boost by replacing the twin SU H4 carburettors with a single Weber 45DCOE carburettor, meaning a little adjustment around the speedo aperture to accommodate the ram pipes and a suitable manifold. The speedo was spaced out with a piece of carefully-carved wood to clear the Weber. The engine produced 125bhp at the flywheel and, with the customary 4.2:1 final drive and weight saving of 100lb, the car was very quick, although without the use of a limited slip differential. The car used Dunlop R7 race tyres throughout.

In addition to an oil cooler, the car ran an auxiliary front radiator, fitted on the right-hand side of the grille – which itself was cut down to accommodate the extra radiator; the grille moustache was also removed. It was, however, a Morris Cooper grille, not an Austin grille, but no front badges were fitted.

For the first time, the four additional lamps were connected via a rubber plug and socket attached to the wing on the left-hand side between the headlight and sidelight. This part was sourced from the Land Rover parts bin and would now be a regular fit on Abingdon Minis. The bonnet was secured by two Moke rubber toggles, replacing the leather strap usually seen, as fitted to the Marathon de la Route cars. On the boot lid, a small Healey sidelight was used as a reversing lamp and it too was held securely shut by a single Moke toggle. As the Alpine was not a rough event, the Moke sump guard and sump plate were fitted but with the addition of a duralumin sheet fixed to the sump guard to further protect the gearbox. A battery guard was also used. The car, now in Group 6 form, was very different in appearance compared to a Group 2 Mini.

The Alpine always had strict time schedules on the road and only those who remained on time would win a coveted Alpine Cup. The timed stages were used only as a means of classification. As speeds had increased, the organisers decided that to keep on time cars had to be within just two per cent of the fastest car in their class. The challenge was daunting and it is easy to understand why BMC decided to build a Group 6 car.

The 1967 Alpine was a five-day, 2300-mile event with just two overnight stops at Alpe d'Huez, and with 110 cols to climb and descend it was a great challenge.

After some very relaxed scrutineering in Marseille, where being a Group 6 car meant almost anything goes, the event got under way. The 79 cars set off on Monday evening on 4

The walking wounded. The four works cars, including JBL 172D, being towed on A-frames to be transported home by rail from their attempt on the 1967 Alpine Rally. GRX 310D and GRX 311D both retired, and JMO 969D was a recce car. All broke.

September, for the first leg to Alpe d'Huez – a 24-hour, 900-mile blast over the Alps with 18 tightly timed road selectives, interspersed with four épreuves (timed-to-the-second hillclimb stages). This first leg included the very tight and twisty selectives between Quatre Chemins, Sigale, Entrevaux and Rouaine, the Col D'Allos, the Col de Cayolle and the dangerous Col de Lombarde.

Elford's Porsche was soon leading but the Minis were close by. Aaltonen was fifth fastest on the first épreuve at Logisneuf and was the leading Mini. But soon the pace was becoming too high for Aaltonen's transmission, when the idler gears broke near Sigale and he was out. Fall was also to soon depart, when he slid off and damaged the front suspension irreparably. Within the 24 hours, the four works Minis were down to just two. Mäkinen retired on the last leg, whilst in the lead, also with idler gear problems, which left Hopkirk to take up Abingdon's challenge – and he did, by winning overall, and one of only 20 cars to wind their way to Monte Carlo.

The final Abingdon event for this car was the Tour de Corsica, held on the island of Corsica at the beginning of November. This was renowned as being a very fast, tight, twisty rally using narrow mountain roads that were slippery and potentially dangerous – it was often called the rally of 10,000 corners, which was actually an underestimate…

Abingdon knew it had to build a very powerful car to stay in touch with the threat from the Porsche 911, Alpine Renault and now Lancia with its Fulvia. It was by then the twilight years of the Mini's dominance, as the car was now nearing the end of its development. Undeterred, BMC built a very powerful and lightweight Group 6 Cooper S for Rauno Aaltonen and Henry Liddon for this event.

Built by Johnny Organ, the 1293cc engine was fitted with a full-race camshaft and a high-compression Downton cylinder head giving 12.6:1 compression ratio. For the tight, twisty roads, the straight-cut close-ratio gearbox was fitted with a 4.2:1 final drive with large driveshafts. Being a Group 6 car, where the inlet manifold was free, a large 45DCOE Weber was fitted with 40mm chokes bearing a 190mm main jet and 170mm air correction jet. Slow running was a 45 F9 with a F2 emulsion tube, 0.45 pump jet and 3.5 auxiliary venturi, and finally 5mm float level. These were established by Cliff Humphries on Abingdon's rolling road, where the car produced 104bhp at its wheels.

To keep the engine cool – always an issue with a highly-tuned Cooper S engine – the car ran a small front-mounted radiator on the right-hand side behind the fog lamps, meaning the front grille had to be cut down. Additionally, an 1100 radiator was fitted, and as it was physically a little taller and wider, a small bulge had to be let into the bonnet to accommodate it, with the body pressed out inside. An 11-blade fan was being tried for the first time.

The body was stripped of bumpers and chrome trim around the doors, and all of the glass, bar the front laminated windscreen, was replaced with Perspex. The bonnet, boot and doors were made of aluminium, and internally, the rear seat was removed, as was the headlining; both were covered in lightweight carpet.

All lines were run inside the car and the twin fuel pump fitted under the rear seat. The two hammers to undo the wheel spinners were also under the rear seat – not on the rear

The start of the 1967 Tour de Corsica, with JBL 172D behind GRX 5D. Both were special lightweight Group 6 cars.

JBL 172D was fitted with a front-mounted radiator. The light steady bars clearly seen, held fast with wing nuts.

Liddon checks his paperwork on the roof of JBL 172D. The bulge in the bonnet is for a larger radiator and the bracket is for the mounting of the aluminium bonnet.

Knock-off Minilites to speed up wheel changes. This made little difference, as Aaltonen retired with a flat battery and an overheated engine due to fan belt failure.

parcel shelf – and their helmets stored on the rear seat. But the modified MGB jack was stored in the normal place behind the driver, fixed to the side companion pocket.

To comply with Group 6 regulations, the car had to have a twin braking system. This was made possible by a makeshift method of using a Bowden cable to the handbrake (which operates the rear brakes) from the brake pedal. This was sufficient to satisfy the scrutineers and, once passed, was quickly 'unadjusted' so as to not affect the rear brakes. Hydrolastic suspension was fitted but with the addition of Koni adjustable dampers (at their softest settings) just to the front. This had proved beneficial to stiffen up the suspension when it was used for the first time on the Southern Cross Rally the previous month by Hopkirk. Another first for the car was the fitting of Minilite wheels with knock-off spinners, which, in theory, made the numerous tyre changes as quick as possible.

The rally started at Ajaccio on the west coast of Corsica on Saturday evening and would end just 22 hours later back again at Ajaccio. Ahead of the 98 entries were 800 miles of sinuous roads that were intermixed with 80 miles of four timed-to-the-second stages. The overall average of near 40mph, having to be maintained for the entire duration, meant many would retire simply because they ran over their one-hour allowable lateness. And it was also raining...

The first stage was very near the start, a 15-mile tight section that Elford's Porsche covered in just over 18 minutes. Aaltonen was not in the top six and was already in trouble with the engine overheating. This was only to get worse. The

WORKS MINIS IN DETAIL

fan belt was tightened, as this was found to be loose, meaning the water pump was not being properly driven; in addition, the alternator was also not charging because of the loose belt and hence the lights were fading. Once tightened, he set off again but the problems persisted and yet again the fan belt was tightened. The problem was not solved, and shortly Aaltonen was out with a completely flat battery and a very hot engine. This very fast event was won by Sandro Munari in a Lancia Fulvia. Only 14 cars made it to the finish.

It subsequently transpired that the trusty Ferodo fan belts, used without problems for so many years, had been sourced from a faulty batch. This was a sad and frustrating end for the team and for the car, which in four headline events had failed to finish any. It was also just a little embarrassing for Browning to explain away to BMC management – a retirement due to a failed fan belt!

JBL 172D was one of several cars sold to Mike Wood at the garage, Tillotson's, where he worked.

Outside Tillotson's Garage, two works cars for sale, one of which was JBL 172D.

Competition Record

Date	Event	Crew	Number	Overall result	Class result
May 1966	Acropolis Rally	Rauno Aaltonen/Henry Liddon	77	DNF	
July 1966	German Rally	Tony Fall/Henry Liddon	49	DNF	
May 1967	Police Rally	Cliff Wrigley/Michael Wise	16		
Sept 1967	Alpine Rally	Rauno Aaltonen/Henry Liddon	106	DNF	
Nov 1967	Tour de Corsica	Rauno Aaltonen/Henry Liddon	106	DNF	

Registration Number	First registered	Chassis number	Engine	Engine number	Model
JBL 493D	June 1966	KA2S4 851272	1275cc	9F-SA-Y 41301	Morris Cooper S

Timo Mäkinen, crash helmet in hand, leaves his hotel for the start of the 1966 Czech Rally, whilst Paul Easter sits patiently in JBL 493D's passenger seat.

JBL 493D was from a batch of three JBLs registered in early summer of 1966: two were Austins and the third a Morris, which was this car. Built by Mick Legg and Peter Bartram for Timo Mäkinen and Paul Easter (Mäkinen always drove a Morris for personal contractual reasons), JBL 493D was a Group 2 car for the 1966 Czech Rally, also known as the Rallye Vltava (and, locally, the Moldau Rally).

As was customary, the fresh engine was bored 0.020in to give 1293cc. There was a lightened steel flywheel and an AEA648 race camshaft, also with lightened timing gears. The cylinder head had a relatively low 11.7 compression to help with the lower-octane fuel available in Czechoslovakia. After dyno testing, the twin SU H4 carburettors were fitted with AZ needles rather than the normal BG. Mäkinen, as always, requested a very short 4.26:1 diff ratio for the straight-cut close-ratio transmission, which was protected by a very heavy-duty spring-steel Scandinavian pattern sump guard, which had been developed for the rough Acropolis rally. Cooling was without a thermostat, with the bypass hose blanked off and using a four-bladed fan on the 16-fin Cooper S radiator.

The car was built with Hydrolastic suspension, with single-blue and double-blue displacers front and back, much to Mäkinen's displeasure, as he preferred dry suspension. The rear suspension was strengthened using modified brackets for the radius arms and plating to the top of the rear subframe. It also ran Aeon bump stops and was set to give approximately 13in from the wheel centre to the edge of the wheelarch. It's also noted that the front tie bars and track arms were secured by castellated nuts and split pins to ensure they stayed in place. Further, protection plates were provided at the front of the tie bars onto the front subframe and the flexible brake pipe, onto the brake calliper, also had a fabricated protection plate.

The exhaust also had a protection plate welded to its lower edge and the joints had locating bars welded to them to ensure they were not torn apart on rough ground. The car ran 4½J steel wheels, which meant that the body was fitted with black fibreglass wheelarch extensions needed to cover the wider wheels. Brakes had racing Ferodo DS11 pads and VG95 brake linings, with a 325psi rear limiting valve to allow more rear braking.

All of the standard electrics were removed and replaced by an individually made wiring harness, constructed over many hours, by the resident Lucas Racing mechanics, either John Smith or Stan Chalmers. These were works of art and although similar on many cars, all were just that little bit different – largely brought about by a driver's preference of controls and switch positions, plus the individual hallmark of anything entirely handmade. All of the electrical cables were cloth-covered, with the spade terminals made of copper and all joints soldered. The entire loom was then tightly hand-bound, in situ, with looming tape. The end result was always a joy to see.

The car was fitted with a Lucas 11AC alternator with a remote 4TR regulator, which generated sufficient power for the four auxiliary lamps, secured on the lamp bar low down by the bumper. The front slam panel was modified to accommodate the alternator and as a result the Cooper S diagonal stiffener plate was relocated into a vertical position adjacent. Special black crackle-finished alloy panels, crafted by Abingdon, were fitted in front of the driver and navigator with all of the necessary switches, controls, navigation and timing equipment. An additional switch panel was provided in the navigator's door pocket and the navigator also had a foot-operated horn button on the front bulkhead.

All lines were run inside the car, with the twin SU fuel pump now placed under the rear seat; there was now a larger T-piece joining the twin tanks, as flow was being restricted

Mäkinen so nearly won the Czech Rally but a broken rocker on the very last vital test dropped him to third place.

with the standard-diameter pipe. The battery was reversed, with the terminals facing away from the sides of the fuel tanks, which were protected by thin asbestos sheet glued to their sides. The fuel tank strapping now reverted to the standard position – on the outside – on the fuel cap side, not inboard as on earlier cars.

Mäkinen had a fibreglass bucket seat, whilst Easter had a special Abingdon-fabricated more comfortable reclining seat, with lap-and-diagonal and full-harness Irvin belts respectively. The crew also had the use of an intercom, and a modified MGB jack was fitted inside the car behind the driver on the side of the rear door pocket. Additional padding was supplied to the door pockets, B-post and door locks, and Mäkinen had a thick-grip Moto-Lita steering wheel.

The Czech Rally was contested by 82 cars on a 1570-mile two-day thrash centred around Prague. The route consisted of 14 special stages, making up 144 miles of tough competition – and this in addition to two regularity races at the very start and finish that would ultimately, as it transpired, decide the outcome of the rally. Connecting the stages were loose-surface roads both twisty and demanding, and because of the Czech authorities abandoning speed limits at night, very tightly timed: 26 time controls had to be visited, and with long, tightly timed sections during both nights, these alone would see off 20 cars into retirement on both nights.

The first regularity race, where six laps of the Strahov Stadium's perimeter road were tackled, saw Bengt Söderström in a works Cortina just ahead of Aaltonen and Mäkinen in third. At the first service, just after the noon start, both of Mäkinen's fuel tanks had moved inside the boot, with the result that the fuel caps were jammed in the body. This was probably a throwback from the tank strapping being relocated into the standard position and not fully tightened. The fault was quickly remedied and Mäkinen was on his way, then continued to post very fast times on the stages as night fell and the fast road sections began to take their toll on others. Mäkinen, however,

Mäkinen took Pekka Keskitalo on the 1966 1000 Lakes Rally with him, looking for a second win on his home event.

clawing back his lead and was credited with ten out of the 14 fastest times.

By the time they reached Prague for the final time, Mäkinen was in the lead as Aaltonen had also dropped time by a short off-road excursion and running out of fuel. Onto the last test, the rerun of the regularity race where cars had to equal or better their time set two days prior, Mäkinen hit trouble on the very last lap when a rocker broke and he had to limp back on three cylinders. This disaster resulted in him dropping sufficient time to allow Aaltonen back into the lead, and Mäkinen had to content himself with third place, just behind the works Cortina of Söderström. Mäkinen was of the mind to protest the results of the race, as the leading times were considered suspect, but in the absence of Stuart Turner, no protest was lodged. BMC had won the rally and the team prize (with Sobieslaw Zasada coming home fourth in EBL 56C), so Abingdon honours were upheld and nothing was to be gained by the protest, other than personal pride.

For the car's next event, the 1000 Lakes Rally in Finland in August, Mäkinen retained the car and, as the 1000 Lakes didn't allow practice in 1966, he relied heavily on local knowledge. Mäkinen took local navigator Pekka Kestikola, whilst Easter was dispatched to recce the forthcoming Alpine Rally with Henry Liddon.

The Group 2 car was again fitted with a 1293cc engine and was essentially unchanged from the Czech Rally. The only addition was the fitting of mud flaps all round, as required by Finnish traffic laws. It was also required to have a wing mirror on the driver's side for much the same reason. The cars also, rather uniquely for the time, were bedecked with sponsors' decals supplied by the organisers.

However, the major change on the car was instigated by Mäkinen when the Mini arrived in Finland. Being a Hydrolastic car, Mäkinen was determined that it should be a dry car for the many jumps found on the rally. JBL 493D was therefore swiftly taken off to the local Morris importer, for which Mäkinen worked when not rallying, where the Hydrolastic suspension was removed and replaced with dry cone units – much to Stuart Turner's displeasure. The dry suspension, as it transpired, raised the car too much for Mäkinen's liking, so the Abingdon mechanics then set about removing the cones and shortening them – twice – until he was entirely satisfied.

Inside the car Mäkinen also abandoned the Abingdon fibreglass bucket seat in preference for a more comfortable and more compliant reclining seat. Mäkinen had been complaining that the tight-fitting bucket seat had been giving him back troubles and with the forthcoming pounding on the Finnish jumps, it was likely to only make matter worse – so the bucket went.

At Jyväskylä were 115 cars lined up for this two-day rally, which contained 27 relatively short stages amounting to just

was clean throughout, with no loss of time.

The next day saw Mäkinen relinquish his lead to Aaltonen when his car's fuel pump failed on the sixth stage. A swift-acting Easter, striking the pump with a large spanner, temporarily cured the problem but the resulting time loss saw Mäkinen down in third place. Mäkinen then set about

Mäkinen put up impressive times on all of the stages in JBL 493D keeping clear of Aaltonen, his teammate and rival.

Mäkinen and Keskitalo jumping high on one of the many jumps found in the Scandinavian forests. Mäkinen would win the rally by a clear two minutes.

JBL 493D was kept in Finland and loaned out to Mäkinen (who eventually bought the car) to compete in events in Finland. The car received numerous modifications by his mechanics in Finland; note the odd central lamp and the extra supports to the lamp bar.

100 miles of competitive motoring – all except one on loose surfaces. The transit roads between the stages were timed at a very low average speed, primarily due to police restrictions, meaning the rally became somewhat processional between the stages. The short stages did, however, mean those with problems were generally not penalised so heavily had the stages been longer.

Being a secret and therefore non-practice rally, local knowledge was much in demand, especially as the route information issued on the day of the rally consisted only of a sheet of tracing paper showing the route without controls or stages being marked. This meant, unless you knew otherwise, the locations of stages and controls were a matter of stumbling upon them. Mäkinen and Keskitalo, of course, knew a good number of the stages, so were better off than some.

The rally started at midday in Jyväskylä and Mäkinen was showing a fast and furious pace straight away, battling with Bengt Söderström's works Lotus Cortina. This was a grudge match between these old sparing partners. By midnight Mäkinen was lying second to his Ford rival but by the morning Mäkinen was in the lead, as Söderström slowed during the night.

After the breakfast halt, Mäkinen pulled a master stroke as the next stage was a five-lap tarmac race around a park perimeter track: he had deposited a set of his own race tyres at the start, whilst everyone else was on forest tyres – including Aaltonen, much to his annoyance. Despite Mäkinen and Aaltonen being teammates there was a good deal of healthy rivalry between these two star drivers. This time Aaltonen lost out.

Mäkinen was now building up an unassailable lead, which became much easier when Söderström retired the Ford with a broken gearbox. The second night saw more fastest times by Mäkinen and despite Aaltonen by now also posting top times, he couldn't catch Mäkinen; at the finish he had won by two minutes and beaten his teammate by three minutes. This did, however, mean they won the team prize, with Jorma Lusenius in the other works Mini coming home third in class.

JBL 493D was initially loaned out to Timo, as the car stayed in Finland after the 1000 Lakes. The car was eventually sold to Timo Mäkinen and he continued to use it on numerous events in Finland with Pekka Keskitalo.

Competition Record

Date	Event	Crew	Number	Overall result	Class result
July 1966	Czech Rally	Timo Mäkinen/Paul Easter	77	3rd	2nd
Aug 1966	1000 Lakes Rally	Timo Mäkinen/Pekka Keskitalo	45	1st	1st

WORKS MINIS IN DETAIL

Registration Number	First registered	Chassis number	Engine	Engine number	Model
JBL 494D	May 1966	CA2S7 851190	1275cc	9F-SA-Y 41279	Austin Cooper S

Rauno Aaltonen and Henry Liddon in JBL 494D blast off the line on one of the speed tests on the 1966 Czech Rally.

The second JBL car to be prepared in early summer 1966 was JBL 494D, being an Austin Cooper S. Built by Roy Brown and Robin Vokins, it was prepared as a Group 2 car for the Czech Rally in June of that year. The car was assigned to Rauno Aaltonen and Henry Liddon; with Aaltonen's long-time co-driver Tony Ambrose deciding to retire and Henry Liddon and Paddy Hopkirk deciding to split, this relatively new partnership of Aaltonen and Liddon, of just two rallies, was working well, and the Czech would be their third.

The car was built to identical specification to its sister car, JBL 493D, in almost every way. Nevertheless, Aaltonen was always looking for an edge over his rival teammate Timo Mäkinen and as such was closely involved in the build to ensure that he got just what he wanted.

Because of the anticipated poor fuel being available in Czechoslovakia, the compression of the 1293cc engine was reduced to 11.7:1 with the Downton cylinder head having 19.2cc combustion chambers. The car was fitted with a 4.26 final drive and carried a heavy-duty sump guard for the poor-quality roads ahead. The car ran the latest enlarged driveshafts with Hardy Spicer couplings.

Unlike Mäkinen, Aaltonen was happy to run with Hydrolastic suspension. The car was fitted with double-blue and single-blue displacers with additional bump stops and the rear subframe was strengthened, as were the locating brackets for the rear radius arms. The front tie bars were protected with a fabricated bracket fitted to each front corner of the subframe; this also added much strength. The exhaust was skidded and the joints secured with a joining bar, and it was secured to the car with modified mountings on the rear subframe, with the bolt passing through the rubber – because of that it was never fully tightened but held securely with an interference stiff nut. Additionally the brackets on the exhaust were welded to the system – this exhaust was never going to fall off!

All the lines were run inside the car, with the fuel pump now being fitted under the rear seat, away from the old location in the harsh environment on the rear subframe. The battery was reversed in the boot, with the terminals safely away from the side of the metal fuel tank. The 11 AC alternator powered the four auxiliary lamps mounted on the badge bar by the front bumper. These lamps, all fitted with iodine bulbs, were individually switched, with the two middle driving lamps able to operate with or without the headlights' main beam via a three-way switch. The headlights were fitted with European lenses, giving a vertical dip for the 60/40W dipping bulbs. Aaltonen had a small Healey 3000 side lamp fitted low down on the boot as a reversing lamp, switched via the gearbox. The car was fitted with a two-speed wiper motor with deep-throated wheel boxes, which were much stronger than standard Mini parts.

Externally the car had fibreglass wheelarch extensions covering the wide 4½J steel wheels. These were from Dunlop stock and were unfinished, appearing in brown primer paint, with Dunlop R7 tyres fitted for the early tarmac race.

Internally the car was fitted with Aaltonen's much preferred fibreglass and cloth-covered bucket seat. Liddon was using one of Abingdon's fabricated and comfortable reclining seats. Both had the use of an intercom, with the box fitted to the roof of the car. All the glass, carpet and other trim was retained (being a Group 2 car) and Aaltonen also had an asbestos blanket placed under the carpet at the front to keep as much heat out of the car as possible. All of the usual extra padding to the door pockets, lock and B-post were provided – all made in the MG trim shop. To ensure the car stayed dry, all of the bung holes in the floor were stuck down and sealed. These used to be welded over but this was an area of concern within the new regulations, so this practice was abandoned. The car, as usual, was presented and delivered in immaculate condition to Prague.

Eighty-two, mostly local, crews descended on Prague for the start of the Czech Rally, which as it was a round of the European Championship saw BMC, Ford and Saab in attendance ready to tackle the 1570-mile event. In front of them lay 14 stages of 144 miles, two regularity races and 26 time controls. The road timing was tight, made especially so as no speed limits were in force at night. The timed road sections were nothing short of a hard road race, much of it at night, on tight twisty and often unsurfaced roads. These alone contributed to over half of the entry falling by the wayside.

Scrutineering was uneventful, but with the relatively new FIA rules in place everyone was still feeling anxious. The event started with the first of the two regularity races around the perimeter roads of the local stadium, with the race being for eight cars setting off at ten-second intervals for six laps. The Ford of Bengt Söderström was fastest, with Aaltonen close by. On into the afternoon, the stages began with Aaltonen lying third behind Söderström and Mäkinen after the first three stages. Into the night and Söderström slowed, and as the pace picked up on the timed road sections many lost time, but Aaltonen was still clean on the road as the second day began.

Aaltonen was in the lead after the sixth stage, when Mäkinen was delayed by a fuel pump problem. Despite Mäkinen posting many fastest times, he was still 15 seconds behind Aaltonen. With the pressure on, Aaltonen briefly left the road for one-and-a-half minutes but with no loss of road time.

All was going well until the 13th stage, when Aaltonen ran out of fuel. This was initially blamed on Liddon for not monitoring their fuel closely enough but it soon became apparent that the fuel gauge had failed. Aaltonen was now behind Mäkinen with only the final regularity race to complete, where drivers had to beat or equal their time set on the first race. Luck swung back to Aaltonen as Mäkinen, on the very last lap, had an engine problem and had to coast around, losing nearly a minute to Aaltonen and hence his lead. Aaltonen was declared the winner ahead of Mäkinen, who was relegated to third place, with the Ford of Söderström in second place. But with Sobiesław Zasada coming home fourth in EBL 56C, BMC also collected the team prize.

At the completion of an event, drivers were often asked to complete a competition report to allow Abingdon to see what perhaps needed to be changed or improved by the crew. Reports were generally completed by the co-driver on the driver's behalf, and do make interesting reading. Liddon's report, using Aaltonen's findings for the car on the Czech, tell us that the power of the engine was satisfactory but that it dropped towards the end, and ran well on the low 86-octane fuel. Petrol consumption for the 2700 miles was normal but embarrassingly they ran out of fuel (as noted above) with the faulty fuel gauge. The oil used was Castrol Liquid Tungsten but the consumption wasn't noted and the oil pressure remained normal. Their clutch needed adjusting once and the gearchange was fine, as were the gears – although Aaltonen commented that Zasada's gearbox (in EBL 56C) was very noisy. Aaltonen complained that he still

Aaltonen and Liddon would win the Czech Rally, which was a mixture of regularity speed tests and special stages - they beat Mäkinen on the last test to win the event.

found excessive heat by his clutch foot.

The roadholding was described as excellent, Aaltonen commenting that it was the nicest car he'd ever been issued with. Little tyre wear was found, and they used Dunlop R7s and SP44s. Aaltonen said he didn't have enough rear braking and wanted a different limiting valve fitted for his next event – which would be their recce for the Polish Rally. All the electrics were reported as fine with no problems but the delay in the electric washers working was an annoyance and Aaltonen questioned the accuracy of the rev counter – and of course that fuel gauge. Liddon also requested a shield for the Halda to prevent its light shining up onto the screen and distracting Aaltonen at night.

No water leaks were noted on the body but the draughts, being summer, were said to be welcome. The new seat covering was said to be excellent but the seat belts should have a strap fixed to the back of the seat to prevent the shoulder straps falling down, and further the strap adjusters fitted away from the collarbone. Aaltonen did complain that although the car was very good, he felt preparation suffered due to a shortage of time. He also wanted a better jack, rather than the modified MGB jack, preferring the VW monkey-on-a-stick quick-action jack. Aaltonen was, however, delighted with the car and the event, having won.

After the rally, the car was used by Paddy Hopkirk and Chris Nash to do their recce for the German Rally, an event on which they would use GRX 311D. It is likely that as the Czech Rally and the German Rally were less than two weeks apart, JBL 494D stayed in Europe, with Hopkirk and Nash

Jorma Lusenius and Klaus Lehto took JBL 494D to the 1966 1000 Lakes Rally in Finland, the car carrying local registration A-1445.

joining the car to do their practice.

For the car's next event, the 1000 Lakes Rally in Finland in August, Aaltonen's winning car (and Hopkirk's recce car) was handed to Jorma Lusenius, who was being offered his second drive for Abingdon after his fine showing on the RAC Rally the previous November. Lusenius also gave Mäkinen a run for his money on the 1000 Lakes Rally the previous year, so was drafted in as the third member of the Abingdon team. He would also take local navigator Klaus Lehto with him. With the rally being a secret event and therefore practice not being possible, local knowledge was a valuable asset.

The Czech car was rebuilt and prepared for the 1000 Lakes by Johnny Organ, and it had numerous changes, notably the cylinder head was of a higher compression at 12.6:1 but the diff ratio selected was slightly longer, at 4.2:1. To increase engine breathing, the oil filler cap had its internal hole increased in size to 5/16in, and numerous 1/8in holes were drilled into the air vents in the cap's side.

The engine remote shift had a Mitchell mounting rubber with a strengthened remote mounting bracket and further strengthening and strapping inside the car – all to ensure the mounting or rubber didn't fracture with the pounding the car would receive in Finland over the many jumps. The Hydrolastic suspension remained unchanged (unlike Mäkinen's car, which reverted to dry suspension). Along with the heavy-duty Scandinavian sump guard, almost mandatory for Finland, the car was also fitted with a protection shield below the battery box, which spanned the rear subframe.

Other changes of note were that the fibreglass bucket seat for the driver was porta-powered apart, to allow a little more room for a larger posterior than Aaltonen's. The car was also secretly strengthened by the fitting of a double-skinned box section across the car where the seats mounted. This added much strength and rigidity to the car but was sufficiently disguised that no scrutineer ever found it. One final change was the car had its Abingdon number plate taped over and a local registration attached: A-1445.

Lusenius was the third member of the BMC team for the 1000 Lakes, along with Aaltonen and Mäkinen. Records show that only Scandinavian drivers ever had much success on this their home international, so these three lined up with a great number of local drivers, making up the 113 starters from Jyväskylä on this two-day event. The format was of three loops around Jyväskylä with around 100 miles of stages, all on loose surfaces and relatively short in distance; there were 27 in all but joined together on rather slow interconnecting roads where the police were enforcing a low average speed.

With a midday start the early stages were in daylight, where Lusenius stayed outside the top ten, and it wasn't until nightfall that he got into his stride with a fastest time on the sixth stage, and from then on started to feature in the results. However, with Mäkinen and Aaltonen posting fastest times between them on a regular basis on the second day and night, Lusenius was left in their wake and finished in sixth place overall, over seven minutes adrift of the winner Mäkinen – but still third in class and allowing BMC to take the team prize. Sadly, he was unable to recreate his previous year's form of chasing Mäkinen so hard.

The Munich-Vienna-Budapest Rally was the next event for the car, in October 1966, when JBL 494D was handed to Tony Fall, who on this occasion had Henry Liddon as co-driver. The car was reprepared by Johnny Organ as a Group 2 car, much as it had been for the 1000 Lakes. It is noted that the car was now fitted with special oil control piston rings, as high oil consumption had started to become an issue with the oval pistons. The car was also fitted with the latest strengthened

Lusenius and Lehto would finish in sixth place behind the two Abingdon starters of Mäkinen and Aaltonen.

engine block, and the cylinder head now used MGB head studs tightened down to 50lb.ft to ensure the head gasket stayed intact. Cylinder compression remained at 12.6:1 with the 16.4cc Downton cylinder head.

The starter motor received attention by spraying liberally with Molyslip to ensure the pinion remained free; in addition, a hole was drilled in the flywheel housing to allow more lubricant to be applied in situ. This modification was done primarily because, after hard use, clutch dust was contaminating the pinion, which sometimes prevented the starter working properly. It was also noted that all of the electrical switches were routinely changed to ensure reliability – after every event – and there was Isopon on alternator bolts to ensure they stayed in place.

As the Munich-Vienna-Budapest Rally was a round of the European championship for Group 1 and Group 2 cars, a healthy entry of 104 arrived at Munich for the start, but only 58 would make it to Budapest. BMC, Saab and Lancia sent works cars. BMC with Mäkinen, Fall and privateer Bob Freeborough made up the team in his 970S. The event, often more easily known as the Three Cities Rally, had a reputation for a complicated marking system, which this year was simplified by having all seven stages decided on scratch times. Many rallies were by now abandoning the unpopular class improvement system, which was both complicated and subject to careful manipulation by the smarter teams (BMC being one).

The early morning start saw Fall safely through the first all-tarmac stage on wide but damp tarmac – Mäkinen being the fastest. The route then headed towards the Czech border for the second test in the Hinterschmiding forest – which Fall never made, as his engine seized just before the start and he was forced into retirement. BMC was rewarded, however, with Mäkinen's outright win, helping his points haul for the European Championship, but this was no consolation to Tony Fall. It should be noted that by this time, BMC as a company was no more, as at the end of September BMC had amalgamated with Jaguar Cars and Pressed Steel to form British Motor Holdings Limited, with George Harriman being in overall control. The company would from then be known at BMH.

The RAC Rally in November 1966, Abingdon's home event, was next on the list for JBL 493D. Once again, the hard-pressed car was preprepared for this most demanding event, and a new car was not built. The car was assigned to BMC Sweden driver Harry Källström, who would take his usual co-driver, Ragnvald Haakansson with him, rather than a British navigator, which Stuart Turner was favoured to do. Källström was really in the second division of the works entries, along with Marjetta Aaltonen (Rauno's sister) and Simo Lampinen. Källström was on his fifth drive for Abingdon and hadn't fared well so far, retiring on all – but history will show he redeemed himself in fine style, coming home in second place.

The 1966 RAC Rally saw JBL 494D handed to Harry Källström and Ragnvald Haakansson. This would be the fifth drive the Swede had for Abingdon over a two-year period, and he hadn't finished any...

The car was prepared by Robin Vokins, with a fresh engine after its premature failure the previous month, and would follow the same specification of the other eight works Minis entered. All of the cars (bar Mäkinen's) ran the standard Cooper S AEG510 camshaft, instead of Abingdon's normal AEA648 race camshaft. This was primarily because Abingdon was seeking to get as much low-down torque as possible, in an attempt to combat the slippery muddy conditions that were expected in the forests up and down the country in November. It did, however, rob the car of much horsepower, as it achieved only 75bhp on the Abingdon rolling road – around 15bhp down. The 1293cc engine had slightly lower compression at 11.4:1 with the Downton cylinder head, but rapid acceleration was guaranteed by the fitting of a 4.2:1 differential.

One new feature inside the car was a roll cage – the first time fitted to a works Mini. The cages were produced by John Aley and were made from lightweight aircraft-quality aluminium in the form of a simple loop behind the B-post and single backstay onto the rear parcel shelf – nothing like the structural roll cages fitted to competition cars today.

Another addition for the RAC was a pair of forward-facing mud flaps fitted to the front corner of the bumper, designed to prevent muddy water from splashing up onto the headlights and windscreen – a problem due to the close proximity of the front wheels to the nose of the car. However, the flaps were less than successful as they tended to restrict airflow to the already-overworked front brakes. Protecting the engine and gearbox was a new Scandinavian sump guard made from spring steel. With the front of the guard extending up to almost the bumper, the quick-lift jacking brackets had to be moved to the leading edge of the sump guard.

Early in the RAC Källström was putting up steady times just outside the top ten.

Harry Källström waits at the control whilst Ragnvald Haakansson gets his time card stamped.

Other changes to the car were the headlamp washers – rather crude affairs of simply a Bundy metal brake pipe with a capped end, which sprayed water onto the headlamps. The car was also now fitted with a heated front windscreen and, of course, the heavy-duty Scandinavian sump guard. To keep out the worst of the weather, the front grille was fitted with a grille muff, manufactured by the MG trim shop and attached around the grille moustache with Lift-the-Dot fixings. To ensure reliability, all the light switches were replaced; this would now be standard practice every time a car was reprepared. The final change was to replace the kph speedo used in Europe for one reading in mph for the UK.

The RAC Rally in 1966 was sponsored by the *Sun* newspaper and because of that the public interest in the rally was high, with a reported million spectators seeing the rally. Huge crowds greeted the cars at the Excelsior Hotel at London Airport to see the 144 crews depart on their five-day competition to Scotland and back. Ahead of the crews was a route of some 2400 miles, incorporating 67 stages of 400 stage miles, mostly on forest roads. The challenging route went from West London to the West Country and into Wales for the first night out of bed, through the Midlands and up into Northern England for the second night without sleep to arrive in Aviemore in Scotland for one night in bed. From Aviemore the field journeyed down the east side of the country to Northumberland and Yorkshire, over the next two days, then back to London Airport. Only 63 exhausted crews would make it back five days later. Of the eight Abingdon

Once the rally turned south from Scotland Källström's constant fast times saw him up into fifth place.

Minis entered, only four would finish.

Once under way, Källström started steadily as they headed westwards, setting times outside the top ten but still in contention. As the field entered Wales for the first night, Källström began setting quick times and was soon within the top ten, setting a fastest time in Taliesyn just before breakfast. Top ten times continued on many of the stages as they headed north and, after a trouble-free run, they were lying in fifth place at the much needed overnight halt in Aviemore. By now the field had lost 52 cars after they had tackled the 38 stages, and only 92 cars restarted the next day.

On the return south, Källström kept the pressure up, continuing to set times in the top ten on many stages. The rates of attrition continued as the tired crews battled over the remaining 25 stages, seeing another 29 cars retire. With the rough Scottish stages behind them the fast Yorkshire stages and the Lake District awaited. With consistently fast times and others dropping by the wayside, Källström found himself in second place at Barnby Moor, with just Sherwood Forest and Silverstone to the finish. With no let up, Källström consolidated his position and finished back at London Airport in a fine second place, a minute ahead of Tom Trana's Volvo – and the best works Mini, albeit some 13 minutes behind the leading Lotus Cortina of Bengt Söderström.

After the rally, JBL 494D was road tested by *Autosport* magazine's resident tester, John Bolster who reported that the car was a joy to drive and with the standard Cooper S camshaft fitted, it could be used comfortably in London traffic. Against the stopwatch, on wet roads, the car showed 0-to-60mph in 9 seconds and with the very short 4.26 diff, 100mph was easily achieved but at 7200rpm. Despite the hard life it had experienced on the RAC, the brakes, clutch and handling were reported to be superb. A testament indeed of Abingdon's fine build quality.

Having finished its works career, the car was finally sold to Adrian Boyd, the well-known Irish rally driver, who went on to use it to great effect in Ireland.

By the end of the 2400-mile RAC rally Källström and Haakansson had got themselves up into second place on the final stages, breaking his long non-finishing record in fine style.

Competition Record

Date	Event	Crew	Number	Overall result	Class result
July 1966	Czech Rally	Rauno Aaltonen/Henry Liddon	75	1st	1st
Aug 1966	1000 Lakes Rally	Jorma Lusenius/Klaus Lehto	27	6th	3rd
Oct 1966	Munich-Vienna-Budapest	Tony Fall/Henry Liddon		DNF	
Nov 1966	RAC Rally	Harry Källström/Ragnvald Haakansson	66	2nd	1st

Registration Number	First registered	Chassis number	Engine	Engine number	Model
JBL 495D	May 1966	CA2S7 851189	1275cc	9F-SA-Y 41212	Austin Cooper S

JBL 495D was the last of a trio of JBLs registered in May 1966. This Austin Cooper S was prepared by Nobby Hall for Paddy Hopkirk and Terry Harryman to do the Geneva Rally the following month. It was built as Group 2 car, despite the Geneva Rally favouring the more standard Group 1 cars.

The engine was bored to 0.020in to give 1293cc, just within the up-to-1300cc class, but of course by this time the Mini was primarily concerned with overall wins rather than class wins. Class wins were nevertheless still very much valued by Abingdon and would be advertised widely.

The engine was fitted with a lightened steel flywheel and timing gear along with the near-universal-fit of the AEA648

Paddy Hopkirk with Terry Harryman took JBL 495D on the 1966 Geneva Rally.

race camshaft. Compression was high at 12.6:1 on the Downton cylinder head with 16.3cc combustion chambers. Breathing through twin SU H4 carburettors with BG needles, the engine produced 92bhp at the wheels on Abingdon's rolling road. A very short 4.26:1 final drive was fitted, and the entire engine and gearbox was protected by Abingdon's RAC-pattern sump guard. The exhaust was skidded and had the tailpipe turned up, with the joint fitted with locating bars welded on.

Running Hydrolastic suspension, the car was fitted with double-blue displacers at the rear and single-blue on the front. In addition there were modified struts and orange helper springs plus Aeon bump stops – all to try and prevent the pitching experienced with Hydrolastic fluid suspension. The rear radius arm brackets on the subframe were modified, which involved a double-welded plate and additional metal let in to prevent premature failure of this much-stressed item. The car ran Dunlop R7 race tyres and had fibreglass wheelarch extensions to cover the wider 41/2J steel rims. The suspension was set to show 13in from the wheel centre to the edge of the wheelarch. Brakes used DS11 racing disc pads with hard VG95 rear shoes and a 325psi limiting valve.

The electrics received the usual Abingdon attention by the resident Lucas Racing technicians who did their masterly job of completely wiring the car from scratch. It was fitted with an 11AC alternator with a remote 4TR regulator, two-speed wipers and a foot-operated co-driver horn. Various additional switches were added, at the crew's request, on black-crackle aluminium instrument panels in front of both crew members. The co-driver also had an additional switch panel in his door pocket.

Lighting was now the standard Abingdon fit of four auxiliary lamps, all Lucas 700s. The two middle lamps were driving lamps, with two fog lamps on each end. These lamps, all with iodine bulbs and individually switched, were fitted to a long lamp bar just above the bumper, which was fabricated out of cut-down angle iron, shaped to the front of the car's profile and chrome-plated.

Inside the car Hopkirk had a fibreglass bucket seat trimmed in cloth, whilst Harryman had an Abingdon reclining seat. Both used Irvin belts, only Harryman's was a full harness whilst Hopkirk had a more simple lap-and-diagonal belt. The heater had larger-diameter demister pipes to direct more warm air onto the non-heated front 'screen. Additional padding was fitted to the door pockets and door locks plus the door pillar and the edge of the co-driver's rear seat companion box. All glass, trim and carpet was retained, and an asbestos blanket placed under the front carpet to keep out heat. The crew used an intercom, which was fitted to the roof of the car.

All lines were run inside the car, with the twin SU fuel pump located under the rear seat. The fuel tanks were protected by thin sheets of asbestos glued to their exposed sides in the boot and, just to be safe, the battery was reversed, with its terminals away from the fuel tank.

The Geneva Rally, a round of the European Championship, saw just 61 starters line up on the June evening in Geneva to tackle this relatively short rally of just two legs: one to the north and west of Geneva, of 15 hours and 500 miles; the second, after a day's sleep, to the south and west of Geneva of 20 hours' duration and just over 600 miles, including many of the favourite Alpine passes. Interspersed were ten flat-out selectives, three hillclimbs and fast average road speed, which produced a hard, challenging event.

The event's marking system favoured Group 1 cars due to the handicap system – an outdated idea that was rather at odds with most European championship rounds, which now favoured scratch times (just the hillclimbs were on scratch as tie deciders). Because of this, Abingdon also entered Tony Fall in a Group 1 car. Nevertheless, Hopkirk in a full Group 2 car still had a good chance of an outright win.

From the start, Hopkirk was in contention, and as the first night wore on was in third place after the first hillclimb. The fast road timing was just achievable on the dry road but as dawn broke, where Hopkirk found himself by now in the lead, he was soon in trouble. On the start line of the selective over the Col de l'Aiguillon, his gearbox broke, yet he managed to find second gear and it just held long enough for him to get to the top of the climb, which allowed him to freewheel down on what was fast, wide tarmac. He was fast enough, despite only having second gear, to just clean the selective and hold

CHAPTER 3: THE MK 1 MINI COOPER S

Hopkirk and Harryman were to retire from the lead of the rally when the gearbox failed, leaving him with only second gear.

The Gulf London Rally of 1966 saw Paddy Hopkirk reunited with Ron Crellin for this mammoth rally around the UK. Because manufacturer's support was not possible due to SMMT stipulations, JBL 495D was a private entry for Paddy Hopkirk, not BMC.

onto his lead. Now however, service was a way away and time was fast disappearing. Hopkirk didn't make it in time, despite physically hauling the car uphill pulling on the tow rope. He was desperate to get to the top of another col so that he could freewheel down to service. It was to no avail, and he was forced to retire from what was a leading position.

At the finish, as expected, the first six places were all Group 1 cars. Gilbert Staepelaere, in a works Lotus Cortina won, finishing just ahead of Fall in the second Mini. BMC won the team prize, plus two class awards, so was well rewarded for its efforts, despite losing Hopkirk's car from the lead.

For JBL 495D's next event, the Gulf London Rally, which took place less than two weeks after the Geneva Rally towards the end of June, the car was quickly reprepared – notably with a new gearbox – and dispatched for Paddy Hopkirk, this time with Ron Crellin, to do the London Rally. This rally was a relatively new event in the calendar, in only its third year as a full international. It was also different in that it was not permissible for UK manufacturers to have trade support because it was not on the list of Society of Motor Manufactures and Traders (SMMT) accredited events, so BMC could not officially enter – instead supporting private entrants who just happened to have been loaned a works car.

The second works Cooper S, DJB 93B, was 'loaned' to Tony Fall and Mike Wood. BMC service was likewise, in theory, not to be in evidence – although clearly a covert facility was provided for the two 'private' works Minis, the Abingdon mechanics looking after these two cars whilst on holiday from their day jobs. This was all rather unfair to British entrants, as the SMMT rules didn't apply to foreign entrants – so a heavy works contingent was entered by Saab, Renault and VW all hopeful to beat the British crews on their home turf.

The Gulf London was designed to be a very tough rally. The route traversed most of Great Britain, much as the RAC Rally of the day. The event ran continuously for three days, with only two one-hour breaks – it was the British equivalent of the Liège Rally.

It was run and devised by David Seigle-Morris, once a BMC works team driver in the Healey days, who was a great exponent of long endurance rallies. The event sponsor, Gulf Oil, also supplied free Gulf fuel and oil to all competitors, which was a massive attraction to proper private entrants. Gulf tankers were to be seen dispatching free fuel in addition to providing free fuel at the company's petrol stations along the 1200-mile route.

The itinerary, starting and finishing near London Airport, saw the crews head north until they reached Kielder Forest. The event had 34 stages totalling 300 miles, one of which was 40 miles long in Allerston Forest – a real challenge. The road timing was also very high as the organisers had devised a timing system that encompassed 50mph stage timing into the road schedule, and with little rest, it was a challenge to keep on time. The 120 starters were largely British clubmen, attracted by the free fuel and low entry fee. The many stage miles and furious pace took a heavy toll on cars, with just 44 cars making the finish line.

Hopkirk was running well – and up with the leading crews – but having to give second best to Fall, who was lying in second place behind Roger Clark (in a loaned works Cortina) in the early stages. Up in the Lake District and into Kielder Forest, Hopkirk made his mark but still trailed Fall. Nearing Chester before the tough section in North Wales, Hopkirk was forced to retire with both a cracked sump – with which he could continue – and a seized engine – with which he couldn't.

269

Challenging the leaders, Hopkirk and Crellin were forced to retire with a seized engine and cracked sump.

Rauno Aaltonen and Henry Liddon had a new JBL 495D at their disposal for the 1966 Alpine Rally, seen here at the start in Marseille.

Fall went onto so nearly win but a massive roll in the Forest of Dean near the end saw him out too. Ake Andersson in a works Saab won convincingly once Fall had been sidelined.

After the damage sustained to the car's bodyshell on the rough and demanding stages of the Gulf London Rally, a body swap was in order for the car's next event – the Alpine Rally in early September 1966. The fresh car was now assigned to Rauno Aaltonen and Henry Liddon and built by Roy Brown to Group 2 specification.

The engine was to a very similar specification, running at a high compression, which again produced 92bhp at the wheels on the rolling road. The only change to the engine specification was the provision of lightweight tappets, and to the gearbox where the final drive was dropped to 4.2:1.

Because the Alpine was not a rough event, a lighter sump guard arrangement was fitted, this being the short RAF guard, commonly known as the '13-hole guard' because of the number of air holes along its front edge. To this was fitted a Dural plate extending rearwards to cover the gearbox, in addition to a Moke sump plate screwed to the bottom of the gearbox. The remote shift was fitted with a Mitchell mounting and a strengthened bracket.

The car remained on the same-specification Hydrolastic suspension. It is noted that the car now had a double-skinned box section running across where the seats' brackets mounted, intended to add strength and rigidity to the bodyshell. This would have involved a good deal of cutting and re-welding to fit inside the existing box section. It was actually not permitted under the Group 2 regulations (as it was strengthening) but it was well hidden and was never discovered at any scrutineering inspection.

The brakes, which received so much hard work up in the Alps and especially with Aaltonen's technique (and Mäkinen's) of left-foot braking, received careful attention. To help dissipate the heat built up from the often red-hot disc brakes, Abingdon manufactured asbestos blocks that were fitted into the brake calliper piston, which just touched the brake pads rather than the piston. This helped to keep heat transference away from the calliper and its brake fluid. In addition, the rear brake drums were drilled with air holes and the backplates also had a multitude of holes drilled to let out hot air. The final modification was to thread the boss of the rear wheel cylinder, where the retaining circlip usually goes, and bolt the wheel cylinder solidly to the backplate, which allowed the backplate to act as a heatsink for the hot wheel cylinder. With DS11 brake pads and VG95 brake shoes, plus the use of racing brake fluid, the onset of brake fade through overworked brakes was averted. Further still, Aaltonen had asked for air scoops to be fitted below the bumper to feed cool air to the front brakes but this was not done - as it definitely would have raised the eyebrows at scrutineering.

This thinly disguised road race, namely the Alpine Rally, was always an Abingdon favourite. Run over three 24-hour legs, which started in Marseille, went over to Aix-les-Bains for two visits and then finished in Cannes, was a huge 2400-mile challenge. Each leg of around 800 miles, interspersed with a rest day, was very tightly timed, with scant opportunity for service let alone a break. Many crews struggled to keep to the high average speed.

In addition were 14 stages, timed to the second to decide the winner, also to be tackled using the very best climbs in the Southern Alps. So tough was the event that of the 80 hopefuls

CHAPTER 3: THE MK 1 MINI COOPER S

Aaltonen and Liddon were hunting an Alpine Cup for a clean run on the road and the pace, even through villages, was high.

Aaltonen and Liddon lost their clean time sheet due to numerous electrical problems; despite this, they finished third overall.

Simo Lampinen and Tony Ambrose took JBL 495D on the 1966 RAC Rally where the car, for the first time, was fitted with a roll cage.

that started in the sunshine in late September, only 19 crews made it to the finish. Of these, just seven were awarded their coveted Coupe des Alpes for not collecting any road time penalties (a clean sheet) – in itself a tall order.

Aaltonen started well and was up the leaderboard after the first-leg stop at Aix-Les-Bains. The attrition had been high, however, with 26 cars failing to make it this far and only 16 cars still holding onto a clean sheet. The second leg, a circular route to Aix and back, saw Aaltonen up to third place behind the works Lotus Cortina of Roger Clark and the works Alfa GTA of Jean Rolland. By now just 28 cars were left running and the clean sheet count was down to 11. Aaltonen was still one of them, with his Alpine Cup in sight. At the end of the leg, again in Aix, the BMC service crew, in the allocated 20 minutes' service time, replaced, as a precaution, the entire front suspension of JBL 495D.

The third and final blast down to Cannes, over yet more climbs, saw Aaltonen's Cup evaporate by just 15 seconds when he clocked in late at the Isola control near the French-Italian border, just after dawn. Having had intermittent electrical trouble throughout the rally, the SU twin fuel pump decided to pack up and then the starter motor promptly jammed. Aaltonen and Liddon put this right and were soon mobile again and had a race against time, when they hit more trouble with the needle jet in one of the carburettors jamming open, flooding the engine with fuel. They finally got going but were just over time at the next control, and their Coupes des Alpes was gone. However, they held onto their third place but still behind the Ford and victorious Alfa. It had not been a great Alpine for Abingdon, with Aaltonen being the team's lone finisher.

Prior to the car's next event, the RAC Rally, JBL 495D was pressed into service as a practice car for Graham Hill, the Grand Prix driver, to use with Paddy Hopkirk at the Ministry of Defence proving ground at Bagshot. The Mini used was actually Hopkirk's Gulf London Rally car, which he had used in the summer and retired with a seized engine. Fitted with a new engine, the car had a standard Cooper S camshaft, which was to be used on Hill's car on the RAC. Hill was unused to rallying and had been entered by BMC on the RAC Rally as a publicity stunt. Ford had signed up Jim Clark to drive a Lotus Cortina, so BMC followed suit and signed up Graham Hill, who would drive GRX 309D. Hopkirk was assigned to teach Hill the rudiments of fast driving over loose surfaces. Hill was never really at home with the front-wheel-drive car nor on the loose surface but by the end of the day, despite numerous visits to the scenery, he was improving considerably and posting quick times.

Aaltonen's Alpine car was reprepared for the RAC Rally of Great Britain and handed over to Simo Lampinen and Tony Ambrose to contest BMC's home event. This was Lampinen's first drive for BMC. He was a very successful rally driver in his homeland of Finland, being the national champion in 1963 and 1964. By contrast, this was to be Tony Ambrose's final event for the BMC team as he was retiring from competition after the RAC Rally. It had been ten years since he won his first RAC and had been European champion with Rauno Aaltonen in 1965. He was probably one of the very first professional co-drivers and one of the best at BMC.

JBL 495D was one of eight works Minis entered on this much-publicised event. With Rauno Aaltonen having won for BMC the previous year, they were keen to repeat the feat in 1966 and assembled a very strong team of cars and drivers. The Alpine car was rebuilt by Tommy Eales and Johnny Organ. It was entered as a Group 2 car but was detuned for the rally by the fitting of a standard Cooper S road camshaft instead of the usual race cam. This was fitted to all of the works Minis (except Mäkinen's car, which, on his insistence, was fitted with the usual camshaft). The thinking behind this move was to get as much low-down torque as possible in the muddy and slippery conditions found in the British forests in November. Whilst this extra torque was welcomed, it came at the cost of a loss of around 15bhp, dropping the power to just 75bhp at the wheels. A slightly lower-compression Downton cylinder head was also fitted but with a customary very short final drive in the transmission to give maximum acceleration.

Also new for the RAC Rally was a roll cage in the car, this being the first time any works Mini had been fitted with one. Only Mäkinen went without. The cage would prove its worth, particularly for Lampinen, who rolled the car comprehensively in Wales and was quite unscathed – which was more than could be said of the car. Also new was a very substantial Scandinavian sump guard, which being made from spring steel was both lighter and stronger than the previous heavy-duty guard. This new guard is easily distinguished with the front quick-lift jacking brackets fixed to its leading edge and extending up to the underside of the bumper.

Forward-facing mud flaps were also fitted to try and keep the windscreen and headlights clear of muddy spray. Their downside was they tended to restrict the air to the front brakes, which soon overheated on longer stages. Headlight washers were fitted and a grille muff added to the front grille moustache to keep out possible snow and raise the engine temperature. This standardised item, made in the MG trim shop, meant that the leather bonnet strap on JBL 495D had to be relocated from its previous location on the passenger side (on the Alpine) to the driver's side, now in common with the other cars. Also fitted on the grille moustache was a pair of lamp steadies for the two centre driving lamps, intended reduce vibration.

Sponsored and heavily publicised by the *Sun* newspaper, spectators were very much in evidence on the RAC Rally. They lined much of the route, witnessing the 144 cars tackle the 2400-mile rally, which contained 67 stages, amounting to almost 400 miles of mostly loose-surface forest tracks. The five-day event covered most of the country: starting from London Airport, it headed for the West Country, onto Wales and up through the Midlands, the Lake District and Northern England, onto Scotland and then to Aviemore for the one-and-only night in bed. After a night's rest, more rough Scottish stages were followed by fast, demanding Yorkshire stages, and the route headed south down the east side of the country to finish back at London Airport. Just 63 cars would make the finish.

Lampinen's RAC Rally would, however, be relatively short-lived, as after a steady start and outside the top ten, on the second day in Wales, he came to grief on the Coed-y-Brenin stage, when he majestically and irretrievably rolled the car. On a fast downhill section, the car came to a crest, which he flew over to be greeted by a right-hand bend. The end was

The new roll cage saved the crew from harm when Lampinen rolled the car convincingly in Wales.

JBL 495D was considered far too damaged to continue and was withdrawn before too many people saw the badly deranged Mini.

Yet another new JBL 495D appeared on the 1967 Swedish Rally for Aaltonen and Liddon. The snowbound event was one Abingdon had not had great success with over the years.

obvious. Despite the car being severely deranged, the crew miraculously continued and, thanks no doubt to the new roll cage, both were unharmed. The car was patched up but was soon retired, being unsuitable to continue. There was scarcely a straight panel on the car.

After the severe damage inflicted on the car by Lampinen on the RAC, a new car appeared on the Swedish Rally in February the following year for Rauno Aaltonen and Henry Liddon, built by Dudley Pike. This Group 2 car was fitted with a 1293cc engine in the latest strengthened block, machined down to 0.010in off the piston crown to achieve maximum compression – 12.6:1 with a Downton cylinder head that had 16.4cc chambers. The customary AEG648 camshaft was fitted and the engine showed 90bhp on the rolling road, which was probably 5bhp down on expectations. However, with the 4.2:1 final drive, acceleration would have been considerable. A straight-cut close-ratio gearbox was used, fitted with large driveshafts and Hardy Spicer couplings.

The suspension was Hydrolastic, fitted with blue displacers and orange helper springs. The Swedish Rally was similar in many ways to the RAC Rally, so the subframes were strengthened by double-skinning the top of the rear and security-welding the front. Further, the centre crossmember inside the car was double-skinned. The car was also fitted with a heavy-duty Scandinavian sump guard and a battery box guard.

For an anticipated rough event, the exhaust also received special attention. It was skidded under the silencer and the hanging bracket's rubber drilled and a bolt placed right through it. All the joints were welded, and there were welded clips instead of Jubilee clips. To ensure that the remote gearshift did not part company with its overworked rubber mounting, it was replaced with a Mitchell mounting – and should this almost-indestructible mounting fail, a metal safety strap was made and fitted under the remote shift.

The electrics, as always, received much attention, being completely rewired. The car was fitted with an alternator to power the four additional lamps and the power-sapping heated front 'screen. Headlamp washers were fitted in addition to Perspex protectors. These washers were simple Bundy brake pipes with a restriction in the end to spray water onto the headlamps. Aaltonen had the headlight dip switch moved from its standard position on the floor to a new stalk on the steering column. He also used a new thick-rimmed Moto-Lita steering wheel with thumb pads, preferred from the thin steering wheel used in the past.

Another addition to the car for the Swedish was the fitting of a short metal plate onto the lower edge of the standard fuel tank to protect it from damage from the vicious spiked tyres carried in the boot. The sides of each tank were further protected in the boot with a thin sheet of asbestos glued to its exposed face.

Inside the car, an alloy roll cage was again fitted, as would now be a permanent fitting to all works Minis, having proved their worth in saving Lampinen and Ambrose from injury when they rolled the car. All lines were run inside the car and the twin fuel pump fitted under the rear seat pan. Much care was also taken to exclude all draughts from the car.

The Swedish Rally had not been a happy hunting ground for Abingdon in recent years, with a succession of non-finishes in 1965 and 1966. The rally was similar in many ways to the RAC Rally, with a large content of forest mileage to challenge the car and drivers plus the added Scandinavian attraction of ice racing on frozen lakes and rivers. With the event being dominated by Scandinavia drivers – due to the prevailing

BMC service attending Aaltonen's car in the sub-zero temperatures found in Sweden.

Aaltonen went off and rolled the car into a snowbank and badly damaged the car; the service crew changed the steering arm by the side of the road. Aaltonen would eventually finish in third place.

winter conditions – Aaltonen was best placed to do well, with his obvious experience on such roads and having one of the best-prepared cars available.

This event was marked as Peter Browning's first event at the Abingdon helm, after Stuart Turner's departure to Castrol (en-route eventually to Ford's competition department). Everyone knew Turner would be a hard act to follow, including Browning, but it soon became clear that he too proved to be a formidable competitions manager.

The format of the Swedish consisted of two loops centred on the timber-producing town of Karlstead. The first loop, of 23 hours, contained 16 stages, mostly in forests. The second loop – the same as the first but effectively in the opposite direction – was 31 hours in duration and contained 21 stages. In total there were 820 miles of flat-out stages within a route of just 1750 miles.

The stages were based on scratch time, meaning for every second spent on the stage, time was accumulated. The road sections, between the stages, were relatively relaxed (in most cases). Before the start, however, tyres, so important on this snow-and-ice-covered event, became an issue. Aaltonen wanted to use specialist narrow high-profile Hakkapeliitta tyres with Kometa 5mm studs. BMC, being contracted to Dunlop, which only made a Hakka-type tyre remoulded onto a Dunlop carcass with Secomet studs, was not happy. However, common sense prevailed and Aaltonen was able to use his preferred tyres in exchange for carrying Secomet adverts on the car.

The 121 crews started at 8pm on the Thursday evening, with the first show stage a race around an ice-covered trotting track. The first 16 cars were all amateur drivers acting as ploughs to carve their way for the seeded drivers to follow.

Then followed the first of three forest stages, all of which Aaltonen had practised and had pace notes for. This caused a rumpus between some competitors, because the route was supposed to be secret in order to enable the owners of the many forests, the Billerud Paper Company, to carry on their logging work undisturbed. At the last minute, Billerud and the organisers relented and allowed practice for those able to.

Aaltonen was well up the field, but trailing Björn Wäldegard's Porsche and eventual winner Bengt Söderstrom's Lotus Cortina. A long road section followed, into three further forest stages, two of which had to be scrubbed due to missing direction arrows, which caused many to take the incorrect route. With his pace notes, Aaltonen was second-fastest on the fifth and only stage to count – but by now, he was driving on sight as he had no notes for the remaining stages.

As dawn broke on the Friday, three more stages were undertaken, joined by two very fast road sections (timed at 55mph average). This meant a flat-out charge of over 190 miles without respite. Aaltonen was, on aggregate, 39 seconds faster than the next man Wäldegard and was now up to fourth place overall.

However, his luck was about to change, as on the last stage of the day Aaltonen went off and rolled the car and into a snow bank. He badly damaged the car, and whilst extracting it saw little loss of time, the resultant time loss of eight minutes on the following road section took its toll. The service crew changed a damaged steering arm by the side of the road and sent him on his way, but this loss of road time saw him relegated into sixth place on the return to Karlstead.

The following morning, at the restart, Aaltonen was determined to claw back as much of the lost time as possible but it was a forlorn hope. Try as he might, he could not redress all of the lost time and had to settle for third place behind the Ford and the Saab of Simo Lampinen – the man who had wrecked the previous JBL 495D.

On its return to Abingdon, the rather bent body meant that it was never used again. However, the number was transferred onto another car, as it was used by Paul Easter as a recce car for the 1967 Tulip Rally that was to be held in April 1967.

Paul Easter with a rebadged JBL 495D during a break in recce work with Mike Wood for the 1967 Tulip Rally.

Competition Record

Date	Event	Crew	Number	Overall result	Class result
June 1966	Geneva Rally	Paddy Hopkirk/Terry Harryman	50	DNF	
June 1966	Gulf London Rally	Paddy Hopkirk/Ron Crellin	6	DNF	
Sept 1966	Alpine Rally	Rauno Aaltonen/Henry Liddon	62	3rd	2nd
Nov 1966	RAC Rally	Simo Lampinen/Tony Ambrose	29	DNF	
Feb 1967	Swedish Rally	Rauno Aaltonen/Henry Liddon	26	3rd	2nd

Registration Number	First registered	Chassis number	Engine	Engine number	Model
JMO 969D	July 1966	KA2S4 850926	1275cc	9F-SA-Y 40958	Morris Cooper S

JMO 969D was registered in July 1966 and unusually was not part of a block of cars assigned to the competition department, as was often the case. The car was built to Group 2 specification by Tommy Eales and Nobby Hall and assigned to Timo Mäkinen and Paul Easter to compete on the Alpine Rally, scheduled for September 1966. It was one of four similar works Minis entered for Abingdon's favourite rally but was the only one that was new for the event.

Built with an overbored 1293cc engine, which produced 90bhp at the wheels, the engine was fitted with the almost-standard race camshaft, the AEA648. With a high-compression Downton cylinder head, with 16.4cc combustion chambers, the resulting compression ratio was a healthy 12.6:1. The clack valve on the inlet manifold was blanked off and holes cut in the hose for breathing. The cylinder block was machined to within 0.010in of the special forged piston crowns to increase the compression to as much as was safely possible. The crankshaft was double drilled to increase oil flow and the flywheel was made of steel and lightened, as were the duplex timing gears. Lightened tappets were also fitted. Cooling the engine was a four-blade fan pushing air through a 16-fins-per-inch radiator, secured with ¼in bolts rather than small screws.

Because the Alpine Rally was not a rough event, a lightweight sump guard was used – the RAF guard, more commonly known as the 13-hole guard (because of the number of holes in the front edge). This was supplemented by a Dural sheet fitted onto the guard and extending over the gearbox, which also had a Moke sump plate screwed onto its base. An additional shield was also fitted onto the rear subframe to protect the vulnerable battery box.

Timo Mäkinen and Paul Easter with JMO 969D before the start in Marseille before the 1966 Alpine Rally.

On the starting ramp of the Alpine Rally with many spectators. The crew only completed one stage, which they won, but soon after they were out with a blown head gasket.

The suspension was Hydrolastic with double-blue displacers at the rear and single-blue at the front, together with orange 30lb helper springs and heavy-duty Aeon bump stops – all in an attempt to prevent the car pitching on its fluid suspension. The swinging arm locating brackets on the rear subframe were modified and strengthened, and the top of the rear subframe was double-skinned. A set of 4½J steel wheels were fitted, along with fibreglass wheelarch extensions that were now required to fully cover these slightly-protruding wide wheels. The car sat on Dunlop R7 race tyres, which Abingdon was now using for most tarmac events and even when smooth gravel roads were encountered. The brakes used racing DS11 front disc pads and hard VG95 brake shoes at the rear, with a 325psi limiting valve – brakes were always overworked on the Alpine Rally.

As was standard Abingdon practice, the car was completely rewired with a wiring harness unique to the car. The four auxiliary lamps on the front were fixed to a lamp bar, which was cut from 1¾x½x3/16in angle iron and now fixed to the car with a stronger centre bracket, in an attempt to prevent lamp vibration. Mäkinen elected to use a rear-mounted Lucas fog lamp as a reversing lamp, fitted to the boot lid, rather than a Healey 3000 sidelight, which meant a more powerful 48w bulb could be fitted. An 11AC Lucas alternator with a remote regulator was fitted, which meant the oil cooler and its fixing brackets had to be moved over to allow clearance, and the diagonal stiffener bracket refixed in a vertical position.

Two-speed wipers were used, fitted to deep-throated wheel boxes. These were used more or less universally, as the standard items were liable to breakages, especially if sweeping off heavy snow from the windscreen. Maserati air horns were used, which were additionally operated by a foot switch on the co-driver's side.

Inside the car, the box section between the seats was double-skinned to help strengthen the car and also to aid rigidity to the shell. This was contrary to the current regulations and, although becoming almost standard practice with Abingdon, was never discovered by scrutineers – fortunately. All of the lines were run inside the car and padding was fitted to the door locks, door pocket sides and the B-post; a grab handle, from an Austin 1800, was fitted above the co-driver's door opening, and the interior mirror was from an MGB. In front of the driver and navigator were the customary additional instrument panels that housed the Halda distance recorder and stopwatch and clock, together with numerous control switches. The driver, in addition to his extra control switches, had a large rev counter. Irvin seat belts were used, with a lap-and-diagonal for the driver and a full harness for the navigator, who also had a special Abingdon-fabricated reclining seat. Mäkinen, who had a fibreglass bucket seat, had it porta-powered apart to give his larger frame a bit of comfort.

The 1966 Alpine Rally, starting in Marseille in brilliant late September weather, was a unique and very tough event and one for which Abingdon always fielded a strong team. Run over three blistering fast legs, with a day off in between, it saw 80 crews attempt the 2500-mile road race. Ahead lay 14 timed-to-the-second hillclimbs over some of the best climbs that the Alps had to offer. For those who kept to the tight time schedule it meant a clean sheet and a much-valued Alpine Cup. So tough was the event that only 19 cars finished the event and of them a mere seven Coupe des Alpes were awarded.

Mäkinen wasn't one of the few who made it to the finish in Cannes. In typical style, Mäkinen was flat out from the start and took the lead on the very first stage – but that was as far as it went, as the car was soon out with a blown head gasket, which saw streams of water coming out of the exhaust pipe – but at least he could say he was leading when he retired.

For JMO 969D's next event, the car was handed to Paddy Hopkirk and Ron Crellin for one of BMC's most important events, the RAC Rally of Great Britain. The car was built by Nobby Hall as a Group 2 car but with a difference, in that it was detuned by the fitting of a standard AEG510 Cooper S camshaft rather than the customary AEA649 race cam. This change robbed the car of around 15bhp, down to just 75bhp at the wheels, but it was hoped the extra low-down torque that this road camshaft offered would benefit the car in the slippery muddy conditions in the British forests. Another change for the RAC Rally was the fitting, for the first time on a works Mini, of a roll cage. This was manufactured by John Aley in aircraft-quality aluminium and was a simple loop behind the crew with a backstay fitted onto the rear parcel shelf. Protecting the engine and gearbox was a new Scandinavian sump guard, which was now lighter and stronger than the earlier heavy guard. Made from spring steel, it proved most effective. With the front of the guard extending up the front panel to almost the bumper, it necessitated the quick-lift jacking brackets to be fixed to the leading edge of the sump guard.

Other additions on the car for the RAC were the provision of headlight washers, which were simple Bundy brake tube with an end that allowed water to be sprayed onto the lamps – quite novel for the day. Also to try and keep the lights and 'screen free from muddy splashes, the car ran with front-facing mud flaps on the front corners. These, however, did overheat the brakes due to interrupting the airflow.

A heated front windscreen was fitted to the car and a more powerful heater was inside. To keep out the worst of the weather from the engine and help raise the temperature a grille muff was added to the front grille around the moustache and fitted with Lift-the-Dot fixings. To ensure reliability of the lighting, all light switches were renewed and, of course, the speedometer and trip meter were recalibrated to read in mph rather than kph as used on the Alpine Rally.

The 1966 RAC Rally, held in November, was a challenging event, one of the toughest, with over 2400 miles and 67 stages coving 400 miles to tackle, nearly all on loose-surface forest roads. A reported million spectators turned out to watch the event, no doubt boosted by the event's sponsor – the *Sun* newspaper. The route covered most of the United Kingdom. Starting from the Excelsior Hotel at London Airport it took in the West Country, Wales, the Midlands, Northern England and the Lake District, then up into Scotland and Aviemore for the only night in bed in five days. From Aviemore the field journeyed down the east side of the country, back to London Airport, to the finish five days later. At the start were 144 crews, but the hard route meant only 63 would make it back to London.

Prior to the event, Hopkirk was detailed to instruct Graham Hill, the Grand Prix driver, who would also be competing on

Paddy Hopkirk and Ron Crellin took over JMO 969D for the 1966 RAC, here at the start at London Airport.

the RAC in a works Mini, GRX 309D. Hopkirk and Hill were sent to the military testing ground at Bagshot, along with the TV crew from *Wheelbase*, where Hill tested in Hopkirk's car from the Gulf London JBL 495D. Hill was struggling with front-wheel drive and, despite Hopkirk's instruction, was never at home in the Mini, as results proved.

Hopkirk started the rally at a steady pace; no doubt the car's lack of power compared to Mäkinen's car was not helping. It was not until reaching the Lake District that Hopkirk's times started to get into the top ten as he got used to getting the

A steady start by Hopkirk with JMO 969D fitted with a standard Cooper S camshaft, rather than a race camshaft, robbing it of much power.

At the Aviemore night halt, Hopkirk was lying in fifth place as he pulled into the time control.

Severe overheating, due to a lost fan belt and then a stuck thermostat, saw Hopkirk slip down the order, only to retire with a broken driveshaft in the Lake District.

most from the car and others started to fall by the wayside. At the Aviemore night halt, Hopkirk was lying in fifth place, but well behind Mäkinen who was leading, with Fall in fourth place. On the Glentrool stage, out of Aviemore, the car lost its fan belt and Hopkirk drove eight of the ten-mile stage without cooling, with the car overheating badly. A new belt, at the next service, failed to cure the overheating and the car got even hotter on the next stage, even blistering the paint on the cylinder head. At the next service point, Mäkinen diagnosed a stuck thermostat, so it was bypassed and the car then ran perfectly – perhaps even better than before, as Hopkirk thought the 'cooking' allowed the engine to loosen up a bit.

However, it was not to last, as on the last night in Yorkshire he retired. Hopkirk went off on a corner on the fast Yorkshire forests and shot up the escape road (where others had been before). He spun the car around, put the car into first and the driveshaft broke as they tried to accelerate away. He was out.

The next appearance for JMO 969D was the Swedish Rally in February 1967. The plan had been for JBL 494D to enter the event but it is likely that the car, having finished second on the recent RAC Rally at the hands of Harry Källström was rather tired, so a new car was built and entered as JMO 969D.

The car was to be driven by Timo Mäkinen and Paul Easter and, although the Swedish Rally was not dissimilar to the RAC Rally in that it had a high concentration of forest on the route, it is unlikely that Mäkinen would have been offered a car used on the RAC. Built by Mick Legg, the Group 2 car was fitted with a powerful 1293cc engine with a high-compression Downton cylinder head, coupled to a straight-cut close-ratio gearbox with a 4.2: final drive. Hardy Spicer needle roller universal joints were fitted to special driveshafts.

The suspension was Hydrolastic, despite Mäkinen's preference for dry cone suspension. Uprated displacers were fitted to try and stop the to-and-fro pitching often experienced with hard-driven Hydrolastic cars. As the Swedish was very similar to the RAC Rally, being a forest event, the car was built with additional strengthening to the front and rear subframes by additional plating to the top of the rear frame and additional welding to the front.

The front tie bars were protected and strengthened by additional brackets. The rear radius arm brackets were also reinforced. Inside the car, the crossmember was double-skinned. The engine and gearbox were protected by a heavy-duty Scandinavian guard, crafted from spring steel, which had the car's front jacking points fitted to its leading edge. A steel battery guard was also fitted and all lines, battery, brake and fuel were run inside the car, keeping them out of harm's way.

Another addition to the car for the Swedish was the fitting of a short metal plate onto the lower edge of the standard fuel tank to protect it from damage from the vicious spiked tyres, needed on the event and carried in the boot. The sides of the tank were further protected in the boot with a thin sheet of asbestos glued to the exposed face. Headlamp washers were fitted with simple, but innovative, washers for the time. The headlights were also protected by Perspex covers.

The car was fitted with an alternator to power the four additional lamps and the power-sapping heated front 'screen, and the car was rewired from scratch to ensure reliability. Inside, an alloy roll cage was again fitted, which would now be a permanent fitting to all works Minis, having proved their worth in saving Lampinen and Ambrose from injury when they rolled their car.

The Swedish Rally had not been kind to BMC, with all of its cars retiring in the two previous attempts, but this was an event dominated by Scandinavians particularly used to driving on ice-covered forest roads. Mäkinen was therefore hoping to do well, as was new competition manager Peter Browning, this being his first event in charge, having taken over from Stuart Turner.

The 1967 Swedish, based in Karlstead, was mostly forest stages but with the added attraction of ice racing on frozen rivers and lakes. The 1750-mile route consisted of two loops from Karlstead, one clockwise and the other mirroring the first loop but anticlockwise, meaning many stages were attempted twice but in the opposite direction. The first loop saw 16 stages covered in 23 hours and the second, after a day's rest, 21 stages in 32 hours. A total of 820 miles of flat-out stages were interspersed with relatively relaxed road sections.

However, before the start, trouble was brewing with tyre selection, which was so important on this snow-and-ice-covered event. With BMC contracted to Dunlop, only Hakka-style tyres were available, remoulded onto a Dunlop carcass with Secomet studs – but Mäkinen wanted to use special narrow high-profile Hakkapellitta tyres with Kometa 5mm studs. In the end, Dunlop relented and allowed Mäkinen to have his way, in exchange for carrying Secomet adverts on the car.

The event attracted 121 crews, lined up on Thursday evening for the first show stage – a race run on a frozen floodlit trotting track. The first 16 cars, all amateur drivers, acted as way-finders, carving out a path for the following seeded drivers to speed along. It was then onto the first group of three stages, all of which Mäkinen had practised, even though the event had, up until the previous week, been a secret route. The owner of the majority of the forests, the Billerud Paper Company, had then relented and allowed practice through the forests.

Mäkinen was second fastest to eventual winner Bengt Söderstrom's Lotus Cortina on the first of these three forest stages. On the second, he burst a rear wheel brake cylinder when leaving the stage, but was still fourth fastest. This was replaced by the attendant BMC service crew. Unfortunately, the same fate befell him in the middle of the third stage, when the other wheel's cylinder failed, and he was out. Yet again, the Swedish Rally jinx had struck and Mäkinen was again thwarted.

The car's next appearance was on recce duties for the 1967 Acropolis Rally in May, where Abingdon had entered three cars for Timo Mäkinen, Rauno Aaltonen and East African driver David Benzimra. Paul Easter used the car with Henry Liddon to produce notes for the other two cars, and the rough roads meant the car was fully rebuilt on its return to Abingdon. The car was also used for the recce for the Alpine Rally held in early September.

Mäkinen and Easter were back in a new JMO 969D for the 1967 Swedish Rally. Two failed rear wheel cylinders, in quick succession, saw the car retire after just three stages.

The next event scheduled for the car was to be the *Sun*-sponsored 1967 RAC Rally of Great Britain, which was cancelled less than 15 hours before the start of the rally due to an outbreak of foot-and-mouth disease in the UK. The car was to be driven by Tony Fall and Mike Wood and was a powerful lightweight Group 6 fitted with a 45DCOE Weber carburettor. Although a lightweight car, it did retain its bumpers but no door chromes nor opening rear side windows. Large front mud flaps were fitted and it also ran wide Group 6 wheelarch extensions, which were subtly

JMO 969D was prepared for Tony Fall and Mike Wood for the 1967 RAC, which was cancelled at the very last minute - the car here is driven away to fight another day.

Paddy Hopkirk took JMO 969D to the Ministry of Transport in London to demonstrate seat belts to the then-Minister for Transport, Barbara Castle.

The Circuit of Ireland during Easter 1968 saw Paddy Hopkirk and Terry Harryman use JMO 969D on his home event, trying to repeat his win the previous year.

wider that those fitted to Group 2 cars. A grille muff was supplied but no heated 'screen was fitted. The four auxiliary lights were wired to a rubber plug and socket rather than bullet snap connectors. Because the event was always rough, the very strong but heavy Scandinavian guard was fitted. All of this, however, was to no avail and the car was saved for another day. Hopkirk was to use the car for publicity purposes when he took the car to the Ministry of Transport to publicise the use of seat belts for the then-minister of transport Barbara Castle.

Easter 1968 was a busy time for Abingdon with 1800s on the Safari Rally in East Africa, and the Circuit of Ireland the same weekend. Paddy Hopkirk and Terry Harryman were back in the car and JMO 969D was again in Group 6 specification. Prepared by young Michael Hogan, an MG apprentice, it was very similar to the car that appeared on the abortive RAC Rally. Rather than running split Webers as the cars were now doing when in Group 2 specification, Group 6 rules allowed for a long, non-standard inlet manifold, so a single 45DCOE Weber was fitted. This actually needed some minor panel-bashing, as the carburettor, which protruded into the speedo aperture, was relieved to allow the Weber to fit and clear the front bulkhead. The speedo was also moved out slightly by the use of a wooden spacer. The 1293cc engine ran the standard Abingdon full-race camshaft with a high-compression Downton cylinder head. A short 4.2:1 final drive was fitted to the straight-cut gearbox and this was now fitted with straight-cut drop gears. The engine showed 92bhp at the wheels.

Despite the Circuit of Ireland being mostly a tarmac special-stage rally, some forests were used and the roads were often very bumpy, so the heavy-duty Scandinavian sump guard was fitted, despite its obvious weight penalty. To save weight, all the glass was replaced with Perspex (except the laminated front windscreen), the door chrome was deleted and the side rear window had neither a chrome surround nor opening. The grille surround was removed but the grille and bumpers remained. The bonnet, boot and doors were in aluminium, and as much trim as possible was removed from inside the car. The rear seat was removed and the exposed metal was covered in lightweight carpet, along with the headlining.

The suspension was Hydrolastic and the subframes were plated and rewelded. The car was also fitted with negative-camber bottom arms on the front suspension. Inside, the box section across the car was double-skinned and the floor strengthened, including around the gearstick to take the Mitchell mounting for the remote gearchange.

The main visual differences from how the car appeared in November were the removal of the forward-facing mud flaps and the larger black wheelarch extensions that were now painted in red body colour. The number plate was painted on a rectangle on the offside of the bonnet, which was now retained using Moke rubber toggles, as was the boot lid. The car was virtually unchanged for the abortive RAC Rally but much changed from its previous outing on the Swedish Rally, now being a Group 6 car.

The brakes were improved by fitting asbestos inserts in the pistons to try and keep some heat away from the brake fluid

Hopkirk and Harryman have the rear brakes adjusted by Bill Price at the car's service stop.

Hopkirk, lying in second place, threads the car between the gate posts only to retire on the Lough Eske stage when the car's differential broke.

and, for the same reason, the rear wheel cylinders were held to the backplates with a large nut rather than the standard circlip – this acted as a heatsink. Below the front panel, in line with the wheels, an air duct hole was cut to channel cool air onto the front brakes. The rear brake drums and backplates were also drilled to allow heat out of the brakes.

The four auxiliary lights on the low lamp bar were connected to the car with a rubber plug and socket located just below the offside headlight. The middle two were held steady with adjustable rods secured to the front panel and the top of the lamp. Inside the car, the wheel braces were now housed under the seats and the crash helmets in boxes where the rear seat sat. A first aid kit was also there too. The modified MGB jack was fitted to the driver's-side rear pocket.

Starting at number one, in recognition for his win the previous year, Hopkirk (and Harryman) lined up on Good Friday evening at the Gallaher factory in Ballymena with 122 other starters for their four-day blast around Ireland. The route contained 400 miles of stages, mostly on closed public roads and a few forest stages thrown in for good measure. The average speed set for the stages' target times was indeed very high, of over 60mph. These were interspersed with tight road sections, which didn't allow for too much service and refuelling time, although adequate service time was provided at the end of each leg prior to the cars being locked away in parc fermé. Then the nighttime partying and revelry began, as only the Irish can supply.

The route headed out for a night of hard rallying with 11 stages before breakfast at Blessington near the Wicklow Mountains; the first two being loose surfaces saw forest tyres quickly swapped for race tyres for the remaining stages. These often narrow, bumpy and dusty early stages were demanding, and straight away Hopkirk was locked in a battle with Roger Clark in the new Ford Escort Twin Cam. After a short forest stage, it was back to tarmac and the long 24-mile Sally Gap stage where Clark's much more powerful Escort stormed the wide tarmac stage. At the two-hour breakfast stop near Dublin, Hopkirk held second place 30 seconds adrift of Clark.

Then followed ten more stages to Killarney on Easter Saturday, a loop around the mountains near Killarney and the overnight halt; most again were tarmac, including the wonderful Healy Pass. Hopkirk took his lamps off the car to save them from damage and to save weight, plus he needed to get as much air into the engine as possible as it was starting to overheat and would need constant topping up at every opportunity.

Clark would again lead Hopkirk on most stages but he was certainly close, and on several beating the Escort, when the stages were better suited to the Mini. Arriving at Killarney for the night stop the Mini was still causing worries with its overheating, but constant topping up was keeping it under control. The first stage on Easter Sunday, where just 75 cars had restarted, was the very fast ten-mile Moll's Gap stage, when again the Escort proved unbeatable. But Hopkirk was still second, albeit a good way adrift. Clark continued to extend his lead; Hopkirk continued to have overheating issues but was still in a creditable second place.

By their return to Killarney the field had reduced further but Clark was now in an unassailable position. The next morning, JMO 969D refused to start, and in parc fermé Hopkirk and Harryman had to resort to bump-starting the car to get it to eventually splutter into life. The route headed up to Northern Ireland to Enniskillen and into the night in Donegal, the sting

JMO 969D was entered for Lars Ytterbring and Lars Persson for the 1968 Scottish Rally, seen here in a typical slide through a gateway.

comprehensive roll on the 1966 event in GRX 55D.

Just 50 cars made their way to the finish at Larne, where Clark was a clear winner by 20 minutes, despite having slackened his pace after Hopkirk's retirement. This was the shape of things to come, as the Mini struggled to match the power of more modern machinery.

The final outing for JMO 969D was on the 1968 Scottish Rally, held in early June. With both Rauno Aaltonen and Timo Mäkinen in Greece for the Acropolis Rally and Paddy Hopkirk in Canada for the Shell 4000, Lars Ytterbring and Lars Persson were brought in to drive the car.

Fully rebuilt after the Circuit of Ireland and prepared as a Group 6 car by Peter Bartram, the car was again using a 45DCOE single carburettor, carried lightweight panels, Perspex windows and the very necessary heavy-duty Scandinavian sump guard for the rough Scottish forest stages.

The Scottish Rally was always a very hard event on the cars, and the 1968 edition was no exception, with 400 stage miles on invariably rough, hard, summer-baked forest roads greeting the 92 starters who lined up on Sunday morning in Glasgow's Blythswood Square start. The five-day rally saw the cars travel on the first leg over 1000 miles in the next 36 hours to their overnight stop on Monday evening in Grantown, which would be their base for the next three nights. Here they would have three days to and from Grantown and finish back there on Thursday afternoon. The meat of the rally was undoubtedly the first leg, where 240 miles of those stages were tackled in hot, sunny weather. It would also decimate the field by over half.

in the tail of 16 stages of over 100 miles. Hopkirk's struggle with overheating had continued but it all ended on the Lough Eske stage when the car's differential broke and he was out whilst in a strong second place behind the Escort. Ironically, this occurred on the same stage and only a few miles from the

Seeded at number three, Ytterbring was up against the now all-conquering Ford Escort Twin Cam of Roger Clark, plus a pair of works Saabs. Ytterbring started steadily but by the sixth stage was onto the leaderboard with some fast times. Two very long stages, separated by just 200 yards, amounting to 33 miles of fast forest saw Ytterbring fourth overall on both stages.

Towards the end of the day he lost only 16 seconds to Clark on the last five stages and arrived at the Dumfries dinner halt in fourth place overall. He was behind the Saab and Escort and the very rapidly driven Hillman Imp of Colin Malkin. Ytterbring and Malkin would have a close fight with each other to the very last mile of the rally.

Into the night and 20 cars had already retired. At Balloch for breakfast, Ytterbring was holding his fourth and would hold it to the end of the leg at Grantown where the car was serviced and put away in parc fermé.

The second leg, the next day, was tame by comparison, with eight stages of 60 miles to tackle. Malkin broke a fan

Overheating of the car saw the lights removed, and the front-mounted radiator can clearly be seen as the car receives a tyre change and service; also seen here are the air ducts feeding air to the front brakes.

belt on the Imp and was delayed but was still just ahead of Ytterbring. At the end of the day, a further five cars were out, including the leading Saab, so Ytterbring was now up to third place but still pressing the works Imp, only seconds ahead.

For the third leg of 12 stages of 50 miles, the heat of the day was causing overheating problems for the car and it soon sprouted a small front-mounted radiator (perfectly legal for a Group 6 car) to lower the water temperature. Malkin was delayed by a puncture, where he drove six miles to the loss of 80 seconds to Ytterbring, elevating the Mini to second place. On the final day, of just five stages and 45 miles, Clark now comfortably in the lead eased off, which coincided with Ytterbring throwing caution to the wind to fend off the hard-changing Imp and netting him four stage wins.

Just 40 cars were classified as finishers, with Clark winning comfortably by over ten minutes. But Ytterbring was a wonderful second place, and it was a fitting end for the car.

Ytterbring and Persson would finish the Scottish Rally in second place - the only finish recorded for JMO 969D.

JMO 969D was sold to Rob Lawrence, a successful and well-known club rally driver who went on to use the car very successfully in numerous events.

Competition Record

Date	Event	Crew	Number	Overall result	Class result
Sept 1966	Alpine Rally	Timo Mäkinen/Paul Easter	68	DNF	
Nov 1966	RAC Rally	Paddy Hopkirk/Ron Crellin	10	DNF	
Feb 1967	Swedish Rally	Timo Mäkinen/Paul Easter	22	DNF	
Nov 1967	RAC Rally	Tony Fall/Mike Wood	27	Cancelled	
April 1968	Circuit of Ireland	Paddy Hopkirk/Terry Harryman	1	DNF	
June 1968	Scottish Rally	Lars Ytterbring/Lars Persson	3	2nd	1st

Registration Number	First registered	Chassis number	Engine	Engine number	Model
LBL 6D	Dec 1966	KA2S4 956052	1275cc	9F-SA-Y 43705	Morris Cooper S

LBL 6D was one of four brand-new Cooper Ss delivered to Abingdon and registered in December 1966 in preparation for the January 1967 Monte Carlo Rally. Two were Austin and two were Morris Cooper Ss, of which LBL 6D was the latter. LBL 6D would go on to become one of the most famous works Minis, and resides today in the British Motor Heritage Museum in Gaydon, Warwickshire.

This famous car, built by Roy Brown for Rauno Aaltonen and Henry Liddon as a 1293cc Group 2, followed what was now standard practice of fitting the most powerful but reliable engine they could build. The extra power largely came from a full-race camshaft, the well tried-and-tested AEA648, along with a high-compression and gas-flowed Downton cylinder head (12.6:1), which was held down with MGB cylinder head studs. Carburettors were twin SU H4s with BG needles and blue springs. The ignition was provided by Champion N60Y spark plugs from a Lucas 40979 distributor. The crankshaft was double drilled for extra oil feed and the flywheel was

Rauno Aaltonen and Henry Liddon in LBL 6D on the 1967 Monte Carlo Rally - a car which has achieved iconic status.

lightened steel with an orange diaphragm – all this was carefully balanced.

Keeping the engine cool was a six-blade export fan and a standard Cooper S radiator. Transmission saw special straight-cut close-ratio gears with a short 4.2:1 final drive to give maximum acceleration rather than top speed. Enlarged driveshafts were also fitted.

The car ran Hydrolastic suspension, with single-blue and double-blue displacer units, front and back, with orange helper springs at the rear together with additional heavy-duty bump stops. The car was fitted with lightweight magnesium Minilite wheels for the very first time. These, just homologated before the Monte, were produced by Tech-Del and saved around 50lb in total – all the wheels were fitted with bolt-in racing inner tubes; they were also immensely strong and would allow the car to run on the rim, should they need to, without breaking up.

Brakes, so important, especially with Aaltonen's left-foot braking technique, were served by standard Cooper S disc brakes fitted with Ferodo DS11 racing pads and hard VG95 rear linings. The brake servo was retained and the handbrake was modified to be a fly-off type.

The customary rewiring of all the electrics was undertaken by the resident Lucas Competition technician crafting an entirely new and unique loom for the car. For the high demands placed upon the electrical system (from the four extra lamps and heated front windscreen) a high-output Lucas 11AC alternator was fitted on a heavy-duty cast-iron bracket. The additional lamps were fitted on the now-standard-for-Abingdon four-lamp bar secured by three brackets along the lower front panel. The two centre driving lamps were made secure by fabricated steady brackets fixed to the top of the lamps and to the grille moustache, which stopped vibration of the rather heavy lamps.

Inside the car were crackle-black dashboards in front of each crew member. Aaltonen's housed the rev counter and additional control switches, with Liddon's fitted with a Halda Twinmaster distance recorder and a set of Heuer watches. Also in front of Liddon was a bank of four fuseboxes and, in his door pocket, another switch panel with his map reading light. He also had a foot-operated horn button to ward off errant spectators – and perhaps other slower cars in front. Padding was supplied to the door pockets, door locks and B-post and the alloy roll cage was also padded, as was their intercom box secured onto the roll cage.

A lightweight bucket seat was provided for Aaltonen and a modified high-back reclining seat for Liddon. Both seats sat on modified seat brackets. The full harness seat belt was, for the Monte, mounted from the rear parcel shelf rather than between the rear seat cushions – this to accommodate two extra spare wheels. Securing the extra wheels also entailed some additional fabrication. Whilst two wheels and tyres were easily accommodated in the boot, as they usually were, two additional wheels and tyres were accommodated where the rear seat squab usually sat, but not before various other locations were tried – by the co-driver's feet proved very unpopular! The wheels were secured to the seat pan with a clever over-centre clamp, designed by Terry Mitchell. This allowed the wheels to be quickly removed but securely stowed. Because the car was in Group 2, and therefore had to retain all of its trim, the relocated rear seat squab was fixed to the rear seat back with long leather straps. As always, the car appeared at scrutineering in pristine condition.

LBL 6D was trailered down to Monte Carlo for the start by Roy Brown, who built it. He was joined by mechanics Mick Legg, Dudley Pike and Ron Shepherd, and the Mini was towed by their Austin A110 estate. This barge would go on to service the rally car on its journey.

Despite most professional drivers preferring other rallies, in the public's eye, the Monte Carlo Rally was still the rally that captured their imagination. The motor manufacturers knew that only too well, especially BMC, which is why the firm put such great effort into trying to win the Monte for the third (really the fourth) time. Entering five works Minis (four of which were brand-new cars) entailed 18 mechanics with six service barges and two vans, eight ice note crews, one doctor and one secretary, together with management staff, plus supplying and looking after seven recce Minis that were scattered all around the Alpes Maritime.

Aaltonen, along with most of the team drivers and co-drivers, had been practising and tyre testing in the Alps since November. Tyres received particular attention. New regulations for the 1967 event meant cars had to be entered in one of two categories: category 1 would allow free use of any number of tyres on each of the two competitive legs but the downside was they would have their stage times handicapped by 12.5 per cent; those in category 2 would be restricted to just eight tyres on each of the two legs of the rally. Stuart Turner, along with almost everyone else, calculated that a 12.5 per cent handicap was too much to win back, so elected to use just eight tyres per leg. Cars within category 2 were identified by having yellow door squares, to which their numbers were affixed, rather than the normal white. Only 17 cars elected to run in category 1, so almost everyone was restricted to the eight-tyre rule.

This tyre-restricting rule was designed to help private entrants, with the organisers assuming, incorrectly, that works cars would elect to have no restriction on tyre numbers. However, the timing handicap was just too high, so none did, nor did hardly any private entrants either.

Before the start, the scrutineers at Monte Carlo were insisting that all of the competitors' rally plates were to appear vertically and not fixed to the bonnet as was customary. This involved fixing the rally plate vertically above the windscreen on brackets off the drip rail and secured rearwards onto the roof. The cars also had to be fitted with the mandatory rear mud flaps. BMC had prepared the cars to conform to the regulations in every detail, through feared being excluded yet again on a minor technicality, like the previous year.

The format for the 1967 Monte Carlo Rally saw 185 cars starting from eight locations around Europe who would all, after several days' continuous driving, descend on Monte Carlo, where after a night's rest they would undertake the loop from Monte Carlo to Chambéry and back. After another day's rest, the top 60 would attempt the mountain circuit, finishing the next morning. The start venues, as always, were a gamble as some would be an easy run, others less so, and some would drive almost twice the distance of others. Turner decided upon four starting points, to increase publicity and hedge his bets with the weather.

Aaltonen would start from Monte Carlo, along with 48 others. The car carried four spare wheels, two on the rear seat platform and two on the roof rack. He ran on Dunlop SP3s with two plain SP44 tyres and two lightly-studded SP44s – just to be sure – should the weather deteriorate over the Alps. His route would see him travel out westwards to Bayonne in the south-west corner of France, almost on the Spanish border, and then drive up the west of France through Bergerac, La Rochelle and Poitiers before heading back south to Monte Carlo. His route would be undertaken in relatively clement weather and he, along with 176 others, arrived in Monte Carlo in early afternoon. He had been on the road for just over 50 hours but arrived on time and without penalty, with the car still in good health.

Two competitive legs were then to be tackled after all of the cars had arrived in Monte Carlo. They would do a 24-hour 850-mile loop from Monte Carlo to Chambéry and back, and within that tackle six flat-out timed stages of around 75 miles. The second leg would be restricted to the top 60 cars still running and they would tackle what became known as the mountain circuit – a 12-hour, 380-mile loop, at night, from Monte and back again. This amounted to another 75 miles of torturous stages up and down the Alps.

Tyres for each of these two loops had to be selected in a restricted tyre area, and once chosen were painted with radioactive yellow paint and branded with the car's number. Severe penalties were to be meted out should tyres not be with the car when checked or crews were caught using tyres that hadn't been branded. Once the choice had been made, the cars were put into parc fermé and no changes were possible.

So weather-watching and good reconnaissance were essential to ensure the right choices of tyre were made. It also had to be remembered that all eight wheels and tyres had to be with the car, so the additional weight of the extra wheels and tyres was also a consideration. The roof rack that was used for the run down to Monte Carlo, to carry the extra wheels and tyres, was discarded for the stages because of its weight and wind resistance. Also to save weight, the heavy and comfortable reclining co-driver's seat was removed at Monte Car-

Aaltonen and Liddon at full speed, with both headlight protectors loose. The rally plate on the roof was a later Monte Carlo requirement to be placed vertically.

Service for LBL 6D, clearly showing the battery box cover over the carburettors retaining warmth, also the sound proofing under the bonnet and bulkhead all retained.

Hard cornering in a very travel-stained LBL 6D showing rear mud flaps fitted and the large Lucas reversing lamp.

A motor-drive sequence of Aaltonen and Liddon around an open hairpin on the snow and ice.

lo, in preference for a lighter seat. There would be no sleeping or relaxing in the car from then on. The front mud flaps were also removed, to allow more cooling air to the front brakes.

Needless to say, this tyre restriction put much pressure on Dunlop, which was responsible for supplying tyres to BMC. Numerous batches of different-compound tyres were manufactured and transported for the team to test in France long before the rally. It is to Dunlop's credit that it manufactured a special hard compound for the SP44 Weathermaster tyre in an attempt to make them last. The likes of Aaltonen and Mäkinen could easily destroy a soft set of SP44s in less than 20 miles. So it was that after testing and despite the restrictions, Turner drew up a shopping list of 420 tyres, 380 of which were to allow sufficient choice once at Monte Carlo for the two competitive legs for his five cars. In the interest of economy only 152 Minilite wheel rims were purchased... It should also be said that the previous year, in 1966 where no tyre restrictions were in place, BMC had at its disposal close to 2000 tyres.

With the common run from Monte Carlo to Chambéry due to start the following day, Aaltonen, along with others, headed up into the mountains behind Monte Carlo in recce Minis to see the prevailing conditions. Once returned, and after consultation with Turner and Aaltonen's experienced co-driver Liddon, it was time to select his tyres for the following day. These had to be fitted and stowed, branded and checked in the available 20 minutes or time penalties were dished out. Aaltonen selected four Dunlop SP3s and four partially-studded SP44s. The car was then locked away for the 11.30am start the next morning.

Ahead of Aaltonen were six stages within the 785-mile route. The average speed needed to keep on time was not high

Aaltonen in the driving seat of LBL 6D with his Abingdon-built bucket seat with a large jubilee clip steadying the seat runner; also the very comprehensive dashboard and (just seen) the light reflection shade over Liddon's dashboard.

but to allow time for service and tyre swapping, the pace was quick. The tyres were regularly swapped over, with SP3s being used more or less exclusively for the road sections and dry stages, and the SP44s being reserved for icy stages. This was where the Abingdon ice-note crews were so valuable: going over the stages at the very last moment, before the roads were closed, the ice-note crew marked a copy of Aaltonen's pace notes to show areas of snow and ice. This was handed to him before the start of the stage, so that he could select his tyres and be warned of areas where ice had formed.

The first stage was the St Auban stage, which was mostly dry and clear of snow. Here Aaltonen was tenth fastest with his customary steady start. The Lancia Fulvia of Cella was fastest and the feared Porsche 911 of Elford in the middle. The famous Mont Ventoux hillclimb followed, and it was now into darkness. The stage was again dry and even clear at the observatory at the summit, with just a smattering of ice; Aaltonen was sixth fastest; Elford fastest.

Elford would again be fastest on the next stage, the Col De Rousset, which had black ice over part of the road to catch the unwary; Aaltonen was fourth. Then it was the long Col du Granier Stage, all 28 miles of it, which was in reality three cols joined into one long stage. Aaltonen had spent nearly two weeks practising the stage and, despite the road being in parts heavily rutted ice, he was rewarded with the fastest time, just ahead of a hard-charging Hopkirk. The fifth stage, in early morning at Gap was mostly dry, free of snow and ice, and was extremely fast. It was to the Mini's credit that they all got into the top ten; Aaltonen was ninth but none could catch the fast Lancia of Cella.

It was now daylight for the last stage of the common run, a relatively short one at Levens. With the stage completely dry and free of ice, it saw Aaltonen finished in fourth place – with Elford being fastest, stamping his mark on the hillclimb in the powerful Porsche.

Aaltonen returned to Monte Carlo, in common with most, with totally worn-out tyres, which called into question the wisdom of the regulation that put unnecessary risk on driv-

Aaltonen just crosses the finishing line victorious in Monte Carlo, winning by a slender margin on the last night in the mountains above Monaco.

ers. At the Monte Carlo check-in, 101 cars made it in time, meaning 75 had fallen by the wayside. All were now classed as finishers, and the top 60 were prepared for the final night on the mountain circuit above Monte Carlo the following night. Aaltonen, with his consistent performance, was now lying in fourth place overall and still very much in contention – although he was nearly penalised at the final control for not having one headlight working. Fast talking by blaming the scrutineer for breaking the lamp when he went to check his engine security seals saved the day. Elford was leading, with Aaltonen just 48 seconds adrift of the Porsche.

Once again, whilst many went to bed, Aaltonen went up into the mountains with a recce car to see for himself the conditions of the so-important Col du Turin stage, which would be tackled no less than three times. The tyre choice for the mountain circuit would prove critical, as although the weather had been unusually dry and mild, slight rain was starting to indicate there could be snow on high ground. Tyre choice could wait until the next day with the question mark hanging over the deteriorating weather.

Despite the stages near Monte Carlo still being dry and, after much deliberation with Liddon and Turner, Aaltonen decided upon four normally-studded SP44s and four specially-studded SP44s of a harder compound. These hard SP44s had special longer studs in an asymmetric pattern, further into the tyre, in the hope of retaining most of them as they wore down.

The next evening, 60 cars started at 7pm for their 380-mile dash around the Alpes-Maritimes to tackle six decisive stages. Once again the average speed was not too high, but to stay on time and allow an extra five minutes' service at the start and/or finish of the stages meant, in practice, it was to be very fast night.

The first stage, the Gorges du Piaon, starting at Sospel, was mostly dry but icy on some of the hairpins. Elford extended his lead, with Aaltonen fourth fastest. By now it had start-

CHAPTER 3: THE MK 1 MINI COOPER S

ed to rain, which meant it would likely be followed by snow on higher ground. The second stage, the first run up the Col du Turini, in the northerly direction, had ice at the very top where huge crowds gathered in party mood to greet the car, with floodlights, camera flash bulbs and bonfires ablaze; wild cheers greeted the cars as they slithered over the summit – a magical place for any rally enthusiast.

Aaltonen was again fourth fastest, with Elford still holding the lead but now with Ove Andersson, in his Lancia, making a big push. Still on mostly-dry roads, tyres were beginning to wear badly, and before the third stage his tyres were swapped front to back. Aaltonen was also experiencing electrical problems, with the dip switch failing. The Col de Couillole stage followed and, as predicted, it was snowing at the summit. Andersson was now charging hard and Aaltonen could do no better than seventh fastest, just a second slower than Elford's Porsche. A second visit to the Turini, this time heading south, saw more snow and Aaltonen stormed the stage, fastest on his better tyres.

So close were the times, it was becoming unclear who was in the lead but it was now a three-way fight between Aaltonen, Andersson and Elford. The next service in St Sauveur saw Aaltonen swap his tyres again and have his fan belt replaced. He was now using his worn studded SP44s for the road section, swapping for his special studded tyres for the stages. A second visit to the Col du Couillole, which was now mostly under snow, saw fortunes change.

By then Elford had completely run out of studded tyres and could no longer master the 200bhp Porsche in the snow. Aaltonen came fourth, just behind Andersson, and although Elford held a slender one-second lead over Aaltonen, he was powerless to hold off the Mini. Andersson, still hard charging, was in third spot. The sixth, decisive and final stage awaited – a third run up the Col du Turini from the north.

Things were now about to play into Aaltonen's hands as they arrived at the stage start. They found the start delayed due to a spectator's car having fallen onto the stage. In the 20 minutes it took to extricate the car, snow fell relentlessly and left Aaltonen with the best tyres to tackle the Turini. However, Aaltonen nearly didn't finish the stage. Driving flat-out in blinding snow, he slid off on one of the many downhill hairpins that was covered in sheet ice, but miraculously trundled down and rejoined the road below without damage to the car, nor loss of time. Andersson won the stage but with Aaltonen in second place, 20 seconds adrift, Anderson was unable to close the gap on Aaltonen.

Although it would take several hours to check all of the times, by early afternoon it was announced that it was Aaltonen who had won the 1967 Monte Carlo Rally by a slender 13 seconds.

BMC was delighted to have won again, and the team's three star drivers now had one Monte victory apiece. BMC had a big party at Menton and even Alec Issigonis flew over for the celebrations. The victorious Minis and crews were flown back to England in a Carvair but it was a bittersweet return as it had been announced that Stuart Turner, the mastermind of so much that Abingdon had achieved, would be leaving to join Castrol. Peter Browning, his very capable deputy, would be taking over on the Tulip Rally in April. He would be a hard act to follow.

Despite this car, in recent times, being held in the highest regard, when it returned from the Monte win, it was not cos-

Aaltonen and Liddon with the spoils of their victory outside Monaco Palace.

289

WORKS MINIS IN DETAIL

Returning to the UK in the BUA Carvair, Aaltonen, Liddon and Mäkinen await the welcome party - and the ramp.

Celebration champagne for Aaltonen and Liddon for their win on the Monte Carlo Rally on their return to the UK, with many press and notorieties in attendance.

seted away. Although it was not used in competition again, it was unceremoniously parked outside at Abingdon for long periods of time.

LBL 6D eventually found its way to the motor museum in Syon Park, housing the British Motor Museum collection of cars. It was then partially restored, as a project, by BL apprentices at Marshalls of Cambridge during 1979 and 1980. Finally it was moved, in 1993, to its present facility in Gaydon. Those wishing to study this car should be aware that the car now sadly lacks numerous period details from that Monte win, not least of which it is now devoid of its Monte engine.

Competition Record					
DATE	EVENT	CREW	NUMBER	OVERALL RESULT	CLASS RESULT
Jan 1967	Monte Carlo Rally	Rauno Aaltonen/Henry Liddon	177	1st	1st

REGISTRATION NUMBER	FIRST REGISTERED	CHASSIS NUMBER	ENGINE	ENGINE NUMBER	MODEL
LBL 66D	DEC 1966	KA2S4 956051	1275CC	9F-SA-Y 43701	MORRIS COOPER S

LBL 66D was the second of four new Cooper Ss delivered to Abingdon that were all destined for the 1967 Monte Carlo Rally in January. The car was registered in December 1966. As this car was assigned to Timo Mäkinen, it was naturally a Morris Cooper S because of Mäkinen's personal contractual arrangements. He would be sharing the car with his long-term co-driver Paul Easter. The Group 2 car was built by Johnny Evans and would follow very similar lines to the other Monte cars now in preparation.

Built almost identically to its sister cars, this new Mini was entrusted to Johnny Evans. The 1293cc engine produced 94bhp on the Abingdon rolling road, so it was one of the most powerful produced by Abingdon to date. Fitted with a high-compression Downton cylinder head, with 16.4cc combustion chambers and AEA648 race camshaft, with the short 4.2:1 final drive fitted to the straight-cut close-ratio transmission, it gave the car superb acceleration. Forged pistons with special piston rings were used in the latest strengthened engine block, and were fitted to a cross-double-drilled and balanced crankshaft. The Cooper S crankshaft, at that time, was one of the strongest production crankshafts made. A lightened steel flywheel and backplate were also fitted.

Carburettors were twin SU H4s with BG needles and blue springs, with float chamber extensions and fork-and-peg linkage. Ignition was from a Lucas 40979 distributor through Champion N60Y spark plugs. A six-blade fan was fitted and ,to keep things cool, a Cooper S radiator was used; it also ran a thermostat with the bypass hose retained. A distinguishing feature of the engine for the Monte Carlo Rally was the scrutineer's security tag, which was fixed onto the engine by the engine number to ensure that the unit was not replaced during the event

Despite Mäkinen's preference for dry suspension, LBL 66D was built with Hydrolastic, with single-blue and double-blue displacer units, with orange helper springs at the rear together with additional heavy-duty bump stops. The suspension was set at a standard ride height, at 13in from the wheel centre to the edge of the wheelarch. Special Timken wheel bearings were fitted to the rear hubs, and the front tie rods secured with castellated nuts and split pins.

Newly-homologated lightweight, and very strong, magnesium Minilite wheels were used, which offered 50lb saving over standard steel wheels. Brakes, which Mäkinen was very hard on due to his left-foot braking technique, were standard Cooper S disc brakes but fitted with Ferodo DS11 racing pads and hard VG95 rear linings. The handbrake was modified to be a fly-off type, and the brake servo was retained under the bonnet.

The bodywork had quick-lift jacking points front and back, with towing eyes fitted to the front subframe lower mounts. The bonnet was held shut securely with the addition of a leather strap, and the boot lid by a rubber toggle. The car ran fibreglass wheelarch extensions to cover the slightly protruding wheels, and also had rear mud flaps, together with larger front mud flaps fitted to the front corner by the bumper, which prevented water spraying up onto the headlights and 'screen (to a certain degree). Domed Perspex covers were fitted over the headlights to protect them from stone damage. Also, to keep driving snow out of the engine and to keep things warm, the front grille was covered by a removable grille muff, which was secured to the grille moustache with Lift-the-Dot studs.

The car's electrics were completely rewired and, because of the demands on the system from the heated front 'screen and extra lamps, a high-output Lucas 11AC alternator was fitted. The extra lamps consisted of four large Lucas 700 units: two fog lamps on the outside and two driving lamps in the middle;

LBL 66D, in the hands of Timo Mäkinen and Paul Easter, tried one of its spare wheels rather uncomfortably by Easter's feet for the 1967 Monte Carlo Rally. The square taped to the door card is a list of fuses.

these two were held securely with lamp steadies. The lamps were fixed to a chromed lamp bar on the lower front panel above the bumper. A rear-mounting Lucas 576 fog lamp was additionally fitted to the boot lid to act as a reversing lamp. A two-speed wiper motor was fitted with special deep-throated wheel boxes; the car also had electric washers.

Inside were two aluminium dashboards, one in front of each crew member, housing the rev counter and additional control switches, with Easter's fitted with the distance recorder and a set of watches. There was also an additional switch panel in his door pocket for his map light and other switches.

The crew had the security of an alloy roll cage, and Easter had a full-harness Irvin seat belt, attached at the back onto the rear parcel shelf. Mäkinen had a simple lap-and-diagonal Irvin belt (which he rarely used). Crew comfort was important on a long, cold event. Easter had the benefit of a cloth-covered relining seat – which Mäkinen often occupied on the long road sections. However, for the relatively relaxed run down to Monte Carlo, the driver also had the comfort of a reclining seat. Both were replaced, once in Monte Carlo for the competitive sections, with lightweight seats. Padding was supplied to the door locks, door pockets and door pillar, and great care was taken to exclude draughts. The battery, brake and fuel lines were run inside the car and the twin fuel pump was situated under the rear seat pan.

Another feature of the car was the need to carry four spare wheels. One was fixed rather uncomfortably by the co-driver's feet; the others on the rear seat pan. This also meant that rear seat cushion needed relocating. As it had to be carried in the car, it was strapped to the rear seat back. The extra wheels were retained with a quick-release clamp, fixed to the seat pan and the floor. Tyres, as always, would play a vital part on the Monte.

Having won the 1965 Monte so convincingly in atrocious conditions, and also having won but then disqualified on a lighting infringement in 1966, Mäkinen was looking for another win in 1967 – for his hat-trick. Along with the other drivers and co-drivers, he had been practising, tyre testing and making pace notes in the Alps since early November.

Stuart Turner had planned for every eventuality and had produced a 17-page confidential document outlining everything the team needed to know about plans for the Monte Carlo Rally. This was issued to all the Abingdon staff involved in the Monte – which was for the day, an army of people. Apart from the ten drivers and co-drivers, 18 mechanics were on duty to service the five cars. The all-important ice-note crews, who would give up-to-date reports on the condition of the roads and mark the pace notes accordingly, numbered another eight people. As well as management staff, including Turner and Peter Browning, Turner also had his secretary, who was permanently manning a special direct telephone line in their Monte Carlo hotel. There was also a doctor in attendance to monitor the heart rates of the crews under the stress of competition. Fortunately or otherwise, Mäkinen and Easter were not considered suitable for this experiment! All these people needed travel arrangements, hotels and instructions of their required movements throughout the rally; it was all very much Turner's speciality, the master planner and tactician.

Added complications in the planning for the 1967 Monte were the tyre restrictions, in which the organisers devised two categories for tyre choice. Category one would allow free choice of any number of tyres on the two competitive legs, which they expected all works cars to enter. Category two, which restricted the cars to just eight tyres on each of the two legs, it was hoped would be filled with private entrants. However, the 12.5 per cent handicap on stage times, for those electing to run in category one, was thought too heavy a burden. So the vast majority entered in the restricted tyre class, despite the added encumbrance of having to carry four spare wheels in the car. This, however, did mean that Dunlop had to develop suitable tyres able to withstand the punishment that a hard-driven works Mini inflicted on them. Dunlop sent numerous batches of tyres over to France for Mäkinen and the other drivers to test until they arrived at a compromise tyre that would likely last and not affect grip too much. Dunlop supplied 420 tyres of various patterns and compounds for the five Minis – which was about 20 per cent of the number of tyres supplied to Abingdon for the Monte in 1966.

Mäkinen and Easter started their Monte Carlo Rally challenge from Lisbon and had Bill Price and Johnny Evans to service the car on their way to Monte Carlo. Turner had spread his works cars around Europe at the various starting points to achieve maximum publicity and also hopefully ensure that not all of his cars were troubled by possible adverse weather. However, before the start, word had come through from Turner at Monte Carlo that the scrutineers were insisting that the cars' competition rally plates had to be fixed in a vertical position. This necessitated hurried work on the car. The rally plate was fixed vertically on brackets on the right-hand side of the bonnet. This obscured the number plate, so that too had to be remade, the bonnet repainted and the registration number repainted on the left side.

Only a dozen other cars joined Mäkinen at the Lisbon start. Their route headed illogically south from Lisbon to Seville before turning north through Madrid and up into France, joining the Monte Carlo starters at Bayonne to jointly travel up the west side of France before turning south at Poitiers and descending on Monaco some 50 hours later. Mäkinen arrived fresh and relaxed whilst Easter was very tired and not in the best of moods, having driven most of the way whilst Mäkinen slept. Of the 185 starters, 176 made it to Monte Carlo – for some that was achievement enough.

Once in Monte Carlo, Mäkinen headed straight for the mountains, in a recce Mini, to survey the roads in the Alpes Maritime before he decided on his selection of tyres that evening. With information from the ice-note crews and Turner plus his own inspection on the unusually mild weather, Mäkinen decided upon his tyres for the first competitive section. This would be from Monte Carlo to Chambéry and back, a loop of over 785 miles with six stages of around

Mäkinen and Easter started from Lisbon on their long run to Monaco some 50 hours later.

75 miles, all hillclimbs up and over the Alps in 24 hours. Mäkinen chose four Dunlop SP3 tyres, two plain SP44s and two lightly-studded SP44s. His tyres were painted with yellow radioactive paint and branded with 144, his start number. The SP3s were fitted on the car and LBL 66D was locked away in parc fermé.

The next day, at mid morning, the common run began. Mäkinen headed for the first stage at St Auban. This was mostly dry and Mäkinen stamped his mark with third fastest. Mäkinen had his brakes bled before the next stage, the famous Mont Ventoux hillclimb, where even that was ice free, apart from at the very top; Mäkinen was again third, with the much-feared Porsche 911 of Vic Elford being fastest.

By the time the Col du Rousset stage was tackled, it was dark with black ice much in evidence. Once more Mäkinen was third fastest but again Elford was fastest. As the night wore on, the longest stage beckoned; three cols joined together to make one long 30-mile stage culminating on the Col du Granier. Mäkinen had spent much time practising this important stage and had even found a little short cut. Here they stationed Tony Ambrose in a recce Mini on the night, with its bonnet up, blocking the short cut to all bar the works Minis. Despite this, Mäkinen, on this often-ice-rutted stage, saw him only fourth fastest but he had now beaten Elford.

As dawn broke, the stage at Gap was free of ice and mostly dry, and Mäkinen came fifth. The final stage at Levens, being completely dry, was very fast and rewarded Mäkinen with second fastest, just behind that man Elford again. As predicted, Mäkinen had made good use of his tyres but he, like most others, arrived back at Monte Carlo with eight very worn-out tyres. Mäkinen, however, was still not happy with his brakes and so the rear brakes were changed before Monte Carlo. Elford unsurprisingly was leading but Mäkinen was laying third overall, and if the weather turned the Mini would be better placed in the snow.

Upon arrival at the Monte time control, to book in and have his tyres inspected (to see if they were all present and correct) he parked the car and again headed off to the mountains above Monte Carlo to review the road conditions. He would once more have to select his tyres for the mountain circuit the following evening. This leg, only open to the top 60 cars, again included six stages of around 75 miles including three runs up the Col de Turini. This 12-hour race over the mountains, although just over 385 miles in length, meant, to allow time for numerous tyre swaps and service, the pace was to be fast and furious. Once again, after much deliberation, Mäkinen selected four plain SP44 tyres and four half-studded SP44s for the mountain circuit.

At 7pm the first car left Monte Carlo for the mountains. The first stage near Sospel, through the Gorge De Pion, was dry but with many hairpin bends with some ice, it caught out several. Mäkinen was second, just behind Elford, but was now having brake troubles and had a rear wheel cylinder changed

Mäkinen and Easter were keen to avenge their 1966 lighting disqualification, and put up blisteringly fast times.

by the service crew.

By then spots of rain were falling and that could only mean snow was on its way on high ground. The first of three trips up the Col de Turini was next and, despite some fog at the top, Mäkinen was very fast and took 23 seconds off Elford to claim his first stage win. However, the mostly dry roads were still taking their toll on the tyres, with Mäkinen still trying to look after his studded tyres. With continued brake problems Mäkinen had another wheel cylinder changed at the next service. The Col de Couillole stage followed and by now it was snowing, but with his brake problems still not cured, he finished the stage tenth – albeit only 11 seconds down on Elford. Mäkinen was now in the lead.

The snow was now becoming heavier and as Mäkinen headed for the second run at the Turini, disaster struck. A huge boulder, possibly dislodged by the rain (or possibly not...) crashed down in front of the car; it initially missed the Mini but it hit the retaining wall and then bounced into the front of the car. It was impossible to avoid at what was 75mph. In a split second the oil cooler, starter motor and distributor were damaged. Hasty repairs, in the snow and dark, bypassing the oil cooler and refitting a repaired distributor, eventually got them going again but the half-hour lateness allowance had evaporated and they were out. They made it down the hill to the waiting service car and retired to the nearest bar.

Elford ran out of tyres and a late charge by Ove Andersson, in a works Lancia, came just a little too late, leaving Rauno Aaltonen with the win by a scant 13 seconds. Mäkinen's 'third' win had evaded him.

Disaster struck LBL66D on the second of their trips to the Col du Turini when a dislodged bolder crashed down in front of the car, smashing the oil cooler, starter and distributor. Repairs to get them going saw them still classified as finishers but down in 41st place.

By the final night of the 1967 Monte Carlo Rally, Mäkinen and Easter found themselves into the lead with three trips to the Col du Turini to undertake on the final mountain circuit.

The car was loaned out after the Monte to the BMC publicity department – even in its initial damaged condition – and was displayed in the window of BMC's showroom and head office in the West End of London, complete with mocked-up large snowball in front of the damaged car. The car was returned to Abingdon during the following November.

The next event for LBL 66D was the Tulip Rally held in late April 1968. During the intervening 15 months since its last appearance on the 1967 Monte, much had changed – not least, the Mk2 Mini was introduced at the Earls Court Motor Show in October 1967. There were also new masters at the head of the company. At the end of January 1968, BLMC was formed with a merger of British Motor Holdings (as BMC had become a year earlier) and Leyland Motor Corporation, which included Triumph and Leyland Cars. Although George Harriman was chairman (a strong supporter of Abingdon), Lord Stokes was appointed as managing director (who was not) and would, over time, see a redirection in Abingdon's activities and then ultimate closure.

A Mk2 Cooper S was built up by Gerald Wiffen for Timo Mäkinen and Paul Easter as a powerful Group 2. This was not a Mk1 that was trimmed and badged as a Mk2, as some were, which is evident by the car having a larger rear window. Mk2s were only slightly different from the Mk1s they replaced and were mechanically identical; the changes were only cosmetic, being mainly a new front grille, badges and a wider rear screen (which this car did have) and large rear lights. Internally, however, the cars appeared quite different, with a now-all-black interior.

Abingdon at this time was losing the power battle, with strong opposition from Porsche and Alpine Renault. To try and arrest this power difference, Abingdon, with help from Mäkinen – who found a pair of modified Weber carburettors in Finland – tried them on the works cars. They were a pair of Weber 45DCOE carburettors, which had one choke machined off each, then had a stub tube welded to the carburettor to allow it to be mounted directly onto a Mini inlet manifold. Cliff Humphries, who was Abingdon's engine man, set about testing and devising a way these split carbs could legally be fitted to a standard Cooper S inlet manifold, which under Group 2 rules they were obliged to use. He came up with what Abingdon called a 'prototype carburettor', the result of

LBL 66D was loaned out to BMC publicity and was shown, complete with damaged front, at BMC's main showroom in the West End of London.

CHAPTER 3: THE MK 1 MINI COOPER S

LBL 66D now appeared in Mk2 form. This was not a cosmetically converted Mk1. We now see body-coloured wheelarch extensions and square number plates on the bonnet.

Scrutineering in Noordwijk in Holland for the 1968 Tulip Rally. LBL 66D for Mäkinen and Easter is car 73; the car in the foreground, number 74, is for Julien Vernaeve and Mike Wood.

LBL 66D with ORX 707F line up before the start of the 1968 Tulip Rally with their gold-painted 5½J Minilite wheels.

which was a gain of 7bhp and more mid-range torque, giving 93bhp at the wheels.

The powerful 1293cc engine was fitted with a high-compression Downton cylinder head giving 12.6: compression ratio, forged pistons and an AEA648 race camshaft. The engine was now fitted with straight-cut drop gears with a roller bearing on the idler gear, replacing the standard helical transfer. The inlet manifold was located to the cylinder head by standard locating rings rather than being pegged. Engine cooling was by a Cooper S radiator, a four-blade fan and an MG Midget water pump. A straight-cut close-ratio gearbox with a 4.2:1 final drive plus enlarged diameter drive shafts was fitted. Underneath, the engine and gearbox were protected by a 13-hole Moke sump guard and a Moke plate screwed to the base of the gearbox. Hydrolastic suspension, with a rear anti-roll bar, was used with single-blue and double-blue displacers front and back, without front dampers but with orange helper springs at the rear.

The brakes were improved, with the callipers having asbestos blocks fitted into the pistons to take excess heat away from the brake fluid; the rear wheel cylinders were threaded so they were fixed to the backplate with a large nut rather than a circlip, also to take heat away from the brake fluid. As the Tulip was an all-tarmac rally, for the first time the car was fitted with 5½J Minilite wheels and these, to ease identification, were painted gold; they were fitted with Dunlop R7 race tyres. To cover these wider wheels, even wider wheelarch extensions were fitted to the car, painted red. The bonnet had the number plate painted on the offside, and the rally plate fixed to the other side of the bonnet.

Lucas wired the car to the usual high standard; it ran an alternator, largely because of four additional lamps: two fog lamps and two driving lamps were fixed to a lamp bar, connected by a five-pin rubber socket and the two driving lamps secured by steady bars. European headlamps with Perspex protective covers were fitted with iodine bulbs, as were the extra lamps.

The driver's auxiliary dash panel had the oil pressure gauge moved next to the rev counter and in its place in the binnacle was the water temperature gauge, which gave its previous position to a circular fuel gauge. The co-driver's instrument panel housed his usual Halda distance recorder, a pair of Heuer clocks and numerous other controls; he also had a switch panel

295

in his door pocket. As he now had an expansion tank from the radiator by his feet in the footwell, the Tudor electric screen washer bottles were moved to the rear of the car on the driver's side. The co-driver also had a foot-operated horn switch.

A fibreglass bucket seat, covered in black cord material for the driver and a reclining high-back seat for the co-driver, were fitted on modified seat brackets. An Irvin lap-and-diagonal seatbelt for Mäkinen, which he hardly ever wore, and a full=harness Irvin belt for Easter were also fitted. All standard trim and glass had to be retained under Group 2 regulations, including the carpets. Padding to the door pockets, door locks, co-driver's rear pocket bin corner and door pillars added to crew comfort. The roll cage, which also housed the intercom box, was also padded. All lines were run inside the car, with the fuel pump located under the rear seat.

Starting in Noordwijk on the west cost of Holland, the route of some 2200-mile went to Annecy in France via the Ardennes, Vosges and Jura Mountains, and back four days later to Holland. The route, very similar to 1967, attracted just 77 starters who had eight special stages ahead of them with target times (many of which were cleaned by top crews), and two very important eliminating tests decided on scratch times. These stages and tests were interspersed with many quickly-timed road sections, and were particularly demanding on the mountain circuit from Annecy to Rumilly.

An early morning start saw the cars head for the first test at the Zolder race circuit, where the powerful cars headed the list. Then followed a long run to the Vosges and the St Odile hillclimb, which was better suited to the Mini, where Mäkinen was sixth fastest. The fast road sections that followed saw everyone, other than Mäkinen and Roger Clark in the works Escort Twin Cam, drop time. The next two stages were cleaned by Mäkinen and many more, so proved of no value.

Into the night and there was another long haul to the Jura Mountains on the route to Annecy. Service before Annecy saw Mäkinen have fresh tyres and his clutch adjusted before heading for parc fermé and a ten-hour rest during the day before setting off again the following evening, along with 67 other cars. He was now lying in fourth place overall and leading the touring car class behind the two works Escorts and a Renault Alpine.

The second night saw a 300-mile six-hour fast section to Rumilly, where only ten cars arrived without time loss. Mäkinen was still without any time penalties. Snow had blocked a pass near Thono and many cars took the wrong route, costing them time. Service at Rumilly, in time for breakfast, and Mäkinen had the timing adjusted as he was complaining the car was down on power. He collected a rear puncture on the Mont Clergeon stage, which was over 12 miles long, and he carried on for over eight miles on the rim, arriving at the end with the carcass shredded around the destroyed Minilite. Miraculously, he lost only 44 seconds and was still fourth fastest.

The early-season fine, warm weather was by then deteriorating into rain. This was actually welcome by Mäkinen, as apart from reducing the advantage that the more powerful cars had on what were now slippery roads, the lower air temperature meant the engine, which was susceptible to overheating, was running cooler.

The weather deteriorated further as the route headed back to the Jura Mountains and then onto to Vosges. Very uncharacteristically Mäkinen left the road on stage 12, on the Col du Brabant. Strangely, this was a relatively easy stage where he was not driving flat-out, but he misjudged the road, flew off down a bank and into a field. Unable to drive back, the Mini was stuck. Easter headed back to the start to inform the marshals they had gone off, and on his return found Mäkinen had summoned a small army of locals to manhandle the car back onto the road. In return, assuming they were out, he gave them their rally plates. They had been off the road for just over an hour.

Once mobile again, Easter calculated that if they drove flat-out they might just get to the next time control at Sarrebourg in time. This was 65 miles away, which they made just in time and convinced the marshals that their rally plates had been stolen by locals when they went off. They had averaged well over 60mph to get there.

Several stages were cleaned by many and with Mäkinen's time loss of over an hour it was all rather academic. Into the last night, the leading Renault Alpine of Andruet retired, leaving the two Escort TCs of Roger Clark and Ove Andersson in an unassailable position. Back at Noordwijk, the next morning, Mäkinen found himself again in 41st place, just as in the Monte after the accident, but it was calculated by Easter that if they hadn't gone off nor had the puncture they could have won the Tulip by a scant single second.

LBL 66D was kept at Abingdon well past the normal

Mäkinen and Easter were setting their usual fast pace in the mostly wet conditions. Uncharacteristically Mäkinen left the road on the Col du Brabant and lost an hour extracting the car. Driving flat out, he made the next control just in time but was again placed 41st.

CHAPTER 3: THE MK 1 MINI COOPER S

time when used rally cars were moved on. It was used for recce work and met its end when Paddy Hopkirk and Tony Nash used the car for their recce for the 1969 Tour de France. Travelling quickly on the Chamrousse hillclimb near Grenoble and on racing tyres, a gravel-strewn hairpin caught Hopkirk out and, on full lock, the fat racing tyre jammed in the wheelarch, spun the car around, sending it over the edge; the car ended up wedged upside down between a rock face and a tree. With fuel spilling out, they quickly kicked the screen out. However, the car was perilously unstable and they had to hold the car until help arrived. John Handley and Paul Easter were soon on the scene and, with the help of a local with a tractor; the car was righted and pulled back up to the road. An adventurous end to the car.

LBL 66D was sold to Les Lambourne, who was the MG plant director at Abingdon

Paddy Hopkirk and Tony Nash used LBL 66D for their recce for the 1969 Tour de France but went off the road near Grenoble with dire results.

Competition Record

Date	Event	Crew	Number	Overall result	Class result
Jan 1967	Monte Carlo Rally	Timo Mäkinen/Paul Easter	144	41st	
April 1968	Tulip Rally	Timo Mäkinen/Paul Easter	73	41st	

Registration Number	First registered	Chassis number	Engine	Engine number	Model
LBL 666D	Dec 1966	CA2S7 956254	1275cc	9F-SA-Y 43696	Austin Cooper S

LBL 666D, an Austin Cooper S, was the third of the new batch of Cooper Ss delivered to Abingdon for the 1967 Monte Carlo Rally in January. Abingdon had, for many years, managed to get consecutive numbers for works Minis from the local registration authorities, and this one was registered in December 1966 as the third in the line as LBL 666D.

The car was assigned to Paddy Hopkirk and Ron Crellin. The Group 2 car was built by Gerald Wiffen and followed very similar lines to the build of its sister cars, as standardisation was now becoming very prevalent. This helped on event servicing, when multiple cars were being entered and the build could also be standardised.

The heart of the car was a 1293cc engine, overbored by 0.020in to get to the near limit of the 1300cc class. Abingdon by then was primarily interested in overall positions, rather than simply class wins. Fitted with a high-compression gas-flowed Downton cylinder head, this with the pistons machined to within 0.010in of the top of the engine block, gave a high 12.6:1 compression ratio. The by-now-almost-

LBL 666D in which Paddy Hopkirk and Ron Crellin were entered in for the 1967 Monte Carlo Rally, with the rally plate initially fitted to the bonnet.

297

Boot detail of LBL 666D showing the twin tanks protected by asbestos sheet, a rubber fuel bag held secure by a bungee strap and the Tyre-and-Fire tyre inflater by the right-hand tank.

The rear seat squab of LBL 666D held vertical by leather straps so that two spare wheels can be clamped to the vacant seat pan. The tool roll hangs over the seat and the fuel pump under the rear seat.

Interior of LBL 666D showing dashboard arrangement typical of the layout of that time. Windscreen washer bottle lower left.

The respective seats fitted to LBL 666D. Both red and grey cloth covered, a fibreglass bucket seat for Hopkirk and a modified high-back recliner for Crellin.

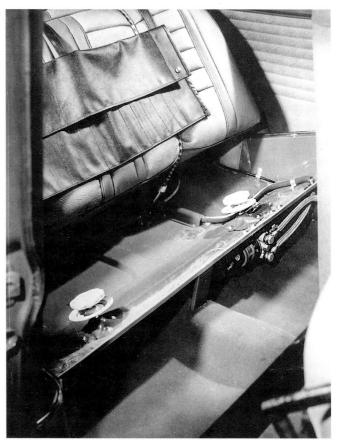

standard full race-camshaft gave power at the wheels of 95bhp (one more than LBL 66D had at its disposal). The twin H4SU carburettors had a modified fork-and-peg linkage to remove the strain on the throttle cable, and the fuel delivery banjo bolts were wire-locked to prevent them loosening and pumping fuel over the hot exhaust manifold. The gearbox was straight-cut close-ratio, but with helical drop gears, and the remote gearchange used a Mitchell mounting, designed to be indestructible. The diff ratio was 4.2:1, using a special enlarged driveshaft. An oil cooler was of course fitted but was relocated further over on its mounting platform to clear the large alternator; this in turn meant that the front panel diagonal stiffener plate had to be repositioned into a vertical position adjacent.

Suspension was Hydrolastic, with single-blue displacers for the front and double-blue units on the rear. The rear had orange helper springs and heavy-duty bump stops, and the front end also had heavy-duty bump stops – all designed to stiffen the suspension and reduce the tendency to pitch, which was an affliction associated with Hydrolastic suspension. A standard ride height was set.

All wheel bearings used high-temperature grease and the rear bearings were Timken roller bearings rather than the standard ball race bearing, which had, on occasions, proved troublesome in replacing. Brakes were standard Cooper S but with the use of high-temperature disc pads and rear linings; the brake servo was retained and fitted in the standard position under the bonnet. New for the Monte were Minilite wheels, cast in magnesium for light weight and strength, offering a considerable weight saving over standard Cooper S steel wheels.

To accommodate these magnesium wheels, which had a similar offset to the wide Cooper S steel wheels, fibreglass wheelarch extensions were fitted to the car. Rear mud flaps were a mandatory requirement for the Monte and the car also had large forward-facing mud flaps fitted to the front panel by the bumper corners – designed to keep muck off of the 'screen and headlamps. The headlamps were also protected by Perspex covers, held in place by straps onto the wing and front panel. Quick-lift jacking points were fitted front and back to quickly raise the car with the racing jack that the service crew carried around. Tow eyes were fitted to the front of the car but not to the rear.

To keep snow (and cold) out of the engine, a grille muff was made in the MG trim shop at Abingdon, and this was fitted to the grille moustache with Lift-the-Dot studs. It had opening flaps for the oil cooler and to allow more air to the engine.

Four extra lamps were fitted to the car on a badge bar crafted from a heavy angle iron, which was chrome-plated and fitted low by the bumper on three quick-release fixings. These four lamps, all separately switched, consisted of two fog lamps and two driving lamps. Hopkirk always had his fog lamp beams crossing in front of the car, rather than outwards. All lamps

A fully-studded Dunlop Weathermaster SP44 tyre on 4½J magnesium Minilite wheel under black fibreglass wheelarch extensions; also the fuel filler cap secured by a chain.

had quartz iodine bulbs, as did the European headlamps, which had a vertical dip. To power these extra lamps and the heated front windscreen, a high-output alternator was fitted.

The car was completely rewired from scratch to ensure everything was as reliable as possible. All electrical connections were both crimped and soldered. A large-capacity battery was fitted with its terminal away from the side of the fuel tank should this be moved over in a side impact; it was also insulated from the cold, in its battery box, with a foam lining. The battery cable was run inside the car, as were the fuel line and brake line. The twin fuel pump was located out of harm's way (and the cold) underneath the rear seat. Twin tanks were fitted with their filler caps held on with small chains; the interconnecting pipe between the tanks was enlarged to encourage a faster flow between the tanks and the pump. The tanks were protected from damage from carrying studded tyres by sticking thin asbestos sheets to the sides of the tanks.

Inside the car, dashboards faced each crew member. Hopkirk's housed the rev counter, a special switch to operate the heated front 'screen and numerous switches and controls. Crellin had his distance recorder and watches, with additional switches. The distance recorder and speedo were calibrated to read in kilometres. He in addition had a foot-operated horn button and another switch panel in his door pocket for his map light and more switches.

A comfortable high-back reclining seat was supplied for Crellin, whilst Hopkirk had a cloth-covered bucket seat.

WORKS MINIS IN DETAIL

Hopkirk and Crellin on their journey to Monte Carlo in LBL666D from their difficult start from Athens. The roof rack and tyres were removed once the serious competition started. The yellow door square indicates they were restricted to eight tyres per competitive section.

Crellin had a full harness belt and Hopkirk a lap-and-diagonal belt, both made by the Irvin Parachute Company. There was padding supplied to the door pillar, door locks and pocket side and the alloy roll cage. Their crash helmets were stowed on the rear parcel shelf.

The car had to be adapted to carry four spare wheels because of the tyre restriction class they had entered (see below). Provision therefore had to be made for two wheels and tyres to be housed inside the car. They were fitted on the rear seat pan, which meant that to comply with Group 2 regulations they had to retain the rear seat cushion somewhere, so this was fixed onto the back of the seat with long leather straps. A roof rack was fitted for the long run down to Monte Carlo and this housed two extra wheels and tyres. It was removed once they arrived at Monte Carlo for the competitive stages, as were the front-facing mud flaps. The high-back reclining seat, which weighed some 41lb, was also removed at Monte Carlo, replaced by a standard Mini seat, with a supportive seat cover, which weighed in at just 18lb.

The final piece of car preparation happened just before the start in Athens, when word came down from Stuart Turner that the organisers were insisting that front-facing rally plates had to be fixed vertically. Den Green with Gerald Wiffen, who built the car and would service it on its way to Monte Carlo, quickly got to work. The rally plate was relocated from the bonnet and fixed vertically on the front bumper. This partially obscured the oil cooler but with the prevailing cold weather it was not considered detrimental.

With one Monte win under his belt, in 1964 with 33 EJB, Hopkirk was hopeful for another. And after the disappointment of the disqualification last year he, along with the rest of the Abingdon team, was determined to win again. With the five-car team being sent to four different locations around Europe for their respective starts, Hopkirk, it was decided, should start from Athens. This was by means of a publicity appeasement after his problems with the organisers of the Acropolis Rally in 1966 (see GRX 311D). It was also to help relations with the local BMC agent in Athens, Ducas Brothers. As it transpired, Hopkirk and Crellin were made to feel very welcome and he received a great reception from everyone in Athens.

The Monte for 1967 was to be different as far as tyres were concerned: the organisers put in place two categories. The first allowed free choice of any number of tyres throughout the rally. The second would mean cars were restricted to just eight tyres on each of the two competitive legs of the rally; these when they had reached Monte Carlo. The problem was if a crew elected to have unlimited tyres, they had a handicap of 12.5 per cent added to their stage times. This, everyone

Tyres, for those electing to be restricted to eight tyres, were branded with hot irons. These were checked at random points to see the car still had all eight tyres and also at the finish.

concluded, was too big a handicap to overcome and so all bar 17 cars entered the restricted-tyre category. This, however, only applied on the two competitive loops once in Monte Carlo; the route to Monte did not have tyre restrictions, so extra wheels and tyres were carried on a roof rack on the car. Cars in the restricted-tyre category all had yellow door squares, rather than white, to distinguish them. The other downside of the eight-tyres category was that the car had to have all eight wheels and tyres with them, meaning most cars had to accommodate at least two extra wheels and tyres (and the extra weight).

For BMC, the added problem was the simple fact that a hard-driven works Mini could destroy a set of front tyres in no time at all, especially if they were incorrect tyres for the prevailing conditions. Dunlop therefore spent a lot of time developing tyres that would hopefully last the distance. Tyre testing had been carried out extensively with BMC works drivers in the Alps for several months prior to the rally, along with their normal recce and practice. Despite the restrictions, Dunlop still provided over 400 tyres for the five works Minis, which was actually a fraction of the number supplied in 1966, when no restriction on tyres was in place.

Stuart Turner's task in the organisation of five works cars and all of the many personnel scattered around Europe, their travel, accommodation and itinerary was considerable. This was, however, to be Turner's last big event for the team as he was moving to Castrol in the next few months, handing over to Peter Browning. It was indeed a baptism of fire for Browning, learning what he would then be expected to do. Accounting for over 40 people and 20 vehicles was no mean task.

As it transpired, Hopkirk's start from Athens was not an inspired choice, as the Athens starters encountered very severe weather in their journey to Monte Carlo. Of the rally's 185 entrants, only ten had elected to start from Athens and, because of the terrible weather, only three cars made it to Monte Carlo. Fortunately, Hopkirk was one of them.

After an early morning start from Athens they soon found the road blocked by heavy snow and abandoned trucks near Larissa, so were forced to turn around and take a long detour via Volos, approaching a control from the wrong direction but unpenalised. Much snow was found in Yugoslavia – it was so deep that at one point that they had to dig at the snow for 20 minutes, then charge the Mini at the snow drift to clear a path through. Another road blockage saw them convince a rather idle snowplough driver to get to work and open the road. They were joined by the Oslo and Warsaw starters in northern Italy, where they still encountered freezing fog and ice until the weather eased as they neared Monaco. Hopkirk arrived with a clean time card, which in the circumstances was a great achievement.

Then Hopkirk had to consider what tyres he would take on the first competitive leg the next day, the 24-hour loop to Chambéry and back. The 785-mile loop contained six stages, and tyre choice would be important. With Hopkirk's experience in actually getting to Monte Carlo fresh in his mind, his tyre choice was cautious and so he decided to take four plain SP44s and four half-studded SP44s. These tyres were painted and branded, so they could be checked at any point, and the car put away in parc fermé.

The next day, the 173 survivors set off on the common run. The first stage, St Auban, was dry and Hopkirk, with his SP44s was not in the top ten. Mont Ventoux followed and that too was dry apart from ice at the very top. Hopkirk was fifth but the car's engine was running hot, so the grille muff was removed to try and lower its temperature. Black ice was in evidence on the Col du Rousset stage and Hopkirk swapped his tyres front to back; with the good tyres he was second only to the powerful Porsche of Vic Elford.

Hopkirk would again be second on the very long fourth stage culminating in the Col du Granier. This much-practised stage by Hopkirk saw rutted ice on the higher ground but his studded tyres served him well. The Gap to Valserres stage was free of snow and ice but still Hopkirk recorded second fastest, beating Elford by 10 seconds. The final stage, the very twisty Levens stage, which was completely dry, saw Hopkirk down in sixth place with what were now very worn-out tyres. No spare tyres were carried by the service crews, through fear of accusations of cheating; they were, however, allowed to carry wheel rims and inner tubes – which were not restricted. However, Hopkirk was still having cooling problems, so the

Hopkirk and Crellin descending the Col du Turini on the last night's snowy conditions.

thermostat was changed before Monte Carlo.

Once checked in back at Monte Carlo, he joined other BMC crews in numerous recce cars to investigate the condition of the roads in the mountains above Monaco, which would be used the following night for the mountain circuit. The 12-hour thrash was only open to the top 60 cars, so 40 cars, now classified as finishers, had to sit out the last night. Six stages were again to be tackled, three of which were on the Col du Turini. For the final night Hopkirk again selected four plain SP44s and four half-studded SP44s with the hope that the weather would produce snow and allow the Mini to outstrip the Elford Porsche, which was now leading Hopkirk by just 27 seconds.

The following evening, Hopkirk set off on the 380-mile mountain circuit. However, he was still having problems with an overheating engine. Once again the thermostat was changed and he only just made the next time control at Sospel. Hopkirk could not improve his position on the first stage, the Gorge de Pion, which was mainly dry and despite the numerous hairpin bends, had to concede another ten seconds to Elford.

Rain had started to fall as he approached the Col de Turini and by now Hopkirk's studded tyres were being ruined (as indeed were Elford's). Hopkirk could do no better than ninth.

The Col de Couillole stage was next, which was mainly dry, with some snow at the top, but with his tyres suffering he was still fourth. The second visit to the Turini followed and saw Hopkirk slip further back with seventh fastest, and it was now snowing. Stage five, a second visit to the Couillole, saw it snowing very hard, with 2in lying on the road. Hopkirk, now with virtually useless tyres, spun twice.

The final stage, the last trip to the Turini, saw all hope lost as he again spun twice and had, despite having high hopes going into the last night in second place, to settle for sixth overall. Consolation was that Aaltonen, in the other team car, had won, so BMC had won and avenged its disappointment from the previous year.

After the Monte Carlo Rally, LBL 666D was shipped off to the BMC publicity department to be used as a display car to promote the Monte success of LBL 6D. It was used on numerous publicity shots, and LBL 666D was returned to Abingdon towards the end of the year.

Its activities during 1968 are not recorded and it may well have been used as a recce car, but by the time 1969 came along many changes had taken place at Abingdon. With the new company (BLMC) now being headed by Lord Stokes, severe financial cuts were placed on the competition budget. Stokes was not a fan of motorsport, nor did he see its value in selling cars. He decided that Abingdon should concentrate on racing rather than rallying, in his view it being more in the public eye. BMC, as it was, had been racing Minis successfully with John Cooper for many years. Stokes saw no reason to continue that relationship, so cancelled Cooper's contract, deciding that Abingdon would now represent BLMC on the racetrack.

Browning managed to secure John Rhodes's signature to drive for Abingdon, attracting him away from Cooper. John Rhodes was of course no stranger to racing Minis; he had raced F3 Cooper single-seaters but was more successful racing in spectacular tyre-smoking style in Minis for the Cooper Car Company. He had won the 1300cc class in the British Saloon Car Championship from 1964 through to 1968 and he also won the 1968 European Saloon Car Championship for Cooper, so he was a big scalp for Abingdon. He would be partnered by the experienced John Handley, a great test driver, who had raced for British Vita. Cooper would continue racing with Minis, now sponsored by Britax and Downton, and would appear in striking bright yellow paintwork, driven very effectively by Gordon Spice and Steve Neal.

Internally things at Abingdon also changed. Den Green was made responsible for building and maintaining the race Minis. Doug Watts would look after the diminished rally programme and Tommy Wellman took over responsibility for the rallycross cars. At the same time, Bill Price was promoted to assistant competitions manager and would be in control of the race programme. It would prove a testing year for Abingdon.

LBL 666D, as a Mk2 Group 5 race car, had its first race in the Martini International at Silverstone in May, which was the fifth round of the British Saloon Car Championship (BSCC). Although Abingdon was not a contender for overall race wins, the BSCC was decided on class wins, so if Abingdon was consistently successful in the class it could win the

Hopkirk and Crellin cross the finish line having overcome numerous problems, mostly running out of tyres, to finish in sixth place.

championship, as Cooper had for the past five years.

Testing, the week before at Silverstone, saw Rhodes at the circuit with GRX 310D to try different suspension setups and wheel and tyre options. The car, with a similar engine, ran dry suspension but with Hydrolastic top arms, Mini van rear struts and adjustable bottom arms. It ran 2 degree negative camber at the front, with 0.5 degree at the rear. It also used lightweight Minifin rear brake drums. Cooper Rose Petal 7J wheels were fitted to the front and 6J to the rear, needing 7/8in spacers. Quick-lift jacking points were fitted to the car, painted in body colour.

The car appeared for the race with the following specification: its 1293cc engine was dry decked with a Mk2 Weslake cylinder head with 13:1 compression. This was fuel-injected with Lucas throttle slide and with splayed BMC pipes. An auxiliary radiator was fitted to try and keep the water temperature under control.

The car was fitted with a 3.765:1 Salisbury limited-slip diff, which was set at 115lb.ft. The suspension was by rubber cone with Hydrolastic top arms and Hydrolastic trailing arms and fitted with Koni shock absorbers set at half-a-turn off their maximum. It also ran a rear anti-roll bar. Front negative camber arms were set at 1 degree with 2.5 degrees castor angle and 0.5 degree negative camber at the rear. The front negative camber had been reduced on the front, after practice, as the temperature of the tyres' outside edges was too high.

A Group 6 dual-circuit tandem braking system was fitted, with DS11 brake pads and VG 95 brake shoes. Wheels and tyres were 7J Minilites on the front and 6J on the rear, with Dunlop D22-232 tyres set at 50psi front and 45psi rear, which were covered by wide wheelarch extensions with a chrome finisher strip. The fuel filler neck was set into the bodywork, as this was required by the regulations, where the cap was considered too vulnerable in the event of an accident. The car, when weighed with a full tank of fuel, was 1393lb (633kg).

Practice for the 20-lap race, on a dry track on the fast Northamptonshire circuit, saw Rhodes on the third row of the grid just ahead of his teammate Handley on the fourth row. Both, however, were headed by the Britax-Coopers of Spice and Neal. Come race day, the track was wet, which was hoped would favour the Mini.

The track had started to dry after the preceding sports car race and Rhodes was quickly put on dry race tyres for the race; many stayed on intermediate tyres. This proved to be a wise choice. As the flag dropped for the 38 cars, Rhodes had a good start but was still behind Spice and Neal, who promptly obliged him by hitting each other on the first lap. Neal went for the inside of Spice at Club corner, went sideways and Spice clobbered him. The result was that Spice rolled into retirement and Neal was delayed with a badly-damaged car and struggled home in 14th place. Rhodes was now up to eighth place and hard-charging. He collected body damage on the front corner but this did not stop him recording the

John Rhodes with LBL 666D, now as a Mk2 race car, at Silverstone for the Martini International, round five of the British Saloon Car Championship. The car now fitted with 12in Minilite wheels, homologated a few weeks prior.

Rhodes lost a wheelarch extension with a clash with another car but still finished sixth overall.

class lap record and he finished a fine sixth overall and second in class, which was won by Chris Craft in his Broadspeed Escort 1300GT. The overall winner was Roy Pierpoint in a big Ford Falcon.

The next round of the BSCC, round six, followed a week later, at the lovely circuit just outside London at Crystal Place. This challenging but rather narrow circuit meant that the race was divided in two, with the first race being for larger-capacity cars and the second, the Anerley Trophy, for up-to-1300cc cars. At least the Minis would not be outshone by the bigger cars on their race for a change.

Rhodes would be using LBL 666D virtually unchanged from the specification used at Silverstone. Visually the only

Rhodes at the London Crystal Palace race for the sixth round of the BSCC. The car is little changed bar for the front jacking points now painted white.

A race-long battle with the Broadspeed Escort, which would repeat for most of the season. Rhodes finished well in fourth place.

minor differences were the quick-lift jacking points were of a different type and painted white. The practice didn't go well for Rhodes as he had a persistent misfire, which resulted in number three and four plugs becoming oiled. He did, however, still beat the class lap record, but had to settle behind the two Britax cars of Spice and Neal, along with that of Handley in the sister Abingdon car. After practice it was decided to change Rhodes's engine for the spare, which was R4 – he had been using R8. Therefore, the engine was likely to have been an older unit. Significantly, the unit was fitted with a 3.9 final drive and after the race Rhodes conceded that a 4.1 would have been a more suitable choice for the circuit, negating the use of second gear on some corners.

With Spice on pole (in his spare car after his Silverstone accident) he was alongside two Broadspeed Escorts, and at the start he roared ahead with Neal and Handley close by, and with Rhodes trailing the leading five cars. Rhodes eventually passed Handley and then Neal, and was soon up to third place as the Broadspeed Escort of Fitzpatrick dropped back. Rhodes was now catching Spice and up to second place, having passed the second Broadspeed Escort of Craft, when his replacement engine also started to lose power and noticeably burn oil. He started to fall back, eventually being overtaken by Handley and having to settle for fourth place with a rather sick engine. Spice won the class, a whisker ahead of the Craft Escort.

Mallory Park in Leicestershire was the next time LBL 666D was raced, again with John Rhodes at the wheel. The Guards 4000 Guineas International, round seven of the BSCC, was held over 20 laps on 29 June. The engine was the same unit as used at Crystal Palace the previous month, albeit rebuilt after its previous plug-oiling episode; it was unchanged in specification, as was the setup, other than the adjustable bottom arms were now at 1 degree negative, not 1.5 degrees. This was in an attempt to reduce tyre temperature.

Like the Crystal Palace meeting, there were two races for the saloon cars, where all the Minis were in the up-to-1300cc race, with larger cars scrapping amongst themselves in their own race, both held over 20 laps. Practice was again problematic for Rhodes when the car developed severe clutch slip after 19 laps, which meant a new clutch for the race. Nevertheless only one second separated the two Abingdon cars from the Britax Coopers of Neal and Spice, but as was customary the two Britax cars headed Rhodes and Handley on the starting grid.

At the end of the first lap Rhodes lay ahead of Handley but behind Spice, Neal and the Escort of Chris Craft. As the race wore on Handley retired and Rhodes started to experience tyre problems. Rhodes had to settle for fourth place, much as where he started and just behind Neal, with Spice and Craft finishing in a dead heat some way ahead. Post-event showed that the Dunlop D22-232s had shown severe cracking of the tread, with the Britax cars experiencing a similar fate with their D15-232s. Dunlop would have some work to do to satisfy these two tyre-hungry teams, where again tyre

CHAPTER 3: THE MK 1 MINI COOPER S

Rhodes in a virtually unchanged LBL 666D at Mallory Park for the seventh BSCC round, seen here with Fitzpatrick ahead, with Neal, Enever and Handley behind him.

Rhodes finished behind the two Britax cars, being slowed by excessive tyre temperature.

In the paddock at Silverstone with LBL 666D for Rhodes with Handley's sister car, LRX 827E with the bonnet up behind with the eight-port head just visible.

Rhodes in LBL 666D at Silverstone, showing the number plate at its usual angle. Also the recessed fuel filler cap and the breather pipe routed up the rear seam and the electrical cut-out on the rear apron.

temperature seemed to be their undoing.

The support race at the prestigious British Grand Prix at Silverstone was the next race on 19 July. This was the ninth round of the BSCC, and the works Minis were still struggling to come on terms with the two Britax-Coopers, and all were bested by the 1300 Ford Escorts. This would continue throughout the season. John Rhodes was again at the wheel of LBL 666D, where the car was little changed from Mallory Park, the Group 5 car being fuel injected and with a Weslake crossflow cylinder head. For Silverstone a 3.9:1 Salisbury diff was used, set at 115lb. The car was still running on dry rubber suspension, albeit with Hydrolastic top arms. For Silverstone

WORKS MINIS IN DETAIL

Oulton Park, for round ten of the BSCC, sees LBL 666D now fitted with extra-wide wheelarch extensions without chrome trim and rally-style front jacking points.

Rhodes was to finish a disappointing 12th place and by now the championship had been won by Alec Poole in the one-litre Mini.

Minis, who by lap seven were all very close when they all came together at Copse Corner. Rhodes escaped relatively unscathed, other than a dent to his bodywork just behind the driver's door, but Handley and Neal lost time regaining the track. Spice went on to finish clear of Rhodes, who finished in eighth place and fourth in class, one place behind Spice. The class was won by Chris Craft in a Broadspeed Escort 1300.

The next round of the BSCC, round ten, held at Oulton Park on 16 August was the support race to the Formula 1 Gold Cup meeting and Rhodes was in the car again. With the championship drawing to a close, Abingdon was still scrapping with the Britax-Cooper team but it was Alec Poole who, in the Arden eight-port one-litre Mini, was leading the championship due to his multiple class wins.

Weslake had done more work on the eight-port engine in an attempt to get on terms with the Britax cars. The rather special engine had the bore and stroke changed to give 1299cc – it being almost a square engine, with a bore of 74mm and special steel crank with a stroke of 75.5mm. Standard bore and stroke on a 1293cc engine is 71.12mm (0.020in) with a stroke of 81.28mm – so it was quite special. It was fitted with titanium conrods and used special slipper pistons. A windage plate was fitted between the engine and gearbox to reduce drag caused by oil spray flung up from the rotating gears below.

The new engine did have more power, and LBL 666D was now using a Salisbury 3.7:1 final drive. Cooling, which had been an issue, also received much attention with rerouted water pipes and an auxiliary radiator. The suspension, tyres and brakes remained unchanged but the car was now fitted with wider wheelarch extensions without a chrome finishing strip, and the front jacking points again changed to body-coloured rally type.

Practice had been hampered with intermittent rain, which upset the predicted grid. Rhodes was on row five alongside Spice but Neal was ahead on row three with Handley four rows further back. Neal, with the entire BSCC on the grid together, was after the opening lap, up to the ninth place, with Spice and Rhodes fighting out 13th and 14th places, with Handley a lowly 20th. On the dry circuit the larger-capacity cars were soon streets ahead and the Minis fell back.

Towards the end of the 19-lap race the four Minis started to bunch up, with Neal finishing in 12th place, heading off a hard-charging Rhodes in 13th place. Spice, with virtually no brakes, was close by, followed by Handley, who was just lapped by the leaders. Alec Poole, as predicted, won the championship by yet again winning his class. Abingdon and Cooper would have done well to have pooled their resources, rather than fighting each other, and foreseen the relatively easy path the one-litre car of Alec Poole had to championship laurels.

It was off to Brands Hatch in Kent on 1 September for the 11th round of the BSCC, and with the championship already won by Alec Poole, the race was of little consequence. Nevertheless, Rhodes was once again in LBL 666D, which was

the car ran Dunlop D22-232 tyres, with Koni adjustable dampers with camber set at 1 degree negative at the front and 2.5 caster angle.

The 20-lap race saw 30 saloon cars out on the Grand Prix circuit, with the front of the grid dominated by the bigger-capacity cars. Rhodes was, after practice, on the fourth row of the grid just behind the Britax-Cooper of Spice but ahead of Neal in the sister Britax car, with Handley in the other Abingdon car just behind.

From the flag, Spice headed Handley, who had started well, getting just ahead of Rhodes, with Neal two places further back. Spice started to pull away from the other three

CHAPTER 3: THE MK 1 MINI COOPER S

LBL 666D seen at Brands Hatch outside the Drivers' Club prior to the final round of the BSCC.

The car was little changed from how it appeared at the last race. Rhodes had a good race on the two-heat meeting, beating Spice around the last bend to finish just ahead of the Britax car claiming tenth place.

The final outing for Rhodes in LBL 666D was in Austria at the Salzburg ring. The car was converted to Group 2 with bumpers and other regulation requirements, seen here on the far right of the grid.

little changed from how it appeared at Oulton Park two weeks prior. Still with its very special short-stroke 1299cc engine, a successful finish at the end of the season was hoped for. The race was run over two 15-lap heats with the result decided on the cumulative times of the two. The starting order for the first heat was by normal practice lap times but for the second heat starting order was to be the finishing order of the first.

With a large field of 31 saloon cars using the very fast full Grand Prix circuit, the Evening News Trophy attracted a large crowd for this late-summer penultimate round of the championship. Rhodes qualified on the fifth row of the grid ahead of both the Britax-Cooper cars, which didn't have the advantage of the short-stoke engine that Rhodes had at his disposal. Spice, trying exceptionally hard in qualifying to get on terms, clipped the kerb at Paddock Bend and deflated the tyre, which jettisoned him into the bank, damaging the car considerably. He would take over Neal's sister car and start at the back of the grid.

In the first heat, Rhodes was initially running in 14th place and the leading Mini but behind the three class-winning Escorts. As the race wore on, he started to pick up places and at the flag finished in 11th place, with Spice four places back in 15th. Handley, in the other team car, had already retired with electrical problems. He would be destined to start at the back of the grid for the second heat.

The second heat, under damp conditions, saw Spice fit experimental grooved tyres to help in the slippery conditions and the ploy paid off, as he held off Rhodes until the very last lap, when his tyres started to go off on the now-dry track. Rhodes put in a supreme effort and passed Spice at Clearway, the final bend, to finish a foot ahead of the Britax car. Rhodes would finish in tenth place overall but still fourth in class behind the Escorts, the class again being won by Chris Craft's 1300 Escort.

This was the end of Abingdon's attempt to win the BSCC championship, as it would not contend the last round at Brands Hatch in late October. Rhodes would finish the championship in 18th place and fifth in the 1300 class, behind the Britax-Cooper pair of Spice and Neal in fifth and 15th place overall, which also meant they were second and fourth in their class. Clearly, Abingdon could not get on terms with the much more experienced Cooper Car Company team. With hindsight, Abingdon should have kept to rallying where its experience lay, but neither Abingdon nor Cooper expected the 1300 Escorts to be their beating either.

The final race outing for 1969 and the last race for LBL

WORKS MINIS IN DETAIL

LBL 666D looking quite different as a Group 2 car, with chrome bumpers but still fitted with extra-wide wheelarches. Rhodes would win the race and it was a good end to a troubled year, with teammate Handley in second place.

666D was held in Austria. The car was taken to Salzburg for the support race for the Donaupokal Race for Group 4 sports cars, held on 12 October at the high-speed Salzburgring. The support race was for Group 2 and Group 5 cars, so the Group 5 LBL 666D had a distinct advantage over many other cars, although it now was fitted with bumpers to the front and rear and appeared as a Group 2 car, and devoid of quick-lift jacking points. BL Austria had requested Abingdon contest the race for publicity purposes and the company was happy to oblige, sending two cars and a full support team. They were supported by another Mini, prepared by Don Wooding from Hamburg, who was an ex-Nuffield Exports agent, and his tuning shop prepared its own Mini, which was strongly challenging Rhodes.

In unseasonably warm weather, practice went well and a large crowd turned up for race day. Rhodes had qualified on the front row of the grid with the Wooding Mini alongside, and they were both joined by a very potent 1300 Alfa Romeo. Handley in the second Abingdon works Mini was right behind the trio on row three, with ten other Minis further back.

The race was very close, with the Alfa pressing the Minis very hard. At the flag, Rhodes had pulled clear, and with Handley following him to the flag, it was a satisfying end to what had been a troublesome race year for Abingdon.

LBL 666D was sold to Don Wooding in February 1970, and the car continued to be raced quite successfully in Europe.

Competition Record

Date	Event	Crew	Number	Overall result	Class result
Jan 1967	Monte Carlo Rally	Paddy Hopkirk/Ron Crellin	205	6th	
Feb 1967	*Transferred to BMC publicity department*	*Returned November 1967*			
May 1969	BSCC Silverstone	John Rhodes	17	6th	2nd
May 1969	BSCC Crystal Palace	John Rhodes	134	4th	4th
June 1969	BSCC Mallory Park	John Rhodes	118	4th	4th
July 1969	BSCC Silverstone	John Rhodes	16	8th	4th
Aug 1969	BSCC Oulton Park	John Rhodes	75	13th	4th
Sept 1969	BSCC Brands Hatch	John Rhodes	244	10th	4th
Oct 1969	Salzburgring	John Rhodes	30	1st	1st

Registration Number	First registered	Chassis number	Engine	Engine number	Model
LBL 606D	Dec 1966	CA2S7 956238	1275cc	9F-SA-Y 43741	Austin Cooper S

LBL 606D was the last of the four new Cooper Ss that arrived at Abingdon to be prepared for the 1967 Monte Carlo Rally. The car was registered in December 1966 and the preparation and build was undertaken very similarly to the other three team cars freshly-built for the event.

The new car was assigned to Tony Fall and Raymond Joss. Joss was a television producer and this fourth team car was supported by Associated Television, his employer, which was wishing to cover the rally from first-hand experience. The car was also the first 'new' car that Fall had been given and, although he had been rallying with BMC since the end of 1965, he had always used reprepared cars. Fall was always in the shadow of Mäkinen, Aaltonen and Hopkirk, and this was his chance to shine, with a brand-new works Austin Cooper S at his disposal.

A powerful and reliable engine was built to comply with Group 2 regulations. This saw a 1293cc engine put together with great care, with a race camshaft, special high-compression Downton cylinder head, twin SU H4 carburettors and a straight-cut close-ratio gearbox. With a short differential giving maximum acceleration, the car was indeed both very quick and powerful.

Protecting the power unit and gearbox was a short Moke guard, distinguished with 13 air holes at the front edge, and to this was fixed a duralumin sheet extending rearwards. The sump was further protected by screwing a Moke sump plate directly to the underside. This protection was relatively light, as the Monte was not a rough loose-surface event. The special centre exhaust, with its swept-up tailpipe, was protected with plates welded to its underside and all joints were security bolted. It was held to the car with special mountings to ensure they did not fail.

The car used Hydrolastic suspension with single-blue displacers on the front and double-blue units on the rear. Red displacers had originally been specified but testing had indicated that the blue units produced a more compliant ride. Both types, however, eased the front-to-back pitching, which was often found on hard-driven Hydrolastic cars. A big saving was made in the unsprung weight of the car, as for the first time, it was fitted with lightweight magnesium Minilite wheels. Combined, they saved 50lb on the car over their steel counterparts. The handling was also significantly improved with these very light wheels, and they also allowed more air to the hard-working brakes. The brakes had to be standard, other than allowing the use of improved disc pad material. Ferodo supplied racing brake pads and linings.

Wheelarch extensions were fitted to the car, along with quick-lift jacking points front and back, to speed up tyre changes. Front towing eyes were fitted and there were forward-facing mud flaps by the front corner of the bumper. Rear mud flaps were required to be fitted but no rear tow eye was used. The bonnet and boot were secured additionally with a leather strap on the front, and a Moke rubber toggle on the boot lid. The boot lid also housed a reversing lamp on the right-hand side, which was a Healey 3000 sidelight.

Because the car was running in the restricted tyre class (see below) the customary white door square with a competition number painted on was to be painted yellow to distinguish it from those who had unrestricted tyre usage. The rally plate, on the front of the car, was initially fixed vertically onto the bumper in the middle but once under way, it was refixed to the roof gutter above the windscreen. A roof rack was fitted to the car for the long run down to Monte Carlo, carrying two extra wheels and tyres; this was removed as soon as they reached Monte Carlo to save weight. At the front of the car were four additional large Lucas lamps on a lamp bar low by the front grille. The grille had a grille muff fitted to its surround to keep snow and the cold out of the engine. This was removable and could also be partially opened. Power for these extra lamps and the heated front 'screen was from a high-output 11AC alternator. A large-capacity battery was also installed. The car was completely rewired by the resident Lucas Racing mechanic at Abingdon.

Inside the car, the lines were run for battery, brake and fuel. The twin fuel pump was also housed safely, away from the wet and cold, underneath the rear seat pan. Two additional dashboards were fitted to the car, with the driver's housing the rev counter, heated front windscreen switch and numerous control switches; it also had a route card holder above, which would contain route notes, written on postcards, to help the driver on the long drive whilst perhaps the other crew member slept – be that Fall or Joss. The card holder was illuminated by aircraft lamps for night use. The co-driver's dashboard held a Halda Twinmaster distance recorder and a pair of Heuer watches consisting of a clock and stopwatch; these too were illuminated externally by aircraft lamps. He also had various control switches, along with a second switch panel in his door pocket that also housed his map light.

For the run to Monte Carlo, the co-driver had an armchair-style reclining seat, which was comfortable but very heavy. This was replaced, upon reaching Monte Carlo, by a standard Mini seat with a Karobes supportive seat cover because of the weight saving. The driver sat in a cloth-covered fibreglass bucket seat. Both seats were made at Abingdon.

Because of the need to carry two extra wheels and tyres inside the car on the two competitive sections, the rear seat pan had two mounting plates made to hold the wheels securely in place, so the removed seat cushion was secured to the rear seat by long straps from the parcel shelf. All the trim and carpets had to be retained in Group 2 and were added to with additional padding to the door pocket side, door pillar and locks, plus an asbestos blanket laid under the front carpet to keep the manifold and exhaust heat out of the car. The car was fitted with an alloy roll cage, and this too was also padded. To the cage was secured the car's intercom box.

Fall would start his Monte Carlo Rally from Dover, along

Tony Fall and Raymond Joss took LBL 606D on the 1967 Monte Carlo Rally. Here starting from Dover with Fall in the passenger seat.

with Simo Lampinen in another works Mini. They would be accompanied by Brian Moylan and Robin Vokins, who would be servicing them en-route, along with Doug Watts. At the ungodly hour of 3am, Fall – along with 34 other starters, mostly British – set off and drove a matter of yards and onto the cross-channel Ferry to Boulogne, where they could catch up on missed sleep. Their route headed out to Liège, where Fall had the only drama on the entire journey when just outside Mons, driving very fast, he collided with a petrol pump on a garage forecourt while going straight on at a T-junction. No lasting damage (other than to the petrol pump), and they were soon on their way to Amsterdam, where the route then turned back along the coast all the way back close to Boulogne via Antwerp. From there they headed out westwards to Rennes, then south through Limoges and then eventually to Monte Carlo, some 57 long hours at the wheel later.

Their rather circuitous route was an attempt to equalise the time and distance each competitor had to travel from the numerous start locations around Europe. Stuart Turner had spread his five works Minis around Europe to increase local press coverage and also to ensure not all of his eggs were in one basket should the weather be bad at one location. This, of course, made the planning and logistics of such a large undertaking a headache. With 40 personnel, six service vehicles, two vans, five works Minis and seven recce cars to look after, along with all of their hotel and personal travel arrangements, Turner had to not only be a master tactician but also a good planner. Fortunately at least, all of Fall and Joss's hotel arrangements were taken care of by Associated Television.

Fall now at the wheel on the way to Monte Carlo with roof rack with spare tyres. This was removed once they arrived at Monte Carlo.

Another major headache for Turner on the 1967 Monte was one of tyres. Whilst in the past the choice of tyres was free and with that a huge expense in providing so many, for this year, to curb costs and hopefully attract more private entrants, the organisers devised two categories by which cars could enter. Category one would, as usual, have free choice of any number of tyres on the two competitive sections. The second category would be restricted to just eight tyres on each of the legs. The sting in the tale was that those who wanted free use of tyres would suffer a 12 per cent handicap on their stage times. This large time addition was considered by almost everyone to be just too much, so the entire entry of 185 cars (all bar 17) ran in category two of eight tyres – all of which had to be with the car at all times, so entrants had the extra burden of stowing at least two extra wheels and tyres, plus the extra weight.

It therefore became very important that the correct tyres were selected for the two legs, after which they couldn't be changed; and to check conformity, the selected tyres were painted with radioactive paint and branded with the car's number. Dunlop had spent a lot of time developing tyres that would hopefully last the distance and had been testing with BMC up in the Alps for several months to design a suitable compound for the tyres. Nevertheless, despite the restrictions, Turner had specified 420 tyres for his five works Minis (a mere fraction of 1966's). To help decide on which tyres to use, up-to-the-minute information was very important, so weather watching was vital – but nothing beats first-hand knowledge, so as soon as he was in Monte Carlo, Fall went to have a look at the roads in the mountains above Monaco to decide which tyres to take the next day.

Fall, along with the other works Minis (other than Hopkirk, who was more conservative with his choice, having gone through bad weather from Athens) selected four SP3s and four lightly-studded SP44 tyres. The weather looked set to be dry with just some ice at high level.

At 11.30am the next day, the 176 cars that had safely made it to Monte Carlo set off on the common run, which was a loop to Chambéry and back in 24 hours of some 780 miles. They would tackle six stages, all timed to the second, that were hillclimbs of various lengths, amounting to 75 miles of competition. The first was St Auban, which was mostly dry, and saw Fall eighth fastest. The next, the climb up Mont Ventoux, was also dry apart from some ice at the observatory at the very top, and Fall recorded seventh fastest.

As night started to fall, the Col Du Rousset was tackled, where black ice was found, but Fall was still in contention, coming eighth on this stage. Next was the longest stage, some 28 miles of three cols joined together, finishing with the Col du Granier; and with rutted ice in places, Fall was outside the top ten. As dawn broke, the stage from Gap to Valserres was dry but icy in parts, and Fall was back up to speed and came seventh. The final stage, the twisty Levens stage, was completely dry and Fall was seventh. The very fast Porsche

CHAPTER 3: THE MK 1 MINI COOPER S

Fall would slip one place on the mountain circuit and would finish in tenth place overall.

Raymond Joss collects their tenth place award, whilst Fall remains at the wheel.

Fall understeering in the snow with LBL 606D on the common run from Monte Carlo to Chambéry and back. He returned to Monte in ninth place.

911 of Vic Elford was now leading as the cars headed back to Monte Carlo after the common run; the three works Minis were right behind him, and Fall was ninth overall.

Once again, it was tyre choice time. Back in Monte Carlo, the tyres for the mountain circuit the following evening had to be selected but not until once more Fall headed up to inspect the roads for himself. With the dry weather forecast to end, Fall selected four plain SP44s and four half-studded SP44s. The next evening saw the top 60 cars begin the mountain circuit, which was a 385-mile loop from Monte Carlo and back taking in six stages, three of which were trips up the Col du Turini.

The first stage, the Gorge de Piaon, was dry with just a little ice and the second, the first trip up the Turini started dry but rain had begun and saw ice forming at the top. The Col de la Couillole saw snow in evidence at the top, coupled with fog. Fall's tyres were now being compromised on the dry sections, and it was compounded by him loosing time when he had to stop and have his tyres checked at Sospel on his way to the Turini.

On the Turini it was snowing, and even worse on the following second visit to the Col de la Couillole, where deep snow lay. The final stage, once more up the Turini, saw Fall battle the conditions with his badly-worn tyres. At the finish, Fall had slipped to tenth overall after having been 13th fastest on the mountain circuit. Elford faded with completely worn-out tyres, which saw Aaltonen win by a slender 13 seconds – and BMC was delighted to have avenged the disqualification the previous year.

It was also a fitting end for Turner, who would be leaving Abingdon for pastures new in a few months – the running of the competition department now falling to Peter Browning. To put this team achievement into perspective, 28 BMC Minis had entered the 1967 Monte and only seven would finish – five of those were works Minis.

WORKS MINIS IN DETAIL

Tony Fall and Mike Wood used LBL 606D for their recce for the 1967 Alpine Rally, seen here on Mont Ventoux.

LBL 606D was used for the next year on various recce duties before its next competitive event towards the end of 1968. The first of these was for the 1967 Acropolis Rally in May and the second was when Tony Fall and Mike Wood used the car for their recce for the 1967 Alpine Rally in September. Rauno Aaltonen and Henry Liddon used the car for their recce for the 1968 Monte Carlo Rally, and again in February 1968 for their recce for the San Remo Rally. The car was always fully prepared and fitted with a large roof rack for four extra tyres but invariably with an engine that was closer to standard than their normal rally engine – to ensure some reliability, as time wasted with a broken car on a recce was very disruptive.

The Portuguese Rally, handsomely sponsored by the national airline (Transportes Aéreos Portugueses) thus became known as the TAP Rally. With Paddy Hopkirk now being the only surviving Abingdon team member on a full-time contract and with BLMC being seriously constrained in its rally programme since the Leyland takeover – and more significantly most of Abingdon's efforts being concentrated on the London to Sydney Marathon only six weeks away – Hopkirk was the single BLMC entry on this rally. Built as Group 6 car, Hopkirk elected to take Tony Nash as co-driver, this being their second event together. Ron Crellin, who was Hopkirk's regular co-driver, earlier in the year had decided to retire to concentrate on his business. However, he was coaxed out of retirement by Tony Fall for this very rally – and they went on to win in a Lancia Fulvia.

LBL 606D, being a Group 6 car, was fitted with lightweight panels and Perspex windows; it also ran a 45DCOE carburettor on the 1293cc engine. The car now appeared as a Mk2 Cooper S with larger Mk2 rear lights and Mk2 badges and with black interior trim. It was fitted with an extra radiator on the front of the car between the two driving lamps and the front grille was removed. It was also fitted with the heavy-duty Scandinavian sump guard, extra-wide wheelarch extensions (now painted red body colour) and gold-painted 5½J magnesium Minilite wheels. With the very stiff opposition the Mini was now facing, a Group 6 car was the only sensible choice if it was to get on terms with the current crop of rally cars.

With the aforementioned high level of TAP sponsorship, the event attracted 174 starters for this late-October traditional rally. Free entries for foreign crews, plus free hotels, a lucrative prize fund and also 100 litres of fuel assured a large entry was assembled from the 12 starting points around Europe, with all to descend on Madrid where the competition really began. The concentration routes were for some a three-day tour of some 1300 miles; for others less than 400 miles and just one night out of bed.

Hopkirk selected a short run and started from Lisbon, where he had an uneventful run and arrived in Madrid without loss of time. The common runs starting from Madrid consisted of three legs of 400, 600 and 550 miles to decide the winner, the first of which was a relatively easy route to Lisbon where the first stage was a ten-lap race around Jarama race circuit, which unsurprisingly was a Porsche 911 benefit. The second

LBL 606D now as a Mk2 Cooper S and a Group 6 car for Paddy Hopkirk and Tony Nash for the 1968 TAP Rally in Portugal. They would finish in second place behind Tony Fall in a Lancia.

As a publicity stunt, LBL 606D was used by Inter City Rail in an advertising film of a car racing a train. Seen here in snow conditions in Scotland.

TV presenters Gordon Wilkins and Michael Frostick took LBL 606D on the 1969 Monte Carlo Rally, entered in the veterans' class where they finished in third place.

stage was a blast around a banked track at a football ground near Lisbon, where Hopkirk recorded fourth fastest time.

The second leg, from Lisbon to Porto, was very difficult and demanding and saw the entry decimated. Seventy time controls, which were very tightly timed, and three stages lay ahead. Hopkirk undoubtedly benefited from completing a full recce of this defining leg – only 42 of those who set out from Lisbon made it to Porto. Hopkirk was fastest on the first stage, with Tony Fall second, and the places were reversed on the next stage.

The final stage was another blast around the banked football stadium, where Hopkirk was fastest and now led Fall into Porto for the last leg to the finish in Estoril. This section was equally punishing, with 78 controls and two more stages. The field was again cut by a huge margin, with only 13 cars making it to the finish. Hopkirk was second to Fall on both stages but despite this, he was unfortunately delayed by a full four minutes when a level crossing barred his route and his two-minute lead was lost to the Lancia. With so few finishing from a field of 174, it indicated just how tough the rally was – albeit it was only the last two legs that were so demanding.

There was one non-competition-related interlude for LBL 606D when it was taken to Scotland in the winter of 1968 for a publicity film advertising InterCity Rail, where it represented a race between a train and car. It was filmed by French expert Patrice Pouget, who filmed the acclaimed *Une Homme et Une Femme* (*A Man and Women*), which was an iconic rally film. Abingdon was delighted to co-operate with the project and happily loaned LBL 606D, where the car was driven in great style by club rally driver and the man commissioned by British Rail to produce the advert, Jeremy Hunter.

There was one final outing for LBL 606D as a rally car, when it was used on the 1969 Monte Carlo Rally by TV presenters Gordon Wilkins and Michael Frostick. These two gentlemen hosted the BBC *Wheelbase* programme, the forerunner to *Top Gear*, and were loaned the car to enter the Veterans' Competition, which ran alongside the main event. The car, as a Mk2, was a Group 2 car, so it is highly likely not to have been the same car that Hopkirk used on the 1968 TAP Rally the previous October, that being a Group 6. The crew started from Lisbon and were credited with third place in this veterans' category. The car was next used in the summer of 1969 when John Handley and Paul Easter used the car for their recce for the Tour de France Auto.

The next and last appearance of LBL 606D was as a race car in the summer of 1970, when it was entered for John Handley and Alec Poole to compete in the Spa 24-hour saloon car race. It is possible that this car was indeed the Group 2 Mk2 LBL 606D last seen on the Monte Carlo Rally in 1969: there is evidence that an external power socket was fitted alongside the offside headlight, indicating that a four-light lamp bar and plug had been used on the car, adding to this possibility. The

LBL 606D, now as a Mk2 race car, was entered in the Spa 24-hour saloon car race for Group 2 cars, for John Handley and Alec Poole. Here on the starting grid with a change onto wet race tyres as the weather changed.

LBL 606D ran for 11 of the 24 hours, covering 1000 miles, only for a conrod to let go and the car was out.

car was also fitted with rally-style quick-lift jacking plates and in addition was still wearing a GB plate on the bootlid, which all adds up to the possibility of the car being a rally car.

As a Group 2 car, it ran with bumpers and all of its standard trim and glass, making it much heavier. The new European Touring Car Championship (as it was called from 1970 onwards, and not Challenge) was run under new Group 2 rules that had just come into effect.

The race, run continuously for 24 hours, meant nighttime running needed to be catered for. The car therefore carried two extra driving lights mounted on brackets secured to the lower panel and bumper. It also had a coloured identification light placed at the front edge of the roof. It had a number plate light fixed to the door to illuminate the competition number on the door. A roundel was also painted centrally on the bonnet. In addition it had its competition number stuck above the driver's door on the roof. Two additional driving lamps were fitted to the car on individual brackets; the headlights were also protected by Perspex clip-on covers. Handley and Poole's car was also quite distinctive from the rear, as it had three broad bands of tape across the rear window to act as a deflector for other cars' headlights dazzling the driver at night.

The car ran aluminium panels and the bonnet was secured with two Moke rubber toggles and a central leather strap. The car sat on wide 12in Minilite wheels with wide wheelarch extensions without chrome trim.

The engine was not fitted with an eight-port cylinder head (unlike Rhodes's car) but a five-port head, so Handley ran the car on split Weber carburettors rather than fuel injection – he deeming that a more reliable option for such a long race. On a circuit where a high top speed is vital, a rather long 3.3:1 final drive was fitted. The car would need to lap at around 100mph to be in contention.

The Spa Francorchamps race was one of the most important saloon car races on the calendar and BL was keen to be seen there. Held between 25 and 26 July, the race had a full field of 60 cars turn up for practice. Two sessions were scheduled, one of which was in the hours of darkness and compulsory. After two days of trouble-free practice, Handley and Poole were classified in 43rd place (one behind teammate Rhodes).

Despite the two team cars working together, slipstreaming each other, the large number of big-engined and more powerful cars entered meant they were well into the back half of the grid – but with a long endurance race ahead this was not as important as in a sprint race.

Overnight storms had saturated the track, and come the start at 3pm, although it had stopped raining, the track was still very wet. Handley decided to start on intermediate racing tyres, being Dunlop R7s on 10in Minilites, as the forecast was not favourable. However, after half an hour, a dry line started to appear and he was soon suffering with his tyres. Handley pitted early, had a quick top-up of fuel, changed onto dry racing tyres and stormed back into the field. He had not been alone being caught out with an incorrect tyre choice.

At the four-hour mark, with the weather now settled into a fine evening, Handley was laying in 29th place, eight behind his teammate but now in the top half of the field. At the six-hour mark, the pair had pulled up four more places and were now up to 25th overall. The pace had been relentless and retirements were being posted as the night set in. The car was, however, running well and starting to close the gap to Rhodes as his engine started to go off-song. At 1.30am, Rhodes was out with a damaged cylinder head. Handley pressed on, only

CHAPTER 3: THE MK 1 MINI COOPER S

to put a rod through the side of the block just before 2am. The car had nevertheless lapped at close to 100mph and had covered nearly 1000 miles before it all went wrong.

The race car was bought by Jim Whitehouse when Abingdon disposed of all of its cars when its closure was announced in August 1970. Whitehouse was a renowned engine builder, who always managed to get as much power as possible from the Mini's engine, and the man behind the Arden name – he built Mini engines that brought victory for John Rhodes and Gordon Spice, and Alec Poole won the 1969 British saloon title using Whitehouse's Arden eight-port head.

LBL 606D was, however, never repainted in Arden colours and ultimately never used by Arden in competition before being sold on.

Competition Record

Date	Event	Crew	Number	Overall result	Class result
Jan 1967	Monte Carlo Rally	Tony Fall/Raymond Joss	32	10th	
Oct 1968	TAP Rally	Paddy Hopkirk/Tony Nash	71	2nd	2nd
Jan 1969	Monte Carlo Rally	Gordon Wilkins/Michael Frostick	240	3rd Veteran	
July 1970	Spa 24 hours	John Handley/Alec Poole	73	DNF	

Registration Number	First registered	Chassis number	Engine	Engine number	Model
LBL 590E	Jan 1967	CA2S7 956239	1275cc	9F-SA-Y 43789	Austin Cooper S

LBL 590E was unusual in that it competed in only one competition for Abingdon, a distinction shared by very few other works Minis. It did, however, carry on in the background being used for recce work on several occasions and used on three internationals as part of the BMC team with David Friswell driving.

The car may well have been part of the new delivery stock for the 1967 Monte, when all were registered in December 1966 with sequential numbers. LBL 590E was not registered until January the next year, in readiness for the Rally of the Flowers in late February. The car was allocated to Paddy Hopkirk and Ron Crellin, built by Robin Vokins and entered as a Group 2.

As was by now customary, the 1293cc engine was fitted with Abingdon's 'standard' full-race AEA648 camshaft and coupled with a high-compression 12.6:1 Downton cylinder head; breathing through a pair of SU H4 carburettors, the car showed 90bhp at the wheels on the Abingdon rolling road. Special oval forged pistons were fitted to a double-cross-drilled crankshaft, to which was fitted an extra-lightened steel flywheel with an orange diaphragm spring. The latest Lucas 40979 distributor was used, with a special-heavy duty condenser.

A straight-cut three-speed synchromesh gearbox was fitted with a 4.2: final drive running out through enlarged driveshafts with Hardy Spicer couplings. All of this was protected by a large heavy-duty Scandinavian sump guard with an alloy extension to the end of the remote shift, which was itself secured using a special Mitchell mounting rubber to a strengthened bracket. The sump guard also had front quick-

Paddy Hopkirk and Ron Crellin assemble in San Remo with LBL 590E for the start of the 1967 Rally of the Flowers.

lift jacking points fixed to the protruding front edge. Keeping the engine cool was a four-blade fan, with ¼in removed from the end of the blades to aid fan belt changes; no thermostat was fitted, just a blanking sleeve.

The Hydrolastic suspension was fitted with single-blue and double-blue displacers front and back, with orange helper springs to the rear together with Swedish bump stops. The rear subframe was double-skinned along its top and it, and the front subframe, was rewelded for added strength. The tie rods, for added security, were secured with castellated nuts and split pins, as were the steering arms. Brakes were fitted with DS11 racing disc pads, VG95 linings and a 325psi limiting valve to apportion more braking to the rear. The brakes' lines were run inside of the car and a servo was also fitted in the standard position under the bonnet.

Electrics were served by an 11AC alternator, with the main battery cable run inside the car and the battery reversed to allow the terminals to be away from the side of the fuel tank. The battery box was protected from the outside with a steel plate spanning the rear subframe. The car was equipped with vertical-dip Lucas European headlamps with 80/60w double-filament iodine bulbs. The four auxiliary lamps fitted to the lamp bar consisted of two Lucas 700 fog lamps and two Continental headlamp units in the middle with steady brackets – all with iodine bulbs. The reversing lamp consisted of an Austin Healey side lamp, fitted low down on the right-hand side of the bootlid.

A two-speed wiper motor was fitted with stronger deep-throated wheel boxes, which dealt better with snow loads and were far more reliable. Maserati air horns replaced the feeble standard offerings and were operated from the standard horn push in the steering wheel plus a foot-operated button by the co-driver's feet.

The twin SU fuel pump was fitted under the rear seat but only one pump was wired – the second was there as a back-up should the first fail. Driver and navigator had their respective additional alloy dashboards: the driver's panel housed a 0-10,000rpm rev counter and numerous additional switches and controls. For the navigator, there was a Halda Twinmaster distance recorder (calibrated in kilometres) and a pair of Heuer watches, illuminated by external P-lights, along with a two-pin socket and control switches for wipers, washers and such like.

Crew comfort included padding to the door locks, side pockets, B-post and for safety's sake, the roll cage was also padded. Hopkirk sat in a lightweight bucket seat and Crellin in a high-back reclining seat. Hopkirk had an Irvin lap and diagonal seat belt whereas Crellin had a full-harness Irvin belt. Hopkirk used a thick-grip Moto-Lita steering wheel. A grab handle, taken from an 1800, was fitted above the door on Crellin's side of the car. An intercom was used between the two of them, with the intercom box secured to the top of the roll cage. A modified MGB jack was fitted behind Hopkirk, secured to the side of the rear companion pocket. Being a Group 2 car, all carpets, trim and glass were retained.

Externally, the car ran large front-facing mud flaps fitted where the overriders would have been. It also used a radiator muff, fitted around the grille moustache. This helped to keep the engine warm, keep out snow and rain, should it be needed. Fibreglass wheelarch extensions were riveted to the body to cover the now-standard fit lightweight Minilite magnesium wheels. These proved a revelation in reducing unsprung weight and dissipating heat, and had the added bonus that they were strong enough to run on should a tyre be lost – and they looked great.

For the Flowers Rally provision was made to fit the front rally plate vertically. This was fitted on brackets on the right-hand side of the bonnet with the painted square number plate located on the other side. Reflective Scotchlite tape was placed on the rear bumper and door shuts, as a safely measure at night.

Before the car's first event, the Rally of the Flowers, it appeared in a film about the 1967 Monte Carlo Rally where it was mocked up to be LBL 66D, Timo Mäkinen's car on the event.

The Rally of the Flowers didn't start well for Hopkirk and Crellin, due to their planned recce being interrupted by heavy snow in the week before the rally. This meant the closure of the many of the roads that were to be used for the stages. Luckily, just before the start, the weather eased and thawed, allowing for some frenetic practising. The weather had damaged many of the roads, making the already poor roads even rougher and, as many of these were being used multiple times on the very compact route, conditions were going to be hard on the cars – and tyres. Tyre choice was therefore exclusively Dunlop SP44s, most of which were lightly studded for the snow-covered roads on the higher hills – plus they worked equally well on the very rough roads.

Based in San Remo, the intertwined 1000-mile route, broken down into 25 timed road sections, had to be covered in just over 30 hours and was a tough rally. Most of the roads in the hills around San Remo, hewn into the rock face, were very poor with steep drops, most unguarded, to catch the unwary, making a good recce vital. However, with generous road timing, the rally was decided on the 12 timed stages. This meant around 100 miles of flat-out driving over very rough tracks, resulting in many cars being retired damaged or broken in some form or another. Oddly, each of the 12 stages had a flying start and a flying finish, and records show that only the first stage had its target time beaten.

The rally was very fast on particularly rough roads, where Hopkirk was soon into the lead.

Snow had made the already poor quality roads even worse and many were still snow-covered. The car here can be seen with the large competition number required to the rear.

Driveshaft failure just 12km from the end of the rally, which was mostly downhill, saw the car pushed by the following service barge to the last control, which went unnoticed but his lead had gone and Hopkirk finished 2nd. The car was towed away by Tony Fall in GRX 195D.

Hopkirk had a long battle with Jean Francois Piot's Renault R8 Gordini and had a slight lead on his French rival at half distance, after fighting his way back from sixth place, having looked after the car on some of the early particularly rough stages. Despite the expected relaxed road timing, the conditions meant Hopkirk was the only car with a clean sheet on the road by the halfway mark. Hopkirk held his lead until the very last stage – the 19km stage from Badalucco to Vignai – and then to the finish in San Remo. Fortunately, this stage was mostly downhill, as were the roads onto San Remo and the events unfolded into one of rallying's great tales of resilience and indeed 'rallymanship'.

With just 5km to the end of the final stage, Hopkirk came upon a large farm vehicle on the stage (which should have been clear of other traffic), indignantly blasting past it with lights and horn blazing. He sped by unabated, only to succumb to a terrible vibration, which could only mean a failed driveshaft coupling. With no drive, the car coasted to a halt. Hopkirk, quick as a flash, leapt from the car and started to wave down the vehicle they had passed a few moments ago. He asked the driver of the vehicle to push him to the top of the hill, from where he hoped he could freewheel down to the end of the stage, where the BMC service crew would be stationed and could hopefully patch the car up. But with little time in hand, this was perhaps a forlorn hope, with the finish control still 12 miles away – although fortunately mostly all downhill.

The car freewheeled to the end of the stage to collect its time but so slender was the lead that the delay had cost Hopkirk his first place, relegating him into second. The car left the control, rather slowly, still pointing downhill, feigning clutch slip and into the waiting arms of Doug Watts and Peter Browning, manning the service point in their trusty Vanden Plas Princess R. With no time to effect a proper repair, despite a new shaft being available, Watts reconnected the drive coupling but warned that starting off may just break it again.

Hopkirk set off gingerly, trying to not put too much torque through the wheels, hoping desperately that the anticipated traffic into San Remo would not cause a problem with stopping and starting. With the Princess R right behind, the car freewheeled down the hills into San Remo. On the few level pieces of road, where the car slowed, they received a friendly nudge from the service barge; fortunately both cars had bumpers of a similar height, so damage was not severe and the car kept descending onto San Remo and the finish control.

Both cars had a hair-raising journey down through the many hairpin bends, and with no drive, nor any retardation from the engine, bends were taken at breakneck speed, trying to keep up as much momentum as possible. With the Princess not being as agile as the Mini, Duggie Watts was also driving like a demon. The Mini was now overheating badly, despite changing the earlier broken fan belt, and there was a passage control that still had to be visited – again, fortunately, it was still downhill. So they checked in and slowly departed with the same feigning of clutch slip, and were soon nudged on their way by the ever-present service barge.

The final drama occurred a few-hundred yards from the final control, which was situated in a large car park at the exit to a long tunnel. The Princess R got up to top speed in the tunnel, pushing the Mini through the tunnel; just before the exit, Watts braked and the Mini shot out on its own, screamed past the waiting photographers, TV crews and policeman, and with his lights and horn blazing again, Hopkirk completed a perfect handbrake turn into the car park, stopping right by the control table in a shower of dust. He clocked in, to rapturous applause from all the spectators and the entire

317

organising team. Nobody was surprised, or bothered, that the car had just broken its drive coupling and could travel no further. Hopkirk and Crellin received their second place and nobody protested their assisted passage to the finish.

The event was kind to BMC, with Tony Fall coming home in fourth place. It was a fitting end to Stuart Turner's very successful reign at the helm of Abingdon. Peter Browning would have big boots to fill. It would also be the end of LBL 590E as a competition works Mini, although it would be pressed into recce and other duties on several occasions.

Its first recce was on the 1967 Acropolis Rally, three months after returning from the Rally of the Flowers, where Paddy Hopkirk and Ron Crellin used the car. Suitably repaired with a new boot lid and some panel beating to the rear end, the car was also to be loaned to Phil Jones, a *Motor* journalist, to cover the Acropolis for the magazine. Trouble was, Timo Mäkinen had blown the car up practising on one of the hillclimbs. Undeterred, the BMC team, assisted by the local BMC agent in Athens, rebuilt LBL 590E with the engine from another recce car and the suspension from another, and the car was ready for the journalist to cover the event the next morning. It was a remarkable effort, especially as they had three rally cars to attend to for the rally itself.

The next outing for the car was for BMC Austria, which was running a competition-driving training course outside Vienna. LBL 590E was sent to Vienna on a trailer behind a Princess R, with Bill Price and Dudley Pike in attendance. Rauno Aaltonen and Paddy Hopkirk were there using the car, giving instructions and demonstration runs, as it was considered a good promotional opportunity for the local BMC agent.

LBL 590E was shipped to Vienna at the request of BMC Austria. Rauno Aaltonen and Paddy Hopkirk gave driving instruction and demonstration runs to invited BMC guests.

Tony Fall and Mike Wood recceing for the 1968 Monte Carlo Rally in LBL 590E, seen here practising at full speed at the top of the Col de Turini.

David Friswell and Mike Merrick entered the 1968 Acropolis Rally with LBL 590E as a works-supported entry. They rolled the car very heavily.

The car's final outings for Abingdon were when Tony Fall and Mike Wood used it for their recce for the 1968 Monte Carlo Rally. For this recce, the car reverted to a standard engine rather than a full competition Group 2 powerhouse, as Fall preferred the reliability that a standard power unit gave him, negating the frequent attention a competition engine often needed, especially without a full service crew in constant attendance. The car was left in France at a local BMC dealer to be used as a practice car and ice-note car for the 1968 Monte. It was subsequently used for Fall and Wood to recce the 1968 Flowers Rally, the car having been retained in Southern France.

The car was sold to David Friswell for the sum of £500. David, an accountant, was a keen enthusiast who had achieved much in road rallying and was trying very hard to become a professional rally driver. He was offered a contract by Peter Browning to undertake three events with his ex-works car and be part of the BMC team. He entered the 1968 Circuit of Ireland with the car, where it was prepared and serviced by the special tuning team, but that didn't go well when he lost first gear and then retired with clutch failure.

On the 1968 Tulip Rally he was again co-opted into the BMC team, this time retiring with a failed wheel bearing. His final event with the car was on the 1968 Acropolis when he was again co-opted into the BMC team; this time the car retired after a heavy roll. BMC kindly took the car back to England but it was never used again in international rallies. Friswell was given a spare rally car's bodyshell that was no longer needed by the competition department as compensation for his team efforts.

Competition Record

Date	Event	Crew	Number	Overall result	Class result
Feb 67	Flowers Rally	Paddy Hopkirk/Ron Crellin	67	2nd	2nd

Registration Number	First registered	Chassis number	Engine	Engine number	Model
LRX 827E	March 1967	KA2S4 956685	1275cc	9F-SA-Y 44642	Morris Cooper S

LRX 827E was the first of a crop of four new cars delivered to Abingdon and registered early in 1967. This Group 2 car was assigned to Timo Mäkinen and Paul Easter for the Tulip Rally in April.

The latest strengthened engine block, bored to give 1293cc, was fitted, with a race camshaft (the AEA648), forged oval pistons and a lightened steel flywheel. A Downton high-compression cylinder head was used, as were twin SU H4 carburettors with ram pipes and float bowl extension. A straight-cut close-ratio gear set was used and the idler transfer gear was now fitted with a special bearing, as it had caused issues in the past. A 4.2:1 final drive was fitted with the latest Hardy Spicer shafts and joints, and a Mitchell mounting was used to secure the end of the remote-control gearchange. The oil cooler was relocated a few inches further over, and the diagonal stiffener removed and placed vertically to clear the alternator.

The suspension was Hydrolastic, despite Mäkinen's preference for dry cone suspension. This was fitted with single-blue and double-blue banded displacer units at the front and back, plus orange helper springs. The subframes were strengthened and the rear radius arm bracket also double-plated. The ride height was set at 13in and as the Tulip was not a rough rally, the car was fitted with a short 13-hole guard protecting the front of the sump. In addition, a Moke sump plate was screwed to the bottom of the gear

Timo Mäkinen and Paul Easter took the new LRX 827E on the 1967 Tulip Rally; this all-tarmac event saw Mäkinen driving the car very hard and ran into piston trouble very early on.

case, machined flat to securely mount it. The standard brakes, with servo, were fitted with DS11 racing brake pads and hard VG95 brake shoes.

The bodywork had black fibreglass wheelarch extensions covering the Minilite magnesium wheels, which were fitted with Dunlop R7 race tyres. The boot lid had a back-mounted Lucas 576 fog lamp as a revering lamp. At the front, the four auxiliary lamps – two fog lamps on the outside and two

WORKS MINIS IN DETAIL

Mäkinen and Easter leave service, where the car was topped up with oil and extra taken on board, such was the car's consumption, needing regular top-ups.

driving lamps in the centre – were fixed to a heavy-gauge lamp bar. The front grille moustache had Lift-the-Dot fixings for a grille muff. The iodine European headlamps had Perspex covers to protect them during the day but were discarded at night. Quick-lift jacking points were fitted front and back. The number plate, on a black square, was painted on the offside of the bonnet, itself held shut with a leather strap.

Inside, the car had an alloy roll cage, as fitted to all works Minis since the last RAC Rally. Mäkinen had a lightweight cloth-covered bucket seat, which was stretched with a hydraulic jack to give him a little more room (the seat, brought over from Finland by Aaltonen, was fine for him, but a little snug for Mäkinen). Easter had a more comfortable but less supportive reclining seat, also cloth-covered. Mäkinen had an Irvin lap-and-diagonal seat belt but hardly ever used it; Easter had a full-harness Irvin belt. Two additional dash panels were fitted – Mäkinen's having a rev counter and numerous switches, and Easter's the Halda Twinmaster and a pair of Heuer watches illuminated by external aircraft P-lamps. He also had an additional switch panel in his door pocket for a map light and more control switches. Being a Group 2 car, all of the carpets and trim had to be retained. Padding was fitted to the door lock, door pockets and pillars, and care taken to exclude all draughts.

The car was completely rewired throughout by Lucas Racing's resident technician at Abingdon. A twin fuel pump was located under the rear seat, all lines were run inside the car and a modified MGB jack secured against the driver's rear companion bin. The windscreen washer bottle was located in the footwell, along with a foot-operated horn switch for Easter and an intercom.

The 1967 Tulip Rally, held in late April, was a popular event for many UK privateers and had been so for many years. It was a relatively easy rally, and using its famous Tulip navigation method, which has since become universally accepted as the way rally road books are put together, helped navigation enormously. Now run on scratch timing, in line with most European rallies, the class improvement scheme was no longer used as the rally modernised.

On offer for 108 competitors was a route of some 2000 miles from the Dutch coast, through Belgium, Luxembourg and on into the French mountains to Annecy. After a 12-hour rest at Annecy, the route meandered back to Noordwijk but not after an event-defining night loop from Annecy to Rumilly.

Mäkinen blasts off the line with a cloud of blue smoke. The ritual being to top the car with oil at the start of every stage, which meant they were good for around 30 miles of hard driving.

Sadly, heavy snow a week before the rally had meant much of the route had been changed in Eastern France. So, along the way only 18 tests, timed to the second, had to be tackled; all bar two were classic hillclimbs. These tests were interspersed with numerous timed selectives with a bogey time to beat. It was still a challenging event.

Despite the earlier snow, the event started on a fine, sunny morning. Mäkinen was expected to do well but was wary of the threat of the powerful Porsche 911 of Vic Elford, so well suited to the all-tarmac rally. So it proved to be, with Elford fastest on all stages bar one (which Mäkinen won). Elford was soon building up a small but comfortable lead. Mäkinen was close behind but leading the touring car class as the first night wore on, and still setting very fast times within the top five. Trouble was, however, brewing, as the engine started to run badly and was diagnosed as a burnt piston. This resulted in frequent changes of spark plugs and copious quantities of oil being consumed. The procedure at the start line of each test was that they had to change plugs and fill up with oil – the car was then very quick for just about 30 miles. Despite this setback, Mäkinen continued his rapid pace, the engine running better higher up in the rev range.

Into Annecy for a well-earned 12-hour rest, there was much service activity but no rectifying Mäkinen's ailing engine. Ninety cars set off in the evening for the Annecy-to-Rumilly loop on a cold but clear night. This was to be a defining section, which contained many short, fast sections, where any mistake would result in penalties.

So it was in the Croix Fry tunnel, which had an unforgiving fast left-hand bend in the middle; snow had melted, which ran across the road, and in turn frozen in the cold night air. Elford, the first to arrive, smacked the outside rock face with the Porsche and collected a puncture, which delayed him enough to give the lead to Mäkinen. Mäkinen miraculously managed to just avoid the rock face – many didn't, including Aaltonen, his teammate, who clobbered the rear end as he threw the car sideways. He too collected a puncture for his trouble. The three-hour stop at Rumilly the next day was well received.

Eighty-three cars then set off on the last leg back to Holland. Elford turned up the wick and grabbed back his lead, continuing to set fastest times. Mäkinen was still hard-charging with his ailing engine, beating Elford on the Route de Mont climb and equalling him on the penultimate test, the Vlasakkers army ground test, and so secured the touring car win. Just 60 cars had made it back to the Dutch coast. Elford won, Mäkinen the class, and BMC won the team price with Julien Vernaeve and Mike Wood in Vernaeve's private Cooper S.

The next event for the car was the Geneva Rally in Switzerland. This rally was a round of the European Championship and the organisers were allowing only cars in Group 1 and 3 to score points – this in an attempt to encourage more standard cars to compete. BMC was not, in 1967, very interested in this championship, so elected not to enter any Group 1 cars, sticking to Group 2 cars, which was where the team's strengths lay. Fortunately, the organisers ran another rally concurrent with the Geneva called the Criterium de Crans-sur-Sierre – the Criterium for short – which did cater for Group 2 cars, amongst others, and this is what LRX 827E was entered into.

Despite their continual engine problems, the engine held together and Mäkinen and Easter finished a remarkable second overall and won their class.

Tony Fall and Mike Wood took over LRX 827E for the 1967 Geneva Rally, seen here before the start with Julien Vernaeve's car, LRX 830E, behind.

Tony Fall and Mike Wood were handed the car for the Criterium, it being little changed from when it appeared last on the Tulip Rally. Because the Criterium had some forest mileage, the car was initially fitted with its short 13-hole sump guard alloy extension plate but this was replaced with a heavy-duty Scandinavian sump guard later in the event for the forest stages. The car also had the addition of a battery box guard underneath. The brakes were upgraded by drilling the brake drums and their backplates to aid cooling, and the wheel cylinder bosses were threaded, replacing the circlips, which this acted as a heatsink. The front brakes weren't neglected either, as the pistons had an asbestos block fitted, again to take heat away from the brake fluid.

The Criterium attracted 76 hopefuls. Ahead of them were some 1250 miles, including around 100 miles of tests, mainly on French roads and consisting of mostly tarmac hillclimbs and one very challenging forest test. This test, in the Jura Mountains north of Geneva, in the Gimel St-George forest, was to nearly see the end of both the works Minis.

Starting on 15 June from Crans, 15 miles north of Geneva, the route consisted of two legs, one of 500 miles and with six tests; the second of 750 miles held the other six tests. The first leg looped southwards around Annecy and included that Gimel forest test; the second loop was a figure of eight south of Geneva, tackled after an 11-hour rest halt.

Before anyone set off, they had to pass scrutineering, where they insisted all cars had to have a minimum of 10cm ground clearance; to test it, cars had to drive over a 10cm lump of wood. BMC was soon to be seen pumping up Fall's Hydrolastic suspension – other cars were changing springs to try to comply, and those that couldn't be made high enough were withdrawn from the entry. Another peculiarity of the rally was the marking: it was not on scratch timing as most rallies now were (meaning the fastest car won) but on a class improvement scheme with each class having its own bogey times to beat. This often led to difficulties knowing exactly who was beating whom.

The first leg got under way and three short hillclimbs were the first offering. These were all on slippery tarmac and immediately Vic Elford, in the very fast Porsche 911, took fastest time on all three. Fall was sixth, fourth and sixth respectively, and well in the hunt despite spinning at the last hairpin on the first climb. Snow on Col de Joux Verte meant it was blocked and so was cancelled.

As the day wore on and into the night, Sandro Munari in his Lancia Fulvia was leading, despite Elford being fastest overall – such were the class improvement system peculiarities. A fast night section, as they neared Aix Les-Bains, had many short, sharp sections and this saw many losing road time. Fall, however, was still on time and would keep his clean sheet to the end.

Nearing the end of the first leg, the Gimel forest lay ahead. This ten-mile test was a typical forest, which Fall was only too familiar with from his experience in British rallying but it nearly turned to disaster when he spun and slid off, putting a bolder-sized dent into the offside of the car. Despite this, he was still sixth fastest and it would also be the only test Elford wasn't fastest on – but was second, all the same.

At the end of the first leg, near Geneva, activity was taking place on many cars after the damage in the forest. There was a one-hour service just before the parc fermé, then an 11-hour rest stop. Many used all of that time. Fall was lying in fourth

LRX 827E being serviced, where the ride heights had to be raised before they were allowed to start, having to pass over a 100mm block of wood, meaning the Hydrolastic suspension had to be pumped up.

Fall's car was tipped onto its side to attend to the underside to investigate damage caused by going off on one of the forest stages. Despite this, Fall and Wood won the Group 2 section of the Geneva Rally, actually called the Criterium Rally.

place at halfway, but Munari still led. Fifty cars restarted that evening for the second leg with six more tests, which saw Elford steadily pull away and win them all. Fall was once again knocking on the door, with very high placings on all of the tests. At the finish in Geneva, Elford was deservedly declared the overall winner, with Fall being credited with third overall on the Geneva and winning the Criterium Rally. With his two lots of prize money, he won more than Elford.

The Alpine was, at the time, one of the last great road races left in the rally calendar and a favourite amongst the BMC team – Hopkirk in particular. Run in early September, the Alps were free of snow and slippery conditions and were relatively free of tourists. Paddy Hopkirk was again teamed with Ron Crellin for this epic rally. He was assigned LRX 827E, which was much changed from the Geneva/Criterium Rally as it was prepared as a lightweight Group 6 car. BMC viewed that this year's Alpine would be extremely fast, and in attempt to keep pace with the Porsche 911s and Alpine Renaults, the car had to shed much weight.

The car was fitted with lightweight aluminium panels to the bonnet, boot lid and doors. All of the glass, save the front laminated 'screen, was replaced with Perspex. The bumpers were removed, as was the chrome trims around the doors. The rear side windows were fixed, with no hinge nor metal frame. As much trim as possible was also taken out. Rivington thin carpet was laid where the rear seat once was. The engine also received a power boost by replacing the twin SU H4 carburettors with a single Weber 45DCOE – this necessitated a bit of fettling around the speedo aperture to accommodate the ram pipes and a suitable manifold. The speedo was also spaced out into the cabin with a piece of carefully carved wood. The engine reputedly now produced 125bhp at the flywheel, and with the customary 4.2:1 final drive and weight saving of some 100lb, the car would have been very quick to accelerate and climb, but without the use of a limited slip differential. The car ran Dunlop R7 race tyres throughout but Dunlop had, in the truck, SP44 Weathermasters should the weather turn.

To keep things cool, in addition to an oil cooler, the car ran an auxiliary front-mounted radiator (fabricated from a Mini heater matrix), which was fitted on the right-hand side of the grille. The front grille was cut down to accommodate the extra radiator and the grille moustache also deleted. For the first time, the four additional lamps were connected via a rubber plug and socket attached to the wing on the left-hand side between the headlight and sidelight. This part, sourced from the Land Rover parts bin, would be a regular fit on Abingdon Minis from then on, which made removing the lamps much quicker. The bonnet was held down by two Moke rubber toggles, replacing the usual leather strap; they were first seen on Marathon de la Route cars. On the boot lid, a small Healey sidelight was used as a reversing lamp and it too was held securely shut by a single Moke toggle.

LRX 827E was converted to a lightweight Group 6 car for Paddy Hopkirk and Ron Crellin for the 1967 Alpine Rally, seen here near Abingdon before its departure to France.

As the Alpine was not a rough event, the Moke sump guard and Moke sump plate were employed but with the addition of a duralumin sheet fixed to the sump guard to further protect the gearbox. The car, in Group 6 form, was very striking and purposeful in appearance compared to a Group 2 Mini. However, all was not well in Hopkirk's eyes, as he felt that the Group 6 car was sluggish – until it was discovered that the mandatory dual braking system that Abingdon had fabricated had the cable attached to the rear brakes too tightly; once slackened off (negating the dual braking system) all was well.

The Alpine of old had strict time schedules on the road and only those who remained on time would win a coveted Alpine Cup. The timed stages were used simply as a means of classification. Now as speeds had increased, the organisers deemed that to keep on time cars had to be within just 2 per cent of the fastest car in their class. The challenge was daunting and explains BMC's need to build a Group 6 car. The Mini was indeed as fast as anything on the road downhill but had to give best to more powerful cars going uphill. Only three cars would remain clean on the road this year, one of which would be Hopkirk's.

Starting from Marseille on 4 September, after some very relaxed scrutineering, where being a Group 6 car meant almost anything goes, 79 cars set off on Monday evening for the first leg to Alpe d'Huez of this 2300-mile event, with 110 cols to climb and descend. This leg was a 900-mile blast over the Alps with 18 tightly timed selectives on the road, interspersed with four épreuves (timed-to-the-second hillclimb stages). Old Alpine favourites in that breakneck first leg included the very tight and twisty selectives between Quatre Chemins, Sigale, Entrevaux and Rouaine, the Col D'Allos, the Col de Cayolle and the dangerous Col de Lombarde. Elford's Porsche was

The blistering pace of the Alpine Rally saw Hopkirk always up with the leaders, having practised the entire route and having made pace notes for most of it.

soon leading but Hopkirk was running steadily and arrived in the evening for a night's rest at Alpe d'Huez in seventh place; Mäkinen was third behind two Alpine Renaults. Elford had fallen to fifth.

The next morning, the second leg, the easiest of the three, started. In front lay 450 miles of tortuous Alpine roads in 13 hours, with 13 selectives but no classification épreuves. It was all about fast continuous speed. Hopkirk, who had practised the entire route at least once, had pace notes for the entire route and Crellin was forever reading reams of notes to keep the car on time. He was rewarded by clawing their way up to fourth at their return to Alps D'Huez despite losing their fan belt at the start of the Chamrousse. The 20-minute service at the end of the leg was well used by everyone, where Hopkirk needed a new brake servo.

The third and final leg – the sting in the tail – was a 29-hour bash to Menton, near Monte Carlo. This section was just over 1000 miles long, with 18 selectives and six épreuves to tackle. It was demanding and, with difficult navigation skirting north around Chambéry, it would prove defining.

Hopkirk was now pressing the leading Alpine as hard as he could. He was second fastest on the Notre Dame Des Fres épreuve and fastest on the foggy Col de L'Iseran épreuve, no doubt due to good pace notes. Hopkirk sensed his chance of victory and pressed on with two more fastest times on the last two épreuves.

At Guillestre the leading Alpine blew up, promoting Mäkinen temporarily into the lead but he too was soon to retire. Hopkirk flew over the 7000ft Allos but there were still three difficult selectives to go: the Rouaine to Quatre Chemins selective and two tight selectives over difficult mountain roads between Puget-Théniers and Nice.

Hopkirk came through unscathed and still on time, took the win and cruised into Menton victorious. Only 20 cars followed him to the finish line. Abingdon won this gruelling event but it was to mark the very last international rally

A relentless battle with the works Porsche and Renault Alpines was to prove defining as Hopkirk kept his clean sheet and found himself at the top on the leaderboard.

At the finish Hopkirk and Crellin are greeted by the press and public. This win would be marked as the last international win for the works Minis.

win for the Mini, as more powerful cars slowly but surely overhauled the Mini and ended its long dominance.

After that Alpine win in September 1967 and until a new race car appeared some 18 months later, the rally-winning car was used by BMC as a publicity machine, being touted around BMC dealerships as the Alpine winner and acting as a shop window for BMC cars.

There were great tides of change at Abingdon in 1969. BMC had become BLMC and was headed by Lord Stokes, who had little time for motorsport, nor indeed rallying, viewing it as not helping car sales. The competition budget, once always rubber-stamped, was severely slashed by Stokes. It went further, as he decided that Abingdon would concentrate on racing rather than rallying, as this had a wider public appeal.

This was all very well and good but the racing side of BMC had, for years, been covered very successfully by John Cooper with his green-and-white Cooper Car Company race Minis. They had won the British Saloon Car Championship from 1964 to 1968, so the team knew what they were doing. Stokes promptly cancelled the contracts with John Cooper and instead charged Abingdon with the responsibility of entering the British Saloon Car Championship. There were also resulting changes at Abingdon: Den Green was put in charge of building and maintaining the race cars whilst Doug Watts handled the small rally programme and Tommy Wellman found himself looking after the rallycross cars. Meanwhile, Bill Price had been promoted to assistant competitions manager and would be in control of the race programme for 1969. Abingdon was fortunate to entice John Rhodes away from Cooper and also signed John Handley from British Vita to accompany him in the two-car team. Beating Cooper would be a tall order.

The first round of the championship at Brands Hatch two weeks earlier had been a disaster for the new Abingdon race team. Rhodes wrote off a brand-new OBL 45F on a start-line crash, then Handley wrote off the sister car OBL 46F on the last lap of the race. Much work was needed to prepare new cars for Handley and Rhodes for the next round at Silverstone. Handley would have a new LRX 827E, which was now prepared for a season of racing. The Alpine Rally-winning car was retained at Abingdon.

It is highly likely that Abingdon had prepared complete spare cars for the assault on the 1969 BSCC series and, despite the loss of two new cars only two weeks prior, LRX 827E was probably complete and ready to go and of very similar specification to its predecessor. The engine was 1293cc with a dry-decked block and fitted with Lucas slide-throttle fuel injection. The necessary fuel injection metering system meant the dynamo was relocated high up on the right-hand side of the bulkhead. The car ran a Salisbury limited-slip 3.7:1 diff, which was set to 66lb.ft. The car ran on rubber cone suspension, fitted with Koni shock absorbers. The car was also fitted with a rear anti-roll bar, and negative camber was set on all four corners.

John Handley at the wheel of LRX 827E at Silverstone for the second round of the British Saloon Car Championship, seen here with 10in wheels, awaiting homologation of 12in wheels.

A Group 6 dual-circuit tandem braking system was fitted. The fuel filler neck was set into the bodywork on the offside and the overflow pipe was run externally up the rear finisher seam. The left-hand filler neck was blocked off. Despite Abingdon's best efforts, it was forced to race with 10in wheels, as the much awaited 12in wheels were yet to be homologated – this again meant overheating tyres and severe wear rate on the hard-worked Dunlop race tyres.

The car was again in red and white and now sported numerous trade sponsorship decals on the rear, together with a large metal BL badge on the front wings and white door roundels plus one on the bonnet for its race number. The bonnet was held securely by two Moke rubber toggles at each corner. Handley's car, in addition, had an identification marking on the front of the roof just above the mirror. The front quick-lift jacking points were painted body red, unlike the rally cars, which were white. No bumpers were fitted either; a rubber strip covering the protruding edge.

The second round of the British Saloon Car Championship was held over 29 laps of the Silverstone Grand Prix race circuit on 30 March. Handley would again be teamed with Rhodes and these two BL drivers would again take the battle to the two Britax-Downton-Cooper Minis of Spice and Neal.

Practice, of two one-hour sessions, had not been without its problems. Handley had his engine changed after the gearbox broke and he was three places behind Rhodes, who in turn trailed Gordon Spice but was ahead of Steve Neal in their

Handley would use the car again at Thruxton for the next round, seen here right on the tail of one of the Ford Falcons.

Britax cars. Spice had also broken the lap record in practice.

Come the race, where the track was wet and oily after the main sports car race, Spice shot ahead and soon opened a healthy gap on Rhodes, who was just ahead of Neal and Handley. Handley, however, started to close on Rhodes and Neal as Rhodes slowed. With the track drying, the slight advantage the Minis had over the bigger cars soon evaporated and the class was won by Fitzpatrick in a Broadspeed Escort 1300GT. Handley led Rhodes to the flag but behind the Britax pair, and the two Abingdon cars were the last not to be lapped by the winning Broadspeed Escort TC of Frank Gardner. Handley finished tenth overall and fourth in the up-to-1300 class.

The fourth round of the championship was held on the Easter Monday at the Thruxton Circuit and Handley again had LRX 827E at his disposal, having missed the previous round on Good Friday at Snetterton. These two races, over the Easter weekend, were overseen by Peter Browning as Bill Price was in attendance on the Circuit of Ireland with Paddy Hopkirk.

The car was now fitted with the long-awaited 12in wheels, freshly homologated only days before, where it was hoped they would both improve grip and handling plus reduce the high wear rate due to excessive tyre temperature. The car was fitted with 12in Cooper Rose Petal wheels and wide wheelarch extensions with a chrome edge finisher to accommodate the fat 6J and 7J wheels. The car appeared much as at Silverstone, with the only visible addition of the bonnet being held down with a central leather strap in addition to the two Moke toggles at each corner.

In practice for the 25-lap race, Handley qualified 13th in a field of 28. Not great but ahead of Rhodes who was three places back, but both were behind the two Britax-Coopers of Neal and Spice in eighth and tenth place. Spice was in a spare car, having damaged his race car. Handley had a hard race and sustained frontal damage nudging another car, and finished well in ninth place but again behind the Britax cars of Spice and Neal in sixth and seventh. The class was won again by Craft in the Broadspeed 1300 Escort. Rhodes trailed home a distant last place with severe oil surge problems, three laps behind the overall winner, Pierpoint in a Ford Falcon.

Handley would use LRX 827E again for round five but before the next round at Silverstone, Abingdon tested with Rhodes at the circuit with GRX 310D to try different suspension setups and wheel and tyre options. The car ran dry suspension but with Hydrolastic top arms and rear struts and adjustable bottom arms. It also ran 2 degree negative camber at the front with 0.5 degree at the rear. There were lightweight Minifin rear brake drums, Cooper Rose Petal 7J wheels at the front and 6J to the rear, needing 7/8in spacers. The tyres ran at 50psi.

For the Silverstone race the following week, LRX 827E ran a 3.765 differential with the limited-slip diff set at 115lb.ft. It also now used Minilite wheels, not Cooper Rose Petal wheels. The bonnet roundel was now placed centrally rather than half on the bonnet and wing – probably due to a new bonnet being fitted, replacing the damage from Thruxton.

The Silverstone Martini International held on 17 May was a 20-lap race on the very fast Northamptonshire circuit, and the Minis, not unsurprisingly, were down on the third and fourth row of the grid with the two Britax-Coopers ahead of the Abingdon pair. After the 20-lap practice the negative camber on the front wheels was reduced to 1 degree, due to very high temperature on the outside edge of the tyres, which were Dunlop D22-232s.

The circuit had been wet for the previous sports car race and a dry line was just appearing, and Abingdon decided at the last minute to start Handley on dry tyres. As the 38 cars shot away, Handley, on a damp circuit, made good progress through the field but the Britax-Cooper pair came together on the first lap, with the result that Spice rolled but Neal

LRX 827E was now fitted with 12in wheels and, as can be seen here, the car received a punch in the nose. He would finish in ninth place.

It was back to Silverstone for Handley and LRX 327E for round 6 of the BSCC, the car now fitted with 12in Minilite wheels rather than Cooper Rose Petals seen at Thruxton.

Handley with LRX 827E on the starting grid in front of a packed crowd at the South London Crystal Palace race circuit.

Cosmetically the car's only change for the sixth round of the BSCC at Crystal Palace was the white front jacking points. Handley would finish a fine third place on the tight, twisty circuit.

continued albeit with a badly-deranged car. Handley, with the correct tyres, was locked in a race-long battle with Fitzpatrick in his Broadspeed 1300 Escort, who between them posted the fastest lap for the class. Handley just led the Escort to the flag but 13 seconds adrift of Rhodes. Chris Craft won the 1300 class, with Rhodes and Handley second and third and a creditable sixth and seventh overall. Pierpoint's Falcon won the race outright.

Round six of the BSCC was held on 26 May at the lovely London race circuit at Crystal Palace, a narrow picturesque track that often punished those who slid off in the wrong place. Handley would again use LRX 827E, which was little changed from Silverstone other than the front jacking plates were now a different type and painted white.

The fuel-injected dry-decked engine, fitted with a 13:1-compression Weslake cylinder head and a 1241 camshaft produced 112bhp at the wheels on the Abingdon rolling road. Rubber cone suspension with Hydrolastic arms was used before but the rear anti-roll bar was disconnected during practice and the diff ratio changed to 4:1 after practice to improve acceleration, to the detriment of some top speed. The adjustable bottom arms were now set at 1 degree negative, not 1.5 degrees, to help reduce tyre temperature, which was causing issues. Practice went well for Handley, shaving 1.5 seconds off the class lap record and he was ahead of Rhodes on the grid for the 15-lap race. Both cars beat the 1968 lap record.

The round at Crystal Palace was divided into two races, the first for the larger-capacity cars and the second for the smaller classes for the Anerley trophy. So for a change the Minis were not overshadowed by the big-capacity cars. Handley had qualified on the second row, still behind Spice on the front row but alongside Neal. Spice, from pole, was in his spare car after his roll at Silverstone the week before. Spice led, with Handley in a strong fourth place, battling hard with Neal until the inevitable happened: Neal and Handley touched and both spun off, but without much damage and both continued with little time lost.

Handley was still fourth and was soon closing on Rhodes, whom he overtook on lap 11 and headed his teammate to the flag. Spice won from Craft's Escort, with Handley third. It was a much better race for the Minis.

Mallory Park in Leicestershire was the next round of the BSCC. The Guards 4000 Guineas International was held over 20 laps on 29 June. LRX 827E was again little changed, other

Handley's LRX 827E for Mallory Park and round seven saw the car with a broad red identification stripe appear on the front grille, and extra-wide wheelarch extensions.

than Handley's car had a broad red vertical stripe painted centrally on the front grille to aid identification, but still retaining the identification mark on the roof. The car was now fitted with wider Group 5 wheelarch extensions, without a chrome strip finisher. The engine was the same unit last used at Crystal Palace the previous month but now fitted with a longer 3.9:1 diff.

Two races were again scheduled, where all the Minis were in the up-to-1300cc race and the larger cars in their own race, both held over 20 laps. Practice saw Handley just behind Rhodes on the time sheets, and only one second separated the two Abingdon cars from the Britax works Coopers of Neal and Spice. So both the Britax cars headed Rhodes and Handley on the starting grid.

The first lap saw Handley chasing hard just behind Rhodes

Handley approaches Shaw's Corner at Mallory Park, clearly showing the rear number plate at an angle, the electrical cut-out on the lower right and the recessed fuel filler cap.

but both behind Spice and Neal and the Escort of Chris Craft. As the race wore on, Handley started to experience overheating problems and it soon saw the car into retirement with a blown piston, which was actually the first mechanical failure of the race season. Rhodes had to settle for fourth place behind Neal, with Spice and Craft finishing in a dead heat some way ahead.

The next race meeting scheduled for LRX 827E was the very popular saloon car race that accompanied the British Grand Prix at Silverstone in Northamptonshire, held on 19 July. This was the ninth round of the British Saloon Car Championship and attracted a huge crowd. John Handley was again assigned this potent Group 5 car to hopefully get on terms with the Britax-Cooper cars, which had got the better of the Abingdon cars for much of the season.

The specification of the car was again little changed from the previous rounds, running fuel injection on a Weslake Mk1 crossflow cylinder head at 13:1 compression with an auxiliary radiator to try to keep things cool. The car was again running dry suspension but using Hydrolastic top arms and adjustable tie rods. The Koni dampers were set at just half a turn off their maximum. The car sat on wide wheels, being 7J at the front and 6J at the rear – all 12in Minilite magnesium wheels. Dunlop D22-232 tyres were at 48psi and 44psi front and back. Cambers was set at 1 degree negative at the front with 2.5 degree caster. The 3.9:1 Salisbury diff was set at a very high 115lb and the car weighed in at 625kg.

Thirty cars contested the 20-lap race, where Handley found himself starting from the fifth row behind Rhodes and the two Britax cars of Spice and Neal, these all behind the now-dominant 1300 Broadspeed Escorts of John Fitzpatrick and Chris Craft.

Once the flag dropped, Spice led the Minis and Handley found himself in 13th spot just ahead of Rhodes, with Neal two places behind them. The trio of Handley, Rhodes and Neal continued to circulate in close quarters until disaster struck on lap seven when the three collided at Copse Corner. Rhodes managed to escape with little damage from the fracas but Handley and Neal lost time untangling themselves and getting going again. Handley sustained a deranged bonnet and grille for his troubles.

Neal would go on to finish just ahead of Handley, and both continued their battle to the flag. They finished ninth and tenth respectively, behind Spice and Rhodes in seventh and eighth. But the two Escorts were yet again ahead at fifth and sixth, being class winners. It was now evident that the works Minis would struggle against both the Fords and the Britax cars, even though Handley's best lap time was only tenth of a second off that of the class-winning Escort's fastest lap.

Thirty-one cars turned up for the 11th round of the BSCC, which was held on 1 September at Brands Hatch. The race would be decided over two 15-lap heats of the full Grand Prix circuit, the cumulative time of the two races deciding the winner. The starting order of the first race decided on practice

Handley in the thick of it at Silverstone in LRX 827E, with Gordon Spice right behind in the Britax car followed by John Rhodes in the other Abingdon car.

The coming-together of Handley and Steve Neal's Britax car at Silverstone saw Handley recover to finish seventh in round nine.

LRX 827E at Brands Hatch for round 11 saw the car revert to different jacking points on the front yet again. He was classed as a non-finisher due to electrical problems.

time but the second heat's starting order was the finishing order of the first heat.

Handley was in LRX 827E, which was little changed from its last outing, other than losing the marking on the front of its roof and the front jacking points reverting to how they appeared way back in May. It is possible this was a car swap, though no evidence exists to support this summation, other than the jacking points details. Handley did not have the new more-powerful 1299cc short-stroke engine that Rhodes had at his disposal, and was behind his teammate in practice for the first race. However, with the championship already won by Alec Poole in his one-litre Arden Mini, Abingdon was still hoping for a good finish to the season. Spice would uncharacteristically find himself at the back of the grid, having badly damaging his Britax-Cooper at Paddock Hill Bend. He would commandeer Neal's car for the race.

Despite the woes of the opposition, Handley's race did not go well, as he was forced to retire after just seven laps of the first heat when his electrics shorted out. He would start at the back of the grid for the second heat. This he finished in 15th place, just behind Alec Poole, but would not be classed as a finisher, having failed to complete the first heat's full distance. Rhodes would finish in tenth place overall but still fourth in class behind the Escorts.

This would bring a premature end to Abingdon's attempt to win the BSCC, as it would not contend the last round at Brands Hatch in late October. Handley would finish the 1969 BSCC 23rd overall and seventh in the 1300 class. Not what Abingdon had hoped for but it was a clear indication that it could not, in just one season, hope to get on terms with the vast racing experience that the Cooper Car Company of John Cooper and Ginger Devlin had developed over many seasons' racing.

The final race outing for LRX 827E and Handley for 1969 was in Austria on 12 October at the Salzburgring. This was a Group 2 race as part of the support programme for the high-profile Donaupokal Race for big sports and GT cars. BL Austria requested Abingdon contest the support race to increase its publicity; Abingdon was happy to do so and sent two works cars and a full support team.

With LRX 827E being a highly-developed Group 5, it was hastily put into Group 2 trim, sporting bumpers for the first time in the season. The car lost its quick-lift jacking points and Handley's distinctive roof identification marking. Nevertheless, the car did have an advantage over most of the grid, which apart from a couple of quick Alfas, consisted of ten other homegrown Mini race cars. Abingdon was supported in

WORKS MINIS IN DETAIL

LRX 827E appeared in Group 2 form for the race at the Salzburgring in Austria. The car lost its front jacking point and would finish a fine second place just behind Rhodes.

The Spa 24-hour race saw LRX 827E handed to John Rhodes who would share the drive with Geoff Mabbs. Seen here on the starting grid hastily swapping off wet race tyres, gambling the track would soon dry.

its team by another Mini prepared locally by Don Wooding, an ex-Nuffield Exports representative, who had his own tuning business in Germany. He would offer a strong challenge to the two works cars of Handley and Rhodes.

Practice went well in front of a large crowd, and saw Rhodes qualify on the front row of the grid alongside Wooding and a 1300 Alfa Romeo. Handley, in the second Abingdon works Mini was behind on row three, with ten other Minis further back. The rest of the grid had a few NSUs and Fiats to make up the numbers. Nevertheless, the race was hard fought, with the Alfa going very well but as the race wore on, the Abingdon pair pulled away. At the flag, Rhodes won, with Handley following close by. This marked a pleasing end to a rather unsuccessful race year for Abingdon and the team celebrated in fine 'end of term' style.

Leaping forward to the summer of 1970, Abingdon decided to enter the very prestigious 24-hour saloon car race at Spa Francorchamps. This was probably the most important saloon car race of the year, so BL entered for all the right corporate reasons. LRX 827E was prepared for John Rhodes and Geoff Mabbs within the new Group 2 rules for 1970. The Spa race was round seven of the newly-renamed European Touring Car Championship – the same initials as before, but the ETCC was previously known as the European Touring Car Challenge. It was, however, now open only to Group 2 cars. It is possible that the Group 2 LRX 827E that competed in Salzburg was rolled out again for Spa but it is also possible the car could have been previously used as a rally car. There is evidence that an external power socket was fitted alongside the offside headlight, indicating that a lamp bar and plug was once fitted but now blanked off. The appearance of a GB plate on the bootlid would also support the notion that the car was an ex-rally car.

Being a Group 2 car, the Mini carried its trim, a heavy heater and glass (not Perspex); it also had to run with bumpers. As Spa was a 24-hour race and run in darkness, the car was fitted with an identification lamp on the front of its roof. It also had a number plate lamp secured to the door to illuminate its competition number at night. Numbers were stuck on the roof above the driver's door, and it also had a broad red vertical mark in the centre of the grille. This marking, during the 1969 season, was the preserve of John Handley in 'his' LRX 827E. It ran two additional driving lamps, secured to the front panel and bumper on individual brackets, rather than on a detachable lamp bar favoured by the rally cars. The headlights were protected by a Perspex snap-on cover but not the type seen on rally cars.

The engine was a powerful crossflow eight-port engine where Rhodes had elected to have the car built with fuel injection, in an attempt to get as much power as possible, especially on a circuit where speed was crucial. Accordingly, a rather long 3.3:1 final drive was fitted to the car to get as much top speed as possible but to the detriment of acceleration.

The Spa race between 25 and 26 July attracted a full entry of 60 cars (59 started). Two practice sessions were scheduled, one of which (compulsory) was in the hours of darkness. After an uneventful two days of practice, Rhodes qualified in 43rd place, despite working with Handley towing each other around by slipstreaming. It, however, has to be remembered that the majority of entrants were big, high-powered cars and even the class Rhodes was competing in was for up-to-1600cc cars.

Come race day, after storms throughout the night, it was still wet and overcast at the scheduled 3pm start but not raining and Rhodes decided to gamble and started on dry 12in race tyres. The gamble paid off and the track soon began to dry on the race line, and those who decided to start on intermediate tyres were soon pitting early to change onto dry tyres. After four hours' running and a driver change, the car was up into 21st place; at the six-hour mark, it was up into 17th place.

So far all the pit stops had been scheduled and routine with a simple driver change, new tyres, fuel and oil replenished. As darkness fell and the night wore on, the engine started to sound rough and they were losing power and starting to drop places. At just before 1.30am, the car came into the pits on three cylinders. It had destroyed a valve and its seat. With very little compression, the car was withdrawn, much to Rhodes's displeasure as he urged the mechanics to try and rectify the car from what had been a strong finishing position. Just 30 cars made it through to the 3pm flag. The class-winning 1300 Alfa completed nearly 2400 miles in 24 hours.

Peter Baldwin bought the race car soon after the 1970 Spa and continued to use it in club races.

LRX 827E was trimmed as a Group 2 car for Spa and also carried an identification lamp on the roof. Rhodes and Mabbs retired the car in the middle of the night with a dropped valve.

Competition Record

Date	Event	Crew	Number	Overall result	Class result
April 1967	Tulip Rally	Timo Mäkinen/Paul Easter	64	2nd	1st
June 1967	Criterium Rally	Tony Fall/Mike Wood	79	1st	1st
Sept 1967	Alpine Rally	Paddy Hopkirk/Ron Crellin	107	1st	1st
March 1969	Silverstone	John Handley	15	10th	4th
April 1969	Thruxton	John Handley	24	9th	5th
May 1969	Silverstone	John Handley	16	7th	3rd
May 1969	Crystal palace	John Handley	135	3rd	3rd
June 1969	Mallory Park	John Handley	117	DNF	
July 1969	Silverstone	John Handley	15	10th	6th
Sept 1969	Brands Hatch	John Handley	245	DNF	
Oct 1969	Salzburgring	John Handley	31	2nd	2nd
July 1970	Spa 24 Hrs	John Rhodes/Geoff Mabbs	72	DNF	

Registration Number	First registered	Chassis number	Engine	Engine number	Model
LRX 828E	March 1967	CA2S7 956612	1275cc	9F-SA-Y 44521	Austin Cooper S

LRX 828E was the second of a crop of four new cars delivered to Abingdon and registered early in 1967. This Group 2 car was assigned to Rauno Aaltonen and Henry Liddon for the Acropolis Rally in May.

Build started by Bob Whittington early April; as usual, the 1293cc engine featured the Abingdon staple of the AEA648 full-race camshaft. An extra-lightweight steel flywheel was fitted, and the high-compression Downton cylinder head had slightly lower compression to reflect the often lower-quality fuel available in Greece at that time. New for the engine was a large-bore exhaust manifold of 1¾in. Carburettors were twin SU 1½ H4s fitted with BG needles and blue springs along with float chamber extensions. The gearbox, with straight-cut close-ratio gears, was fitted with a 4.26:1, with the casing machined to take a Moke sump plate.

The car, because of the anticipated rough terrain, was fitted

Rauno Aaltonen and Henry Liddon in Athens with LRX 828E just prior to the start of the 1967 Acropolis Rally.

Liddon facing the camera as Aaltonen attends to the car whilst in service on the opening day of the rally.

with a heavy-duty Scandinavian sump guard and tie-bar protectors. Hardy Spicer drive couplings were fitted to larger-diameter driveshafts but no limited-slip diff. An additional metal safety strap was fitted to the car, screwed through the floor, under the remote gearshift to secure it in case the locating bracket or rubber was to fail. A skid was fitted under the battery box, and the front brake hoses also had protection plates fixed to the callipers to stop them from being torn off.

Hydrolastic suspension was fitted, which Aaltonen favoured, with single-blue and double-blue displacers and orange helper springs plus Aeon bump stops. Again, because of the rough roads, the rear subframe was double-skinned and rewelded, with reinforced radius arm brackets also added.

The electrical system was rewired throughout by the Lucas Racing technicians resident at Abingdon. Aaltonen had fitted to his car a dip switch to the left-hand side of the steering column, preferring this to the cumbersome standard dip switch, on the floor, by his clutch foot. This switch, from the Lucas parts bin, was from a Riley Pathfinder. All four auxiliary lamps, on the chrome badge bar, were fitted with steady brackets to prevent the lamps from vibrating. These stays were fitted to the top of the lamps and secured to the grille moustache. The boot lid carried a Healey 3000 sidelight, used as a reversing lamp.

The twin fuel pump was located under the rear seat but only one pump was wired. All lines were run inside the car. An expansion tank from the radiator and a washer bottle, were located in the co-driver's footwell, while an intercom box was fitted to the roll cage, above the crew's heads, by the interior light.

LRX 828E was fitted with fibreglass wheelarch extensions, covering wide Minilite wheels, and was fitted with large front-facing mud flaps, secured to the corners of the bumper and front panel. Another distinguishing oddity of this car was the leather bonnet strap, which was fitted centrally under the Austin Cooper badge. The front number plate was affixed to a black-painted square on the right-hand side of the bonnet, with the rally plate fixed to the other side of the bonnet. Inside was a padded roll cage.

Tyre choice was both Dunlop SP44s and R7 race tyres. The brakes, as had become custom, were modified by the use of asbestos blocks in the calliper pistons, and the rear brake drums and backplates were drilled to aid cooling; further, the wheel cylinders were bolted to the backplate to help dissipate heat. DS11 racing brake pads and VG95 brake shoes were used; such were the demands on the brakes, brought about, largely, by Aaltonen's habit of left-foot braking.

Based in Athens, the Acropolis Rally was a hard, demanding rally and one that needed a fast and reliable car. The roads were hot, dry, dusty and of poor-quality tarmac (bar two loose-surface stages). These roads were scattered around the many hills in Greece, and although not high in altitude, they did have severe drops. The 2000-mile route, spanning two days and two nights non-stop, included 220 miles of stages and hillclimbs. The stages all had a target time to beat to stay clean.

As it turned out, many of the fast cars achieved their target time and so it was down to just four 'impossible' stages and the three hillclimbs, timed on scratch, to decide the winner. Seventy-two cars lined up in the evening by the Acropolis for the start; only 18 would make it back to the capital two days later, so tough was the rally.

During the first night, Aaltonen hit trouble and collected a puncture early on one of the stages – but he was so fast that he and Liddon changed the wheel and lost only four seconds against their target time.

Then disaster struck near Thessalonica the following day. A competitor in a Renault Gordini, just ahead of Aaltonen, slid off the stage and plunged 150ft down the side of the hill. A spectating doctor saw it in the distance and instinctively jumped into his VW and shot off down the stage to see what he could do. Trouble was, he was now driving against the rally traffic and Aaltonen was next on the stage. A huge collision was inevitable, and as Aaltonen rounded a blind left-hand bend he was confronted by the errant VW. When Aaltonen got out of the car to remonstrate with the driver, he promptly collapsed. The impact completely destroyed the Mini and put Aaltonen in hospital for two days with concussion and amnesia. Liddon was spared serious injuries, confined to just cuts and bruises.

LRX 828E was trailed back to Abingdon, where it was stripped of all of its useable parts and a new car was built. Abingdon was, however, rewarded by Hopkirk winning the rally, avenging his relegation from the top spot the previous year for a servicing infringement.

The new LRX 828E was built by Gerald Wiffen as a Group 2 car, with work starting in early July for the next event, the Danube Rally at the end of the month, where again Aaltonen and Liddon would take over the car.

It was built to an almost identical specification to the car it replaced – and it should be noted that a first-aid kit was now to be fitted in the rear of the car, no doubt as a direct result of Aaltonen's accident in Greece. Spinner-type wheel braces were supplied and fitted under the seats on the floor – again, probably due to Aaltonen's need to replace a flat tyre, on a stage, in a hurry, as he had to do on the last event.

Other minor cosmetic changes were that only the two middle auxiliary lamps now had lamp steadies fitted – probably reasoning that fog lamps needn't be so rigid. Aaltonen also had an 1800 indicator stalk, which incorporated a headlamp flasher; it replaced the headlamp flasher stalk customarily fitted to the fascia of the driver's auxiliary dash panel.

Abingdon was by now starting to standardise certain aspects of a car's build, one of which was to fit a five-pin socket for the quick removal of the lamps in situ on the lamp bar. However, despite it being noted as a requirement for this car's build, LRX 828E reverted to the rather clumsy and occasionally temperamental cluster of bullet connectors for the lamps. It is possible, therefore, that this car was not a new build but another earlier car with its identity changed. One last detail was that the front mud flaps disappeared and the bonnet strap reverted to the right-hand side of the bonnet.

The Danube Rally was part of the European Championship; despite that, the rally attracted only 63 starters for a 2000-mile high speed event, which had to be completed in just 50 hours virtually non-stop. The route loosely followed the line of the Danube River from Germany, Austria and Hungary, then on to the Black Sea in Romania.

Two starting points were on offer: Germany and Prague. Aaltonen elected to start in Prague, with the two routes converging on the Austrian border. Nine fast and dusty stages in the mountains, mainly in Romania, formed the meat of the rally. In between were 41 tightly timed road sections, which only 11 crews completed without time penalties – some were set as high as 60mph average. Servicing was also a problem, as the route was in a general straight line, making

A new LRX 828E was built for Aaltonen and Liddon for the 1967 Danube Rally, seen here ready to go on one of the very fast and dusty stages.

The result of a doctor travelling down the stage, against rally traffic, to attend to a car that had gone off the road. Aaltonen was hospitalised for two days.

Despite leading the rally for much of it Aaltonen, was refused entry into Hungary, only having a Finnish passport, and had to retire on the spot.

leap-frogging almost impossible for the single BMC service barge. Thick dust was a major problem for the competitors, making overtaking, especially on the longer stages, difficult and dangerous.

However, Aaltonen, leading, was unable to show his prowess any further, being refused entry into Hungary. Having only a Finnish passport meant he didn't have the necessary Hungarian visa, and he was forced to retire on the spot.

Only 36 crews made the finish. All was not loss for BMC, however, as against all of the odds, Tony Fall won the rally, driving an Austin 1800.

LRX 828E was next shipped to Australia at the request of BMC Australia to compete on the Southern Cross Rally. The car left Abingdon, having been thoroughly checked with the engine producing 83bhp on the Abingdon rolling road prior to dispatch. The car had to be registered in Australia and carried the number EPX 813, whilst still clearly displaying its LRX 828E number on the bonnet behind. BMC Australia requested Paddy Hopkirk drive the car on the Southern Cross, as he was already in Australia racing in the Bathurst race; the local team would service the car on the rally. He was paired with local navigator Garry Chapman. Timo Mäkinen was also there with a sister car.

The Southern Cross was now an event very similar to European rallies with forest and mountain stages, all of which were tackled at night. At the start in South Eastern Australia for the first leg to Canberra were 84 cars. The initial stages were rocky, and fog was an issue on higher ground. The forests west of Canberra followed, which were very fast and more to Hopkirk's taste, where he dropped no time. Hopkirk was lying in third place when 73 other cars arrived in Canberra for their day's rest.

The route then headed south west from Canberra to Bairnsdale. Just past Kiandra in the Snowy Mountains, Hopkirk had gearbox problems and he was out. Mäkinen had already retired earlier with similar problems. A mere 39 crews made it to the finish in Sydney, where the event was won by a Volkswagen driven by Barry Ferguson.

The car remained in Australia and became the property of BMC Australia.

LRX 828E was shipped to Australia for the Southern Cross Rally for Paddy Hopkirk and local navigator Garry Chapman and re-registered EPX 813. They would retire whilst lying in third place with a broken gearbox.

Competition Record

Date	Event	Crew	Number	Overall result	Class result
May 1967	Acropolis Rally	Rauno Aaltonen/Henry Liddon	92	DNF	
July 1967	Danube Rally	Rauno Aaltonen/Henry Liddon	34	DNF	
Oct 1967	Southern Cross Rally	Paddy Hopkirk/Garry Chapman	14	DNF	

CHAPTER 3: THE MK 1 MINI COOPER S

Registration Number	First registered	Chassis number	Engine	Engine number	Model
LRX 829E	March 1967	KA2S4 956691	1275cc	9F-SA-Y 44695	Morris Cooper S

LRX 829E was the third of a crop of four new cars delivered to Abingdon and registered early in 1967. This Group 2 car was assigned to Rauno Aaltonen and Henry Liddon for the Tulip Rally in April. It was built by Roy Brown.

The new car was fitted with the latest strengthened block, bored to give 1293cc and with Abingdon's standard-fit race camshaft, the AEA648. A high-compression 12.6:1 Downton cylinder head was fitted with 16.4cc combustion chambers, held firm by MGB studs. Forged oval pistons and a lightened steel flywheel were fitted. Carburettors were twin SU H4s, fitted with BG needles and blue springs along with float chamber extensions. A Lucas 40979 distributor was added. The emissions clack valve was blanked off and holes cut in its hose.

Transmission was by straight-cut close-ratio gears and the idler transfer gear was now housed in a special bearing within the casing, as this had started to seize under heavy use. The bottom of the gear case was machined flat to enable a Moke sump plate to be securely screwed to its underside. A 4.2:1 final drive was fitted, along with the latest Hardy Spicer shafts and joints. A Mitchell mounting was used to secure the end of the remote-control gearchange. Even though this was virtually indestructible, a safely strap was made up and secured through the floor to the underside of the remote control. Because of the large alternator, the oil cooler was also relocated a few inches further over and the diagonal stiffener removed and placed vertically.

The suspension was Hydrolastic with single-blue displacers at the front and double-blue displacers on the rear, with orange helper springs. The subframes were both strengthened and the rear radius arm bracket also modified with an extra metal block welded into place to add strength. The ride height was set at 13in wheel centre to the wheelarch. Because the Tulip was an all-tarmac rally, the car was fitted with a short 13-hole guard protecting just the front of the sump plus the Moke sump plate. A battery box guard was not fitted.

The brakes were all standard, including the retaining of the servo but using DS11 racing brake pads and VG95 brake shoes. Aaltonen had a special 450psi brake limiting valve, putting more braking to the front wheels. His left-foot braking technique played heavily on the brakes.

Outside the car, fibreglass wheelarches were fitted, covering the Minilite magnesium wheels, first seen on the Monte Carlo Rally earlier in the year. These were exclusively fitted with Dunlop R7 race tyres throughout the rally. The boot lid was held securely with a Moke rubber toggle strap and had a large back-mounted Lucas fog lamp to act as a revering lamp. It also carried rear mud flaps.

At the front, the four auxiliary lamps (two fog lamps on the outside and two driving lamps in the centre) were fixed to a heavy-gauge badge/lamp bar. The two driving lamps were held firm with fabricated steadies just under the front grille. The front grille moustache had Lift-the-Dot fixings for the grille muff, which could be fixed on to keep out the cold

Rauno Aaltonen and Henry Liddon with LRX 829E blast off the line in the early stages of the 1967 Tulip Rally.

Stuart Turner and Doug Watts examine the Amplivox intercom used on LRX 829E - which can just be seen fixed to the roll cage in the previous picture. Numerous types were used on the cars.

Aaltonen would have a long battle with Elford's works Porsche 911 despite never being far behind the German car.

or snow if it were encountered. The iodine headlamps were protected by Perspex covers held on by straps fixed to the wing and front panel. Quick-lift jacking points were located front and back. The number plate was now on a black square on the offside of the bonnet, and the bonnet was held securely by a leather strap.

Inside the car was an alloy roll cage, as first seen on the previous year's RAC Rally. Aaltonen sat in a lightweight cloth-covered bucket seat and Liddon in a more comfortable but less supportive reclining seat, also cloth-covered. Aaltonen used an Irvin lap-and-diagonal seat belt, and Liddon a full-harness Irvin belt. Each of the crew had a black crackle-finish additional dashboard housing instruments, switches and navigational and timing equipment. Liddon also had an additional switch panel in his door pocket for his map light and more control switches.

A clear view demister panel was fitted to the rear 'screen but there was no heated front windscreen. All carpet and trim was retained, with an addition of an asbestos blanket to keep out exhaust heat. Padding to the door lock, door pockets and pillars was fitted, covered in red vinyl.

The electrical system was rewired throughout by the Lucas Racing resident at Abingdon. The twin fuel pump was located under the rear seat but only one pump was wired. All lines were run inside the car, and a modified MGB jack secured inside the car against the driver's rear companion bin. The windscreen washer bottle was located in Liddon's footwell, along with a foot-operated horn switch. An intercom was also fitted, with the control box fixed to the centre of the roll cage, and their crash helmets were stowed on the rear parcel shelf.

The Tulip Rally was a popular all-tarmac event, which started way back in 1949 and was the instigator of the now-universally used Tulip-designed road book navigation system. The event was once run on the class improvement system but by now, to fall in line with the majority of European events, ran on scratch times, meaning basically the fastest won.

The 1967 rendition, held between 24 and 30 April, consisted of 18 timed-to-the-second tests and all bar two were classic hillclimbs. These tests were interspersed with numerous timed selectives with a bogey time to beat, mostly set at 45mph. The 2000-mile route wound its way from its start at Noordwijk, on the Dutch coast halfway between Amsterdam and The Hague, on to Belgium, into Luxembourg, then to the western mountains of France and on to Annecy where the crews had a 12-hour rest. The route then returned to Noordwijk via a three-hour stop at Rumilly on a northern route, mirroring the outward-bound southern path. Heavy snow, a few weeks prior, had unfortunately meant some drastic rerouting, to the detriment of the rally's competitive content, particularly in the area south of Geneva near Annecy. Nevertheless, 108 starters lined up on Monday morning, in fine sunny weather, to take on what was on offer.

With his high-powered and brand-new Cooper S, hopes were high for Aaltonen, but all knew the threat would be coming from Germany with Vic Elford in the fast and reliable Porsche 911. And so it proved: Elford was fastest on all bar one stage, which went to Aaltonen's teammate, Mäkinen.

However, despite the Porsche domination, Aaltonen was never far from the top of the time sheet. The first test, at Zolder race track, saw Aaltonen sixth fastest (but it was otherwise a Porsche benefit). As the route trudged on and into the night, the Charbonnière climb was undertaken, where Aaltonen was again sixth. Elford was beginning to build up a comfortable lead, but Aaltonen was still in touch and second in class behind his teammate.

The 12-hour rest at Annecy on Tuesday was welcomed and the one-hour service before parc fermé was well used by many. Fresh racing tyres were seen on most top cars.

Ninety cars restarted the night section from Annecy to Rumilly – a loop that would be decisive for many. In six hours were 17 short sharp sections in the mountains between Geneva, Chamonix and Annecy. With a cold night, patches of ice were there to catch the unwary and the Croix Fry tunnel caused havoc. A left-hand bend in the middle had a cascade of water across the road, which had frozen just before the apex; the first car through, Elford, clobbered the outside of the rock face, collecting a puncture (and much body damage), losing his lead and three minutes. Aaltonen, like many others, would not escape unscathed. He smacked the rear wing as he put the car sideways to avoid understeering into the rock face, fortunately with little time loss.

Many wounded cars pulled into Rumilly for a three-hour rest – again much servicing activity was in evidence. The route back to Noordwijk was restarted by 83 cars, and another 20 would fall by the wayside. Elford started to claw back his lost time and Aaltonen set after his teammate, beating him on the later stages. He so nearly came to grief when he spun backwards and into a ditch, but with no damage. He was soon on his way to the last test at the Zandvoort circuit but

CHAPTER 3: THE MK 1 MINI COOPER S

Aaltonen took evasive action on some unseen ice and to save understeering into a rock face he put the car sideways and hit the rear wing - with little time loss.

Aaltonen and Liddon had to settle for third place, such was the pace of the rally, here at the finish at Noordwijk.

had to settle for second in the touring car class and, more significantly, third overall behind the very rapid Porsche. A fine result.

The second event for LRX 829E is often referred to as the Geneva Rally but it's more correctly the Criterium de Crans-sur-Sierre that was open to Group 2 cars, which the car was entered as. The Geneva Rally was a round of the European Championship, where this year only Group 1 or Group 3 cars could score championship points. As BMC was not chasing the European Championship in 1967, it was decided to enter the Criterium Group 2 category, where there was the best chance of a good result. A trio of privateers, in their Group 1 cars, was also enlisted to try and win the Geneva team prize.

The Criterium was in effect a rally within the Geneva Rally, as they both shared the same route and timetable. For the Criterium, the Group 2 car was handed to Julien Vernaeve, who would have Henry Liddon as his navigator. Vernaeve was a Belgian Mini race and rally driver, who won the Belgian Saloon Car Championship in 1964 and the rally championship in 1962 and 1963. He regularly supported the works teams, when called upon, with his own private Cooper S and helped in winning the team prize on numerous occasions. This was to be his first of several drives for Abingdon and he would have at his disposal a full works Mini. His car was built as a Group 2 by Nobby Hall, one of the true craftsman mechanics at Abingdon.

The engine bay of LRX 829E taken after the rally for a magazine article. Details of the carburettor fire plate can be seen and of note is the car is fitted with all of the sound-deadening material.

337

The boot detail of LRX 829E taken at the same time, showing the spare fuel lines, inner tubes, fuel bag and the tool bag with assorted spares and tools carried with the car.

RALLY EQUIPMENT

Tool bag	Schrader valve kit
Tool roll	Barnacle mirror
1 D.E. Spanner 1/4" x 5/16" AF	Holts screen wash
1 D.E. Spanner 3/8" x 7'16" AF	4 qts. Castrol XL oil
1 D.E. Spanner 7/16" x 1/2" AF	Ball pins and shims
1 D.E. Spanner 9/16" x 5/8" AF	2 ft. plastic tubing and clips
1 D.E. Spanner 15/16" x 1" AF	4in. adjustable spanner
1 D.E. Spanner 11/16" x 19/32" AF	Chisel
1 ring Spanner A.F. 1/2" x 19/32"	Sparking plugs
Foglamp spanner	Top water hose
Mole wrench	Bottom water hose
Adjustable spanner	Fan belt
Screw driver, medium	Molyslip E
Screwdriver, electrical	Accelerator spring
Screwdriver, medium (Phillips)	Radiator cap
Screwdriver, small (Phillips)	Distributor, complete
Plug spanner	Nuts, bolts and washers
Pair pliers	Bleeder tube
Ball pein hammer, 1 lb	Rubber bands
Tyre gauge	Set of bulbs
Wheel brace	35 amp fuses
Jack modified	50 amp fuses
Length locking wire	Wiper arms
Length electrical wire	Wiper blades
Roll insulating tape	Speedo cable
Tow rope	Halda cable
Fire extinguisher	Brake pads DS11 (faded)
First aid kit	Caliper pins
Triangle sign	Front brake hoses
Torch	Rear brake hoses
Accelerator cable (special)	Set brake shoe springs
Hand cream and wiper	Brake fluid - Disc
Roll masking tape, 1 in.	Tins Rad Weld, large
Carb. repair kit	Tins Gun Gum Bandage
Elopress	Tins Gun Gum
Wheel nuts	Petrol bag
Inner Tubes	Set fuel pipes
Sponge	Clutch hose
Leather (in plastic bag)	WD-40 silicone spray

The comprehensive list of spares, tools and equipment often carried in a works Mini in the tool bags in the boot and the tool roll on the rear seat back. This must have added considerable weight to the car.

The car was little changed from the Tulip Rally, fitted with a 1293cc engine of exactly the same specification as previously. The major changes were underneath the car, as the Criterium, although not a very rough event, was certainly not smooth tarmac either. The lightweight 13-hole guard with an alloy extension plate was initially fitted but changed to a Scandinavian guard for the forest stages, while the engine was still fitted with a Moke sump plate screwed to the bottom of the sump. In addition to the sump guard, the battery box also had a steel battery guard, which spanned the rear subframe and protected the vulnerable battery box.

The brakes also received added attention. The backplates were drilled, as were the brake drums to allow additional cooling to the rear brakes. The rear wheel cylinders were also threaded, rather than held in place by a circlip. This added as an additional heatsink for what were often very hot brakes. The rear brake limiting valve returned to the normal 325psi. The front brakes also received attention, with asbestos blocks being fitted in the pistons, intended to keep some of the intense heat away from the brake fluid. The last modification for the Criterium was the fitting of a rear anti-roll bar.

Held between 15 and 18 June, the rally started in Switzerland, 80 miles east of Geneva. Some 76 cars had entered for this 1250-mile event, most of which were on French roads and comprised 11 tests totalling just under 100 miles, consisting mostly of hillclimbs but with one notoriously difficult forest stage north of Geneva in the Jura mountains. This stage, in the Gimel St-George forest, was to be the undoing of many, including nearly both BMC works Minis.

The route was divided into two legs. The first, of 500 miles with six tests, where the route looped southwards around Annecy and including the Gimel forest; the second of 750 miles and the remaining six tests, tackled after an 11-hour rest stop. This second loop was a figure of eight south of Geneva. However, before any cars could set off the scrutineers had to be satisfied. They insisted that all cars had to have a minimum of 10cm ground clearance – tested by driving over a 10cm lump of wood. BMC would be found hastily pumping up the cars' Hydrolastic suspension sufficiently to clear the obstacle. Others had to change springs, and some were simply unable to achieve the required ground clearance and were denied a start.

Once under way, the first three relatively short tests were attempted, which soon showed Vic Elford in the Porsche 911 was the car to beat, as he was fastest on all three. Vernaeve

LRX 829E was handed to Julien Vernaeve and Henry Liddon for the 1967 Geneva Rally (the Criterium Rally for Group 2 cars).

Vernaeve slid off on a forest stage, damaging the suspension and steering rack, which the mechanics here changed in under half an hour.

Vernaeve and Liddon would finish a creditable second overall, and as a result this would be the first of several drives for Abingdon.

LRX 829E with LRX 827E in the background get serviced together where the Scandinavian guards (in the foreground) were changed for the forest stages.

was not far behind on these early tarmac short hillclimbs – they were, however, all very slippery. Snow still prevalent high in the hills meant the Col de la Joux Verte test had to be cancelled, losing 12 miles of competitive motoring. The marking of the Geneva and Criterium was not on scratch timing (meaning the fastest car won) but was on a class improvement scheme, and with each class having their own bogey times to beat, it was often difficult to know exactly who was leading whom. Oddly, Elford was lying in second place to Sandro Munari in his Lancia Fulvia, despite Elford being fastest overall.

Into the night towards Aix-Les-Bains and some fast tight road sections tested many, and few cleaned the road times set. Vernaeve, however, was still clean on the road, and would remain so – just.

As dawn broke, the Gimel forest loomed. Ten miles in length with a few bad bumps, it was also rough in parts. Vernaeve had a big moment, when he slid off comprehensively, bending the suspension and – more seriously – the steering rack. The car was barely drivable but he limped it into service at the end of the first leg. Here the organisers had fortunately allowed an hour's service time prior to parc fermé for the 11-hour stop. Much activity was witnessed all around the car park – except the five works Porsches, which sat together untouched. Five BMC mechanics descended on Vernaeve's car and miraculously they changed the steering rack in just 27 minutes. A remarkable achievement.

Once the long second leg was under way, Elford found himself in the lead and steadily pulled away from Munari. With six more tests ahead of him, he would win every one of them, other than the Gimel forest stage, where he had to settle for second place; he was the deserved winner of the Geneva Rally. Vernaeve would bring home the car in second place on the Criterium and would be credited with fifth place overall on the Geneva Rally (but without European Championship points, as he was in a Group 2 car). This was a creditable result, which repaid Peter Browning's trust in him and would mean Vernaeve would be given further works drives over the next few years.

After the Criterium Rally, LRX 829E was transformed into a lightweight Group 6 car for the 1967 Alpine Rally, now registered and appearing as GRX 311D. Another LRX 829E was soon to find its way to Australia: this was not the car that did either the 1967 Alpine nor the 1967 Geneva but likely a new car or another car with that registration. LRX 829E was shipped to Australia for the Southern Cross Rally, which took place in New South Wales in early October. Timo Mäkinen, with local co-driver Bob Forsythe was to drive the car, taking advantage of being in Australia to also compete in the Bathurst 1000 race. The car was serviced by BMC Australia on the rally. To comply with Australian laws, the car had to be reregistered and carried the number plate EPX 812 on a vertical plate on the front of the bonnet, but with its UK plate clearly still visible.

LRX 829E was replated as GRX 311D as a Group 6 lightweight car for Mäkinen and Easter for the 1967 Alpine Rally, seen here at Alpe d'Huez.

Timo Mäkinen and local navigator Bob Forsythe would see another LRX 829E transported to Australia for the Southern Cross Rally, where the car was reregistered EPX 812. Mäkinen retired with a broken gearbox.

This was a major international rally held over five days, mostly at night, and was a fast event in a similar style to European events with the fastest car winning – and not based on the endurance to sustain rough roads and creek crossing as in the past. Forest stages and mountainous roads were scheduled for the 84 starters. The first night saw numerous stages on mountain roads on a demanding route to Canberra from the Bankstown start. After 250 miles, and four stages, Mäkinen was in the lead and Hopkirk third.

Already 11 cars had retired on the damaging rocky roads, not helped by foggy conditions. Mäkinen too struggled in the conditions when he misjudged a corner, leapt a gully and just missed numerous rocks and trees, cutting the route and rejoining the road several 100 yards further on – he probably saved several seconds in the process… The forests west of Canberra followed, which were very fast and more to Mäkinen's liking, where he dropped no time and led into the Canberra rest halt with Hopkirk still third.

After a day's rest, the route headed south west from Canberra to Bairnsdale. On the road near Kiandra, Mäkinen's gearbox broke and threw a gear through the case, which quickly deposited all of its oil onto the road and he was out. Just past Kiandra in the Snowy Mountains, Hopkirk too had gearbox problems and he too was out. Just 39 crews made it to the finish in Sydney, where the event was won by Barry Ferguson in a Volkswagen.

LRX 829E remained in Australia and became the property of BMC Australia. The car that had been entered on the Tulip, Criterium and Alpine Rallies remained in the UK and was sold to an Abingdon employee.

Competition Record

Date	Event	Crew	Number	Overall result	Class result
April 1967	Tulip Rally	Rauno Aaltonen/Henry Liddon	65	3rd	2nd
June 1967	Criterium Rally	Julien Vernaeve/Henry Liddon	80	2nd	2nd
Sept 1967	Alpine Rally	(as GRX311D) Mäkinen/Easter	103	DNF	
Oct 1967	Southern Cross Rally	Timo Mäkinen/Bob Forsythe	76	DNF	

CHAPTER 3: THE MK 1 MINI COOPER S

Registration Number	First registered	Chassis number	Engine	Engine number	Model
LRX 830E	March 1967	CA2S7 956615	1275cc	9F-SA-Y 44525	Austin Cooper S

LRX 830E was the last of the four new cars registered in March 1967. It was built by Robin Vokins as a Group 2 car for Paddy Hopkirk and Ron Crellin to do the Acropolis Rally.

By then, Abingdon was starting to standardise the building of cars, especially when a trio of cars entered the same event such as this Acropolis. However, there were always additional changes and preferences that each driver wanted on their cars.

This car's engine, bored to 1293cc, was fitted with a full-race camshaft, and coupled to a high-compression Downton cylinder head, bolted down using 1800 head studs. The engine produced 88bhp at the wheels on twin SU H4 carburettors. The oil cooler, from an MGB, sat a little further over than on a standard car, needed to clear the large 11AC alternator. This also meant that the diagonal stiffener was removed and fitted vertically.

Keeping the engine cool saw a four-blade fan fitted, and to help secure the radiator, the bottom was bolted down solidly, forsaking the standard rubber mountings. No thermostat was fitted – only a blanking sleeve. In addition, the bonnet was seen to be wedged slightly open, by the use of a rubber block screwed down by the bonnet safely catch. To increase the effective water capacity, an expansion tank was housed in the navigator's footwell.

A straight-cut close-ratio gearbox was used with a 4.2:1 diff, the casing of which was machined flat to enable a Moke sump plate to be fitted. Enlarged driveshafts and Hardy Spicer couplings were added, these being far more reliable in hard use. In addition to the sump plate, a Scandinavian guard was also fitted for maximum protection. Tie bar protection plates were also fitted and bolted to the front and side of the subframe – these not only protected the tie bars but also added strength. Both subframes were strengthened, plated and rewelded. Heavy-duty engine mountings were used and the top engine steady had a bolt inserted, replacing the stepped stud to allow for easy replacement of the rubbers.

The suspension was Hydrolastic, and double-blue and single-blue displacers were fitted with orange helper springs. The ride height was measured as 13in from the wheel centre to the wheelarch – good ground clearance being imperative in Greece with its poor roads. All lines for fuel, battery and brake were run inside the car, while the exhaust was skidded and used mounting rubbers with bolts passed through in case they were to fail.

Hopkirk decided to have a large reversing lamp fitted to the boot, rather than the smaller Healey sidelight so often used. The two front driving lamps, with Continental lenses, had steady bars fitted, being crafted from bicycle brake

Paddy Hopkirk and Ron Crellin on the starting ramp in Athens with LRX 830E for the 1967 Acropolis Rally.

levers. Two large front-facing mud flaps were fitted to the car to keep mud off of the windscreen and headlights. For the Acropolis, in addition to rally plates and numbers on the doors, the cars additionally carried large black numbers on the bonnet. Minilite wheels were used throughout, with either Dunlop SP44s or R7 race tyres; two spare wheels were carried in the boot. The car was fitted with black fibreglass wheelarch extensions, designed to cover the wider wheels. The brakes were improved by an asbestos block in the pistons to keep heat away from the fluid. Additionally, the rear wheel cylinders were bolted to the backplates to add as a heatsink. The brake drums were also drilled to seep heat away (and reduce weight). DS11 pads and VG95 brake linings were fitted front and back.

Hopkirk used a thick-grip leather steering wheel and sat in a lightweight red and grey corded seat. Crellin had the comfort of a high-backed reclining seat, also covered in red and grey corduroy. They used a lap-and-diagonal and full-harness Irvin seat belt respectively. Each had additional dash

WORKS MINIS IN DETAIL

The traditionally rough roads and hot weather tested the car to the full, seen here with the auxiliary lamps removed to improve airflow to the engine; the bonnet was also propped open with a small block of rubber.

LRX 830E was tipped onto its side to replace the rear remote mounting and have the rear subframe rewelded.

Hopkirk and Crellin pull into a time control on the Acropolis Rally; they were always in the top places and would win the rally – revenge for their exclusion the previous year.

panels in front of them housing extra instruments, controls and switches. The car was also fitted with a roll cage – well padded, and additional padding was fitted to the door locks, pockets and B-post. An intercom was used by the crew. As always, the car was presented in immaculate condition, but it was not to last – the Greek roads would see to that.

The 1967 Acropolis Rally was as tough as any year, always hot and dusty with poor surfaces and 2000 miles of motoring over two days and nights to sort the winner. There were 220 miles of stages on offer to the 72 starters, who lined up at the foot of the Acropolis for their first of two nights out of bed. The stages, in the hills all around Greece, had target times to beat before penalties were given but all bar four of these were cleaned by the faster cars, leaving the three hillclimbs (which were timed on scratch and driven blind without the co-driver) to decide the winner. Only 18 cars would make it back to Athens for the 30-minute circuit race to conclude the event.

Hopkirk had a score to settle on the Acropolis, having been relegated from the top spot last year after being unfairly penalised for servicing just a few feet inside a control area. He, along with the two sister works Minis, were setting a fast pace and keeping clean on the road.

With the start of the second day, when the hillclimbs and stages really started to count, he was lying third but he was playing a waiting game. First Aaltonen departed after a bad accident, leaving Hopkirk and Mäkinen in the chase.

On the second night Mäkinen's gearbox started to fail, and by morning he too was out, leaving Hopkirk in the lead, but the rough event was taking its toll. Service saw the car tipped onto its side, having the remote mounting changed and the

Seen here the Scandinavian sump guard with an extension plate; also just visible is the safety strap fitted in case the rear remote failed.

Hopkirk and Crellin with a washed and polished LRX 830E arrive at the award ceremony with shirts and ties to collect their winners' trophies.

LRX 830E along with GRX 5D were prepared for the gruelling 72-hour Marathon-de La Route. LRX 830E was fitted with a one-litre engine and seen here near Abingdon before leaving the UK.

LRX 830E returned onto its wheels after the repairs, showing fuel leakage from tipping the car onto its side.

The second event for the car was the Marathon de la Route, held at the end of August. This odd event was halfway between a race and a rally and was in essence a regularity event on a racetrack. The car was assigned to a three-driver team, as they would each have to drive over the three-and-a-half days and nights around the daunting and demanding Nürburgring. A team of three experienced race drivers were assembled: Alec Poole was a former MG apprentice with a successful career in his own BMC cars, who went on to win the 1969 saloon car championship; Roger Enever was also associated with MG, as his father was an MG designer and also had a successful career in racing MGBs; Clive Baker was

subframe restitched together. The Hydrolastic suspension was also pumped up again. By now Hopkirk was also complaining of clutch slip but still going strong and won all of the hillclimbs. He just had to nurse the car back to Athens and tackle the half-hour race around the Tatoi Airfield the next day. This had no bearing on the results, providing the car finished the race – which was just as well, as Hopkirk's car lost all of its oil pressure and ran its bearings after just three laps. He had to wait at the finishing line to allow him to just crawl across the line, in last place, but still first overall on the rally. His disappointment from last year was avenged and they duly received their winner's trophies from King Constantine of Greece at the Acropolis.

LRX 830E was driven by Alec Poole, Roger Enever and Clive Baker. They ran as high as third overall before Poole rolled the car and they were out.

Prior to the 1967 RAC a press day was organised and LRX 830E, which was used as a recce and practice car for the Tour de Corsica, was driven by several works drivers, including here Doug Watts. Also noticeable is the air vent to the brakes.

the third member, and he raced for BMC in MGBs and Austin Healeys at Le Mans and Sebring. He and Enever had won the Marathon de la Route in a works MGB the previous year, so were experienced in this quite different event.

LRX 830E was considerably different from how it appeared on the Acropolis Rally. There was an absence of chrome surrounds to the doors, and the rear side windows were non-opening. Perspex windows were fitted, replacing the heavy glass. The car was built more as a race car than a rally car for this 84-hour marathon. The engine was built as a 970S, bored 0.040in to give 999cc, the capacity limit for the up-to-one-litre class that Browning decided to enter.

Inside the car most of its trim was removed, including the rear seat, which had carpet laid over the bulkhead. Padding was fitted to the driver's door pillar, door lock and pocket pad, along with the roll cage. A clear view was fitted to the rear 'screen and the front laminated windscreen had an electric heater bar fitted by the driver's side to help keep it clear.

Externally the car's appearance was quite striking. The bumpers were removed and the fixing lip cut off the front panel. A large 16-row oil cooler was fitted prominently where the grille was once fitted, and there was also an auxiliary radiator alongside the oil cooler. To help keep the oil filter cool, two large air holes were punched into the lower panel.

The car ran four auxiliary lamps: two small Lucas spot lamps and two fog lamps where the grille moustache was fitted. These lamps and the headlights were protected by covers during the daylight hours. Quick-lift jacking points were fitted but painted red, rather than white as they customarily were. To help speed up refuelling, quick-release Aston petrol caps were fitted to the twin tanks. Large white roundels were painted onto the doors rather than the usual white door squares; the bonnet also had a large roundel and was held down by two Moke rubber toggles. The registration number was painted low on the bonnet.

The format for this rather complicated event was to see who could travel the furthest within the three-and-a-half days around the race circuit. Each class had its own target time for one lap, and provided they did that time, they were credited with one lap; if not, no lap was credited. One-litre cars were allowed 18 minutes to complete each 17.5-mile lap. To allow for refuelling, an extra three minutes every 12 laps were allowed, and for periodic service, an extra ten minutes every 75 laps were allowed. Further still, in darkness, an extra two minutes per lap were allowed. If any car was more that 30 minutes late on one lap, he was excluded; likewise if a car had accumulated 60 minutes' delay. Yes, it was complicated, but Peter Browning was not only the BMC competition manager but also an accredited RAC timekeeper, so he was well placed to keep a careful watch on progress.

Browning had entered LRX 830E in the up-to-one-litre class because the target lap times were more generous than the 1300 class. He was also hoping that poor weather at night, which the Eifel Forest was renowned for, would hopefully equalise the car's lack of overall speed. As it transpired, only one night was foggy and it was sadly the undoing of the car. The event started in Chaudfontaine, some eight miles from Liège and then travelled 80 miles onto the Nürburgring, where some even got lost or broke down en route. Those still running drove back to Chaudfontaine three-and-a-half days later.

The marathon started at midnight on the Tuesday and would not finish until Friday lunchtime. The schedule was to have the drivers at the wheel for a three-hour stint and then have a six-hour rest.

After the first full shift, the car was lying in fifth place overall. The car ran very well for over 48 hours continuously, lapping about two-and-a-half minutes below their bogey time but exactly on their own schedule. After 24 hours they were up to third overall.

However, during the foggy Friday morning, where visibility dropped to around 10m, with Baker at the wheel and by now lying second overall, the car broke its throttle cable way out on the circuit. Unfortunately, it took 21 minutes for him to fix a temporary repair and get it back to the pits. Despite it only taking five minutes in the pits to rethread the new cable they had been penalised 26 minutes, and with 30 minutes maximum allowed, this was a close call.

Poole took over driving duties and was told to go as fast as he possibly could to try and get back some of those lost laps. Up until then they had been restricted to using around 5000rpm, as this had proved sufficient to achieve their lap times and preserve the engine. Unfortunately, a slight misjudgement on his fifth lap of his session saw Poole roll the car, and that was the end. Porsche won by 12 laps but Abingdon was delighted to see the sister car, GRX 5D, come home second overall and win the one-litre class.

LRX 830E was used as a recce car for the Tour de Corsica, which was held in September 1967. The car was now much changed and was likely a different car; it was fitted with air ducts below the bumpers, where the front panel was much like a full-skirt early edition. It also ran a larger radiator with a bulge on the bonnet to accommodate its extra size. The Tour de Corsica, as the records show, was a disastrous event for Abingdon, where the two cars GRX 5D and GRX 172D (for Hopkirk and Mäkinen respectively) retired very early on with defective fan belts – perhaps they should have used their recce cars…

A press day for the forthcoming RAC Rally was organised by Abingdon, in a field just outside Abingdon, where numerous cars were on display and rides given in the works cars to those brave enough. Hopkirk drove LRX 830E with great verve and impressed everyone in attendance.

The final outing for the car was as a recce car for the 1968 Monte Carlo Rally. LRX 830E joined a fleet of other works cars being used as recce cars for this prestigious event. It, and the other cars, were left in France after the initial recce to be used again as ice-note cars during the event.

LRX 830E was sold to Irish rally enthusiast Ronnie McCartney, who would go on to use the car to great effect in his home country on numerous Irish road and stage events.

LRX 830E was used as a recce car for the 1968 Monte Carlo Rally, seen here in the backstreets of Monte Carlo. Running with steel wheels, the air duct can just be seen below the bumper.

The car was also used for testing for the Monte Carlo Rally; the two crew here are unknown.

Competition Record

Date	Event	Crew	Number	Overall result	Class result
March 1967	Acropolis Rally	Paddy Hopkirk/Ron Crellin	89	1st	1st
Aug 67	Marathon-de La Route	Alec Poole/Roger Enever/Clive Baker	40	DNF	

CHAPTER 4:
THE MK 2 MINI COOPER S

The Mk1 Mini, come September 1967, had been in production for eight years and was due a facelift to keep the model fresh in the customer's eye. The problem was, at the time, British Leyland was in dire trouble financially and the resultant new car was little more than cosmetic tinkering.

The only significant change to the body was the slightly wider rear 'screen aperture, which was hardly noticeable. The rear light clusters were larger and certainly more visible. The cost cutting meant both Austin and Morris variants now had the same front grille and the overrider corner bars were dropped. Badges did vary between the marques but were both very similar and it was now difficult to tell them apart.

The interior trim was also standardised as plain black. The boot lid was now double-skinned (as indeed were late Mk1 boot lids). There were other very minor changes but none of any great note. The Mk2 would only stay in production for just over two years before the Mk3 appeared, but by that time, January 1970, Abingdon was building few cars and took delivery of only one Mk3 Cooper S.

Abingdon, for its part, corporately, had to be seen in the new Mk2 car, so – when it was introduced in October 1967 – the team took delivery of a batch of cars, destined to be registered in OBL sequence, but were all actually Mk1s that Abingdon would change to appear as the new Mk2s. It is assumed there was a surplus stock of Mk1s sitting awaiting buyers that were hard to move with the new car now in the showrooms. It was therefore a matter of expediency that Abingdon would be allocated these surplus cars for competition.

They were not converted initially but over time they morphed into Mk2 cars. This, of course, because of the less-than-radical facelift, meant the only bodywork change Abingdon would undertake would be the fitting of larger rear lights. The bigger rear 'screen was never used – all retained the smaller Mk1 rear windscreen. The change to the external brightwork was a simple matter. Interior trim was an oddity because early Mk2 cars still retained red-and-gold brocade trim.

The first actual Mk2s delivered to Abingdon were the ORX series of cars built for the 1968 Monte Carlo Rally.

Mechanically there was no difference between the Mk1 and Mk2 cars: suspension (all Hydrolastic), engine and gearbox were all unchanged. All retained the big-valve AEG163 cylinder head. The 12G940 cylinder head would not appear until almost the end of Mk2 production. The gearbox was still only fitted with synchromesh on three gears; It would not be for another year that the car got a four-speed synchromesh gearbox. None of this, of course, was of much concern to Abingdon, as engines and gearboxes were built to the team's own standards and specifications

Registration Number	First registered	Chassis number	Engine	Engine number	Model
ORX 7F	Jan 1968	KA2S6 1068931A	1275cc	9F-SA-Y 47692	Morris Cooper S Mk2

ORX 7F was one of four new cars delivered to Abingdon in November 1967 for the Monte Carlo Rally in January. These cars were all Mk2s and the first of their kind to be prepared at Abingdon. The Mk2s were not significantly different from their predecessors, other than cosmetic changes – notably larger rear lamps, a different front grille, and interior trim that was now black. The rear window was slightly wider, but they were otherwise basically the same as Mk1s.

The car was built for the Monte by Bob Whittington as a Group 2 car for Rauno Aaltonen and Henry Liddon, who were also last year's Monte winners. As the power and speed of the opposition had increased, with the major threat coming from Porsche, Renault Alpine and Lancia, Abingdon was now on the back foot in the power race. It was the flexibility to enter a highly-modified Group 6 car that was keeping Abingdon still a force to be reckoned with, but this was not an option for the Monte Carlo Rally. With often poor weather, which tended to favour the front-wheel-drive and nimble Mini, Abingdon was hoping it would still be able to win this winter classic.

Cliff Humphries, who was continually trying to squeeze as

The offending split Weber carburettors that nearly caused all of the works Minis to be excluded from the results of the 1968 Monte Carlo Rally.

much power from the A-series engine as he could, had fitted new carburettors to the engines, which replaced the trusty twin SU H4 units. Mäkinen had seen these on a car in Finland and had brought a set back to Abingdon to test. They were based on a pair of Weber 45DCOEs but one choke of each had been machined off and a short extension welded onto the carburettors to allow them to be fitted to the standard Cooper S inlet manifold – which under Group 2 rules had to be maintained. Fortunately, carburettors were always free under these rules. Abingdon stated that the modified Webers, with their welded extension and cut-off chokes, were a prototype carburettor, details of which had been sent in advance to the Automobile Club de Monaco (ACM). These split Webers gave an extra 7bhp, boosting the power to around 93bhp at the wheels.

Once again the engine was 1293cc, with a high-compression Downton cylinder head giving 12.6:1 compression ratio, forged pistons and an AEA648 race camshaft. A lightened and balanced flywheel was used, and an orange diaphragm. Helical transfer gears were fitted but a straight-cut close-ratio gearbox with a 4.2:1 final drive and enlarged diameter driveshafts. Keeping the engine cool was a Cooper S radiator, a four-blade fan and a 72C thermostat. An oil cooler was fitted. A provision also had to be made to fit a bracket to the engine for the seals that the ACM would fit to the engine to ensure it wasn't changed. The engine was protected by a 13-hole Moke sump guard with the addition of an alloy extension plate. It was also fitted with a battery box cover, and the front tie bars had protection plates added to the subframe.

The suspension was Hydrolastic with single-blue and double-blue displacers front and back, without front dampers but orange helper springs at the rear. It was, however, fitted with a rear anti-roll bar. No subframe strengthening was carried out.

The brakes also received attention, with the callipers having asbestos blocks fitted into the pistons in an attempt to take excess heat away from the brake fluid. Additionally,

Rauno Aaltonen and Henry Liddon near the end of their long journey to Monte Carlo from their start in Athens where heavy snow in Yugoslavia nearly prevented them even getting to Monaco. The roof rack full of spares and studded tyres was removed on arrival.

the rear wheel cylinders were threaded so they were fixed to the backplates with a large nut rather than a circlip; this also served to take heat away from the brake fluid. The brake servo was retained in its standard position under the bonnet.

The electrics were completely rewired by Lucas to the usual high standard. The car ran an alternator for the four auxiliary lamps and the heated front 'screen. These lamps – two fog lamps and two driving lamps fixed to a lamp bar – were connected by a five-pin rubber socket, and the two driving lamps secured by steady bars. A two-speed wiper motor was used with deep-throated wheel boxes. European headlamps with Perspex protective covers were fitted with iodine bulbs, as were the extra lamps; headlamp washers were also fitted. A Lucas 576 fog lamp was fitted to the boot lid as a reversing lamp.

Provision was made for a grille muff to be fitted around the front grille to keep out snow, should it be needed. The car was also fitted with forward-facing front mud flaps below the sidelights and it also carried mandatory rear mud flaps. For the first time, the wheelarch extensions were painted body colour and not left in black.

Inside the car, the oil pressure gauge was moved next to the rev counter on the driver's dashboard and in its place was the water temperature gauge; in its place was a circular fuel gauge – the original gauge now inoperable in the speedo. The co-driver's instrument panel housed his usual Halda distance recorder and a pair of Heuer clocks but it was getting crowded down by his feet, as in his footwell was an expansion tank from the radiator. The Tudor electric screen washer bottles were moved to the rear of the car on the driver's side, along with the jack by the rear pocket. Seats were a black cord-covered bucket seat for the driver and a reclining seat for the co-driver. Once the competition element of the Monte Carlo Rally started, the heavy reclining seat was replaced with a standard Mini seat, which was covered in a Karobes seat cover to save weight. There was an Irvin lap-and-diagonal seat belt for the driver and an Irvin full harness for the co-driver. An intercom box was fitted to the padded alloy roll cage.

All standard trim and glass was retained, and the carpet in the front was insulated underneath with an asbestos blanket to keep heat away. Padding to the door pockets, door locks and door pillar helped to add to crew comfort. All lines were run inside the car, with the fuel pump located under the rear seat. In the boot the twin fuel tanks were protected from damage from studded tyres by sticking asbestos sheet to the exposed sides of the tanks.

The Monte Carlo Rally of 1968, held between 20 and 25 January, was in many professional drivers' eyes a tiring three-day drive through Europe to arrive at Monte Carlo before the rally properly started. Once in Monte Carlo, there was a 24-hour common run with seven special stages to Aix-les-Bains and back, covering some 900 miles using the Ardèche and the Alpes Maritime. The top 60 were then confronted with the famous mountain circuit as a classification run, with six special stages and 390 miles in a 12-hour blast over the mountains north of Monaco – a route virtually unchanged since its inception in 1965. Nevertheless, the Monte was still the event to win for any manufacturer.

BMC had been practising before and after Christmas, compiling detailed pace notes of all of the stages and, in what were then snowy conditions, tyre selection was also prevalent. BMC had no less that five recce cars left in France for this purpose. These pre-used rally cars were fully prepared but generally with rather standard engines, so as to keep them reliable. Breakdowns on recces were time-consuming and disruptive.

Dunlop supplied – for Abingdon's use and carted all over Europe – a selection of 750 tyres of 13 various types; as it transpired, with the dry conditions that year, R7 racing tyres were the most in demand. Dunlop provided 14 mechanics and five trucks. On top of all of this, Abingdon had seven service cars, one transporter, one van, four ice-note crews plus half-a-dozen office personnel, whilst Castrol had two complete service crews in attendance.

There were eight starting points across Europe, with 200 cars. Aaltonen would start from Athens, which was always a bit of a gamble as the weather could be very unpredictable. Sure enough, before the rally had even started there was trouble with the weather. The two cars for Aaltonen and Mäkinen, on their way to the Athens start in a transporter, become stuck in heavy snowdrifts and it was only the hard-working Robin Vokins and Den Green who managed to dig their way through and catch the latest ferry to Athens. If they had missed it, neither car would have made the start.

Once under way, Aaltonen from Athens experienced thick, rutted, snowbound roads, particularly in Yugoslavia. Near Sarajevo the road was completely blocked but, with the help of others, they dug their way through. Aaltonen was also suffering from his carburettors freezing.

At Monte Carlo, 153 cars made it for a well-earned 24-hour rest, and all the works Minis had arrived with no time penalties. As the works Minis arrived, they were stripped of their roof racks and all other items of unwanted impedimenta, then a list of items to be attended to were given to the mechanics, and finally the cars were all washed and taken to parc fermé. All four cars retained the half-studded Weathermaster tyres they had started on, delaying their tyre decision for the next leg until the next day. This was to prove rather crucial.

Aaltonen took a recce car out to investigate the roads near the principality, but trouble was brewing with the split Webers after the ACM's technical inspection. They were having misgivings about the carburettors and told Peter Browning they had doubts about their eligibility. The letter of the rules was discussed in detail and it was accepted they were fitted in good faith but their opinion was that a protest may be lodged by other competitors – and if so they would have to review the situation and likely uphold any protest. It was therefore very likely that the car may now effectively have been disqualified and not be allowed to start the next leg.

The ACM then offered to allow the car to be worked on in parc fermé to allow mechanics to replace the split Webers with twin SU carburettors. This, Browning decided, after consulting with Longbridge, not to do. At the last moment, the ACM allowed BMC to continue on the common run but with the cloud hanging over that the cars may eventually be disqualified if protests were lodged. This long, protracted delay, which had indicated the cars were already disqualified and not allowed to restart, meant the service crews (particularly those from Dunlop) were not prepared and ready to go, being scattered away from Monte Carlo, assuming they were not needed.

A hurried call to arms by Browning meant a scrabble to get things reorganised. Unfortunately, by the time Aaltonen had set off, the Dunlop tyre truck was not in position for the first stage. He was therefore obliged to do the first stage using badly-worn half-studded tyres used on the long haul from Athens – far from ideal, when race tyres were the covers to use.

The same happened on the next stage and it was now dark, and once again Aaltonen arrived at the start where neither the

Service for ORX 7F. Henry Liddon, Bill Price and Rauno Aaltonen stand by as the mechanics work. The carburettors are covered with a battery box – not to hide them but to keep heat from the exhaust around them, preventing them from icing.

service crew nor the Dunlop van had caught up. He decided he had enough time in hand and decided to wait, but when the service crew turned up, the Dunlop van was still not with them – so he continued on the same even-more-worn-out tyres. Nevertheless, despite not having the best of tyres, his times were still creditable, being just tenth on the St Auban

Aaltonen and Liddon power ORX 7F onwards. They would be in fifth place after the common run, despite being hampered with the correct tyres not being in the right place.

WORKS MINIS IN DETAIL

The final night of the Monte, the mountain circuit saw Aaltonen claw back to third place, unable to beat the power of the two works Porsches ahead of him.

Another service shot with Den Green at work. Liddon sits passively still belted in his seat, showing the Karobes seat cover. Of note are the twin washer bottles fitted below the driver's rear side window and his seat belt mounting.

ORX 7F washed and cleaned for the prize-giving, where Aaltonen and Liddon received their third-place awards.

stage and fifth on Le Moulinon.

He changed onto the race tyres for the third stage – the notorious Burzet stage – but once the road conditions deteriorated on the Le Madeleine stage, he reverted to studded tyres again, and posted sixth fastest. Aaltonen had been in been in the top ten times on five of the six stages and arrived back in Monte Carlo in fourth overall. The rally was being headed by Gerard Larrousse in the nimble Renault Alpine.

Only 78 cars arrived back at Monte Carlo to be classified as finishers within time, and just 27 were unpenalised. The top 60 would then, after a 12-hour rest, tackle the mountain circuit. Once more, they headed off in a recce car into the mountains to check the condition of the roads and, with the weather relatively mild, most roads were found to be dry with very little ice, so race tyres would be the order of the day for most. The mountain circuit, all in darkness, consisted of six stages within the 390 miles to be covered in 11-and-a-half hours, meaning an average of 34mph. To allow time for service and tyre changes, the pace would indeed be very fast. Ahead of them were three runs over the Col du Turini and two over the Col de Couillole plus the Gorges de Piaon.

Aaltonen started to close ground on the cars ahead of him and was fifth fastest on the opening Sospel to Mentour stage. The top of the Turini was icy, where the racing tyres struggled for grip, but still he recorded fifth fastest behind the Porsche 911 pair and the pair of Alpine Renaults. The leading Alpine went off on the second assault on the Turini, reportedly on snow thrown onto the bend by spectators, leaving Elford's Porsche now in an unassailable position; Aaltonen was again fifth fastest, and fourth fastest on the last run over the famous of all Monte stages.

With consistently fast times, albeit no match for the Porsches', Aaltonen had clawed himself up to third overall by the time he returned to the principality. At the finish in Monte Carlo at the final scrutineering, the ACM went back on its word and decided it was not going to allow the result to stand because of the split Weber carburettor. After much badgering by Browning to the sporting commission, it was agreed to let the carburettors pass. A repeat of the 1966 disqualification rumpus was not being relished by anyone. It remains to be seen if the sporting commission would have relented had BMC won.

Despite the works Minis not winning, they were not disgraced, only being headed by two much more powerful Porsche 911s. Between them, the four Minis were in the top ten on every one of the 13 stages.

CHAPTER 4: THE MK 2 MINI COOPER S

Timo Mäkinen borrowed ORX 7F for his own use back home in Finland, seen here on the Salpausseklä Rally. The car was returned to Abingdon badly damaged, and rebodied.

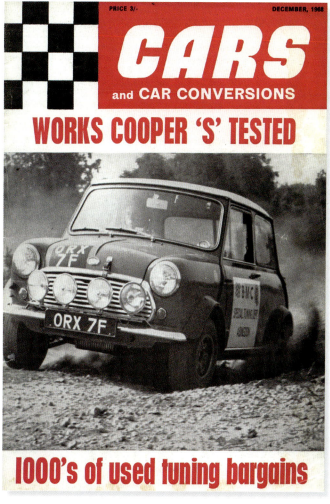

A new ORX 7F was rebuilt and used by special tuning as a demonstrator and shop window for Basil Wales' ST department.

After the Monte Carlo Rally the car was loaned out to Timo Mäkinen to use privately in Finland. It was returned in July that year badly damaged and then rebodied to become a demonstrator for the special tuning department, used as a mobile shop window for all of the numerous special tuning parts that were being offered to the public by Basil Wales from Abingdon, right next door to the competitions department. The car was widely publicised and featured in numerous magazines at the time, publicising special tuning. It was later sold to W Andrew & Co Belfast and campaigned on many events in Ireland.

Competition Record

Date	Event	Crew	Number	Overall result	Class result
Jan 1968	Monte Carlo Rally	Rauno Aaltonen/Henry Liddon	18	3rd	1st

Registration Number	First registered	Chassis number	Engine	Engine number	Model
ORX 77F	Jan 1968	KA2S6 1068932A	1275cc	9F-SA-Y 47690	Morris Cooper S Mk2

ORX 77F was the second of four new cars delivered to Abingdon in November 1967 for the Monte Carlo Rally in January 1968. All were the first batch of Mk2s to be prepared at Abingdon. The car was built for the Monte by Brian Moylan as a Group 2 car for Timo Mäkinen and Paul Easter.

With the days of the Mini's domination being severely challenged by Porsche, Alpine and Lancia, Abingdon was trying to squeeze as much power as possible from the ancient A-series engine. The flexibility afforded by building highly-modified Group 6 cars was the preference now, but this was not an option for the Monte Carlo Rally – it had to be a Group 2 car. A new pair of Abingdon-built carburettors was the answer. Mäkinen had seen a similar setup on a car in Finland, and took a set to Abingdon to let Cliff Humphries test. They were based on a pair of Weber 45DCOEs but one choke of each was machined off and a short extension welded onto the carburettors, to allow them to be fitted to the standard Cooper

Engine bay of ORX 77F showing, amongst other things, the split Weber carburettors.

The interior photos of ORX 77F showing the dashboard detail with the oil pressure gauge moved to beside the rev counter, two fuseboxes below the navigator's panel and the expansion tank by his feet.

S inlet manifold – mandatory under Group 2 rules. These split Webers, as they later became known, produced an extra 7bhp and an increase in mid-range torque. Now the car had around 93bhp at the wheels. Abingdon stated, importantly, that these modified Webers, with their welded extensions and cut-off chokes, were a prototype carburettor, details of which had been sent in advance to the Automobile Club de Monaco (ACM).

The car's engine was bored to 1293cc and fitted with forged pistons, a high-compression Downton cylinder head giving 12.6:1 compression ratio, and an AEA648 race camshaft. Helical transfer gears were fitted but there was a straight-cut close-ratio gearbox with a 4.2:1 final drive. A Cooper S radiator, a four-blade fan and a 72C thermostat was used. The fan had 1/4in machined off its ends to aid fast fan-belt changing; there was also a spare fan belt carried around the timing cover.

There was a bracket secured to the engine for the seals that the ACM would fit. It was protected by a 13-hole Moke sump guard with the addition of an alloy expansion plate, and it also had a battery box cover. The front tie bars were protected by plates added to the subframe, which added strength but were accepted purely as skid protection, which was permitted in the regulations (whereas strengthening wasn't).

Much as Mäkinen preferred dry suspension, Hydrolastic was fitted, using single-blue and double-blue displacers front and back, and only orange helper springs; it was, however, fitted with a rear anti-roll bar. No subframe strengthening was carried out (as was customary) through fear of the ACM disqualifying the car.

The brake servo was retained in its standard position under the bonnet. Racing Ferodo DS11 brake pads were fitted, with VG95 rear linings, and the callipers had asbestos blocks in the pistons in an attempt to take excess heat away from the brake fluid; to take heat away from the rear brakes, the rear wheel cylinders were threaded and secured with a large nut rather than a circlip.

The car ran an alternator, essential for the four auxiliary lamps and the heated front windscreen. These lamps – two fog lamps and two driving lamps, fixed to a lamp bar – were connected by a five-pin rubber socket, and the two driving lamps secured by steady bars. A two-speed wiper motor was used with deep-throated wheel boxes. European headlamps with Perspex protective covers had a vertical dipped beam and were fitted with iodine bulbs, as were the extra lamps. Headlamp washers were also added. The ACM had insisted that no advertising was to be permitted, so the normal Lucas motifs on the lamp covers were replaced with plain black. The electrics were completely rewired by Lucas to the usual high standard.

The Mini's magnesium wheels were covered by wheelarch extensions, painted in red body colour and not left in black. The car was fitted with forward-facing front mud flaps below the sidelights; it also carried mandatory rear mud flaps, and a grille muff was fitted around the front grille.

All lines were run inside the car, with the fuel pump located under the rear seat. All standard trim and glass was retained, and the carpet in the front insulated underneath with an asbestos blanket to keep heat away. An intercom box was fitted to the padded alloy roll cage. The driver's alloy instrument panels had an oil pressure gauge next to the rev counter, and in its place in the oval binnacle was a water temperature gauge. In its previous position was a circular fuel gauge, with the gauge in the speedo now redundant. The co-driver's instrument panel housed his usual Halda distance recorder and a pair of Heuer clocks illuminated by aircraft P-lamps. The washer bottles were at the rear of the car on the driver's side, as the co-driver's footwell housed an expansion tank from the radiator. The seats were in red and grey cord material, not black, as the seats were likely recycled.

Held between 20 and 25 January, the Monte Carlo Rally of 1968 began with a three-day drive through Europe before the rally really started in earnest from Monte Carlo. Once in Monte Carlo, the next day there was a 24-hour common run with seven special stages to Aix-les-Bains and back, covering some 900 miles over the Alpes Maritime and the Ardèche. The top 60 survivors were then sent off the following evening on the famous mountain circuit as a classification run of some 390 miles in just under 12 hours, with six classic special stages over the mountains north of Monaco.

Mäkinen and Easter had been practising before and after Christmas, compiling detailed pace notes of the stages, which were mostly snow covered so tyre selection would be important. Dunlop had supplied BMC a selection of 750 tyres of 13 various types but because of unseasonably mild weather, R7 racing tyres were best suited over much of the route. The BMC team was provided with 14 mechanics and five trucks to move tyres and service the cars. Abingdon itself had seven

The beautifully made and trimmed works bucket seat and high-back recliner seat. The very heavy navigator's seat was swapped for a lighter standard seat, with supportive cover, once the car arrived at Monte Carlo.

ORX 77F being loaded into the BMC transporter for its journey, along with ORX 7F, to their respective starts in Athens. The rear anti-roll bar can be clearly seen here.

Timo Mäkinen and Paul Easter in ORX 77F cutting a corner on the 1968 Monte Carlo Rally.

Service stop for ORX 77F; Paul Easter attends to the contents of his briefcase, Mäkinen looks on as the mechanics attend to the car.

service cars, one transporter, one van, four ice-note crews plus half-a-dozen office personnel and five recce Minis in attendance in France for this classic rally.

Before the rally had even started there was trouble with the weather. The two cars for Aaltonen and Mäkinen, on their way to the Athens start in a transporter, become stuck in heavy snowdrifts, and it was only the hard-working Robin Vokins and Den Green who managed to dig their way through and just catch the latest ferry to Athens. If they had missed it, neither car would have made the start.

From their eight starting points across Europe, 200 cars started on their long, often tedious respective journeys to Monte Carlo. Mäkinen from Athens experienced thick, rutted, snowbound roads, particularly in Yugoslavia; he even resorted to fitting chains to his tyres. Near Sarajevo the road became completely blocked but they dug their way out. He also had minor brake problems and had the brake servo changed as a precaution.

Mäkinen arrived in Monte Carlo without loss of time, along with 153 others who trickled into the principality for a day's rest. Before heading for parc fermé, the car was serviced and the roof rack was removed, along with the front mud flaps and any extra sleeping material. The car was washed and headed for scrutineering still with its half-studded tyres fitted – awaiting Mäkinen's final choice for the next day.

At the technical inspection, trouble was brewing with the split Webers. The ACM's scrutineers were having misgivings about the fitting of the carburettors on all four works Minis and told Peter Browning they had doubts about their eligibility. The rules were studied and discussed in detail and it was accepted they were fitted in good faith but the ACM's opinion was that a protest may be lodged by other competitors – and if so they would have to review the situation and likely uphold any protest.

Facing disqualification, the ACM offered to allow all four Minis to be worked on in parc fermé to allow the split Webers to be replaced with twin SU carburettors. This, Browning decided (after consulting with Longbridge) not to do. However, the ACM relented and at the very last moment did allow BMC to continue on the common run – but with the cloud hanging over the team's head that they may eventually be disqualified, if protests were lodged. It was not a good feeling, and a repeat of the 1966 lighting disqualification was looming.

This protracted delay meant the service crews and particularly those from Dunlop were not prepared and ready to go, being scattered far and wide, assuming they were not needed. A hurried call around by Browning to everyone meant a mad rush to get things reorganised. Unfortunately, by the time Mäkinen had set off the Dunlop tyre truck was not in position for the first stage, St Auban, so he had to do the first stage using the worn half-studded tyres he'd used since Athens.

At the Le Moulinon stage start, again neither the service crew nor Dunlop van had caught up, so with time in hand Mäkinen decided to wait. However, when the service crew appeared, the Dunlop van was still not with them, so Mäkinen again continued on the same worn-out tyres but was still sixth fastest.

Once on race tyres for the Burzet stage, Mäkinen was plagued with a tyre problem, unable to bed them in properly and acclimatise to them, but managed eighth place on the following Col de Party stage. However, once the road conditions deteriorated on the 30-mile-long Barcillonnette stage, using studded tyres again, he posted a second-fastest into Gap.

But it was all to no avail, as when leaving the Levens control, on one of the long sections over the Alpes Maritimes, the bolt holding the crank pulley came adrift, leaving Mäkinen with no fan, no water pump and no alternator. But in true Mäkinen style he continued on and did the final Levens hillclimb test, boiling up but freewheeling downhill to arrive at Monte Carlo

Mäkinen and Easter were destined not to finish the Monte Carlo Rally, despite being very fast. The crank pulley bolt was lost and the engine soon became red hot with no circulating water, and they retired.

ORX 77F was handed to Rauno Aaltonen and Henry Liddon for the 1968 Rally of the Flowers – seen here much travel-stained, pulling out of service along with Tony Fall and Mike Wood in ORX 777F.

only seven minutes late and to qualify as a finisher. When the bonnet was lifted, the engine was literally glowing cherry red, it was so hot. It was a miracle it had not seized – such are the merits of forged pistons.

Just 78 cars arrived back at Monte Carlo and classified as finishers, and only 27 were unpenalised. The top 60 would now, after a 12-hour rest, tackle the mountain circuit.

To everyone's surprise, the next evening Mäkinen's car, unprepared having been abandoned in parc fermé, started first time, so Mäkinen and Easter promptly shot off to the start, so that they could be classified as a finisher – and then retired immediately.

Elford's Porsche won the Monte, with another driven by Toivonen in second spot. The other three Minis eventually worked themselves up to third, fourth and fifth overall – Aaltonen, Fall and Hopkirk respectively, behind two Porsche 911s. It was not all over, however, as at the finish final scrutineering, the ACM back-pedalled and decreed it was not going to allow the results to stand because of the split Weber carburettors. After much arguing, some quite heated by Browning to the sporting commission, they eventually changed their minds and agreed to let the carburettors pass. Despite the works Minis not winning, they showed well – between them the four Minis were in the top ten on every one of the 13 stages, only being beaten by two much more powerful Porsche 911s.

After the Monte Carlo Rally the car was rebuilt by Bob Whittington for Rauno Aaltonen and Henry Liddon to do the San Remo Rally, previously known as the Rally of the Flowers. The Monte Group 2 car, driven then by Timo Mäkinen, had a fresh engine for the San Remo, having been cooked on the Monte. It was indeed general practice for engines to be completely rebuilt and in many cases replaced after hard use on just one event. However, the car was basically unchanged from how it appeared on the Monte.

One significant change was that the engine was now fitted with straight-cut drop gears with a roller bearing on the idler gear, replacing the standard helical transfer gears – these were not as power-sapping at their helical counterparts. The other minor change to the engine was in the inlet manifold, which was mated to the cylinder head by locating rings rather than being pegged as previously, meaning a new inlet manifold and new cylinder head. The car retained the short 4.2:1 final drive and straight-cut gearbox – all rebuilt.

It was now fitted with a heavy-duty Scandinavian sump guard, replacing the Moke guard, as the event largely took place on loose-surface roads. However, the subframes remained unstrengthened. On the Abingdon rolling road, the engine, still with its controversial split Webers, showed 90bhp at the wheels, a few bhp down on the Monte engine but not significant. Cosmetically, Aaltonen's rally plate was secured vertically on the nearside of the bonnet, much as the Monte plate was.

Although the San Remo Rally was in effect only 31 hours in duration, the route was so tough and demanding that more effort was needed to get the car to the finish than much longer events such as the Monte Carlo Rally. It was a hard, rough event, held in early March, in the mountains above the Italian Riviera of the Flowers, just along the coast from Monaco, where roads were very minor and largely carved out by the Italian Army before the war; and whilst the lower roads were tarmac, once they climbed, the surface deteriorated to loose surface with no barriers and many 'fresh air' bends.

Because of the compact route on offer, many of the 19 stages, amounting to 80 miles of competition, were visited twice and invariably in opposite direction. This made practising and making pace notes difficult and dangerous, in not knowing if another entrant was charging fast in the opposite direction. Two works Lancias had been written off in such circumstances.

Henry Liddon checks his paperwork whilst ORX 77F is serviced and tyres changed on the Rally of the Flowers.

Tony Fall looking at ORX 77F with Aaltonen in the background as ORX 77F is serviced during the night.

The only way for Aaltonen to safely complete a recce was to do it all at night, which he did in early February straight after the Monte.

At the start were 72 competitors, after a day of scrutineering. Once again the split Webers came under close examination but were eventually accepted, and Aaltonen was allowed to start. Although the entry was low in number, eight works teams took part – one of which was Ford, and it marked the very first appearance of the Ford Escort TC and the beginning of what became a very successful rally car. Driven by Ove Andersson, it would come home in third place – a great achievement.

Controversially, the entry was not seeded; cars were simply grouped in capacity classes, which meant some balking on the longer stages. Rain the week before the rally meant many roads were in even worse condition than when they were practised – one stage was abandoned due to it being simply washed away. Despite the rain, snow was evident on high ground; Aaltonen used Dunlop SP44 tyres throughout and lightly-studded tyres on the three snowy stages.

The first stage of ten miles over the Passo di Teglia was after a long run out, where Aaltonen was sixth fastest despite the snowy descent and was just ten seconds over the bogey time. This was also causing some moaning from competitors as it was felt, despite the demanding terrain, the target times were often not fast enough. Aaltonen, along with the other top runners, cleaned the third stage, then was seventh and sixth on the following two.

It was now past midnight after six stages and the first hint of trouble befell Aaltonen as the engine started to consume a lot of oil, and with that was starting to overheat. Aaltonen pressed on, still recording competitive times, and was well up with the leaders. But it was not to last, as after the 12th stage, he was forced into retirement with a near-seized engine. Only 31 cars arrived back at the finish, where Pauli Toivonen in the Porsche 911T was declared the clear winner. Porsche was now the car to beat – which for Abingdon was to prove a tall order.

The last event for ORX 77F was in August 1968 for Finland's Rally of 1000 Lakes. The curtailed plans for Abingdon's activities in 1968, brought about by its new Leyland master, had not included the this rally. However, once Castrol and BBC Television had announced they would be filming the rally, they hastily changed their plans. Abingdon also agreed to loan the film crew Timo Mäkinen's practice car, ORX 707F, and they included a wonderful in-car sequence of Mäkinen driving on one of the stages during practice. It is a film well worth watching, even today.

The troubles at Abingdon caused by the merger of BMC and Leyland Cars into BLMC had far-reaching effects, notably because the new company was headed by Lord Stokes, who was not the least bit interested in motorsport and definitely not rallying. It also didn't help that the Mini was now right at the end of its dominant reign and Stokes wanted results for little money, and was cutting costs at every opportunity. Abingdon was very much on the list.

As it transpired, ORX 77F needed little preparation for the 1000 Lakes as it had already been prepared for the Geneva Rally in late June, but that event was postponed and moved to late October – so the fresh car was already available for the Rally of 1000 Lakes. It was prepared as a Group 2 car by Dudley Pike for Timo Mäkinen and Pekka Keskitalo; Mäkinen preferring to take a local experienced co-driver rather than Paul Easter. The records show the rally had never been won by a non-Scandinavian driver, so experience on this specialised event was paramount. Mäkinen had been practising for two weeks since the route was published, using his Mercedes towing a caravan and his practice car behind. However, strict speed limits were in force on the forest roads used for the stages, as these loose-surface roads were all public roads. Many a speeding ticket was issued, both during practice and on the interconnecting roads during the rally.

ORX 77F was little changed from how it appeared on the San Remo Rally in Italy. The engine and transmission specification was the same and it once again ran split Weber carburettors. Where things were different was the car was much stronger because of the many heavy landings the car was due to experience. A heavier-gauge rear subframe was specially manufactured by the press shop, and it also had extra plates welded on.

The car also ran shock absorbers on the front but it was still Hydrolastic. A rear anti-roll bar was again fitted, and 5½J magnesium Minilite wheels were accompanied by Dunlop SP44 tyres for the forests and Dunlop R7 race tyres for the tarmac tests, meaning the Mini also had extra-wide wheelarch extensions. Another noticeable addition was the fitting of huge forward-facing front mud flaps, which extended up to the wheelarch extensions.

The rally started in Jyväskylä and straight away the car was in trouble at scrutineering – not because of the infamous split Webers, but because of the lights. It was deemed the car had to have lights that complied with Finnish traffic rules, so they were all changed, until it was pointed out that FIA rules allowed a British car to use lights that complied with British traffic laws – so they were changed back again. One other addition was the car being plastered with sponsors' adverts placed liberally on the car at scrutineering. This, in the early days of motorsport sponsorship, was an unusual sight.

Ninety-five starters headed off for the first of 40 stages, 38 of which were on 200 miles of fast forest stages, and all of which were on scratch time, meaning the fastest car would be the winner.

The first stage was an around-the-houses tarmac sprint near the start before they headed off in the evening for the first forest stage. Mäkinen was on the pace straight away, being fifth fastest on the tarmac and second on the first short five-mile forest stage.

Into the early night and the rain began, making the slippery stages even worse, but now Mäkinen was in alternator trouble. This was quickly changed at his service by the side of the road, but nearing the next stage the problem persisted, so he elected to go back to the service barge for more attention and valuable time was lost incurring 14 minutes of road penalties, dropping him from a commanding second place down to 38th. The problem was eventually found to be incorrect wiring to the alternator.

Once fixed, Mäkinen set about clawing back the lost time. All through the first night he recorded fast stage times, winning the fifth stage and always in the top few. Come dawn and early morning, after the breakfast stop at the Hämeenlinna race circuit, three laps of the figure-of-eight circuit was the next stage and it was still raining. With race tyres, Mäkinen was dismayed to strip first gear as he shot off the start line; he was still credited with fifth fastest but he was to go no further and retired.

The rally was won by Hannu Mikkola in an Escort TC, who would go on to have a long and distinguished career with Ford and other marques.

It was a sad end to Mäkinen's long and distinguished career with the team, as this rally marked the last drive he would have with the works Minis. Still probably the fastest rally driver ever, and his win on the snowbound 1965 Monte Carlo Rally was probably his greatest drive.

The car was sold to Jack Grundy, a very successful clubman, who went on to use the car on numerous rallies to great effect.

Fast as always, Mäkinen was beset with early electrical problems, dropping out of contention, only to retire on the last stage where he stripped first gear and the transmission failed.

Competition Record

Date	Event	Crew	Number	Overall result	Class result
Jan 68	Monte Carlo Rally	Timo Mäkinen/Paul Easter	7	55th	
Feb 68	San Remo Rally	Rauno Aaltonen/Henry Liddon	40	DNF	
Aug 68	Rally of 1000 Lakes	Timo Mäkinen/Pekka Keskitalo	47	DNF	

WORKS MINIS IN DETAIL

Registration Number	First registered	Chassis number	Engine	Engine number	Model
ORX 777F	Jan 1968	CA2SB 1068930A	1275cc	9F-SA-Y 47693	Austin Cooper S Mk2

Paddy Hopkirk and a rather fed-up-looking Ron Crellin in Lisbon just before their start with ORX 777F for the 1968 Monte Carlo Rally.

ORX 777F was third of four new cars delivered to Abingdon in November 1967 for the Monte Carlo Rally in January 1968. These cars, all Mk2s, had sequential registration numbers, as Abingdon had a good relationship with the local registration authority – which was why in 1968 the Monte cars all had '7' digits, in 1967 they had '6' and in 1965 '5's.

These cars were the first Mk2s to be prepared at Abingdon. Mk2 cars had only minor cosmetic changes from Mk1s, such as larger rear lamps, a wider rear screen, new badges and a new front grille, plus the interior trim was now black. Otherwise they were basically the same as their predecessors.

The car was assigned to Paddy Hopkirk and Ron Crellin for the 1968 Monte and was built by Gerald Wiffen as a Group 2 car, despite Abingdon's preference, in these latter years of the Cooper S, for Group 6 cars (if the regulations allowed) because the opposition was getting stronger. Nevertheless, with the often poor weather on the Monte, which tended to favour the front-wheel-drive and nimble Mini, Abingdon was hoping it would still be able to win this winter classic.

A new development on the car, which would cause much controversy, was the fitting of new carburettors that became known as split Webers. Timo Mäkinen had discovered a Mini in Finland using such a setup and decided to take a pair to Abingdon to let Cliff Humphries, the engine guru, see if any extra power could be squeezed out of the engine. These carburettors were found to give an extra 7bhp, boosting the power to around 93bhp at the wheels. They were based on a pair of Weber 45DCOE but with one choke of each unit machined off and with a short extension welded onto them, which allowed them to be fitted to the standard Cooper S inlet manifold. Abingdon informed the Automobile Club de Monaco (ACM) of the intention to use these units and stated that these carburettors, with their welded extension and cut-off chokes, were a 'prototype carburettor' – but this, as events unfolded, would prove a bone of contention.

This powerful engine was 1293cc with a 12.6:1 high-compression Downton cylinder head, fitted with forged pistons and an AEA648 race camshaft. Helical transfer gears were fitted with a straight-cut close-ratio gearbox with a 4.2:1 final drive and enlarged-diameter driveshafts plus a lightened and balanced flywheel with an orange diaphragm. The provision also had to be made to fit a bracket to the engine for the seals that the ACM would fit to the engine to ensure it wasn't changed.

The engine was protected by a 13-hole Moke sump guard with the addition of an alloy extension plate and it was also fitted with a battery box cover. The cooling system consisted of a Cooper S radiator, a four-blade fan and a 74C thermostat; this temperature was established by Humphries as the optimum temperature to run the engine for maximum power by extensive tests on the rolling road. A grille muff was fitted around the front grille, which could be used should the outside temperature be exceptionally low.

Hydrolastic suspension was used with single-blue and double-blue displacers front and back but without front dampers and only orange helper springs at the rear, although a rear anti-roll bar was being used. No subframe strengthening was carried out but the front tie bars had protection plates added to the subframe, which did add strength.

The brakes with its servo retained in its standard position under the bonnet used Ferodo DS11pads and VG95 shoes. The brake callipers had asbestos blocks fitted into the pistons to take excess heat away from the brake fluid. The rear wheel cylinders were also threaded where they were fixed to the backplate and held fast with a large nut - this also served to take heat away from the brake fluid.

Lucas Racing, invariably resident at Abingdon, rewired the new car completely to include the requirements of the driver and equipment. The car was fitted with an alternator needed for the four auxiliary lamps and the heated front windscreen. These lamps were connected by a five-pin rubber socket just below the offside headlamp. A two-speed wiper motor was fitted with deep-throated wheel boxes, which were stronger and coped better with heavy snow loads. European headlamps, washers and Perspex protective covers were fitted, along with iodine bulbs, as were the extra lamps.

The driver's instrument panel had the vital oil pressure gauge moved next to the rev counter, and in its place was the water temperature gauge; in its previous place was a circular fuel gauge. The co-driver's instrument panel housed his usual Halda distance recorder and a pair of Heuer clocks, while near his feet was an expansion tank from the radiator and a foot-operated horn switch. Two Tudor electric screen washer bottles were fitted to the rear of the car on the driver's side, along with the jack by the rear pocket. Seats were a bucket seat in red and grey cord for the driver and a reclining high-back seat for the co-driver, both on modified seat brackets. An Irvin lap-and-diagonal seat belt was supplied for the driver and a full-harness Irvin belt for the co-driver.

Being a Group 2 car, all standard trim and glass had to be retained. Under the front carpet was an asbestos blanket was placed to keep heat away. Padding to the door pockets, door locks, co-driver's rear pocket corner and door pillar helped to add to crew comfort. The alloy roll cage was also padded, as was the intercom box attached to it. All lines were run inside the car, with the fuel pump located under the rear seat. In the boot the twin fuel tanks were protected from damage from studded tyres by sticking asbestos sheets to the exposed sides of the tanks.

Outside the car, a rectangle number plate was painted on the offside of the bonnet and it was secured by a single leather strap underneath; the rally plate secured vertically alongside. For the run to Monte Carlo, the car was fitted with a roof rack for two additional spare wheels and a Lucas 576 fog lamp on the boot lid as a reversing lamp. The boot lid was secured with a Moke rubber toggle. The car was also fitted with forward-facing front mud flaps below the sidelights, and it also carried mandatory rear mud flaps. The wheelarch extensions were painted red.

The 1968 Monte Carlo Rally was held between 20 and 25 January and started with a rather tiring three-day drive through Europe to arrive at Monte Carlo before the rally really began. On arrival in Monte Carlo, after a full day's rest, there was a 24-hour 900-mile common run with seven special stages to Aix-les-Bains and back. Then, the following evening, the top 60 tackled the famous 12-hour 390-mile mountain circuit as a classification run, with six special stages over the mountains north of Monaco to find a winner.

BMC had been practising the stages before and after Christmas, writing detailed pace notes of all of the stages. During the recces the weather had been very cold and snowy, so tyre selection was to be important. BMC had five recce cars in France; these, used rally cars, were fully prepared but with rather standard engines to keep them reliable because

Crellin at the wheel of ORX 777F on their long three=day journey to Monte Carlo whilst Hopkirk tries to sleep in the passenger seat.

breakdowns on recces were time-consuming.

Dunlop supplied a huge selection of 750 tyres of 13 various types for the four works Minis. However, once under way, an unseasonal thaw in the weather descended, which meant dry conditions over most of the important stages, so R7 racing tyres were those most in demand. Dunlop provided 14 mechanics and five trucks. Abingdon's transport fleet consisted of seven service cars, one transporter, one van, four ice-note crews plus half-a-dozen office personnel, and of course four brand-new rally cars.

From their eight starting points across Europe, 200 cars set off on their various journeys; some would be relatively easy, and others more demanding. Hopkirk started from Lisbon along with just a dozen other cars. Once under way, Hopkirk was not without problems: he experienced freezing fog through the Massif Central but his heated 'screen was much appreciated.

Bigger problems occurred when the pipe from the radiator to the expansion tank detached itself and deposited boiling hot anti-freeze over the crew. There was also a scare when Hopkirk was reported, in error, to have missed the time control in Aurillac. A reassuring phone call to Peter Browning allayed his fears.

At Monte Carlo, 153 cars made it for a well-earned 24-hour rest, and all the works Minis arrived with no time penalties. As soon as Hopkirk arrived just outside Monte Carlo, the car was divested of its roof racks and all other items of unwanted bits of extraneous travel rubbish. Crellin handed a list of items required to be attended to by the service crew, and finally the car was washed and driven off to parc fermé. However, Hopkirk's car stayed on his rather worn half-studded tyres that had been on the car since Lisbon, as he was delaying his

Overheating problems and being initially on the wrong tyres meant Hopkirk and Crellin arrived in sixth place after the common run.

Crellin checks his pace notes with the ice note additions for the mountain circuit defining stages.

tyre choice for the next leg until the next day.

Trouble was, however, brewing with the split Webers. Scrutineering was taking place in Monte Carlo, and after the ACM's technical inspection they were clearly having misgivings about the fitting of the carburettors to Hopkirk's and the other three works Minis, and informed Peter Browning they had doubts about their eligibility. The letter of the rules was discussed in detail and, although it was accepted they were fitted in good faith, their opinion remained that a protest may be lodged by other competitors – and if so they would have to review the situation and likely uphold any protest. Browning was now faced with a dilemma as it seemed very likely that the cars would be disqualified and not be allowed to start the next leg.

In an attempt to resolve the issue and not have a repeat of the 1966 disqualification rumpus over their lighting, the ACM offered to allow all four Minis to be worked on in parc fermé to allow mechanics to replace the split Webers with twin SU carburettors. This, Browning decided after consulting with Longbridge, not to do. The press even reported that Hopkirk was seen swapping over his carburettors but this proved unfounded. However, at the last moment the ACM decided to allow the car to start and continue on the common run, with the ever-present cloud hanging over his head that he may eventually be disqualified.

This long delay meant the service crews (particularly those from Dunlop) were not prepared and ready to go, being scattered away from Monte Carlo assuming they were not needed. A hurried series of phone calls by Browning meant a scrabble to get things reorganised. Unfortunately, by the time Hopkirk had set off, the all-important Dunlop tyre truck was not in position for the first stage to change Hopkirk's tyres onto the race tyres that the now-warmer conditions demanded. He therefore had to do the first stage, St Auban, using badly-worn half-studded tyres and was outside the top ten.

Hopkirk was more fortunate on the stage, Le Moulinon, as the Dunlop tyre truck arrived just as he did, so he was able to have a long-awaited change of tyres onto racers and he just got into the top ten, being tenth again on the famous Burzet stage. Nevertheless, he was not entirely happy as the car was overheating, and at the service in Gap he had water added, as coolant in the expansion tank (which had soaked them earlier) was not flowing back to the radiator and hence it was running too hot.

He would record two other tenth places and arrived back at Monte Carlo the next day in sixth place overall. The rally was being headed by Gerard Larrousse in the nimble Renault Alpine.

Back at Monte Carlo, just 78 cars arrived to be classified as finishers and only 27 were still unpenalised. Hopkirk soon headed off in a recce car into the mountains to check the condition of the roads, and with the weather now relatively mild (most roads were dry with very little ice), race tyres would be the order of the day. The top 60 would, after a day's rest, tackle the mountain circuit the following evening. This famous route, unchanged since 1965, consisted of six stages within the 390 miles and were to be covered in 11-and-a-half hours, meaning an average of 34mph. Three runs over the Col du Turini and two over the Col de Couillole plus the Gorges de Piaon meant that to allow time for service, tyre changes and refuelling, the pace would indeed be very fast.

The first stage from Sospel saw Hopkirk sixth fastest in dry conditions. The top of the Turini was icy, where Hopkirk struggled on his race tyres for grip but was rewarded with

The last night of the Monte and the mountain circuit saw Hopkirk eventually finish in fifth place.

Hopkirk and Crellin at the finish in Monte Carlo. The threat of exclusion due to the controversial split Webers carburettors evaporated - it may not, had the Mini won...

seventh fastest, and seventh on the Couillole that followed. The leading Alpine went off on the return visit to the Turini, reportedly on snow thrown onto the bend by spectators, leaving Elford's Porsche in an unassailable position. Hopkirk was sixth. With just two stages remaining, Hopkirk consolidated his position and finished in fifth place.

At the final scrutineering in Monte Carlo, the ACM went back on its word and decided it was not going to allow the results to stand because of the carburettors. After much badgering by Browning to the sporting commission, it was agreed to let the carburettors pass. Quite what the decision might have been if Hopkirk had won is perhaps open to debate…

This Monte was also to be the last event for Ron Crellin, who had decided to retire and concentrate on his business. Hopkirk and Crellin had been a successful partnership, which over two years had seen them compete in a dozen internationals together, with three overall wins to their credit.

Paddy Hopkirk had returned ORX 777F to Abingdon relatively unscathed after the Monte Carlo Rally, but the car was nevertheless rebuilt by Brian Moylan for Tony Fall and Mike Wood to take on the San Remo Rally, previously known as the Rally of the Flowers. The engine was of the same specification to that used on the Monte, including the controversial split Weber carburettors. A major change was the replacement of the power-sapping and often unreliable helical transfer gears with straight-cut gears with a roller bearing for the idler gear. The inlet manifold was changed slightly, as it was now fixed to the cylinder head with locating rings and not pegs as was customary.

The car retained its short 4.2:1 final drive and a straight-cut gearbox. It was fitted with a heavy-duty Scandinavian sump guard, replacing the Moke guard, as the event was mainly on loose-surface roads. However, the subframes remained unstrengthened, which was to prove a problem. On the Abingdon rolling road, the engine, still with its controversial split Webers, showed 92bhp at the wheels. However, the car was basically unchanged from how it appeared on the Monte, with Fall's San Remo Rally plate now fitted onto the middle of the bonnet rather than in a vertical position.

The San Remo Rally was a short and sharp event but the route was tough and demanding. Run in early March, in the mountains above the Italian Riviera of the Flowers, along the coast from Monaco, the roads were mostly unsurfaced. Whilst the lower roads were tarmac, once they climbed, the surface deteriorated into rough, loose surface with no barriers.

The compact route, of 19 stages of just 80 miles of competitive motoring, meant numerous visits to the same stages, tackled often in both directions, meaning practising and making pace notes was difficult and dangerous. The uncertainty of not knowing if another entrant was charging fast in the opposite direction was unnerving. Lancias lost two cars in head-on accidents in practice. Fall therefore decided to only practice at night – it being considered much safer. Rain the week before the rally meant many roads were in even worse condition than when they were practiced, and one stage was abandoned due to it being washed away.

Eight works teams took part, one of which was from Ford and marked the very first appearance of the Escort TC – the start of what was to become a very successful rally car. Driven here by Ove Andersson, the new Escort would be raced home into third place.

The low entry of just 72 starters headed off after scrutineering, where once again the split Webers came under

Mike Wood sitting on the wing of ORX 777F with Tony Fall looking on at the start of the 1968 San Remo Rally.

Henry Liddon compares stage times with Mike Wood sitting in ORX 777F whilst both cars are serviced on the San Remo Rally.

close examination. Eventually the technical commission decided to allow the carbs and Fall was flagged away. Controversially, the entry was not seeded – cars were simply grouped in capacity classes, which meant some balking on the longer stages and Fall found himself in the latter half of the field. Despite the earlier rain damaging the roads, snow was evident on high ground, so Fall used Dunlop SP44 tyres mostly, and lightly-studded tyres on several of the snowy stages.

After a long run out of some 30 miles, the first stage over the Passo di Teglia of ten miles saw several cars clean this and the next stage. It was felt by some that the target times were perhaps too generous. Fall started to make his mark, recording fifth fastest on the next two stages and sixth on the sixth stage, well up with the leading cars.

As night fell, the first sign of trouble appeared on the car, as the engine was running very hot and although not losing water initially, it was difficult to find a solution. The event wore on during the night, and Fall's troubles were to get worse when the pounding from the rough stages had started to show: the rear subframe was beginning to fracture. It had not been strengthened, which was perhaps an error. Fall nevertheless continued to post quick times but was losing lots of water as the persistently hot engine continued to boil over.

He was ultimately forced into retirement with an incurably overheated engine after 12 stages. Only 31 cars were classed as finishers, and the event was won by Pauli Toivonen in a Porsche 911T.

The final event for ORX 777F was the Rally of 1000 Lakes held in Finland in mid-August 1968. By now the merger in January 1968 of the then-British Motor Holdings (as BMC had become) and Leyland Motor Cars was starting to bite hard. The new company, BLMC (British Leyland Motor Cars) was headed by the ex-Leyland Cars chairman Lord Donald Stokes, and he was not that interested in motorsport – and certainly not rallying, so the plans set out by Peter Browning for the 1968 season were being seriously cut back.

ORX 777F was initially prepared for the Geneva Rally in late June but that event was postponed and moved to late October, so the car, unused, was fresh and ready for the Rally of 1000 Lakes. The car was again prepared by Brian Moylan as a Group 2 car but this time the car was handed to Lars Ytterbring and Lars Persson, the competitive Swedish pair, to try their luck on this specialised Finnish rally. At that time, no non-Scandinavian driver had ever won the 1000 Lakes. Rauno Aaltonen did not relish competing in Finland because of the country's rather draconian attitude towards speeding drivers and preferred to keep his licence clean and so stayed away.

Abingdon had initially decided not to enter the rally but once it discovered it was being filmed by Castrol and BBC Television, the managers changed their minds and entered. They loaned ORX 707F to the film crew for their use after it had been used as a team practice car. The resulting movie on the Rally of the 1000 Lakes became a famous film depicting Timo Mäkinen hard at work in his practice car and is a fine record of the event.

The car was little changed from how it was prepared for the San Remo Rally but it was substantially strengthened this time, having suffered badly in Italy. Rather than a standard subframe, a heavy-gauge subframe was fabricated by the press shop. The car also ran adjustable shock absorbers to the front but none on the rear. It again sat on Hydrolastic suspension and now also had a rear anti-roll bar fitted. The remote-control mounting bracket was modified and strengthened with strips of steel inside the car where it bolted through the floor.

The freshly built engine, it was noted, was run-in using twin SU H4 carburettors before the fitting of the split Weber carburettor setup. Otherwise, the engine and transmission specification was unchanged. One noticeable alteration to the car was the fitting of very large forward-facing front mud flaps, which extended halfway up the wide front wheelarch extensions. The car ran 5½J magnesium Minilite wheels and used Dunlop SP44 tyres for the forests and Dunlop R7 race tyres for the tarmac tests. Also of note was the car was adorned with sponsors' adverts placed liberally on the bodywork at scrutineering once in Finland. Being the early days of motorsport sponsorship, it was unusual for this to be seen.

The 1968 Rally of 1000 Lakes was mostly run on closed public roads. These Finnish roads, however, were all loose-surface forest roads with many blind crests to catch out the unwary. Practice and detailed pace notes (or very good local knowledge) was essential.

Starting in Jyväskylä, in mid Finland, saw scrutineering problems for the car when the British lights were refused and so were hurriedly changed to those conforming to Finnish traffic laws. However, it was then pointed out that under FIA rules, it was quite correct for British cars to only comply with British lighting regulations – so the lights were changed back.

Ahead of the 95 starters, nearly all of whom were Scandinavian, were some 200 miles of forest stages with a smattering of tarmac tests, all of which were based on scratch time – the fastest car wins. The route had been announced at the end of July, and from then on practice was allowed but all 38 of the forest stages all had a low mandatory speed limit, which was rigorously enforced for the duration, and speed traps caught out many whilst practising and on the interconnecting roads on the rally (hence Aaltonen's reluctance to enter the event).

The cars headed off early evening for the first round-the-houses spectator stage, and then it was straight into the forests. Ytterbring started steadily and although he hadn't featured in any of the top six stage times, it all came to a sudden end when he flew off the road on the fifth stage. He damaged the front suspension sufficiently that he couldn't continue and he was out. It was a sad end to what was to be

Nighttime service stop with ORX 777F's bonnet up; Aaltonen talks to Fall whilst Peter Browning tops up the car with fuel from the fuel bag; Mike Wood supervises. Fall would retire with an incurably overheated engine.

his last event for the team. The event was won by up-and-coming star Hannu Mikkola, in a Ford Escort Twin Cam; it would be the first of many for him.

The car was sold to former MG apprentice and Dublin race driver Alec Poole, who in 1969 went onto to win the British Touring Car Championship in an Arden-entered one-litre Mini Cooper S.

Young boys fascinated by Lars Ytterbring and Lars Persson's ORX 777F awaiting the start of the 1968 1000 Lakes Rally. Peter Browning sits on the front wing. Ytterbring would retire when he left the road.

Competition Record

Date	Event	Crew	Number	Overall result	Class result
Jan 68	Monte Carlo Rally	Paddy Hopkirk/Ron Crellin	87	5th	3rd
Feb 68	San Remo Rally	Tony Fall/Mike Wood	44	DNF	
Aug 68	Rally of 1000 Lakes	Lars Ytterbring/Lars Persson	41	DNF	

Registration Number	First registered	Chassis number	Engine	Engine number	Model
ORX 707F	Jan 1968	CA2SB 1088682A	1275cc	9F-SA-Y 47762	Austin Cooper S Mk2

Tony Fall and Mike Wood descend the starting ramp at Dover in ORX 707F on their long journey through Europe bound for Monte Carlo.

ORX 707F was the last of four new cars delivered to Abingdon in November 1967 in readiness for the Monte Carlo Rally in January 1968. This car was one of the first four Mk2s prepared at Abingdon. The Mk2 cars were only slightly different from the Mk1s they replaced and were mechanically identical; changes were only cosmetic, being a new front grille, badges, larger rear lights and a wider rear 'screen. Internally, however the cars appeared quite different, with an all-black interior.

The car was built for the Monte by Roy Brown, as a Group 2 car, for Tony Fall and Mike Wood. Abingdon at this time was losing the power battle, with strong opposition from Porsche and Alpine Renault, which explained the preference for building Group 6 cars – which could be both lighter and have a more powerful engine, unrestricted by constraining rules. However, the Monte was only for Group 2 cars.

Help was at hand when Timo Mäkinen brought into Abingdon a pair of carburettors he had seen in Finland fitted in a successful Mini. They were a pair of Weber 45DCOE carburettors, which had one choke machined off each and were mounted onto a manifold to suit the Mini, allowing the charge to go straight into the cylinder head. Cliff Humphries, who was Abingdon's engine man, set about testing and devising a way these split carbs could legally be fitted to a standard Cooper S inlet manifold, which under Group 2 rules they were obliged to use. He came up with what Abingdon called a 'prototype carburettor', which entailed welding an intermediate stub tube to the cut-down Weber to allow it to fit directly onto the standard inlet manifold. The result was a gain of 7bhp and a more mid-range torque, giving 93bhp at the wheels. Importantly, Abingdon sent details of these prototypes in advance to the Automobile Club de Monaco (ACM) to ensure it was happy with them and it seemed, at the time, all was well.

The all-new and powerful 1293cc engine was fitted with a high-compression Downton cylinder head giving 12.6:1 compression ratio, with forged pistons and fitted with an AEA648 race camshaft. A straight-cut close-ratio gearbox with a 4.2:1 final drive plus enlarged-diameter driveshafts was fitted, ideal for climbing cols. Engine cooling was by a Cooper S radiator, a four-blade fan and a 74C thermostat. An oil cooler was fitted. The engine was also equipped with a bracket for the seals that the ACM would fit to ensure the engine wasn't replaced.

Underneath, the engine and gearbox was protected by a 13-hole Moke sump guard with an alloy expansion plate. A battery box cover was fitted and the front tie bars also had protection plates added to the subframe (which also added some strength to the subframe, even though it was prohibited by Group 2 rules). Hydrolastic suspension, with a rear anti-roll bar, was used with single-blue and double-blue displacers front and back; they were without front dampers but had orange helper springs at the rear. No subframe strengthening or rewelding was carried out through fear of the strict ACM scrutineers.

The brakes were improved, with the callipers having asbestos blocks fitted into the pistons to take excess heat away from the brake fluid, and the rear wheel cylinders were threaded so they were fixed to the backplate with a large nut rather than a circlip, also to take heat away from the brake fluid.

Lucas completely rewired the car to the usual high standard, as indeed it did to every works Mini, largely to ensure total reliability. Because of all of the additional equipment, such as the heated front windscreen and four extra lamps, the car ran an alternator. The lamps – two fog lamps and two driving lamps fixed to a lamp bar – were connected by a five-pin rubber socket, and the two driving lamps secured by steady bars. European headlamps with Perspex protective covers were fitted with iodine bulbs, as were the extra lamps; headlamp washers were also fitted. A Lucas 576 fog lamp was fitted to the boot lid as a reversing lamp.

The driver's auxiliary dash panel had the oil pressure gauge moved to beside the rev counter, and in its place in the binnacle was the water temperature gauge, with its previous position taken by a circular fuel gauge (the original gauge now inoperable in the speedo). The co-driver's instrument panel housed his usual Halda distance recorder, a pair of Heuer clocks and numerous other controls; he also had a switch panel in his door pocket. As he now had an expansion tank from the radiator by his feet in the footwell, the Tudor electric screen washer bottles were moved to the rear of the car on the driver's side. The co-driver also had a foot-operated horn switch.

A fibreglass bucket seat, covered in red and grey cord material for the driver, and a reclining high-back seat for the co-driver were fitted on modified seat brackets. An Irvin lap-and-diagonal seat belt for Fall and a full-harness Irvin belt for Wood were also added. All standard trim and glass had to be retained under Group 2 regulations, including the carpets; the front had an asbestos blanket underneath to keep heat away from the hot exhaust. Padding to the door pockets, door locks, co-driver's rear pocket bin corner and door pillars added to crew comfort. The roll cage, which also housed the intercom box, was also padded.

All lines were run inside the car, with the fuel pump located under the rear seat. In the boot the twin fuel tanks were protected from damage from studded tyres by sticking asbestos sheet to the exposed sides of the tanks. Outside the car, provision was made for a grille muff to be fitted around the front grille to keep out snow, should it be needed. The bonnet had the number plate painted on the offside and the nearside had the rally plate fixed vertically. The car was fitted with forward-facing front mud flaps below the sidelights and it also carried mandatory rear mud flaps.

On 20 January the Monte Carlo Rally of 1968 began from eight locations, and 200 cars started on their long circuitous drive through a wintry Europe before the real competition started three days later from Monte Carlo.

Once in Monte Carlo after a day's rest, there was a 24-hour common run with seven special stages of over 100 miles to Aix-les-Bains and back, covering 900 miles over the Alpes Maritime and the Ardèche. The top 60 then tackled the famous mountain circuit as a classification run. This contained six special stages of 75 miles within 390 miles, which had to be driven at night in just less than 12 hours. This challenging dash over the mountains north of Monaco was mostly unchanged since its inception in 1965 and was a great spectacle.

Another Monte win was much in Abingdon's sights and Fall, along with the other three works drivers, had been practising before and after Christmas, compiling detailed pace notes of

Fall and Wood on the rural roads of France on their way to Monte Carlo. It would not be an easy journey for the 30 cars that left from Dover, and many would lose time penalties along the way.

At the end of the 24-hour common run, Fall and Wood were lying in seventh place, able to be fitted with the correct tyres, unlike the other works Minis.

Full service for ORX 707F near the end of the common run.

The mountain circuit for the top 60 cars saw Fall running well; here he is chased by the ex-works Mini DJB 92B, driven by Cresdee and Philips who didn't finish.

all the stages in what were then snowy conditions. BMC's effort for the Monte was huge. The team had five recce cars in France – all old rally cars but mostly with standard and hence reliable engines. For the rally there were seven service cars, one transporter, one van, four ice-note crews, half-a-dozen office personnel plus four brand-new Mk2 rally cars. At the team's disposal was a selection of 750 tyres of 13 various types, all supplied by Dunlop, which itself had 14 mechanics in five trucks to move and service the cars with fresh tyres.

Fall, along with 30 other crews, started from Dover, no longer having to endure the long haul from Glasgow. Once under way, Fall experienced many delays, mostly around Lille when arriving in rush hour and having difficulty locating the all-important time control on schedule – he did but many didn't, and only six of the 30 Dover starters arrived in Monaco without time penalties.

At Monte Carlo, 153 cars made it for a well-earned 24 hour rest, and all the works Minis arrived with no time penalties. As soon as Fall arrived at the service point just outside Monte Carlo, the roof rack and all other items of unwanted junk accumulated over the three-day journey were removed. The car was serviced, washed and sent off to scrutineering before parc fermé. Significantly, the car stayed on its half-studded Dunlop tyres used since Dover, delaying Fall's tyre decision for the next leg until the following day.

However, all did not go well at scrutineering, as the new carburettors were being questioned by the ACM. The scrutineers were having doubts about the legality of the carburettors and told Peter Browning they were considering disqualifying the car. The letter rules were examined in detail and it was accepted the carbs were fitted in good faith but their opinion was that a protest may be lodged by other competitors – and if so they would have to review the situation and likely uphold any protest. The ACM then offered to allow all four Minis to be worked on in parc fermé to allow mechanics to replace the split Webers with twin SU carburettors. This Browning decided not to do, after consulting with Longbridge. However, at the last moment, the ACM allowed BMC to continue on the common run but with the question that the Minis may eventually be disqualified if protests were lodged.

This long delay meant the service crews and particularly those from Dunlop were not prepared and ready to go. Most were in hotels outside Monte Carlo and had to be quickly summoned and told to swing into action. Unfortunately, by the time Aaltonen, Mäkinen and Hopkirk had set off in the sister cars, the Dunlop tyre truck was not in position for the first stage. All three had to do the first stage using badly-worn half-studded tyres used on the long haul from their starting points. Fall, however, running later in the field, did meet up with the Dunlop tyre truck and was fitted with fresh racing tyres for the first stage. Fall continued to post good times, being seventh fastest on the Le Moulinon and Burzet stages and consolidated his position, despite a wrong tyre choice on the next stage – staying on racers when light studs would have been preferable – but dropping no road time and arriving back at Monte Carlo in seventh place, where the rally was being led by Gerard Larrousse in an Alpine Renault.

Back at Monte Carlo, just 78 tired crews arrived to be classified as finishers and only 27 were unpenalised. The top 60 would, the following evening, tackle the mountain circuit. Fall headed off in a recce car into the mountains to check the condition of the roads and, with the weather now relatively mild (most roads were dry with just some ice at the very top of some climbs), race tyres would be the order of the day for most. The mountain circuit saw three runs over the Col du Turini and two over the Col de Couillole plus the Gorges de Piaon. Seventy-five miles of flat-out motoring, all at night, would be challenging.

The top of the Turini was icy where the Minis struggled for grip on their racing tyres but Fall was still sixth fastest. On the second run over the Turini, Fall was eighth but then the leading Alpine went off on snow thrown onto the bend by spectators; this left Elford's Porsche in a clear leading position. Fall's best stage time was on the Col de la Couillole where he was third fastest behind the two much more powerful Porsche 911s. After the third and final blast over the Turini, where Fall simply maintained his position, he came safely back to Monte Carlo in fourth place overall, just ahead of Hopkirk.

At the finish in Monte Carlo, at the final scrutineering, the ACM decided it was not going to allow the results to stand because of the split Weber carburettors, much to Browning's

The Col du Turini on the last night, full of spectators, saw Fall consolidate his strong performance to finish in fourth place overall just ahead of teammate Hopkirk but behind Aaltonen who was third.

Julien Vernaeve and Mike Wood took ORX 707F to The Hague for the 1968 Tulip Rally. The car now fitted with 5½J Minilite wheels and extra-wide wheelarch extensions.

disgust. After hours of arguments to the sporting commission, the representatives changed their minds and agreed to let the carburettors pass. Nobody really wanted a repeat of the 1966 disqualification rumpus and, as none of the works Minis had actually won, a pragmatic solution was reached and the results stood. Even so, between them, the four Minis were in the top ten on every one of the 13 stages, and in the final results were only beaten by the two much more powerful works Porsche 911s – so they were not disgraced.

The next event for ORX 707F was the 1968 Tulip Rally, held at a busy time for Abingdon. April that year saw the team on the Safari Rally in East Africa with 1800s and on the same weekend in Ireland for the Circuit of Ireland, then a week later in Holland for the start of the Tulip Rally. Any signs that things were being cut back under the new BLMC management were certainly not felt that spring.

After the Monte the car was rebuilt by Robin Vokins for Julien Vernaeve, the very successful Belgian race and rally driver. He would be teamed with Mike Wood, where Tony Fall, his regular driver, was in Africa with the 1800. The car was very similar in specification to the Group 2 that Fall and Wood had taken to fourth place on the Monte.

Notable changes were the fitting of straight-cut transfer gears, which replaced the previous helical gears. The water pump was changed to an MG Midget type. The car again ran split Weber carburettors but with larger chokes and jets. The heated front 'screen disappeared, as did the forward-facing mud flaps. The interior now saw black corduroy-covered driver and navigator's seats, a single Tudor washer bottle, and crash helmets stowed in a box rather than on the rear parcel shelf.

Externally, the biggest difference was (for the first time) the use of 5½J Minilite wheels, painted gold to ease identification. Red paint had been tried but aesthetically this was not considered very attractive. As the Tulip was an all-tarmac rally, getting as much grip as possible was essential – hence the wider wheels and Dunlop R7 race tyres. To cover these wider wheels were wider wheelarch extensions, also painted red. The suspension and brakes remained the same, including the rear anti-roll bar.

Starting in Noordwijk near The Hague on the west cost of Holland, the 2200-mile route journeyed over to Annecy in France via the Ardennes, Vosges and Jura Mountains before returning to Holland four days later. The route, very similar to 1967, attracted just 77 starters who faced eight special stages with target times (many of which were cleaned by the top crews) and two very important eliminating tests, decided on scratch times. These stages and tests were interspersed with many quickly timed road sections, reminiscent of British road rallies, and were particularly demanding on the mountain circuit from Annecy to Rumilly.

At 8.30am the cars set off for the first test at the Zolder race circuit, where the powerful cars headed the list. Then followed a long run to Vosges and the St Odile hillclimb, which was better suited to the Mini, where Vernaeve got on the score sheet. The fast road sections that followed saw everyone bar two cars drop time. The next two stages were cleaned by Vernaeve and many more, so proved of no value.

Much rubber being left on the corners of this all-tarmac event meant racing tyres were used throughout. Vernaeve was putting up fast times on the important classification tests.

Queuing for the start of a speed test on the Zolder race circuit; Vernaeve's speed and Wood's careful navigation of the difficult sections resulted in a win in the touring class and third place overall.

It was then into the night and another long haul to the Jura Mountains on the route to Annecy. Service before Annecy saw Vernaeve have his clutch adjusted and fresh tyres fitted before heading for parc fermé and a ten-hour rest during the day. Setting off again the following evening, along with 67 other cars, saw a 300-mile six-hour fast section to Rumilly, where only ten cars arrived without time loss. Snow had blocked a pass near Thono and many cars took the wrong route, costing them time.

Service at Rumilly, in time for breakfast, witnessed Vernaeve having the timing adjusted as he was complaining the car was down on power. It also saw the fine warm weather deteriorate into rain. This was actually welcome by Vernaeve, as apart from reducing the advantage that the more powerful cars had on what were now slippery roads, the lower air temperature meant the engine, which was susceptible to overheating, was running cooler.

The weather deteriorated further as the route headed back to the Jura Mountains and then onto to Vosges. Several stages were cleaned by many and Vernaeve was by now leading the touring car category, behind the leading Escort TCs and Alpines.

Into the last night, the leading Renault Alpine of Andruet retired, leaving the two Escort TCs of Roger Clark and Ove Andersson in an unassailable position. Back at Noordwijk, the next morning, Vernaeve would indeed win the touring class and finish a very creditable third overall, behind the Escorts. Clearly the Mini was now struggling against much more powerful cars.

ORX 707F was used for recce work after the Tulip Rally and was also used as a practice car by Timo Mäkinen for the 1968 Rally of 1000 Lakes. It was then used by the Castrol film unit to film the rally. The car was eventually sold to Mike Wood in October that year.

ORX 707F was used as a recce car for Timo Mäkinen and as a film car for the Castrol Flying Finns film of the 1968 1000 Lakes Rally. Seen here with a heavily-laden BMC service barge.

Competition Record

Date	Event	Crew	Number	Overall result	Class result
Jan 68	Monte Carlo Rally	Tony Fall/Mike Wood	185	4th	2nd
April 68	Tulip Rally	Julien Vernaeve/Mike Wood	74	3rd	1st

Registration Number	First registered	Chassis number	Engine	Engine number	Model
OBL 45F	Sept 1967	CA2S7 1012033A	1275cc	9F-SA-Y 46140	Austin Cooper S Mk1

OBL 45F, although registered as a Mk2 Austin Cooper S, was initially a MK1 Cooper S in its first incarnation at Abingdon and used as such. It is likely that as Mk2 production officially came on stream in October 1967, there were numerous unsold Mk1s still to dispose of and the competition department would have been a willing recipient of such cars. In several cases they converted to Mk2s with the simple expediency of changing the rear lights and fitting Mk2 grille and badges. The slightly smaller rear screen was an unnecessary step too far. OBL 45F was, however, not a car that was initially converted.

OBL 45F's first foray as a works car was as a recce car for the 1968 Monte Carlo Rally, where such a car was not in the public view. The car was used by Timo Mäkinen and Paul Easter and they encountered very snowy conditions on that recce where the car was fitted, as they usually were, with a roof rack for additional tyres and a reliable engine rather than a high-performance unit, as breakdowns and constant servicing was very time-consuming and disruptive on a recce.

The second outing for the car, still as a Mk1, was on the Gulf-London Rally in July 1968, where Tony Fall and Mike Wood entered this superb event. OBL 45F was built as a Group 6 car with a very powerful engine. The build is shrouded in mystery as no records exist, but it likely that it was using split Weber carburettors on a five-port cylinder head, although it could be that the car ran an eight-port engine and fuel injection, similar to that built for Mäkinen for the ill-fated 1967 RAC the previous November. Contemporary reports of the rally say the car was never seen with its bonnet open, not even at scrutineering, which adds to the rumours. It was, however, using a limited-slip differential as its failure was listed as the reason for the car's demise after only two stages of this most tough of all the home internationals.

The Gulf-London Rally was the brainchild of David Siegel-Morris, an ex-works BMC and Ford driver. His aim was to produce an event as tough and challenging as the by-then much-missed Liège Rally. The event was without doubt a demanding challenge. Starting and finishing in Manchester, it ran for four days and three nights continuously, over the length and breadth of England, Scotland and Wales, more or less non-stop, with only five short one-hour breaks. The route covered more than 2000 miles of Great Britain, with 79 stages amounting to over 400 miles, nearly all on forest tracks. It was indeed a hard event, which put many European events to shame.

It attracted many entrants from Scandinavia, as Gulf Oil was based in Sweden and financially encouraged the

Paddy Hopkirk and Tony Nash stand by a Mk1 OBL 45F, which oddly has had its S badge removed from above the Mk1 Cooper badge.

nation's entrants. Gulf also supplied free fuel and oil to every competitor, dispensed mostly from fuel tankers at convenient locations around the route. Even service crews received fuel at a discount.

However, because the event was solely sponsored by Gulf Oil and these were early days of any sponsorship in motorsport, the SMMT (Society of Motor Manufacturers and Traders) did not recognise the event, which meant factory entries and support could not be accepted. This resulted in Tony Fall 'borrowing' a car from the factory and entering the rally himself. It also meant trade support suppliers, such as Dunlop and Ferodo, were moving around in hired white vans. All very strange.

At the 2 July start, 106 cars lined up in the pouring rain for a short run to the first stage at Oulton Park racetrack. The Oulton Park stage consisted of 15 laps of the circuit, with cars being dispatched at one-minute intervals in groups of 30 cars, timed from their exit and re-entry into the paddock gates. Much sliding and many spins were encountered on the soaking wet tarmac and indeed numerous accidents.

The same Mk1 OBL 45F was used by Timo Mäkinen and Paul Easter for their recce for the 1968 Monte Carlo Rally, seen here with others recceing in deep snow.

Fall set down a marker by recording the fifth fastest time. After service at the track, removing race tyres, the cars headed off for their long journey over to North Wales and the first of the many forest stages. Dyfnant Forests would, however, be the first and last forest stage that Fall would tackle, as the limited-slip differential shed a bolt and threw it out of the casting, with the result of losing most of his oil. A temporary repair failed to stem the flow of oil, and with the differential now badly damaged, the car was retired.

Fall had attempted all four editions of the Gulf-London and had failed to finish any of them. Only 39 cars arrived back at Manchester four days later at the finish, the rally being won by Ake Andersson in a Porsche 911. Significantly, 29 Minis had entered and only four finished this extremely tough event. It was not best-suited to the Mini.

Tony Fall and Mike Wood used OBL 45F, still as a Mk1 but with the number plate moved over, for the Gulf London Rally. They retired early on this epic rally when the differential failed.

In 1969, Abingdon was being forced to seriously cut back its motorsport activities. Lord Stokes, now at the head of the company, did not believe motorsport (and certainly not rallying successes) sold cars. So in 1969 the budget for such things was drastically cut. Stokes decided Abingdon would enter its own cars on the British and European race championships and concentrate on racing. Some restructuring at Abingdon took place, where Den Green would be responsible for race car preparation and Doug Watts would concentrate on the limited rally entries. Tommy Wellman was assigned the rallycross cars. Bill Price was promoted to assistant competitions manager and would oversee the 1969 racing programme.

BLMC, as it now was, would no longer be represented on the racetracks by the green-and-white Cooper Car Company Minis as the contract with John Cooper, which had been in place and reaped great benefits for so many years, was cancelled. This meant that John Cooper, if he wanted to continue racing Minis, would need alternative backers – in the form of Britax and Downton Engineering sponsorship. His cars would be painted in bright yellow with black roofs, driven by Gordon Spice and Steve Neal.

In reality, neither Abingdon nor Cooper could expect to win any of the BSCC races outright, but the championship was decided upon class wins, so if either team consistently won their class they could end up overall championship winner, much as had been the case since 1964 with Cooper. However, neither had anticipated just how well the 1300GT Ford Escort would perform.

Abingdon for its part managed to sign John Rhodes from Cooper and also secured John Handley from British Vita to race in the new two-car team. However, for Abingdon to build race cars capable of beating the experienced Cooper Car Company would be a tall order – and so it proved to be.

Rhodes was duly handed a brand-new OBL 45F, as a Mk2 Cooper S, for the first round of the British Saloon Car Championship. This first race, of a 12-round series, was held at Brands Hatch on 16 March as the main support race for the Formula One Race of Champions, called the Guards Trophy Race. This was a two-heat 20-lap race on the full Grand Prix circuit, with the aggregate of the two races to find a winner over 106 miles of racing at the Kent circuit.

Much testing had been carried out at Thruxton in early February on Abingdon's race cars' build and specification. Back-to-back tests were carried out with Group 2 race car running an eight-port Weslake head and Hydrolastic suspension against a lightweight rallycross car running a conventional 1293cc engine but with fuel injection and a limited-slip differential, sitting on dry suspension. The conclusion was the eight-port Group 2 car was one second per lap faster than the rallycross car. They also tried 10in and 12in wheels (Minilites and Cooper Rose Petals) and although the 12in tyres ran cooler and were therefore a better option, neither driver preferred the handling. As these 12in wheels would not be homologated until 1 April, the first two rounds would mean using 10in tyres, these being Dunlop CR81 Mk2 tyres. However, Perspex windows and negative-camber bottom arms had been homologated for Group 2 on 1 January so could be freely used.

The new OBL 45F had initially proved disastrous. The car was neither quick, nor did it stop or handle very well. However, after many changes and subsequent testing, the car was near where it needed to be. The engine was 1293cc with a dry-decked block and cylinder head and was fuel injected with Lucas slide-throttle, a high-pressure pump and ram pipes. The fuel injection metering system meant the dynamo was now relocated high up on the right-hand side of the bulkhead. The car ran a Salisbury limited-slip 3.7:1 diff, set to 80lb.ft.

Despite Hydrolastic suspension being used extensively by Cooper, for this first event the car was on rubber cone suspension and fitted with Koni shock absorbers, as Abingdon could not get the pitching on the Hydrolastic suspension sorted out. The car was also fitted with a substantial rear anti-roll bar plus negative camber was set on all four corners. A Group 6 dual-circuit tandem braking system was fitted and lightweight panels and Perspex glass were used. The fuel filler neck was set into the bodywork on the offside, as a safety requirement, and the nearside tank hole was blanked off; the overflow pipe was run externally up the rear finisher seam. The car ran on wide 10in magnesium Minilite wheels with equally wide Dunlop race tyres.

The new car appeared on the track with various adverts, reflecting Abingdon's trade sponsors. An over-large metal British Leyland badge adorned the front wing where the evocative Safety Fast rosettes had once appeared.

Practice and qualifying on a damp Saturday flattered the Mini's performance and Rhodes found himself on the middle of the third row, having qualified eighth but still nearly two seconds adrift of the Britax-Downton-Cooper of Gordon Spice ahead of him.

Come Sunday and race day, the first of the two heats saw disaster for Rhodes. With a blistering start from the flag, Rhodes shot past Crabtree's Escort and was level with Brian Muir's Ford Falcon. Seconds later, Crabtree's Escort bounced off the Falcon and they were now in the way of the hard-charging Mini. This then triggered a coming together of Rhodes and Chris Craft's Escort and the two cars were swiftly destroyed on the infield to Paddock Hill Bend. OBL 45F was now destined for the cutting torch. This, with Handley in the sister car also being destroyed at the end of the race, meant Abingdon's first foray into saloon car racing had been an unmitigated disaster, with two brand-new cars written off.

For the next round at Silverstone, just two weeks away, Abingdon would have much to do. The race was won by Roy

OBL 45F was built as a Mk2 race car for the 1969 British Saloon Car Championship. The fuel-injection engine with throttle slides was used by John Rhodes for the first round at Brands Hatch.

Rhodes about to start the race alongside Brian Muir's Ford Falcon. The race would not end well as he and Chris Craft, in the Escort behind Muir, collided and both cars were destroyed.

Rhodes inspects the aftermath of the accident with the Craft Escort. The car would not appear again.

Tony Nash with Paddy Hopkirk in his race suit with OBL 45F at Silverstone for testing the car prior to the 1969 Tour de France.

Engine bay of OBL 45F for the Tour de France, with the unmistakable fuel injection at the front of the eight-port cylinder head.

Pierpoint in his 4.7-litre Ford Falcon but Gordon Spice in the Britax-Downton-Cooper finished a superb fourth overall and would be the car Abingdon had to beat as the season progressed.

The Tour de France Auto was the next event for OBL 45F, where Paddy Hopkirk would again be co-driven by Tony Nash. After the heavy damage the car sustained at Brands Hatch earlier in the year, a new car was built up, retaining the same registration but in a Mk2 Cooper S bodyshell.

The new car was tested at Silverstone prior to the Tour Auto, where the press were also in attendance. The main aim was to decide wheel and tyre combinations for the rally. It was decided to use 12in Minilite wheels with knock-off hubs and race tyres, although 10in wheels and tyres were also made available should they be needed. This would mean wide Group 5 arches would be fitted to cover the 6J rims. Hopkirk's engine would reflect the racing experience Abingdon had gained during 1969 and so it would be fitted with fuel injection. The engine, although being as powerful as possible, also had to be built to run for over 3000 miles on this event.

Built as a Group 5 car, OBL 45F was halfway between a race car and a rally car, this reflecting the nature of the event. Externally the car looked very purposeful and was fitted with two Lucas 700 fog lamps on a long lamp bar; these were accompanied by two Mixo horns on the bar, which was fitted with an external socket below the offside headlamp. The headlights were fitted with Perspex covers.

Inside the car was a bucket seat for Hopkirk and a high-back reclining seat for Nash. A padded roll cage and 'screen demister were fitted, along with two auxiliary dash panels. The car carried numerous trade adverts and white door roundels for its competition number. OBL 45F also had a red vertical stripe painted on the front of the grille to aid identification during the race.

The Tour de France Auto had not been run for the last four years, and this year's event (between 18 and 26 September) was a revival of much the same, in that it was a gruelling eight-day 3000-mile tour around most of France with nine races and a dozen hillclimbs.

The route was split into six legs, the first of which was a 28-hour slog from Nice to Nancy of some 1000 miles. Six hillclimbs were tackled, including Mont Ventoux and the Chamrousse (where Hopkirk went off badly on his recce in LBL 66D). There was also a timed tarmac special stage just before Nancy, which only differed from the hillclimbs in that it didn't go up a mountain. Here Hopkirk charged through the twisty 12-mile stage and was fifth fastest overall.

The second leg to Reims restarted at 2am and the cars headed for Germany for the first race, an early morning six-lap blast around the Nürburgring. This race was split, as most were, between the big Group 3, 4 and 6 sports cars and the saloon cars in Group 1, 2 and 5. This was where it

CHAPTER 4: THE MK 2 MINI COOPER S

Paddy Hopkirk and Tony Nash took a new OBL 45F on the 1969 Tour de France Auto, seen here with a model on the roof of the car before the start in Nice.

for an evening race at Le Mans Bugatti circuit.

By the time Hopkirk was racing, it was dark. Hopkirk was keeping the revs down on the car as the engine was starting to show signs of stress. A broken valve spring was detected and, with no provision to remove the cylinder head – as the entire engine had been sealed by the scrutineers – the only choice was to try to change the spring in situ. With judicial use of a bent screwdriver, the spring was replaced and most of the offending spring was removed.

Hopkirk in OBL 45F at the Francorchamps race circuit with John Handley in URX 560G in hot pursuit.

Hopkirk and Nash ascend a hillclimb in a misty early morning, clearly showing the knock-off Minilite wheels the car was using.

was hoped Hopkirk would do well. It was then on to Spa for a 20-lap race, where Hopkirk and his teammate Handley worked together slipstreaming each other to good effect until Hopkirk was forced into the pits desperately low on fuel. His fuel-injected car was consuming more fuel than Handley's Weber-fed sister car. Forty seconds were lost but Hopkirk still finished sixth, just behind Handley.

After a welcome night's rest, leg three headed for Rouen. The route started with a 30-lap race at the road circuit at Reims just down from the start. Here just the Group 2 and 5 cars were together and Hopkirk finished in tenth place, a few back from Handley. The Rouen race, also for just Group 2 and 5 cars, saw Handley briefly leading but Hopkirk finished ahead after 20 laps when Handley experienced clutch issues that delayed him.

The fourth leg was a long trudge up to Dieppe with no circuits or hillclimbs, just miles of timed road section. From Dieppe, the fifth leg headed to Vichy with an all-day journey

WORKS MINIS IN DETAIL

Hopkirk at the Rouen race circuit. Hopkirk and Nash would win the touring car class and finish in 14th place despite numerous time-consuming problems.

A broken dynamo bracket had to be repaired at the roadside, with no time lost after the Col du Minier hillclimb, where Hopkirk was again in eighth place. Nearing Albi, Hopkirk lost time when the heater hose came adrift. Worse was to come, as the bolt in the lower arm came adrift, and between them Hopkirk and Nash fixed it themselves but with the loss of 23 minutes' road time – and with that, ten places down the overall classification.

The final leg was from Albi to the finish in Biarritz. An early start saw less than half of the original 106 starters still running. With just two hillclimbs and a very twisty race to go, Hopkirk was hoping to improve his standing. Low oil pressure was starting to be a concern, due to broken pieces of valve spring being ingested into the engine, and before the Nogaro racetrack (the very last test) and after a long road section, the car was losing power.

The engine would get worse but Hopkirk still recorded sixth fastest on the tarmac stage at Cap Fréhel. Onto Magny-Cours race circuit, where the strain was showing on his engine, he still squeezed into tenth place. The sixth leg from Vichy to Albi started with a race around the Clermont-Ferrand Circuit de Charade, which really suited the Mini and Hopkirk, despite suffering oil surge in the race, was running eighth overall and fourth in class.

At the last race, Hopkirk blasted off the line only to return after one lap to change an oiled plug. He rejoined and stormed through the field, only to get a puncture. Quickly changed, he again rejoined and continued his pursuit of the field, finishing leading his class. The end result was a fine 14th place overall and a win in the class.

The car was sold to Phil Cooper, a very successful privateer, who used the car to great effect – although it's unknown if the car was sold with the fuel-injection engine.

Competition Record

Date	Event	Crew	Number	Overall result	Class result
July 1968	Gulf-London Rally	Tony Fall/Mike Wood	7	DNF	
March 1969	Brands Hatch BSCC	John Rhodes	125	DNF	
Sept 1969	Tour de France	Paddy Hopkirk/Tony Nash	57	14th	1st

Registration Number	First registered	Chassis number	Engine	Engine number	Model
OBL 46F	Oct 1967	CA2S7 1012035A	1275cc	9F-SA-Y 46183	Austin Cooper S Mk1

OBL 46F all dressed up and nowhere to go. The car was prepared for the aborted 1967 RAC Rally for Paddy Hopkirk and Ron Crellin to drive, seen here at the London Airport start.

Like its four OBL sister cars, OBL 46F, was in fact a Mk1 Morris Cooper S and carried a Mk1 chassis plate. It appeared in its first two outings, the aborted 1967 RAC Rally and 1968 Circuit of Ireland, as a Mk1 Mini but by the time in early 1969 that it appeared on the race circuits, it was a Mk2 Cooper S.

The first event scheduled for the car was to be the *Sun*-sponsored 1967 RAC Rally of Great Britain in late November – which was cancelled less than 15 hours before the start of the rally due to an outbreak of foot-and-mouth disease in the UK.

The car, as a Mk1 Cooper S, was to be driven by Paddy Hopkirk and Ron Crellin, and was a powerful Group 6 fitted with a 45DCOE Weber carburettor. Although a lightweight

OBL 46F was handed to Lars Ytterbring and Lars Persson for the 1968 Circuit of Ireland, seen here in the Berkshire countryside prior to shipping to Ireland.

Ytterbring and Persson slide through a gateway near Carnearney.

car, it did retain its bumpers but no door chromes nor opening rear side windows. Large front mud flaps were fitted and it also ran wide Group 6 wheelarch extensions, which were subtly wider that those fitted to Group 2 cars. A grille muff was supplied but no heated windscreen was fitted. The four auxiliary lights were wired to a rubber plug and socket rather than bullet connectors. Because the event was always rough, the very strong (but heavy) Scandinavian guard was fitted. All of this, however, was to no avail and the brand-new car was saved for another day.

The next event for OBL 46F, still as a Mk1 Cooper S, was the 1968 Circuit of Ireland held over the Easter weekend – a busy time for Abingdon with 1800s on the Safari Rally in East Africa and the Circuit of Ireland the same weekend. Lars Ytterbring and Lars Persson were to drive the still-unused OBL 46F on the event. This was the first of three drives the Swedish pair would have with the team.

OBL 46F was again in Group 6 specification, and although split Webers were now being used on Group 2 cars, Group 6 rules allowed a long inlet manifold to be used, so a single 45DCOE Weber was fitted as it produced similar power. The front bulkhead needed some minor panel bashing, as the carburettor, which protruded into the speedo aperture, was relieved to allow the Weber to fit and clear the bulkhead. The speedo was also spaced out slightly by the use of a wooden spacer. The 1293cc engine ran the standard Abingdon full-race camshaft with a high-compression Downton cylinder head. A short 4.2:1 final drive was fitted to the straight-cut gearbox, and this was now fitted with straight-cut drop gears. The engine showed 92bhp at the wheels.

The Circuit of Ireland was mostly a tarmac special stage rally but with some forest stages, and as these roads were often very bumpy, the heavy-duty Scandinavian sump guard was retained, despite its obvious weight penalty. To save weight, all the glass had been replaced with Perspex (except the front laminated windscreen). The bonnet, boot and doors were in aluminium and as much trim as possible was removed from inside the car. The rear seat was removed and the exposed metal covered in lightweight carpet, along with the headlining.

The box section across the car was double-skinned and the floor strengthened around the seats and gearstick, to take the Mitchell mounting for the remote gearchange. An emergency strap was made up and also fitted under the remote, just in case the special rubber mounting did fail. Inside the car, the wheel braces were housed under the seats and the crash helmets in boxes where the rear seat sat. A first-aid kit was fitted there too. The modified MGB jack was fitted to the driver's side rear pocket.

The suspension was Hydrolastic with negative-camber bottom arms, and the subframes were plated and rewelded. The brakes were improved by fitting asbestos insets in the pistons to try and keep some heat away from the brake fluid; for the same reason, the rear wheel cylinders were held to the backplates with a large nut rather than the standard circlip – this acted as a heatsink. Below the front panel, in line with the wheels, an air duct hole was cut to channel cool air onto the front brakes. The rear brake drums and backplates were also drilled to allow heat out of the brakes.

The four auxiliary lights on the low lamp bar were connected to the car with a rubber plug and socket located just below

Persson attends to the tyre as Ytterbring hands over the Tyre-and-Fire to inflate the tyre. The single 45DCOE Weber can be clearly seen under the bonnet.

Ytterbring went off the road on the Cadgers stage and deranged the front corner. Despite the setback and a long battle with Roger Clark and Paddy Hopkirk, he retired near the end when he comprehensively rolled the car.

Good Friday evening at the Gallaher factory in Ballymena with 122 other starters for their four-day blast around Ireland. The route contained 400 miles of stages, mostly on closed public roads and a few forest stages thrown in for good measure. The average speed for the stages was very high, averaging over 60mph. They were interspersed with tight road sections, which allowed for little service time, although adequate service time was provided at the end of each leg, prior to the cars being locked away in parc fermé.

The route headed out for a night of hard rallying with 11 stages before breakfast at Blessington near the Wicklow Mountains. The first two were loose surface and saw forest tyres quickly swapped for racer tyres for the remaining stages. These often narrow, bumpy and dusty early stages were demanding, and straight away Ytterbring was battling with Hopkirk in a sister car, and Roger Clark in the new Ford Escort Twin Cam.

After a short forest stage, it was back to tarmac where Ytterbring collided with the scenery on the Cadgers Road stage and badly bent the front wing. It was then onto the long 24-mile Sally Gap stage, where Clark's much more powerful Escort stormed the wide tarmac stage. Ytterbring went off again, clouting a bank on the Serrell Hill stage but continued unabated. At the two-hour breakfast stop near Dublin, Ytterbring held third place behind Clark and Hopkirk but still close by.

Then followed ten more stages to Killarney on Easter Saturday, a loop around the mountains near Killarney and the overnight halt; most again were tarmac, including the wonderful Healy Pass. Ytterbring, like many, took his lamps off the car to save them from damage and to save weight. Clark would again lead Ytterbring on most stages but he was certainly close, and beating the Escort on several when the stages were better suited to the Mini.

Arriving at Killarney for the night stop and the inevitable Irish party, the Mini was serviced where new headlights were put on and rudimentary repairs carried out to the damage; OBL 46F was then put away in parc fermé. In the morning (many entrants with sore heads), Ytterbring's car refused to start and it took a full 20 minutes before it would fire up; they left on Easter Sunday in a rush, and just 75 cars restarted.

The first stage was the very fast ten-mile-long Moll's Gap stage when again the Escort proved unbeatable, but Ytterbring was still third on a stage not best suited to a Mini, albeit a good way adrift. Ytterbring was holding third place overall behind Clark and Hopkirk. It was not to last, as on the fifth stage of the day Ytterbring savaged a bridge and rolled the car several times and into retirement. The much-deranged car was dragged away.

Just 50 cars made their way to the finish at Larne, where Clark was a clear winner by 20 minutes despite having slackened his pace towards the end. This was the shape of things to come, as the Mini struggled to match the power of

the offside headlight. The middle two were held steady with adjustable rods secured to the front panel and the top of the lamp. The main visual differences from how the car appeared in November was that the larger black wheelarch extensions were now painted in red body colour. The RAC car had the number plate painted on a rectangle on the offside of the bonnet, which was retained using Moke rubber toggles, as was the boot lid. The car was virtually unchanged from the abortive RAC Rally.

Ytterbring was seeded at number three and lined up on

CHAPTER 4: THE MK 2 MINI COOPER S

Onto the race circuits of the 1969 BSCC series sees John Rhodes teamed with John Handley, here with OBL 46F at Silverstone testing pre-season.

more modern machinery.

After the destruction of the car on the Circuit of Ireland, and because Abingdon was being forced to cut back on its rally programme – instead headed for the racetracks – a new OBL 46F Group 5 race car was built for the first round of the RAC British Saloon Car Championship; this time it was as a Mk2 Cooper S. Held at Brands Hatch on 16 March 1969, the Race of Champions Formula One support race on the full Grand Prix circuit drew exactly the public attention the new Leyland masters were after.

It has to be remembered that until 1969, all of the Mini factory racing activities (of which there were many) were dealt with by John Cooper and his beautiful dark green-and-white Cooper Car Company race Minis. They were without doubt highly successful, yet the Leyland management decided that Abingdon should now take on that role and cease financial help for the John Cooper race team. This left John Cooper to seek other financial backers, enlisting the support of the Britax Seat Belt Company and Downton Engineering. He forsook their normal livery and the cars were presented in striking yellow-and-black paintwork, ready to lock horns with Abingdon. It was a tall order for Abingdon to challenge the Cooper Car Company team, which had years of experience building winning Mini race cars and engines.

Nevertheless, a beautiful new OBL 46F was presented at scrutineering and there were many who were pleased to see the lovely red-and-white cars on the race circuit, especially when their days of dominance in rallying was being eclipsed by much more powerful cars.

The engine was 1293cc with a dry-decked block and cylinder head, and fuel injected with a Lucas slide throttle, with a high-pressure pump fitted under the car at 100psi minimum pressure. It was very crowded under the bonnet because the fuel-injection metering unit sat where the dynamo was normally fitted – this was now relocated high up on the right-hand side of the bulkhead. Large breather pipes were fitted to the engine.

The car was fitted with a Salisbury limited-slip 3.7:1 diff set at 80lb.ft, and the suspension was by rubber cone and fitted with Koni shock absorbers plus a rear anti-roll bar. Negative camber was set on all four corners. A Group 6 dual-circuit tandem braking system was fitted, as needed by the regulations. Lightweight panels and Perspex windows were used, and the car was devoid of any bumpers. The fuel filler neck was set into the bodywork, as this too was required by the regulations, where the cap was considered too vulnerable in the event of an accident.

The car ran on 10in magnesium Minilite wheels with 8in rims on the front and 6in on the rear and equally wide Dunlop race tyres. The hoped-for 12in wheels, used in rallycross, had yet to be homologated, so the car was restricted to the smaller and hence hotter 10in tyres; the 10in tyres required a running pressure of around 55psi and the tyre temperatures reached some 120C, so the larger 12in versions were eagerly awaited. Numerous trade adverts were now also filling space on the side of the car.

OBL 46F was to be driven at Brands Hatch by John Handley, who was a very experienced race driver, particularly in Minis, and had raced for Broadspeed, Cooper and British Vita, where he won the 1968 European Saloon Car Championship. Abingdon was obviously keen to sign him up for the new race team as he was also a very good test driver and probably did more miles testing for Cooper than actually racing. He would be teamed with John Rhodes throughout the 1969 season but

Handley with OBL 46F at Brands Hatch for the first round of the BSCC Championship, seen here still with 10in wheels, as 12in wheels were yet to be homologated.

377

Handley ran strongly after the early demise of Rhodes in the sister car. It was not to last, as Handley too destroyed the car near the end of the race. Abingdon lost two brand-new cars in one weekend.

would be in a supportive role where Rhodes was the number one driver. This would often include assisting Rhodes in qualifying by slipstreaming with him to improve his lap times.

Nevertheless, the Mini Cooper S was now confined to fighting for class awards, as the British Saloon Car Championship (in which it was entered) catered for much more powerful cars, notably big American Fords and numerous Escorts.

The Guards Trophy race was run over two 20-lap heats decided on aggregate times. The Saturday afternoon practice was on a damp circuit and was in parts foggy, which helped the lower-powered Minis over the bigger cars. Handley qualified in 13th place and trailed Rhodes, Gordon Spice and Steve Neal in their Britax cars, some three seconds adrift of Spice and two seconds from Rhodes.

Once the race was under way, Handley soon settled into a race-long battle with Neal, between them running eighth and ninth. Neal slowly pulled away towards the end of the first heat until Handley, on the very last lap, had his own accident when he put a wheel onto the grass at Southbank and crashed the new car very heavily. He was unhurt but the car would take no further part, resulting in another car being needed for the next round, just two weeks hence, at Silverstone.

With Rhodes's car also destroyed in a start-line fracas, it had not been a successful weekend for Abingdon, losing two brand-new cars. However, the 1300cc class lap record fell during the race, but not to the Abingdon cars: Gordon Spice in the Britax-Downton-Cooper finished a superb fourth overall, with the aggregate of the two races going to Roy Pierpoint in a 4.7-litre Ford Falcon.

A radical change now befell OBL 46F as a brand-new Mini Clubman was built for John Handley and Paul Easter to undertake their recce for the forthcoming World Cup Rally. It was decided, as they would be using a Mini Clubman on the event (XJB 308H) that they should also use a very similar car for the recce for this epic rally. It would also allow them to suggest changes to the build of their new car, test the engine specification and trial the timing schedule of the event. The car was also unusual in that it was painted beige (but still with a white roof) – Antelope, to give it its BL paint name. The Clubman had just been launched and the bodyshell was a pre-production shell, which had numerous odd features not found on production cars.

The car was built up by Brian Moylan and was equipped with a 1293cc engine, which was fitted with split Webers and was also dry decked. This was a race car innovation, which aided cooling to the cylinder head with a separate water supply, at the opposite end to the water pump, directly into the cylinder head water jacket. Straight-cut close-ratio gears with a 3.9:1 final drive were used.

The suspension was Hydrolastic with red displacer units. The interconnecting pipes, run inside the car, had isolating taps fitted to allow the front and rear to be independent and also stiffen up the suspension when needed. In addition this stopped the pitching often experienced with this fluid suspension. Front shock absorbers were fitted, along with a rear anti-roll bar. The car sat on 12x6J magnesium wheels and had wide wheelarches. The brakes were standard Cooper S, other than the fitting of racing pads and linings, but there

OBL 46F now prepared as a 1275 GT Clubman, built for John Handley and Paul Easter to undertake a recce for the forthcoming World Cup Rally - the car was painted beige.

was a tandem brake master cylinder and a servo. This tandem master cylinder supplied separate feeds front to back and was used should one line fail.

Because of the anticipated rough roads, the front and rear subframes were rewelded, gusseted and double-plated. The car was also fitted with a magnesium Tech-Del sump guard, which was immensely strong in addition to being lightweight. A battery guard was also fitted at the rear and all lines (battery, fuel, brake and Hydrolastic) were run inside the car.

To save weight, aluminium doors and boot lid were fitted but a steel bonnet was retained. Perspex replaced the heavy glass, and inside the car the rear seat was dispensed with, the space being taken by two spare wheels. The car was equipped with many spares and tools and the jack was of the Bilstein monkey-up-a-stick type, adapted to be used on a Mini. This was not only quick to raise the car but also let it down even quicker.

As the car was a Clubman, the traditional works Cooper S dash panels were not used but a fabricated full-width dashboard was supplied, containing the additional switches, controls, navigational equipment and instruments. Four extra lamps were fitted to the front of the car: two 7in Lucas Continental driving lamps and two rectangular Lucas Square 8 FT8 fog lights. The car did look quite different from any car Abingdon had built thus far.

Much testing of the car was undertaken at the Bagshot military testing ground and at Finmere Airfield. Handley was also keen to test tyres in a road environment, so testing, at night, was carried out in Wales on little-trafficked road. He was keen to try the new Dunlop MP27 rallycross tyre on tarmac and compare it to Dunlop R7 race tyres. He also tested SP44s and SP68s. As it transpired, the rallycross tyre was around three seconds per mile faster than the R7. It was therefore decided that if the wear rate was acceptable, these were the tyres he would use on the tarmac timed sections, with SP68s on the roads, and SP44s being reserved for loose-surface sections.

Handley and Easter started their recce in mid February just two months before the 16,000-mile event was due to start in April. They followed the rally route through France, Germany, Austria, Hungary, Yugoslavia and Bulgaria to Sofia on mostly good roads and reported the time allowed by the organisers was generous. The first loose surface was not encountered until near the Yugoslavia border. They did, however, have some confusion with the route to Pec, where they were uncertain if a northern or southern route was correct. They attempted the southern route but it was blocked with snow and was also rough going. The northern route was on better roads but longer and they arrived slightly late.

The first prime (or timed) stage at Montenegro of just 50 miles in length (almost the shortest of the event) was snow-free initially and on good loose surface. It then deteriorated with large snowdrifts as they climbed and the road got

The engine bay of OBL 46F showing split Webers and the twin-circuit brake master cylinder. The car would revert to SUs for the rally.

Interior of OBL 46F with the speedo in front of the navigator and the Halda distance recorder in the middle. Also seen is the cranked gear lever.

WORKS MINIS IN DETAIL

TV presenter and Grand Prix commentator Murray Walker dons his crash helmet for a hot-seat ride in the car, it being sponsored by BBC Television's Grandstand programme.

Handley and Easter's recce was beset with weather problems. The early year recce meant many roads were snow-covered and many were blocked. The recce was aborted early.

rougher, only to smooth out for the last half, which they then unfortunately found blocked with snow. They had to take a long detour to pick up the finish at Titograd and journey in the reverse direction to complete their notes. This meant missing out about 12km of the route and reporting it very rough in places. They were also becoming very concerned about the heavy oil consumption of the car.

The second prime, of some 120 miles in Serbia, still in Yugoslavia, was aborted due to it being virtually impassable because of snow and abandoned lorries. The decision was made to abandon any further recce work in Yugoslavia, reckoning it was either freak weather or too early in the year. However, valuable conclusions were still drawn from the exercise. They recommended that the service crews should carry a spare sump shield for the Mini, as they felt the stages could easily damage it with a heavy landing. It was also suggested that two service points be scheduled in the middle of each prime, as the main service between the primes at Titograd may not be sufficient.

They also came back with many suggestions to improve their rally car. Handley wanted the roll cage padding to be reduced near his shoulder, a switch panel for washers/wipers and lights in his door pocket, a flick-type dip switch and the flasher moved to the left of the column, and also a 1in crank put into the gear leaver. Easter wanted his seat moved further forward and the roll cage further back, with the Halda moved further to the left and his map-light switch moved to the floor. They both complained of not being able to reach all of the switches when strapped in, and they wanted a large-capacity washer bottle and round fog lights, not liking the rectangular lights on the recce car.

As for the engine, a more responsive camshaft with lower pick-up was asked for. They asked for 12in Dunlop SP44s for both primes but also to have a half-studded set made available should snow be encountered. The fuel consumption was approximately 20mpg whilst touring but dropped to 10mpg when flat-out, so they thought they would need extra fuel tanks for the longer primes. Oil consumption was also an issue. All of this was to no avail, as they blew a hole in a piston in XJB 308H on the World Cup Rally, on only the third prime, much to their bitter disappointment.

The car was sold to Norman Higgins, who was the chief accountant at the MG factory and a great ally of the competition department.

Competition Record

Date	Event	Crew		Number	Overall result	Class result
Nov 1967	RAC Rally	Paddy Hopkirk/Ron Crellin		26	Cancelled	
April 1968	Circuit of Ireland	Lars Ytterbring/Lars Persson		3	DNF	
March 1969	Brands Hatch BSCC	John Handley		126	DNF	
Feb 1970	World Cup recce	John Handley/Paul Easter	*Clubman shell*			

CHAPTER 4: THE MK 2 MINI COOPER S

Registration Number	First registered	Chassis number	Engine	Engine number	Model
OBL 47F	Oct 1967	KA2S4 1012089	1275cc	9F-SA-Y 46165	Morris Cooper S Mk1

OBL 47F was one of four OBLs sent to Abingdon and registered in October 1967. This Mk2 car, in common with the other OBLs, was in fact a Mk1 bodyshell (and it carried a Mk1 chassis plate) that had been cosmetically changed to that of a Mk2. OBL 47F simply had the rear light clusters changed and the badges, trim and grille also changed to Mk2 pattern. The larger Mk2 rear screen was, however, not fitted. The reason for this economic deception was that Abingdon needed to be seen in Mk2 cars when the car was launched in October 1967, and with a surplus stock of Mk1s to move plus Mk2s in demand by the public, it was expedient for these Mk1s to be used for competition and cosmetically changed.

The car was officially noted to be a special tuning demonstrator, which fell under the jurisdiction of Basil Wales. It is, however, considered as a works Mini as Abingdon requisitioned the car from special tuning when a recce car was needed for an event. OBL 47F was indeed used for the recce for the 1968 Monte Carlo Rally, as one of a good number of cars for the recce for Abingdon's four-car entry with brand-new Mk2 ORX-registered cars. The car was at this stage still a Mk1 Cooper S.

It was not converted to appear as a Mk2 Cooper S when it was taken to Denmark, where it was used for a special tuning demonstration run at the request of the Danish Austin importer in Odense. Basil Wales took the car, in late February 1968, by ship to Esbjerg, where he visited the Morris importer in Copenhagen on the way to meeting up with Timo Mäkinen. The car was then taken to the Roskilde Ring for the demonstration, which entailed numerous laps, at high speed, on snow and ice, demonstrating the car to the invited guests. The car was fully rally-prepared. It was well received.

In September 1968 the car was entered for the Scottish Rally, sponsored by Autocar magazine for journalist Nick Brittan and navigated by Hamish Cardno. The Scottish Rally was always a very hard event on the cars, and the 1968 edition was no exception, with 400 hard stage miles within the 1000-mile route, and for a driver whose experience was largely in racing, this was a tall order.

The meat of the rally was in the first leg of 36 hours, where 240 miles of those stages were tackled in hot, dry conditions – it would also decimate the field by over a half, including

Timo Mäkinen drifting ORX 47F through the Pirelli bend as a public relations exercise at the Roskilde Ring Circuit in Denmark, once the location for the Danish Grand Prix.

OBL 47F. Pressing the car hard, the crew left the road and, whilst the car was relatively undamaged, the landing burst a Hydrolastic suspension unit.

Once extracted by a local tractor, the crew in their otherwise-unscathed car skipped seven special stages in a vain attempt to keep on time and locate the BMC service crews to try to effect a repair. They never found them. With no suspension on the driver's side and just 2½in of ground clearance, they continued on the rough tracks, scraping along on the underside of the car. Through the night they pressed on, and with only one headlight and at best two of the four auxiliary lamps working, they eventually located the BMC service crews at breakfast time (who were extensively servicing Lars Ytterbring's car JMO 969D). However, by the time the replacement displacer was fitted, they were outside their maximum lateness and excluded.

The car was bought by Tony Fall, who soon sold the car on and it was then used successfully on numerous rallies in private hands.

Competition Record

Date	Event	Crew	Number	Overall result	Class result
Sept 1968	Scottish Rally	Nick Brittan/Hamish Cardno		DNF	

WORKS MINIS IN DETAIL

Registration Number	First registered	Chassis number	Engine	Engine number	Model
OBL 48F	Oct 1967	KA2S4 1012091A	1275cc	9F-SA-Y 46159	Morris Cooper S Mk1

OBL 48F as a Mk1 Cooper S, tyre testing at Silverstone before the Tour de France, seen here without wheelarch extensions.

Like its four sister cars, OBL 48F was in fact a Mk1 Morris Cooper S and carried a Mk1 chassis plate. This car, however, unlike its three sister cars, was not converted to appear as a Mk2 Cooper S whilst at Abingdon.

The car, like the other new OBL cars, was used for the recce for the 1968 Monte Carlo Rally, primarily by Timo Mäkinen and Paul Easter. Once the recce was over, the car was left in France as a spare car and to be used by other team members as a recce car. It was also used on the event for the ice-note teams.

OBL 48F was also used for tyre testing at Silverstone prior to the 1969 Tour de France. Here, extensive testing was carried out with the car on narrow 3½J wheels and Dunlop R7 race tyres. It was a concern that the tyres would not be effective with such narrow wheel rims. Brian Culcheth was to use URX 550G as a Group 1 car, on 3½J wheels for the Tour de France, hence the need to establish if the tyres would work on the car.

OBL 48F was then used by Culcheth and his navigator Johnstone Syer for their full recce for the 1969 Tour de France. The car was subsequently loaned out to Johnstone Syer. The car was eventually bought by Johnston Syer and by now was to appear in Mk2 form.

Competition Record
None

Registration Number	First registered	Chassis number	Engine	Engine number	Model
RBL 450F	May 1968	KA2S4 111643A	1275cc	9F-SA-Y 48921	Morris Cooper S Mk2

Rauno Aaltonen presents RBL 450F for scrutineering at the start of the 1968 Acropolis Rally, seen here with large front-facing mud flaps and wide wheels and arches.

RBL450F was registered in May 1968 as a Mk2 Cooper S and was, unlike the OBL series of cars, built as a Mk2. There has been some debate if these relatively early cars, in the Mk2 timeline, were built from Mk1 body shells and converted to appear as Mk2. However, close examination of the rear screen aperture clearly indicates that this, and the two subsequent RJB cars, were all Mk2 cars with a wider rear screen. To mimic the wider rear screen would be a complex operation but the changing of the rear lights and of course the addition of Mk2 grille and badges and trim was indeed a straight forward task. Here we see a Mk2 car, not a converted Mk1.

RBL 450F was built early 1968. Its first event was the very tough Acropolis Rally, held at the end of May. Built as a Group 2 car, the 1293cc Morris Cooper S ran split Weber carburettors, as Abingdon struggled to keep up with more powerful cars, especially the new Ford Escort Twin Cam. They were what Abingdon called prototype carburettors, being a pair of Weber 45DCOEs with one choke of each machined off and the remaining choke on each welded to a tube, which allowed it to be bolted directly to a standard Cooper S inlet manifold. This was necessary as Group 2 regulations dictated that the inlet manifold could not be changed. With these new split Webers, as they became known, an extra 7bhp was found and a little more mid-range torque, meaning the car now produced 92bhp at the wheels.

With the Abingdon almost-standard-fit full-race AEA648 camshaft, a high-compression Downton cylinder head and a short 4.2:1 final drive, the car was indeed very quick but sadly, as time will show, not quick enough to keep up with the opposition. The engine was fitted with straight-cut transfer gears in addition to a close-ratio straight-cut gearbox. These new transfer gears were used to increase reliability; they also had the advantage of having a roller bearing fitted on the idler gear, which had been prone to early failure.

Underneath, the engine and gearbox were protected by a heavy-duty Scandinavian guard with the jacking points welded to its front edge. A wide battery box cover was also fitted at the rear of the car. Hydrolastic suspension, with a rear anti-roll bar, was used with single-blue and double-blue displacers front and back, without front dampers but orange helper springs at the rear.

The brakes were improved, with the callipers having asbestos blocks fitted into the pistons to take excess heat away from the brake fluid and the rear wheel cylinders being threaded, so they were fixed to the backplate with a large nut rather than a circlip to also take heat away from the brake fluid.

Even wider wheelarch extensions were fitted to the car, now painted red. It was also fitted with forward-facing mud flaps under the headlights, in addition to rear mud flaps. Lucas wired the car, which ran an alternator, largely because of having four additional lamps: two fog lamps and two driving lamps, fixed to a lamp bar, connected by a five-pin rubber socket and the two driving lamps secured by steady bars. European headlamps with Perspex protective covers were fitted with iodine bulbs, as were the extra lamps.

The driver's auxiliary dash panel had the oil pressure gauge moved next to the rev counter, and in its place in the binnacle was the water temperature gauge, now replaced by a circular fuel gauge. The co-driver's instrument panel housed his usual Halda distance recorder, a pair of Heuer clocks and numerous other controls, and he also had a switch panel in his door pocket. As he had an expansion tank from the radiator by his feet in the footwell, the Tudor electric screen washer bottles were moved to the rear of the car on the driver's side. The co-driver also had a foot-operated horn switch.

A fibreglass bucket seat, now covered in black cord material for the driver, and a reclining high-back seat for the co-driver were fitted on modified seat brackets. An Irvin lap-and-diagonal seat belt for Aaltonen and full-harness Irvin belt for Liddon were also fitted. All standard trim and glass had to

Aaltonen with Henry Liddon pull into a time control where Aaltonen appears to be showing some concern.

be retained under Group 2 regulations, including the carpets. Padding to the door pockets, door locks, co-driver's rear pocket bin corner and door pillars added to crew comfort. The roll cage, which also housed the intercom box, was also padded. All lines were run inside the car, with the fuel pump located under the rear seat. The number plate was now painted on the offside of the bonnet, which was held fast with a leather strap.

The Acropolis Rally was a demanding 2000-mile event, very similar to that of the previous year. Twelve stages, all on scratch time, totalling 180 miles with 42 time controls, were on offer plus three tests that were rather meaningless, the first of which was used simply as a tie decider should it be needed. Severe weather the previous week, washing away some remote roads, had meant the loss of three stages and a 100-mile loop around Volos. The rally was somewhat relentless, being 56 hours non-stop from Thursday lunchtime to Saturday evening. No service time, let alone any rest halts were scheduled; the only downtime was the ferry crossing of the Corinth Bay, where it was considered dead time.

Scrutineering, the day before starting, was straightforward, with even the car's split Webers not causing any issues. The only rumpus was due to the low entry: classes were amalgamated and this was causing some complaints, especially within classes, as the seeding was on drawing lots. This also meant a good number of cars being bulked later in the event.

So it was that the low entry of 60 starters lined up at the foot of the Acropolis in blazing heat. Even before that, Aaltonen was having the Hydrolastic suspension hastily pumped up to increase its ground clearance, and he only just made the start. The first test, a simple one-mile sprint up the road, saw Aaltonen ninth fastest. Onto the first six-mile stage at Souli, where Aaltonen was seventh, and already a pattern was being set, with three works Escort Twin Cams and two works Porsche 911s in the lead. On the second stage Aaltonen was third at Kastanea, and his teammate Mäkinen was out before the next stage.

The rough stages and roads saw Aaltonen unable to get on terms with the more powerful cars; overheating was also hampering the car.

Servicing for RBL 450F where Dan Green attends to the exhaust mounting, the rear anti-roll bar clearly visible. Henry Liddon looks to the camera.

With these early stages, all on closed tarmac roads, the Mini was struggling against the much more powerful cars. But Aaltonen was seventh on the long third stage, as the best of the rest. The ferry crossing at Patras, at dawn, gave some respite and it was then onto stages at Bralos, where Aaltonen was experiencing overheating problems but continued on a long haul across to Grinion. These stages were all becoming an Escort benefit.

The rally went on to Thessaloniki, with its many rough roads, where Aaltonen, in the heat of the day, was running the heater blower to take some heat off the engine. By breakfast the next day, just 22 cars remained – but Aaltonen continued, despite his very hot engine, leading his class but behind the overall leaders. He was, however, never lower than eighth on any of the stages.

At the service before the last two stages, he removed the heavy sump guard, the lamp bar and the front mud flaps, and recorded his best times, coming second on each of the last two. These measures not only reduced the weight of the car but also allowed more air into the very hot engine. All that was left was the ceremonial blast around Tatoil airfield and the rally was over. Aaltonen finished fifth overall and won the 1300 class but it was a measure of things to come, where the Mini simply could no longer beat top cars.

RBL 450F would next officially appear over a year later, not as a rally car but as a race car and also as a new Mk2. There is no doubt that the RBL 450F Acropolis car, after such a hard rally, would not have been converted to a Group 5 race car. Much had changed at Abingdon that year: BMC had been gobbled up by Leyland Cars and become BLMC, headed by Lord Stokes. Further still, Stokes was not a fan of rallying, nor motorsport in general, but did decree that Abingdon should concentrate its efforts on the racetracks during 1969, and curtailed much of Peter Browning's planned rally programme.

The result was that Stokes cancelled the long-standing contract with John Cooper, who had happily and successfully represented BMC on racetracks for many years. Abingdon now had to learn fast to produce and run race cars. The cars were entrusted to Den Green to build and maintain, whilst Bill Price, now elevated to Browning's assistant, had overall control of the race programme.

The 1969 season so far had not been a blistering success, as Abingdon had to play catch-up against the more experienced Britax-Cooper-Downton race Minis that John Cooper was now fielding with Gordon Spice and Steve Neal. However, both Cooper and Abingdon were unable to beat the more powerful Broadspeed 1300 Escorts of John Fitzpatrick and Chris Craft. None of this was welcome news to Lord Stokes, who wanted results.

RBL 450F was built as a Group 5 race car (sporting numerous sponsors' decals), something Abingdon was getting to grips with, as the race season was in full swing. The car was entered for the Six Hour European Touring Car race at Brands Hatch on 22 June and was the be driven by John Handley and Roger Enever. The engine was 1293cc dry-decked with Lucas slide-throttle fuel injection with splayed inlet pipes on a Weslake Mk2 eight-port cylinder head, with a 1247 camshaft. The cylinder head had 14.9cc combustion chambers but the pistons were run slightly down the bore. The conrods and crankshaft were standard Cooper S but with forged Hepolite pistons with special rings. Keeping the water cool involved modified waterways within the cylinder head and the fitting of an auxiliary side-mounted radiator. Running on Champion RGY101 plugs, the engine, for longevity, was restricted to a maximum of 7200rpm.

The gearbox was a three-speed straight-cut close-ratio 'box, forsaking the four-synchromesh gearbox as the three-

CHAPTER 4: THE MK 2 MINI COOPER S

The final stage at the Tatoil Airfield saw the car stripped of its heavy sump guard and lights. Aaltonen would finish fifth place on the rally.

A new RBL 450F was built for the 1969 ETCC six-hour race at Brands Hatch, where John Handley and Roger Enever shared the car.

Minilite 12in knock-off wheels were used for this endurance race to speed up tyre changes. Also seen here is the recessed fuel filler cap for the long-range tank. They would finish fourth overall.

speed ratios were considered more suitable. A competition clutch was fitted and special Deva bush drop gears used. For Brands Hatch the final drive selected was 3.7:1 and a Salisbury limited-slip differential was a Ford unit modified to fit the Mini.

The brakes had a dual brake master cylinder fitted but without a servo. The disc pads were Ferodo DS11, with VG95 brake shoes at the rear. The suspension was by dry rubber cone but with Hydrolastic top arms and adjustable bottom arms and tie rods, being set at 1.5 degrees negative camber and 2.5 degrees caster angle. The rear was set at just 0.5 degrees negative and it too used Hydrolastic radius arms with dry rubber cone suspension. Adjustable Koni shock absorbers were used all round.

Wheels were 12x6J magnesium Minilites with knock-off hubs to make tyre changes quicker, fitted beneath wide wheelarch extensions with a chrome strip. The Dunlop D15 race tyres were run at 50psi at the front and 46psi at the rear. For the long-distance race, the car carried 17.5 gallons of fuel in a steel tank plus an extra rubber tank – as the fuel consumption was around 7mpg when racing. The car ran with a chrome bumper on the front but not the rear. It was identified as Handley's with a red flash on the front of the roof just above the interior mirror; it also wore a large number 5 race number on the boot lid.

For the six-hour race, a crowd of 10,000 were there to watch. Ten Minis were on the grid where Handley and Enever had qualified in a respectable 13th place but behind his teammates Rhodes/Hopkirk, the Cooper of Spice/Neal and also the two Broadspeed Escorts. Handley would do the first two hours, when the front tyres would then be changed and the car refuelled. Enever would take over for the next two hours, with Handley taking the last stint.

After two hours Handley was running in seventh place after Spice lost time with a fuel pump change and would eventually retire with numerous time-delaying problems, from a dynamo belt change to eventually erratic handling. Cooper had a troubled weekend as Neal had rolled his car in practice when it jumped out of gear.

At the handover, Enever held station despite the car starting to use a lot of oil. For the last stint, Handley got the car up into fourth place overall, which he just held to the finish with failing oil pressure and a virtually flat tyre, with which he struggled to the finish. They were rewarded with a fine second in class behind the Broadspeed Escort of Fitzpatrick. After the race it was noticed that the dynamo bracket on the thermostat housing had fractured and the small-end bearings had also failed on the engine due to oil starvation, which showed up as low oil pressure. The engine had consumed nearly a gallon of oil over the 184 laps of the six-hour race.

The following month RBL 450F was entered for another long-distance race, the 6 Hours of Nürburgring, which was a round of the European Touring Car Challenge. Held on 6

RBL 450F was next used at the six-hour European Touring Car Challenge at Nürburgring, where Handley and Enever retired after five hours, having led the class, with no clutch and broken suspension.

July, the car was again assigned to John Handley and Roger Enever. With no Britax-Coopers to challenge the works Minis, a good class result was hoped for.

A very powerful engine was built, with a very high compression ratio of 14.5:1, meaning the combustion chambers in the Weslake Mk3 cylinder head were at 13.5cc. The Weslake head now had modified waterways to assist cooling and, because of the length of the race and with Hepolite pistons tending to consume oil, an oil container with a pump was fitted to the parcel shelf. The crossflow head was fed by Lucas fuel injection and Weslake slider with splayed inlet pipes. The engine was, for reliability, restricted to 7200rpm. Fuel for the race was via a standard 5½-gallon steel tank, supplemented by a 12-gallon flexible tank fitted across the boot area.

The car was fitted with Armstrong adjustable dampers and Hydrolastic suspension with fixed bottom arms but with adjustable tie rods. The Hydrolastic fluid was pumped up to 250psi. The brakes were fitted with DS11 front disc pads and VG95 rear shoes. No servo was fitted but there was a tandem brake master cylinder. Knock-off Minilites were fitted to the car to speed up wheel changes, and Dunlop D15-232 tyres were used. These tyres had a stiff sidewall, so the normal pressure was dropped slightly to compensate.

In practice, the recoded fuel consumption was down to 7.6mpg, so the refuelling and driver change schedule could be established by Peter Browning. Handley's car had, in addition to the identification mark on the roof, a broad red stripe in the centre of the grille; the wheelarches were wider and without a chrome finisher strip.

Practice also showed up problems with the new knock-off wheels, which were not seating properly on the locating peg – it being too tight, resulting in the wheel jamming before it was properly home and tightened. This had resulted in wheels becoming loose, but it was rectified before the race.

After practice, the engine was removed to rectify a clutch and a primary gear problem, which had started to move. Whilst the engine was removed, the diff ratio of 3.7:1, fitted to achieve high top speed on the fast German circuit in the Eifel Mountains, was changed to a lower 3.9:1 for the race.

Come race day at the 11am start, Handley took the first stint. After 90 minutes he was leading the class and handed over to Enever. Enever held station and brought the car back at the three-hour mark still with the class lead. Handley took the wheel, only to make an unscheduled stop at around 4pm with a collapsed offside radius arm strut. A new strut was fitted and Handley sped back into the race, having lost the class lead to a 1300 Alfa.

Enever took the car over at the next stop but by now the clutch was all but gone. He didn't complete one lap before the nearside radius arm strut collapsed and the car was out, stranded four miles away out on the circuit. The car was classified as being 35th overall and eighth in class, having run for five hours and completed 28 laps but not running at the finish. This was a rather disappointing end to a race that started with much promise. It was likely that the Nürburgring, being a fast but bumpy circuit, resulted in the radius strut arm failure, exacerbated by the stiff sidewalls of the Dunlop D15 tyres. Abingdon planned to fit solid shafts in future.

Spa-Francorchamps was the destination for the next round of the ETCC, over the weekend of 26 and 27 July. This was a 24-hour endurance race held on the 8.75-mile circuit in the Ardennes Forest of Belgium. Weather often played its part in disrupting the race, with mist and rain, especially at night, being a persistent worry to most, even though the race was held in the height of summer.

Since the previous year the circuit had been substantially resurfaced and more Armco barriers appeared, largely to ensure that the Grand Prix could continue to be run there. Uncharacteristically, Abingdon had left its entry late, as the team wasn't contesting the entire series. The result of which was that both cars were placed on the reserve list and vying for a place in the 65-car maximum grid. As it transpired, only John Handley and Roger Enever made the start; Rhodes and Mabbs missed the cut. Handley and Enever were again using their RBL 450F.

The car was prepared for reliability and as a result the compression of the fuel-injected Weslake eight-port engine was dropped to 12:1. To achieve as much top speed as possible, the car was fitted with a long 3.3:1 final drive (without a limited-slip diff) but still with the much-preferred three-speed straight-cut close-ratio gearbox. This allowed the car to lap at very close to an average of 100mph on this very fast circuit.

CHAPTER 4: THE MK 2 MINI COOPER S

The Spa-Francorchamps pits sees RBL 450F with its yellow identification nose for the 24-hour endurance race, where Handley and Enever again used the car. RJB 327F is in the foreground.

Only RBL 450F was allowed to start, RJB 327F being refused due to being a late entry.

Knock-off Minilites were retained, which were 6J wide, and the car sat on Dunlop D15-236 tyres with Dunlop R7s reserved should it be wet. The car ran Hydrolastic suspension, pumped to 250psi, it had negative-camber bottom arms set at ¾ degrees, with adjustable tie bars to accurately set the caster angle. As was common for endurance race cars, it was fitted with a long-range fuel tank in the boot, with the filler cap let into the bodywork for safety.

To help identify the car at night, the car had a distinctive broad yellow stripe across the bottom of the bonnet and a matching yellow identification light above the windscreen. In addition, it also carried a broad red vertical strip in the centre of the grille. Two additional driving lamps were fitted to the car on individual brackets; it also had quick-lift jacking points and it ran chrome bumpers front and back.

Scrutineering did not go well, as the organisers decided that the wheelarch extensions were each 1cm too wide, so the mechanics had to hack off the extra fibreglass. Further, the in-car oil replenish system, consisting of a reservoir and a hand pump for the driver to pump in oil on the move, was also deemed illegal and had to be removed – even though it had been used in the past.

Two qualifying sessions of three hours each had to be completed, with one during the night. Fortunately, both were carried out in dry weather. Handley qualified in 43rd place but seventh behind a gaggle of Alfa Romeo 1300 GTAs in the 1300 class. Fuel consumption was recorded at 11.6mpg. With most entrants being large sports cars, the position was creditable.

Come race day the weather had changed and it was wet.

The race began in damp conditions and Handley, who started, was put on Dunlop R7 intermediate race tyres. After half an hour he returned to the pits to change onto Dunlop D15 race tyres. Handley and Enever slowly but surely started to claw their way up through the field. The pace had started to take its toll on many, and come nightfall they were contending the class lead, being in second place. Miraculously, they had

Handley and Enever hauled RBL 450F into 12th place overall but the engine let go just 90 minutes from the end of the 24 hours.

clawed their way up to 12th place overall, so reliable had the car been, with little time lost at pit stops. The only minor issues that night were a damaged battery cable and the rear exhaust Jubilee clip that needed replacing – both of which were quickly repaired.

Come daylight, they were soon leading the 1300 class after overhauling the impressive 1300 Alfas. The crew continued to circle around but oil consumption within the engine had become an issue, it needing two pints at each pit stop. With no means to top up on the move, as had been planned, oil surge and the resultant lack of oil pressure in the corners was a concern on the life of the engine. It all fell apart at La Source hairpin with just 90 minutes of the 24-hour race remaining, when due to oil starvation a conrod let go and destroyed the engine block. With well over 2000 miles completed and so near the finish, it was a bitter blow.

Post-event analysis showed that the conrod bearings had failed, probably due to fuel contaminating the meagre oil supply, plus some of the oilways had also become blocked with loose debris that was found in the engine. Lessons learnt.

The car was sold to engine guru Jim Whitehouse of Arden in late 1969 and was reprepared by Arden to compete in the 1970 British Saloon Car Championship, painted in its blue and silver colours for Gordon Spice to drive.

Competition Record

Date	Event	Crew	Number	Overall result	Class result
May 68	Acropolis Rally	Rauno Aaltonen/Henry Liddon	73	6th	1st
June 69	ETCC Brands Hatch 6 hr	John Handley/Roger Enever	5	4th	2nd
July 69	ETCC Nürburgring 6 hr	John Handley/Roger Enever	74	35th	8th
July 69	ETCC Spa 24 hr	John Handley/Roger Enever	78	DNF	

Registration Number	First registered	Chassis number	Engine	Engine number	Model
RJB 326F	June 1968	CA2SB 1129435A	1275cc	9F-SA-Y 48920	Austin Cooper S Mk2

This car is an odd one, in that it arrived at Abingdon along with its sister car RJB 327F and was registered, after being built in June 1968, but never used in anger by the factory team. The question has to be asked why it was supplied to Abingdon in the first place.

It is possible that the car could have been used for recce work by Hopkirk for the Portuguese Rally, which was due to take place in October. It could also have been used as a test mule, but none of this can be confirmed. With Abingdon at this time concentrating on the London-to-Sydney Marathon, due to take place at the end of November 1968, and the 1969 season seeing virtually no rallying for the team – its efforts being on the racetracks – it is clear that RJB 326F was rather surplus to requirements.

It has to be assumed that the car was built into a Group 2 rally car when it was sold to successful privateer Phil Cooper in October 1968, who would be the recipient of other works cars. Virtually unused at the time, Cooper immediately entered RJB 326F on the TAP Rally in Portugal and then the Firestone Rally in Spain, just weeks before the RAC Rally.

Cooper would use the car on a dozen internationals and national rallies over the next year, and notably to great effect on the 1968 RAC Rally. With no Abingdon cars on the home international (due to the funds and time-sapping Marathon) the fine result Cooper achieved on the RAC cannot be understated. From a huge field, Cooper finished fourth overall in his Group 2 car. Two Group 6 cars, which ran alongside the main event and were not part of the FIA European Championship, were ahead of him, which relegated him to sixth place, but the records nevertheless show he was fourth on 1968's RAC Rally of Great Britain.

It is worth briefly describing the 1968 RAC Rally to

RJB 326F was acquired by Phil Cooper from Abingdon, unused, where he entered the car for the 1968 RAC Rally. He, with Mike Bennett, took the car to a superb fourth overall, rewarding Abingdon's faith in letting him have the car.

CHAPTER 4: THE MK 2 MINI COOPER S

reinforce the achievement of Phil Cooper and the obvious fine build of the car by Abingdon. The 1968 RAC was reported as being the toughest RAC Rally ever, covering the entire British Isles in a clockwise direction starting and finishing at London Airport.

The 2500-mile route, over five days with 87 stages of some 500 miles to tackle, most on forest tracks, was a formidable challenge. Only one night in bed was programmed, when the route reached Edinburgh on the third day. Only two one-hour food stops had been scheduled in between. The return two-day run back to London had but a one-hour stop. Of the 120 cars that started, only 35 cars made it safely home, such was the rate of attrition, due to mechanical incidents, accidents or plain exhaustion.

Cooper did a remarkable job, which was not without its problems. He had a litany of suspension problems, from collapsed Hydrolastic units to broken subframes and wheel bearings. He went off the road in Yorkshire but recovered thanks to the many spectators along the route. The weather in late November was cold, wet and foggy, and to his credit he posted five fastest times on the stages and numerous others in the top three.

For a private entry, albeit with a fresh factory-built car, the result of fourth overall was a superb achievement. This leaves one to wonder what result Abingdon might have achieved if it had entered the rally in Minis for one last time – and not forsaken it for the London-to-Sydney Marathon. Timo Mäkinen and Paul Easter were in a Ford Escort on the RAC, Rauno Aaltonen and Henry Liddon were in a Lancia Fulvia, and Tony Fall was Porsche 911-mounted. So we will never know.

Competition Record

Date	Event	Crew	Number	Overall result	Class result
No Abingdon works competition history.					
Nov 1968	RAC Rally	Phil Cooper/Mike Bennett	28	4th	

Registration Number	First registered	Chassis number	Engine	Engine number	Model
RJB 327F	July 1968	KA2S6 1116764A	1275cc	9F-SA-Y 48915	Morris Cooper S Mk2

RJB 327F, a Mk2 Morris Cooper S, was built and registered in summer 1968 but it was not until April 1969 that the car was seen in competition. During those fallow months the car was used as a development test mule for the 1969 race season.

With the Britax-Coopers having many seasons' racing experience, they were Abingdon's main opposition. Abingdon had a lot to learn, and was on a steep learning curve. As history will show, Abingdon failed to beat the Britax team, and both struggled against the very quick Broadspeed 1300 Escorts.

The car was built as a Group 5 racer with at its heart a very powerful fuel-injected crossflow eight-port engine of some 125bhp. The cylinder head was crafted by Weslake from its factory in Rye in Kent, which had a close association with Abingdon. The car clearly had the tell-tale signs of being a rally car, having been fitted with Perspex headlamp protectors, quick-lift jacking points and a dipping interior mirror. It is not clear if the car had actually been used as a rally car but it is probable, with the reduced rallying programme and attention diverted to racing, that it was initially built as a rally car, then converted into a race car.

Testing during the winter of 1969 saw RJB 327F out at Thruxton circuit, where John Rhodes was assigned testing duties. Rhodes had been wooed away from the Cooper Car Company's race team when Abingdon was charged with taking on the British Saloon Car Championship. BL management decided they would dispense with the long-term tie-up with John Cooper and build the Minis internally. John Cooper for his part had lost valuable financial support from BL and hence became involved with Britax so that he could continue racing. He would now be fighting Abingdon rather

John Rhodes testing the new RJB 327F at Brands Hatch early in the season still on 10in wheels.

Fuel-injected crossflow eight-port engine being tested in RJB 327F at Brands Hatch by John Rhodes and John Handley.

Interior of RJB 327F showing the large brake pedal, the air hose for face-level cold air and the vent hole in the floor for fresh air, all of which was asked for by Rhodes.

than collaborating. Perhaps if they had joined forces they may have beaten the Broadspeed Fords, but it wasn't to be.

On a cold and frosty February, Rhodes completed 22 laps of the circuit until the engine broke with a suspected flywheel failure. The engine strip-down revealed the centre main bearing in the block had broken.

Prior to the failure, the day hadn't begun well when the car refused to start. New plugs and a new battery saw it out onto the circuit to warm up before tyre testing. These were Dunlop CR81s running at 55psi on the front and 48 at the rear, on 6J and 5½J magnesium Minilite wheels respectively, covered by wide wheelarch extensions with a chrome finishing strip. The car, at that time, was fitted with standard body panels and glass (lightweight panels were still to be homologated). The straight-cut close-ratio three-synchromesh gearbox had, for Thruxton, a 3.765 final drive fitted. It was on Hydrolastic suspension and had a rear anti-roll bar.

After some early laps Rhodes asked for the shock absorbers to be fully unwound and then fully wound up to gauge the difference. The car was around 1.5 seconds faster with the harder damper settings. He was, however, still not happy with the engine, feeling it was sluggish, especially at high revs. He suggested numerous changes to the car – notably larger pedals and an early solid gearstick (still favoured by most of the rally drivers). He also wanted a lightweight fibreglass bucket seat.

Further testing took place with the car at Brands Hatch in March, where Rhodes and John Handley were present for evaluation. This time the car was fitted with a Salisbury limited-slip differential set at a modest 66lb, and again with a 3.7 final drive. Overheating was a major issue all day, with the car running at boiling point most of the time. The system was bled and then they tried isolating the auxiliary radiator, all to no avail, and at lunchtime the head gasket was changed. Rhodes continued to do more laps in the afternoon, getting

Rhodes used RJB 327F on the third round of the BSCC at Snetterton, now with 12in wheels. It saw Rhodes the first Mini home, in 12th place overall.

similar times to the morning and then in late afternoon handed the car over to Handley (who had also been testing with OBL 46F) who did just one lap before the gearbox broke. It was another frustrating test session.

RJB 327F was first used in anger for the third round of the British Saloon Car Championship (BSCC), the Good Friday meeting at Snetterton for the Guards International on 4 April. Rhodes was effectively without Handley, as he did not run in the race.

Now built as a new Group 5 race car, with numerous trade sponsor decals on the bodywork, the 1293cc power unit produced 128bhp on the Abingdon test bed and had a 13:1 compression-ratio Weslake cylinder head running Lucas fuel injection with slide throttle and a 1247 camshaft. Special idler gears were fitted to the close-ratio straight-cut transmission and the limited-slip differential was set at 65lb. The suspension, with special tie rods, was fitted with Koni dampers together with Hydrolastic top arms and Hydrolastic rear struts, but by dry rubber cone. Negative camber of 2 degrees was on the front wheels and 0.5 degrees negative to the rear. The brakes had alloy Minifin brake drums fitted to the rear with VG95 rear linings and Ferodo DS11 disc pads.

The car was fitted with 12in wheels, which were of the Cooper Car Company Rose Petal design, not Minilites, and fitted with wide wheelarch extensions with a chrome finishing strip. The 12in wheels, homologated on 1 April, allowed for cooler running of the larger 12in tyres. A 12.5-gallon flexible fuel tank was fitted in the boot, with the fuel filler neck let into the bodywork. The car also had aluminium panels to the bonnet and doors, plus a fibreglass boot lid.

The 15-lap race saw Spice shoot ahead in the Britax car, only to get a 60-second penalty for jumping the start; he eventually retired after ten laps with a broken gearbox. His teammate Neal, being delayed with a coil coming adrift on the fifth lap and with Handley not competing, left Rhodes the first Mini home, albeit fourth in the 1300 class and 12th overall behind three hard-charging 1300 Ford Escorts headed by Chris Craft. The round was won by Roy Pierpoint in a mighty Ford Falcon.

The car next appeared as a Group 5 race car at Spa for John Rhodes and Geoff Mabbs to race. The Spa-Francorchamps race, held over the weekend of 26 and 27 July, was a 24-hour endurance race on an 8.75-mile circuit in the Belgium Ardennes Forest, and a round of the European Touring Car Challenge. The car was built with reliability in mind, so the compression of the Lucas fuel-injected Weslake eight-port engine was dropped to 12:1. Top speed was also a necessity at this fast circuit and to try to achieve that the car was fitted with a long 3.3:1 final drive (without a limited-slip diff).

Knock-off Minilites were fitted to speed up pit stop tyre changes, in 6J width; the car sat on Dunlop D15-236 tyres and had wider wheelarch extensions without a chrome trim finisher on their edges. The car ran Hydrolastic suspension,

RJB 327F at the Spa 24-hour race where the car sported extra-wide wheelarches devoid of chrome trim and knock-off Minilites. The car could only practice as the late entry meant they missed the cut, although Handley in the sister car in RBL 450F did race.

pumped to 250psi, with negative-camber bottom arms set at ¾ degrees and fitted with adjustable tie bars. A long-range fuel tank was to be found in the boot, with the filler cap let into the bodywork for safety. To help identify the car at night it had a broad light-green stripe across the bottom of the bonnet and a matching identification light above the windscreen; also a number plate lamp was fixed to the door to illuminate the race number.

Uncharacteristically, Abingdon had left the entry late, as it wasn't contesting the entire ETCC series – but with one eye on a potential class win as the Britax Coopers had not entered, a late decision was made to take part. The outcome of this late entry was that both BL cars were placed on the reserve list.

As it transpired, Rhodes and Mabbs were frustrated and were not allowed to start as the maximum grid of 65 cars had been filled, so they were reduced to a spectating role. This left teammates John Handley and Roger Enever, who made the cut, to uphold BL honours on their own. Sadly, whilst leading the 1300 class, their car was forced to retire with a blown engine with just 90 minutes of the race remaining, having covered over 2000 miles of hard racing. It was not a happy weekend for Abingdon.

Better luck was hoped for when the car was entered, this time for John Handley, for round ten of the BSCC at Oulton Park on 16 August. This was the support race to the Formula 1 Gold Cup meeting at the picturesque Cheshire circuit. The championship was drawing to a close and it was all set for Alec Poole as the likely winner with his one-litre eight-port Arden Mini because of his class winning rate; he would beat both the Britax-Cooper team and that of British Leyland.

Abingdon was still trying to get more power out of its

Oulton Park for round ten of the BSCC saw John Handley in RJB3 27F, where Handley could only finish in 15th place, the championship now being won by Alec Poole in the Arden one-litre Mini.

RJB 327F still carried its Spa 24-hour race identification light on the roof but now bumpers and knock-off Minilites were not used.

Geoff Mabbs took RJB 327F to Thruxton for a non-championship race, where he was the BBC camera car - the camera being massive compared to modern units. Mabbs, after an early accident, finished in fourth place.

cars, even though the championship was lost. Weslake had done more work on the eight-port engine used for the abortive Spa 24-hour race. It had more power and was now running a Salisbury 3.7:1 final drive. Cooling also received much attention with re-routed water pipes and an auxiliary radiator. The big difference in the car was that the Hydrolastic suspension was replaced with rubber cone suspension, which was considered to be a better option. Koni shock absorbers were used but without a rear anti-roll bar. Tyres were changed to Dunlop D22-232 on 7J and 6J Minilites. The car still appeared with its distinctive Spa identification light on the roof and its bonnet stripe but had lost its bumpers and resorted to normal wheel hubs, forsaking the knock-off hubs.

Despite the upgraded engine, Handley qualified behind the two Britax-Cooper cars of Spice and Neal and behind Rhodes in the sister car. The practice had been hampered with intermittent rain, which meant tyres were proving crucial. With the entire BSCC field being on the grid (unlike several other rounds when the smaller cars were in a separate race of their own) the lead Mini of Neal was on row three and Spice back on the fifth row, with Rhodes four rows further back still.

Come the flag drop, Neal, after the opening lap, was up to the ninth place, with Spice and Rhodes fighting out 13th and 14th places, and Handley a lowly 20th. The bigger cars were soon charging, and at the finish, the four Minis all came in very close together, with Neal in 12th place heading off Rhodes and Spice close by, followed by Handley. Craft won the class in his 1300GT Escort in eighth place and Poole won the championship by yet again winning his class.

The next appearance of RJB 327F was at Thruxton circuit at the end of August, where the car was assigned to Geoff Mabbs. This was a round of the BARC Championship (British Automobile Racing Club) and sponsored by BBC Television. The car appeared the same as it did at Oulton Park, other than the illuminating light for the race number on the driver's door had been removed and the space covered by a large BARC sticker. It is likely that Mabbs was using the

Mabbs bounces over the kerbs in a valiant attempt to catch the leaders after his early accident with Richard Longman's Mini.

race as a test session and also for publicity, as Abingdon was not contesting that championship; and, more importantly, the car was equipped with heavy BBC camera equipment to broadcast in-car race footage to the BBC viewers.

The race was for Special saloons, which were more highly modified than the more stringent BSCC regulations, and it was for cars up to 1300cc. Richard Longman was on pole with his Downton Mini and the race was not without its dramas, as Mabbs collided with a spinning Longman on the opening lap and sustained body damage to the nearside front of the car. Longman got a puncture for his trouble. No doubt it made good television viewing, as Mabbs charged through the field trying to catch up, bumping over Club Chicane and getting all four wheels off the ground – the result of which was a headlight rim fell off. He finished a creditable fourth place.

RJB 327F would then find itself transported to Australia for the Southern Cross Rally. With the no race programme planned for 1970, it has been suggested that the race car was rebuilt to compete in the rally but this is very doubtful. It is possible that a surplus rally car was rebadged but far more likely is that an entirely new bodyshell was built up for RJB 327F. However, the car nearly didn't make it to Australia, as the closure of the Abingdon competition department, due on 31 October, meant all proposed events were to be cancelled (and cars disposed of). It was only saved by BL Australia offering to finance the entire entry, so the car was duly sent to Australia for Brian Culcheth and local navigator Roger Bonhomme to compete on this very hard rally.

The new car was built up as a Mk2 Cooper S with a 1293cc engine with a five-port cylinder head and running large twin SU 1¾in HS6 carburettors. Four auxiliary Lucas 700 lamps were fitted on a lamp bar on the front of the car and two small MGB reversing lights fixed to the bootlid. The car ran 10in Minilite magnesium wheels with Dunlop SP44 tyres and wide wheelarch extensions. It was also fitted with a magnesium sump guard.

RJB327F was immediately reregistered with Australian number BLA 532 on its arrival, to comply with Australia's legal requirements. Soon after arrival, a press day was organised by BL Australia to display the two Abingdon works cars that had been sent over and that the team would soon own. Culcheth was demonstrating the car with one of the BL directors on board, when on a sharp turn the tyre dug in and he rolled the brand-new car.

It transpired that the Dunlop SP44 tyres that had been supplied were not fitted with tubes, and the tyre coming off the rim meant it instantly deflated. The car was very badly damaged with both wings, bonnet and roof very deranged. It looked a mess and a certain write-off. Miraculously, with a new bonnet and some skilful panel beating and pulling, the car was straightened and made it to the start a week later (with the RJB 327F plate on the bonnet now no more).

The rally was centred around Port Macquarie, which was adjacent to thousands of square miles of forests in the Blue Mountains region of New South Wales. Starting and finishing in Sydney, the three-day event from 7 to 11 of October consisted of three loops, all centred on the resort of Port Macquarie. Some 78 cars headed off from Sydney at noon to the first of 20 stages. Culcheth cleaned the first five stages. As

RJB 327F was now transported to Australia for Brian Culcheth, with local navigator Roger Bonhomme, for the 1970 Southern Cross Rally. The pair were lying second when the head gasket failed.

Culcheth and Bonhomme would use RJB 327F again, now registered as BLA 532, for the 1970 Rally of the Hills in the hot, dusty weather.

RJB 327F as BLA 532 being serviced with the other works entries. Culcheth and Bonhomme would finish fourth after a navigational error dropped them from the lead.

the event wore on through the night, he held a slender lead of two minutes and arrived at Port Macquarie with a loss of just eight minutes after the first day and a lead of a minute.

The second loop day, heading north, restarted with a 15-minute maximum service stop, which was insufficient for many and some lost road time getting to the first stage. Again Culcheth was setting fast times and cleaned the very arduous 40-mile climb west of Kempsey.

Two narrow, twisty forest stages followed, where Culcheth lost time to his closest rivals. Hard charging to pull back time, the following difficult stage near Dorrigo saw numerous cars off the road. With dust and blockages causing delays, this saw Culcheth drop seven minutes.

After a service point in Dorrigo came the long Corfes Road stage, which was narrow and rough. Here Culcheth dropped a little more time to the leaders (and teammate Cowan). A rest halt at Grafton and the pressure eased, but the difficult stages were soon to follow. However, Culcheth, with fast consistent times, finished the second leg in second place, two minutes down on leader Cowan in the other Abingdon Cooper S.

A generous one-hour service was allowed at the start of the third loop day, which headed out westwards, and was appreciated by many. The first stage, a long 28 miles, saw Culcheth fastest, but still drop seven minutes and into the lead. But it was not to last. On a very rough stage, he landed heavily and the impact fractured the water pipe to the auxiliary radiator. Carrying on, he soon lost most of his water, and with that the head gasket failed.

He struggled on, refilling the radiator until getting back to Port Macquarie where the car had to go into parc fermé. The decision was taken to remove the car from parc fermé, under severe penalty, and change the head gasket. The resultant three-hour time penalty ruled the car out of contention.

Determined nevertheless to carry on and finish the rally, they started the final day with the engine back to full health. However, later in the day when they came across teammate Cowan (now in the lead) at the roadside with a broken driveshaft, Culcheth offered his car's driveshaft. Unfortunately, they had incompatible fixings, so both cars were out, and both from leading positions.

Soon after the disappointment of the Southern Cross, Culcheth and Bonhomme would again use the RJB 327F on the Rally of the Hills. This would mark the very last event that Abingdon took part in. The car was reprepared by BL Australia mechanics to a high standard. They fitted new engine mountings, as it was discovered that these mountings had been weakened when Culcheth rolled the car – and had been the reason the engine moved sufficiently on the previous rally when the car landed heavily on the rough track, leading to fracturing of the water pipe.

Held on 24 to 25 October, the rally used many of the hill and forest roads in the Blue Mountains area of New South Wales. Starting just outside Sydney, the two-day event's first special stage was held in a valley running steeply down the right-hand hillside for about two miles, then returned up the opposite side. A single practice run was allowed; Culcheth and Bonhomme made full use of it and made pace notes on their single pass. Needless to say, they were fastest on the stage. The route then went into the hills with an unusual feature that cars with odd starting numbers went off in one direction and the even numbers in the opposite. This was novel, and after the first run, Culcheth was in the lead by three minutes.

The procedure was then reversed and unfortunately Culcheth missed a turn, which was allegedly arrowed. In retracing their steps, four minutes were lost. Ironically, if they

CHAPTER 4: THE MK 2 MINI COOPER S

had continued down the 'wrong' road, they would have cut off several miles of track. The delay meant they never fully recovered the time lost, and finished fourth overall. Sadly, the last outing for an Abingdon-prepared car did not end with a win. The Abingdon competition department closed a week afterwards.

The car was sold to BMC Australia after the Rally of the Hills, which continued to use it on selected events.

Competition Record

Date	Event	Crew	Number	Overall result	Class result
April 69	BSCC Snetterton	John Rhodes	125	12th	4th
July 69	ETCC Spa 24hrs	John Rhodes/Geoff Mabbs	79	Did not race	
Aug 69	BSCC Oulton Park	John Handley	74	15th	6th
Aug 69	BSCC Thruxton	Geoff Mabbs	176	4th	3rd
Oct 70	Southern Cross Rally	Brian Culcheth/Roger Bonhomme	12	DNF	
Oct 70	Rally of the Hills	Brian Culcheth/Roger Bonhomme	10	4th	

Registration Number	First registered	Chassis number	Engine	Engine number	Model
URX 550G	June 1969	KA2S6 1289172A	1275cc	9F-XE-Y 53028	Morris Cooper S Mk2

The 1969 season saw Abingdon concentrate largely on the racetrack. BMC had in the past always been ably represented on the track by John Cooper but now BMC had been consumed by Leyland Cars and become BLMC under the control of Lord Stokes; he decided he would sever ties with Cooper and that Abingdon should race its own cars. So Abingdon now had to quickly adapt to building race engines and race cars.

Two new cars were delivered to Abingdon in early summer of 1969. One car was built for John Handley, it being URX 550G, and John Rhodes would have its sister car, URX 560G. The first race for the cars was at the German track of Hockenheim on 15 June. Den Green was now responsible for the race car builds, and Bill Price, now promoted to assistant competition manager, was in charge of the race programme; both would be in attendance in Germany with the cars.

Built as a Group 2 car, URX 550G had a 1293cc engine with a very-high-compression Downton cylinder head of 13.4:1 and used an AEA648 full-race camshaft. The crankshaft and conrods were all standard but balanced. Forged Hepolite pistons were fitted and it ran a competition clutch. The engine had breathers into a catch tank similar to those used on Group 5 race cars. Trying to keep things cool was an 11-blade plastic fan but no auxiliary radiator was permitted.

Split Weber carburettors were fitted to a standard inlet manifold, needed for a Group 2 car, but with O-rings fitted. Champion N57R spark plugs were used and the engine rev limit was set at 8000rpm. Special drop gears were fitted with roller bearings. A straight-cut close-ratio gearbox was used and fitted with a long 3.65:1 final drive to get as much top speed on the very fast high-speed track.

The suspension was by Hydrolastic units with single-blue displacers at the front, blanked off and run at 250psi. They now, however, could fit shock absorbers to the front, as they had been homologated. The rear displacer units were double-blue, also blanked off at 250psi. Armstrong adjustable dampers were fitted, with the suspension set with 1½ degrees negative on fixed arms. The brakes were effectively standard, without a twin braking system. Ferodo DS11 disc pads and VG95 rear brake shoes were used – both designed for high-heat race application.

URX 550G was entered for John Handley to drive an ETCC round at Hockenheim, which saw the car in Group 2 form, meaning 10in wheels among many other things. The car finished fifth despite overheating problems.

Brian Culcheth was teamed with Johnstone Syer, where they would use URX 550G in Group 1 form for the 1969 Tour de France, seen here at Silverstone for testing and press duties prior to the event.

A very standard-looking Group 1 URX 550G without wheelarch extensions and standard steel wheels. Reliability and class awards were the aim.

Being a Group 2 car, the Mini had its carpets, trim, heater, bumpers and safety glass retained. It also had standard twin fuel tanks and was forced to run 10in wheels: 5½Jx10in Minilite magnesium wheels with CR81 Mk2 Dunlop race tyres run at 50psi at the front and 45psi rear. It was fitted with extra-wide wheelarch extensions, without a chrome strip.

Practice was fraught for Handley, with overheating problems. The ambient temperature was very high and the car initially ran at 110C. Handley was then sent back out with the bonnet open on the safety strap. After two more laps he returned, where the temperature had dropped to a just-acceptable 95C. Now the heater was turned full on to try and dissipate some additional heat. Handley was assisted by Rhodes with a tow for a couple of laps, where the long-geared car reached over 120mph.

After the practice the grille slats were flattened to increase airflow still further and the thermostat was removed and replaced by a blanking sleeve. It was also discovered that the nearside wheel had been fouling the radius arm, so a small spacer was fitted. The scrutineers also insisted that the car carry a spare wheel and jack for the race.

Come the race, the weather was still very hot and concerns still persisted as to the temperature of the engine. Handley started from the fourth row of the grid, behind Rhodes on row three. The 15-lap race of some 60 miles settled down with the very powerful Alfa GTA Juniors heading the field. Help, however, was at hand by German driver Christian Schmarje in his Cooper S, who had been persuaded by Abingdon to act as a tow car for Handley, allowing him to use the slipstream to increase his speed. This he did for several laps, helping Handley climb up the field and close to the Alfas, until with two laps to go, the toughened 'screen on the German's car shattered and he was forced into the pits, unable to see out. As a result, Handley dropped back and finished fifth in class and eighth overall behind the winning Alfa that always dominated German 1300cc saloon car races.

The Tour de France Auto in September was the next event for URX 550G, where Brian Culcheth and Johnston Syer would be entered in the now-Group 1 car. This was in the hope of securing a good class win. Two other team cars were entered by BL, both Group 5 cars: one for John Handley and the other for Paddy Hopkirk. BL would also have Julien Vernaeve with Ivo Michielsen in the works team, driving his own car, also a Group 1.

The Group 2 car that appeared at the race at Hockenheim in June would have needed considerable detuning to allow it to be entered as a Group 1 car, including work to the bodywork, such as removing the wheelarch extensions. It is unclear if this was the case or indeed a new Group 1 car was built up.

Being in Group 1, the car ran on standard 3½J steel wheels, without wheelarch extensions. Testing at Silverstone had shown the car to be 18 seconds per lap slower than the Group 5 sister cars on their wide Minilite wheels and much more powerful engines. Standard glass and trim was also retained. The car did, however, have two auxiliary Lucas 700 fog lamps fixed to a four-lamp bar and Perspex headlamp covers. It also carried numerous trade sponsor adverts on the side.

This was the first Tour de France for a number of years, due to lack of sponsorship. However, the revived format for 1969 was similar to previous editions, in that it was a 3000-mile tour around much of France and beyond, between 18 and 26 September, using race circuits and hillclimbs. The 1969 event started in Nice, and ahead for the 106 entrants was an energy-sapping first leg to Nancy of some 900 miles, to be covered in just 28 hours, and included seven tests, six of which were hillclimbs.

After the first of six legs, Vernaeve was leading Culcheth in the Group 1 class – a situation that would continue, with Culcheth complaining that he felt Vernaeve's car was perhaps not entirely within the Group 1 rules, as it seemed to have more power than his Abingdon car.

The second leg from Nancy to Reims saw two circuit races at Nürburgring and Spa-Francorchamps. Culcheth was fifth in Group 1, just one place behind Vernaeve in Germany and likewise in Belgium. Here in Spa they, like Handley and Hopkirk, worked together slipstreaming each other to improve their positions.

On the third leg to Rouen there were two more circuit races: one at the Reims road circuit just after the early start, and one at Rouen near the end of the leg. However, Culcheth was experiencing piston troubles and the engine was starting to make unpleasant noises, but with little option to do much about it, he continued on, hoping it would last.

The fourth leg from Rouen to Vichy saw them at the Le Mans Bugatti circuit for a 30-lap race, where even against other Group 1 cars, Culcheth could not improve his position. Into the night and a tarmac special stage at Cap Fréhel, the rally then went onto Magny-Cours for another race, where again Vernaeve headed Culcheth (now in his sick-sounding car) in fourth place.

From Vichy, the now much-depleted field, which was reduced by almost half, headed for Albi and the first race at Clermont-Ferrand, where the Circuit Charade suited the Mini well. Both Vernaeve and Culcheth did well, and as a result Vernaeve was now leading the class, with Culcheth not far behind despite his ailing engine.

One more hillclimb and then a circuit race at Albi saw the penultimate leg completed with their position maintained. The final leg to the finish at Biarritz had two hillclimbs and one circuit race to complete before the finish. The final race at Nogaro, a tight, twisty circuit made for the Mini, saw Culcheth briefly leading the race but he had to succumb to the more powerful Group 2 and 5 cars – but he did indeed win the last race for the Group 1 class. However, it was not sufficient for him to overhaul Vernaeve, who ran out as the class winner, with Culcheth having to settle for second place in the Group 1 category but a superb fifth in the Touring class and 28th overall. Only 49 cars finished the gruelling event.

The car was bought by Brian Culcheth and it continued to be used in competition, including the 1971 Monte Carlo Rally when it was driven by Andrew Cowan and still with Johnston Syer in the navigator's seat. It changed in appearance, as it was repainted white to reflect its Scotsman newspaper sponsorship.

The Tour de France being a cross between a series of races and rallying hillclimbs saw many circuit races around France and beyond. Culcheth lines up URX 550G alongside Julien Vernaeve's car, who was also in the BL team.

Culcheth and Syer brought the Group 1 car home in fifth place in the touring class and second in their group, it being won by Vernaeve in his own car.

Competition Record

Date	Event	Crew	Number	Overall result	Class result
June 1969	Hockenheim ETCC Race	John Handley	2	8th	5th
Sept 1969	Tour de France	Brian Culcheth/Johnston Syer	12	5th	2nd

Registration Number	First registered	Chassis number	Engine	Engine number	Model
URX 560G	June 1969	KA2S6 1289173A	1275cc	9F-XE-Y 53068	Morris Cooper S Mk2

John Rhodes testing URX 560G at Thruxton prior to its race at Hockenheim, running without the benefit of fuel injection, being a Group 2 car.

Two new Minis were sent to Abingdon in the spring of 1969 to be built as Group 2 race cars. John Rhodes was assigned one, URX 560G, with John Handley the other, URX 550G. By then, Abingdon's attention was focused away from rallying and concentrating mainly on racing. With the Leyland takeover and Lord Stokes heading the company, he decided BLMC should enter races itself rather than rely on John Cooper, whose long-standing (and very successful) contract, was cancelled.

Abingdon would have to learn quickly how to build and race Minis. This responsibility fell to Den Green, who would have the responsibility of building the cars, whilst Bill Price would oversee the entire race programme.

The first race for URX 560G was to be in Germany at the Hockenheim racetrack on 15 June. This was part of the German Group 2 touring car series and Abingdon was likely doing some flag-waving to the German market. Being a Group 2 car, the Mini had to retain its carpets, trim, heater, bumpers, twin tanks, safety glass and so on; this was no stripped out racer and, as it transpired, the heater was much needed.

The 1293cc engine had split Webers, a high-compression Downton cylinder head of 13.4:1 compression ratio, and an AEA648 race camshaft, which produced 131bhp at 7000rpm. A competition clutch was fitted in the transmission, which was through a straight-cut close-ratio gearbox running a relatively long 3.65 final drive for the fast Hockenheim circuit. Straight-cut roller bearing drop gears were also fitted.

At pre-event testing at Silverstone, the side exhaust was changed for a straight-through pipe, which gave another 150rpm on the long straight – however, after ten laps, the crankshaft let go. The new car was also tested at Thruxton with a rear anti-roll bar fitted.

Hydrolastic suspension had to be used with single- and double-blue displacers. These were blanked off, front to back, and set at 250psi. The front camber was simply set with 1½ degree negative-camber bottom arms. No other adjustment was permitted other than the fitment of a rear anti-roll bar and front shock absorbers (which had recently been homologated for Group 2 in May). Standard brakes were used but fitted with competition pads and linings. In addition, 10in wheels and tyres had to be used as the preferred 12in wheels were not permitted either. Wide 5½J magnesium Minilite wheels, painted gold, were used, for the first time with extra-wide wheelarches without chrome trim. These were termed Group 5 arches although they seemed to be acceptable to run on a Group 2 car. Dunlop CR81 race tyres were run at 50psi on the front with 5psi less at the rear.

Practice, the day before the race, had shown that the car was seriously overheating in the very hot weather. The engine was running at over 110C, and with no auxiliary radiator being allowed and just a standard 11-blade plastic fan, the bonnet was propped slightly open on the safety strap and Rhodes was sent out again. He returned with the engine running at a just acceptable 95C. The heater was run on full in an attempt to remove more heat, and practice continued. Rhodes was assisted by Handley who used his slipstream to tow the car along to get a bit more top speed, reaching over 120mph on the long straight. Rhodes had qualified on the third row, ahead of Handley.

After practice, to get more air into the engine, the grille slats were flattened. In addition, the thermostat was removed from the cylinder head and a blanking sleeve fitted in its place to increase the flow of water around the engine. It was hoped this would be sufficient to keep the water temperature within safe limits for the 60-mile race.

The next day, it was blisteringly hot for the 15-lap race and Abingdon hoped for the best. As the flag dropped, Rhodes, with a good start, was close to the dominant and powerful Alfa GTAs. He was soon up to third place, thanks to the assistance of German race driver Christian Schmarje in his Cooper S, who had agreed to assist Rhodes in slipstreaming him to help him climb up the field.

Rhodes was now challenging the Alfa, following in its slipstream, and nipped out to overtake on the fifth lap; with Schmarje close behind he too was able to follow through and

Rhodes mixing it with the other Minis at Hockenheim where he used Christian Schmarje's Mini to slipstream, until Schmarje's 'screen broke.

Rhodes understeering the Group 2 Mini to sixth place overall at Hockenheim.

both took the Alfa. It seemed this strategy would work well, with Rhodes up into second place in the class. Sadly, on the very last lap Schmarje's windscreen shattered and he had to pull into the pits, being unable to see forward. This meant Rhodes too slipped back and had to settle for third in class as the Alfa again swept past. Hockenheim is not a track best suited to a Mini, and the result was much applauded by the German crowd.

It was off to France for the next event for the car, where John Handley and Paul Easter would use URX 560G on the Tour De France Auto. This was a mammoth eight-day event, covering most of France and a mix of race circuits and hillclimbs, with many road miles in between and not much sleep.

Testing had been carried out prior to the rally, at Silverstone, to establish the best combination of wheels and tyres. Handley would use 6Jx12in knock-off Minilite wheels with racing tyres on the race circuits and 5½Jx10in Minilites on the hillclimbs. Extra-wide Group 5 arches were fitted to cover the wheels to keep the car within legal limits on the road. It was also decided to run the engine with split Webers and not fuel injection, which Paddy Hopkirk would be using.

URX 560G, built as a Group 2/5 car, was a cross between a rally car and a race car and it carried a T2/5 decal on the left-hand door to signify this grouping. This was an oddity that only seemed to exist in France.

With Abingdon's race experience from the 1969 season, the engine was as powerful as possible but it had to withstand the high mileage the event demanded. The car was fitted with a short 13-hole sump guard with a light duralumin extension plate, Perspex headlight protectors and quick-lift jacking points. It also carried, for the night sections, of which there were many, two Lucas 700 fog lamps at each end along Abingdon's customary four-lamp bar on a detachable plug.

The competition door numbers were on a white roundel rather than a white door square.

Inside, the car was equipped as a rally car, with two auxiliary dash panels and a bucket seat for Handley plus a high-back reclining seat for Easter, a padded roll cage and a demister panel in the rear 'screen. Finishing off the car's race appearance were numerous trade sponsor adverts on the rear side panel.

Held between 18 and 26 September, the Tour de France Auto had not been run since 1964, due to lack of sponsorship, but for 1969 the event was revived and was much as before – a massive hike mostly around France of over 3000 miles, taking in nine race circuits and 11 hillclimbs. It was divided into six legs, starting from Nice, where the first leg was 28 hours of driving, over 900 miles in length, to Nancy, taking in six tough hillclimbs and one chronomètre section (a twisty tarmac special stage without the climb). These hillclimbs were classic climbs, including Mont Ventoux, the Chamrousse, Mont Revard and the Ballon.

Handley, in his first full-length rally in a Mini, acquitted himself well on these demanding climbs, particularly when they were tight and twisty and the big-engined cars were unable to use all their power. Although the Mini was up against numerous high-performance sports cars, it was in the touring class that a good result was hoped for.

On the forthcoming race circuits, where Handley's racing experience would shine through, the big sports cars would race amongst themselves and then a separate race for the touring cars would follow, giving many chances for the Mini to show itself well. Handley was fourth overall on the tight last chronomètre Rainkopf stage into Nancy and was also lying fourth in class.

The restart, at 2am, saw the crews head for Reims for the

An early departure from Reims for Handley and Easter.

URX 560G mixing it with the big boys at the Reims Circuit, where Handley finished strongly.

Handley's racing experience stood the car in good stead and his performance on racetracks pulled the car eventually to eighth place overall, seen here at Magny-Cours.

Handley and Easter in URX 560G on the Chamrousse hillclimb. Handley acquitted himself well on the stages – this being his first rally.

second leg. This leg opened in Germany with six laps of the full Nürburgring. Handley's race experience showed here, and in the Group 1, 2 and 5 race he was an amazing seventh overall and fourth on the Group 2/5 class.

It was then onto Spa-Francorchamps for 20 laps round the classic Belgium circuit of some 175 miles. Handley and Hopkirk worked together here, assisting each other with slipstreaming on this very fast circuit, with Handley coming out on top in fifth place. After a night in bed at Reims, the first race was at the Reims circuit nearby. Here Handley ran well and finished in sixth place after 33 laps of this classic road circuit.

Onto Rouen, where Handley briefly led the 20-lap race due to some fearsome out-braking at the hairpin. However, all was not well with the clutch, which was starting to slip. Unfortunately the engine had been sealed by a scrutineer at the start, so it was not possible to change the clutch. So the mechanics resorted to a quick dose of fire extinguisher blasted into the housing. This would be a constant problem, with the mechanics even draining oil from the bottom of the clutch housing whenever time allowed.

The next leg from Rouen to Vichy saw a day-long run down to Le Mans where everyone joined for an evening race of 30 laps on the Le Mans Bugatti Circuit. Here again, Handley was very fast as they raced into the darkness. He was now just into the top ten overall, and on into the night was seventh fastest on the Cap Fréhel chronomètre.

There was then more racing at the Magny-Cours circuit, where yet again Handley's clutch was delaying him, having to pit during the 25-lap race to have it adjusted. The fifth leg from Vichy to Albi opened with a superb race at Clermont-Ferrand Circuit de Charade, where Handley stormed around revelling in this Mini-favoured circuit. His performance had him now up to seventh place overall – and considering the opposition of Ferraris, Porsches and GT40s it was very creditable. Another hillclimb was followed by a race at Albi, which saw Handley slide to eighth. And with just two more hillclimbs to go, he was determined to pull the place back.

The sixth and last leg from Albi to the finish at Biarritz, after a 4am start and the Col d'Aspin, saw it all come to an end on very next and last climb, the Col du Tourmalet. Handley misheard a pace note from Easter and took a tight right-hand bend just too fast, and they bounced heavily off a very stout parapet wall. The Mini was out, despite the best efforts of the BL mechanics who tried in vain to get the very-badly-damaged car patched up. It was cruel luck so close to the end from a potential eighth overall. Only 49 cars finished this gruelling event and it's a great shame URX 560G wasn't one of them.

The car was bought by Peter Browning, the Abingdon competition manager

Handley and Easter tackle the Aspin hillclimb after which they badly damaged the car against a bridge parapet on the Tourmalet stage.

The BL service crew desperately try to get URX 560G drivable, but it was a lost hope and the car was retired from eighth overall, to their disappointment.

Competition Record

Date	Event	Crew	Number	Overall result	Class result
June 1969	Hockenheim ETCC Race	John Rhodes	1	6th	3rd
Sept 1969	Tour de France	John Handley/Paul Easter	56	DNF	

CHAPTER 5:
THE MK3 MINI COOPER S & MINI CLUBMAN

The Mk2 Cooper S had a short lifespan over just 18 months before it was replaced by the Mk3 Cooper S, which was officially launched in October 1969. However, Mk3 Cooper S production did not commence until March 1970 and the first cars were not dispatched until the beginning of May.

The new car was structurally different, as the external door hinges disappeared in preference to flush internal hinges, and with that came wind-up windows. The door height and side window increased slightly up to the roof gutter line. The boot lid now had a light housed above the number plate and it reverted to single-skinned. The suspension still remained as Hydrolastic, despite the standard Mini reverting to the more desirable (by enthusiasts) dry cone suspension. Gone too was the duo-tone paintwork, all cars now appearing in monotone finish.

The engine was different in the Mk3: gone was the expensive nitrided crankshaft, to be replaced by a cheaper Tufftrided version. The big-valve Cooper S cylinder head was replaced with a smaller 12G940 cylinder head. These new BL engines were also painted black, not mid-bronze green as they had been since the early days. The gearbox at least now had the benefit of synchromesh on all four gears, which had appeared at the end of the Mk2 line.

Trim and internal fittings were slightly revised but not significantly. The grille was now common to all Minis. BL dropped the Austin and Morris names on the cars and they were now simply Mini Cooper Ss. The car was visually now so close to the standard Mini that a casual observer would not see the distinction other than a Cooper S badge on the boot and vented wide wheels.

The Mk3 Cooper S also had a short life, ceasing production in June 1971. This sad end to the Cooper name was another BL cost-cutting measure when Lord Stokes severed all ties with John Cooper, deciding he would no long pay royalties to John Cooper for the pleasure of having his name on the BL car.

It would, however, be a better story for the Mini Clubman and the 1275 GT, which were also introduced at the same time as the Mk3 Cooper S. The Clubman bodyshell was the same as the Mk3 Mini other than a complete change to the front end. The square front design gave more room around the engine but it added weight and was less aerodynamic. The 1275 GT version of the Mini Clubman was built as a replacement to the Mini Cooper (not the Cooper S). It had a single-carburettor 1275cc engine, pulled from the Austin-Morris 1300 range, with 59bhp. The car was fitted with Cooper S brakes and Hydrolastic suspension (initially at least). The four-speed synchromesh gearbox lost the heavy remote-change casting and this was soon replaced by a rod-change system. The standard Mini Clubman was fitted with a 1098cc engine from the Austin-Morris 1100 range.

Abingdon was now being seriously restricted in its motorsport activities. The 1969 racing season had not been the success that is BL masters had hoped for and the plans for 1970 reflected a loss of faith and interest in competitions by British Leyland. Other than the World Cup Rally in April 1970, the competition programme looked sparse compared to former years. Nevertheless, five Mini Clubmans would pass through the gates of Abingdon and just one Mk3 Cooper S. All of these cars were effectively Cooper Ss, built to the highest specification as they had always been. Certainly the extra room around the larger square front on the Clubman was welcome for fitting auxiliary front-mounted radiators and for additional space for forward-facing carburettors fitted to crossflow cylinder heads. It is interesting to note that the single Mk3 Cooper S that was built at Abingdon, YMO 881H, still retained sliding widows, as did all of the works Clubmans and 1275GTs. This had the benefit of forsaking the heavy winding mechanism in the doors. The doors were, however, devoid of external hinges.

Of the five Clubmans built, one was a rebodied Mk2 for the World Cup recce (this being OBL 46F), two were noted as Mini Clubmans (YMO 885J and its sister car YMO 886J) and the other two (XJB 308H and SOH 878H) as Mini Clubman 1275GTs. These last cars have to be considered as the pinnacle of the Mini's development by the competition department at Abingdon.

CHAPTER 5: THE MK3 MINI COOPER S & MINI CLUBMAN S

Registration Number	First registered	Chassis number	Engine	Engine number	Model
XJB 308H	Jan 1970	XA2 S2 34034A	1275cc	99H35 BHE 19539	Mini Clubman 1275GT

XJB 308H was part of a large BL effort on the London-to-Mexico World Cup Rally but it was the only Mini – the other BL works cars were four Triumph 2.5 PI Mk2s and a couple of Austin Maxis. The car was assigned to John Handley and Paul Easter.

From the outset, the car was destined to go as fast as possible to Lisbon, in the hope of chasing the pack falling by the wayside. It was a plan that didn't go well. The car was undoubtedly faster and more nimble than any of the other BL entries but it was not as strong and certainly not an endurance car. The car was, in truth, very much the poor relation in the BL assault on the World Cup Rally and its development and testing was often at the back of the queue. It is said that the car was not expected to finish, and the proof of that was there were little spares provisions in the huge BL manifest for the Mini for the latter half of the route.

XJB 308H was built into a new Clubman bodyshell (rather than that of a Mini), which had just been launched, so it was with good publicity in mind. It did, however, with its elongated square front, allow just a bit more room around the engine. The car was built with a five-port 1293cc engine with Downton cylinder head coupled to a straight-cut close-ratio gearbox with a 3.9:1 final drive. The engine was run on twin 1½in SU H4 carburettors rather than a single Weber or indeed split Webers. It produced 115bhp at the flywheel on the dynamometer. It ran an auxiliary radiator behind the front grille in addition to the standard side-mounted unit.

The car ran Hydrolastic suspension rather than dry cone and had special taps to isolate the front suspension from the back. This not only tended to stop pitching, it also served to stiffen up the suspension should it be needed. To aid the Hydrolastic suspension, front shock absorbers were fitted in addition to a rear anti-roll bar. It sat on wide 6J Minilite wheels covered by wide wheelarch extensions.

The bodyshell had aluminium doors and fibreglass bonnet and boot lid. Inside was equipped with a very special full-width dashboard, roll cage, high-back reclining seat for Easter and a supportive bucket seat for Handley. To contend with the high mileage between refuelling and the car's high consumption, an extra 11-gallon fuel safety cell was fitted into the boot well. The car now carried 22 gallons of fuel.

Externally the car ran huge front-facing mud flaps in addition to four rear-facing flaps (required by the rally's regulations). It ran four extra lights on a four-lamp bar with an external plug and socket, and wire mesh headlight protectors. Finished in traditional red-and-white paintwork, the car also carried large BBC TV adverts on the rear panels,

Paul Easter with John Handley consulting the road book with XJB 308H in front of a packed crowd at Wembley Stadium for the start of the 1970 World Cup Rally.

which denoted its sponsorship from the BBC Grandstand TV programme.

The World Cup Rally was the second of the really big rallies, the first being the London-to-Sydney Rally in 1968 where BMC came home in second place. The company was hoping for more this time. The logistics of Abingdon building and supporting seven cars on a 16,000-mile route to the other side of the world was a huge task, which Peter Browning masterminded. Bill Price, as his right-hand man, reported that he took 44 separate flights on 11 different aircraft, leapfrogging the route to oversee service and ensure the vast array of spares and personnel were in the right places at the right times.

The rally, held between 19 April and 27 May saw 96 cars travel from Wembley Stadium in London all the way eastwards through France, Germany and Yugoslavia to Sofia in Bulgaria and then back westwards through Italy, France and Spain to Lisbon on the Portuguese coast. A long boat trip from Lisbon (and a welcome break) took the remaining cars to Rio de Janeiro in South America. The rally continued down to southern parts of Argentina and then up northwards through Chile, Peru and Columbia to finish in the Aztec Stadium in Mexico five weeks later.

So it was that the cars were flagged away at 10am from Wembley for their big adventure by Sir Alf Ramsey, the then-

The rough early primes saw Handley and Easter continue to post fast times despite XJB 308H having an engine that was showing signs of failing.

Handley and Easter descend the starting ramp at Wembley on their hoped-for 16,000-mile journey to Mexico.

The early primes in Yugoslavia saw Handley posting competitive times, with the aim that the car should race as fast as possible to Lisbon.

Football Association manager and ironically, Lord Stokes – BL's Chairman, who would soon be wielding his axe over Abingdon's competition department. Start numbers were simply drawn out of a hat (but they would be reseeded from Lisbon onwards).

Once across the channel the Mini of Handley settled into the task of eating up the miles through France and Germany for breakfast at Munich. They would arrive in Sofia the following morning, where by now the Mini was showing signs of problems. The engine was consuming a lot of oil and starting to oil plugs and misfire under heavy load – and not sounding very healthy at all – even though the rally's competitive mileage had yet to start… The fault could not be rectified by the attendant service crew.

The first prime (special stage) was to be held later that afternoon in Yugoslavia from Pec to Titograd. However, it had to be rerouted because the prime was snowbound. This came as no surprise to Handley and Easter as they had failed to recce the stage a month earlier because of the snow.

The organiser (John Sprinzel) rerouted the cars to Titograd and ran the first prime from Titograd to Kotor. This change had been given in good enough time to allow Mike Wood to do a full recce of the new prime, make pace notes and hand them to Easter at the Belgrade control well before they arrived in Sofia. This 50-mile prime, now renamed the Montenegro Prime, started on tarmac but was soon on mostly narrow loose-surface mountain roads that were not closed to traffic. Here incidents with lorries caused delays and obstructions were common.

The route, at its end, saw a series of endless tight hairpin bends into Kotor. With a bogey time of 65 minutes, Handley – even with his misfiring engine – revelled in this prime that really suited the Mini. He dropped just two minutes and was in equal 11th place.

The second prime that night, still in Yugoslavia, was from Glamoc to Bosanska Krups and was over 100 miles long, with a bogey time of 2 hours, 50 minutes. With the misfire getting steadily worse, Handley and Easter pressed on. The prime was on gravel and rough in parts and also had some snow and ice in places. A diversion, because of roadworks,

saw some divert and others press on through. The diversion was for a broken bridge: some turned back and one, Hannu Mikkola, the eventual winner, took a run at it and leapt the void! By the time Handley had arrived, previous competitors had laid planks across the gap and they passed without delay. Again, despite a now sick engine, Handley came ninth on the prime but still dropped 27 minutes.

The route continued to head north into Italy and the first rest halt after over three days of driving at Monza (and it would be the only one until Lisbon). With a possible six hours' service allowed if needed, the BL service team tried in vain to fix the ailing Mini. It was diagnosed that the misfire had caused piston damage due to fuel starvation – the probable cause being a restriction between the hastily-installed bag tank and the twin steel tanks. The engine was simply just not getting enough fuel. This also meant that the car was constantly oiling plugs as the piston started to fail. There were not high hopes of the car going much further, let alone making it across to Lisbon.

After a night's rest, Handley and Easter headed for the third prime at San Remo. This would be familiar territory for Easter, the roads being Rally of the Flowers territory, but it all came unstuck – to nobody's surprise – when the engine let go on the San Remo prime and Handley and Easter were posted as the first BL retirement. They had barely scratched the surface of this rally, albeit they had already covered 2500 miles in the Mini.

Despite heavy fuel consumption on their recce in OBL 46F, fuel starvation on the event put paid to the engine. The plan had always been for the car to act as a 'hare' and go flat-out to Lisbon; sadly it only got as far as Italy and retired after just four days' rallying. They were lying the eighth place overall at the time.

XJB 308H having already retired, the mechanics try to get the car to run, to no avail. The car was the first of BL's retirements, having not even got out of Italy.

Fast forward to the end in Mexico and Abingdon was rewarded with much publicity, with Brian Culcheth finishing in second place in his Triumph PI, and Hopkirk fourth in his Triumph. In the end, the cost to BL was never established, although it must have been a big number. Norman Higgins, the company accountant, never added up all the bills and nobody ever asked…

After the disappointment of the World Cup Rally for XJB 308H, the car was soon returned to the UK and Cliff Humphries set about building a new engine for it. It had been entered for the Scottish Rally in early June, which was due to start just ten days after the World Cup had finished. Quite what would have been left of the car had it completed the 16,000-mile rally is open to debate. Nevertheless, the car was

Handley surveys XJB 308H's engine, which failed with a holed piston at San Remo.

Paddy Hopkirk and Tony Nash, who dashed back from the finish of the World Cup Rally, took a rebuilt XJB 308H on the 1970 Scottish Rally.

WORKS MINIS IN DETAIL

After starting on 12in wheels, Hopkirk soon changed these to 10in wheels but the lowered ride height on the rough roads took its toll. Here the damaged gearchange is being investigated.

Much welding to the damaged remote shift still saw Hopkirk up with the leading cars, despite only having second gear until it could be repaired.

reprepared and the first thing to go was the offending fuel cell in the boot, which had likely caused the fuel starvation that crippled the car. It still, however, retained its World Cup aluminium boot lid with its little bulge to clear that fuel cell. Also ditched from the World Cup car were the twin SU 1½in H4 carburettors, replaced with a set of split Webers.

The car was to be driven by Paddy Hopkirk and Tony Nash and they would be joined by Brian Culcheth, straight from second place on the World Cup Rally, in a lightweight Triumph PI running on triple Webers (contrary to BL management's dictate). Culcheth would go on to win the rally, despite protests from Lancia when Harry Källström was heavily penalised for late arrival at a number of stage starts.

Run from 6 to 12 June, the Scottish was always a tough rally, especially on the hard, dry, rough forest tracks – but was usually blessed with good weather. Starting from Glasgow, 143 cars faced nearly 36 hours of motoring (with a few short breaks for sustenance).

Setting off on Sunday morning, the rally ran continuously until arriving in Grantown-on-Spey late Monday afternoon. Hopkirk started well enough but the car was still running on its World Cup 12in Minilite wheels, which Hopkirk was sceptical about using, especially with a limited-slip diff and the forest roads.

Come Sunday afternoon, Hopkirk had had enough of the unpredictable handling of the car on 12in wheels and swapped over to 10in wheels. The car was now handling much better, albeit it was now lower and more susceptible to damage than on the taller wheels. Hopkirk set about making up lost time through the Sunday night and Monday morning stages.

By the time of an early breakfast at Bathgate, with 22 stages completed, he was lying sixth. The night had taken its toll, with 30 cars already having fallen by the wayside. The route now headed across the central lowlands of Scotland and 11 more stages before a brief lunch stop at Aberfeldy, where Hopkirk had pulled back to fourth place. However, the next five rough stages started to take their toll on the car and a damaged remote shift meant the car was stuck in second gear. At the Grantown night halt, the car was tipped onto its side by the BL service crew and they set about welding the damaged remote and linkage. Nevertheless, Hopkirk was still in fourth place.

The next three days saw the rally base itself at Grantown, running only during the day, with bed and revelry each night.

Hopkirk comes into service to attend to a slipping clutch; seen here is the bulge in the boot for the World Cup fuel cell. Hopkirk and Nash finished a fine second place. This would be the last works Mini appearance in the UK.

406

CHAPTER 5: THE MK3 MINI COOPER S & MINI CLUBMAN S

Heading out the next morning, Hopkirk was in trouble again, as the welding soon failed and he was once again having difficulty changing gear. He came out of the Blackhall stage stuck in second.

At the lunch halt at Potarch, after nine more stages, the car was again tipped onto its side. Jumbo-sized aluminium rods had been purchased from a tractor repair agent and the BL mechanics set about welding the remote again. All of this took time and Hopkirk only just made it to the next time control, with just two minutes to spare before being excluded.

Wednesday morning saw the car refuse to start, so Hopkirk and Nash had to push it out of parc fermé and solicit the BL service crew to bump start them down the road. The route headed westwards and Hopkirk was up to third place as more and more cars dropped out due to damage.

So to the final day and Hopkirk's problems were still not over, as the car started to develop clutch slip. They continued and, despite having to be careful with the clutch, they arrived at the finish that evening in Grantown in second place. It was a testament to Hopkirk and the Mini that the car could still, in the right hands, be competitive on tough events.

This was to be Hopkirk's last drive for BMC/BL and the last works rally for the Mini in the UK. Hopkirk tried to buy XJB 308H after the rally, to keep it as a memory of one of the last works Minis. He was disappointed, because the car was sold to Phil Cooper, who continued to use it to good effect.

Competition Record

Date	Event	Crew	Number	Overall result	Class result
April 1970	World Cup Rally	John Handley/Paul Easter	56	DNF	
June 1970	Scottish Rally	Paddy Hopkirk/Tony Nash	14	2nd	1st

Registration Number	First registered	Chassis number	Engine	Engine number	Model
YMO 881H	June 1970	XADL 131159A	1275cc	249	Mini Cooper S Mk3

For Abingdon, 1970 was a demanding time. Most of the team's efforts and resources were employed on the London-to-Mexico Rally, scheduled for April. However, dark times were just around the corner, where in October, Abingdon would see the closure of the competition department. Nevertheless, plans and budget had been in place for a minimal programme of events (apart from the London-to-Mexico) for the coming year, and cars were supplied and being prepared.

YMO 881H was the first and only Mk3 Cooper S that Abingdon had been supplied with, and the car was prepared for the Southern Cross Rally in Australian in early October. It was to be driven by Andrew Cowan and Bob Forsyth. Cowan had won the event the previous year and was keen to repeat the win, and Forsyth, being a native Australian, was well-versed in navigation and rallying in that country.

The car, being a Mk3 bodyshell, had lost its distinctive external door hinges but was not fitted with wind-up windows. So it was converted to have sliding windows, being of considerably less weight. However, as the Mk3 Cooper S was yet to be homologated, it is likely the car may have needed to fall under Mk2 homologation and hence sliding windows were fitted. Most of the trim was removed to make the car as light as possible.

Four auxiliary Lucas 700 lamps were fitted on a lamp bar on the front of the car but it is noted that the car carried a Cibié advert for its far superior lights. The car ran 10in Minilite magnesium wheels fitted with Dunlop SP44 tyres. It was also fitted with a magnesium sump guard, mud flaps behind the front wheels but none at the rear.

The engine was a 1293cc with a five-port cylinder head and twin SU 1¾in HS6 carburettors. Once shipped to Australia, the car, to comply with local laws was immediately reregistered BLA 523 and this number plate was fixed vertically above the front grille, partially masking the YMO881H number – which was not removed.

It is probable that the car also received additional preparation when it arrived in Australia as it was effectively under the control of BL Australia, which was financing the entire entry. This, as it transpired, was the salvation of the entry, as by the end of August, when the announcement of the closure of Abingdon was made public, all projects were stopped, but this BL Australia-financed entry went ahead.

The Southern Cross Rally, run between 7 and 11 October, started and finished in Sydney. The New South Wales resort town of Port Macquarie, with thousands of square miles of adjacent forests, was host to 78 crews for three nights of the rally. This would see a great seesaw battle between Andrew Cowan and Brian Culcheth, in their respective works Cooper Ss.

A large crowd saw the cars depart from Sydney at midday, heading for a rallycross at Windsor raceway but it was

WORKS MINIS IN DETAIL

Andrew Cowan with Bob Forsyth lead the Southern Cross Rally in YMO 881H but were forced to retire when the brakes failed and the resulting damage took too long to repair.

cancelled. An easy section to Newcastle saw the crews tackle 20 sections to Port Macquarie. The first stage saw Cowan clean the stage, along with many of the front runners. After six stages, he had dropped only one minute. Cowan continued to clean stages but, as the night wore on, he and others began to lose time as the forest roads became more demanding. At his arrival at Port Macquarie he was in third place.

The second day, running northwards, saw some frantic activity with only 15 minutes allowed for service after the restart. Some crews would lose time on the road north to Kempsey, where the serious competition began with a long, climbing stage of almost 40 miles. Cowan was again clean. Two forestry stages on narrow and somewhat overgrown tracks saw Cowan drop only a single minute. The stage west of Dorrigo was nine miles in 12 minutes with some very deceptive tightening bends and Cowan dropped five minutes – but others did far worse.

After a service point in Dorrigo came another long stage, which was narrow and rough, but Cowan only dropped three minutes, plus another three on the next before the rest stop. More demanding stages followed, with Cowan dropping nine minutes on a difficult 28-mile stage. However, on his return to Port Macquarie, Cowan found himself with a lead of two minutes ahead of Culcheth.

The third leg began heading westwards from Port Macquarie with a generous one-hour service period, which allowed for a lot of work on the cars. The field then headed to Wauchope and to the first stage. At almost 28 miles in 39 minutes, the Kerriki Creek stage saw Cowan drop eight minutes. The next, tight stage saw Cowan respond, dropping just three minutes – the tight conditions suiting the Mini perfectly. Cowan continued to set fast times but at the return to Port Macquarie he was four minutes adrift in second place.

Sixty-odd cars headed out for the fourth and final leg to tackle the remaining 400 miles of competition, of which a final 120-mile stage would be the roughest and toughest. The first 20-mile stage was cleaned by Cowan, then a 43-mile stage followed, with Cowan dropping just three minutes.

Cowan then moved into the lead with a ten-minute buffer but it was not to last, as on the next stage his brakes failed. Cowan flung the Mini sideways but it hit a bank and ripped off a front wheel and broke the driveshaft. It took an hour to make repairs (with parts cannibalised from Brian Culcheth's car, which had already retired) and the car was out. The accident handed the win to Brian Ferguson's Holden. It had been a hard rally and it was disappointing that Cowan, with the lead, had his trouble so near the end.

The car was sold to BL Australia, which continued to use it, with Cowan, on several events in Australia.

Competition Record

Date	Event	Crew	Number	Overall result	Class result
Oct 1970	Southern Cross Rally	Andrew Cowan/Bob Forsyth	10	DNF	

Registration Number	First registered	Chassis number	Engine	Engine number	Model
YMO 885J	Aug 1970		1275cc		Mini Clubman

YMO 885J, and its sister car YMO 886J, were the very last two works Minis ever built at Abingdon. It was registered in early August 1970, when it was already common knowledge that Abingdon was to close in the very near future. The closure was officially announced on 25 August; Peter Browning had already resigned in protest about the cutbacks wielded in July, only to find, a few weeks later, that Lord Stokes had decreed that the department was to close at the end of October.

The new Mini Clubman was built up for Brian Culcheth and Johnstone Syer to compete on the Sherry Rally, to be held in Spain between 8 and 10 September. The car was fitted

CHAPTER 5: THE MK3 MINI COOPER S & MINI CLUBMAN S

Interior of YMO 885J with its full-width dashboard and sliding windows on MK3 doors. The car was never used by Abingdon, having been built for the Sherry Rally from which the BL masters withdraw the entry.

with a 1293cc Cooper S engine, which was dry-decked and fitted with a Weslake cast-iron eight-port crossflow cylinder head. This was fed by twin 45DCOE Weber carburettors. An auxiliary front-mounted radiator also aided the cooling.

The car was fitted with a straight-cut close-ratio gearbox and, running with 12in Minilite wheels, it was fitted with a 3.9:1 limited-slip final drive.

The suspension was Hydrolastic with the addition of Koni dampers at the front and heavy-duty competition bump stops. The subframes were strengthened and plated. As the Sherry Rally was using loose-surface roads, the car was fitted with a Tech-Del magnesium sump guard. Being a Group 6 car, YMO 885J was fitted with aluminium doors and boot lid plus a fibreglass bonnet. Perspex replaced the heavy glass.

Inside the car, a fibreglass bucket seat and a high-back reclining seat were supplied, all in black cord trim, and an alloy roll cage. A full-width dashboard was crafted, containing the instruments. The Halda distance recorder was now located in the middle of the dashboard and alongside, to the left, a small speedo; to its right, two fuseboxes. In front of the driver, the rev counter had three additional gauges to its left: a dual oil pressure and water temperature gauge, a circular fuel gauge and a battery condition gauge. It was not fitted with a heated front windscreen.

Despite Culcheth and Syer completing a full recce, the entry was not allowed to go ahead by the BL masters and the car sat unused. It was sold in October as part of Abingdon's forced clear-out sale, reputedly with just 200 miles on the clock, for £1500. It immediately went to the Isle of Man to its new owner and the Berkshire registration ceased. The car continued to be used to good effect in its post-Abingdon life.

YMO 885J was sold with only test mileage and went to the Isle of Man, lost its Berkshire registration but was used to good effect on the island.

Competition Record
None

WORKS MINIS IN DETAIL

Registration Number	First registered	Chassis number	Engine	Engine number	Model
YMO 886J	Aug 1970	XA2S2 148800A	1275cc	9FSAY 35826	Mini Clubman

YMO 886J has the distinction of being the very last works Mini built at Abingdon. Registered in August 1970, along with its sister car YMO 885J, the car was already on borrowed time because the competition department was due to close at the end of October. Lord Stokes had decided that he no longer needed professional rally drivers to test his cars and saw no need for the expense of a competition department.

The closure was announced, officially, at the end of August but the news was already widely known by Abingdon staff. Nevertheless, the build for the car continued as the car was to be entered for Paddy Hopkirk and Tony Nash for the Sherry Rally in Spain in early September. Despite completing a full recce of the event, the entry was pulled by British Leyland bosses and the car was never used in competition by Abingdon.

Built into a new Mini Clubman body, YMO 886J probably represented the very pinnacle of what could be achieved with the now rather aged Mini. Lest we forget, the Mini design was now 11 years old – but it had also come a long way in that time. Fitted with a 1293 Cooper S engine, it had a Weslake eight-port cylinder head with twin Weber 45DCOE carburettors in preference to fuel injection. The engine block was also dry-decked, which aided cooling, and was further helped with an extra front-mounted radiator. The car had a straight-cut close-ratio gearbox and a Salisbury limited-slip differential running with 6Jx12in Minilite wheels.

The suspension was Hydrolastic with Koni dampers and heavy-duty bump stops. Being a Group 6 car, both the front and rear subframes were strengthened, and the car was also lightened. It was fitted with Perspex windows together with aluminium doors and boot lid and a fibreglass bonnet. On the front of the car were four Lucas 700 lamps on a lamp bar, fitted with a rubber lamp socket. It also had two MGB reversing lamps set into the boot.

The car today with its beautifully restored engine bay showing the crossflow cylinder head and twin Weber carburettors.

CHAPTER 5: THE MK3 MINI COOPER S & MINI CLUBMAN S

Inside the car, a padded alloy roll cage was fitted and the trim, being all black, had a lightweight bucket seat and a high-back recliner, both with Britax full-harness seat belts. A quick-lift (and descend) monkey-up-a-stick jack was fitted behind the driver's seat. A full-width alloy dashboard was fabricated, quite different to that found in the other works Minis. This had the Halda distance recorder centrally mounted, with a speedo to the left and a couple of fuseboxes to the right. The driver had a rev counter and three auxiliary gauges: a combined oil and water gauge, a fuel gauge and a voltage gauge.

The unused car was loaned out to George Forbes who used it on the Snowman Rally, the Seven Dales Rally and the Welsh International Rally in 1971. Quite why the car was on loan is unknown, especially when its sister car and numerous others were disposed of in short order under the edict from Lord Stokes. It was sold a year later in August 1971, by the factory, to Malcolm Patrick, who was often to be seen competing in national and international rallies, to great effect, in various cars.

YMO 886J, built for the aborted entry for the Sherry Rally; the car was loaned to George Forbes and he used it on numerous events including the Welsh International. The car was returned to Abingdon and sold on.

Competition Record
None at Abingdon

Registration Number	First registered	Chassis number	Engine	Engine number	Model
SOH 878H	Jan 1970	XAD2 405A	1275cc	114	Mini Clubman 1275GT

By early 1970, much if not all of Abingdon's efforts and resources were concentrated on the London-to-Mexico Rally to be held in April. It was to be a six-week-long rally with BL fielding seven cars. Nevertheless, a minimal programme of rallies, rallycross and just a few races were still on the books.

The storm clouds were, however, gathering, as BL management became more disillusioned with the notion of funding a competition department. This came to a head in July when Peter Browning gave up the inevitable struggle to get a sufficient programme approved by the Longbridge management and offered his resignation. This culminated in BL deciding, a month later, that the competition department would be closed at the end of October. It was officially announced on 25 August and was a terrible blow. Events already in the programme would, however, remain, which meant the entry for SOH 878H on the Marathon de La Route would continue.

A new Clubman 1275 GT, already well under way when the axe fell, was built up for this gruelling 84-hour race around the fearsome Nürburgring. The car would have a crew of three race drivers: John Handley, Alec Poole and Julien Vernaeve. Built very much as a race car, it was an ultra-lightweight Group 6 car but not fitted with an eight-

John Handley, Alec Poole and Julien Vernaeve drove SOH 878H on the Marathon de La Route, which was effectively a three-and-a-half-day race around the Nürburgring.

port crossflow cylinder head and fuel injection – it being considered more reliable to use a five-port cylinder head and Weber carburettors.

The car was painted white with an identification light on the contrasting roof. This was a change from the normal red-and-white livery – perhaps viewed that a white car was more visible at night. It also had two additional fog lights and a number plate lamp on the door to illuminate its race number. The car ran 12in knock-off Minilite wheels and wide wheelarch extensions.

News of the impending closure of the competition department, although not officially announced, had been broken to the team as they headed out to Germany on the ferry, and it was a moral deflater. Nonetheless, Abingdon planned to go out in style. The Marathon de la Route, which ran for 86 hours between 5 and 8 August, meant the Mini would have to travel well over 300 laps of the 17.68-mile circuit – at least 5300 miles. It would be a tall order at race speeds. Consistent lap times were also required. The cars had to complete at least the same number of laps in the last 12 hours as they did in the first 12 hours – disqualification being the result of this transgression. Stopping in the pits for more than 15 minutes also resulted in exclusion – but a capable driver could, if he was able to, repair the car himself opposite his pit but away from the attendant mechanics. However, he still only had 24 minutes to complete his task. Further still, for each minute spent in the pits, other than a minute allowed to change drivers, a lap was deducted from the total. Trouble-free consistent runs were the key to winning.

Sixty-four cars lined up at the ceremonial start in Liège for the neutral run out to the race circuit. In fine weather the flag dropped at 1am and immediately the Mini screamed off. Ahead was the other BL entry in the shape of a potent Rover V8, which also took off at an incredibly fast pace. After the first lap, the Rover V8 was running well ahead of the field by a considerable margin of nearly two minutes.

Eventually the second car came into view, which to everyone's surprise was the Mini Clubman. With John Handley at the wheel, he was heading the chasing pack and, with the field full of much more powerful BMWs and Porsches, it was clear BL wanted to make a statement of intent. The Rover was starting to build up a big lead, which was soon to stretch to six laps, but the Mini continued to hold second place on the road.

Through the night, the BL pair continued onwards, trouble-free still in first and second places. Come dawn, the Mini was starting to experience overheating problems and was becoming difficult to restart at driver change-overs.

At 9am, with Vernaeve at the wheel, the decision was made to bring the car in and attempt to change the head gasket. With only 15 minutes allowed to complete the job, they ran out of time. Nevertheless, ten minutes later the car was indeed fixed and running again. One more lap, under exclusion, was completed just to make the point. It had been a remarkable performance, albeit for only eight hours of running. The Rover ran on until 5pm that first day and had built up a three-lap lead but had to be withdrawn with a badly vibrating propshaft, preventing further damage and a resultant oil spill on the circuit.

It was unlikely Abingdon would have got to the finish of the race with the Mini, running at the pace that it was. The lead of the Rover and Mini was masked by others being careful on the opening 12 hours, mindful of the requirement to complete the same number of laps in the last 12 hours as the first. Abingdon probably threw caution to the wind. Only 24 cars finished this most demanding of all races.

With Abingdon's closure now imminent and with instructions to dispose of all of the works cars, it wasn't long before John Handley bought this little-used car.

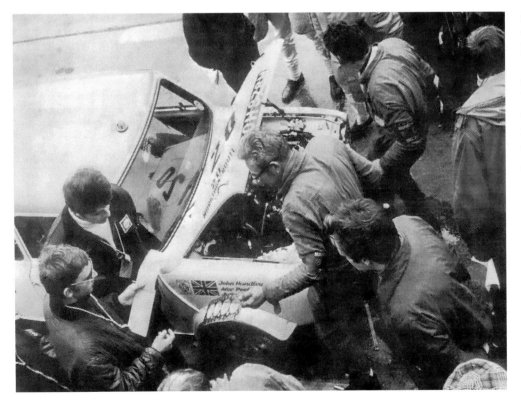

The car ran strongly into second place but a failed head gasket after just eight hours saw the car out, despite the gasket being changed in under half an hour, with only 15 minutes' service allowed.

Competition Record

Date	Event	Crew	Number	Overall result	Class result
Aug 70	Marathon de La Route	John Handley/Alec Poole/Julien Vernaeve	20	DNF	

CHAPTER 5: THE MK3 MINI COOPER S & MINI CLUBMAN S

Registration Number	First registered	Chassis number	Engine	Engine number	Model
OBL 991F	Nov 1967	CA2S7 985611A	1275cc	9F-SA-Y 45967	Austin Cooper S Mk1

Although catalogued in Abingdon's records as a Mk2 Cooper S, OBL 991F, like all of the other OBL cars, was a Mk1 Cooper S. And despite it being registered in November 1967, a month after the Mk2 Cooper S was introduced, the car was prepared and appeared as a Mk1 Cooper S.

OBL 991F was only ever used for recce duties, and one of those was for 1968 Rally Fiori (San Remo Rally), held in February that year. The car was fully prepared and used by Tony Fall and Mike Wood for a full recce. They would do the event in ORX 777F but retired.

OBL 991F was sold to the MG plant accountant Norman Higgins in September 1968. He was a great ally of the Abingdon Competition department and was always available to help with the thorny problem of budgets and expenditure.

OBL 991F used by Tony Fall and Mike Wood for their recce for 1968 San Remo Rally, with the new autostrada in the background. The car was never used in competition.

Competition Record
None

Registration Number	First registered	Chassis number	Engine	Engine number	Model
NBL 126E	July 67	CA2S7 956996	1275cc	9F-SA-Y 44911	Austin Cooper S Mk1

This car was another late Mk1 Cooper S that was assigned to Abingdon. NBL 126E, however, differed in one particular aspect, in that it was finished white with a black roof and not the usual Abingdon warpaint of red and white.

The car was assigned to Cliff Humphries, who was largely responsible for building the engines of many works cars used by Abingdon. The car was prepared very much in the vein of a works Mini and, apart from being used as a mobile engine test-bed by Humphries, it was also extensively used to evaluate modifications that Abingdon was experimenting with, in a desperate attempt to keep ahead of the fast-closing opposition. The car was fitted with an early pawl-type limited-slip differential to test just how reliable and easy it was to use.

It is very likely that the car was also used for recce duties whilst at Abingdon but no records exist to confirm this.

NBL 126E was never used in competition and was painted white and black. It was primarily used as a development car and seen here in the yard at Abingdon with many other works Minis held at that time by the competition department.

Competition Record
None

CHAPTER 6: RALLYCROSS

Timo Mäkinen with Tony Fall as passenger in GRX 311D on the Camberley TV special stage after the cancellation of the 1967 RAC Rally in November. This is often considered the start of rallycross.

The first Rallycross meeting at Lydden Hill in February 1967 saw Bob Freeborough severely damage GRX 310D - it would pave the way for many rally cars to end their days in rallycross.

The first organised rallycross event took place on 3 February 1967 and was run by the 750 Motor Club at Lydden circuit, near Canterbury in Kent. Originally intended as a one-off and conceived by a producer on TV's *World of Sport* programme, the event was a huge success and more TV coverage would soon follow.

Abingdon entered this inaugural event in GRX 310D, which was written off by Bob Freeborough. He was sharing the drive with Tony Fall, who was credited with taking third place. The event was won by Vic Elford in a Porsche 911. Interest by the public was capitalised on by the British ITV company, which broadcast a rallycross championship season through the winter of 1967 and 1968. Robert Reed, the then-ITV *World of Sport* Producer is credited with inventing rallycross. This was followed, the following year, when the BBC hosted a championship season from Lydden Hill in Kent. ITV held a championship at Croft circuit near Darlington and later added events at Cadwell Park in Lincolnshire.

The birth of rallycross is often wrongly connected with the cancellation of the 1967 RAC Rally due to the foot-and-mouth epidemic in November 1967. A single televised special stage was put on outside Camberley on Ministry of Defence land for the sake of the disappointed television companies. This was won by Swede Erik Carlsson in his Saab and the iconic picture of Timo Mäkinen with Tony Fall in the passenger seat in GRX 311D is often published. This was about ten months after the maiden event at Lydden Hill.

The sport of rallycross, in essence is a cross between racing, rallying and autocross. These events took place over the winter months on various racetracks, which were modified to include an off-road section as well as tarmac. The form was generally to have four cars race against each other over three laps. There were mostly three rounds where cars competed against different opponents each round. The winner was the one with the lowest aggregate time over the three rounds. Sometimes, however, the rounds were run on an eliminator basis and a final decided on the winners of each round. It was always dramatic to watch and ideally suited to television coverage.

The BL Abingdon competition department became involved in rallycross from late December 1968 until its closure on 31 October 1970. This was viewed by Lord Stokes, the boss of British Leyland, as a low-cost high-publicity way of getting TV coverage. With rallycross becoming a regular feature on British television on Saturday afternoons it was watched by millions.

Peter Browning had secured the signatures of John Rhodes and John Handley for the forthcoming 1969 race car season, as this was where Abingdon would be concentrating its efforts in 1969 – again at the direction of BL, which wanted Abingdon to take on John Cooper on the racetracks rather than paying him to do the racing. With two top-class racing drivers signed up, they were the obvious choice for rallycross. When the programme was expanded to a four-car team the following year, Jeff Williamson and Brian Chatfield, who were both experienced rallycross drivers, joined the ranks.

The preparation of the rallycross cars largely fell to Tommy Wellman (with Den Green now responsible for the race cars under Bill Price's leadership). However, the pressure on the department in the build-up to the 1970 World Cup Rally in April meant they could no longer support four rallycross cars. Williamson and Chatfield were told they were welcome to take their Abingdon rallycross cars away and prepare them themselves and Abingdon would supply all of the parts necessary. This was an amicable agreement that worked well and allowed Abingdon to field a strong team on limited resources.

All of the cars were heavily modified and ran as Group 6 cars. This meant lightweight panels were fitted and glass replaced with Perspex, trim removed, headlights were blanked over and highly-modified engines used. These engines were always fitted with extremely low final drives to ensure lightening-fast acceleration.

Rallycross by some, especially Paddy Hopkirk, was viewed as a 'destruction derby' and a great abuse of the cars. It is unlikely Abingdon ever built new rallycross cars – they were all either old rally cars at the end of their lives or old race cars suitably reprepared for rallycross. As these cars hardly ever carried any registration number plates, it is difficult to establish with any certainty which cars were used. By careful observation of period photographs, it is however possible to identify a couple of cars.

John Rhodes and John Handley in GRX 5D do battle at Croft in December 1968, both cars showing dented doors for their trouble. This was John Rhodes's first stint at rallycross.

1968-TO-1969 WINTER SEASON

Abingdon stuck its toe in the water of rallycross at the end of December 1968 when entering the ITV rallycross meeting at Croft. The late December weather had not been kind and the icebound track succumbed to heavy snow as the day progressed, and those who had early runs benefited. Both Rhodes and Handley were entered in Mk1 Minis and Abingdon was encouraged with the pair coming home third and sixth respectively.

Handley was in GRX 5D as a fuel-injected Abingdon Mini, whereas John Rhodes was in a fuel-injected British Vita Mini. Despite Rhodes's considerable circuit racing experience, this was the first time he had competed in rallycross for BL, although he had done so previously for British Vita in very special lightweight Minis. Here his third place was testament to his ability. Handley, although sixth overall, was credited with the fourth fastest time of the day.

Into 1969 and the next round of the televised championship was held at Lydden Hill in early January, where the chalky clay was always a challenge. Abingdon fielded two cars: a fuel-injected Cooper S for Rhodes and an experimental Austin 1300 for Paddy Hopkirk. When Rhodes broke the diff of the powerful Cooper S in practice, he took over the Austin 1300 from Hopkirk, who was then roped in as a commentator.

Rhodes finished sixth on the day with the rather unsorted car. Four weeks later, the next round of the ITV World of Sport Championship was held at Croft, where Rhodes would again have the Austin 1300, and Handley had a fuel-injected Cooper S with 12in wheels. Handley had mixed fortunes, coming last in one heat and winning another. He would finish fifth overall on the day.

John Handley at Croft in February 1969 in a typical full slide on the slippery surface – the car is clearly a Mk1.

John Rhodes at Croft in April 1969 in the fuel-injected Mini was lying second in the championship with the hope of securing it at Croft, but his eagerness earned him a ten-second penalty for a jump start and his championship hopes were gone.

One month later, in early March, it was back to Croft for the next round, with Handley again in the fuel-injected Cooper S with 12in wheels on the front but 10in on the rear. Rhodes would be in the Austin 1300 and they were all challenged by a four-wheel-drive Ford Capri driven by Roger Clark. Abingdon was stepping up its presence as Geoff Mabbs was also there with a Rover 3500 and Brian Culcheth in a 4WD Austin 1300. Peter Browning was in attendance, also with Den Green, overseeing their four different cars.

The championship organisers were now getting concerned with accepting 4WD cars, and machines, although in Group 6, beginning to appear with much-modified bodywork. The result was that there was a tentative agreement between the organisers, Ford and BL that the cars' silhouettes should remain unchanged – Browning feeling the cars should look the same as the cars that customers could buy and drive home. Handley had a good meeting, winning the second heat and coming second behind Rhodes on the third heat. He would, however, finish fifth overall on aggregate time.

The winter was turning to spring and the final round of the championship was held on 12 April at Croft, where again Abingdon had four cars entered – but only one was a Mini. Rhodes had the only fuel-injected Cooper S. He was lying second in the championship, and with double points on offer for the final, there were high hopes of a championship win. Having been behind the wheel of an Austin 1300 for most of the season, he elected to swap with Handley and drove the fuel-injected Cooper S for the final round.

The Mini was still sporting a bonnet hump despite the undertaking on silhouettes taken four weeks earlier. Rhodes won the first heat but received a ten-second penalty for jumping the start and with that his championship hope was gone. He would nevertheless finish fourth overall on the day. Jeff Williamson won best clubman in the championship with his Cooper S-powered Elf, and this no doubt helped considerably when Abingdon went shopping for additional drivers for the 1969-to-1970 winter season.

The following day the entourage would head for High Eggborough in North Yorkshire for more. This was actually an autocross event and a curtain-raiser for the 1969 National Autocross Championship. It can only be assumed that as the Abingdon cars were at Croft, a dash to Yorkshire the next day was a swansong for its season of rallycross – especially if Rhodes had been crowned champion.

March 1969 saw Handley at Croft once more, the car showing the large box out for the fuel injection on the crossflow cylinder head.

Handley would drive the fuel-injected Cooper S, sharing the car with Geoff Mabbs, as the Rover 3500 wasn't entered. Rhodes would revert to the Austin 1300, and Culcheth would roll the 4WD Austin 1300 whilst leading his run when the suspension broke. Handley won the last qualifying run of the day in the Mini but finished seventh overall on aggregate. However, the Mini was pressed into service for the last eliminating round when Jeff Williamson's engine in his Elf went off song and Peter Browning generously loaned him the works Mini that Handley had been driving. He rewarded Browning by getting fastest time of the day and only just losing out to Rhodes on the line in the Austin 1300, in a car he had never sat in. It had been a learning season for Abingdon; the following season would see serious participation with a four-car team of Minis.

1969-TO-1970 WINTER SEASON

The '69-to-'70 winter season started with the opening round in early October at Lydden Hill; this was a televised meeting that the BL masters were keen to be seen at. Only two cars were entered for this first meeting, for John Rhodes and John Handley, although for all of the remaining rounds a four-car team would represent BL.

Rhodes, in an eight-port fuel-injected car, was handicapped by having a TV camera strapped to his roll cage. This, to BL's embarrassment, showed him struggle off the line in his heat against two one-litre Minis and a Lotus Europa, only to charge through to second place and then pull off before the finish with failed transmission. The car took no further part.

Both the BL works cars had 12in wheels on the front and 10in rims on the rear. Handley, also in an eight-port fuel-injected car, was having problems with the engine refusing to run cleanly all day and he was handicapped accordingly, finishing a rather lowly eighth overall in what was a very wet and muddy opening round.

The second round on 1 November saw a four-car team assembled by Abingdon for the meeting at Cadwell Park, which was again a televised meeting. Rhodes was joined by Jeff Williamson and Brian Chatfield, both very experienced and successful rallycross drivers in their own Minis. Brian Culcheth stood in for John Handley, and whilst Rhodes had

Brian Culcheth at Cadwell Park in LBL 606D had to give best to the other three BL team drivers and had to settle for seventh place.

The BL works line-up at Cadwell Park, from left to right: John Rhodes, Jeff Williamson, Brian Chatfield and Brian Culcheth, standing in for John Handley, with the BL transporter as a backdrop.

November 1969 and the new season championship under way. Cadwell Park saw BL field a strong four-car team.; Rhodes, in RJB 327F, ran out the winner.

Cadwell Park again in late November, where John Rhodes took LBL 666D to fifth place on the round where only Group 1 to 4 cars were permitted; BL had been entering Group 6 cars, so the cars ran split Webers.

John Handley took LRX 827E to the restricted Cadwell Park round where he could do no better that tenth place without the benefit of fuel injection and crossflow cylinder head.

the benefit of an eight-port fuel-injected Mini, Williamson, Chatfield and Culcheth had to make do with five-port engines with split Webers.

Rhodes's Mini was clearly an ex-racing car, having chrome around the door and retaining its front bumper lip, a large metal BL badge on the wing plus a clearly recessed fuel cap on the driver's side (now blanked off). It is very likely this car was RJB 327F. Culcheth's car, also with chrome around the door and a bumper lip, was an ex-rally car as the body showed evidence of Lift-the-Dot fixings for plastic headlight covers and also a blanked-off light plug socket; it was probably LBL 606D.

Williamson's and Chatfield's cars appeared very similar with the bumper lip removed but Williamson's car was a Mk1 and Chatfield's a Mk2, believed to be LBL 666D. All the cars wore front and rear mud flaps but they also used different wheel and tyre combination over the day. Rhodes used 12in wheels throughout, with newly designed Dunlop MP27 tyres specially formulated for rallycross. Culcheth used 10in wheels fitted with Dunlop R7 race tyres. Chatfield and Williamson tried 12in wheels on the front and 10in on the rear; he tried Dunlop SP44s and Dunlop R7s but ultimately decided on using 10in R7s like Culcheth.

Both Chatfield and Williamson had acquitted themselves well, with Browning having signed them up for the year. Williamson won one of his rounds, as did Chatfield and Rhodes.

The last race decider therefore saw three works Minis line up: Rhodes, Williamson and Chatfield against Rob Chapman's Escort. A battle between Chapman was settled with Rhodes having more traction and power with the eight-port engine, taking the Escort on the finish line. Chatfield was a strong third, whilst Williamson spun himself out of contention. Rhodes ran out the overall winner on the day's aggregate times and also claimed the fastest time of the day. Chatfield came home fourth, Culcheth seventh, and Williamson eighth after his spin.

An unseasonal sunny Lydden Hill was the next televised round the following week. Williamson was absent this time as his engine was still not running well and the car had been slightly damaged the previous week at Cadwell Park. A returning Handley shone, winning on aggregate and also claiming fastest time of the day; Chatfield was close by in second place. This time all the cars ran on 12in wheels with the new Dunlop MP27 rallycross tyre, but only Rhodes had the benefit of a fuel-injected eight-port engine.

Chatfield won his first round, as did Handley. Rhodes hit a bank on his first round, coming last and damaging his car, needing new steering arms, but won his second round, as did Handley. The final saw Handley win, with Chatfield finishing third, spinning just after his start. Rhodes would finish seventh overall on the day.

At the end of November, Cadwell Park hosted the next ITV televised round and, in attempt to attract more rally cars for the television audience, the meeting was open only to Groups 1 to 4. This meant the cars that Abingdon had been using as Group 6 cars were not permitted. Nevertheless, Abingdon turned up with two Group 2 cars, with Rhodes in LBL 666D and Handley in LRX 827E. Williamson and Chatfield would still race but not in works cars on this occasion.

The weather was atrocious, with a snow-covered track, which with heavy snow later meant a trying day – so much so that the organisers reduced the heats by a lap. Being a Group 2 entry, Ford had Timo Mäkinen and Roger Clark there in works TC Escort rally cars, and Lancia had Tony Fall present his RAC Rally Lancia Fulvia. Tyre choice was crucial in the snowy conditions, where Rhodes elected to run 10in tyres with SP44s on his five-port split Weber car. Handley, with a similar engine, chose 12in tyres and Dunlop came up with another new block-tread snow tyre for the cars.

Handley won his first round and Williamson burnt out a piston on his car. Rhodes narrowly won his round and also his second round, but the times the opposition were recording meant the Mini was not on the top of the score card. Once the snow came, the last races were in very difficult conditions and were a question of who didn't make a mistake. Mäkinen won the day, with Clark a close second. Rhodes had to be content with fifth place and Handley tenth.

The next week, the cars returned to Lydden Hill, for the BBC-covered meeting, where the TV viewer witnessed a mud-bath at the Kent circuit. A full-strength Abingdon team was entered. Rhodes had a fuel-injected eight-port engine; Handley, Chatfield and Williamson had five-porters and split Webers. Handley's car, because of all of the mud, had a large Perspex screen on the bonnet to deflect the mud. Williamson removed his front and rear windscreens and suffered numerous cuts and abrasions for his trouble. All four cars were running narrow-width 10in rims with Dunlop block-tread tyres.

On their first rounds, Rhodes and Williamson won whilst Handley was second. Chatfield won his second round, ahead of Handley. Rhodes, however, retired with a slipped fuel-injection timing belt on his second round. Handley also retired on his third round, which Williamson won. Rhodes, with his timing issue fixed, came second on his third round, hampered by failed wipers. The aggregate times found Williamson in second place overall but the other three Abingdon cars were not in the top ten due to their various maladies.

Jeff Williamson at Croft just before Christmas 1969, where Williamson removed the front 'screen to help his vision and got cuts and abrasions for his trouble, but still finished second overall.

A few days before Christmas, the team headed for Croft for the last of ITV's coverage of rallycross, where foggy and icy conditions greeted the cars. The meeting was curtailed after only two runs, which had also been shortened to only two laps. The conditions suited the Minis and Williamson came home in second place, one ahead of Rhodes. Handley had an eight-port engine at his disposal this time around, but as Rhodes had problems in practice with his fuel-injected car's engine failing, he used Handley's car for the race, and he in turn was to share Williamson's car, which had its usual five-port split Weber engine. Chatfield didn't have a good day, tipping his works car onto its side on his first round. Handley was second on his first run, with Rhodes and Williamson winning their first rounds. With Williamson winning his second round from Handley, back in his eight-port engine, Williamson's place was secured.

The first round of 1970 on 10 January was held at Lydden Hill, where Abingdon fielded the same four-car team of cars and drivers. Williamson carried on where he left off before Christmas, by winning this BBC TV round, whilst Rhodes got the fastest time of the day in his eight-port fuel-injected car. The weather was again atrocious, with constant rain and deep mud, so only two runs were scheduled. But Williamson revelled in the conditions – and again ran the car without any windscreens. Chatfield, however, didn't have a good day, as he lost the transmission on his car on his first run whilst racing against Handley. Rhodes set such a fast time on his

John Rhodes at Lydden Hill in January 1970 scored the fastest time of the day in the eight-port fuel-injected car but ran out seventh overall, seen here with a deflector screen on the car.

Jeff Williamson was the overall winner at the January Lydden Hill meeting, where the conditions were atrocious. Williamson removed the 'screen for the second heat.

The two works Minis of Handley and Rhodes receiving attention between races at Lydden Hill in February 1970. Handley's car in the foreground, being LBL 606D, has a deflector screen whereas Rhodes's behind does not.

John Rhodes won the February 1970 round at Lydden Hill and it would be a fitting end to his rallycross with BL.

Brian Chatfield, in March 1970 at a snow-covered Lydden Hill was with Williamson, the only pair to represent BL as Abingdon was busy with the World Cup Rally. Neither would finish and it brought a sad end to BL's rallycross involvement.

first run that everyone else was trying hard to better his time, but as the conditions worsened, he was safe. Rhodes, on his second run, after a terrible start, finished a distant last - but seventh overall on aggregate time.

Four weeks later in early February, once again at Lydden Hill and televised, Williamson's fortunes were reversed when his car went onto three cylinders on his first run (but he didn't finish last) and didn't take part in the third run when the clutch failed at the end of his second run.

The four-car BL team was structured a little differently here, as only Rhodes and Handley would have cars prepared and maintained by Abingdon. Pressure on resources in preparation for the World Cup Rally, now only a few months away, meant the team could not look after Chatfield and Williamson's cars; instead, their cars were loaned to the pair and they would prepare their works cars themselves – but Abingdon would foot the bill. Chatfield had two cars at his disposal but Williamson just one.

Rhodes ran out the winner, having had three comfortable wins on his rounds. Handley was leading after the first rounds and Chatfield had better luck in second place after the first runs. Handley, however, struggled in the later rounds. Rhodes only just missed out on fastest time of the day, giving best to

Hugh Wheldon, who was touting for an Abingdon drive in the summer's European rallycross season.

The final round at Lydden Hill, a month later, where double points were on offer, saw only Williamson and Chatfield representing Abingdon. The impending World Cup meant that neither Rhodes nor Handley were entered. It would not be a great last round, where both of the cars retired. Williamson had an accident big enough that meant the deranged car could not continue, and Chatfield broke a driveshaft, also into retirement.

This would be the end of Abingdon's involvement in rallycross. With the Abingdon competitions department's closure on 31 October 1970, a day after the 1970/1971 rallycross season started at Lydden Hill, special tuning, under the management of Basil Wales, would continue a much-reduced rallycross programme.

RALLYCROSS RESULTS

Date	Rallycross	Crew	Car	Number	Result
Feb 67	Lydden Hill	T Fall	GRX 310D		
		B Freeborough	GRX 310D		DNF
Nov 67	Camberley TV stage	T Mäkinen	GRX 311D	18	
Dec 68	Croft	J Rhodes	Vita car	11	3rd
		J Handley	GRX 5D	7	6th
11 Jan 69	Lydden Hill	J Rhodes			DNF
08 Feb 69	Croft	J Handley		66	5th
08 Mar 69	Croft	J Handley		70	5th
12 Apr 69	Croft	J Rhodes		51	4th
13 Apr 69	High Eggborough	J Handley			7th
		G Mabbs			
04 Oct 69	Lydden Hill	J Rhodes			DNF
		J Handley			8th
01 Nov 69	Cadwell Park	J Rhodes	RJB 327F	2	1st
		J Williamson		3	8th
		B Chatfield	LBL 666D	10	4th
		B Culcheth	LBL 606D	31	7th
08 Nov 69	Lydden Hill	J Handley		16	1st
		B Chatfield		27	3rd
		J Rhodes			7th
29 Nov 69	Cadwell Park	J Rhodes	LBL 666D	2	5th
		J Handley	LRX 827E	5	10th
06 Dec 69	Lydden Hill	J Rhodes			Not in top 10
		J Handley			Not in top 10
		J Williamson		68	2nd
		B Chatfield			Not in top 10
20 Dec 69	Croft	J Rhodes		2	3rd
		J Handley			Not in top 10
		J Williamson		68	2nd
		B Chatfield			Not in top 10
10 Jan 70	Lydden Hill	J Rhodes		15	7th
		J Handley			Not in top 10
		J Williamson		68	1st
		B Chatfield			Not in top 10
07 Feb 70	Lydden Hill	J Rhodes		27	1st
		J Handley	LBL 606D	16	Not in top 10
		J Williamson			Not in top 10
		B Chatfield			Not in top 10
07 Mar 70	Lydden Hill	J Williamson			DNF
		B Chatfield		7	DNF

CHAPTER 7: EPILOGUE

August 2017 saw the largest collection of ex-works cars amass outside the old Abingdon competition department, the premises now owned by UK Mail. Will there ever be a bigger display?

This story of the works Minis would not be complete if the closure of Abingdon was glossed over. This was regarded by everyone as a travesty and a very short-sighted view from the British Leyland management. Lord Stokes officially disbanded the competition department on 31 October 1970 with a simple statement that, "A disproportionate amount of management time in the area of design development and engineering has had to be devoted to competition at a time when the corporation's forward model programme is being rapidly formed. It is now felt that the new model programme must take precedence in the immediate future." This had been a long time coming.

As far back as early 1968, Peter Browning was aware that for BL and Abingdon to remain competitive, against what was becoming fierce opposition, they needed a proper and well-funded development programme. He had proposed that the competition department and special tuning should merge, with the proposal that a dedicated development section, housed in the adjacent special tuning workshop, should to be put together. Cliff Humphries would head up a small team permanently undertaking development work. This would still leave special tuning to serve customers' cars and the competition department would then reap the benefits of development work.

Sadly, this did not come to pass and Peter Browning became ever more frustrated trying to work within even tighter and restrictive budgets, and with that a restricted competitions programme. It was destined to fail, with BL management being indifferent to the needs of the competition department. When the axe fell, the only survivor was special tuning, which under Basil Wales's management, was making a good profit from selling competition-approved parts to the public – the profits of which were happily supporting much of Abingdon's competition budget.

The net result was that a team of 30-plus specialised technicians at Abingdon had no future. Peter Browning had already resigned in July that year, having given up the unenviable struggle to have a sensible competitions budget approved for the following season. He agreed to stay on until a successor could be found.

So the competition department at Abingdon, which was once a revered name that put fear into others, was no more. Abingdon's reputation had been built up over the years due to the standard of preparation and professionalism within the team, and was one of the reasons it was so successful. This was unequalled by any manufacturer at the time and the envy of many.

The early days of gentleman drivers, with numerous MGs and assorted other cars from the BMC range, was soon surpassed when the Big Healey became the weapon of choice. Under Marcus Chambers, the competition department grew, and once Stuart Turner took the reins and the Mini Cooper became available, things really took off.

For over four years, the Cooper S reigned supreme and was the car to beat. Stuart Turner, ever canny, left the department to Peter Browning when the Cooper S was starting to feel the challenge from much more powerful machines from other manufacturers. In truth, by late 1967 the Cooper S as an outright winner was fading but Abingdon persevered with its loved one right to the bitter end.

The 1969 season in racing and rallycross, away from rallying, had not been the success that the Leyland bosses had hoped for and that Abingdon needed. Their last hope was the World Cup Rally, which had they won, other than being the first of the rest, could possibly have saved Abingdon and perhaps made it publicly more difficult for Lord Stokes to shut the doors – but with the head of the company having zero interest in competition, the writing was on the wall as soon as he took the chair.

The careful selection of events (and more development) may just have given the Mini an extended life but Abingdon's future, if it had one, lay in other cars. The final Abingdon display on the 86-hour Marathon de la Route, where the lone Rover V8 led on the fearsome Nürburgring by three laps from factory Porsches, only to retire with a failed propshaft, showed great potential. Plus the singleton Mini putting up an equally impressive show, before it too retired, showed Abingdon was still a force to be reckoned with.

With development, the Rover V8 could have been a challenger. However, without the will and a workable budget to go forward, Abingdon was being backed into a corner. The resignation of Peter Browning was therefore inevitable before the curtain finally came down.

So the Abingdon team was broken up, to be either dispersed around other departments or made redundant. Doug Watts went to rectification and road testing of cars. Brian Moylan and Gerald Wiffen moved next door to special tuning under Basil Wales. Engine guru Cliff Humphries was dispatched to the trim line, of all things! Others went to work on the MG line and a few took redundancy. Bill Price also went to special tuning but that relationship didn't last two weeks and he too left the company. As to the drivers and navigators, all had been let go, other than Brian Culcheth.

As a team of managers, mechanics, drivers and navigators, they had all worked together, always stayed in the same hotels on events and always ate and celebrated together. It was a team bond that was unbreakable.

You can break up a team but you can't kill its spirit. It is testimony to that statement that even to this day, there are annual reunions of the competition staff and numerous veterans from the era attend BMC-related events as guests; many also make a point of attending the Mini Cooper Register's National Mini Day at Beaulieu each year, to the great interest of club members. There is still great camaraderie amongst the Abingdon team, even after 50 years.

A tribute event was staged at Abingdon in 2017, when as many ex-works Minis as could be mustered attended a reunion, and the cavalcade of red-and-white Minis drove to the site of the old Abingdon competition department (at the time of the visit owned by UK Mail). It was a spectacular occasion and a fitting testament to their survival, their success and the strength of the competition department at Abingdon – and, of course, that of the Mini.